World History

World History

A Concise Thematic Analysis
VOLUME ONE

Steven Wallech
Long Beach City College
Craig Hendricks
Long Beach City College
Touraj Daryaee
California State University–Fullerton
Anne Lynne Negus
Fullerton College
Peter Wan
Fullerton College
Gordon Morris Bakken
California State University–Fullerton

Brenda Farrington, Developmental Editor
Chapman University

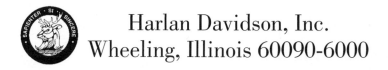
Harlan Davidson, Inc.
Wheeling, Illinois 60090-6000

Library of Congress Cataloging-in-Publication Data

Wallech, Steven.
  World history : a concise thematic analysis / Steven Wallech, principal author and editor ; Gordon Morris
Bakken, project founder and coordinator [and] U.S. specialist ; Peter Wan, Chinese and Japanese specialist ;
Craig Hendricks, Latin and Native American specialist ; Anne Lynne Negus, African specialist ; Touraj Daryaee,
Persian, Greek, and Roman specialist ; Brenda Farrington, developmental editor.
      p. cm.
  Includes bibliographical references and index.
  ISBN-13: 978-0-88295-244-4 (alk. paper)
  1. World history. 2. Civilization—History. I. Bakken, Gordon Morris. II. Farrington, Brenda. III. Title.
  D20.W355 2007
  909—dc22

                        2006030630

Cover photograph: "The Treasury at Petra," Jordan, built c. 300 BCE. Photograph by Mike Lopez,
www.vagabum.com.
Cover design: Chris Calvetti, c2itgraphics.

Manufactured in the United States of America
09 08 07 06 1 2 3 4 5 VP

TABLE OF CONTENTS

INTRODUCTION

Teaching a course in World History at the college-level presents an instructor with an especially difficult challenge. Unlike most historians who conduct courses in the study of a particular culture, nation, or region, those who teach World History ostensibly must have familiarity with the history of all the earth's peoples. As daunting as such a proposition is, the matter is even more complicated. Because imparting the history of humanity within the confines of a college-level course is, of course, impossible, world historians must convey to their students an appreciation of the short- and long-term effects of human practices on local and regional environments, the interdependencies of humans, animals, plants, and pathogens, and the diffusion of ideas, technologies, and disease through trade, migration, war, empire building, and human resistance—phenomena that create crosscultural, transnational, and transregional patterns over time.

To make things even more difficult, much of the historical literature on world history emphasizes the differences between regional cultures and local histories, leaving the instructor scrambling to find the similarities that might produce a lucid global narrative. In particular, the current generation of world history textbooks fails to succeed in conveying a unified, coherent account. Indeed, linear surveys lack a central storyline, with any potential core narrative submerged under a sea of details that simply overwhelms the student reader.

What probably explains this bleak state of affairs is the fact that as a distinct discipline, World History is only about six decades old. Begun in the 1960s as part of a slow shift from Western Civilization, World History gradually became a subdiscipline as increasing numbers of historians recognized the usefulness of a global perspective to understand humanity's past. Developing steadily despite the vast amount of material that had to be digested and the necessary development of new mental habits of synthesis, World History finally achieved recognition as a discipline in 1982 with the establishment of the World History Association. Since then, the WHA has grown to 1,500 members,

World History has become a standard general education requirement at the college level, and several major universities now offer advanced degrees in the field. Nonetheless, no one, until now, has written an accessible, concise world history textbook.

With decades of combined experience teaching World History—in community colleges and four-year institutions—we have witnessed firsthand the frustration instructors and students of world history experience with current survey textbooks. Deeming a new approach necessary, even overdue, we spent the last several years conceiving of and writing *World History: A Concise Thematic Analysis*.

It will be immediately apparent to anyone familiar with the full-length or even so-called concise world history surveys currently on the market that this book stands alone: its interesting and recurrent themes—conceptual bridges that span the many centuries—give it a unique voice. Its format helps the reader see the larger picture, to conceptualize patterns over time by importing concepts from one unit to another. And while this book might not offer flashy four-color maps and illustrations, its length and price speak for themselves. Too often students are required to pay a great deal of money for books they have no hope of finishing, let alone comprehending or remembering long after they turn in the last exam.

To achieve the brief but coherent account of global events, *World History: A Concise Thematic Analysis* comprises four complete units: the first is long (ten chapters); the second, short (six chapters); the third, long (again, ten chapters); and the fourth and last is short (seven chapters).

Unit One covers the ancient world, using two scientific themes: symbiosis to explain agriculture, and parasitism to account for eras of sudden death. Coupled with these two biological themes are several geographic concepts that facilitate an understanding of the movement of plants, animals, tools, ideas, and germs from one of the world's major cultural hearths to another. Equally important is the condition of geographic isolation, which denied such movement. Finally, this unit introduces the concept of culture, explaining how it organized human creativity in response to the circumstances of life in the ancient world.

Unit Two, the middle years of world history, develops further the concept of culture, elevating it to the central theme that governs the six chapters that consider the years 500 to 1000 [1500] CE. Culture serves to explain how the dominant human communities of the globe expanded to their limits, while only one of them developed the potential to change world events. Hence, a broad analysis of each major civilization reveals why most of them preferred stability to change, even as one of them broke the mold of tradition to set in motion a whirlwind of change that laid the foundation for globalism and the modern era.

Unit Three addresses the modern era, 1492 to 1914. Its major themes are modernization, the differential of power, and globalization. Focusing on European culture as the one [that] proactively transformed the world, this analysis of modernization considers the key institutional changes that created the nation-state in the West. Using a comparative cultural analysis of political, economic, and military institutions to demonstrate the growing material might of Europe in contrast with the waning power of non-European societies, Unit Three outlines the material advantages that Western peoples and cultures enjoyed as they expanded outward—and were themselves transformed by the peoples, ideas, and resources they encountered in the Western Hemisphere, Africa, and Asia. Next, the theme of globalization helps explain how other cultures of the world imported many of the Western institutions, adapting them in an effort to survive, but ultimately sought to expel Europeans from their territories through the long and difficult process known as decolonization.

Unit Four considers the postmodern world, 1914 to 2006. It begins by showing how global warfare, a harvest of violence set in motion by the empire building of Unit Three, destroyed Europe's hold over its colonies, protectorates, and spheres of influence and shifted dramatically the global differential of power. At the same time, we approached Unit Four in a unique way. Given that 1914 to 2006 constitutes slightly less than one hundred years of world history, we strived to maintain an appropriate balance between its content and the remainder of the text. In other words, the last 93 years established the contemporary world but deserve no more space then any other period of global history. Accordingly, the content of Unit Four is as concise as possible, even as we show that its tumultuous events and the state of the world today are the product of, and the conclusion to, the preceding three units.

The advantage of this long-, short-, long-, short-unit presentation is that it allows for a logical division of the text for use in either the semester or the quarter system. For those on the semester system, the completion of Units One and Two bring the reader to the modern age (1500 CE), the classic stopping point for the first half of world history. Units Three and Four complete the story in the second semester. For those on the quarter system, Unit One covers the ancient world, the standard stopping point in a ten-week class. Unit Two and the first half of Unit Three link the middle years to the early modern era (1000–1750 CE) and bring the narrative up to the formation of nation-states, the standard stopping point for the second ten-week period of study. Finally, the second half of Unit Three and all of Unit Four cover modernization and the postmodern age.

As mentioned, each unit features a dominant set of themes. Not only do these themes make up the thesis for the unit under consideration, but they also reappear throughout the text, providing cohesiveness and unity where none otherwise exists and making World History accessible and meaningful to student readers. On the other side of the desk, both experienced and inexperienced instructors, eager to find footholds as an otherwise unwieldy narrative unfolds, will find the use of overriding themes helpful. In short, the introduction of themes in a world history text eliminates the problem of presenting an isolated and seemingly endless list of facts, figures, and dates: the "one darn thing after another" phenomenon that gives World History a bad name.

Themes also help build a comparative analysis of regional histories. Such comparisons help students grasp how human creativity produces a unique stamp on the development of distinct cultures, even as people everywhere struggle with a common set of problems. Finally, themes highlight contrasts between cultural hearths, making the text relevant to an increasingly diverse student population, as well as useful in the new comparative World History courses.

Whether you are new to the field of World History or have taught the subject for years, it is our hope that you will give our approach a chance-and that you will agree that a thematic analysis goes a long way toward making a complicated compendium of human numbers, economies, and cultures meaningful to student readers.

Steven Wallech
Craig Hendricks
Touraj Daryaee
Anne Lynne Negus
Peter Wan
Gordon Morris Bakken

Themes   *Unit One*
The Ancient World

The theme of Unit One is the role biology played in world history. Our approach will be to link the symbiosis of agriculture to the parasitism of sedentary life and show how both combined with human creativity. The integration of all three factors into one story underscores the biological basis of the oldest cities in the world. Then we will examine a comparative study of the original *cultural hearths* (places of cultural origins) of the ancient era that produced the first urban centers located in different agricultural sites around the world. These urban centers will be further analyzed to show how scribes, artisans, merchants, soldiers, kings, and priests—the agents of human creativity—produced writing, metallurgy, trade, war, and religious ideas belonging to unique locales, which emerged from the first economies generated in the great river basins of Eurasia. Here, the role played by geography, trade, and humans explains how the cultural diffusion of domesticated plants, animals, and local pathogens, plus the movement of agricultural technology, commercial goods, and religious and philosophical ideas offered Eurasians a distinct advantage over peoples located elsewhere in the world. Furthermore, this analysis is extended to Mesoamerica, the Andes, and sub-Saharan Africa to reveal the geographic and biological differences under which the urban centers of these three regions labored. There, conditions spawned the development of fewer cities, which in turn resulted in fewer plants and animals available to feed urban dwellers, a smaller urban elite to perpetuate skilled occupations, and the absence of contact with other cultures due to geographic isolation. Finally, by linking the initial dates for the domestication of plants and animals in these various global cultural zones and cataloging the variety of plants, animals, and germs available to each civilization, Unit One will: 1) explain the role that food production played in the development of all these ancient urban centers; 2) describe these cities as generators of urban skills between 10,000 BCE* and 500 CE*, and 3) measure their effect on outlying nomadic peoples.

*BCE = **Before the Common Era**; CE = **the Common Era**

The symbiosis of agriculture and the parasitism of sedentary life combined to create a biological equilibrium between food production and the development of disease that marked the beginning of human creativity in an ancient urban setting. *Symbiosis* itself is a positive, reciprocal relationship between the populations of two different species. *Agriculture*, in turn, is a unique symbiosis between humans, plants, and animals because cultivation involves a deliberate human selection of specific varieties of omega plants and animals to produce food. *Omega* here refers to those varieties of plants and animals that could not reproduce in the wild without human intervention, which in turn, created a reciprocal dependency between humans, seeds, and livestock. The combination of symbiosis, agriculture, and omega varieties then lifted ancient farmers, domesticated plants, and domesticated animals out of a natural setting and placed them in a new artificial environment called *civilization*.

Parasitism accompanied agriculture because the cultivation of plants concentrated human farming populations and their dependent plants and animals in specific geographic sites which attracted parasitical organisms that could feed off these humans, plants, and animals settled in their "civilization" environment. Parasites then developed complex relationships with their hosts that caused periodic and widespread famines and epidemics that decimated one civilization even as they helped launch another. Parasites specializing in plants and animals denied humans food. Those orgranisms that parasitized humans initiated a micro-evolutionary process that transformed temporary illnesses into endemic diseases that maintained low-level infections in specific populations. Each original cultural hearth that established an urban civilization, therefore, developed its own local diseases that impacted the ancient world through trade. Periodically, parasites from one disease-exporting culture invaded healthy societies along trade routes, causing massive demographic crises in different regions at different times. Such sudden and massive losses of human life upset the delicate balance between agriculture and parasitism and began to erode the foundations of civilization.

Accordingly, if the balance between agriculture and disease tipped the scales of life in favor of food production, human numbers grew, cities developed, a variety of urban skills matured, and political control of geographic space became important. Periodically, when disease struck in the form of epidemic or pandemic infections, human numbers dropped sharply and the foundation of civilization eroded. This unpredictable impact of disease is basic to understanding how stable food production could sustain long continuous civilizations, while sudden, massive die-offs could undermine and upset the delicate internal balance within empires. Furthermore, those geographic zones with longer, more stable food production can stand in contrast to less fortunate cultural sites, which helps explain why some regions produced far more cultural artifacts than did others.

A "healthy" society is one in which food production is stable, epidemics are rare, and diseases take the form of childhood infections that kill the youngest, most vulnerable, and most easily replaced members of the community. The nutrients supplied by cultivation include a wide variety of plants and animals, and agricultural technology is linked to the muscle of large, domesticated mammals, permitting the use of heavy tools like the wheel and the plow to generate the largest harvests possible to sustain cities. The food surpluses achieved, in turn, provided the nutrient base needed to free some people living in urban centers from cultivation, affording them the time necessary to create writing, produce records, establish administrations, run bureaucracies, send out census takers, protect tax collectors, raise armies, and manufacture the weapons needed to command their geographic space.

Three critical but variable factors reinforced this dynamic link between the symbiosis of agriculture, the parasitism of a sedentary existence, and the human creativity stimulated by urban life: 1) the longer a stable agricultural system was able to sustain itself; 2) the greater the number of domesticated plants and animals it could support, and; 3) the more strategic the geographic location of a given civilization; the more plant cultivation supported the development of a rich, urban setting. In turn, the richer this urban life proved to be, the more humans were released from agricultural pursuits to produce the artifacts of civilization. In contrast, the shorter, or poorer, their life proved to be, the less we know today about the events that took place within that specific civilization because fewer people with urban skills left artifacts behind.

A "sick" society is one in which disease was rife, political chaos far outweighed political stability, and contact with other cultures led to the exportation of epidemics that cause demographic crises in foreign lands. In a sick society, living in cities reduces life expectancy, erodes the urban skills needed to create a stable political system, and encourages religious speculation that sustains belief in another world. Furthermore, healthy societies that come in contact with sick ones often suffer an immediate die-off, which may result in the collapse of a particular civilization but may also sustain the microevolution between humans and a new population of micro-organisms that leads to the immunities needed to resist future infections. Hence, healthy societies—just like healthy individuals—may undergo but live through cycles of sickness that make them immune to future infection by new diseases. What follows in such communities is the development of an increased biological arsenal, if you will, of plants, animals, and germs that sets the stage for a new era of world history.

Meanwhile, once a civilization begins, the maturation of local urban occupations and their accompanying skills enables plants, animals, tools, ideas, and germs to travel from one culture to another. The geographic *site*—its location in the world—and the situation of a particular civilization determines whether its culture has access to the developments taking place in other human communities. The *situation* of a culture is its position relative to other civilizations. But the circumstances of site and situation are dynamic and change with the development of transportation. Hence, in the ancient world, Mesopotamia occupied the most strategic location among all the civilizations because of its situation on a land bridge between Europe, Asia, and Africa. This site, with its dearth of local raw materials as well as its strategic situation between Anatolia, Egypt, and India, gave the Sumerians, the first civilization of Mesopotamia, the motivation needed to develop the wheel and load-bearing oxcarts. Trade then stimulated intercultural contact between Sumeria and other local cultures to set in motion a pattern of diffusion that accelerated cultural development throughout Mesopotamia, then the Mediterranean, and eventually much of Eurasia in general. The stimulation of this intercultural communication, and its attendant diffusion of plants, animals, tools, ideas, and even germs, allowed a flowering of civilizations in Eurasia at the fastest rate possible in the world at the time.

In contrast, Mesoamerica and the Andean civilizations of the Western Hemisphere suffered from severe geographic isolation, and the absence there of a large variety of domesticated animals, due to the two massive oceans that framed these civilizations and cut them off from events taking place in Europe, Asia, and Africa. Therefore, ancient Native Americans did not have the geographic or biological advantages of humans living in Eurasia. Consequently, this placed Native American cultures on a different time scale in contrast with Eurasia when it comes to the development of major technologies such as iron, gunpowder, the wheel, and the plow. Thus, Native American civilizations did not have access to the intercultural communication that took place in Eurasia; nor did they have access to the same supply of plants, animals, tools, ideas, or germs.

This lack of access does not mean that Native Americans would not have developed the same level of technology as found in Eurasia given enough time. Yet it does mean that they did not have the same cultural advantages enjoyed by the Spanish, for example, once Christopher Columbus breached the geographic barriers that had isolated the Western Hemisphere from 10,000 BCE to 1492 CE. Hence, when global contacts like the Columbian Exchange are taken into consideration, these differences in situation become significant in world history.

The history of metallurgy, meanwhile, serves as another example of the importance of site and situation. The movement and influence of new kinds of metals, and the subsequent food surpluses generated by the use of metal tools during the ancient era, is hugely important to a particular culture's location and the length of time its people had to develop urban skills. The development of bronze in Mesopotamia, for example, affected urban history there and Mesopotamian contact with alien cultures. Trade diffused the skills of Mesopotamia to many outlying nomadic cultures. The same is true for the history of iron. Simultaneously, the introduction of iron manufacturing radically transformed agriculture in Eurasia by allowing the creation of the first metal farm tools. Iron is far more plentiful than bronze; iron ore is the most common metal-bearing rock on Earth, while the manufacture of bronze requires the proper combination of copper and tin, a far less common metal. Hence, Bronze Age cultures confined precious metal tools to their urban elite, leaving farms with a Neolithic technology. Only the awe of religious beliefs bound the farmer of a Bronze Age culture to his city and maintained the tax-base that fed those with urban skills.

The Iron Age, in contrast, ushered in an era during which metal became far more plentiful. Iron manufacturing allowed blacksmiths to supply farmers with metal plow blades, scythes, and sickles, and created a new bond between cultivators and their cities. In short, the widespread use of efficient iron tools generated massive new food surpluses, but also created a credit-debt relationship that drew farmers into the political affairs of towns. Farmer-soldiers wearing metal armor, carrying metal weapons, and fighting for massive, new political organizations either took up arms as citizens, as in Western civilization, or joined new imperial armies, as in the Ancient Near East, Mediterranean, and Asian empires. Thus, the civilizations of Eurasia that experienced the Iron Age received a major stimulus to agriculture, developed new urban skills, and generated the military resources needed to establish and expand their empires. In contrast, cultures that did not have iron or bronze produced food using a Stone Age technology and suffered a smaller food base and population.

Unit One, therefore, explains how the artificial existence of civilization emerged from the natural consequences of human interaction with geography and biology during the ancient era of world history. The *artificial existence of civilization* refers to the growing distance between living conditions and nature as agriculture separated various peoples in different locations around the world from their passive reliance on the Earth's bounty. The *natural consequences of human interaction with geography and biology* refers to the specific events surrounding the development of ancient cities as these urban centers organized the skills needed to survive using the new food base generated by agriculture. Plant cultivation in turn imposed specific requirements on ancient human life—irrigation, field preparation, seed selection, food storage, rationing, the development of a calendar, the production of new tools, and the explanation of the local rhythms of nature—that elevated humans' consciousness to new levels of awareness of the unique, but increasingly distant relationship to the natural world around them. It is this new level of human consciousness that launched ancient world history when the people who dwelled in the oldest urban centers began to record their struggle to exist in this new artificial setting created by agriculture. This record in turn produced the story that became the core of ancient world history and serves as the heart of Unit One of this text.

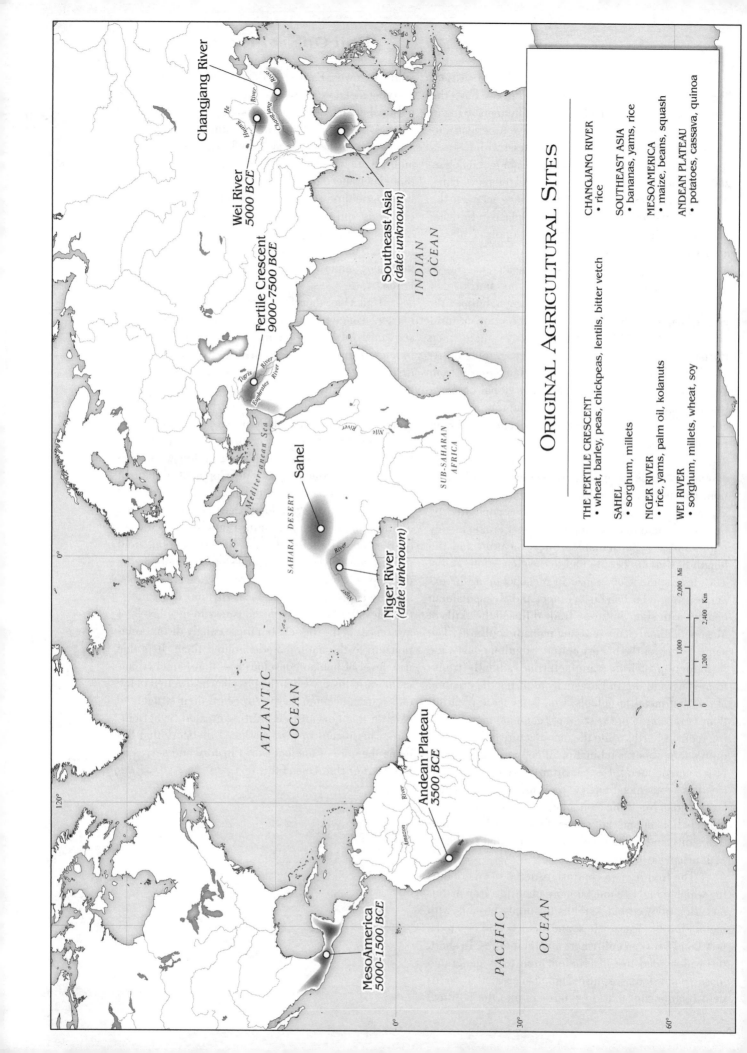

ORIGINAL AGRICULTURAL SITES

THE FERTILE CRESCENT
• wheat, barley, peas, chickpeas, lentils, bitter vetch

SAHEL
• sorghum, millets

NIGER RIVER
• rice, yams, palm oil, kolanuts

WEI RIVER
• sorghum, millets, wheat, soy

CHANGJANG RIVER
• rice

SOUTHEAST ASIA
• bananas, yams, rice

MESOAMERICA
• maize, beans, squash

ANDEAN PLATEAU
• potatoes, cassava, quinoa

Changjang River

Wei River
5000 BCE

Fertile Crescent
9000–7500 BCE

Southeast Asia
(date unknown)

Sahel

Niger River
(date unknown)

INDIAN OCEAN

Tigris River

Euphrates River

Mediterranean Sea

Nile River

SAHARA DESERT

SUB-SAHARAN AFRICA

Niger

ATLANTIC OCEAN

Andean Plateau
3500 BCE

Amazon River

MesoAmerica
5000–1500 BCE

PACIFIC OCEAN

0   1,000   2,000 Mi

0   1,200   2,400 Km

I

BIOLOGY
AND WORLD HISTORY:
Civilization and Nomads

The origins of agriculture mark the boundary between prehistory and history. Before the domestication of plants and animals, humans lived a nomadic existence of hunting and gathering. Since hunting and gathering involves following migratory animals, early humans continuously moved from place to place, which denied them the idle time necessary to develop the skills to produce a written history of their past. Instead, all the earliest humans left behind were fragments of their existence in the form of discarded or lost tools, broken or abandoned artifacts, deserted campsites, and some cave paintings. With the development of agriculture, however, humans finally had the chance to settle down, develop cities, and in time refine an urban division of labor that included scholars able to leave an organized record of their people's past. Thus, world civilization began about the time people opted for plant cultivation over hunting.

Yet the question remains: why would different groups of people at various times and in various places choose to abandon millions of years of living in harmony with the rhythms of nature in order to take up a new style of life based on agriculture? What forced different human populations to forsake a pattern of existence that matched all of their (and our) ancestors' needs and substitute for it the artificial mechanisms that eventually created ever more impenetrable buffers between humankind and nature?

Although not all historians agree on exactly why and how this change occurred, most of them believe that the primary factor common to people everywhere was population pressure. In any given place or time, once human numbers grew beyond what nature's bounty could support through a hunting-and-gathering lifestyle, people turned to cultivation to meet their growing demand for food. Each of these independent developments of cultivation evolved in synchronization with the local circumstances of climate, geographic location, and the numbers of humans, animals, and plants. Yet when and where these events occurred, and how rich a supply of food each one generated, depended on specific local conditions. In addition, the longer this process endured, the greater abundance and variety of foods it produced, and the geographic position of each site in relation to other human communities created great contrasts in the effect of agriculture on local human behavior. As a result, the oldest, richest, most fertile, and most strategically located cultivation sites played the largest role in the way agriculture shaped world history.

Those regions where agriculture started first produced the greatest supply and variety of foods and developed the first cities, therefore dominating the first chapters in the story of humanity. And those regions with the best material circumstances had a better chance of developing at a faster rate than others with fewer natural resources. The contrast between these sites, the consequences of these differences, and the diverse cultures they produced, all help to explain why there is such wide variation in the way early civilizations developed throughout the ancient world. The wealth, or dearth, of food produced, the strategic location, or relative isolation of one human group contrasted with another, and the creative potential fed by local conditions, all played a key role in the development of local culture. Finally, the study of all the local cultures taken together constitute the material for early world history.

Local Circumstances and the Domestication of Plants

To lay a foundation for understanding the part agriculture played in the origins of world history, one must begin with a broad assessment of geographic conditions. Two key themes play a central role in this assessment: *site*, which refers to the actual place where agriculture began, and *situation*, which refers to the relative location of this place in relation to other human communities. The more generous the natural resources of a site, and the more strategic its situation, the greater the impact agriculture would have on a given region.

Another crucial factor in the development of civilizations is a concept known as *land axis*. Given the general topography of the continents, land axis determined whether large sections of the Earth fell roughly within the same agriculturally productive climatic zones. A quick contrast of the three largest land masses will illustrate this point. Eurasia has a broad land axis that runs east and west. Because of the orientation of this axis, and because of a common temperate-zone stretching from Spain in the West to China in the East, much of Eurasia falls within what geographers call the *sunbelt*. If agriculture began in a strategic location on the Eurasian continent, say the Middle East, then domesticated plants and animals easily could spread from their point of origin to other zones of cultivation that shared common seasons, temperature, and moisture levels. The fact, therefore, that many of the earliest civilizations on the Eurasian continents developed a common crop-base using the same plants and animals whose original ancestors came from the Middle East should not come as a surprise.

In sharp contrast, the Americas have a broad land axis that runs north and south. Most of the land distribution in North America, Mesoamerica, and South America lies in such a way as to make a north-south axis dominant, as opposed to the east-west axis of Eurasia. But since the climate zones tend to run east-west, a north-south land axis naturally created a wide variety of agricultural conditions as one moves from north to south. Many of these climatic zones were inhospitable to the original plants and animals domesticated by Native Americans. Consequently, when humans did develop a successful relationship with local plants and animals in the Americas, they found it much more difficult to migrate with these resources to other locations. Hence, the spread of agriculture took much longer in the Americas than it did in Eurasia.

The continent of Africa is roughly 5,000 miles wide and 5,000 miles long. Thus, its land axis should have played a much less significant role in the development of agriculture. Yet the fact that the Sahara Desert begins just south of the Atlas Mountains in North Africa—in which rainfall amounted to less than an inch per year—eliminated many of the advantages enjoyed by Africa's east-west axis. In addition, the Sahara is the largest desert on Earth, with approximately 3 million square miles of sand dunes and wastelands, which precluded the possibility of plants and animals to the south having shared a common ancestry with those in the north. Hence, the lands cultivated in sub-Saharan Africa had plants of different origin to those native to Eurasia and North Africa. This made the African story unique when compared to the rest of the Eastern Hemisphere. And this placed sub-Saharan Africa in a state of isolation similar to that of the Americas.

Having made these broad statements about land axis, we move to an analysis of the sites where agriculture actually began. The point here is to determine why some sites were better suited to agriculture than others. This analysis also includes the relative location of these sites to other potential zones of cultivation once humans learned to live with certain plants and animals.

The original sites for the development of agriculture include the Middle East, the Wei Valley and Changjiang (Yangtze) River of China, the Central Valley of Mexico, the Andean highlands, and the Sudanese Belt and Niger River of Africa. One other possible site is in Southeast Asia. Each site served as the setting for a unique story and supplied a different array of plants and animals that were potential foods for humans. Of these various sites, one is the oldest, has the best location, and enjoys the best situation. This site comprises the Anatolian Highlands of Turkey, the Zagros Mountains of western Iran, and the Levant Coast of Syria, Lebanon, and Palestine. It is known as the *Fertile Crescent*.

The Fertile Crescent, the earliest zone of cultivation (9500–7500 BCE), has numerous advantages for those scholars wishing to study the effect of agriculture on urban society. First the Fertile Crescent is the most studied region in the world when it comes to the development of cultivation; modern researchers have by this time identified the wild ancestors of most of the domesticated plants in this region. The geographic range of the Fertile Crescent's plants also is well known, and the genetic changes these plants underwent in the process of domestication have been thoroughly documented. The result is that the Fertile Crescent serves as an excellent example of a site that provides almost all of the information necessary to gain an understanding of the importance of agriculture in the formation of urban civilization.

One reason for the early success enjoyed by the peoples of the Fertile Crescent in establishing agriculture is that the site featured both a Mediterranean climate and one of the largest and most centrally located land bridges in the world. Mild, wet winters and long, dry summers characterize a Mediterranean climate; such a climate encourages plants that grow rapidly, produce large seeds, and lay dormant until the next growing season. Known as *annuals*, these plants not only produce edible cereals and pulses (i.e., legumes like peas, lentils, and beans), but they also replenish their seeds each year. At the same time, they are self-pollinating, which allows humans to select and control each individual plant's reproductive cycle. Annuals also put more energy into seed production rather than stems, stocks, and plant fibers, and thus generate some of the most nutrient-rich foods in the world. And because their seeds are so large and lay dormant for so long, annuals are easy to store from one growing season to the next. Seed-gatherers in the Fertile Crescent had the extraordinary luck to have access to seven "founder plants" (i.e., the plants that provided sufficient nutritional value to establish the first agricultural communities). These seven founder plants included two different varieties of wheat, einkorn and emmer, and one each of barley, peas, chickpeas, lentils, and bitter vetch (a bean-like fruit of the leguminous plant *Vicia*), plus the fiber-plant, flax.

A second advantage the Fertile Crescent offered its residents was its strategic location in the world. Situated on a land bridge between North Africa, Europe, and Asia, the Fertile Crescent allowed the seven founder plants common to this region to spread far and wide. Given the basic east-west land axis of Eurasia, wheat, barley, peas, chickpeas, lentils, bitter vetch, and flax made their way across the North African coast, throughout Europe as far as Great Britain, and into Iraq, Iran, India, and as far north as Tibet.

In contrast, China, Mexico, the Andes, and the Sudanese Belt and Niger River of Africa offer far fewer advantages. China's size, relative isolation, and ecological diversity when compared to the Fertile Crescent produced a wide variety of human responses to local circumstances. Each of these responses represented how early farmers dealt with the specific climate, soil, and wildlife available for cultivation. The first of these responses occurred in the Wei River Valley around 5000 BCE due to an abundance of *loess*. Loess, an unusually deep and fertile topsoil rich in decayed organic materials, especially the lime produced from the decomposed shells of small creatures, is yellow in color, which gave the Yellow River its distinctive appearance. Deposited by the wind and spread by the flooding of local rivers, loess provides an excellent medium in which to cultivate plants. Spread along the floodplains of both the Wei and Yellow rivers, loess supplied the soil needed to cultivate plants in North China. Those plants first domesticated in North China included soybeans, millets, and sorghum. The Chinese later added wheat to this list of foods, but the DNA (genetic code) of Chinese wheat varied from that of the variety domesticated in the Fertile Crescent. In any event, while the combination of soybeans, millet, sorghum, and wheat provided the original food base for North China, these four crops could not match the immense nutritional output of the seven founder plants native to the Fertile Crescent.

While North China produced the four founder crops named above, South China experienced an independent agricultural revolution. Separated from the North by interior mountain ranges and distinctly different climates, South Chinese farmers could not grow wheat, millets, sorghum, and soybeans. Given an abundance of water due to both the monsoons and the Changjiang River, Southern Chinese farmers had to grow plants that had a high water tolerance. Accordingly, they managed to domesticate rice. As a result, two separate agricultural societies evolved in China as if they were continents apart.

While the internal circumstances of China isolated agricultural communities and denied the internal diffusion of plant species to create a common food base, the Americas developed cultivation under far more secluded geographic conditions. Large deserts transected the northern regions of Mexico and restricted cultivation to Central and Southern Mesoamerica. Also, the land bridge between Mesoamerica and South America proved to be virtually impassible because it is a very narrow isthmus covered with a dense jungle. Furthermore, the Andes Mountains along the west coast of South America rise sharply out of the Pacific Ocean to create a very narrow coastline with isolated mountains and valleys. Finally, both the Atlantic and the Pacific Oceans virtually quarantined the Americas from both Eurasia and Africa.

Beginning with Mesoamerica, the story of the domestication of plants in the Americas remains a long and confusing one. The key founder plant of Mexican agriculture, the wild ancestor of corn, still has not been identified with certainty to this day. Most experts argue, however, that a grass called *teosinte* (*Zea mexicana*), and not wild corn, provided the genetic material that led to domesticated *maize* (corn) from 5000 to 1500 BCE. Teosinte grows all over Central America and has been successfully crossbred with wild corn. This proves that both plants share compatible DNA, which suggests a common ancestry. And like maize, teosinte produces an eatable dry seed one can grind into flour or soften with water. Finally, teosinte, like corn, pops when heated. According to the argument for teosinte, the origins of ancient domesticated corn required constant human intervention to select individual plants that eventually evolved into maize. Once selected, ancient gatherers then preserved the most desirable traits by deliberately planting those varieties of teosinte with the largest cobs.

Arguing against the teosinte theory are some who believe that the original DNA for corn evolved from an ancient variety of popcorn. This argument states that wild popcorn is far more generous as a food than teosinte and would more likely have been selected for consumption. In order to render maize from teosinte, the counterargument continues, humans would have had to conduct centuries of very complicated selective breeding. Finally, the ancient farmers who cultivated teosinte would have had to have prior knowledge of what they were doing in order to produce the maize eaten today.

Despite the ongoing dispute between teosinte and popcorn as the original ancestor of corn, the most recent scenario for the domestication of maize is that an accidental cross-fertilization created a new grain. This most recent argument stated that teosinte serendipitously fertilized a wild grass called *gamagrass* or *tripsacum* to create an unusually hardy plant that also generated a better grain than its parent plants. Furthermore, desperation for food, rather than flavor, encouraged the cultivation of these robust teosinte-gamagrass offspring in a high-risk environment. The constant threat of drought common to the Oaxaca Valley of southwestern Mexico, where the domestication of corn occurred, would have motivated Mesoamerica's earliest farmers to cultivate any hardy plant capable of dealing with a quixotic climate. Over the course of several centuries, rather than thousands of years, as this new theory argues, the teosinte-gamagrass hybrid went from a low-yielding cob into what we now call corn today and would have led to the necessary knowledge of food production to create modern maize.

Separate from the current dispute over the ancestry of domesticated corn is another major flaw in this plant that must have added even more time to the discovery of maize as a reliable source of food. Each kernel of corn contains an indigestible supply of the vitamin niacin. If one consumes mostly corn without having prepared it properly, one will feel satisfied but soon develop a dangerous niacin deficiency that can lead to a disease called *pellagra*, which, unless the host ingests niacin, can be lethal. To make the niacin within the corn digestible, the kernels had to be boiled in a lime-rich water to produce either hominy or dough that could be baked into tortillas.

Despite all the problems associated with the domestication of corn, it became one of the founder crops of civilization. And to this founder crop, Mexican farmers added squash and beans. All three of these plants, combined with the chili pepper, compose "the Mexican trinity"—the three key plants—of Mesoamerica. The protein and carbohydrates from corn, beans, and squash supplied a sufficiently balanced diet to sustain human life, but such nutritional yield did not come close to the generosity offered by the seven plants found in the Fertile Crescent. Furthermore, the north-south land axis of Mesoamerica discouraged diffusion of these foods to other locations. Only after centuries of climatic adjustment did corn eventually make its way north; it did not arrive in the northeastern forests of North America until 200 CE.

Like the farmers of Mesoamerica, the first cultivators of the Andes had a very difficult time domesticating their staple plants, potatoes and beans. Just as the hunters and gatherers of Mexico lived in a harsh environment, the first farmers of the Andes selected beans and potatoes to supplement a scarce food supply. They began this process around 5000 BCE. Living at 8,500 feet, the Guitarrero people gathered fruits, potatoes, beans, lima beans, and chili peppers to supplement a diet of deer and rabbit. In the process of selecting their foods, the Guitarrero gained control over the reproductive cycle of plants capable of living at high altitudes. Grown on small plots of land near rivers and streams, potatoes and beans soon became the most common foods in the Andean diet.

Eventually ancient farmers in the Andes developed different strains of potatoes that could grow at various altitudes and in all kinds of soil and weather. Some of the potatoes they chose evolved into a rich starchy food highly preferred by humans. Others grew well at low altitudes and were selected because they stored water. Some grew fast enough so that they could adjust to the very short growing season found at the highest elevations of the Andes. Still others were chosen because they could be easily stored after they had been pressed and frozen in the cold mountain air. In fact, experts believe that some 3,000 varieties of potatoes exist today because of the careful selection process begun by the ancient South American farmers.

Given the many isolated valleys and mountains of the Andes, a diverse population of farmers slowly evolved in a difficult environment. With the addition of a South American founder plant called *quinoa* (a protein-rich grain the British today call corn), and a tuber called *cassava*, the total supply of cultivated food in the Andes eventually matched that found in Mesoamerica. Caught in the same kind of isolation as experienced in Mexico, however, the potato never made its way north into Mesoamerica until the Spanish Conquest. As a result, both Meso and South America developed independently of one another (5000 BCE–1492 CE), and neither experienced anything near the site and situation advantages of human groups in the Fertile Crescent when it came to plant migration.

The last known region to have domesticated its own founder crops is sub-Saharan Africa. Although sub-Saharan Africa exists in close proximity to the Fertile Crescent, none of the plants selected in this portion of Africa were related to wheat, barley, peas, lentils, chickpeas, or bitter vetch. As already mentioned, the east-west land axis of Eurasia permitted the founder crops of the Fertile Crescent to spread southwest into

North Africa and northwest into Europe, and east into Iraq, Iran, India, and Tibet. At the same time, these same crops diffused up the Nile as far as Ethiopia, where they stopped. The reason these plants were able to travel as far as they did was that much of North Africa, Europe, and Southwest Asia, and the long valley of the Nile as far south as Ethiopia, experienced mild, wet winters and long, dry summers: which happened to be the ideal climatic conditions for Fertile Crescent crops.

Just below the Sahara, however, in a region called the Sahel, the rainy season is exactly the opposite of that of the Mediterranean climate to the north. Rain falls mostly in the summer while the winters are dry. The founder crops of the Fertile Crescent therefore fared poorly in the Sahel; indeed, they drowned there during their dormant phase. But even if these plants could have adapted to this change in the rainfall pattern, there were already annual grasses in the Sahel that could provide the needed food—sorghum and millets. Since both of the latter are founder plants, they provided the necessary calories for the beginning of urban life. The date of their domestication, however, is unknown.

Meanwhile, just south of the Sahel lies a wet zone that would not support either sorghum or millets. Thus, like China, a second, independent process of domestication occurred in Africa, this one along the Niger River. These crops include African rice, yams, oil palms, and kola nuts. While yams and rice were founder crops, the yam proved to be the best at traveling with its farmers. African rice, therefore, remained confined to West Africa and did not accompany yams during the great human trek called the Bantu migration between 3000 BCE and 500 CE.

The last batch of founder plants grown in Africa was not native to this continent; rather they came from Southeast Asia. These include bananas, Asian yams, Asian rice, and taro, all of which traveled with Asian and Indonesian farmers across the India Ocean at an unknown date. Because the DNA of both Asian yams and rice are different from their African counterparts, these plants appear to have been domesticated independently in Southeast Asia at some unknown date. Of these two plants, Asian rice proved far more mobile than the African variety and spread throughout East Africa.

The contrast between the various geographic sites where the original domestication of plants took place, along with the number of founder crops involved in each process, defines the earliest date for the origin of cities and the available food surplus to feed people living in an urban setting. Just as important is the capacity for these plants to travel from one potential cultural hearth to another. Three factors all combined to determine how large the potential food surpluses might be during each harvest: 1) the earlier a plant fell under human control; 2) the greater the predictability of that plant's life cycle as a food source when compared to hunting and gathering; and 3) the total number of plants domesticated as dietary resources. Since a food surplus is defined as the number of seeds not needed by farmers either as the means to generate the next crop or as food itself, then the greater the size of the surplus, the more people it might release from agricultural work to engage in urban occupations and refine their skills. Hence, a large food suplus ensures a greater chance that writing, metallurgy, armies, and recorded religious speculation, philosophy, art, literature, and proto-science, the bases behind the term *civilization*, would appear. Therefore, historians in general agree that the beginning of agriculture marked the beginning of cities, and the beginning of cities marked the beginning of world history.

Given the list of cultural possibilities made available by the domestication of plants, the earlier a group of people began cultivation, and the farther they could travel, the greater their impact on a geographic region. Accordingly, the peoples of the Fertile Crescent had extraordinary advantages over those in China, the Americas, sub-Saharan Africa, and Southeast Asia. The Fertile Crescent, as mentioned, had seven founder crops, occupied the land bridge between Eurasia and Africa, diffused its food supply to India, Iraq, Iran, North Africa, and Europe, and gathered up many useful artifacts through trade with strangers on the fringes of sedentary agriculture. And once cities came into existence, trade joined the list of crucial urban activities and stimulated enormous growth in civilization. As a result, then, one cannot stress enough the advantages acquired by those cultures that founded the first cities in the Fertile Crescent.

Equally important as this history of the domestication of plants, yet subordinate in terms of food value, is the role played by the domestication of animals. The number of domesticated animals found in a region determined the availability of an alternative energy source to do labor for humans in the process of producing food. Also, the types of animals available for domestication determined the number of different uses humans could find to employ such a powerful resource. Yet to maintain an animal required use of land in such a way that denied plant cultivation on that parcel for humans. Furthermore, the ratio of the number of calories of plant matter needed to keep an animal alive, verses the number of calories this same animal represented in terms of meat protein, is 10 to 1; in other words it took 100,000 plant calories to produce 10,000 meat calories. Clearly, it was better to work an animal in the production of plants than to eat it. Hence, the domestication of animals is a subordinate story in the development of cities when compared to the domestication of plants.

The Domestication of Animals

The successful domestication of animals, like that of plants, depended on the available species of animals found in a particular geographic site and the situation of that site. Yet given an abundant variety of potentially domesticated animals, three questions still beg answers: What kind of temperament did these animals have? How social were they? And would they submit to human domination?

Once again, when compared to the rest of the world, the Fertile Crescent proved to have extraordinary advantages in its natural supply of domesticable animals. The superb site and situation of the Fertile Crescent allowed for the easy transfer of any animal species the people living there managed to domesticate. At the same time, the Fertile Crescent was rich in its variety of indigenous animal species. The Fertile Crescent there-

Llamas were useful not only as pack animals but also as a source of wool and meat, providing goods for trade with neighboring, nonnomadic communities. Possessing an even temperament, they were easily domesticated. Sassyhuaman, Incan site near Cuzco, Peru. Photo © 2006 Vagabum Mike Lopez (www.vagabum.com).

fore introduced to human use the greatest number of domesticated animals, which included cows or oxen, sheep, goats, and pigs. Although four species does not seem to be a whopping number, it is when compared to the total number of domesticated animals found in the world today.

Indeed, cows or oxen, sheep, goats, and pigs represent four of the five major animal species that people use throughout the world today. The fifth major species is the horse, which was domesticated in southern Russia and Mongolia. Besides these five, there are only nine other minor species of domesticated animals; these nine, however, did not travel as well as the original five. The minor nine include: the Arabian camel (one hump), the Bactrian camel (two humps) from Central Asia, the Andes camelets (the llama and the alpaca), the North African and Southeast Asian donkey, the north Eurasian reindeer, and the Himalayan and Southeast Asian water buffalo. Two local variations of cattle were distinct enough from those found in the Middle East to be listed separately: the Bali cow from Southeast Asia; and the mithan from India and Burma. In total, this combination of the major five and minor nine constitutes only fourteen animal species selected from a list of 148 potentially domesticated large herbivorous mammals. Native to Eurasia alone, twelve of these fourteen species did not reside below the Sahara Desert or live in the Americas. (Keep in mind that North Africa belonged culturally to the Middle East and is therefore considered part of Eurasia rather than Africa proper.) The remaining 134 potential candidates for domestication did not have the correct qualities that would make them useful to humans.

The correct qualities large herbivorous mammals need to possess to serve as domesticated animals depend on their diet, growth rate, breeding habits, disposition, and temperament, or tendency to panic. Diet refers to the amount of plant calories humans are willing to dedicate to an animal rather than to themselves. Growth rate defines how long it takes an unproductive offspring to reach useful adult maturity. Breeding in captivity is difficult because many species of mammals are too shy to allow humans to intervene in their reproductive cycle; disposition, then, refers to how aggressive a species of mammal might be, whether they will submit to human domination or instead try to injure their captors. Finally, temperament, the tendency to panic, refers to those species of large herbivorous mammals that damage or destroy themselves in captivity; these animals might be useful as game on the open plains but will not tolerate being confined in pens.

To these qualities must be added sociability: does the species in question live in herds; do individual animals within a local population of the species have a social hierarchy; and do these same individuals live in an overlapping range with other species of animals, or are they solitary? If a particular species of mammal lives in herds, it suggests that this species has established a social hierarchy; if a mammalian species lives in ranges that overlap those of other species, it suggests that this species will tolerate strangers. Hence, humans tend to select individual animals from a species that will accept people as a substitute for the dominant member of a herd. At the same time, if these individuals live in overlapping ranges with other species, these animals seem to be tolerant of strangers who seek to be their leader. Accordingly, all fourteen of both the major and minor species found on the list of most useful domesticated mammals in the world today possess both the right qualities and social disposition. And of these fourteen species, the ancient ancestors of four of the major five lived within the Fertile Crescent.

Because the Fertile Crescent included four of the five major species of large herbivorous domesticated mammals, it was twice blessed with exceptional biological resources. Of these four, one was an excellent draft animal, two provided wool, two supplied milk and milk products, and all four provided meat. Also, due to the early date of the domestication there of plants (9500 to 7500 BCE) and animals (9000 to 7000 BCE), the combination of both in the same region led to the possibility of improved farm tools. Oxen (*bos taurus*), usually castrated male cattle, proved to be very powerful, docile, and obedient creatures. Using oxen to pull up the stumps of felled trees, early farmers observed that dragging the roots along the freshly exposed soil prepared the land for cultivation. Hence, the plow came into existence. Yet, the effective use of such a heavy and cumbersome tool would not have been possible without the muscle power of the ox.

The plow itself, once discovered, then spread to wherever Fertile Crescent plants came under cultivation. Since the Mediterranean grasses of the Fertile Crescent traveled as far west as Spain, as far north as Great Britain, and as far east as Tibet, all the farm tools developed for planting arrived in these places soon afterward. Also, since the plow required a draft animal to drag it through the soil, all of the Fertile Crescent's four major species—cattle, sheep, goats, and pigs—spread to all of the above places as well. Combined with flax that produced linen as a fiber for clothing, the wool supplied by sheep and goats completed a list of materials useful both to people living at high altitudes and those engaged in river valley cultivation. Finally, the availability of milk from cows and goats and meat from all four species of domesticated mammals pro-

vided luxury food sources that complemented an overwhelmingly carbohydrate diet in all of the Mediterranean world.

As for China, the original domesticated animals there included the pig, the dog, and the chicken. Bones of these local animals appear in the earliest agriculture sites of Northern China. Still later, the Chinese domesticated ducks and geese as sources of meat and added the silkworm to create a unique fiber, silk, that remained a Chinese secret for centuries. At the same time, because of the east-west land axis of Eurasia, the Chinese ultimately acquired knowledge of the twelve species of large domesticated animals found in Eurasia today. From the major five, and seven of the minor nine (Eurasia did not import the alpaca or llama), the Chinese picked whatever they needed according to regional variations in local climate and the domesticated plants under cultivation. At the same time, the Chinese eventually had access to all of the Eurasian farm tools. To illustrate the power of the plow, in particular, one merely needs to look at the dramatic impact that the relatively late arrival of this tool had on Chinese history.

Chinese cultivation began as an independent discovery; as a result, it did not include knowledge of the Fertile Crescent's plow for 4,500 years (5000 to 500 BCE). Since the Chinese did not develop their own plow, this fact bears testimony to the absence of any large draft animals available for cultivation early in Chinese agricultural history. When the plow finally did arrive, it did so during the Iron Age, around 500 BCE, just as the Chinese had begun a time marked by extreme violence known as the Era of the Warring States (403–221 BCE). Earlier wooden plows probably never made it to China because the Himalayan Mountains and Gobi Desert excluded the use of this farm tool; high altitude and oasis cultivation does not require a plow. Yet once iron technology crossed the Himalayas and Gobi into China, including metal farm tools, Chinese cultivation changed from horticultural to agricultural. Also, by the Iron Age the Chinese had acquired knowledge of the large mammals it had chosen for use in heavy labor. Accordingly, the Chinese employed cattle as draft animals in the north and water buffalo in the south once the plow arrived.

The combination of iron, the plow, and large draft animals dramatically transformed food production in China. And the sudden abundance of new food surpluses in conjunction with the decline of the Zhou Dynasty (1050 to 256 BCE) released a large number of people from agricultural pursuits. Because the Era of the Warring States (403 to 221 BCE) began in nearly the same year as the arrival of the plow (500 BCE), one can conclude that local Chinese rulers chose to use their

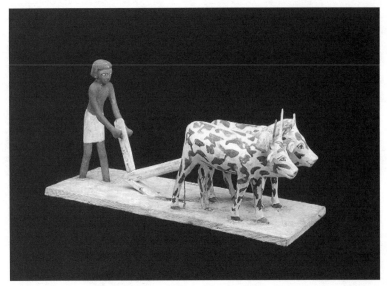

newfound surpluses of food to feed vast armies. At the end of this era of warfare, the victorious ruler, Qin Shih Huangdi (reigned 221–210 BCE), had the means to create the Chinese Empire. This suggests the extraordinary new urban division of labor at his disposal. Therefore, the arrival of the iron plow in Chinese history played a silent but fundamental role—it released enough people to fuel a new political order that converted China from a system of competing kingdoms into a united, fully integrated state.

Although the plow thoroughly changed Chinese history, it never arrived in the Americas or sub-Saharan Africa. In both places, the development of agriculture had to take place without the use of domesticated draft animals or valuable farm tools like the plow. When comparing both regions, however, the Americas represented the most dramatic example of geographic isolation. Therefore, we will consider the Americas first.

Quarantined by two great oceans, the Western Hemisphere experienced the arrival of human migrants very late in world history, near the end of the Pleistocene Era (the last Ice Age). Although currently in dispute by contemporary archaeologists, the route these migrants followed was probably across the frozen Bering Straits (once the Ice Age ended this ice bridge melted, separating the tips of present-day Russia and Alaska by seawater), while their arrival occurred some time between 15,000 to 30,000 years ago. The migrating hunters who crossed the ice sheets covering the Bering Straits found a rich supply of large herbivorous mammals that had never seen humans and did not recognize these newly arrived hunters as a threat. As a result, a mass extinction of indigenous American animal species began and ultimately eliminated nearly all the potential candidates for domestication. Accordingly, Mesoamerica had only three species of animals it found

useful—a hairless dog, later called the Chihuahua, the guinea pig, and the turkey. Clearly, these three animal species could not supply a significant amount of meat, labor, or potential clothing fibers when compared to cattle, sheep, goats, and pigs. Just as clearly, none of these three could pull a plow or a wheel-based cart. Consequently, human muscle had to supply all the labor necessary for food production, and to build cities in both Mexico and Central America.

In contrast, the natives of South America managed to domesticate both the llama and the alpaca—two high-altitude camelets. Because they lived higher than 16,000 feet above sea level, these two camelets probably escaped the mass extinction that had swept away other useful mammals. Like their Eurasian relatives, the Arabian and Bactrian camel, neither the llama nor the alpaca had a suitable body frame or disposition for pulling plows or carts, so neither could be used to enhance plant cultivation. Furthermore, neither the llama nor the alpaca were large enough to match the muscle-power of an ox, nor could either species carry as much weight as their larger Eurasian relatives. Still, the llama and alpaca gave South Americans advantages that Mesoamericans did not enjoy; Native Americans in the Andes had access to these small pack animals that could carry up to a hundred pounds of weight apiece, while supplying an excellent wool fiber useful for high-altitude lifestyles.

In contrast to the Americas, sub-Saharan Africa provided a more complex history of animal domestication, yet it still produced the same results. Given the abundance of large herbivorous mammals living in Africa today, one would expect that several of the major domesticated species available to the world might have come from a sub-Saharan source. In fact, however, sub-Saharan Africa did not produce any major variety of domesticated animals known to the world today. But all of the species native to sub-Saharan Africa were either too aggressive, combative, antisocial, or shy to allow humans to manage their lives. To complicate further the history of domesticated animals in sub-Saharan Africa, the tsetse fly precluded the arrival of foreign livestock. This lethal insect feeds off the blood of quadrupeds and causes a disease called "sleeping sickness" (*trypanosmiasis*). Like the mosquito that fed off humans, the female tsetse fly required blood to ovulate. Thus, each bite stimulated reproduction, so that the more animals a farmer brought into an area, the more flies soon confronted his herds. As a result, the tsetse fly created a disease barrier against the migration of the major five Eurasian species below the Sahara.

Fortunately, the tsetse fly did not live everywhere in sub-Saharan Africa; rather it was confined to the equatorial forests of the continent and spread only where there was enough animal blood, shade, and moisture to sustain its life cycle. Elsewhere, in the grasslands of the Sahel and the Nile Valley of Egypt and the Sudan, this deadly pest did not live. Hence, Eurasia's domesticated animals could penetrate into sub-Saharan Africa, but only in the limited range mentioned above. Accordingly, cattle, camels, and donkeys lived on the Sahel, while horses, cattle, sheep, and goats ventured into Egypt. Furthermore, a major movement of people from a region near modern Nigeria and Cameroon called the Bantu migration (3000 BCE to 500 CE) took cattle, sheep, and goats to South Africa over a 3,500-year trek. This trek took so long because those domesticated animals traveling with the Bantu required 2,000 years to acquire the immunities needed by all mammal species that crossed into tsetse-fly country. The tsetse fly therefore delayed, but did not deny absolutely the entry of domesticated animals into their range. Yet wherever humans took their animals, so the tsetse fly followed. Thus, the tsetse fly spread with the Bantu migrants.

Given these restrictions on animal migration, the plow and the wheel did not penetrate into sub-Saharan Africa—just as they failed to reach the Americas. Yet, the absence of both tools in African history was not caused solely by the absence of suitable draft animals, as in the case of the Americas. Instead, in sub-Saharan Africa there were several good reasons why the plow could not be used. Although cattle migrated into regions of cultivation below the Sahara, camels and donkeys were far more common as draft animals. Neither was suitable to pull a plow. Furthermore, the soils of the African grasslands, the region where cities appeared first, were poor and thin and did not respond well to cultivation with a plow. Indeed, if plowed, these same soils suffered from severe wind and water erosion due to the erratic rainfall in the area. Finally, anyone attempting to bring the plow into sub-Saharan Africa, would have had to cross as many geographic barriers as confronted those trying to bring it to China. So just as the plow awaited the Iron Age before entering China, sub-Saharan Africans acquired knowledge of this tool late in their history, but, for the reasons cited above, still did not put it to use.

In food production, meanwhile, the value of large domesticated animals, especially draft animals capable of pulling a plow, is immeasurable. In combination with the development of irrigation, the role of the plow

The tsetse fly compounded the problems of Africa's food production by carrying disease that killed valuable draft animals needed for heavy agricultural labor. Illustration courtesy Linda Gaio, 2006.

in accelerating efficient agriculture created such happy circumstances that they actually spurred the production of the first cities in world history. On the eastern arc of the Fertile Crescent, where so many founder plants and domesticated animals met, only one section of land could combine irrigation with the use of the plow. This region, the Shot-al-Arab district of Iraq and Susiana plain of Iran, represented only $^1/_{100}$ of the total land space in the Fertile Crescent. But on this relatively tiny patch of arable land, with its high water table, and marshy features, the plow functioned with supreme efficiency; it increased crop yields fifty-fold when compared to cultivation using hoes and pointed sticks. The result was a dramatic increase in food production in a severely restricted area. Such an environmentally attractive region, with an abundance of surplus food, led to an extraordinary concentration of people. At the same time, such a concentration of people resulted in the formation of the first urban hierarchy (the organization of cities, towns, and villages according to their function in the economy) between the years 6500 and 3000 BCE.

Beginning around 6500 BCE, near the ancient city of Susa in semi-arid southeast Iran, a number of residential agricultural villages formed on very small pieces of land. Covering a mere two to three acres, each village housed six or seven families and exploited the floodplains of local streams. Each flood season, fresh water and soil renewed the fertility of the fields and the villages generated rich crop yields using the plow. As population began to grow in response to the abundance of food, more of these villages began to pop up across this same region. Within five hundred years, irrigation began as teams of farmers dug little ditches to feed fields farther and farther away from their water source. Crop yields continued to increase, as well as human numbers, and soon some thirty villages clustered near all the available streams and rivers on the Susiana plain.

Between the years 5500 and 4600 BCE, the demand for water regulation increased dramatically as still more villages appeared in response to the continual growth in human numbers. Irrigation channels now required an organized division of labor, and an urban hierarchy replaced the original haphazard cluster of agricultural hamlets. One town on the site later occupied by Susa became the principal city; it covered some 18 to 20 acres while administering the region under cultivation. Ten larger villages of 7.5 to 10 acres in size provided for the local management of resources. And the remaining 29 villages cultivated the soil to supply this system with food. During this same period, large residences and local ceremonial centers appeared in the original Susa, forming the primary religious center of this new urban hierarchy.

By 4600 BCE, however, the number of settlements had decreased suddenly. Perhaps the population declined as well. Then, a new level of complexity entered the area as three large administrative centers took the place of one. Each new center comprised impressive monumental buildings, elaborate official residences, storage facilities, marketplaces, and large workshops. A system of administrative specialists and bureaucrats seems to have taken up residence in each of these centers, while the urban hierarchy that supported these three cities became more complex as well. No longer organized merely to exploit irrigation and food production, each settlement served as a central city by providing raw materials and manufactured goods, or engaging in commercial exchanges. Large and small cities and towns within the region reflected the availability of native resources and the demand for local services. Finally, by the year 3000 BCE, one city again dominated the Susiana plain, occupied ½ square mile of land, and administered all the large towns, villages, and agricultural hamlets in the area.

As this first urban hierarchy emerged on the Susiana Plain, so Mesopotamia underwent a transformation that paralleled these events; the land between the Tigris and Euphrates rivers built its own urban system 150 miles northwest of Susa. The first principal city to dominate the emerging Mesopotamian system, Uruk, appeared near the Euphrates River, and it grew far greater in size than the original Susa. Indeed, Uruk soon developed into an urban center that housed 30,000 people, covered 1,000 acres of land (approximately 1.55 square miles), featured a major temple, and administered an urban hierarchy that controlled ten times the number of farming villages as found on the Susiana Plain. Uruk continued to grow, becoming a veritable human magnet, as numerous people began to migrate into the region.

The point of this brief urban history is to illustrate that the earlier a city combined the productivity of the plow with a manageable system of irrigation, the sooner people would concentrate in a specific site, and the sooner that city would realize the correct circumstances to propel a human community to form an urban hierarchy. At the same time, the development of an urban hierarchy is a human response to growing population pressures that result in an ever-increasing demand for administrative skills. These skills, in turn, encourage occupational specialization, the development of an urban division of labor, regional exploitation of resources, critical thinking skills, and an impulse to literacy. Nonetheless, the absence of the plow or irrigation does not deny the development of an urban hierarchy; rather, it delays the process and explains, in part, why the people of the Fertile Crescent had such an enormous temporal advantage in the formation of cities.

As a result, similar human concentrations appeared elsewhere in the world, but later because either the food base did not include as many founder plants or domesticated animals or the combination of irrigation and the plow never formed. Thus, the cities of China followed the developmental pattern of Susa and Uruk but did so later because they lacked as rich a food base and the plow. The Valley of Oaxaca, Mexico, had to wait even longer than China because the original farmers in that area lacked domesticated animals, a plow, and irrigation. And even though the people of Cahokia (near present St. Louis, Missouri) enjoyed easy access to the seemingly limitless supply of fresh water from the Mississippi River, they had to wait the longest because they imported their knowledge of corn from Mexico and did not have draft animals or the plow. In each case, the appearance of cities required a concentration of people that depended on the availability of domesticated plants and animals as well as the proper farm technology.

The Biological and Cultural Consequences of Domestication

The domestication of plants and animals linked biology and culture in a reciprocal relationship that lifted humans out of the natural rhythms of hunting and gathering and placed different groups of people in specific artificial settings that became "civilization." The development of this reciprocal relationship between biology and culture that created civilization involved the way population pressures tied humans, plants, and animals to the term, *domestication,* itself. At the heart of domestication is a special relationship between organisms from two different species that requires both to maintain a long and productive association with one another: symbiosis. Agriculture produced many such forms of symbiosis, but it added a separate cultural consequence wherein farmers replaced the *natural selection* of biology with the *artificial selection* of cultivation. In other words, once humans had chosen the seeds they decided to plant, or the animals they decided to breed, they began to change specific portions of specific species' gene pools. The consequences of this artificial selection process then trapped humans, their plants, and their animals in a permanent relationship that spawned the beginning of what we consider world history. To understand this process better, one might well benefit from the consideration of a case study. And since the history of the Fertile Crescent is the most thoroughly explored and best-documented case study, it might be the ideal place to start.

The selection and cultivation of the seven founder plants and four major animal species of the Fertile Crescent led to the first set of symbioses that locked humans into a specific lifeway that ultimately resulted in the creation of urban hierarchies. These urban hierarchies, as mentioned earlier, then generated the administration skills needed to maintain and service an expanding system of agriculture. By selecting wheat, barley, peas, chickpeas, lentils, and bitter vetch, as well as cattle, sheep, goats, and pigs, the people of the Fertile Crescent created the food base of the first cities. And in the process of making these selections, the ancient farmers of the Middle East were the first to impose artificial selection over natural selection. They did so by always picking the seeds that were easiest to find, or the animals that were easiest to tame, thereby substituting human decisions for natural occurrences and forging the link between biology and culture.

A deeper look at this first case study reveals some of the consequences of artificial selection. By consistently choosing the seeds that were easiest to find, humans unwittingly selected those varieties of plants that belonged to the most unsuccessful portion of the gene pool for the seven founder species of the Fertile Crescent. Ironically, the ancient gatherers who collected these seeds picked the ones that remained with the parent plant and, thus, did not scatter and reproduce themselves in a natural setting. The reason these seeds did not scatter is that they were the genetic failures of their species. Since cereals like wheat and barley, and pulses like peas and lentils, use a genetic mechanism to cause their pods to burst and scatter, the seeds gathered for human consumption came from mutant plants that failed to explode properly and cast out their seeds. At the same time, since each of the seven founder plants were members of self-fertilizing species, these mutant seeds preserved the genetic mechanism that caused their failure to burst in the wild. By merely planting these seeds, early food gatherers would have preserved a population of wheat or lentils that should have become extinct in the wild. Thus, these ancient gatherers had selected the *omegas* of the plant gene pool (i.e., the least successful portion of the seed population). Accordingly, this human selection of omega seeds proved to be the critical step in the reproduction of these mutant plants that would have made each individual member of their respective species a failure in natural selection. In contrast, those wild seeds whose pods did burst and scatter, the *alphas* of the species, proved to be impossible to gather. At the same time, these alphas were the most successful individuals among the original wild members of these founder plants. Yet, as these seeds flew away, so did their genetic code.

The seed selection made by humans, therefore, created a gene pool of mutant plants that depended on artificial intervention to secure seed-germination. The success of these mutant plants under the care of humans increased the number of omega members of the founder species grown in the Fertile Crescent. At the same time, the success of farmers in feeding an ever-increasing human population using this omega gene pool caused humans to become dependent on these mutant plants and completed the circle of symbiosis, resulting in a mutual dependency. This process provided the biological basis for survival that defined the role agriculture played in linking humans to specific seeds in the production of food surpluses.

As the numbers of people increased, the combinations of labor needed to cultivate mutant plants also grew more complex. Such combinations of labor relied on the habits of cooperation learned from fishing and hunting but required new organizational systems to meet the needs of agriculture. The new organizational systems, in turn, led to deliberate soil, water, and land management that "closed the trap" of symbiosis between humans, cereals, and pulses. Thus, humans who lived off agriculture could no longer rely on access to fish or game in order to eat and began to poke the soil with digging-sticks, sow selected seeds, weed, and generally supplement their wild diet with ever increasing amounts of domesticated plant calories. Still regarding themselves as hunters or fishers, these humans slipped ever so slowly into farming without knowing it. Living off nature simply became increasingly more remote as grain dependency grew.

The symbiosis between humans and animals followed a similar scenario to that of domesticated plants. To domesticate members of any wild species of animal, a human first had to tame the individual animal and then successfully breed it in captivity. In the case of the first domesticated plants, mutant seeds incapable of flying far away on the wind combined both the taming and reproductive steps in the domestication process when farmers deliberately selected and planted omega cereals and pulses. In the case of animals, these two steps occurred as separate but complementary operations. The process began by selecting those members of the few species of animals capable of tolerating human intervention in their lifestyles. As already mentioned, each species had to have several key characteristics. How much did animal sustenance compete with land dedicated to human food production? How long did these animals take to mature into useful adults? Would these animals breed under the supervision of humans? Did they have an aggressive disposition? Did they tend to panic and destroy themselves in captivity? Did they form social hierarchies that humans could exploit? And did they graze peaceably with other, alien species?

Once humans had selected members of the few species that met these criteria, they then had to eliminate or replace the alpha males and females of a local herd. Those animals least likely to be tamed were the alphas because they had won sexual dominance in the wild; they comprised the most aggressive members of the social hierarchy who resisted domestication with a passion. The omega individuals, on the other hand, tended to be excluded by the alphas from access to sex and reproduction. Thus, the omegas were least likely to reproduce in the wild. Hence, if a human were to intervene and release the omega from the alpha's control, then reproduction in captivity could replace reproduction in the wild. Like the domestication of plants, this process of selection and breeding substituted artificial selection for natural selection and changed the gene pool of domesticated animals by making the tamer animals reproduce. Accordingly, those herds of animals that served humanity as domesticated species began to vary substantially from their wild ancestors.

Many species changed in size. Cows, pigs, and sheep became smaller because humans bred more stunted animals that ate less than did their wild ancestors. Also, because sheep produced wool, humans bred varieties of these animals that did not shed their fleece. Furthermore, since cows and goats produced milk, humans selected individuals that provided the highest yields. And as oxen and horses provided either strength, or served in the military, humans bred them to increase in size in order to maximize their strength and power. This latter example, however, required that humans also develop an easily growable plant fodder to feed larger animals, since most of the land had already been dedicated to producing food to sustain the human population.

In any event, once a band of humans had successfully domesticated a species of animal, its role in the new agricultural community depended on what type of agriculture the humans had decided to practice. If most of the land went to plant production, animals became a source of labor, provided fiber, or served as a luxury food. To reiterate, to produce 10,000 calories of animal flesh required 100,000 calories of plant life. If these 10,000 calories of animal flesh made up the bodies of humans, most of the plants produced in an area fed people; if these 10,000 calories were animals, most of the plants had to be used to feed herds. Hence, land dedicated to plant cultivation could not be used to raise livestock. Furthermore, once human numbers dependent on plant food grew too large for people to rely on animals for meat, then the land could no longer be dedicated to raising livestock. As a result, two types of symbioses marked the beginning of world history: *intensive* and *extensive* agriculture.

Intensive agriculture specialized in plant cultivation and derived its name from the labor required to produce each year's crops. Intensive agriculture yielded

Stonehenge, a massive Neolithic rock construction in England allowed farmers to calculate the angle of the sun as the timepiece for measuring the yearly planting cycle. Such a calendar was a key element of survival for farmers involved in intensive agriculture. Courtesy Anne Lynne Negus.

ten times more calories than did herding, generated a human population ten times as large, but confined the bulk of these people to a specific location (close to their fields) under the control of an urban hierarchy. Consequently, as this style of agriculture grew, so did the demand for management skills. The result was the development of an urban division of labor, the specialization of tasks, concepts of status and authority, calendars, religious explanation of the seasons and forces of nature, and writing. Some or all of these features of urban life eventually emerged if such a culture had enough time to grow and mature.

In contrast, extensive agriculture specialized in animals and derived its name from the amount of land it required to keep large herds alive. Extensive agriculture involved moving a herd from pasture to pasture in order to supply its needed plant calories. This method generated far fewer humans per square mile than did intensive cultivation, and it denied them permanent residence in any one locale, eliminating the possibility of developing urban skills. The result was that extensive agriculture did not produce the types of occupations that required an urban division of labor or a written history.

Thus the domestication of plants and animals set the stage for the dawn of world history. Once agriculture began, especially intensive agriculture, urbanization became possible. When urbanization occurred, writing became a distinct possibility as well. As writing emerged, an explicit record of the past could be developed and maintained. Hence, without agriculture, humanity would still live in a manner consistent with prehistorical times (i.e., the time before written records). For better or worse, the line between prehistory and history was drawn by the domestication of plants and animals. Once that line was drawn, and the supply of food produced by agriculture created the symbioses that brought specific human, plant, and animal populations into a reciprocal relationship that substituted artificial selection for natural selection, then a natural lifestyle like hunting and gathering had to give way permanently to urban existence. Accordingly, the domestication of plants and animals defined the conditions of possibility that humans later exploited to produce the great civilizations of world history.

The Nomads

As mentioned above, the domestication of plants and animals led to two different symbioses that marked the beginning of world history: intensive and extensive agriculture. Intensive agriculture required that people settle down permanently, generate food surpluses suf-

ficient to feed themselves as well as an urban population, expand until management skills produced an urban hierarchy, and resulted in what sedentary cultures call "civilization." On the other hand, the practice of extensive agriculture exploited the food, fibers, and pelts of domesticated animals, forced people to migrate with their herds in search of new pastures, denied the possibility of cities, and resulted in what plant specialists called "barbarism." Significantly, the contrast between these two terms, *civilization* and *barbarism*, suggests a history of hostility between intensive and extensive agricultural societies; this history, in turn, is based on a record of violence that marked the most dramatic and destructive episodes of the ancient world. Understanding what constituted the basis for this violence therefore requires an analysis of both agricultural systems to determine why sedentary peoples came to call people whom continued to practice the nomadic lifestyle "barbarians."

Extensive agriculturists usually traveled through flat, featureless terrain abundant in grasses and rich in wild species of horses. With the domestication of this swift animal, the nomads learned how to regulate the movement of their herds and defend their pastures. The role that war played in nomadic life derived from the fact that herders moved from pasture to pasture in these geographically featureless domains. They left no markers to define the boundaries of their grazing land. The absence of these markers, in turn, caused these nomads constantly to drive other herding communities from their pasturelands. At the same time, since these pastoralists had developed a symbiosis with one or more animal species, both the human and animal herd populations grew rapidly, creating an ever-greater demand for fresh supplies of grass. And with this steady expansion in the demand for more pastures, nomads faced a continual increase in the violence between competing communities as each one struggled to acquire enough food to feed their animals.

In contrast, plant specialists experienced a far more peaceful daily life. Each farming family had to leave its common dwelling, scatter into the various fields, and engage in back-breaking intensive labor. Warlike habits receded as such communities struggled to develop concepts of harmony that placed their members in a productive balance with nature. Also, since these people had taken up residence on permanent fields and lived in densely packed communities that enjoyed ten times the food calories available to nomads, the relationships between individual farming families required that they reinforce harmony to produce stable, sedentary societies. Peace, therefore, was far more practical than war in the normal lifestyle of agriculturalists. However, since sedentary farmers lived in an urban hierarchy capable of producing commodities unavailable to nomadic herders, not only did these cultivators generate attractive stores of food surpluses but they also created urban goods that nomads coveted, prompting nomads to raid sedentary towns. Consequently, plant cultivators made easy targets for the occasional attack generated by hostile nomads.

Because of the potential conflict between these two groups, a delicate balance of power began to develop between farmers and herders. As noted, sedentary cultures sustained far larger populations than did nomadic ones. Therefore, once exposed to the occasional attack by nomads, farmers released increasing numbers of people from agricultural work to develop the urban management skills necessary to design and implement defensive measures that could repulse the hit-and-run raids. For example, part of their urban division of labor supported by food-producing farmers became an occupation called "professional soldiers." Farmers' production also supported masons who built walls to protect cities and outlying farming villages that stored grain. And the fruits of their toil fed soldiers garrisoned in forts or outposts built as strategic defenses along viable approaches to their territory. Ironically, however, such a complex military response to nomadic raids never really created a foolproof barrier to the movement of shepherd peoples. As a result, no clearly drawn frontier existed between herders and farmers during all the years of ancient world history. In fact, no such clearly drawn frontier existed until the modern era had begun (after 1500 CE).

Meanwhile, when a sedentary culture was healthy, prosperous, and led by competent rulers, nomadic herders found their ability to take what they wanted from farmers severely limited. Therefore a second style of interaction developed between plant and animal specialists: trade replaced raids as the principal form of contact between these two types of communities. Instead of trying to snatch grain and other products by force, herders sought to exchange raw materials for the urban goods that the nomads could not produce for themselves. Such commerce proved attractive to plant specialists as well, for farmers tied to permanent fields had lost contact with the territory rich in soft metal ores, timber, and rare stones. Nomadic shepherds who trekked far and wide across the landscape had access to raw materials and attractive wild plants. Their herds also gave them a surplus of leather, pelts, meat, and milk products. The result was the birth and growth of a healthy commerce that often took the place of violence whenever these two groups of people met.

This balance between trade and raiding defined the long history of the interaction between migrating nomads and farmers in all the great eras of world history. Ultimately, huge nomadic raids brought to an end the ancient epoch with the fall of Rome, China, and India. Yet such moments of violence mark the extremes in world history; long before the end of the ancient Eurasian experience, nomads played an increasingly complex role in world history. This role comprised the impact of trade between sedentary and nomadic communities, affected the eras of massive human movement, and caused periodic confrontation between nomadic conquerors and their sedentary victims.

Disease History

Even as the symbiosis of agriculture drove plant specialists to form permanent settlements near their fields and develop cities, a second major biological story began to unfold: the history of disease. The development of local gene pools of parasites that invaded human, plant, and animal hosts linked disease history with geography and human movement to explain the complex relationships between symbiosis and parasitism that shaped Eurasian, African, and American civilizations. Beginning with sedentary cultivation, the combination of symbiosis and parasitism explains how humans, plants, animals, and their pathogens took up residence with one another, and traveled from place to place whenever ancient peoples engaged in trade or migration.

Punctuated with local accounts of how parasites joined the symbiotic relationship between humans and their domesticated species, this second biological story includes short, destructive bursts of epidemics that abruptly changed the course of history in various cultures. How these events came about depended on the immunities particular human groups had developed to their parasites as well as how the pathogens had adjusted to their hosts over time. Also, the site and situation of sedentary peoples helped determine how pathogens traveled from one culture to another.

Isolation reduced human contact and restricted the numbers of living things that took up residence with humans. Life on a land bridge, however, led to the development of a significant number of plants, animals, and pathogens that belonged to a culture's biological gene pool. The size and complexity of such a gene pool played a major role in world history.

Accordingly, this second biological story returns world history to that moment when humans first left Africa. At that moment, they also left behind their ear-

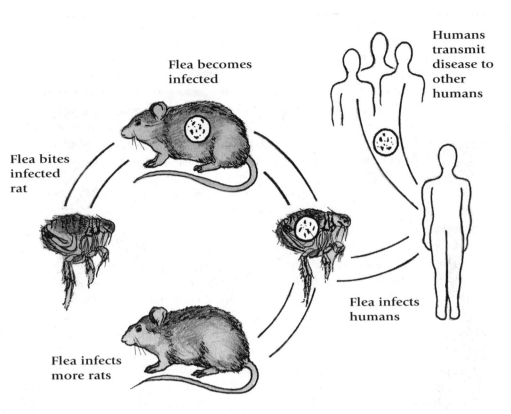

Flea becomes infected

Flea bites infected rat

Humans transmit disease to other humans

Flea infects humans

Flea infects more rats

Bubonic Plague Transmission. Rats infected with *yersinia pestis* are bitten by fleas, which then spread the plague to other rats through their bites. Infected rats traveled from Asia to Europe following trade routes. Infected fleas bit humans who got the disease and then spread it to others through contact. Few people had a natural immunity to the plague—though some did. During the mid– to late–fourteenth century, the plague swept across vast regions of Asia, the Middle East and Europe, killing millions. Illustration courtesy Linda Gaio, 2006.

liest parasites. Hence, hunter-gatherers living outside the boundaries of their original homeland basically led disease-free lives.

The small parasites and microorganisms of Africa's natural environment that created local disease *vectors* (organisms that transmit pathogens—often between species) did not exist in the arid, semi-arid, temperate, maritime, continental, or Arctic zones that migrating humans now occupied. The constant movement of ancient hunters in relatively small familial bands meant that these earliest nomadic communities did not stay long enough in any one region to create a waste problem. In addition, their impact on the environment proved to be relatively light. This impact changed, however, with the advent of intensive agriculture and sedentary life.

Those microorganisms such as viruses, bacteria, and protozoa, and small, visible parasites such as worms, insects, and rodents that enjoyed humans and their plants and animals as a food source, took up residence with the first farmers as all three increased in numbers. Since people became stationary once they became dependent on cultivation, they created a sanitation problem as their waste products accumulated. Hence, the concentration of people living near cities proved to be a very attractive resource to numerous parasites.

Native to the climates suitable for sedentary agriculture, these parasites joined the new urban habitat created by humans and caused numerous diseases.

Water-borne microparasites and worms combined with oral and anal pathogens generated by garbage and human waste to limit the total number of people who could live in the confined space of a city and its attendant farm sites. Airborne viruses carried on droplets of water found in human respiration also caused the spread of disease. Insects who had an appetite for human or animal blood or waste or domesticated plants accompanied farmers, often injecting them with germs through their saliva-filled bites. And due to the long association between domesticated animals and ancient farmers, pathogens that infected herds or beasts of burden also found a host in humans.

The pattern of association between humans and their parasites created a disease history that followed the principles of natural selection. Just as agriculture had changed the gene pool of domesticated plants and animals, so pathogens evolved through a dynamic relationship with their hosts. The key to understanding this pattern of evolution comes from the way two populations of organisms interacted through survival and reproduction.

The principle of natural selection links the existence of a species' populations located in different ecological niches with the possibility of reproduction among its survivors. Survival is necessary if one generation is to reproduce its successor, while reproduction itself determines the size and range of variation within the gene pool of the next generation. In the case of parasites associating with host animals or humans, the host itself functions as the ecological niche. A microorganism that kills its host destroys the niche and also dies. Hence, in the evolution of a disease, natural selection works on both the host and parasite populations at the same time.

New diseases find their hosts and start the process of natural selection. This first encounter is hard on both populations since the consequence is an epidemic. Infected humans die in large numbers; yet, as a host dies, so do their parasitic microorganisms.

Those humans with the capacity to survive this first encounter with an epidemic reproduce, passing on the resistance of both parents to their offspring. Those microorganisms that did not kill their host also survive, reproduce, and pass on to their next generation the common ability to live in but not kill their host. Thus, both populations, human and pathogen, evolve together, forging an equilibrium that keeps both alive through their association. While the human population would still suffer the ill effects of a local disease, after first contact the infection was not necessarily lethal.

Exceptions to this evolutionary process do exist, an example being the Bubonic Plague. This disease proved to be so deadly whenever it appeared that no adjustment was possible between the human hosts and the pathogen populations. Hence, such a disease appeared, killed massive numbers of humans, and then all but disappeared, seemingly waiting for the right conditions to reappear. These conditions involved the rodents and insects that carried the Bubonic Plague; the disease could lay dormant in the digestive tracts of fleas borne by rats and other rodents until the time to attack was once again ripe (meaning it found a host with no immunity). As such, however, lethal pathogens are far less successful in their association with humans then those parasites that evolved with their hosts: again, pathogens similar to those that cause Bubonic Plague wipe themselves out as they kill their hosts and then might lay dormant for centuries without reappearing.

Meanwhile, the more successful pathogens had not only evolved in response to their hosts but also had developed strategies that allowed them to move from one host to another making their victims sick but generally not killing them. These strategies included the production of symptoms such as coughing, skin lesions, diarrhea, and vomiting, which expel germs from one host and are likely to infect another. Furthermore, other pathogens hitched a biological ride using different, larger parasites, such as rodents or insects, so that the smaller microorganisms could make contact with humans through germ-rich insect bites or rodent feces. Accordingly the most successful parasites that caused

extremely deadly epidemics now had evolved into organisms that could feed off humans without destroying fertile adults capable of reproduction; instead, these germs tended to kill mostly children (in biological terms, those members of a gene pool most easily replaced). Simultaneously, those germs that killed mostly children shaped the surviving gene pool of the human population by skipping the most disease-resistant survivors, those individuals with a good chance of surviving into a sexually mature adult capable of reproduction. Together, the parasite and host had made an association that continued from generation to generation.

Hence, a key feature of understanding world history emerges. Civilization became a specific collection of populations—humans, plants, and animals—locked in a local symbiosis called agriculture that had, in turn, attracted an equally specific number of parasites. These humans, their plants and animals, and the parasites that had taken up residence with them frequently developed a successful relationship that kept all four groups of organisms alive—even if periodically ill. In effect, each civilization built up biological gene pools that combined domesticated plants, animals, and parasites that ancient sedentary peoples took with them whenever they traveled. Thus, travel itself became a biological pathway that changed the course of world history.

When humans engaged in trade, travel, or migration, they carried their food supply as well as their pathogens to a new site. Contact with another culture set in motion epidemics and food exchanges that could completely alter the biological basis of a civilization. These changes frequently upset the organization of cities and occasionally redefined a culture entirely. In fact, these changes sometimes changed the local balance of power in a region.

Thus the presence or absence of movement, the frequency of contact between different civilizations, the exchange of foods, urban products and ideas, and the transmission of diseases all profoundly expanded or restricted the biological resources at a civilization's disposal. People from the Fertile Crescent, for example, had an extraordinary number of plants and animals with which they had developed a symbiosis. Their long association with African and Asian cultures contributed both parasites and new foods to their cultural base. They also carried an enormous number of pathogens, parasites, and weeds with them wherever they went.

Therefore, disease history and human movement complete the story of biology as it relates to civilization and nomadism. Mesopotamia was the first site for urban development; its strategic location between three continents made this cultural zone a natural place for the beginning of human civilization. At the same time, the human gene pool of Mesopotamia developed a rich agricultural and disease history. The generous supply of foods and parasites that traveled into the region, and its function as a crossroads for other cultures, made the biology of Mesopotamia, and later, Eurasia very rich. This wealth would play a central role in the fundamental shifts of world history that followed.

Suggested Reading

Aldred, Cyril, *The Egyptians*, Third Revised Edition (New York: Thames and Hudson, 1998).

———. *The Cambridge History of Native Peoples of the Americas*, Three Volumes (1996–2000).

Davies, Nigel, *The Ancient Kingdom of Mexico* (London: Penguin Books, Reprint, ed., 1991).

Diamond, Jared, *Guns, Steel, and Germs: The Fate of Human Societies* (New York: Norton, 1999).

———, *The Third Chimpanzee: The Evolution and Future of the Human Animal*. See especially "Accidental Conquerors," pp. 235–149 (New York: Harper Collins Publishers), 1993.

Eubanks, Mary, "The Puzzle of Corn's Origins Coming Together," Society for American Archaeology Symposium, April 2, 2004.

Fagan, Brian M., *Kingdoms of Gold, Kingdoms of Jade: The Americas Before Columbus* (London: Thames and Hudson, 1991).

Fairbanks, John King and Edwin O. Reischauer, *China: Tradition and Transformation*, Revised Edition (Boston: Houghton Mifflin, 1989)

———, and Merle Goldman, *China: Tradition and Transformation* (Cambridge, Mass.: Harvard University Press, 1999).

Fiedel, Stuart, *Prehistory of the Americas*, Second Edition (Cambridge: Cambridge University Press, 1992).

Gernet, Jacques, *A History of Chinese Civilization*, Second Edition. Translated by J. R. Foster and Charles Hartman (Cambridge: Cambridge University Press, 1999).

Keay, John, *India: A History* (New York: Atlantic Monthly Press, 2000).

Martin, Phyllis M. and Patrick O'Meara, eds., *Africa*, Third Edition (Bloomington, Ind.: University of Indiana Press, 1995).

McNeill, William H., *Plagues and People* (New York: Anchor Press, 1976).

Pollock, Susan, *Ancient Mesopotamia: The Eden that Never Was* (Cambridge: Cambridge University Press, 1999).

Possehl, G. L., ed., *Harappan Civilization: A Contemporary Perspective* (New Delhi: Oxford & IBF Publishing Co., 1982).

Sanderson, Stephen K. *Social Transformations* (1995).

Stiebing, Jr., William H. *Ancient Near Eastern History and Culture* (New York: Longman, 2003).

Streuver, Stuart, ed., *Prehistoric Agriculture* (Garden City, New York: Natural History Press, 1971).

Toussaint-Samat, Maguelonne, *The History of Food* (Oxford, England: Blackwell Publishing, Inc., 2000).

Wenke, Robert J., *Patterns in Prehistory: Humankind's First Three Million Years* (New York, Oxford University Press, 1999).

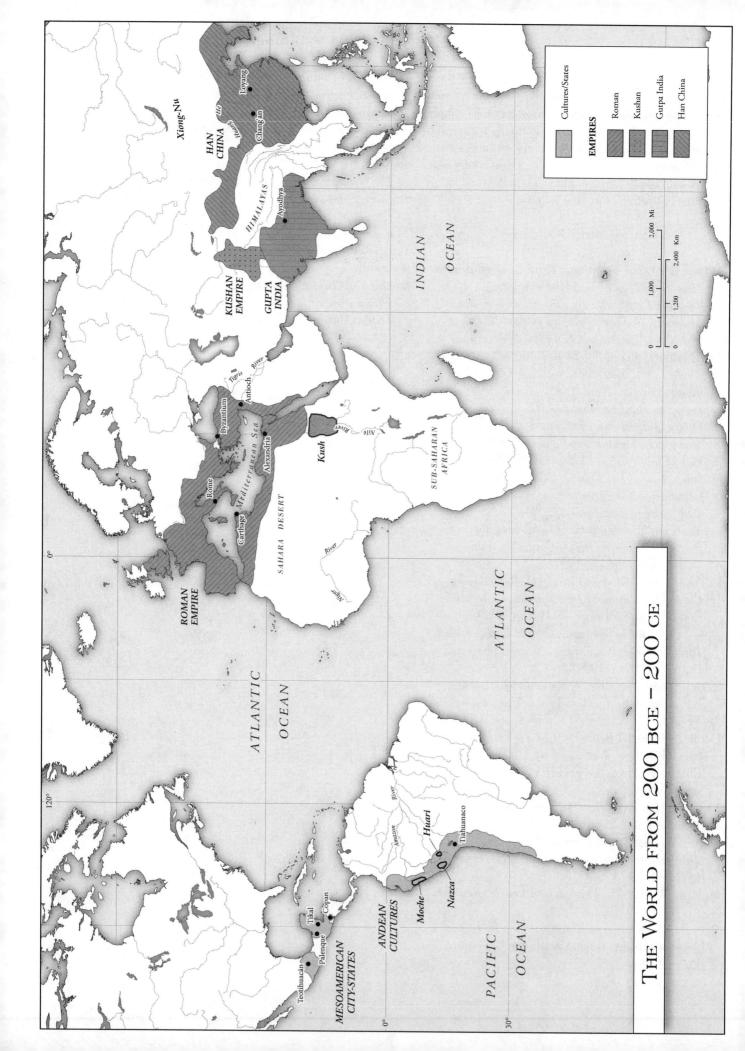

THE WORLD FROM 200 BCE – 200 CE

EMPIRES
Cultures/States
Roman
Kushan
Gupta India
Han China

Xiong-Nu

HAN
CHINA

Loyang

Chang'an

Huang River

HIMALAYAS

KUSHAN
EMPIRE

GUPTA
INDIA

Ayodhya

INDIAN
OCEAN

2,000 Mi

2,400 Km

1,000

1,200

0

0

Tigris River

Antioch

Byzantium

Mediterranean Sea

Alexandria

Nile River

Rome

Carthage

Kush

SUB-SAHARAN
AFRICA

ROMAN
EMPIRE

SAHARA DESERT

River

Niger

ATLANTIC
OCEAN

ATLANTIC
OCEAN

Teotihuacán

Palenque

Tikal

Copan

MESOAMERICAN
CITY-STATES

ANDEAN
CULTURES

Amazon River

Moche

Huari

Nazca

Tiahuanaco

PACIFIC
OCEAN

120°

0°

30°

0°

II

MESOPOTAMIA:
The Land between the Rivers

The Tigris and Euphrates rivers supplied water and nutrient-rich silt to the first permanent fields that fed the first cities in world history. Regularly overrunning their banks, the two rivers' water and mud swept across a broad floodplain called *Mesopotamia* (the Greek word for "the land between the rivers") to produce a complex flood pattern. Breaching their shallow riverbeds, the Tigris and Euphrates sent water rushing across the landscape bringing rich supplies of fresh silt each year to offer ancient farmers an excellent resource to begin their experiment with irrigation. As we have seen, their success with water management led to bountiful rewards by sharply increasing food surpluses while concentrating people on very small plots of land.

Each year the floods deposited on the plain fresh soil that nurtured domesticated wheat, barley, lentils, peas, chickpeas, bitter vetch, and flax. The first farmers, who once burned forests to clear fields to expose the land to both rainfall and sunlight, and then used the ash produced in the fires as fertilizer, now moved to the rivers after deforestation and desiccation had ruined their previous farmland. Caught in the trap of symbiosis, these early slash-and-burn cultivators had no choice but to carry their seeds to local streams and rivers to continue their dependency on the crops that fed their growing numbers.

Once they arrived at the Tigris and Euphrates, these farmers discovered they could significantly increase their food production in the rich, fertile region called the *Shot-al-Arab* (Iraq's marshlands at the Persian Gulf). And with these new agricultural surpluses, a large portion of the population freed itself from farming and took up urban occupations. As a result, a true urban division of labor began to emerge that included artisans, merchants, soldiers, and priests.

Accordingly, village sites at the mouth of the two great rivers in Mesopotamia developed into the first cities, the urban centers of Sumer. Migrating from Anatolia and the Zagros Mountains, the slash-and-burn farmers who created the Sumerian civilization took up residence in these marshlands, where their numbers greatly multiplied. There, by 3500 BCE, they built the first truly urban civilization in world history.

A Temple Economy

The new, nonfarming laborers residing in the first cities of Sumer came about as a result of the earliest form of authority that dominated the ancient urban centers. These administrators managed irrigation, developed a calendar, timed the seasonal steps in cultivation, secured the new food surpluses, stored seeds, and rationed the consumption of food after the harvest. Consequently, this authority produced the means to secure reliable provisions year after year. Yet only one occupation in this urban elite had the time to study nature long enough to acquire the knowledge needed to command and exercise this authority: these were the priests.

Ancient priests decoded nature, communicated with the gods, and sanctified the behavior that commanded local surpluses. Their knowledge of each year's seasonal cycle derived from a lunar calendar that set the rhythm of daily labor. This calendar relied on the phases of the moon to delineate the days of each month and mark the progress of the year. The twenty-eight-day cycle of each new moon created a natural timepiece that captured almost accurately the total number of days in a year. Since the moon fell short several days each year, the priests added a "leap" moon occasionally to reset this timepiece. The priests' acute knowledge of the seasons filled farmers with awe, giving priests significant powers in their agricultural society.

Awe itself functioned as a powerful social and religious force that held together the Sumerian occupational structure. The amazement that farmers felt in regard to the priests' knowledge convinced these food producers that they should fear and respect these "holy men." Awe coupled feelings of personal reverence with the religious magnetism found in the charismatic power invested in the priest's person. The word *charisma* takes its meaning from the original Greek definition, "a divine gift." Thus, the priest had a divine gift to talk to the gods, which gave him a unique command over nature and inspired dread among the local population. Consequently, awe became the sacred glue that bonded Sumeria's rural population to the new urban division of labor to create a coherent occupational system in the Shot-al-Arab.

Because of their apparent control over the forces of nature, priests could attract farmers to sites of worship and receive thanks in the form of food surpluses. This payment became the foundation for taxation and generated the wealth that priests believed they needed in order to please the gods. Regular submission to the authority of priests secured the pleasure of the gods and supported the first full-time urban labor force. Then the priests attracted artisans to their temples to make various items that continued to sustain the gods' good will. Thus did priests develop the authority to run these first Sumerian cities.

As mentioned, priestly authority also supported the artisan specialists who generated the first urban division of labor, which in turn created a temple economy. These temples, called *Ziggurats*, became the dominant structure located at the center of Sumerian cities. Surrounding the Ziggurat were dwellings for priests and the artisans and craftsmen who produced those goods the priests could use in trade. Increased urban production stimulated a growing demand for the importation of raw materials. This demand set in motion the import-export exchange that served as the foundation for regular commerce. Finally, the trade itself became the network through which Sumerian culture spread outward to affect the behavior of Sumeria's neighbors.

Cultural diffusion created the basis for the integration of river cultures with the surrounding rainfall zones. Now the nomads who had relied on a simple symbiosis with herds of domesticated animals began to branch out, seeking raw materials to trade to urban merchants. Staying in one place to satisfy the demand of these merchants caused a pattern of acculturation that partly or completely altered the nomadic lifestyle, causing people to settle down and establish resident marketplaces. These ex-nomads not only learned about urban production, the rewards of grain cultivation, and developed a dependency upon trade, but they also found themselves drawn into a growing matrix of cultures that crisscrossed the Fertile Crescent, which comprised Mesopotamia, southern Anatolia, and the Levant coast (Syria, Lebanon, and Israel/Palestine). This matrix created a general basin of regular contact between different peoples transforming Sumeria into a "mother culture."

The greater the general basin of contact became, the more these ex-nomads found themselves closely tied to civilization and more dependent on Sumerian trade. The reciprocal relationship that developed out of commerce, therefore, alerted ex-nomads to the potential wealth found in urban life. Now, any sign of weakness in Sumeria would undercut this commercial network as well as jeopardize the dependent relationships along the trade route.

The Causes of Trade

The Shot-Al-Arab provided the water and silt needed for cultivation. Yet this marshland did not have ready supplies of the stone, timber, and metal ores needed as building materials and to develop urban crafts. Consequently, while the river supplied the Sumerians with water, fish, fowl, reeds used for small boats, and mud for bricks that they used in their everyday lives, they still lacked critically important raw materials. Hence, the urban Sumerians sent specialists out to look for these raw materials, which suddenly were deemed essential.

The materials required by the new temple economies in Sumeria were imported from different places. Trade to local mountain areas provided stone and timber, but trips to regions as far away as Cyprus, Anatolia, and the Danube River Basin were necessary to acquire the copper and tin ores needed to make bronze. Traveling to these distant locations revealed how much energy the Sumerians had to invest in commerce in order to produce the urban goods they felt were vital to their culture.

In addition, cuprite, azurite, and malachite, the ores needed to make copper, required refinement prior to shipment back home in order to rid the metal of its waste products. Removing this waste material reduced the weight of raw copper by 90 percent and allowed merchants to ship nine times the load back to Sumeria. Such refinement required the concentration of a considerable amount of labor at the site of the distant copper mines. Simultaneously, the same type of labor-investment went into the preparation of cassiterite, or tin ore, prior to its shipment to Sumeria. Thus, both copper and tin demanded that the Sumerians make a major cultural commitment to trade in order to control the production of the vital substance bronze.

Sumerian merchants could not make such commercial trips and do the work themselves. Accordingly, they hit upon the idea of persuading local nomads to provide the required labor. Nomads, however, were accustomed to hunting, and gathering, and/or herding animals for a living and did not like to stay in one place. Thus, if they were to become miners, stonecutters, or lumberjacks to participate in this new trade network, they would have to redefine their lifeways by using the techniques of food production developed by Sumerians. As a result, nomads who accepted goods from Sumeria, gave up their hunting and gathering or herding to mine and refine ores, cut trees, and dress stone. And each ex-nomadic group that changed its labor patterns to engage in some facet of the temple economy of Sumeria found itself drawn away from its pastoral way of life. Thus, they made the transition to a sedentary existence and took up cultivation as they developed a dependency on this trade.

As a result, all the peoples between Sumeria and their trading sites in Cyprus, Anatolia, and the Danube River Basin experienced some degree of change. Those living on the floodplain closest to Sumer, like Akkadia, Babylon, and Assyria, became farmers and discovered that they could imitate the techniques of civilization developed by Sumeria's urban division of labor. Those in rainfall regions of the Fertile Crescent took up agriculture on a smaller scale, developed towns, and engaged in trade through labor invested in the acquisition of raw materials. This network of trade then set up several reciprocal relationships that supported all the participants, yet relied on the continued vitality of Sumerian culture.

In carrying out what had become a vast commerce, Sumerians developed wheeled vehicles that allowed the transport of goods over great distances. The network of culture sustained by this trade supported merchants who, at first, represented Sumerian priests, and later kings, as agents that had made contact with nomads. These merchants transformed the land between Sumeria and the sources of the raw materials needed in the Shot-al-Arab. Such mercantile occupations, however, could not have developed without an efficient Sumerian urban division of labor and a temple monopoly on the goods generated by food surpluses back home.

Kings, War, and Ecocide

Ironically, the success enjoyed by Sumerian cities in both food production and trade created the circumstances that eventually led to the collapse of Sumerian civilization in a terrible struggle over access to fresh water and soil. Sumerian culture matured and spread to produce a set of independent city-states along the Tigris and Euphrates rivers, with each urban center serving a specific god. These cities were independent because of the irregular flood pattern produced by these

two rivers each growing season. Since the rivers draw water from their tributaries located in highlands and mountains situated to the north—where winter snowfall is inconsistent on a yearly basis—every year's floods varied in water-volume.

Raging floods followed by drought also made the Tigris and Euphrates unreliable avenues of communication. Unable to create an urban hierarchy commanded by one universal *centerplace city* (the principal or capital city at the center of culture), Sumeria depended on a system of independent city-states that assembled each harvest at a "congress of the gods" to negotiate the distribution of water and silt. But, years of repeated success in food production and trade had caused the population of Sumeria to grow to the point where it exceeded the available resources; hence, disputes over water rights and silt soon began, driving the various city-states of this successful sedentary civilization to the brink of civil war.

This problem of success becoming failure reflected the consequences of the irrigation used by Sumerian cities to water each year's crops. Sumeria existed in an extremely hot and arid region in which the evaporation rate far exceeded precipitation and caused a sharp increase in the salt content of the local water supply. Given that the Sumerians routinely spread water out over the broad floodplain on which lay their permanent fields, the practice left a residue of salt behind each growing season. Furthermore, given the shallow riverbeds of both the Tigris and Euphrates, the evaporation rate even before irrigation left high concentrations of salt in the water each flood season. Hence, as the Sumerian civilization prospered, and the population grew, the demand on the local water supply caused the increase of both the evaporation rate and salt content in the soil. In other words the Sumerian city-states had begun to poison the land and drive their civilization farther upriver.

Sumeria's success at agriculture had also planted the seeds of destruction for this first and oldest civilization. The number of Sumerians grew beyond the limits of what local harvests could support in the Shot-al-Arab. Competition over water and soil resources among the confederation of cities spawned military rivalry, leading to war and encouraging the development of a new urban occupation: military specialists.

The military specialists were called *kings* and possessed a new charisma that distinguished them from the priests. The kings were warrior-champions who inspired a band of companions to follow them into battle to defend water rights or gain control of desirable land. Successful kings purported—and people believed—

that the gods had favored them with the military victories that secured the food needed to run the city. Given this new charismatic power within the civilization, these king-warrior-champions soon married into priestly families, thereby creating an alliance between religious and political authority. Soon priest/kings emerged, persons who continued to command the awe of religion, but also had the power to mobilize the military resources needed to defend territory and water rights. But since the food base used to support combat was strictly limited, these priest/kings had only a small supply of provisions available to dedicate to war; consequently, conflict was strictly seasonal, with relatively short periods in which to settle disputes.

Rivalries between cities, however, led to a self-destructive form of warfare that eventually weakened Sumeria and exposed it to alien conquest. One of these struggles led to the rise of Sargon the Great (ca. 2334–2279 BCE) who championed the cause of the northern city of Kish against the southern cities of Uruk, Umma, Lagash, and Ur, commanded by a single king, Lugalzagesi. A member of a Semitic linguistic group that had migrated to Sumeria from its homeland in Syria, Sargon and his fellow Semites lived among the Sumerians peacefully. Sargon served as the "cup-bearer" (chief minister) to the king of Kish, Urzababa, whose death at the hands of Lugalzagesi advanced Sargon's career by placing him in the role of Kish's savior. Exploiting this role, Sargon recruited fellow members of his linguistic group, created the first standing army, and relocated his capitol in Akkad, a city situated near the ancient Babylon—slightly north and west of Kish.

As king of Akkadia, Sargon the Great set in motion the first pattern of conquest, which spread his new military techniques throughout Mesopotamia. Sargon mobilized the first year-round standing army by committing all of Akkadia's food surpluses to his soldiers. Investing heavily in his new army, Sargon integrated Mesopotamia into one political system.

Victory, however, set in motion a problem of supply; Sargon needed food to feed his standing army. Since no one had ever before considered the issue of providing a supply system for a year-round mobilized force, Sargon found himself obligated to increase his direct command over the land by conquest as well as by purchase. Yet the price paid the sellers was little more than the value of grain produced for one year, while Sargon and his heirs gained the productive value of the land for four generations. Hence, both conquest and the undervalued purchases of fertile acreage created enormous unrest that increased with the added tribute and taxes paid by defeated subject states. But the constant threat of military action against those who refused

Akkadia's terms produced a condition of general strife that plagued Sargon's empire from its inception. When he died, Sargon's heirs had to maintain this system of royal estates, tribute, and taxation by using the same techniques, even though it was these techniques that enraged the residents of city after city, inspiring rebellion. Thus Akkadia fell to a combined invasion of nomads called the Guti and a rebellious subject-people as the whole region collapsed into chaos. The Guti had left the Zagros Mountains in eastern Iran, invaded Akkadia, and destroyed this first Mesopo-tamian Empire, while the Sumerians rose in rebellion and recovered command of the land.

From this chaos emerged Ur III, the third dynasty of Ur (ca. 2100–2000 BCE), that recovered Sumerian leadership some eighty years after the fall of Sargon's empire. The kings of Ur III created a bureaucracy to meet the problems Sargon's army faced; they planted royal officials and garrisons throughout their domain to administer the territory they had recovered from Akkadia. This bureaucratic innovation required the local royal officials to pay careful attention to tax collection, storage, and rationing. Such attention increased the burden carried by farmers as civilization's resource base. At the same time, the kings of Ur III developed laws to ensure a high level of conformity among their subject people. As this more coherent administrative structure imposed order, however, the strain on local farmers brought Ur III down: raids from a new Semitic group called the Amorites (migrants also from Syria but speaking a different dialect than Akkadian), regional rebellions, and a prolonged drought.

Yet the example that Sargon had set added conquest to trade as a second means of diffusing civilization outward. Every time a sedentary culture reached out to nomads for goods, or to defend themselves from potential attacks, cultural information spread out from one zone to another. Each new group of humans brought into the circle of sedentary life expanded the contacts made between farmers and nomads and compounded the problems of government. Thus, original civilizations like Sumeria shaped the people around them and were, in turn, shaped by the military and biological threats these contacts created.

New cultural hearths, therefore, emerged in regions influenced by Sumeria. This pattern of cultural diffusion slowly integrated local rainfall districts with peoples living upriver from Sumeria until the entire region began to take on a common material stamp. Yet, distance and religious differences set these other, alien cultures apart from Sumeria and encouraged independent urban development based on local agricultural conditions.

In the meantime, peoples living in arid and semi-arid regions like Sumeria, who occupied geographic sites that required similar patterns of human labor to produce food, put lessons learned from Sumeria to good use. Such cultures emerged in Egypt and the Indus River Valley to the west and east of Sumeria, respectively, and adopted similar agricultural methods. Yet both of these new civilizations developed along independent cultural lines. And at the same time, both of these new cultures became parts of an expanding trade network originally set in motion by Sumerian merchants. Now all three civilizations grew in complexity and added to the cultural changes in the surrounding rainfall zones.

The Art of Writing and Hammurabi's Code

As the general complexity of civilization grew in each independent river-based site, a new and highly specialized skill had to be developed to track and manage the allocation of yearly food production. Developed first in Sumeria as part of the political evolution of Mesopotamia, this special skill allowed priests to run their temple economies before the appearance of kings. The addition of kings merely increased the complexity that had required this skill in the first place. In addition, just as this skill had appeared in Sumeria, so it developed naturally in Egypt and the Indus River Valley. This skill was writing.

Writing became a key technical achievement added to the growing urban division of labor found in Sumeria as well as Egypt and India. It established a way to plan the course of an increasingly complex set of yearly transactions. As Sumerian cities expanded production in both agriculture and manufacturing, storage and rationing requirements grew as well. The planning needed for trade expeditions made writing an essential tool to the success of Sumerian culture. These same features drove the Egyptians and Indians to develop their own forms.

An accounting of the resources available to this increasingly complex culture in Sumeria led to a new urban occupation, that of *scribe*. Closely affiliated with priests, the scribes had to keep records of the food surpluses gathered each year that sustained the division of labor found in cities. As urban life and trade grew to encompass more and more people and goods, scribes found themselves encouraged to increase speed and accuracy of their written inventories, accounts, and histories. Such pressure launched an innovative use of *pictographs*, which became simplified into abstract symbols.

An example of cuneiform writing. Essential to trade, writing began as a means to keep a vital inventory. Beginning as pictographs combined with numerals, early lists of a Sumerian city's wealth facilitated rationing the yearly harvest and exchanges with nomads. Later writing used ideograms, or abstract images, and finally words to capture abstract ideas. Courtesy of Touraj Daryaee.

These abstract, simplified symbols tended to reflect the medium in which the records were kept. The Sumerians used soft clay and reed sticks that led them to develop *cuneiform* (wedge writing), while Egyptians used papyrus paper, a quill, and ink. As a result, Sumerian cuneiform was rigid and restricted in the images that it could produce, while Egyptian writing became far more fluid and pictorial. Also, the fact that Sumerian itself was a monosyllabic language encouraged these Mesopotamian scribes to develop *ideograms* in a manner similar to those used in Chinese, another monosyllabic language. Since ideograms captured concepts rather than sounds, this style of writing soon became common throughout Mesopotamia, for while the sounds of Akkadian and Babylonian varied, the concepts in all three cultures did not.

Furthermore, as the pictographs that the Sumerians originally used to capture their ideas slowly evolved into ideograms, scribes generated long lists of nouns in order to keep track of local inventories of goods, which in turn allowed priests and kings to determine what their agricultural surpluses had produced. Finally, these same scribes discovered that they could use homophones (i.e., words with the same sound: to, too, two) as a means to capture the image of action with an ideogram (an abstract picture representing a concept such as $, %). Since some Sumerian nouns shared the same sounds as their verbs, so the ideogram for an object could be substituted for the action of an event within a Sumerian sentence. What the Sumerian scribe did was use the ideogram for the noun in the location of the

Papyrus from the Book of the Dead of Nakht, 1350–1300 BCE. Nakht was a royal scribe and army commander near the end of the eighteenth dynasty. This papyrus demonstrates the use of heiroglyphics as well as scenes to show the afterlife for Nakht. Unlike depictions of royal afterlife, this is more a reflection of an ordinary Egyptian in that the deceased was expected to undertake agricultural activities. Thebes, Egypt. © The Trustees of the British Museum.

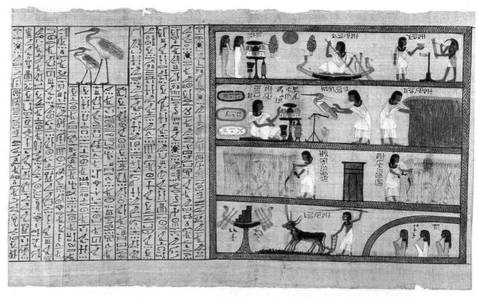

verb within the sentence structure so that the sound conveyed the meaning. In order to differentiate better the noun from the verb, these scribes created a determinate to separate the two words. This change in word usage, and the creation of a determinate, produced the concept of grammar and phonetic symbols. Hence, now a writer could link a subject to a verb and an object to convey a complete thought, while using other symbols to convey sounds rather than concepts.

Rigorous standardization of Sumerian ideograms, and the systematic assembly of these wedges, created a pattern of ancient spelling that all Sumerian scribes had to master. Also, the ridged, pointed sticks and awkward medium of clay used by Sumerians encouraged a system of puns which in turn, led to a style of thought based on analogy (the inference that if two things agree on several features, they must do so on others as well, as in the example of metaphors and similes). Thus, the limitations of the reed stick and clay helped to develop a set of abstract of images and sounds that encouraged a poetic imagination. Accordingly, Sumerian scribes developed the ability to construct complex, rhythmic concepts that functioned to enhance their memory.

Meanwhile, the role of writing in civilization greatly enhanced the ability of kings to command resources and control space. Thus, one of the major cultural developments of the Bronze Age was a complete and coherent written legal code. Developed in Mesopotamia 250 years after the administrative innovations of Ur III, this complex legal code logically extended the Sumerian idea of the law and bureaucracy into its next stage of political development: the first systemic compilation of civil and criminal law.

The creator of this code, an Amorite named Hammurabi, found that he could control his empire centered on Babylon best by dispersing soldiers with bureaucratic officials to staff local garrisons. The complexity of such a system, however, required the keeping of detailed records and the strict conformity of subject peoples. This level of conformity inspired a new system of law as a way of directing positive behavior among peoples of widely different cultural backgrounds. The result was a standardized code of conduct in each garrison town, as well as conformity among the general population.

Hammurabi compiled his code during the eighteenth century BCE and solved the problem of supply identified by Sargon, while also reducing the threat of rebellion that plagued Ur III. His code involved positive law that stated what a person must do. Much more severe than negative law, which states what a person cannot do but leaves everything else open to choice, Hammurabi's code revealed how tightly controlled his command over food surpluses had to be to run his empire. Unless everyone obeyed the law, the system would run short of resources.

Comprised of 282 decrees, Hammurabi's code defined crimes against the state as well as violations of civil law. Crimes against the state were actions by individuals that deprived the king of a valuable person or property. The punishment matched the crime and extracted sufficient pain or wealth to compensate the state for its loss. Civil violations, however, dominated the code by setting standards of conduct for private parties as they carried out their normal daily activities.

At the heart of this code lay harsh standards of justice and public morality designed to impose strict order on an increasingly complex political world. Here issues of marriage, inheritance, family relations, property rights, business practices, and professional competence defined the way society ought to work. These complex social and economic issues determined one's status and value, as well as defined the role of the sexes and described the duty of children to their parents. The goal was to create and maintain a smooth running community with standards of conduct that proved binding for all members. When nobles injured commoners, these aristocrats had to pay a price appropriate to the status of the injured party. When a husband divorced his wife, he had to return the bride's price agreed upon at the beginning of the marriage. When a son disrespected his father, the child lost his inheritance. When women committed adultery, they suffered the death of a witch: they were cast bound into the Euphrates to see if the river accepted them, which proved their innocence. (Unfortunately, the innocent drowned as often as did the guilty.) And if a doctor proved to be incompetent, he lost his hands to prevent him from injuring another patient.

The General Matrix of Civilization

For two thousand years civilization spread from its points of origins outward, with Mesopotamia and Egypt joining with the Indus River Valley to display common features of river-based agriculture. Yet the distance between these cultural zones ensured that separate urban societies would develop along independent lines of tradition. Local traditions created different patterns of behavior based on common agricultural techniques. Diverse geographic circumstances encouraged these local variations and sustained differences in tradition. Hence, the unique cultures that first arose along river basins were able to follow independent developmental paths.

Because of the way these earliest civilizations arose, interacted with their locales, and spread outward in pursuit of raw materials, they drew more and more local nomadic peoples into the circle of sedentary life. Soon the cultural complexity of the zones between Egypt, Sumeria, and the Indus River created an awareness of the wealth that civilization could generate. Yet when compared to Egypt and the Indus, Mesopotamia made the greatest number of contacts with nomadic peoples given the paucity of raw materials in "the Land between the Rivers." The very location of the Shot-al-Arab district, strategically situated on the land bridge of Eurasia and Africa, made Sumeria, and later Akkadia, Babylonia, and Assyria, the principal commercial avenue connecting Mesopotamia to its neighbors. But this location also attracted the greatest number of invaders and nomadic raiders.

Migration, occasional invasions, and the formation of smaller local cultures within a given region punctuated the spread of sedentary civilization. The area stretching between these river-based cultures developed into a complex, vibrant, and dynamic human zone.

In this way, rainfall regions linked with core civilizations to integrate a complex reciprocal system of cultural exchanges.

The basic apparatus of civilization, however, never needed reinvention after Sumeria's beginnings. All of the regions of the Middle East and the Mediterranean proved to be the beneficiaries of these early foundations, with writing, calendars, basic math, irrigation, the potter's wheel, the wheel itself, bronze, and the plow spreading far and wide. And the obvious advantages of civilization served as a model that stimulated concepts of law and exchange.

The Dawn of Religion: Creation Myths

The foundation for the Western religious perspective began in Mesopotamia with an assumption that an understanding of natural events, reason, and divine motivations combined to explain reality. This perspective demonstrated an awareness that agriculture had emerged in an arid setting in which life had become a struggle for existence. This struggle contrasted sharply with memories of the relative ease that hunter-gatherers had enjoyed but then helped to create the image of a paradise lost, a storyline that runs parallel to the parable of The Garden of Eden.

Most people are unaware of the irony that hunter-gatherers led lives of relative leisure, free from disease, and with a low demand for daily labor as compared to their farming descendants. Scholars agree that the earliest *homo sapiens* followed the game each year, carrying with them everything they owned, but had ready access to a bounty of food that cut their working time to only several hours per day. Trace memories of this leisure can be seen in numerous stories like the Garden of Eden that spoke of how the ancestors of farmers had lived in harmony with nature. Men hunted and women gathered because menstruation and repeated pregnancies tied females to local camps. Yearly treks from campsite to campsite, in pursuit of animal herds, caused a high miscarriage rate and extended nursing, which sharply reduced female fertility but kept human numbers in balance with their food supply. Low human numbers and a ready supply of food meant a life free from the backbreaking labor that the symbiosis of agriculture had created with its ever-increasing population pressures on the local environment. Only a shift in climate at the end of the last Ice Age (ca. 14,000 years ago) could change the population dynamics of hunting and gathering and cause people to settle down.

As stated above, when the first cities emerged the complexity of food production increased. Growing populations expanded the demand for more labor to feed the increasing numbers of people. In Mesopotamia, each generation lived off the grain harvested but also had to build, maintain, and repair increasingly more complex irrigation systems. Furthermore, these people had to meet the necessity of storing food surpluses so that humans could eat during those seasons in which wheat did not grow. They also had to develop a religious-political administration system to oversee their combined, cooperative efforts. Life did not get simpler; rather the complexity of civilization expanded the labor requirements of civilization and deepened the trap of symbiosis.

Given the harsh conditions of life in Mesopotamia, a general attitude toward nature developed that diffused from Sumeria to Assyria. This attitude saw nature as hostile, a monstrous realm of chaos that humans and the gods had to defeat in order for civilization to exist. Only constant labor, it seemed, could overcome the obstacles that nature tried to impose on humanity.

The gods were powerful figures who authorized order through their capacity to preside over natural forces. These deities guarded Sumerian cities as patrons whose assembly represented all of Sumeria's combined power. Government and society derived from the authority of the gods. That authority ordained all the offices and occupations that made up the social structure and the division of labor in a Sumerian city.

Believing that humans were given "charisma" as divine gifts, each occupation held a special place in the Sumerian division of labor. As a result, the whole fabric of society became sacred, while the surrounding alien world became profane. Each child born into a family inherited the charisma of its parents and perpetuated the divine order of things. The social hierarchy itself became a consecrated system of status with priests/kings possessing semidivine natures. Every act, skill, and occupation became an integrated tool useful in keeping the gods happy. Hence, society itself existed in alliance with the gods to achieve mastery over nature.

Later renamed Marduk by the Babylonians, Sumerians held that their chief deity, Enlil, defeated a primal female monster that embodied nature and divided her body into numerous parts, which then spread out to create the world. Like the Sumerian Enlil, the Babylonian Marduk organized the world out of a marsh by cutting into the landscape and claiming pieces of earth that humans could put to use. This act shaped islands that rose out of the water-soaked land through controlling the floods that made the environment chaotic.

Throughout Mesopotamian history, Sumerians, Akkadians, Babylonians, and Assyrians believed that irrigation, a floodplain, cultivated fields, cities, and or-

der all derived from a human victory over nature authorized by the gods. Awed by the power of the gods in controlling the forces of nature, Sumerians and Babylonians alike obeyed the authority vested in their social structure. Each of them kept within their appropriate social stations, and stood at the ready to maintain the divine order of their societies. Society itself was a hard-won fight against chaos that constantly had to be maintained.

The design of Mesopotamian towns, featuring carefully laid out grid-patterned streets and walled fortifications spoke of a commitment to order. The repetition of a common layout in both city design and field patterns, both with an emphasis on right angles, spoke to a sensitivity felt by all Mesopotamian cultures that they would keep their land only through ceaseless struggle. Periodically, unreliable and capricious rivers overran their banks, walls of water smashing into sun-baked, mud-brick houses with a vengeance that destroyed much of what had been carved out of nature by civilization.

Only the constant vigilance of regular repairs of irrigation channels and canals saved cities from destruction. Well-built Ziggurats made of baked brick that rose above the highest flood levels served as places of refuge when an extraordinarily bad flood wrecked the network of channels and canals. Finally, intense labor in the orderly and well-kept fields led to rich rewards in the form of food surpluses that sustained urban life and fought the chaos of nature. In essence, as much was invested in the perceived war against nature as was committed to the defense of the town against foreign enemies.

In the worldview of the peoples of Mesopotamia, all that was wild had to be tamed if it was to be of use. Sumeria's list of domesticated animals and plants reveals the energy the Sumerians had invested in manipulating the resources nature had to offer. Once defined by their use to humans, natural things lost their threatening character; they seemingly had been defeated and made submissive. In time those plants and animals that had become useful resources to humans were deemed good, while those that had remained wild were bad. Likewise, an object's usefulness to humanity came to define that object's character in human eyes.

For all their effort, the Sumerians and their heirs lost the struggle with nature. As mentioned above, the high salt content of the water used in their irrigation system left an increasingly thick mineral residue in their fields. Their success in taming the landscape increased the area they irrigated, but thereby pressed their water supply to its limits. The symbiosis between grains, humans, and animals eventually created such a strain on the ecosystem that cultivated fields began to lose their fertility to the mounting levels of salt left in the soil. Ironically, each year of Sumeria's victory over nature marked another season of added salt to the land, which led to their defeat.

Indeed, as soil downstream lost its capacity to produce the rich crops needed to sustain urban life, civilization in Mesopotamia then began a gradual retreat upstream. Sumeria gave way to Akkadia, which in turn surrendered to Babylonia. Finally, Babylonia fell to Assyria, the last of the great civilizations in the land between the rivers. Each step in this migration was a move into the district immediately upstream. Assyria represented the last such step as the entire region became increasingly infertile. Only the discovery of salt-resistant plants such as alfalfa would later restore a degree of fertility to the region.

Iron and Mesopotamia

By 1400 BCE, iron appeared in the ancient Near East, and then diffused outward slowly to reach Europe, Asia, and Africa by 600 BCE. The complicated technique for making iron tools has been credited to the Hittites, a nomadic people who conquered Anatolia in 1600 BCE and subjugated the local population. Originally the Hittites closely guarded the technique for making iron as a state secret, but the Anatolian artisans who had discovered how to produce useful iron tools, and who worked for their Hittite masters neither spoke the same language nor shared the same traditions or culture. These artisans therefore felt no obligation to honor the Hittite demand to keep iron manufacturing a secret.

What these artisans had learned was that common ores like hematite, limonite, biotite, ilmenite, magnetite, and goethite yielded a raw metal when heated in charcoal until red hot and then hammered. The hammering mixed the carbon from the fuel with the metal tool being made, which made iron as hard, flexible, and resilient as bronze when cooled suddenly. This cooling process, called tempering, trapped the carbon molecules within the iron and eliminated the brittleness that plagued cast-iron products. Thus, this useful combination of qualities found in tempered iron made the metal an excellent substitute for bronze.

Because the ores used to make iron happen to be among the most common on the planet, especially when compared to the mixtures of tin and copper required for bronze, every worker or farmer living in a sedentary culture suddenly had access to valuable tools. The general availability of iron made this metal technology both cheap and easy to distribute once the secrets of smelting ores and hammering iron became generally known.

When a major migration of Indo-European nomads destroyed the Hittite Empire in 1200 BCE, refugees scattered the technique for making iron throughout the ancient Near East. The artisans who had developed the method for making tempered iron, now known as "blacksmiths," because of the soot that covered them in the manufacturing process, shared their methods as they fled from the invaders. Thus, iron technology soon became commonplace throughout Mesopotamia.

Between 3500 to 1200 BCE, prior to the common use of iron, the urban products of civilization had essentially bypassed ancient farmers. Even though they served as the tax base that supplied food surpluses to support urban life, farmers had to make their own tools, huts, and clothing without any significant material benefit from their association with urban centers. Connected to cities principally through the awe of religious charisma, farmers developed a material indifference to their urban elite. The rapid adjustment which farmers made to new conquerors who took up residence in local towns and continued taxation revealed this apparent indifference. Since the new conquerors had defeated the old elite, the farmers easily accepted the proposition that the new ruler's gods had to be more powerful. Therefore, transfer of awe to the new masters was a logical transition to make. But this material indifference changed with the introduction of iron.

Once urban blacksmiths could produce iron tools, farmers found themselves drawn more tightly into city life. In Greek and Roman history, farmers began to develop an interest in participating in the defense of towns; in the Ancient Near East, India, and China, farmers felt an even greater demand placed on their productive labor. With iron tools in hand, Greek and Roman farmers could expand their food production, setting aside part of this new produce to pay for new tools and further engage in exchanges as part of the urban market economy. Expanding farm production with the use of iron tools attracted Greek and Roman farmers into towns.

The iron blades that these Western farmers added to their plows expanded the number and size of fields under cultivation. The production of iron sickles and scythes used to harvest crops greatly increased the efficiency of farm labor. Finally, the development of iron rings and plates to reinforce harnesses and the plow extended the efficiency of this tool. Each new development in farm technology gave Greek and Roman farmers a stronger interest in the way urban markets functioned. And this interest drew these farmers into urban politics for the first time in world history.

In the Ancient Near East, India, and China, farm laborers also integrated more tightly with urban life. In

A relief of Assyrian soldiers. Equipped with standardized weapons and organized into standardized units, the Assyrian army carved out the first Iron Age Empire. Courtesy of Anne Lynne Negus.

Mesopotamia, India, and China, however, the farmers found their relationship with cities to be far less voluntary. Often used as conscript labor, or suffering from an increased tax burden, the farmers of Mesopotamia, India, and China served as a new source of labor to supply food for expanded military forces. With the vast new food surpluses these farmers could produce, imperial cultures generated larger armies that built massive empires.

What the kings of these new empires required were passive, obedient subjects who quietly turned over their harvests to their rulers. Thus, the Ancient Near East, India, and China developed along a cultural path that differed quite sharply from the farmer-soldiers found in the West. In the West, the farmer-soldier became the first active political personality, i.e., the citizen. In Mesopotamia, India, and China, the farmer-soldier became a conscript.

Following the Mesopotamian pattern of awe with regard to priests and kings, iron transformed military history by helping convert Assyria into a massive new empire. Indeed, the Assyrians used iron to outfit a new form of military organization. Developing an army that numbered 100,000 to 120,000 men, the Assyrian kings based their authority on exceptional organizational skills.

Unlike a bronze culture that had at its disposal soldiers drawn only from an urban elite, in the Iron Age the Assyrians drafted farmers into military service. This radically expanded the number of men under arms. Since the urban-rural ratio in the Mesopotamia was one city-dweller to every nine farmers, the average size Bronze Age army recruited its soldiers from only a fraction of 10 percent of the total population. As the Iron Age drew farmers into the army, the Assyrian military had access to virtually their entire male population. Hence, Assyrian kings had to figure out a way to manage these new massive numbers.

Their solution was to divide the army into standard formations of 10, 100, and 1,000. Next, they created standardized weapons to outfit all their soldiers. Then, they created a chain of command that selected competent officers to staff their "squads," "companies," and "regiments." The combination of these three decisions created a uniform chain of command, discipline, and function. To these standardized units, the Assyrian kings then added the concept of a "corps," specialized units within the army that provided support to an overall military campaign.

The Assyrian army comprised infantry, engineers, charioteers, archers, an officers' corps, and a small unit of cavalry. Using centralized control through a direct chain of command, Assyrian kings knew their army would respond to their royal will without question. Supporting the military machine with an integrated system of supply, the Assyrian monarchy could rely on a broad agricultural surplus based on iron tools and the labor of subject peoples. Accordingly, the Assyrians had enough men for Mesopotamia to accomplish something unthinkable in the Bronze Age: they conquered not only the Fertile Crescent but Egypt as well. For the first time in Ancient Near Eastern history, "the Land between the Rivers" and the valley of the Nile belonged to one empire.

Engaged in a deliberate policy of deportation and terror, the Assyrian monarchy took the principle of awe to its logical limits. As the last of the Mesopotamia cultures to rule the Ancient Near East, Assyria imposed its will by crushing any opposition. A powerful standing army, an efficient royal administration, the use of positive law, and a determination to eradicate rebellion compelled Assyrian kings to kill defeated urban elites and scatter throughout their empire captured farmers, thereby stripping them of their cultural identity. By overwhelming the victims of conquest, the Assyrians intended to secure a subject labor force to fuel an invincible army.

The Assyrian empire ruled from 747 to 612 BCE. Conquered people were simply uprooted and resettled far from their homeland. Resistance or rebellion led to the same fate: the flaying of opposition leaders, the physical disfigurement of their relatives, and mass impalements. An example would be the ten lost tribes of Israel. In the eighth century BCE, the Assyrians fell upon these ten tribes, killed the elite, and scattered the remainder so that only two tribes of Judah survived to continue the Hebrew tradition, which ultimately led to the first example of *monotheism* (worship of the one "true" god). Assyrian monuments commemorate these violent events as the fierce determination of the kings celebrated the military prowess of the army.

Yet such harsh rule eventually led to the fall of the Assyrian Empire. Three factors combined to destroy Assyria. First Assyria had expanded to the limits of its resources; no other empire had attempted so much. Second, a new military threat appeared from Central Asia, a nomadic cavalry. Discussed in depth later in Chapter Six, cavalry units posed a threat that Assyria simply could not handle: hit-and-run tactics were too much for an infantry-based system to defeat. Third, rebel forces allied and mobilized once it became clear to them that Assyria could no longer quell the mounted nomads sweeping through their empire. Hence, in 612 BCE, a coordinated rebellion in both Egypt and Mesopotamia threw off the yoke of Assyrian rule. Then a combined rebel army placed the Assyrian capital, Nineveh, under siege. Finally, the capture of Nineveh allowed the subject people to impose as violent a fate on the Assyrian monarchy as had been inflicted on the conquered peoples: the victors plowed the land around Nineveh with salt, ruining the soil so that Assyria would never rise again.

The fall of Assyria ended the Mesopotamian era of world history. After its collapse, the center of political and military power shifted east to Persia. Indeed, the appearance of Persian cavalry had changed the nature of warfare in the Ancient Near East. Cultural leadership relocated outside the "Land between the Rivers" as Persia used cavalry to conquer Mesopotamia, Egypt, Anatolia, Macedonia, Iran, Afghanistan, and parts of India. Eventually the Greeks developed a style of infantry warfare that neutralized the threat of cavalry strikes, and Greece defeated Persia in the Persian Wars (490–479 BCE). Next, Macedonia in imitation of Greek tactics, conquered Persia and created the Hellenistic World. Finally, Rome reinvented infantry tactics, captured the Mediterranean Basin, conquered the Macedonian world, and defined the political events for the remainder of ancient world history in the West. Yet all these stories will be told in later chapters.

The Hebrews

The story of the Hebrews reveals the powerful effects of trade and diffusion on a contemporary but minor nomadic culture that came in contact with Mesopotamian civilization and transformed Western history. Combining accounts of the Bronze Age and the Iron Age in their sacred text, the *Torah* (the first five books of the Old Testament), Hebrew history portrays the power of technology, the importance of metal, and the creativity of the human mind. Consequently, the story of this group belongs to this portion of the text as a parallel account of ancient life in the Fertile Crescent.

The Hebrews occupy a unique place in Western history. They, along with the Greeks who will be discussed later, created the ancient Western worldview. The Hebrews contributed the first zealous monotheism, while the Greeks offered the philosophical underpinning that explained the conceptual foundations of Christianity. Hence, each group played a central role in the development of Western civilization and each deserves special attention so that the reader can fully understand how the West viewed nature.

The Hebrews occupied a portion of the Levant coast (modern Syria, Lebanon, Israel, and Palestine), where they composed a culture of relatively insignificant political and military might. Yet it was their vision of God, which they developed over the course of 1,454 years (ca. 2000–546 BCE), that became so compelling during the Roman era when it eclipsed all other Western faiths. How this vision of God matured in the Hebrew imagination requires an understanding of bronze and iron in the context of Hebrew history.

The Hebrews began their history as the "Chosen People" under the authority of a patriarch named Abraham who wandered from the precincts of Ur, in Sumeria, to the Levant around 2000 BCE. Abraham and his heirs lived in the Bronze Age (3500–1200 BCE) without sufficient access to the metals needed to compete with the great sedentary cultures of Mesopotamia and Egypt. Accordingly, the people of Abraham traveled through the wilderness avoiding cities, fighting battles with other nomads—generally eking out a living on the

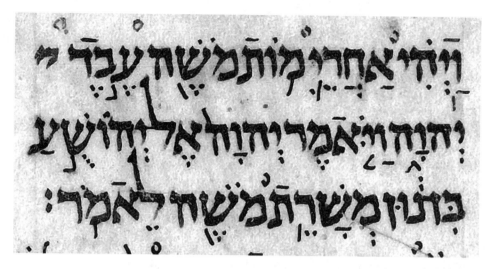

Hebrew writing. The earliest known example of biblical Hebrew manuscript, the Aleppo Codex was written in Palestine in the tenth century. It was later preserved by Aleppo's Jewish community from the fourteenth century on, until its journey from Syria to Israel in the 1950s. Written in approximately 920 CE.

margins of civilization. Meanwhile, the history of the Hebrews during the Bronze Age, as seen in the Torah's *Genesis*, ended with these shepherd people taking up residence in Egypt, where they had gone seeking shelter.

Exodus (ca. 1200 BCE) takes the Hebrew story into the dawn of the Iron Age (also 1200 BCE), when Moses liberated his people from bondage in Egypt and led them into the Sinai Peninsula. The acquisition of Iron technology changed the Hebrews from shepherds into sedentary farmers as this new, plentiful metal armed each member of the twelve tribes of Israel. These twelve tribes themselves descended from Abraham's grandson Jacob, who had sired twelve sons. According to Hebrew history, Jacob changed his name to Israel after having wrestled with an angel, thus demonstrating that God had fulfilled His contract with the "Chosen People," i.e., the First Covenant made in *Genesis*. Moses now prepared the Hebrews for their entry into the Land of Milk and Honey (the Promised Land) as part of the Second Covenant made in *Exodus* and seen in the contract called the "Ten Commandments." A struggle with local Canaanites over the land of Israel marked the evolution of an emerging farming community as Joshua, Samson, Saul, and David redefined the local conditions that shaped a new rural-urban link between Hebrew farmers, their iron plows, their weapons, their farmland, and their cities.

These iron plows and weapons gave the Hebrews the means to establish a stable kingdom even while surrounded by numerous potential enemies. Next, the prophets tell of a struggle to survive in an increasingly hostile world as the kingdom of Israel split into two parts: Judah and Israel. Both confronted the dilemma of loyalty to God, as required by the Ten Commandments, while developing friendly relations with gentile (i.e., everyone outside the Hebrew faith) states who worshipped what the Hebrews considered false gods.

Nonetheless, both Hebrew factions also faced potential annihilation at the hands of the great Iron Age empires of Assyria, Babylonia, and Persia. The Hebrew prophets explained the frequent destruction of Israel's and Judah's cities, their economies, the dispersal of their people, and periods of slavery as failures to keep their Second Covenant with God. The Covenant itself simply demanded that members of the Hebrew community remain loyal to God and his Divine Law, and avoid the corrupting effects that alliances with "pagan" cultures might bring. It was such that the evolution of the Hebrew society within the material realms of metal and politics laid a foundation for the maturation of a religious worldview that shaped the first monotheism.

The Emergence of Monotheism

The first step in the evolution of monotheism began with a growing awareness of God among the Hebrew people as part of their oral tradition. God matured in the Hebrew imagination from one of many shepherd deities into an all-powerful transcendental Being over the course of some fifteen centuries (ca. 2000 to 546 BCE). As a shepherd deity, God led Abraham and his people from Sumeria to the Levant coast probably during the time of Ur III (2100–2000 BCE). On this march, the Hebrews first saw God as a sky deity who defended His people against rival nomads and their divine allies.

The survival of the Hebrews against considerable odds helped them to develop a sense of exclusive loyalty to God as He kept His promises made in the First Covenant that He had struck with Abraham. Settling temporarily near the city of Harren in northern Mesopo-tamia on their way west, Abraham and his descendants continued to follow a nomadic existence and maintained their loyalty to God. He, in turn, they believed protected His Chosen People from hostile neighbors and a violent world as they traveled with their flocks. They crossed the desert seeking water and generally avoided major urban centers. Each move they made reflected divine instructions that protected these Chosen People.

About the time of the Hyksos (i.e., shepherd kings, ca. 1785–1570 BCE), the Hebrews began to move into Egypt. Driven by necessity, they wandered into the Nile Delta seeking food, water, and shelter. Led at the time by Israel, the Hebrews continued to live in uncertainty on Egypt's frontier. Later Israel's son, Joseph, won favor with the pharaoh, who probably was a Hyksos ruler and who allowed the Hebrews to live in peace within his realm. Exclusive worship of one God, without denying the existence of others, had served the Chosen People well but it did not protect them when the Egyptians successfully rebelled against Hyksos rule in 1570 BCE, threw off the foreign yoke, and enslaved all surviving shepherd people. At this point a long period of misery began for the Hebrews, one that culminated in the great Exodus led by Moses (ca. 1200 BCE).

And it was during the Exodus that the Hebrew concept of God matured further in the Hebrew imagination as He apparently had renewed His Covenant with Moses. In the Exodus, God instructed Moses to guide the Chosen People out of Egypt into the Sinai in preparation for entry into the Land of Milk and Honey. The God that inspired this Exodus still lived in a world of rival deities, but now handed down through Moses a set of laws, the Ten Commandments, that became the basis of a new Hebrew society.

These laws told the Hebrews what they must not do, but left all other decisions up to them. Unlike Hammurabi's code, which prescribed conduct through positive laws, the Ten Commandments listed the negative boundaries that God refused the Hebrews to cross. God, therefore, granted the Chosen People free will to act as moral agents. At the same time, the first two Commandments created a *monolatry* (the belief that one true God came before all the rest). Hence, all other gods continued to exist, but the Hebrew understanding of their God had been elevated to a new level of majesty that placed Him above all other deities—a major step in the direction of monotheism.

Upon receiving these laws, the image of God continued to mature in the Hebrew mind. He became an anthropomorphic deity with physical dimensions, emotional qualities, a capricious nature, and wrathful moods. At this time, however, He did not appear to be omnipotent to His people. Instead, God seemed still to be limited to the territory occupied by the Hebrews on their march to the Promised Land. Also, God was not part of nature; rather He existed outside natural events and directed all the forces in His locale.

The Hebrews honored God during the era in which they carved out their homeland in Canaan (1200 to 1000 BCE). Yet they had not by this time completely rejected the possibility of other deities. Directed by the Ten Commandments, the Hebrews worshipped God while developing ethical principles, ceremonial rituals, and feasts of sacrifice. In these celebrations of God's Divinity, the Hebrews reaffirmed their loyalty to the Second Covenant with each generation.

By the time of King David (1012–972 BCE), the Hebrews had won uncontested command over their land against their chief rivals, the Philistines. Yet they still had not managed to maintain a stable record of loyalty to God. Learning cultivation from the Canaanites they had conquered, the Hebrews frequently fell under the spell of the fertility cult of Ba'al. This failure to keep faith with God led to major changes in the Hebrew religion; chief among these changes was the appearance of prophets.

The prophets generated a revolutionary vision in the Hebrew imagination as the image of God reached full maturity. Constantly threatened by more powerful cultures in Mesopotamia and Egypt, the Hebrews incessantly lived in the shadow of destruction. After David's son Solomon ruled Israel (972–932 BCE), the heavy taxes he had assessed to build the temple created such unrest that Israel split into two realms upon his death. The ten tribes of the north followed Jeroboam to form a new kingdom of Israel, while the two tribes of the south formed the kingdom of Judah. This split provoked a war between the two Hebrew states, increased the threat of foreign invasion, and weakened the loyalty of the people to God. The political upheaval inspired religious renewal, for it was at this time that the prophets appeared and became the voice of God, who now revealed the future to reshape the Hebrews' religious imagination.

The prophets established three basic doctrines: God alone rules the universe; God is righteous; and God demands ethical behavior from His Chosen People. As ruler of the universe, God alone commands nature as well as all foreign civilizations to implement His Plan. All other deities are false. As a righteous God, He willed only goodness, for the evil of the world came from humans. As the source of goodness, God expected His Chosen People to keep the laws, for they above all other humans had the privilege of association with Him. Thus, the prophets had declared a thoroughgoing monotheism.

The Hebrew people now worshipped a deity who had become universal, one so powerful that His name could not be spoken. He was invisible, all-powerful, all-knowing, and ubiquitous, or everywhere at once. The Hebrew letters "YY" represented his name, which, as mentioned, could not be pronounced. The reason the Chosen People never uttered these sounds was that they believed no one word could capture the infinite majesty of God. Rather, the Hebrews pronounced several honorific phrases that declared God's glory whenever YY appeared in their sacred texts. The universal nature of this one God now exceeded the boundaries of any possible name and demanded a general obedience under the principle "Love thy neighbor as thyself." Accordingly, each Hebrew person was equal in the eyes of God.

The Hebrews concluded that God cared for all His people. He did not expect ritual and sacrifice to be precise, but He demanded His followers be just, relieve oppression, provide for the poor, and protect the weak. He punished those who abandoned Him, and rewarded the righteous. Those who worshipped false gods like Ba'al, the Canaanite fertility deity, suffered disaster. The prophets Amos and Hosea exhorted Israel to be righteous and forecasted the destruction of the ten tribes of that kingdom at the hands of the Assyrians in 722 BCE (as mentioned above). Still, the Hebrews failed to honor God and met their predetermined fate.

Isaiah and Jeremiah delivered the same warning to Judah, which fell to the Babylonians in 586 BCE. Ezekiel and a second Isaiah told the captives taken from Judah of a new future that included their liberation and redemption. Part of that redemption involved a prophecy of a future role for the Chosen People in which the House of David would provide a religious leader for the rest of the world. Together, all these prophets spoke with one voice of the power and majesty of God.

But, despite the authority of the prophets, the Chosen People frequently failed, or refused, to accept these Divine pronouncements. Accordingly, Israel disappeared, and Judah fell, as greater kingdoms, more powerful empires, and larger armies defined the politics of the Levant coast. Such a heavy price, however, had to be paid in order for the Chosen People to understand fully God's majesty, will, and power.

Given the awe, authority, and goodness of this Deity, as articulated by the prophets, a full grasp of God's omnipotence, omnipresence, and omniscience was now complete. Every animal, plant, or object found in nature became His instrument to reward the righteous and punish the wicked. He used the Heavens and Earth as tools to instruct His worshipers. The natural world became a medium through which God worked His won-

ders. Humanity, the Chosen People in particular, received God's bounty by adhering to His law and honoring Him as the only true Deity. Consequently, the Hebrews believed that all phenomena in nature reflected the will of God. As a result, for the Hebrews the natural course of daily events defined the Divine purpose of God. To understand nature was to decode God's will, while all natural events measured the morality of humanity.

Consistent with the first sentence of the Bible that states, "In the beginning, God created Heaven and Earth," the prophets revealed the full range of God's powers. In this first sentence, "God," as the subject, was the original actor who defined all the actions about to unfold in the remainder of the text. "Heaven and Earth" were the objects acted upon, and, as such, were the passive recipients of God's Will. The infinitive verb, "to create," linked the actor to the action to demonstrate the range of possible events at God's disposal as the history of the universe began. And, finally, the dependent clause, "in the beginning," placed God outside time and space as a Being who existed before all these events on a transcendental plane possessing a boundless potential to act upon the temporal/spatial entities of "Heaven and Earth" and set the stage for human existence.

The depth of meaning implied by this sentence emerged in the imaginations of Abraham, Moses, and the Hebrew prophets. Each was a finite human consciousness struggling to comprehend the infinite. For these Hebrew leaders, God only spoke indirectly through nature to individual human minds that could not grasp the entire message. Each person mastered as best he could, within the context of his own finite world, the awe inspired by his understanding of the Divine. Hence, a sky god became the first amongst all gods, and then finally became the one true God as the Hebrew imagination developed the first monotheism. From this final understanding, achieved in a restored Judah under Cyrus the Great, the founder of the Persian Empire (reigned ca. 549–529 BCE), the Chosen People had become the Jews. The next logical step was to project such a Universal Deity into the rest of the Western world through a prophetic vision of a coming Messiah. This historical step, however, awaited the emergence of the philosophy of the age of Greece and then Rome.

Suggested Reading

Crawford, Harriet, *Sumer and the Sumerians* (Cambridge: Cambridge University Press, 1991).

Hallo, W. W. and W. K. Simpson, *The Ancients' Near East: A History* (New York: Harcourt, Brace, and Jovanovich, 1975).

Jacobsen, Thorkild, *The Treasury of Darkness: A History of Mesopotamia* (New Haven, Conn.: Yale University Press, 1976).

Kramer, Samuel N., *The Sumerians, Their History, Culture, and Character* (Chicago: University of Chicago Press, 1963).

Lloyd, S., *The Archeology of Mesopotamia: From the Old Stone Age to the Persian Conquest,* Revised Edition (London: Thames and Hudson, 1984).

Mallowan, M. E., *Early Mesopotamia and Iran* (New York: McGraw Hill, 1966).

Mellaart, James, *Earliest Civilizations of the Near East* (New York: McGraw Hill, 1965).

Nissen, Hans J., *The Early History of the Ancient Near East, 9000–2000 BC* (Chicago: University of Chicago Press, 1988).

Oppenheim, Stephen K., *Social Transformations* (1995).

Steibin, William H. Jr., *Ancient Near Eastern History and Culture* (New York: Longman, 2003).

Streuver, A. L., *Ancient Mesopotamia,* Second Edition (Chicago: University of Chicago Press, 1977).

III

EGYPT:
The Gift of the Nile

In contrast to Mesopotamia, Egypt produced a civilization that developed a more coherent political history and optimistic view of nature. Thanks to the abundance of water produced by the 4,000-mile-long Nile that linked the tropical south with the arid zones of the north, Egypt enjoyed a rich supply of moisture in the eastern portion of the Sahara Desert. The Nile supplied an abundance of water and fresh silt to a region that received an average rainfall of only one inch per year. The Nile, which flows north from Lake Victoria in tropical Tanzania to its delta in Egypt, carries the monsoon rainfall that feeds its several tributaries. The last 750 miles of the Nile's riverbed, located in Egypt, also ran very deep, which ensured a very low evaporation rate. Thus, the Nile supplied Egypt with fresh, silt-rich, and salt-free water each year.

The length and depth of the Nile also created a gentle flood pattern that made water management in Egypt easy when compared to Mesopotamia. Free from the violent floods that plagued the Land between the Rivers, Egyptians did not have to invest as much labor in repairing irrigation, nor did they have to dig as many channels and canals as their Mesopotamian neighbors. They also had far less fear of an irregular water supply. On average, one out of the five annual Nile River floods was destructively high or low, but usually they were gentle, slow, predictable, and sufficient. Accordingly, Egyptians could rely on a dike-and-canal system that directed water into their permanent fields where saturation irrigation followed. The result was *Kemet*—black, fertile earth—another name for Egypt.

Egyptian statue.
Courtesy Touraj Daryaee.

Saturation irrigation let water sit on the land for long periods, provided deep deposits of fresh silt, turned the soil black, and prepared the land for abundant cultivation. Once the water retreated, Egyptian farmers planted their crops and enjoyed a yearly harvest that proved to be the most generous in Western Civilization. This saturation technique also ensured that any mineral salts that may have remained within the river water leached deep into the black earth, thereby sparing Egypt from hastening the ecocide that destroyed Mesopotamian agriculture. All these factors—the slow rise of the Nile during flood season, the predictable patterns of flooding each year, and the regular supply of fresh water and silt—convinced the Egyptians that Earth was a friendly place.

The Nile flooded its plains annually, beginning in June and ending in October, bringing some 200 tons of fresh soil to Egyptian fields. The contrast between the Nile floodplain and the surrounding Sahara Desert was so extreme that Egyptians concluded that their land truly was the gift of the Nile. The black soil created by the river's water came to symbolize fertility and life, while the red baked lands of the desert represented death and hostility.

Only the red-brown color of blood found in Egyptian art used to mark the skin-tones of native males represented an equal vitality with the black earth watered by the Nile. In contrast, the pale yellow color depicting females denoted a weaker gender, while the occasional representation of black-figured pharaohs denoted the power the monarchy had over its people, the power, in essence, to give them life.

Meanwhile, the Nile saturated a ribbon of land that averaged thirty miles in width within a steep crevasse that, in turn, marked the boundaries between the river and the desert. The prominent cliffs on either bank of the river confined the riverbed to a narrow floodplain, while the first *cataract*, or rapids, located to the south, and deserts both east and west of the Nile, isolated Egypt from invasion on three of its four natural frontiers. Accordingly, 30,000 square miles of black earth

38

cut through the crevasse that the Nile had carved out of the land from the first cataract to the Delta, while the delta itself comprised 40,000 square miles of rich, fertile soil. The abundance of life supported by this black earth created a natural setting for early cultivation and sustained an exceptional urban to rural ratio, estimated at 8 to 2—twice as many people released from agriculture as those in Mesopotamia. Therefore, scholars believe ancient Egypt to have had 100 percent more people freed from agriculture to engage in an urban division of labor or serve as a workforce available to construct the megalithic structures that made this land so famous.

Egyptian attitudes toward nature reflected their appreciation of the gentle and generous features of their river. As deities of nature, Egyptian gods represented the abundance the river and the Earth made available for human enjoyment. The earliest Egyptian cosmology, or creation myth, speaks of an emergence from a watery chaos called *Nun* (nothingness or nonexistence). Like the Nile before the flood, or the sun before it rises, there was only potential. Out of the watery chaos came *Atum* (totality) who began the creation process. First appeared the male principal, *Shu* (dry atmosphere/continuity), and then the female counterpart, *Tefnut*, (wet atmosphere/discontinuity). These two produced the male earth, *Geb*, and the female sky, *Nut*, who in turn produced the male life force, *Osiris*, and the female life force, *Isis*, both of whom embodied fertility, creativity, and sexuality as brother and sister, husband and wife.

Other variations of the creation myth coalesced when three religious traditions synthesized under the authority of kings who unified the Kingdoms of Upper and Lower Egypt by 3100 BCE. The gods remained the same in these myth cycles, but their roles changed, making the final products, Osiris and Isis, and their son *Horus*, who appeared as the king of a united Egypt. Hence, Osiris, Isis, and Horus came to embody the unity of religious and political power as manifested in the person of the king, the living god.

Joined by the life-giving power of the Sun, *Re*, these deities spoke of a regular and orderly universe. Re himself rose in the east each day to bring life to the Nile, and when he set in the west, death walked the land. Each dawn, thus, was a reason to rejoice.

Combined with Re, the mythical life cycle of Osiris explained the origins of agriculture. Osiris, the god of male sexuality and the underworld, brought agriculture to Egypt before his evil brother, *Set* (night) murdered and divided Osiris's body. Isis, Osiris's wife, female sexual counterpart, and sister, then found the scattered body parts and buried these divine fragments in several holy places. Osiris's son by Isis, Horus, avenged

The Egyptian Triad, 237 BCE–57 BCE. This Ptolomeic bas relief is in the Temple of Horace at Edfu. Shown are three significant deities: Osiris (left) merciful judge of death and the underworld; Isis (center), mother of Horus, and wife and sister of Osiris; and Horus (right), ruler of the sky and son of Osiris. Edfu, Egypt. © 2006 Vagabum Mike Lopez (www.vagabum.com).

his father's death, resurrected Osiris's body, and established him as the judge of the underworld. Horus then became a living source of divinity on Earth embodied in the person of the king.

The cyclical story of Osiris connected the rise and fall of the Nile to the life, death, and resurrection. As the creative force in nature, Osiris gave life to seeds, thereby linking him to immortality. His death and resurrection represented the fall and renewal of fertility as each flood renewed life in Egypt. Coupled with the vengeance and justice of Horus, the relocation of Osiris in the underworld explained the origins of political authority.

Meanwhile, the life-giving power of Re showed itself in the fact that the Egyptians developed the first solar calendar to mark the Nile's regular flood patterns. Since the Nile was so predictable, Egyptians noted that the flood began each year when the brightest star in the night sky, *Sirius*, made its annual appearance. Such an orderly universe gave Egyptians comfort as the Sun's yearly trip around the Earth counted the days that led to the return of fertility each growing season. (Peoples of the ancient world, of course, believed that the Earth was the center of the universe.) Consequently, Sirius signaled when the flood would arrive, when fresh water and silt would bring new life into Egypt's black earth, and when a renewed bounty would yield next year's harvest.

While the king (or *pharaoh* in the New Kingdom) represented the living god Horus whose divine presence on the throne of Egypt ensured the life cycle of that culture, Osiris judged the dead in the underworld to determine their fate in the afterlife. Together, these two then joined Re, the giver of life. Consequently, Re, Osiris, Horus, and countless other Egyptian deities represented the eternal aspects of the natural world that made the Earth a friendly place. Alive with divine power, nature's multiple faces represented a pantheon of gods and goddesses who enriched daily life.

In the meantime, since the Nile flowed south to north with a gentle current moving water and silt throughout a well-defined landscape, the river became a natural conduit of commerce. And since the trade winds blew from northeast to southwest, the Egyptians were able to use sails on their river craft to defy the Nile's current and travel south if they wished. Unlike the violent floods that shifted water about along the broad floodplain of the Tigris and Euphrates, denying the formation of a centerplace capital city, the Nile integrated political geography and allowed one ruler to dominate the countryside. Situated in the southern Nile Valley for two-thirds of Egypt's history, this capital allowed the king to rule the land from the first cataracts in the south to the marshlands of the Delta in the north.

Such a ruler could generate a different kind of history than the one experienced in Mesopotamia. Instead of a world rife with numerous languages, civil war, migration, and invasion, Egypt proved to be a stable civilization, its history bearing the relatively peaceful transition of power from one dynasty to the next. Only the occasional era of chaos interrupted a far more serene story than the one found in the Land between the Rivers, while invasions did not commence until relatively late in Egyptian history. Hence, continuity proved far more common than discontinuity as a central government came to rule the land.

Simultaneously, the regularity of the Nile saved Egypt from the ecocide that had destroyed Sumeria. Egypt produced harvest after harvest in an unbroken history of abundance except for the rare periods of invasion and internal unrest. This continued fertility eventually made Egypt the principal grain-exporting region during Greek and Roman times (509 BCE–476 CE).

Such riches led Egyptians to celebrate nature in lavish displays of respect and appreciation. For example, the Egyptians created elaborate gardens with shallow pools of water to decorate their homes. They built luxurious temples and sacred precincts that protected animals and plants that they felt embodied the presence of the gods. Their lengthy history of central authority also spared them the struggle over water rights that plagued Sumeria. Their continual use of saline-free river water never sent their civilization upriver. Their unusually high urban to rural ratio freed far more people from agriculture and allowed the construction of the most impressive stone monuments in the world.

Finally, their optimism toward nature allowed the Egyptians to sustain a rich art that produced paintings, sculpture, and pictographic writing that included numerous details and symbols of nature's bounty.

The Pyramid Age
The Old Kingdom (2700–2200 BCE)

The social structure of Egyptian civilization had developed into a clear hierarchy by the rise of the first kings. These kings occupied the top rung, followed by their royal relatives, and then nobles/aristocrats. Among the latter were the high-ranking military leaders, priests, and bureaucrats, many of whom held titles of multiple occupations. Their complex diet of nutritious foods and a pampered existence, compared to the common farmers, gave the elite long life-spans. Medical attention, highly evolved for ancient times, was readily available and of renowned quality. The art of embalming was equally well developed and underscored the belief in life after death; the privileged believed they could take their wealth and treasured possessions with them.

More then 90 percent of the population, however, were ordinary, hard-working people: peasants, shopkeepers, artisans, and their associates. Their simple diet comprised bread, fish, beer, and vegetables. A farmer in Egypt could produce enough food to sustain twenty people, but the average life expectancy was only twenty-five to thirty-five years during the Old Kingdom. Illiterate, limited in experience, and vulnerable to the vagaries of life, the working people of Egypt died from strenuous labor, accidents, and disease. Trapped through the symbiosis of agriculture in a sandy yet moist environment, they also fell victim to numerous waterborne parasites and sand-related illnesses: parasitic worms such as schistosomiasis (bilharzias), roundworms, tapeworms, and guinea worms came from the water. Blowing sand eroded teeth, abraded the eyes, and filled the lungs.

One of the most hazardous occupations of the time was pyramid building. The Third and Fourth Dynasties, hailed as Egypt's Golden Age, managed to achieve autocratic rule over the land's physical and human resources by focusing the wealth and energy of Egypt on massive pyramid building near the early capital city of Memphis, just south of the Delta. Starting with the first step pyramid and haunting life-size recreation of the administrative center in Memphis in the Third Dynasty to the splendid pyramids and well-ordered towns of the Fourth Dynasty's Giza complexes near modern Cairo, the Egyptian monarchy engaged muscle, mind, and heart in building cities of the dead that took decades of state-paid labor to complete. The great pyramids were tomb complexes for deified royalty. They represented the power of the king to collect taxes through a centralized state that had access to all the food surpluses in Egypt. Given the effectiveness of the Nile as both a source of fresh water and silt and an avenue of commerce and communication, the king of Egypt had ready access to all the rural and urban occupations whose awe his charisma inspired. The pyramids also marked the vast difference in food surpluses, political power, and human labor available in Egypt when contrasted with the unpredictable conditions of life found in Mesopotamia.

Yet, even though these Old Kingdom wonders of the world soared above the desert plateau, they could not mask the forces of decentralization that had begun to emerge from Egypt's political and religious landscape. Just as success had led to failure in Mesopotamia, so the same paradox began to emerge in Egypt. An abundance of food generated by the river sustained a growing population until these human numbers grew large enough to trigger the problem of inheritance; finding jobs for all the surviving children began to undermine the state.

The greater the number of children in the royal family, as well as among the subordinates of the king, the more difficult it was to find suitable employment for all of them. Rival royal family members, jealous Nome leaders (*nomarchs*, or provincial rulers), competing priests, and upstart bureaucrats began to tap into the resource base of Egypt and sap the strength of the state. By the Fifth and Sixth Dynasties, it was clear that the Sun priests of Heliopolis, a city just north of modern Cairo, were able to divert food surpluses from the royal pyramid projects into the Sun temples of their god Re. One priestly family even managed to attain the throne through marriage with the royal heiress. A growing number of cities and towns, established up and down the Nile to enhance the king's position, instead became the power base for provincial nomarchs who sought independence from royal authority. Their tomb inscriptions spoke of serving the king, but the actual events of the day reveal their arrogance and freedom from royal power. To strengthen their own hand, several kings made alliances with priesthood and Nome families, but this only served to enhance the power of the latter. All that remained was for a weak monarch to assume the throne in order for these competing local forces to pull the state apart: this weakness appeared at the end of the Sixth Dynasty in the ninety-fourth year of Pepi II's reign.

A Time of Chaos
The First Intermediate Period (2200–2000 BCE) and the Middle Kingdom (2000–1786 BCE)

Given his advanced age of ninety-four (ca. 2567–2473 BCE), it is not difficult to imagine why Pepi II lost con-

Giza Plateau, located on the west bank of the Nile. Giza is the site of the Great Pyramid and the Great Sphinx, which was carved from a single piece of limestone bedrock. Both were built by Khafre, pharoah of the fourth dynasty. Giza, Egypt. © 2006 Vagabum Mike Lopez (www.vagabum.com).

trol of his kingdom in his waning years. Many historians describe what followed in the Seventh Dynasty as "seventy kings in seventy days," as simultaneous claims to the throne created chaos. Then, a series of disastrously low river levels brought droughts to two-thirds of Egypt, launching famines that eroded the resource base of the state, and encouraging local claims to autonomy. After a brief Eighth Dynasty, a Ninth and then a Tenth claimed power, but both soon had to face an ambitious new rival family that appeared in the southern town of Thebes (the ancient capital for most of the remainder of Egyptian history). This Eleventh Dynasty (Thebes) challenged the Ninth/Tenth Dynasties to the north in a civil war, which, in conjunction with famine brought disease and a demographic crisis (a massive loss of population) that led to political devastation. The integrity of Egypt's frontiers collapsed, foreigners entered the country, and general turmoil reigned. Finally, Men-tuhotep, one of the most imaginative kings in Egyptian history claimed the throne and joined the country together. He refounded the Middle Kingdom on a new principle: royal service and solicitude in return for the allegiance of the humble Egyptian subject.

Mentuhotep accepted the fact that the king could no longer command all the resources made available by the Nile's bounty and that he needed allies among the priests and nobles. Hence, the king had to shed his remote, serene, and divine nature to become an active ruler of his people. Therefore Mentuhotep presented himself in Egyptian art as a careworn shepherd of the land whose subjects came first. Court literature reinforced this image by depicting the king as a haggard, benevolent ruler whose care for his subjects, and their vulnerability to the capricious whims of nature, placed them always on his and his immediate subordinates' minds.

Major state functions no longer aimed to elevate the king but to protect and enhance the lives of the people. As Late Old Kingdom bureaucratic independence ended, a renewed effort to recruit an honest, competent, and faithful staff ensued. Egypt's bureaucracy tended towards an educated meritocracy in which 2 to 5 percent of the population, usually the sons of the literate, discovered that the key to a successful career in government stemmed from a firm command of the language. Higher education took place in the temple House of Life, where students memorized and copied model texts and took part in limited practical workshops in such areas as architecture and medicine.

Sacred *hieroglyphic* script (a hieroglyph is a picture of an object representing a word, syllable, or sound) filled state and religious texts, while *hieratic* script (a form of cursive hieroglyphs useful for daily business) covered the transactions of a normal existence. Later *dernotic* script (the final form of hieroglyphs) and *coptic* script (Egyptian and Greek writing) completed the picture of Egyptian literacy. (Since the earliest hieroglyphs appeared in predynastic records and revealed a rapid development in the art of writing, many scholars argue Egypt's extensive contacts with Mesopotamia inspired the literacy that made Egypt famous during the Middle Kingdom.) Distance and an independent cultural worldview, however, plus the lighter and more convenient medium of papyrus and ink, when compared the clay and reeds of cuneiform, favored the fluid development of hieroglyphs. At any rate, Egyptian civilization excelled in literacy as well as in speculative pursuits about nature.

In mathematics, study of the heavens, and technology, Egyptian civilization emphasized the applied and the practical arts. Their arithmetic, calendar, and tool-making techniques focused on the importance of agriculture and the necessity of linking the floodwaters to the harvest. Farming and irrigation were a year-round concern. Tools were usually made of stone and wood since metals such as copper and later bronze proved too costly for widespread rural use. Thus, like his Mesopotamian counterpart, the Egyptian farmer received little or no material benefit from serving the city other than the awe and knowledge inspired by the king and his priests' command over the Sun and the Nile. Copper and bronze tools did become more plentiful during the Middle Kingdom, given the fact that Egypt had its own deposits of cuprite, azurite, and malachite (copper ores) and cassiterite (tin ore). Throughout Egypt's long history, however, most of the massive megalithic structures were built with the use of stone tools only: copper proved too soft, and bronze too rare. Still, building a pyramid using only a stone technology reveals how much energy and labor the Nile released from agriculture with its abundant harvest. Egyptians de-

veloped a sandstone to cut the large stone blocks used in their monuments. The technique involved a string, sand, and water, which masons drew back and forth across large stones to create their building materials.

In the Middle Kingdom, distressing, variable floods continued, so that the farmers could barely feed the growing population even though they engaged in extensive irrigation projects. These included a massive effort to connect the Nile to the Fayum depression that created an artificial oasis based on the Nile's water and silt. Simultaneously, the frontiers needed fortification to protect a brisk foreign exchange of agricultural products and luxury items. After the Egyptians dug channels in the Nile as barriers, they built more than a dozen fortress towns along the first cataracts near Syene (modern-day Aswan); they also built a great defensive wall and forts to protect the Delta region, Egypt's most vulnerable frontier, in the north.

But, despite all these efforts to meet the needs of the people, protect the state, and compensate for what had become less-than-reliable flood levels, the Middle Kingdom could not match the power concentrated in the hands of the kings of the Old Kingdom. Most of the Middle Kingdom monarchs found themselves incapable of reining in the various nomarchs; and these local rul-

Egyptian monuments were covered with decorative designs and heiroglyphics. Courtesy Touraj Daryaee.

ers retained enough autonomy to maintain private armies and local court privileges, such as passing their status and office to their heirs. The nomarchs were a constant threat, a fact revealed by the arrogance displayed in the monuments they had built in their own honor, which were lavish, self-congratulatory, confident, and militaristic.

One of the most striking features of this change in status between members of the royal household and their subordinates, both nobles and commoners alike, was a shift in belief as to who had access to the after-life. During the Old Kingdom, the Pyramid Texts guided the kings alone in their quest for life after death, while in the Middle Kingdom, Coffin Texts inscribed inside private coffins helped everyone (who could afford it) to achieve the same benefits. The gods of Egypt now seemed to show concern for all the people, not just the divine monarch.

The Hyksos and Second Intermediate Period (ca. 1786–1575 BCE) and The New Kingdom (1575–1050 BCE)

The Second Intermediate Period began with an invasion by the nomadic "shepherd people" (the *Hyksos*) who migrated into Egypt at the end of the Middle Kingdom and took advantage of an air of insurgency among the nomarchs. Realizing the inability of the Egyptian king to control the state, the Hyksos captured the Delta region, where they set up their own kingdom. Humiliation added to decentralization, compounding the sense of chaos that surrounded the Egyptian people. Because of this foreign occupation, when Egyptian rulers rebelled and expelled the Hyksos, all of the New Kingdom pharaohs (kings or "Great House") seemed to have redefined their political-ritual basis of rule. Although each interpreted their ability to rule in a unique, personal fashion, they all claimed the right to engage in military adventures and conquest to ensure against future invasions. Such claims introduced a new universalism to royal authority that reached far beyond the core lands of Egyptian civilization. Earlier familiarity with adjacent cultures had allowed Old Kingdom monarchs to extend contact with foreign peoples through trade, immigration, and military pressures. Now, however, the New Kingdom pharaohs decided to close the avenues of access into Egypt in order to exclude any future humiliation like that experienced under the Hyksos, who had imposed an extended period of foreign occupation. Accordingly, conquest of the Levant to the east and invasion deep into Nubia in the south became state policy, as did the religious sanctions for these operations. Hence, the people believed these military successes were dependent on the effective rituals of the priests in the service of the God Amun (his temple at Karnak near Thebes), and the New Kingdom pharaohs heaped vast rewards and riches onto this priesthood. Yet what started as an invincible alliance between the pharaohs and Amun priests eventually became a deadly rivalry over who controlled Egypt's wealth at the end of the New Kingdom.

Still, the first half dozen rulers of the Eighteenth Dynasty were preoccupied with expelling foreigners, securing frontiers, and extending Egyptian influence and control. One of these half dozen rulers, Tuthmoses, engaged in constant campaigning and set the limits of Egypt's imperial reach: north to what is now Iraq and south to the present fourth cataract of Nubia. Never before had Egypt commanded so much land, maintained a professional standing army, or utilized the key weapon introduced by the Hyksos: the chariot. Military sports, military equipment, battle scenes in Egyptian art, tomb inscriptions of heroic deeds, and stone reliefs detailing major engagements spoke to the new interest in warfare among the pharaohs.

Yet even in the midst of this warlike era, one of Egypt's most unusual political episodes began with the reign of Hatshepsut, the favorite daughter of Tuthmoses I. A willful child of a dynamic father, Hatshepsut could not idly sit by when her father died after a brief but martial reign. Married to a half brother, Tuthmoses II, whose sickly nature did not promise the type of energy needed of a leader in Egypt's new military era, Hatshepsut took advantage of his sudden death to seek the throne. Ignoring her husband's two daughters, and exploiting the youth of his ten-year-old son (the future Tuthmoses III), Hatshepsut began her active political career as a regent. After the first two years of her nearly twenty-year reign (1501–1481 BCE) in this capacity, Hatshepsut suddenly began to present herself as a full-blown co-king, sporting pharaonic regalia and even wearing a royal ceremonial beard. In her own words: "Her Majesty (feminine form) was a maiden, beautiful and blooming. She made her divine form to flourish . . . King of Upper and Lower Egypt."

A reigning female king was not possible in Egyptian ritual, and yet Hatshepsut commanded the lands of the Nile. Only powerful factional support could have enabled her to stay in office for nearly two decades. This support came from the Steward of the House of Amun at Karnak, Senenmut, her advisor, and tutor to the royal children. Hints of a romantic relationship between Senenmut and Hatshepsut permeated her reign, but Senenmut's command over the priesthood at Karnak provided the support she needed to retain power. Her co-king, Tuthmoses III, oversaw military affairs, while his aunt memorialized her achievements on temple reliefs and monuments.

Near her death in 1481 BCE, however, Hatshepsut's name suddenly disappeared from public record, and Tuthmoses III became the sole king. Many years later, a process of defacing her monuments and inscriptions began to wipe out her memory and her access to the afterlife. The perpetrators are unknown, but Tuthmoses III must have been aware of this process. Accordingly, it is highly likely that he ordered this eradication to blot out the memory of Egypt's first female ruler. Hatshepsut was also left out of all the king lists.

Tuthmoses III proved to be a warrior king very much in the mold of Tuthmoses I. Often called the Napoleon of Egypt, Tuthmoses III led seventeen successful campaigns into lands northeast of Egypt. To cement his victories, he married daughters of tributary rulers. Three of these minor wives died young (either in epidemics or by assassination), but their remains (discovered in a once-secret tomb) provide a glimpse into their lives. Their dainty tiaras of gazelle heads and rosettes, hip belts of golden fish, and fine wool shawls to ward off winter chills reveal the luxury and sensuousness of the New Kingdom's court.

The pharaohs after Tuthmoses III maintained the same military posture of this powerful ruler. Dozens of victorious campaigns allowed the pharaohs of the Eighteenth Dynasty to amass untold plunder, much of which went to embellish temples and enrich the priesthood of their patron deity Amun at Karnak. The New Kingdom reached its apex of power and wealth during the reign of Amunhotep III, but, in a recognizable pattern, this would signal a turning point in Egyptian history.

Pharaoh Amunhotep III (reign 1411–1375 BCE) was a family man. Although athletically and militarily active in the early part of his rule, wealth flowing into his treasury seduced him into a life of indolence and self-indulgence. As a patron of the arts, he supported a number of remarkably creative sculptors and poets. He held recreational and ceremonial banquets with free-flowing beer and wine and bevies of women. His sexual interest in women, even several of his own daughters, is documented. The attitude towards royal incest, which we find throughout the dynasties, is still controversial. Royal women stood apart from the nonroyal female population by virtue of the divinity of the queen mother, the principal royal wives, and the concept of the Royal Heiress. Yet rather than legitimizing the rights to the throne or safeguarding property, it may have been that the mere divinity of the royal family required its members to find partners among themselves.

Whatever the case, the women of the New Kingdom played a key role in Egyptian history. Within the royal family, from the celebrated matriarch of the Eighteenth Dynasty, Tetisheri, to Hatshepsut, to Tiye, Amunhotep III's wife and mother of Akhenaton, and the latter's wife, Nefertiti, the role of royal women, while intentionally separate from men's, tended to be equally respected and influential. Among commoners, women received respect and affection from their fathers, husbands, and children. The family was a central institution, with women's principal occupations being childbearing and household maintenance.

Amunhotep III's sensuous reign, however, marked a turning point in the policy of the New Kingdom toward its neighbors. Amunhotep III had two sons, one who died while still quite young and the other, Amunhotep IV, who became very famous for his religious experimentation. Like his father in his laziness and interest in domestic life, the arts, and women, Amunhotep IV turned his face away from conquest and empire. Married in his teens to a lovely young woman his own age, Nefertiti, Amunhotep IV found himself installed as co-king by his father. Then the young Amunhotep IV began to erect a strange ritual complex next to the Theban Karnak temple; a complex that honored a deity named *Aton* represented by a solar disc. Unconventionally, Amunhotep IV had temple statues and paintings made of Nefertiti offering to the god Aton respect and supplication. In addition, statues of Amunhotep IV himself show him as having a distorted, bisexual physique and attitude. Before long, Amunhotep IV left Thebes to begin building a ceremonial city to Aton at Amarna to the north of Thebes in Middle Egypt. The city was ready for residents in record time and became, in effect, a new capital. Now far away from the Amun priesthood, Amunhotep IV changed his name to Akhenaton (i.e., One Who Serves Aton), proscribed the worship of all deities other than Aton, and closed their temples and disbanded their supporters. For seventeen years (ca. 1375–1358 BCE), Akhenaton, Nefertiti, their growing family of girls and pets, and their relatives remained in Amarna obsessed with Aton. More or less ignoring affairs of state, making officials from far away lands like Mesopotamia stand in the hot sun during Aton's ceremonies, Akhenaton slowly lost control of his own kingdom.

Signs of tension within the royal family, as well as within the civilization as a whole, came to a climax with the abrupt disappearance of Akhenaton and most other members of the royal family. Soon vandalism and destruction swept through Amarna. Removed from Amarna, one member of the royal family, Tutankh*aton*, returned to Thebes, was installed as king, and changed his name to Tutankh*amun*. His fabulous tomb, discovered by archaeologists 1922, recorded the resurrection of the priesthood at Karnak and the return of Amun. The priesthood of Amun then set about obliterating the memory of Akhenaton.

Tutankhamun's short reign, and the death of his young wife, brought the Eighteenth Dynasty to an end and the ruler of the Nineteenth Dynasty to the throne. Descendents of commoners who had done well in the military, the Nineteenth Dynasty restored conquest to Egypt's political agenda. Most famous among the eleven rulers of the Nineteenth Dynasty, Ramses II left more traces of himself than did any of his relatives. He was unmatched in energy and bombast, if not in actual accomplishments. At the age of twenty he had already sired ten children; fifty years later, when he died, he left some two hundred male offspring known by name and an unknown number of daughters. He decorated Egypt with countless massive statues of himself, and in his spare time he campaigned as far north as Syria. There he ran into the Hittites, fought a great battle at Kadesh and claimed victory, but found he could not advance any farther. Since the Hittites also claimed victory at Kadesh, most scholars believe the battle must have been a draw.

Perhaps it was Ramses II who was the pharaoh at the time of the Exodus of the Hebrews. Some scholars suggest that at the time the Hebrews would have lived in the eastern Delta city of PiRamses (House of Ramses), approximately where the Hyksos had built their capital Avaris (modern-day Tell el Daba). From there, the Hebrews may have crossed the marshy Reed (Red) Sea to places in the Sinai Peninsula. The only Egyptian historical evidence of the Hebrews at this time is their mention in the Israel Stele (a monumental pillar) of Ramses II's son, Merneptah: "The Canaan has been plundered into every sort of woe . . . Israel is laid waste; his seed is no longer."

Not long afterwards, the last great Egyptian king, Ramses III, came to power, ushering in the Twentieth Dynasty. His achievements were less spectacular than those of Ramses II. Ramses III spent his years fighting against large-scale family migrations and invasions of the Delta from the Sea Peoples and the Libyans. One of the first naval battles recorded in history took place off the Mediterranean coast during his reign. Its depiction on Ramses III's mortuary temple at Medinet Habu shows the progress of the battle almost hour by hour, from the first engagement to the tumbling into the seas of defeated sailors as their ships went down.

As Ramses III lingered after an assassination attempt on his life near the end of his reign, signs of a Third Intermediate period had already surfaced. Decentralization had once again set in: erratic floods had denied the population of Egypt needed food surpluses; and the appearance of a new metal, iron, in Anatolia and then Mesopotamia, threatened foreign invasion. A combination of all these things, plus epidemics, famine, worker unrest, and short-lived kings indicated that Egypt's era of independence and power had ended. The most foreboding of these signs was the introduction of iron; it redefined warfare and excluded Egypt from the ranks of the great powers. Now after nearly two thousand years (3100–1167 BCE), the vast productive potential of the Nile lay open to strangers and invited conquest.

Egypt and the Iron Age

As mentioned in Chapter Two on Mesopotamia, when iron appeared in Anatolia, the widespread diffusion of affordable metal farm tools transformed the farmers' material bonds to the city. At the same time, more efficient plows, scythes, and sickles increased food production. Accordingly, larger harvests, regular exchanges between farmers and urban artisans, and a new tax base redefined the political and military potential of sedentary cultures. The higher annual agricultural yields also released more people to serve the state, while metal armor replaced leather and protected the infantry from archers on the battlefield. Finally, political command over geographic space expanded to meet the needs of one centerplace city in which citizen republics or monarchs governed new empires.

Yet, the Iron Age bypassed Egypt. Unlike Mesopotamia, Greece, Rome, India, and China, where broad floodplains and rainfall districts allowed iron plows to realize their full potential in terms of food production, Egyptian cultivation was confined to: 1) the 30,000 square miles of land bound by the crevasse carved out by the Nile, and 2) the 40,000 square miles of black earth found in the Delta. As a result, the introduction of iron plows could not have increased field size in Egypt, and they could not have opened up adjacent acreage watered by the sparse rainfall of the Sahara Desert. Consequently, iron farm tools, weapons, armor, and the farmer-soldier did not appear in Egyptian history, so Egypt did not experience an agricultural revolution. Furthermore, Egypt was iron-poor, with few iron deposits in the territory.

Suddenly, the abundance generated by the Nile could not compete with the expanded acreage brought under tillage in Mesopotamia or the Mediterranean

Basin. In time, great powers emerged outside Egypt that could not resist the allure of wealth offered by the Nile. First Assyria, then Persia, next Macedonia, and finally Rome captured Egypt and transformed its acreage into a source of food for export. Thus did the Iron Age end native rule over the Nile and integrate the once mighty civilization of Egypt into a larger political landscape governed from the outside.

Suggested Reading

Baines, J. and J. Malek, *The Culture Atlas of the World: Ancient Egypt* (New York: Oxford University Press, 1997).

Grimal, Nicolas, *A History of Ancient Egypt,* Translated by Ian Shaw (Oxford: Oxford University Press, 1992).

Hayes, M., *The Egyptians* (New York: Rizzoli Publishers, 1997).

Redford, Donald, ed., *The Oxford Encyclopedia of Ancient Egypt,* Three Volumes (New York: Oxford University Press, 2001).

Robins, G., *Women in Ancient Egypt* (Stroud: Alan Sutton Publishing, Ltd., 1991).

Romer, J., *Ancient Lives: Daily Life in the Egypt of the Pharaohs* (New York: Holt Rinehart and Winston, 1984).

Silverman, David P., ed., *Ancient Egypt* (New York: Duncan Baird Publishers, Ltd., 1997).

Simpson, William Kelley, *The Literature of Ancient Egypt* (New Haven and London: Yale University Press, 2003).

Strouhal, E., *Life of the Ancient Egyptians* (Cambridge: Cambridge University Press, 1992).

INDIA:
From the Indus to the Ganges

Far to the east of both Egypt and Mesopotamia, the Indus Valley represented the third leg in the three river systems of Eurasia that composed the heartland of the earliest civilizations. Like the Tigris and Euphrates rivers in Mesopotamia, the water of the Indus River carved shallow riverbeds through a vast floodplain, flowed from north to south, and produced violent floods. Unlike the rivers of Mesopotamia, the Indus carried many more metric tons of water, for it was fed by the snow melt of the vast Himalayan Range as well as from that of the smaller local Sulaiman Mountains, and the downpour contributed by the annual summer monsoons.

Indeed, the abundance of water that fed its tributaries, which in turn fed the Indus itself, created a rich source of moisture for agriculture in what scholars call the Harappan civilization (3000–1500 BCE). Named after an archeological site dug on a branch of the Indus, Harappa revealed a city system unique in design. Complemented by artifacts unearthed at other archaeological sites, such as those found at Kalibangan, Mohenjo-Daro, and Lothal, the items produced by the Harappan people paint a picture of a culture rich in casting vessels, statuettes, knives, fishhooks, arrowheads, saws, chisels, sickles, pins, bangles, dishes, bowls, jars, flasks, clay figurines, and extraordinary bricks. We also know that the people of these cities engaged in trade as well as in food production. Yet an understanding of the political organization of these cities and their relation to one another is lost to us because no one has ever figured out how to read their written records.

The reason we cannot read what the Harappan people have left behind is a consequence of the ecological conditions in which they lived. Over the course of many centuries an abundance of water and the accordingly high water table saturated much of India's earliest artifacts. Unfortunately, this blurred a good deal of what the Harappan culture had produced. Archaeologists cannot dig beyond a certain level in this area without releasing water, so the origins of the civilization will always remain unknown to us. Therefore, what

has been unearthed in terms of writing represents only short fragments of twenty-five symbols or less. And even if someone could decipher them, the paucity of information such few symbols would impart would leave scholars seeking more information.

And if we bemoan the high water table of the Indus Valley for the knowledge of which it has deprived us, we can only imagine how these same conditions must have affected the people of this ancient Indian civilization. Their struggle is evidenced by their use of the baked bricks they produced specifically to withstand moisture. Made by master brick makers who produced highly standardized and decorative building blocks, these bricks differentiated architecture in the Indus River valley from that in Mesopotamia, whose structures consisted largely of simple sun-dried blocks of mud and reeds. Baked bricks, however, made water-resistant buildings, so the Indians were able to produce some of the best-planned cities of the ancient world. There was, however, a catch: baked bricks required an enormous amount of fuel to reach the temperatures needed to make them water-resistant.

Given the abundance of meltwater from the Himalayas and Sulaiman Mountains, plus the seasonal rainfall produced by the monsoons, the forests surrounding the upper Indus River valley originally must have been quite lush. More profuse in the north than in the south, where conditions became as arid as Sumer and Egypt, these forests provided the needed fuel for the brickmakers' kilns. But the constant demand for this fuel led to severe deforestation, which ultimately, destroyed India's ancient ecology.

The loss of these trees increased aridity and exposed the soil of the Harappan culture to erosion, which, in turn, increased the violence of floods due to the expanded volume of debris carried in the river waters. These floods also caused the streams feeding the Indus to change their course. Finally, they washed away precious soil, choked irrigation canals, and created vast dust fields between 2000 and 1500 BCE. At the same time, the demand for water, as the symbiosis of agriculture caused human numbers in the Indus River valley to grow, increased evaporation and led to the salination of the soil. To top it all off, the expanding water demand raised the water table, which in turn saturated the roots of the crops needed to feed the residents of Harappan cities. Thus this combination of increasingly powerful floods, course changes of rivers, salinated fields, clogged irrigation systems, dust storms, and a rising water table undermined the Harappans' ability to create food surpluses and forced the retreat of the civilization.

In the classic pattern, this retreat proved to be an open invitation to nomadic invasion. Indeed, just as the Harappan civilization began its downward spiral caused by ecocide around 1900 BCE, warrior cultures using chariots in Central Asia soon began expanding outward. Caught in a cycle of destruction that hit every sedentary culture in Eurasia after 1800 BCE, chariot squadrons of nomads introduced India to the Aryan clans.

The chariot was a devastatingly effective new weapon, the product of a technological revolution that transformed warfare. Overwhelming to sedentary cultures everywhere who had lacked horses for centuries, charioteers successfully invaded Greece, Egypt, Mesopotamia, India, and China from central Asia where these swift animals had been domesticated. In each case, similar tactics were used, except in Greece (see Chapter Six). A fast-moving chariot squadron would drive the infantry defending a city from the field using a shower of arrows that penetrated the leather protection of those foot soldiers who could not afford bronze armor. Since the vast majority of most defending cities' infantry fell into this category, their soldiers soon panicked, beating a hasty retreat behind the city walls. The invaders would then lay siege to the city, surrounding it until the food reserves of the urban culture were exhausted, at which point the starved residents had no choice but to throw open their city walls to the nomads. India proved to be one of the victims of the Aryan charioteers, who overran the Indus River Basin by 1500 BCE.

Ironically, while these Aryan charioteers commanded the battlefield, they could not consolidate their hold over the Indian subcontinent. Clans of nomadic warriors destroyed what was left of the Harappan civilization after the ecocide, but no one single Aryan ruler, or alliance of rulers, emerged to establish a central government. India then plummeted into a Dark Age that lasted from 1500 to 800 BCE. During that time, an oral tradition replaced the writing skills of the Harappan people, and an exact accounting of events became even more difficult to retrieve by archaeologists and histori-

ans. Accordingly, India then experienced a long history of political chaos that made religious events, as opposed to political ones, on the subcontinent far more important as an explanation for the civilization that eventually emerged.

Part of this new religious tradition developed with the *Vedas*, a compilation of epic poems, myths, sacrificial practices, and rituals that offered the Aryans an oral explanation for the origin of the universe. Coupled with the Vedas (which will be more fully discussed later in this chapter), a pantheon of gods and goddesses— similar to those found on Mount Olympus in Greek lore—governed the daily lives of these ancient Indians. Finally, *Brahman* priests became the preeminent local figures that defined human existence for the diverse ethnic groups that lived in India.

The word *Indian* itself belies a sense of unity that did not exist for the people who occupied the subcontinent. Unlike China and the West, where a central government actually came to dominate the political world and produce a common written or spoken administrative language, India never achieved stable or enduring political unity. Instead, hundreds of local dialects and dozens of major linguistic families marked the ethnic diversity of the Indian subcontinent. The absence of a common spoken, written, or administrative language reveals the absence of any significant political order. Indeed, the ruling languages of India of its last five hundred years, Urdu and English, reveal that native political authority was still missing when India entered the modern era.

Hence, religion became the backbone of ancient Indian culture. And, this rich religious tradition rejected a connection between experience and reality as India produced two powerful monisms. The first, *Brahmanism*, which later matured into *Hinduism*, became the religion of the countryside; it explained life in general for most Indians by rejecting a connection between experience and reality. At the same time, *Buddhism* became the religion of India's cities; Buddhism also rejected the world of the senses as an illusion and contended that all of life was filled with suffering. Consequently, both religions held the world of politics as being irrelevant because the imposition of a ruler's will belonged to the realm of illusion and merited only one's scorn. Accordingly, while kings tried to impose their will here and there on the subcontinent, the priests and monks actually dominated the Indian religous imagination. That said, the one moment at which India held the greatest promise of achieving political unification under a native ruler occurred during the Iron Revolution.

India, Iron, and Rice

Although rice had been cultivated on the Indus River floodplain during Harappan times, this grain did not become a major food source there until the start of the Iron Age around 800 BCE. At that time the introduction of iron farm tools and weapons gave would-be Indian kings the means to consolidate political power. Simultaneously, the biological equilibrium between symbiosis and parasitism now tipped in favor of food production, which served as a new tax base for creating the first empires. Thus, India experienced its initial efforts at forming a successful central government.

Rice and iron became common in the Ganges River Basin about the same time that Indian kings and Brahman priests began to consolidate their hold on India. Ironically, just as kings started to acquire the means to establish a centralized government, so their chief rivals, the Brahman priests, attempted to solidify their hold over the imagination of the subcontinent. Hence, even as rice and iron created the food surpluses necessary to underpin the rise of the first extensive Indian kingdom, Magadha (650–320 BCE), the Brahmans sought to implement a powerful religious tradition to fill the power vacuum left by centuries of political disunity. The priests did so when they created their caste system that divided India into ranks with Brahmans first, *Kshatriyas* (kings and warriors) second, *Vaisyas* (merchants, artisans, and farmers) third, *Sudras* (day laborers) fourth, and outcast *untouchables* (those who did all the polluted tasks of society) last. As a result, a rivalry over authority began to develop between priests and kings—a rivalry fueled by rice and iron.

The introduction of rice generated the grain surpluses that made the concentration of political authority possible, while that of iron farm tools expanded greatly the number of fields under cultivation. Thus, the combination of rice and iron created a positive biological foundation to support expanding political systems, a direct challenge to priestly claims to the leadership of society. But at the same time, the combination of rice and iron conjoined to offset still another major factor in India's history of disunity: parasitism became a principal barrier to political unification.

India's first native empire, the Mauryan (320–184 BCE), and its second, the Gupta (320–535 CE), proved fragile, with five centuries of chaos and foreign invasion in between them. Despite the unity they created based on rice and iron, the Mauryan and Gupta empires still had difficulty maintaining the food surpluses necessary to support political centralization. The region where both of these empires began, along the up-per Ganges River, became a dangerous biological zone. While the Ganges was the richest region in food production, it also happened to be a perfect breeding ground for pathogens and the animals that spread them. As the rich agricultural surplus generated a large human population, it also fed the many parasites that exploited people as hosts.

The reason why the Ganges produced so many diseases had to do with its site, one with consistently warm temperatures and abundant water. Unlike the drier and cooler Mediterranean, the Indus River valley, or northern China, the Ganges offered a geographic setting that supported a rich supply of pathogens. The steep Himalayan Mountains sheltered the Ganges from Arctic winds blowing from the north, and the wet riverine environment was warmed by monsoon winds blowing from the south. Because so many pathogens found this region an excellent home, a high incidence of disease reduced the political stability in Indian history; unfortunately, the best place to begin a kingdom and grow rice was also the most dangerous place in which to live.

The power of these biological conditions only became visible once Rome and Han China successfully created commercial links with India between 100 BCE and 300 CE. Covered in detail in Chapter Ten, this semiglobal commercial bond led to an exchange of goods, ideas, and germs that transformed the ancient world. Relevant to this discussion, however, was the effect of India's germs on both Rome and Han China. Exported diseases from India produced a massive die-off in both civilizations that contributed to their internal collapse. Whenever alien peoples invaded India, or engaged in trade with the subcontinent, they exposed themselves to the biological environment that Indians lived with on a daily basis.

Since the emerging caste system placed rigid religious barriers between different occupations and statuses within India, fear of contact with economic inferiors encouraged the rulers to avoid as much as possible their merchants, artisans, peasants, and day laborers. Because this status identity correlated with ethnic variation, the distance the upper castes maintained between themselves and the lower castes (due to the idea of religious "pollution") inadvertently reduced the possibility of disease transmission. The tradition of caste separation might truly have protected the rulers from their far more infectious servants. So while the caste system developed into a functional pattern of social, occupational, and ethnic division, it also may have unintentionally quarantined the rich from the poor.

As far as India's first empire was concerned, the first formation of a centralized government quickly followed the arrival of Alexander the Great when he invaded India in 326 BCE. After conquering Persia, Alexander of Macedonia ventured into India and exposed India's rulers to Western military techniques. One of these kings was Chandragupta Maurya (reigned ca. 325–297 BCE); who was reputed to have had an audience with the Macedonian monarch.

Since Macedonian infantry tactics had successfully defeated India's resistance, the power of this iron-based military system probably impressed Chandragupta Maurya. Learning how to position infantry troops wielding iron weapons, Chandragupta Maurya could have transformed the Macedonian experience into a springboard for creating his own empire. The timing of these events might have been merely coincidental, but Chandragupta Maurya did generate India's largest armies and began his conquest in 322 BCE (one year after the death of Alexander in Babylonia). With these new forces, Chandragupta Maurya captured Magadha in 320 BCE. Then he protected his newly won state by defeating one of Alexander's heirs, the Macedonian general turned king, Seleucus. Having secured his realm in the west, Chandragupta Maurya set out to unify as much of India as he could in his lifetime. After years of struggle, he consolidated his hold on North India to start the Mauryan Empire (320–184 BCE).

Carefully integrating each conquered area into a centralized state, Chandragupta Maurya constructed a vast bureaucracy integrated with direct access to the economic life of his kingdom. Now the state commanded mines, forests, pearl fisheries, farms, shipping, weaving, and salt manufacturing. The surpluses generated from these enterprises along with rice cultivation created the basis for a standing army estimated at 600,000 infantrymen, 30,000 cavalrymen, and 9,000 war elephants.

Sophisticated irrigation systems, a complex matrix of roads, and an elaborate network of spies, informers, and secret police shed light on all corners of the growing empire, so that the emperor could exercise direct control. This attention to the details of power revealed the degree of energy needed to hold together a culture as divided as was India's.

Yet the Mauryan Empire did not last long enough to create a common language, assimilate the diverse ethnic groups of India, generate a universal system of writing, or provide religious unity to the subcontinent. Indeed, the emerging worldview in India rejected the experiences of this world as the basis of reality, which created a widespread indifference among most common people to the political system that Chandragupta Maurya had to control. Hence, if a king wished to command the resources of India, he had to be constantly vigilant and draw his people into a process they seemingly preferred to ignore.

Meanwhile, both Chandragupta and his most talented heir, his grandson Ashoka (reigned ca. 269–232 BCE), rejected Brahmanism as the dominant faith of their empire. Chandragupta Maurya personally retired into the religion of *Jainism* after twenty-eight years of rule. Having invested so heavily in a life of constant action, Chandragupta chose to retire as one who believed that the world comprised numerous souls trapped in all living things by their *karma*, or the deeds that polluted the soul, and kept them here in this world. They were reincarnated again and again until the soul achieved enlightenment.

In comparison, Chandragupta Maurya's grandson Ashoka followed a similar lifestyle by first being extremely active in politics and later retiring into Buddhism. Ashoka spent the first portion of his reign completing the conquest of India. Once done, however, he renounced militarism, began an era of humane rule, and patronized Buddhism. In fact it was Ashoka's long and peaceful reign that secured Buddhism as the most successful rival to the religious authority long claimed by the Brahman priests.

In each case, both great monarchs of the Mauryan Empire rejected the developing dominant tradition of Brahmanism, which was at this time evolving into Hinduism. As India's first great political leaders, they rejected the subordination of kingship to priests as required by the caste system. Such a division between politics and religion, however, continued after the Mauryan Empire collapsed and proved to be central to the developing Indian cultural imagination.

After Ashoka's reign, the assassination of his heir Birhadratha, at the hands of a Brahman priest, sent the Mauryan Empire on a downward spiral toward collapse. India soon returned to political division with only religion as the potential tradition capable of unifying this vast cultural zone. India did not enjoy another period of political unity until the Gupta Empire (320–535 CE—a complete history of the Gupta Dynasty is found in Chapter Ten).

More than five hundred years of division separated the two eras of political empire, which helps to explain why Indians looked to religion rather than politics in order to understand their world. By the time of the Gupta Empire, Brahmanism had fully matured into Hinduism, which became the official religion of the land. Hence, the Gupta emperors accepted the caste system and their subordination to priests, and as a result they produced a political system that came to represent the classical age of Indian history.

Indian Religions

The indifference that most Indians felt toward their local rulers might explain why they did not record any of the major events of their past until near the end of the ancient era. As a result, such indifference may also account for why scholars often have to look elsewhere to fill the gaps in Indian history.

With the exception of much of the Greco-Roman, and some of the Chinese, historical tradition, court officials and the friends of kings usually wrote the ancient histories for political leaders and patrons that glorified their achievements. Hence, history itself came to serve political ends. Yet the first recorded historical event in Indian history occurred in 326 BCE when Alexander the Great invaded the Indus River valley. However, Greek and Macedonian historians recorded this event—not the Indians. Furthermore, the greatest ruler in Indian history, Ashoka, was all but forgotten by those Indians who followed his reign. His story remained unknown until the late nineteenth century, when British amateur historians and archaeologists began reading his name on the rocks and pillars he had left behind during his long reign. Even Ashoka's grandfather, Chandragupta Maurya, the founder of the Mauryan Empire, seemingly died without notice by his contemporaries. The year of his death is merely an educated guess made by modern historians. Finally, the origins of the Gupta Dynasty, the dawn of the classical period in ancient Indian history, can be traced to Chandra Gupta I, but the story of the origins of his family relies on a single ruined Buddhist temple built by his grandfather, Sri Gupta. Sri Gupta had built this place of worship for Chinese monks who began traveling to India in the third century CE as foreign pilgrims seeking the source of their newly acquired faith. Beyond these ruins, however, no mention of Sri Gupta exists anywhere.

As a result of most Indians' indifference to recording history and politics, the formation of Indian civilization represented the survival of a diverse group of peoples, most of whom rejected the world of experience in favor of a transcendental one beyond the senses. Accordingly, Indian culture created a religious tradition that combined the voices of numerous languages, the power of rival political states, and a wide variety of ethnic groups within the context of beliefs that claimed this very mélange itself was an illusion. The evolution of this tradition slowly generated a religious synthesis that took more than 2,300 years to reach maturity (1800 BCE to 535 CE).

During the first millennium of these 2,300 years, between 1800 and 800 BCE, the practice of writing had all but disappeared and a complex oral tradition emerged to sustain a young Hinduism. One thousand years later, Indians continued this oral tradition and shunned writing as a barrier between the power of spoken language and the gods that language petitioned. Thus, no coherent written record of this religious tradition appears until the Gupta Empire (320–535 CE). The Gupta kings therefore represent the first political authority to acknowledge fully the power of the (by now) mature Hindu tradition. Hence, by 320 CE the Gupta Dynasty realized that Hinduism had been firmly planted in India and decided to set down in writing the principal texts of this faith.

Hindu beliefs had become fully integrated into Indian society and offered unity to a civilization that still largely ignored politics. Since most of Indian history reflected political disunity rather than unity, the formation of Hindu beliefs had to develop without the aid of a central government. This religious synthesis had to take into account the vast complexity of heterogeneous ritual practices, and vast linguistic differences, ethnic diversity, and cultural variations within the subcontinent. This variation is reflected in Hinduism's complex responses to the rival religions that developed in opposition to the

A statue of the Buddha. This famous image of Buddha located in Kamakura, Japan, reveals how well this Indian faith traveled. Courtesy of Steven Wallech.

dogma of the Brahman priests. Consequently, the heterogeneous and synthetic nature of the Hindu tradition gave India its distinctive worldview, one that began to change with the Aryan development of the Vedas.

Established after the Aryan invasion, the Vedic tradition was a sacred lore that remained an oral tradition for two millennia (1500 BCE–500 CE) and slowly matured without the aid of writing. As an oral tradition, the Vedas were known for their enormous length, and the heavy investment that the Indian priests, the Brahmans, had to make in exact memorization in order to recite them to followers accurately. The original Aryan language, *Sanskrit*, functioned within this oral tradition as a sacred tongue whose vocalizations generated the power of the Vedas. This requirement to speak the Vedas derived from the belief that the spoken word evoked the divine power embedded in Sanskrit as a sacred language, which carried mystical and magical energy.

The Vedas themselves included four elements: the *Rig Veda*, the *Sama Veda* (a subset of the Rig Veda dealing with ceremony and sacrifice), the *Yajur Veda* (a second subset of the Rig Veda meaning sacrificial prayers), and the *Atharva Veda* (the Veda of the poor composed of the charms and magic of the pre-Aryan peoples called the Dravidians). The first three Vedas are Aryan and are called the *Trayi Vidya* while the fourth Veda is the Veda of the poor that formed in opposition to the Aryans. The Atharva Veda exception to the Trayi Vedic tradition reveals the power of surviving Dravidian beliefs after the Aryan invasions.

Included in the oral tradition of the Vedas was epic poetry. Chief among the poems is the Mahabharata, which is said to be seven times longer than Homer's *The Iliad* and *The Odyssey* combined and reveals again how much time had to have been invested in memorization. The Mahabharata is a complex, rambling tale that has a loose central core about the rivalry between two branches of the same royal family. Rulers of Kurus, this royal family taught by example the lessons of good and evil in a poem rich in ritual, magic, and power. The Mahabharata functions much like The Iliad and The Odyssey to create a unity of belief in a complex culture with no political center.

A second poem, the Ramayana, is shorter and more coherent; it tells of the ideal man and woman. Focusing on the adventures of Prince Rama and his beautiful wife Sita, the Ramayana relates a tale of heroic conduct and love. An incarnation of the god Vishnu, Rama is cheated out of his right to the throne of Ajodhya, and then spends the next fourteen years of his life in exile with his wife Sita. At this point Sita is suddenly carried off by the demon ruler of Ceylon (present-day Sri

Lanka), and is only rescued after Rama enlists the aid of the monkey king, Sugriva, and the wise monkey sage, Humayun. After this victory over the demon ruler, Rama returns to take his rightful place as king of Ajodhya, but wrongfully puts Sita aside due to gossip about her virtue. Sita nevertheless bears twins to Rama, proves her virtue, and her mother, an earth goddess, welcomes Sita's children home. The standards for loyalty, sincerity, virtue, family, love, and duty all appear in this poem alongside the pain and misunderstanding so common to human life.

Both poems, the Mahabharata and the Ramayana, give a human face to the emerging Hindu tradition. Yet at the heart of this tradition lies the mysterious being Brahma. In Sanskrit *Brahma* means devotion. Devotion, however, is not enough to explain the full nature of Brahma that developed over the course of 1,000 years (1800 to 800 BCE). This idea evolved into the concept of an ultimate reality, which became fixed to the idea of Brahma. According to this concept, the apparent diversity of nature was an illusion that masked a hidden unity; this unity manifested itself as a transcendental essence that resided in all things as part of the body of Brahma.

Brahma himself was both the Creator and the creation. Brahma awake, and fully conscious of his own divine, eternal, and transcendental existence, constituted the Creator; Brahma asleep, dreaming of chaotic diversity and the illusions of nature as a temporal, spatial, and evanescent existence, was the creation. Taken together, both awake and asleep, Brahma existed as one divinity. Hence, the image of Brahma as both the Creator and the creation represented the One as found in a monism, the belief that all different things experienced in the universe were in themselves only shadowy aspects of the one, divine Being.

The growing power of the Brahman priests in the absence of political unity defined India's culture as a collection of unequal souls. It was believed that each soul held a different transcendental status that reflected both its location within the universal body of Brahma and its place within the occupational structure of society. Both locations took form at the moment of birth—this is when a soul became a part of a subcaste, or *jati*, that fell within one of the larger four main castes. In turn, each of these main castes composed the parts of the body of Brahma.

Given the political, linguistic, ethnic, and cultural disunity of India, the Brahmanas (i.e., written religious comments on the Vedas compiled by Brahman priests after 800 BCE to explain their authority) concluded that the chaos of experiences in this world of sensation could not be the source of ultimate reality. Instead, ultimate reality had to exist in a realm of transcendental existence (beyond the senses). For the Indians, the notions of time, space, and reason that defined the window into reality for the Greco-Roman worldview became maya (the realm of illusion). Ultimate reality in India consisted of a unity that resided beyond the reach of this chaotic diversity.

The caste system, then, represented all souls in a hierarchy that formed a monistic whole. A person's location in society at birth defined that person's level of preparation to continue the odyssey of discovery each life represented. In each life, a lesson had to be completed in preparation for the next life. During the course of one life, however, a soul accumulated karma.

Karma is Sanskrit for *action*. Since all action, or karma, is based on the deeds of an individual's identity, and since such an identity was an illusion in the sense that a person believed himself or herself to be a separate being apart from Brahma, then all action caused pollution that stained the soul. Such a collection of stains, or karma, assigned the next lesson that the soul needed to learn and determined the location of one's birth in the next life. If one could lead a life as free of karma as possible, he or she might expect to take numerous steps up the caste hierarchy. All karma, then, defiled the soul and dictated the status of the next life. Reincarnation itself returned the soul to the world of illusion as many times as was necessary, in new caste locations, to complete a person's journey until he or she achieved full comprehension of the ultimate reality.

Such an understanding of caste, karma, and reincarnation allowed all ethnic groups within India to find a place in the body of society and created a functional division of labor despite the diversity of languages that filled the subcontinent. Each job, caste, jati, ethnic group, language, and subculture within India secured an occupation that made up the socioeconomic fabric of the community; and all these economic positions received recognition without a central government to provide the legal structure needed to create a sense of order and security. Hence, under the divine image of Brahma, everyone ended up with the means to make a living, even if they could not effectively communicate with their neighbor.

Meanwhile, the origin myth of the "Primal Man" served to shape the image of society as ultimate reality and a manifestation in the body of Brahma. This Primal Man composed the original substance out of which the universe was built. Converted into the image of Brahma, this Primal Man became the monism that existed as the transcendental essence behind the world of the senses.

When the universe began, this Primal Man sacrificed his body to make up the many parts of reality so easily misunderstood by the senses. These parts became a scale of status defined by caste. The priests made up the souls that comprised the Primal Man or Brahma's head. Kings, princes and warriors made up the shoulders and arms. Farmers, artisans, and merchants made up Brahma's trunk. The day-laboring poor (Dravidians) made up his feet. Only the untouchables seemed to be made of a portion of Brahma too profane to mention. By substituting Brahma for the Primal Man, the priests claimed to be the head, and therefore commanded both legitimate knowledge and ultimate authority over the transcendental realm behind the diversity of Indian culture.

Religious Opposition

Complementing the Brahmanas, a second set of commentaries called the *Upanishads* spoke of an independent religious tradition that opposed and enhanced emerging Hinduism. The Upanishads are one of several philosophical systems found in the Vedantas. In Sanskrit *Vedantas* means "after the Vedas," which comprise not only the Upanishads, but also a group of poetic dialogues and commentaries. The Upanishads dealt with ultimate reality like the Brahmanas, but they do so in a way that suggests one could learn about this transcendental realm without having to travel through so many lives or castes.

The Upanishads comprise six systems called *darshanas* that progressively increase one's insight into ultimate reality. Each system depended on its more superficial preceding system and together posited a universal truth (*Dharma*). Dharma accounted for the eternal cycles of growth and destruction in nature and in the regeneration of the human soul. Through these systems, the Upanishads stated that the purpose of philosophy was to end suffering that ignorance (Avidya), a dependency on maya caused. To know reality, and avoid the ignorance inspired by sensation, however, required a specific discipline called Yoga. Yoga prepared the mind and the body for an inward journey that allowed one to deny the illusion of sensation and discover reality through meditation.

The Upanishads define three stages to this discovery of ultimate reality. The first is faith, a state in which one can achieve salvation through acceptance of a disciplined life. The second is understanding, a rational conviction in the correctness of this self-imposed discipline. And the third is realization, the rapture that occurs when the believer becomes one with ultimate reality. This third stage took the form of Nirvana, Sanskrit for Enlightenment, or the bliss the believer experienced when he or she disappeared into a reunion with ultimate reality, the monistic goal of the disciplined life.

What is remarkable about the Upanishads is that they foreshadow Buddhism. The discipline of the Upanishads spoke with same voice that one finds today in the Buddhist worldview. Siddhartha Gautama, the Buddha (ca. 566–486 BCE), born a prince in a royal family near modern Benares, just south of Nepal, developed a similar discipline as the correct path to Enlightenment. His religion, however, created a more fully articulated strategy of how one could achieve Nirvana. Yet, the Buddha came after the Upanishads and required the influence of this philosophical system to permeate India's imagination.

The Upanishads made access to Enlightenment or rapture possible within one lifetime. They also merged with the Buddha as part of a religious rebellion that opposed Brahmanism. This religious rebellion developed alongside emergent Hinduism as a rival tradition. Yet each rival religious movement that developed in opposition to proto-Hinduism eventually found its way into Hinduism as part of ultimate reality. The Brahmans simply claimed that ultimate reality remained hidden from human senses and was easily misunderstood. Thus, these priests stated that any reality revealed by a rival faith was merely a manifestation of a Hindu truth in a different form.

As mentioned, kings and warlords did not like holding second place in the hierarchy of Indian society. So as kingdoms began to form in northern India, it became the zone for opposition to the Brahmanas. The north produced a rich culture of Jainists, Buddhists, ascetics, and mystics. Each of these rival religious traditions rejected castes and the Brahman's wheel of life that justified caste, karma, reincarnation, and priestly authority. Buddhism, asceticism, and mysticism all sought Nirvana as achieved by the inward odyssey of meditation that allowed entry into the transcendental realm of ultimate reality in a single lifetime (similar to the Upanishads).

Buddhism itself emerged in northern India (as mentioned), the product of Siddhartha Gautama, a Ksha-triya youth who rejected politics for religion. Preoccupied with worry over aging, sickness, and death, Siddhartha Gautama experienced a religious awakening that launched him on a life of mysticism and asceticism until he found what he called the "Middle Path." Using a discipline like that recommended in the Upanishads, Gautama realized the Middle Path after a mystical experience achieved from an intense meditative journey. In a trance under a pipal tree one night after years of yogic discipline, Gautama moved

through his past lives to perceive the suffering that came from a karmic outflow of desire that separated human souls from Universal Being. In this trance, Siddhartha Gautama saw that each life he had led had suffered this separation because of the illusions of desire that individual existence used to fuel its false identity. The solution to suffering, therefore, came from rejecting the "I" of individual existence, all castes, and Brahmanism in general to escape the illusion of a separate existence.

When the illusion of the "I" of individual existence ceased, all life reunited as one in Universal Being. With this realization, Siddhartha Gautama set out to help humanity develop awareness about their false identities as separate beings. He thus became the Buddha, or the Enlightened One, and set forth the Four-Noble Truths and the Eight-Fold Path.

To achieve release from this world of illusion, a Buddhist had to begin a religious journey that involved the Four-Noble Truths: 1) life is suffering; 2) the source of suffering is desire; 3) one can escape suffering; and 4) this escape required a disciplined life following the Eight-Fold path. Suffering came from believing that personal identity was real. To escape suffering, the Buddhist must travel through eight levels of awareness and behavior that allowed ultimate rapture to occur. Like the Upanishads, which revealed ultimate reality through three stages (faith, understanding, and realization), the Eight-Fold Path directed the Buddhist to prepare for a religious odyssey. The first two truths developed the mind: Right View and Right Thought. The next four steps converted thought into action: Right Speech, Right Action, Right Livelihood, and Right Effort. The last two steps returned the Buddhist to the mind to achieve realization: Right-Mindedness and Rapture. Hence, Buddhism and the Upanishads belonged to the same developing religious awareness that played a central role in challenging Hinduism.

The Maturation of India's Faiths

Brahmanism fully matured into Hinduism under the pressures offered by these rival faiths, while Buddhism, Jainism, asceticism and mysticism were not the only ideas incorporated into the emerging Brahman tradition. Hinduism also took shape from the addition of foreign ideas. Foreign influences entered India along the trade routes developed between Rome and China between 100 BCE and 300 CE. These routes included not only the Silk Road, but also the sea-lanes that crossed the Indian Ocean.

The trade routes between Rome and China connected the cultural zones of the ancient Eurasian world. These routes allowed an exchange of ideas and diseases that mark the apex of the ancient era (see Chapter Ten). This pattern of exchange created an integration of beliefs that profoundly altered religions found in India and the Mediterranean Basin. Old faiths like Judaism, Brahmanism, and Buddhism developed into new religions like Christianity or Hinduism, or split, as did Buddhism, into two traditions—the *Hinayana* and *Mahayana* variations that migrated out of India to Southeast Asia, China, Korea, and Japan. But all three of these altered religious traditions came to share several important ideas: conversion became the principal avenue of entry for Buddhism and Christianity. All three religions developed the concept of a human-divine savior; the possibility of salvation at the end of this life on Earth; and relocation of the dead believer's soul in a heavenly realm with the divine; and each saw the divine as the ultimate judge in human affairs.

Christianity, Buddhism, and Hinduism then continued to develop independently of one another in the cultural hearths in which they took root. In India, Buddhism and Hinduism continued to test one another as rivals. Buddhism became the religion of northern India, where political unity and religious opposition was strongest. As the religion of the north, Buddhism took up residence in urban centers where the educated created a strong, mobile intellectual tradition among Buddhist monks. These monks then followed the trade routes out of India to foreign urban centers where they sought converts. They spoke of Buddha as a human deity, the savior who made salvation in one lifetime possible.

Traveling into China, Korea, and Japan, Buddhism became a vehicle for transmitting an Indian version of transcendental reality to these lands. This transcendental image appeared to be very much like the message found in the Upanishads. This message spoke of a disconnect between sensation and reality that required an inner journey through meditation to understand the divine. The power of these ideas induced Chinese Confucian scholars to assimilate much of these Indian concepts of transcendental reality in order to compete with this new faith. Buddhism also transformed both the Korean and Japanese societies into strong, independent cultures capable of maintaining their identity in close proximity to a civilization as rich, vast, and seductive as China's. Hence, Buddhism became both a religious tradition and a cultural vehicle for spreading a powerful worldview.

Hinduism remained in India, where it took up residence in the central, eastern, and southern rural provinces to which many Dravidians had fled from the original Aryan invaders. This relocation of a form of Brahmanism into the religious territory rich in Dravidian traditions helped to round out Hinduism by including

some ancient Indus River valley beliefs. For example, the symbolic value of hump-backed bulls, of the pipal tree, and of the swastika all derive from the pre-Aryan traditions that had been spread throughout India by refugees fleeing the chariot invaders. Finally, the deity *Shiva*, and his female consort *Devi*, as well as ritual baths for purification, can be traced to pre-Aryan beliefs. Each of these features joined Brahmanism and the new concepts that entered India along the Silk Road.

At the same time, the Aryan deity *Vishnu* and the Dravidian *Shiva* underwent transformation from gods into saviors. Both Vishnu and Shiva became human incarnations of the divine who traveled the earth offering salvation. A worshipper could in a single lifetime meet one of these incarnations and achieve a mystical breakthrough into the transcendental realm. This person could also escape the relentless wheel of life and enter paradise without having to return to this world of illusion. These saviors then joined a blending of traditions that saw an intellectual reconciliation between Brahman priests and the opposing mystic and speculative traditions represented by the *Upanishads*. This reconciliation completed the emergence of Hinduism as a mature religion.

In this new form, Hinduism reached maturity after more than 2,300 years of evolution. In so doing, Hinduism offered its followers a means to understand the diversity of India by looking beyond the many different ethnicities, statuses, languages, and subcultures of the land to find a transcendental whole that held the fabric of society together. Hinduism also offered a deep psychological sense of satisfaction in the knowledge that all the various peoples that made up the Indian occupational structure be-

This stone statue is of the prominent Hindu god Shiva in his manifestation as Lingodbhava, a human being with multiple arms. The iconography depicts a competition for status between two gods, Brahma and Vishnu. The two were arguing when a shaft of fire appeared between them. Vishnu's boar incarnation investigated the occurrence at the earth (base of the statue) while Brahma went to the skies on the Hamsa bird (seen at the top). From the fire emerged Shiva, to whom they bowed as the most powerful deity. © The Trustees of the British Museum.

longed where they did due to their place within the body of Brahma. Furthermore, a belief in the eternal structure of the community hidden from the senses allowed all Indians, who chose to do so, to ignore the political chaos that surrounded them and lead a meaningful life.

Suggested Reading

Allchin, B. and Allchin, R., *The Rise of Civilization in India and Pakistan* (Cambridge: Cambridge University Press, 1982).

Basham, A. L., ed., *The Origins and Development of Classical Hinduism* (Boston: Beacon Press, 1989).

Bryant, E., *The Quest for Origins of Vedic Culture* (New York: Oxford University Press, 2001).

Conze, E., *Buddhism: Its Essence and Development* (Oxford: Oxford University Press, 1951).

Hardy, F., *The Religious Culture of India* (Cambridge: Cambridge University Press, 1994).

Keay, John, *India: A History* (New York: Atlantic Monthly Press, 2000).

Kosambi, D. D., *Ancient India: A History of Its Culture and Civilization* (New York: Pantheon, 1966).

Possehl, G. L., *The Ancient Cities of the Indus* (Durham, N.C.: Carolina Academic Press, 1979).

Rapson, E. J., ed., *The Cambridge History of India,* Vol. 1 (Cambridge: Cambridge University Press, 1982).

Singhal, D. P., *A History of the Indian People* (London: Metheun, 1983).

Williams, P., *Mahayana Buddhism* (New York: Routledge, 1989).

Woodcock, G., *The Greeks in India* (London: Faber, 1966).

V

CHINA:
The Huang He, Changjiang, and the Dynastic Cycle

China's is the oldest continuing civilization in the world today. The ancient civilizations of Egypt, Mesopotamia, and the Indian Subcontinent all had their day of glory, but each one gave way to other civilizations long before the advent of modern times. The Chinese civilization, however, was unique: it would rise and fall only to rise again like the legendary phoenix out of its own ashes.

Chinese civilization, like the Egyptian, Mesopotamian, and Indian cultures, began with the generosity of a river. In this case, the river was called the *Huang He* (Yellow River), because of the abundance of *loess* (a matter rich in yellow lime dust) suspended in its waters, that gave the river its distinctive color. Loess, one of the most fertile soils on Earth, blessed the floodplain of the Huang He, which sustained extremely productive farms. Yet the Huang He also had a another Chinese name: "China's Sorrow."

This name arose from the fact that the silt-clogged waters of the Huang He produced not only the richest farmland, but also, over time, lured millions of farmers to their death. The headwaters of the Huang He begin in the snowpack of the Himalayas far to the west; the monsoon rains of the wet season in the east add more water. The combination of these water sources, plus the abundance of loess suspended in the river made the Huang He the most soil-rich provider in the world. Yet, once they began to practice irrigation and directed the fresh soil and water of the Huang He to their fields each year, the Chinese also slowed the flow of the annual flood, thereby causing some of the silt to fall into the riverbed during the growing season. Over time this produced a spectacular event: the Huang He's riverbed began to climb above the floodplain.

Eventually the Huang He's riverbed climbed to as much as fifty feet above the floodplain, making effective water management impossible: the river's levees broke, floodwaters swept across the floodplain, the riverbed moved several hundred miles north or south, depending on the site of the break, and thousands of people drowned. Nevertheless, not long after such a catastrophic event, the ancient Chinese, trapped in the symbiosis of agriculture in a dependent relationship with the Huang He, would return to the river valley to grow their crops. No greater source of fresh, fertile soil or water could be found. Hence, in a cyclical pattern the Huang He both gave life and destroyed it. Thus the river had two names: the Yellow River and China's Sorrow.

No greater example exists of the biological deadlock at the basis of agriculture. The symbiosis that ancient farmers created when they first selected omega seeds placed them in a relationship they could not abandon. The Chinese had no choice: they had to use the rich but dangerous waters of the Huang He or find a better and gentler river along which to live.

The only other river that offered the possibility of irrigation was the *Changjiang* (or Yangtze, the Long River). Located to the south of the Huang He, the Changjiang is a potential second site for the origins of agriculture in China. Found in a wet zone, and separated from the Huang He by the Qingling (mountains), the Changjiang provided water for the rice that the Chinese later cultivated when the two rivers were interwoven in one civilization. Yet many years of history passed before Chinese civilization grew large enough to encompass both river systems. In the meantime, a separate Chinese culture existed in the south along the Changjiang, while the cities to the north, known as "the Cradle of Chinese Civilization," existed in a world isolated from events in the south and remained tied to China's Sorrow.

China's Past and Its Impact on the Chinese Imagination

Historians know more about China's past than that of any other civilization. The Chinese people believed that history was a guide to their present and future and developed a deep reverence for it early in their civilization. The Chinese made a greater effort to keep records of their history than did people of any other civiliza-

a

Six Chinese Scripts. *Xie* (to draw, write) is shown here is the six scripts: a) *xiaozhuan* (small seal script); b) *lishu* (clerical script); c) *caoshu* (draft or grass-script); d) *xingshu* (running script); e) *kaishu* (standard script); and f) *jiantizi* (simplified characters). © The Trustees of the British Museum.

b

c

d

e

f

tion. They recorded their activities on oracle bones, bronze vessels, bamboo strips, and paper. Their earliest inscriptions, those on oracle bones, date back one to two thousand years BCE. Their earliest surviving books were written over five hundred years BCE. A long line of great historians left behind vivid and accurate accounts of their history up to their times. In addition, historians can round out their knowledge of China's past by examining numerous archeological findings (including remains of ancient temples, ancient villages, imperial burial sites), literary and nonliterary writings (including poetry, stories, novels, government records, and private account books), and works of art (including paintings, sculptures, and architecture).

The people of modern China take their identity from the past. The first great Chinese imperial era, the Han Dynasty (202 BCE to 220 CE), set the tone for Chinese history. Accordingly, the modern Chinese call themselves the Han Chinese and are overwhelmingly composed of Han people. They call their spoken language *Hanyu*. While Chinese history principally concerns the civilization of the Han Chinese, other ethnic groups do compose a significant part of it. For a long time the Chinese people believed that their country was the center of the world and therefore called it the "Middle Country." The Chinese pictogram for China, *Zhong guo*, still includes this middle image and marks the kingdom that they believed occupied the center of the Earth. They also believed that theirs was the only land of civilized people and that all who lived beyond their borders were unfortunates with no access to the center of the world; hence they considered them "barbarians."

Mythological China

Ancient Chinese creation myths were passed down from generation to generation orally before historians put them down in writing. Although they were often confused and contradictory, a thoughtful examination of the these myths gives us at least a shadowy glimpse of

China's prehistoric past. The central figures of the narratives are often part human and part supernatural beings. Known as "culture heroes," each of these personas represents a murky stage of development in early human society.

The Chinese creation myth begins with the god *Pan Gu*, who created heaven and earth. When he died his limbs and blood became mountains and rivers, his muscles farmland, his left eye the sun, and his right eye the moon. The original female goddess was *Nuwo Shi*. In one version of the myth, she was said to have made humans out of yellow clay. In another version, she slept with her brother and created the human race, after which she banned future marriages between sister and brother. Legends also had Nuwo Shi setting upright a tilted sky, sopping up floods, and killing predatory beasts to create a safe environment in which humans could flourish. The demigod/ruler *You Chao Shi* taught people how to build treehouses to protect themselves from animal attacks. The demigod/ruler *Suiren Shi* taught people how to make fire and cook their food. *Fu Xi Shi* (Nuwo Shi's brother) taught them how to hunt, fish, and domesticate wild animals. *Yan Di*, or *Shen Nong Shi*, was the god of agriculture who introduced cultivation to a hunting and gathering people, teaching them how to make farm tools and clay pots. He also tasted and tested all plants to determine their medicinal qualities. *Huang Di* (Yellow Emperor) invented the calendar and the use of copper. The calendar made it possible to plant and harvest crops at the most favorable times of the year, and copper was used to make musical chimes. Legend has it that Huang Di's descendents founded the Xia and Zhou dynasties. He and Yan Di are sometimes referred to as the first ancestors of the Han Chinese people.

From these origin myths we discern a fishing and gathering people settling down to practice agriculture, with clan-like units gradually evolving from a matriarchal to a patriarchal society. In legendary chronology, the culture heroes were followed by the "Three Kings," King Yao, Shun, and Yu, who were quite likely composite figures of tribal leaders. Tradition has it that Yao and Shun were elected leaders, or kings, of an alliance of tribes, but that Yu was succeeded by his son, thus launching the practice of father-to-son succession to the throne.

These legends laid a foundation for Chinese traditions and rituals. The heroes and gods established a pattern of life in the Chinese imagination that became known as "the Way." Accepted as sacred practices from the past, the Way defined reality, human relationships, and the general practices found acceptable to Heaven (the sacred realm of China's ancestors). Accordingly, the heroes and gods appeared in Chinese philosophy, either directly or indirectly, and held sway over the Chinese imagination. Consequently, myth blended with fact to shape events in China's past.

The Beginning of Verifiable History

The Xia, Shang, and Zhou dynasties belonging to China's traditional mythological past, which was followed by verifiable history, marked by the rise and fall of successive dynasties. A dynasty is a period during which one family continues to rule over the course of time through several human generations. The model of the "dynastic cycle," the rise and fall of one ruling family, is a convenient tool for keeping track of time, regimes, and significant change.

Traditionally, Chinese historians believe that reliable Chinese history began with the three ancient dynasties—the Xia, the Shang, and the Zhou. Although some modern historians remain skeptical about the Xia Dynasty (2205–1766 BCE) ever having existed, an increasing amount of evidence suggests that it did. There is an abundance of information about the Shang Dynasty (1766–1050 BCE), for it left behind the earliest written records (the source of modern Chinese pictograms).

Modern Chinese scholars began studying Shang writings in 1899 when they discovered large deposits of oracle bones in Anyang (a one-time Shang capital). They learned that Shang diviners asked the spirits for guidance on matters of climate and crops, war and peace, and health and childbearing. To put their questions to the spirits they cut pictograms into turtle shells and flat cattle bones and then sent them to the spirits by heating the bones over a fire. The diviners would then examine the heat-induced cracks in the bones to decipher the spirits' answers. Frequently, a priest would preside over the cracking of the bones and let the king interpret the cracks. The reclaimed bones with the inscriptions contain the names of virtually all the traditional rulers of Xia and Shang dynasties and the dates of many eclipses. Shang bronzes bear inscriptions as well.

The characters of the Shang Dynasty have a striking resemblance to modern Chinese characters. Indeed, a modern Chinese person can make an educated guess at the meaning of many of them. This means that Chinese writing began in the distant past and has continued along the same principles today. It is hard for us to comprehend the endurance of Chinese writing, but a western equivalent might be if everyone in the United States and Europe still used a modified cuneiform or hieroglyphics. The fact that the Chinese can trace their

According to Chinese creation myths, Nuwo Shi and Fu Xi Shi are considered the first ancestors of all people. Nuwo Shi is the creator of humankind, whereas her brother and husband Fu Xi Shi, is responsible for introducing writing, fishing, and trapping. This painting on silk is among thousands of cultural relics and documents unearthed from tombs built for nobles of Goaching City from the Western Jin to Tang Dynasties. From the Astana Ancient Tombs, Turpan, Xinjiang Uygur Artman Region. Original from chinaculture.org

writing back to the Shang, and that the West has developed an alphabet instead of using its ancient systems reveals the powerful continuity in Chinese history.

The records and archeological findings reveal much about life in the Shang Dynasty. From them we know that Shang had cities protected by walls, practiced fairly developed forms of cultivation and animal husbandry, used farm tools made of wood or stone, had a written language of pictographs and ideographs, were talented crafters of bronze and artworks, used shells as a kind of primitive money, and had a hierarchically structured society, with kings and aristocrats at the top, multitudes of commoners in the middle, and slaves at the bottom. The gap between ruler and ruled was wide. Even the remains of royal palaces and tombs are impressive in their massive scale, while common people lived in crude pit dwellings.

Yet several other features of Shang life emerge from the absence of certain artifacts. The plow did not arrive in China until the sixth century BCE. Hence all the food for their cities had to come from intensive labor using hoes and pointed sticks. Plows cut land in preparation for cultivation, so those who use the plow are practicing agriculture. Those who prepare the land with only a hoe or pointed stick, however, are practicing horticulture. The difference between the two is estimated by the size of the harvest: agriculture yields fifty times the food that horticulture can, provided irrigation is part of the formula. Irrigation concentrates labor on flatlands near excellent water sources and provides yearly supplies of fresh soil. To produce the surpluses of food necessary to provide for cities using horticulture therefore required extraordinary effort and must have created a huge problem of labor management.

But the Chinese are known for their strict work ethic and emphasis on large families and elaborate internal organizations. And, as mentioned, China was blessed with loess, the richest soil in the world. This is why many scholars believe that the struggle to feed cities through cultivation shaped the Chinese family in the Shang period. This might explain the historic emphasis placed on excellence when it comes to work as well as the role of the ancestors in Heaven, who demanded family and filial piety (respect for elders and the dead).

Shang period bronze works were the possessions of the urban elites only. Bronze was not used to make farm tools that might have helped farmers in their constant toil. This rare and expensive metal was reserved for making weapons and ceremonial vessels. Hence, as mentioned previously, the farmers made all their own tools, clothing, and shelters, while bronze belonged to Chinese art and religion. And the beautiful and technically advanced bronzes of the Shang dynasty have never been surpassed in quality; it is the exceptional Shang bronze works that gives the name to an entire age: the Bronze Age (2000–500 BCE).

The masses of the Shang people lived deeply in awe of supernatural forces. Their kings served as ceremonial leaders who maintained religious harmony on Earth. The Shang people worshiped their ancestors, who probably also served them as demigods. They worshiped Heaven, which, they believed, controlled the forces of nature, human and land fertility, and the fate of humans through the rites performed by the king. They believed in an afterlife, which we know because they buried articles of use and value with the deceased. They practiced human sacrifice in burial ceremonies; aristocrats, commoners, or slaves might be buried with their rulers. Hence, the Shang rulers overawed their people who gladly gave the kings the harvest surpluses each year to maintain harmony on Earth.

The Shang state was a large and powerful one ruled by a king. He was both its head and its high priest. The king's power over his people tended to be absolute, while the tax base allowed him to field armies of three to five thousand men. The king dominated an alliance of vassals, but his was only one domain among those commanded by his local lords. The king had direct control over only his own realm, but he exercised indirect control over the rest of the area through his vassal lords. The local lords exercised autonomy within their own domains but had to pay taxes and provide labor and military service to the king. This system of having one king and his tribe dominate an alliance of tribes with domestic autonomy is often referred to as a *feudal system.*

In the twelfth century BCE, a western Turkish-speaking tribe called the Zhou replaced the Shang by con-

quest due to greater access to horses and chariots. Like the Shang, the Zhou (1050–256 BCE) built a feudal state; both had to distribute estates to loyal subordinates to command all the land that their farmers cultivated. Since the family system served as the basis of order in Chinese culture, feudalism was a natural extension of the family; the Chinese referred to feudalism as "the Cadet Family System." The new king claimed to be the "Son of Heaven" and to rule with the "Mandate of Heaven." He justified his rebellion against the Shang Dynasty on the grounds that Heaven had stripped the last Shang king of the Mandate of Heaven because of his iniquities, bestowing it instead upon the Zhou ruler because of his impeccable virtue. This idea of a transient Mandate of Heaven dominated in Chinese thought down through the ages.

Compared with the Shang, the Zhou practiced a far more developed form of horticulture and a more fully developed urban division of labor. They also built larger cities, and developed a more sophisticated method of writing. Late in the Zhou Dynasty (771–256 BCE), however, the rulers' power suffered a steep decline. Former vassals became ever more assertive; they kept for themselves the taxes (food surpluses) they should have been collecting for the central government, enriching themselves and weakening the state. In this way, the Zhou rulers' command over China declined in much the same way that the kings of Egypt lost control of the Old Kingdom: too many royal offspring demanded suitable employment, population pressure placed stress on food production, violent and unpredictable floods made grain rationing difficult, and disloyal aristocrats separated portions of the realm from the state to create their own fiefdoms.

Zhou aristocrats were constantly fighting one another to extend their own territories, even as their subordinates were plotting to topple them. Consequently, it was a time of endless warfare between and within states that saw widespread human suffering and material destruction. The feudal system was in a state of steep decline. The Late Zhou is also known as the "Spring and Autumn" period (772–481 BCE) and the "Era of the Warring States" (403–221 BCE). Traditionally, Chinese people considered such periods of declining central authority as times of slaughter, destruction, and suffering. But history has shown time and again that the absence of a stifling central authority can also create an environment that fosters great outbursts of energy, growth, and creativity. The Late Zhou was a case in point; even though violence and despair were rampant, it also was a time of rapid and profound change, even of significant progress.

The Iron Age

Iron arrived in China in 600 BCE. It had diffused from Mesopotamia to India by 800 BCE and took the next two hundred years to cross the Himalayan Mountains and the Gobi Desert. When it finally did reach China, iron replaced bronze, as it had elsewhere, spawning the development of a new level of cultivation and military performance. Simultaneously the plow arrived in China in 500 BCE, just prior to the launching by the great aristocrats of the Era of the Warring States (403–221 BCE). Iron, the plow, and warfare tore China apart.

How iron and the plow made this political struggle possible reflects the impact of this new metal and farm technology on Chinese history. Since Shang and Zhou farmers cultivated without a plow before 500 BCE, the food surpluses that fed Chinese cities had to come from the simple hoe and digging stick alone, as we have seen. Since Chinese cities rivaled Sumerian cities in size and complexity, the amount of labor needed to feed this urban population must have been enormous. But because the Chinese work ethic is based on filial piety and demands a very high level of excellence, Chinese farmers somehow managed to produce sufficient surpluses to maintain these great cities using horticulture instead of agriculture. Now just imagine what must have happened to food production in China with the widespread introduction of the plow and iron farm tools.

As mentioned, when used in conjunction with irrigation, the plow generates an estimated increase in yield of fifty fold as compared to a hoe or digging stick. To this sudden increase in farm yields must be added the effect of the iron-tipped plow blades within the context of the Chinese work ethic. This combination released an enormous food surplus that transformed the tax base in Late Zhou society. When the aristocrats simply diverted these new taxes into their own coffers instead of honoring their obligations to the king, the Zhou state crumbled.

At the same time, iron weapons and armor outfitted new armies that could be fed with this newly bloated agricultural surplus. Now, farmer-soldiers swelled the ranks of the military, with Chinese armies undergoing as radical a transformation as had those in Assyria and Greece. Chinese aristocrats declared themselves kings and fought one another to capture wider power. Thus began one of the bloodiest eras of world history.

Fortunately, the unusual combination of iron, the plow, and the Chinese work ethic that fueled the horrors of the wars between princes did not stop the flowering of the greatest era of philosophy in Chinese his-

tory. Indeed, it was during the Era of the Warring States (403–221 BCE) when the most sophisticated thinkers in China created philosophies that effectively governed Chinese standards of conduct all the way to 1905 CE.

As mentioned in past discussions of other ancient civilizations, iron had many advantages over bronze as a metal. Iron was more plentiful, cheaper, and better at holding a cutting edge. In agriculture, iron plowshares could plow deeper than wooden ones, open up more virgin soil, and increase output. This output could release more farmers to become soldiers wearing iron armor as well as creating a surplus that could be traded on the market, giving commerce a boost. In time, even small, closed, and self-sufficient communities began to reach out to engage in interregional activities. People began to make metal currency, and commerce stimulated the growth of towns and cities. Successful merchants became very rich and powerful, with some of them becoming deeply involved in politics. One such businessman, Lu Buwei (?–235 BCE), became a king-maker. Because of the introduction of iron, an economic revolution in both production and commerce dawned.

The Golden Age of Classical Philosophy

Out of all the turbulence of Late Zhou period came an outburst of intellectual energy known as the time when "a hundred flowers bloomed and a hundred schools of thought contended." Now all sorts of men stepped forward with all sorts of reform proposals. These were not dreamers living in ivory towers; most of them were or would soon become hard-nosed realists. They combined philosophy, statecraft, common sense, and often great literary skill to provide answers to the pressing problems of the day. The three main schools of classical Chinese philosophy took shape during this time. Kong Zi (or Confucius, 551–479 BCE) was the founder of Confucianism. Surrounded by chaos and suffering, he wanted to reestablish peace and harmony. His proposed solution was a retrospective one. He believed that there had been a "Golden Age" in early Zhou when the ruler was virtuous and his subjects loyal, when people lived in harmony, followed rituals prescribed by sage kings, and society was stable. He hoped to recreate his version of the Golden Age.

In his philosophy, the model state was an expanded family, a hierarchically structured society in which people related to each other in unequal but reciprocal ways. In a family, the father was the head and had the responsibility of being kind to and caring for his family. Family members on the other hand had the obligations of showing filial respect to their father and of caring for each other. By the same token, the ruler who headed a state had the responsibility of practicing benevolent governance, and had a right to demand obedience from his subjects. His subjects had the obligation to show loyalty to their ruler and to live in harmony with each other. In this arrangement, commoners had to obey their ruler but in turn had a right to expect guidance and protection from him. Maintaining the status quo cemented the social structure: each person had a designated place in the structure and had to stay in his/her place and play his/her role honestly. By following this prescription, all could live in harmony in a stable society; but violating this principle would cause chaos. A benevolent and competent ruler would receive the Mandate of Heaven to rule. The mandate, however, was conditional: a ruler enjoyed the privilege of power only as long as he provided benevolent governance. Should he fail to live up to expectations, the multitudes (commoners) would suffer, Heaven would hear their cries, snatch the mandate from the emperor, and hand it over to a deserving successor. Meng Zi (Mencius, 372–289 BCE), a later philosopher of the Confucian school, put it another way when he asserted that the people were more important than the ruler and declared a popular uprising against a despotic government to be justified.

Statue of Confucius, (551–479 BCE). The most important change in Han government was the adoption of Confucianism as its official philosophy, along with the Confucian idea that government belonged only to the moral, which led to civil service examinations. Another defining feature of the Han was the encouragement of academics. Statue by artist Liu Shih, 1976. Confucius Plaza, New York City, NY. Copyright 2006 by Mark Rifkin/twi-ny.com.

Confucius believed that humans were good by nature, but that their innate goodness could only be brought out through education. In his view it was virtue, not birth, that set the "superior person" apart from the "inferior person." The core of virtue was benevolence, which he defined as the "love of humanity." Therefore a person's first duty is to attend to moral self-perfection, next to run a harmonious household, then to bring the country under good governance, and finally to bring about universal peace. In this system, all persons are duty-bound to practice the rituals prescribed by their names: the king was the king; the subject the subject; the father was the father; and the son was the son.

Confucius served in the government of the kingdom of Lu, one of the states emerging from the collapse of the Zhou. Discontented with having no impact on the ruler of Lu or the human condition, Confucius resigned and traveled from state to state, hoping to persuade one or another of the various rulers to embrace his ideals. But he made no royal converts. By the age of sixty-eight, disillusioned with politics but unshaken in his idealism, he became a private teacher. He took students regardless of their social origins, noble or humble, rich or poor, he would accept them and teach them the "six arts": poetry, history, rituals, music, horsemanship, and archery. He allegedly had three thousand students over the years, seventy of whom became prominent. He also revised the official history of Lu. Known as the *Spring and Autumn Annals*, this became the first chronological history of China. The major source for the study of his thinking is *The Analects*, which is a collection of his conversations compiled by his followers.

The next great figure in classical Chinese philosophy was Lao Zi, the alleged founder of Daoism. Lao Zi's teachings focused on the role of "Dao," or "the Way." The Way was not, Lao Zi asserted, a being with a will to intervene in human affairs, but rather a cosmic force, a set of universal truths or natural laws. His emphasis was on nature and human beings' respect for and harmony with nature. At the core of his thinking were the concepts of nothingness (the void), doing nothing (passivity), and dialectics (the yin and the yang). Lao Zi taught that nothingness was the mother of all things, so that by doing nothing (more precisely, by passively accepting things one was powerless to change) all things could be accomplished. He used parables to illustrate these abstract concepts. A house could be thought of as the empty space between the solid walls. The wheel was the hole that allowed the axle to go through it. Sow the seed, do not interfere, and the plant will grow by itself. Whatever one's goal, be it to rule a country, fight a battle, or survive in adverse circumstances, the one essential principle was to let things take their natural course and to do nothing to interfere with nature. While Confucius tried to create an ideal society through social activism, Lao Zi believed one could achieve his goal only through inaction. In his ideal country, the ruler would be content to control a small territory, keep his subjects physically strong but ignorant, discourage education to prevent ambition, and cut off commerce and travel to holdback greed and cunning. The subjects would toil but live simple and peaceful lives. The ruler would reign but have no need for active intervention: he would reign effectively by letting things take their own course.

Lao Zi also had a keen sense of the dialectical relationship between good and evil, fortune and misfortune, high and low. While the existence of each is dependent of the existence of its opposite, each is defined only in relation to its opposite. Each may also become its opposite. This idea, the ongoing dialect of the *yin* and the *yang* is a core concept in Chinese thinking.

The third school of thought of this classical age, Legalism, was founded by Xun Zi (313?–238 BCE). Xun Zi had been a Confucian disciple but had deviated from orthodox Confucian principles by stating that people are evil by nature and could only be saved by a good education or a very strong ruler. Education created conscious activity by guiding the superior person through rituals to rule the inferior person by law. Thus Confucian concepts became legal principles as Xun Zi converted Confucian philosophy into a new political practice. Legalism was further developed by Han Fei Zi (280?–233 BCE), a disciple of Xun Zi, who emphasized the rule of law. Generally, the Legalists did not believe in personal virtue as did the Confucians, or in doing nothing like the Daoists. Quite the contrary, the Legalists were ruthless activists, their goal to build "a rich country and a strong army." They believed that the ruler should make laws to enhance his power in order to achieve those goals. They also believed that those laws should be equally applicable to all persons, whether noble or common, rich or poor. Believing human beings selfish and evil by nature, the Legalists maintained that the only way to get people to do the ruler's bidding was through a carrot-and-stick system of rich rewards and harsh punishment. Rich rewards would go to those who obeyed the laws and contributed to the state's goals; harsh punishment would be meted out to those who failed to do so.

In an environment in which war and the wealth to sustain war was at the top of any lord's agenda, the Confucian obsession with virtue and the Daoist emphasis on doing nothing held little appeal. But the Legalist goal of "rich country and strong army" fit perfectly with the agenda of the war lords. And they quickly embraced Legalism as their guide to action. It was the state of Qin that successfully implemented Legalist reforms. It became a rich and powerful state that eventually defeated the other lords of the land to unify China under one ruler.

China's First Dynasties: The Qin and the Han

The founder of *Qin* (pronounced "chin"—whence China gets its name) Dynasty, Qin Shihuangdi (221–207 BCE) made history by achieving China's territorial unification and the centralization of governmental power in the hands of one man—an emperor instead of a king. The brief reign of the Qin Dynasty, followed by nearly four centuries of the reign of the Han Dynasty, set the model for China's imperial rule. Yet it was the Qin that mobilized the wealth generated by Iron Age agriculture and the Chinese work ethic to integrate north and south China into one mighty empire.

Qin Shihuangdi (the First Emperor of Qin Dynasty) subscribed to Legalism and was well served by its prescripts. As the head of one of seven states during the Era of the Warring States, he was able to transform his relatively backward land into an example of wealth and military might. He defeated his six rival states through the application of superior military tactics. He executed or exiled the other rulers and aristocrats and then proceeded to tear down their city walls and deprive them of their hereditary privileges. In amazingly short order Shihuangdi established a central government staffed with officials whom he appointed and removed at his pleasure. He also made laws that his officials enforced on the entire empire. This new form of bureaucracy was distinguished both by its appointed officials and centralized power. Shihuangdi essentially wiped out the earlier practice of regional autonomy, creating a central government in which one emperor could impose his will on an entire domain and muster all its resources to drive toward a single goal. For the first time in its history, China had an emperor who exercised direct rule over the entire country.

Once Shihuangdi seized control, he used the power of the centralized government bureaucracy to integrate the various regional states and fend off attacks from barbarian tribes beyond China's borders. To make it possible for his bureaucracy to operate smoothly and efficiently, he set rigorous standards for many important aspects of life. The roads he built radiated out from

Lady Lu: Empress Dowager

In Han China (202 BCE–220 CE), men controlled property, political office, and the network of power that placed them in a position of unquestioned authority. Women, however, commanded the strings of government under the right circumstances. If a woman was politically well connected, and had access to the emperor, then she could wield great influence. One such woman was Lady Lu, wife of Liu Bang, the man who became Emperor Gaodi, founder of the Han Dynasty.

Liu Bang began his political career as a village official during the Qin Dynasty (221–207 BCE). As the Qin spiraled into collapse, however, due to the inept rule of its second emperor, Liu Bang lost his job, beginning a struggle to survive that transformed him from a bandit into a warlord, and eventually allowed him to rise to power as the most successful claimant to the throne. Once he declared himself to be the new emperor in 202 BCE, one of his wives, Lady Lu, became his empress, and her access to power began. Known as Gaodi, Liu Bang ruled from 202 to 195 BCE, then died, and left Lady Lu as the mother of the teenage boy, Liu Ying, who had the best claim as Gaodi's heir.

Lady Lu managed to get her son placed on the throne as Emperor Xiao-Xu with the support of a powerful faction she had cultivated at court during her husband's reign. By successfully installing her son, Lady Lu became the Dowager Empress and Regent, which gave her access to power for fifteen years (195–181 BCE). She proved to be a competent monarch, producing a period of recovery after years of civil war, because she knew that she had to win the hearts of the people to continue in authority.

During her regency, she lightened taxes, removed the severe punishments that the Han had inherited from the Qin emperors, and encouraged the scholarship proposed by the Master Kong's (Confucius') students. She also allowed for the reduction of penalties in capital cases for a specified monetary amount, which eased the cost of government while winning her a reputation for benevolence. Her use of these monetary penalties was appropriately harsh because she kept those capital cases that effectively discouraged the rich from thinking they could buy their way out of any crime. Also, her command over China's affairs was sufficiently effective that there were no revolts during her rule while the nomadic threat from Central Asia receded due to a peace struck with the Xiong-nu (Mongols or Hun). Yet, her command over the strings of power came at a very high, personal price: she had to commit a set of brutal crimes to hold onto power.

Lady Lu's criminal career began when she came into conflict with her son over his preference for his female favorites, the women of the court. One in particular, Lady Qi, used her exceptional beauty to almost unseat the Empress Dowager. Lady Lu, therefore, kept a close watch on Lady Qi, seeking the chance to eliminate her as a challenge. Lady Qi's protection, however, was her ten-year-old son, Liu Ruyi, who had been Gaodi's favorite child, and was under the protection of the young Emperor, Xiao-Xu. So long as Xiao-Xu was vigilant and watched over Liu Ruyi, Lady Qi was safe.

After several months of always keeping the boy at his side, Xiao-Xu made the fatal mistake of going hunting without bringing along his young charge. Lady Lu acted swiftly; she had the boy poisoned before Xiao-Xu's return, and left the young emperor with an impossible conundrum: how do you punish a criminal who is also your mother? Due to his weakness as a monarch, Xiao-Xu found himself unable to match his mother's brutality and felt he could do nothing; thus he allowed Lady Lu to carry on as Empress Dowager.

Then Lady Lu had the dead boy's mother, Lady Qi, mutilated, but left alive. Lady Lu maimed the woman by having her thrown into a sewer outside the court where she lay unattended. Next, the Empress Dowager invited her son to see her disfigured rival, but he did not recognize his ex-favorite, and only discovered the magnitude of this latest crime when an attendant revealed Lady Qi's identity. The young Emperor had a nervous breakdown, did not leave his bed for a year, and left the reins of power in his mother's hands. When he recovered enough to return to court, he abandoned his duties as monarch and wasted the rest of his life in debauchery.

Free to rule as she pleased, Lady Lu amassed a list of personal crimes that kept her in control of the throne for the remainder of her career. She poisoned Xiao-Xu's older half brother. She watched her son drink himself to death, but she adopted a replacement before Xiao-Xu died. She poisoned her new son's natural mother to remove her rival. She elevated members of her family to positions of power in an effort to displace Gaodi's relatives, the Liu family, from reclaiming the throne. And, once her adopted son discovered that Lady Lu had poisoned his real mother, Lady Lu had him pronounced insane and imprisoned until he died. Before his death, however, Lady Lu had found yet another boy to adopt—one with sufficient noble blood to stand in as the future emperor.

This last crime occurred in 184 BCE, three years before Lady Lu's own death. Her grasp on power, though still firm, could not prevent nature taking its course. Hence, in 181 BCE, when Lady Lu died of old age, the Liu family expelled her relatives from power while China's historians did what her son, Xiao-Xu, could not do, condemned her for her crimes. China's historians destroyed Lady Lu's reputation because of all her crimes; this they did despite the fact that she left China in better shape than when she took the reins of power. Lady Lu's career demonstrates that although she was a strong woman with means and opportunity, she had to go to great lengths (as did many men) in order to hold onto power.

Source: Sarah Shaver Hughes and Brady Hughes, *Women in World History, Volume I, Readings from Prehistory to 1500* (Armonk, New York; M. E. Sharpe, 1995), p. 98–105.

The Great Wall, a massive structure that looked out onto the boundless steppes of Mongolia and Russia, replaced the shorter walls of earlier local lords and was designed to protect China's frontiers from attack by nomadic tribes to the north. It also served as a line of demarcation between Han and non-Han peoples and between the agricultural and nomadic ways of life. Courtesy Lynne Blanton.

the capital to the frontiers and used standard gauges that all cart axles had to match precisely. He also set universal standards for measuring length, volume, and weight, and he adopted one standard style of character writing. A daring reformer and innovator, Shihuangdi was also ruthless in the way he enforced his codes. For example Confucian scholars, who adhered to their conservative principles of loyalty, benevolence, and status quo, were fiercely critical of his radical reforms and ruthless ways. In response, Shihuangdi banned Confucianism, burned Confucian texts, and sent students to study under government officials. Those Confucian scholars who resisted the will of the state were thrown into pits and burnt to death along with their books.

It was Shihuangdi who undertook the construction of China's Great Wall in the north and the E-fang Palace in Xiengyang, his capital, located on the Wei River, a tributary of the Huang He. The Great Wall, a massive structure that looked out onto the boundless steppes of Mongolia and Russia, replaced the shorter walls of earlier local lords and was designed to protect China's frontiers from attack by nomadic tribes to the north. It also served as a line of demarcation between Han and non-Han peoples and between the agricultural and nomadic ways of life. These two projects of unprecedented scale took enormous amounts of human and material resources, and they imposed a heavy burden on the population, especially the peasantry.

With Shihuangdi's death, the peasants rejected the burden of taxes and labor service and rose in rebellion against his heir. They were later joined by the ruling families of the local lords Shihuangdi had defeated.

Thus, when the First Emperor died, palace intrigue, reinforced by the uprisings, destroyed the imperial household and ended the dynasty. The title *Qin Shihuangdi* implied that he would be the first of an endless line of descendents who would rule the land forever. But his empire was short-lived. To this day the Chinese people are deeply ambivalent about him. They admire him for his ability to unify the country and make it rich and strong in such a remarkably short period of time, but they abhor him for the ruthless means he employed to achieve his ends.

One of Qin Shihuangdi's legacies was his elaborate mausoleum. A vast structure partly above- and partly underground, he intended it to be a place where he would dwell and be worshipped long after his death. But the surface structures of the mausoleum were burned to the ground and the underground structures ransacked soon after his death. The tomb was all but forgotten by history until a peasant digging in his field discovered it by accident in 1974. Partially excavated, it now inspires awe in people across the world with its thousands of incredibly lifelike terracotta soldiers, numerous weapons, many bronze war chariots and finely crafted luxury goods.

The collapse of the Qin Empire created a huge power vacuum. Men representing different regions and interests rushed in to capture the throne. Out of this chaotic mix, Liu Bang (256–195 BCE) emerged the victor. He founded the Han Dynasty, made Chang'an (today's Xi'an) his capital and took the title of *Han Gaozu* (Great ancestor of the Han Dynasty). Originally a commoner, the emperor Han surrounded himself with ministers and generals who had also risen from the lowly

Terracotta Horses and Cart, 210 BCE. This model was created for the vast tombs of Qin Shihuangdi, the First Imperial Emperor of China. Representative of early horse-and-cart technology, the purpose of this model was to convey the emperor into the afterlife. The same single-axle technology was widely used in various types of agricultural equipment in addition to modes of transport. Tomb of Qin Shihuangdi, Xi'an, China. © 2006 Vagabum Mike Lopez (www.vagabum.com).

from sinking vast resources into large-scale construction and overly ambitious conquests, which in turn allowed them to reduce taxes and labor services.

More than seven decades of governmental restraint gave the people of China an opportunity to recuperate from the harsh treatment of the Qin regime and the ravages of long years of war. The country gradually regained vitality and eventually became strong and prosperous. Then came Han Wudi (Martial Emperor of Han Dynasty, 156–87 BCE). Taking advantage of the accomplishments of his predecessors, he rebuilt the Han regime into a centralized empire of unprecedented wealth and power. Han Wudi increased the power of the emperor and reduced that of ministers and generals, placed all government power in the hands of officials, and all but eliminated the hereditary powers of aristocrats. Han Wudi subjected government officials to the oversight of inspectors, established a standing army directly controlled by the central government, state monopolies to run the salt and iron businesses, and an agency to buy high and sell low in an effort to regulate market prices. While these policies opened up new sources of revenue for the government and restrained powerful landowners and merchants, they were highly controversial, not only at the time but in the eyes of the people of later dynasties.

Now Han Wudi needed a grand ideology to match the reality of his great empire. He made Confucianism the official state ideology, relegating all other philosophies to a back seat. But this was not his forefathers' Confucianism. Although classic Confucianism had much to offer to an empire at peace, Confucian principles alone could not complete the ideology of a martial emperor. The Legalist school of thought was still vital to the primary task of running a government, even though its name had been tarnished by Qin Shihuangdi. The Daoist teachings of restraint and passive aggression continued as a useful supplement, even though their general tenets were ill suited to an ambitious emperor ruling over an expanding empire. Nevertheless, the three philosophies once integrated complemented one another. Indeed, down through the ages the emperors of China would make use of this eclectic mix of Confucianism, Legalism, and Daoism, even if the amalgamation was officially called Confucianism.

strata of society. Unlike that of the Qin, the Han Dynasty lasted for four centuries.

While fighting to win the throne, Liu Bang had shown total disdain for Confucianism. But now his advisors cautioned him that he could seize an empire on horseback (meaning by the use of force), but could not govern in the same manner. They pointed out the inadequacies of Legalism in the example of the short-lived Qin Dynasty. By appealing only to people's base instincts of greed and fear, Qin Shihuangdi had failed to establish a sustainable regime and society. His excesses in military conquest, construction, and grandiose ceremonies had also exhausted the country's wealth and turned the people against his dynasty. The Han, they counseled, would have to avoid this style of rule, and their arguments prevailed. Early Han emperors retained the essentials of Qin's Legalist ways but eased its harshness. Eventually they adopted an eclectic approach to statecraft, combining the best of Legalism, Daoism, and Confucianism, in a manner similar to Xun Zi's writings. Legalism provided the tough guidelines for running an efficient government. The Confucian emphasis on the supremacy of an emperor in a hierarchical order and harmony among his subjects offered a formula to consolidate and sustain a regime and society. The Daoist dictum of restraint discouraged emperors

Han Wudi also founded a state-run university to teach Confucianism, the qualified graduates of which were assigned government positions. Thus began China's imperial examination system for entrance into the civil service. Henceforth, scholars flocked to government and private schools to study Confucianism in the hope of entering a position in government and thereby gaining a degree of wealth and power. This new route of upward social mobility—based on the merits of the individual—became a unique feature of Chinese culture.

Dong Zhongshu (179–104 BCE) was one prominent Confucian scholar of the era. It was he who stepped forward to revise Classical Confucianism to meet the needs of the day. According to his postulation, Heaven, the emperor, and the populace formed a hierarchic entity—the "grand unity." Heaven was above the emperor and the emperor was above all men. From this Dong extrapolated a fundamental rule for social behavior: the emperor would dominate the minister, the father would dominate the son, and the husband would dominate the wife. Although Confucius had said explicitly, "Show respect to gods and spirits but keep [them] at a distance," Dong put forth the doctrine of the "interaction between heaven and man." He was obsessed with omens, indulged in divination, and developed elaborate rituals. He believed that Heaven sent omens to inform the emperor about performance as the "Son of Heaven." In short, Dong managed to transform Confucianism from a philosophy into a religion and transformed Confucius from a man into a demigod. Incidentally, the Daoist religion, which should not be confused with the Daoist philosophy, was also founded around this time.

Han Wudi was not one to be restrained by Confucian teachings of benevolence or Daoist urgings of restraint. The increased wealth and power of his empire tempted him to make war. During his long reign he expanded China's territory in all directions beyond its former borders, launching more than a dozen wars in which he mobilized some 2 million troops. Some of these military campaigns were justifiable; others were not.

The Han Dynasty had long been threatened by the Xiongnu, a nomadic tribe that carried out frequent raids along China's northern frontier. To seek out allies to fight the Xiongnu, the Han imperial court sent envoys to the non-Han tribes that lived to China's north and northwest. The envoys also had the mission of establishing trade relations with those tribes. Han Wudi's emissary, Zhang Qian, probed far into central Asia on this mission. In the first century BCE, Han troops drove Xongnu tribes from the deserts north of China. The expelled tribes then went on to ravage central Asia, Russia, and Eastern Europe, establishing an empire of their own based in Europe during the fourth and fifth centuries CE.

It was these activities that opened international trade along the Silk Road, which linked China with central Asia and Europe, reaching as far as Rome. Indeed, the wearing of silk became a status symbol in Rome at this time. The contact of the Chinese Empire with the Roman Empire was, however, an indirect one, Persian merchants being the main intermediaries. Though mainly a trade route, the Silk Road also served to facilitate the exchange of people and ideas. China's main export was silk, while it imported horses and jade from central Asia, and iron, glass, and precious metals from Rome. China's methods of papermaking, and later of printing and making gunpowder, were introduced to the Near East and then the West via this road. The religions of Buddhism, Islam, and Christianity also traveled eastward on this road to China. Dunhuang, a way station along the road, housed a treasure trove of Buddhist manuscripts discovered accidentally in the early twentieth century.

The greatest of the Chinese historians lived in the Han Dynasty. Sima Qian (145–85 BCE) was the emperor's court historian and chief of the Imperial Secretariat. His *Historical Record* covered Chinese history from its mythological beginnings to the Han Dynasty of his day. In 130 chapters Sima Qian presented the past from three perspectives: a chronological narrative of political events, topical accounts of key institutions, and biographies of individuals. Interestingly, these biographies included as subjects men and women ranging from emperors to commoners, from great generals to merchants, artisans, bandits, great scholars, and outstanding entertainers. Sima Qian's work was so well liked that later emperors would sponsor the writing of the history of their own dynasties on the same model. His character portraits were so vivid that the *Historical Record* can also be read as literature.

The Dynastic Cycle

Ultimately, the Han Dynasty declined and fell, disintegrating into regional fiefdoms until another dynasty rose to rule a reunified China. The rise and fall of dynasties constituted the "dynastic cycle," with the decline of the power of the central government triggering the emergence of new centers of power. Many other factors in the dynastic cycle also played out respectively.

First, apart from the emperor, court officials were usually the most powerful men in a dynasty. Under a strong emperor, their existence was capricious, often ending in exile or execution. But under a weak emperor, the power of the court could grow to overshadow him, as happened in the Late Han.

Second, the empress dowager, one of the emperor's many wives, would receive her esteemed title because she was the mother of the direct heir to the throne. The empress dowager often came from a powerful household. In the absence of a strong emperor, she and her family members might rise to dominate the court. This happened repeatedly in the Han Dynasty (see page 64).

Third, court eunuchs, men who had sacrificed their genitals to become guardians of the emperor's harem and acquire power, usually came from impoverished families, enjoying a close association with the emperor, his wives, and his sons. The royal family would often use the court eunuchs to counterbalance other forces, such as court officials and military commanders. But sometimes the eunuchs themselves would exploit their influence and grow so strong that they essentially dominated the royal family.

Fourth, frontier generals, far removed from the central authority and in command of large armies, sometimes became strong and relatively independent forces. Sometimes the general's position even became hereditary instead of appointed. In turbulent times, a weak emperor might completely lose control over his generals. Although they may not have been able to seize the throne for themselves, they did often manage to tear the empire apart, as happened in the Late Han.

Fifth, over many generations, large landholders used their growing influence to obtain tax exemptions or evade taxes altogether. As the tax base shrank, the government lost revenue and increased the taxes on smaller landholders and free peasants. Unable to bear the staggering tax burden, many small landholders were forced to give up their lands to the privileged large landholders to escape government taxation and persecution. This in turn further reduced government revenue and further increased the tax burden on the remaining farming population. The outcome of such a situation was predictable: once the burden of government taxation and oppression became unbearable, widespread peasant rebellions broke out. The rebellion of the Yellow Turbans in the Late Han Dynasty was one such example.

And sixth, the tension between barbarian invasion and Han expansion was an ever-present reality in Chinese history. A weak Han regime would often embolden nomadic tribes on China's northern and western borders to launch mounted raids into Han territory. These operations could be hit-and-run raids or sustained campaigns. In either case, they were ruthlessly devastating to Han lives and property. Invasions by nomadic tribes played an important role in weakening the Han Dynasty.

The First Empire, including the Qin and Han dynasties and the "Three Dynasties" that preceded them,

shaped the broad outlines of Chinese civilization. Their fundamental characteristics would survive the next two millennia. The English words "China" and "Chinese" are derived from the Chinese word "Qin." China's majority ethnic group, the Han people, derived their name from the Han Dynasty.

Accordingly, China represented one of the most successful stories of the ancient world. The People of Han assembled the resources of the Huang He, horticulture, the Chinese work ethic, Filial Piety, a priest-king, feudalism, Chinese pictograms, the iron plow, an agricultural revolution, warfare, and philosophy to produce one of the most stable systems in world history. Unlike the peoples of Mesopotamia, Egypt, and India, the Chinese never gave up their ancient forms. Mesopotamia and Egypt fell under of the sway of the Persians, Macedonians, and the Romans, while India never achieved a stable, long-lasting, political order. China, in contrast, produced the Dynastic Cycle, returned to its original forms, and maintained a relatively unbroken history from 202 BCE all the way to 1905 CE.

Suggested Reading

De Bary, William Theodore, *The Trouble with Confucianism* (Cambridge: Harvard University Press, 1991).

———, William Theodore, Chan Wing-tsit, and Burton Watson, *Sources of Chinese Tradition* (New York: Columbia University Press, 1964).

Elvin, Mark, *The Pattern of the Chinese Past* (Stanford: Stanford University Press, 1973).

Gernet, Jacques, *A History of Chinese Civilization*, Second Edition (Cambridge: Cambridge University Press, Reprinted 1999).

Hucker, Charles O., *China's Imperial Past: An Introduction to Chinese History and Culture* (Stanford: Stanford University Press, 1975).

Lao Tzu, *Tao Te Ching: The Chinese Book of Integrity and the Way*, Translated by Victor Mair (New York: Bantam Books, 1990).

Loewe, Michael, *The Pride That Was China* (New York: St. Martin's Press, 1990).

Reichauer, Edwin O., and John K. Fairbanks, *China: Tradition and Transformation*, Revised Edition (Boston: Houghton Mifflin Company, 1989).

Twitchett, Denis, and Michael Loewe, eds., *The Cambridge History of China, Volume One: The Ch'in and Han Empires,* (New York: Cambridge University Press, 1986).

Wei-mung Tu, *Confucian Thought: Selfhood as Creative Transformation* (New York: SUNY Press, 1985).

VI

THE NOMADS' TRADE
and the Great Migrations

As mentioned in Chapters Two and Three, to build the great cities of Mesopotamia and Egypt, people had to import raw materials not native to either geographic region. While Egypt turned out to be wealthier in terms of these natural gifts, the people of Mesopotamia had to range far and wide to discover the location of essential resources. Timber, stone, and metal ores were far more difficult for them to acquire, yet given the strategic site of Mesopotamia on the Fertile Crescent, access to strangers with whom to conduct trade proved much easier. As a result, merchants from Mesopotamia made contact with a far greater number of nomadic peoples than did their Egyptian counterparts. This does not mean, however, that Egypt did not engage in extensive trade; rather, it means that Mesopotamian merchants had greater influence on the nomads (and engaged in more cultural exchanges) than did their Egyptian counterparts. For the most part, such trade shaped the behavior of the nomads, spreading knowledge, urban skills, and sedentary practices that transformed nomadic life, rather than the other way around. And knowledge of specialized skills and sedentary practices provided nomads with the means to neutralize many of the military advantages previously enjoyed only by intensive agriculturalists (farmers). Therefore, the spread of plant cultivation, metallurgy, and urban technologies to nomads near and far became a major element in the development of ancient world history.

Two stories emerge from the development of trade. One tells of the spread of sedentary life among those nomads living in the rainfall zones adjacent to Mesopotamia, and the other tells of the spread of strategic urban skills to herders who lived much farther from this river-based civilization. Both stories impacted the delicate balance between trade and raid that characterized the relationships between intensive (farmers) and extensive (herders) agricultural communities.

As mentioned in Chapter Two, due to a demand for raw materials, merchants from Mesopotamia's most ancient civilization, Sumeria, began a process of diffusion that continued throughout world history. Using bronze acquisition as an example, Sumerian merchants sent out numerous commercial expeditions seeking the specific copper ores cuprite, malachite, and azurite, and the tin ore cassiterite used in its production. Sent by royal monopolies from their city-states, each of these expeditions exploited the urban products collected by a local ruler who used them to facilitate exchanges with nomads living in the Fertile Crescent and adjacent lands. Once at a valuable site rich in desired resources, Sumerian merchants traded their urban products to local nomads for essential ores, cut stone, and harvested trees. The copper and tin mines they oversaw in the highlands of Anatolia, Cyprus, modern-day Afghanistan, and the Danube River Basin reveal how far these Sumerian merchants traveled.

As these Sumerian merchants could not mine the ore themselves, their ability to persuade local nomads to become miners caused a change in local lifestyles. Nomads who took up such sedentary occupations as mining soon agreed to refine the ores as well. Since stones like azurite or cassiterite contained 90 percent waste material, Sumerian merchants could not afford to ship these raw ores home intact. Instead, they encouraged the nomad miners to smelt the ores at the mine sites. Thus, these nomads soon found themselves so busy mining and refining raw materials that they no longer had time to tend their herds. Consequently, those nomads who accepted the urban goods from Sumeria found themselves slowly drawn into a sedentary way of life. At the same time, these ex-nomads also had to take up plant cultivation to make up for their loss of animal calories. Hence, the trade between a sedentary culture like Sumeria and local nomads who occupied pastures situated near desired natural resources eventually caused plant cultivation to spread into rainfall zones.

All the land between Sumeria and their trading sites in places such as Cyprus, the Danube, and Afghanistan experienced some degree of change as well. Those former nomads closest to Sumeria, and also situated on the Tigris and Euphrates rivers, such as Akkadia,

"War," The Standard of Ur, about 2600–2400 BCE. This panel is one of the earliest representations of a Sumerian Army. War carts (which pre-dated chariots) trample enemies; cloaked infantymen carry spears; enemy soldiers are killed with axes; others are paraded naked and presented to the king who holds a spear. From Ur, southern Iraq. © The Trustees of the British Museum.

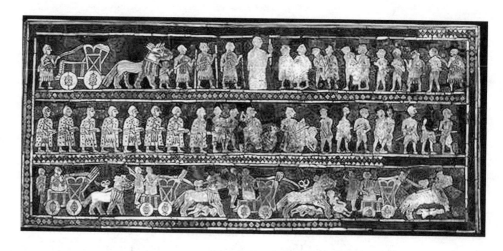

Babylonia, and Assyria, became farmers, imitated the urban division of labor created in Sumeria, and developed cuneiform (the Sumerian script). Those ex-nomads in adjacent rainfall districts took up intensive agriculture on a smaller scale, developed towns, and engaged in trade of raw materials. This network of commercial exchange supported several reciprocal relationships between the participants, but all of these commercial relationships relied on the continued vitality of Sumerian culture. Should something happen to this system, such as internal strife or the outbreak of a major epidemic, the network might suffer a collapse, triggering economic hardship throughout the entire commercial system Sumeria had constructed.

At first, long-distance commerce between Sumeria and the various nomadic communities that mined essential ores depended on Sumerian transport. As this commerce developed and spread, however, a second pattern of cultural exchanges commenced. The carts and harnesses used to carry urban goods to and from distant nomadic regions attracted local attention. Built with heavy wheels, employing two axles, and manufactured to carry high-bulk cargoes, these vehicles traveled a slow but steady pace to their destination. Put into use early in Sumerian history, these carts became common throughout Mesopotamia by 3000 BCE, were found in Syria by 2250 BCE, in Anatolia by 2000 BCE, and on mainland Greece by 1500 BCE. This pattern of technological diffusion reveals that even those nomads beyond the range of overland trade but having a partner in Mesopotamia proper slowly acquired knowledge of key urban tools such as the wheel, the axle, the cart, and the harness. Once in the hands of those distant nomads not yet drawn directly into Mesopotamian trade, these urban tools underwent important refinements that reflected local needs, led to the creation of new types of vehicles, and had a major influence on ancient Eurasian history.

The First Wave of Mass Migrations
The Wheel, the Chariot, and Nomads

As mentioned above, even those nomads who lived beyond direct participation in the Mesopotamian commercial network benefited from the knowledge acquired through this exchange process. Situated on the grasslands of Central Asia were one such people, the Indo-Europeans, who acquired the wheel and cart through Mesopotamia's ancient commercial network. But instead of using domesticated donkeys and oxen to pull their vehicles, these distant nomads had domesticated horses. Used to control the movement of their herds, and to defend their pastures, the horse served as a potential source of power. Indo-Europeans, therefore, reasoned that if these animals could be harnessed to a new type of light and speeding cart, then they might develop a powerful new weapon that could be used in defense of their herds as well as in war. It is probably no accident that the refinement of the wheel, axle, and cart coincided with the first great era of mass migration of nomadic Indo-Europeans (2000 to 1400 BCE).

While the precise factor that launched this migration remains unknown, one can speculate. Most likely success among herding societies led to a sharp rise in population pressures, which naturally increased competition for grass among Indo-European nomadic communities. At the same time, a shift in climate could have caused a cycle of droughts that destroyed pastures just when the demand for new grazing land had become critical in Central Asia. At any rate, Indo-Europeans began a massive migration that severely endangered all the established civilizations living in Eurasia. Synchronized with this massive migration was the refinement of the wheel, which led Indo-Europeans to create a new and devastatingly effective war-cart: the chariot.

Indo-European nomads from Central Asia had acquired knowledge of the wheel from the Sumerians long before the appearance of the chariot. Consequently, they took some time redesigning Sumeria's original heavy, load-bearing wheels and axles to create a light, fast-moving military vehicle capable of withstanding great speeds. Developing a well-balanced, truly circular, and sturdy lightweight disk with a hub, spokes, rim, and bronze tire was no easy task. Such a wheel was necessary because nomads needed speed in order to protect their pastures from rivals. Replacing the solid wooden block disks that Sumerian merchants had used on their commercial carts with a lightweight, rugged wheel capable of carrying a driver and archer at high speeds without shattering on the open plains, these Indo-European nomads created a well-balanced and remarkably sturdy new vehicle. Mounting two of these new wheels on a single axle set beneath a woven wicker cart, these nomads then harnessed a team of two horses to the first chariots. The combination of all these features: the new wheel, the light cart, and a team of horses, resulted in the completed chariot.

Adding the compound bow—a short wooden bow with expandable sinew on one side and bone on the other—these chariots then became highly effective weapons of war. By firing arrows from compound bows, archers could kill an enemy at long range, even as the chariot driver steered the craft across the plain at high speed. The perfection of this war vehicle over the course of two hundred years, allowed the nomads to invade sedentary cultures beginning around the year 1800 BCE.

In the centuries that followed, a process of conquest began that changed the face of Eurasia's sedentary cultures. One civilization after another fell to the might of the chariot, or had to acquire this weapon for its own armies in order to survive future invasions from marauding nomadic tribes. Each assault by a chariot culture spelled a change in the way Eurasian civilizations allocated their food surpluses. The role the army played in political life increased in importance, and armies began to receive a far larger share of a society's food supply. Now the demand for increased central control by a sedentary culture's principal city over its far-flung towns, villages, and hamlets could only spread.

The land from Turkey to the Fertile Crescent was the first to fall under the influence of chariot invaders. Credited as being the earliest to use the horse in conjunction with the chariot, the Kassites conquered Babylon in 1800 BCE. These Indo-European nomads included tribes from both the Zagros and Armenian mountains who moved into Mesopotamia after 2000 BCE as part of the general migration occurring throughout Eurasia. Even though the Kassites settled down in Babylonia to learn the art of sedentary agriculture, they still maintained access to their pastures located north and east of the Fertile Crescent to ensure a steady supply of horses. Once established in Babylon, the Kassites then began a rule that lasted four-and-a-half centuries—one of the longest eras of political stability in Mesopotamian history.

To the northwest of the Kassites, the Indo-Iranian Mitanni, an eastern Indo-European group, established a kingdom in Syria. Like the Kassites, the Mitanni were chariot warriors who took up residence on farmland. As Indo-European nomads, the Mitanni were an aggressive people whose survival depended on speed and skilled archery. Once established in the Levant, they achieved a balance of power with the Kassites that lasted until the Egyptians and the Hittites acquired the chariot.

Like the Kassites and Mitanni, the Hittites were Indo-Europeans who migrated into the Anatolian Highlands of Asia Minor from an area between the Black and Caspian seas around 2000 BCE. Also like the Kassites and Mitanni, the Hittites made this trek in an effort to find a new land in which to settle down. Learning the art of chariot warfare from the Mitanni, the Hittites used this new weapon to build a powerful government centered on Hattusas, its capital, around 1500 BCE. The political system they developed followed a Mesopotamian model, which included a standing army, garrison towns, and local commanders. Using the chariot, the Hittites conquered the Mitanni and then challenged Egypt for control of the Levant Coast (Syria, Lebanon, and Palestine/Israel). This challenge occurred during Egypt's rise to imperial power under the New Kingdom, a political system that was itself responding to nomadic invaders (Chapter Three). Meanwhile, the

Assyrian Wheels, 717 BCE–705 BCE. Iron wheels with bronze hubs were discovered at the site of the capital city of Khorsbad. In 1705, King Sennacherib abandoned Khorsbad relocating the capital to Nineveh. Any unused equipment, including these wheels, were left behind. Oriental Institute Museum, Chicago, IL.

Hittites had developed an empire capable of forcing Ramses II (1292–1225 BCE), one of Egypt's greatest military figures, to settle for a peaceful division of Syria. Compelled by the circumstances of war to agree to this peace, Ramses II also accepted a marriage proposal between his daughter and the heir to the Hittite throne to seal the agreement. Yet soon after this triumph against Egypt, the Hittites themselves fell to another mysterious group of Indo-European invaders that Herodotus (a Greek, and the first Western historian) called the Phrygians ("a people of unknown origin").

While chariot warriors overran Asia Minor and the Fertile Crescent, the Middle Kingdom of Egypt (2000–1786 BCE) suffered an internal collapse and military pressures exerted by the Hyksos (after 1730 BCE), Semitic nomads who entered Egypt from the east. After learning the secrets of the chariot from their Indo-European neighbors, the Hyksos captured the rich Delta of the Nile forcing the native Egyptian rulers to retreat upriver. As mentioned in Chapter Three, the Hyksos (shepherd people) were probably an amalgamation of Semitic tribes originally from an area along the Levant Coast who had wandered into Egypt peacefully. Once there, they used the chariots they had acquired from the Kassites and Mitanni to impose their command over the mouth of the Nile, where they ruled for 155 years (1730–1575 BCE). Meanwhile, when the Hyksos controlled Lower Egypt, they unintentionally revealed to the Egyptians the secrets of the chariot. At the same time, the Hyksos also unintentionally taught the Egyptians to hate foreigners, such as the Hebrew Semites living in their kingdom, which created a form of prejudice that led to both rebellion and the enslavement of any Semitic peoples who remained in Egypt after 1575. The ensuing Egyptian rebellion resulted in the creation of the New Kingdom of Egypt (1575–1050 BCE).

The New Kingdom began as a chariot monarchy whose pharaohs seemed determined to close any avenue of approach to the Nile River valley against future invasion. Having enjoyed 1,370 years (3100–1730 BCE) of relative isolation and freedom from foreign incursion, the Egyptians found rule under the Hyksos a severe shock. Combining the chariot with a new fighting spirit, the pharaoh Ahmose, founder of the New Kingdom, created an absolute government based on the power of the army, conquest, and the priests of Karnak. The Egyptian pharaohs who succeeded Ahmose marched south and pushed their command of the Nile to the frontiers of Kush, at which point they turned their attention east and north to take control of the Levant Coast and Lydia. These pharaohs gained free reign over land as far north as the mouth of the Euphrates River until they ran into the Hittites, who refused to yield the Levant. As mentioned above, the Hittites had taken over Asia Minor and fought Egypt for control of Syria. In the process, the Hittites had destroyed the Mitanni, Egypt's ally. Meanwhile in Egypt, a Semitic people who had remained after the Hyksos withdrew, the Hebrews (Chapter Two), fell from a favored relationship with the pharaohs to one of enslavement under the command of the New Kingdom.

While Egypt struggled to build its first empire, India underwent the Aryan invasions. Yet another Indo-European migratory group, the Aryans (Chapter Four), represented numerous nomadic tribes who filtered into India around 1800 BCE. Like the Kassites, Mitanni, Hittites, and Hyksos, their movement was at first more a migration than an invasion. Yet they brought with them the chariot and soon learned that they held a military advantage over local farmers. Using this advantage, they turned to violence and conquered a well-established, but declining sedentary culture, the remains of the Harappan civilization (2500–1500 BCE).

Because these Aryan tribes destroyed well-established, if retreating, cities and for centuries did not replace them with another urban culture, India entered a Dark Age. Much of what the Harappan civilization had recorded about its past was lost, and the rest of India descended into an era where only an oral tradition maintained the history of the local people. The result was a reconstruction of Indian culture based on the Aryan *Vedas* (the sacred lore, poems, and songs of Brahman priests). This sacred lore was latter joined by surviving Dravidian traditions (the beliefs of the fleeing Harappan peoples). Together, Aryan and Dravidian oral traditions combined, evolving into India's principal religion: Hinduism.

The impetus behind the rise of this combined oral tradition is that the Aryans found that they could conquer the land but could not consolidate their hold over the Indian subcontinent. Unable to impose a system of taxes on a scattered and fleeing population, the Aryans had turned India into a hopelessly confusing and divided realm. Independent regional communities, who spoke widely different languages and comprised unique ethnicities, maintained their own memory of the past. Meanwhile, as the most powerful group, the Aryans tried mightily to impose an emerging religion—Brahmanism (pre-Hinduism)—on the people immediately under their control. At the same time, the Dravidians, as well as other indigenous Indian peoples, maintained their own oral traditions beyond the reach of the invaders. From 1500 to 800 BCE, until new food surpluses generated by a combination of the introduction of rice and iron tools (Chapter Four) allowed certain kings to assert their authority and impose political order.

Just as the rest of Eurasia experienced the power of the chariot, China, too, fell under the sway of this new weapon. The first Chinese to use the chariot were rulers of the Shang Dynasty (Chapter Five) which was originally believed to be a mythical kingdom. Though claimed by Chinese tradition as real, there was no physical evidence of the existence of the Shang Dynasty until 1923, when archeologists began to uncover numerous gravesites of kings as well as the ruins of the Late Shang capital, Anyang, all of which reinforced the truth of Chinese tradition. As a result, a dispute over the origins of the Shang emerged, so two dates have been posted for the beginning of this Dynasty, 1766 BCE and 1523 BCE. The former date conforms to Chinese tradition, and the latter matches the physical evidence.

The dispute over these two dates encouraged archeologists to look beyond their discovery of Anyang to see if the thirty Shang monarchs claimed by Chinese tradition were real. Happily, the tradition that had led to the discovery of Anyang continued to prove an accurate guide. More recently, in 1959, archeologists have unearthed artifacts at Erlitou (near the modern city of Yanshi) that revealed a much longer history for the Shang than the date 1523 BCE. These new archeological discoveries include evidence showing that the Shang capital had been moved from time to time, contained thousands of oracle bones filled with archaic Chinese writings, and identified the very kings named in Chinese tradition. Such evidence indicated that the Shang were indeed much older than originally believed; in fact, artifacts located at Erlitou have been carbon dated to 2100 BCE. Hence, some scholars have even proposed that a prior mythical dynasty, the Xia, was as real as the Shang. Accordingly, they believe the Shang people had emerged from the Xia and later matured into the kingdom ruled from Anyang.

In any event, the Shang itself produced a city-state system commanded by an aristocratic elite whose familial ties to the king justified their political posts. The king was the first among equals who controlled the largest city, which comprised public buildings, altars, and residences for his direct subordinates. These subordinates were the aristocracy who ruled in lesser city-states and formed a chariot elite in the Shang army. The absence of any monumental architecture as found in Mesopotamia and Egypt, as well as the fact that each capital was surrounded by a sea of Neolithic tribal villages, implied that the Shang did not have access to food surpluses as abundant as those found in the Fertile Crescent and Egypt. While the Fertile Crescent and Egypt had provided enough food to generate integrated urban hierarchies called "empires" by 1700 BCE, the Shang were still forming a city-state system somewhat more centralized than early Sumerian times due to the chariot and a Chinese version of feudalism.

Meanwhile, the military aristocracy that served the Shang kings went to war in chariots supported by small levies of infantry, whose weapons—spears and compound bows—had a range matching those of their nomadic neighbors. Armies usually did not exceed 3,000 to 5,000 soldiers, but did grow to 13,000 during times of crisis. Their enemies were usually the nomadic ancestors of the Turks and Mongols who wandered into Shang territory periodically and posed a continuous threat to the Chinese throughout their long history. One of these early Turkish-speaking tribes, the Zhou, defeated the Shang and established the next great era of political development in Chinese history. Evidently, the Zhou had greater access to horses than did the Shang and could mount a more extensive chariot assault. As a result, the Zhou replaced the Shang in 1027 BCE.

Before their fall, while the Shang were fighting to protect their frontiers against nomadic incursions, they assimilated methods of warfare that raised a question: who, exactly, were these people called the Shang? The answer reflects a combination of guesses. We know that they used a rammed-earth technique to build the walls of their fortified cities, employed a system of fired-oracle bones for the art of divination, and reproduced a style of pottery common to Neolithic Shandung sites, which suggest that the Shang had matured out of one of China's eastern farming communities. Yet their use of chariots and archery in warfare, especially the development of a powerful compound bow, suggest nomadic antecedents as well. Whoever the Shang rulers might have been, the most common scenario offered for their origins is that they were Neolithic farmers from the Lungshan (Shandung) culture who slowly moved their capital from east to west as their food surpluses grew. There they encountered nomads whose warlike character and superior weaponry impressed them, teaching these ancient Chinese farmers how to fight and survive. Assimilating the chariot and the compound bow, the Shang rulers then settled along the eastern arm of the Huang He just west of its junction with the Wei River. From this site, they conquered much of northern China based on the advantages acquired with their nomadic weapons. Like the New Kingdom of Egypt, the Shang Dynasty therefore illustrates a sedentary culture's response to contact with shepherd warriors.

Even as the Hittites, Mitanni, and Kassites brought the chariot to Asia Minor and the Fertile Crescent, another new chariot culture appeared in ancient Greece. Between 2000 and 1400 BCE, a Greek-speaking population moved into mainland Greece via northwestern Asia Minor and the Balkans and began to acquire the secrets of plant cultivation from Minoan Crete. Reflecting more an Egyptian influence than a Mesopotamian one, because of the development of trade based on Egyptian ship-and-sail technology, Minoan Crete produced a maritime commercial network that became the principal conduit for the transmission of urban civilization to the Aegean region and its adjacent mainland zones. A beneficiary of this commercial island, Mycenaean culture began a process of maturation that resulted in the first Greek cities between 2000 and 1450 BCE.

By 1450 BCE, however, the Mycenaeans felt strong enough not only to break their cultural dependency on Minoan Crete but to rule this island as the commercial and martial masters of the Aegean world. Capturing the Minoan capital, Knossos, in that year, the Mycenaeans set out to take control of shipping lanes between mainland Greece and the ancient urban centers of Anatolia, the Levant, Egypt, and Mesopotamia. Pirate kingdoms appeared on the Greek mainland as a network of city-states developed a method of hit-and-run raids from the sea, even as they exploited the horse and chariot on land. Related to one another by a common culture and complex kinship ties, these respective Greek-speaking city-states could function independently or in alliance in massive military projects like the capture of Troy in 1200 BCE. Made immortal by Homer's epic poems, *The Iliad* and *The Odyssey*, this assault on Troy tells of how the Mycenaeans employed the chariot as a vehicle to allow great champions to confront one another on the battlefield.

The Mycenaean Greeks (1450–1100 BCE), however, developed a style of chariot warfare that differed from every other chariot culture. Living at the fringe of civilization in the West, the Mycenaeans used the chariot more as a means of transporting champions in heavy bronze armor to points of combat rather than as a swift-moving platform for archers. Once they arrived at a point of confrontation, these champions would dismount and fight an engagement in which specific individuals would confront one another. This tactical style did not have the same impact as the combination of the swift moving archer and driver, which restricted the range and power of Mycenaean rule. Confined more to raids rather than conquest, the Mycenaeans left behind destruction instead of a wave of new empires.

A Second Wave of Migrations
The Iron Age

Like the chariot's effect on the first wave of migrations, the second great age of human movement coincided with the manufacture of iron, the major technological revolution that changed the metallurgy of the ancient world. As already mentioned, iron production originated in Eurasia with the Hittites and spread to settled peoples. Now, however, the technology behind the manufacture and the products thereof had diffused to the nomads who refined iron's uses. Like chariot warfare, iron tech-

nology redefined combat and changed the face of Eurasian civilization.

Once combined with the chariot, iron armor and weaponry allowed the Hittites to hold their own against the New Kingdom of Egypt, to function as a major military power along the Levant Coast, and to invade Mesopotamia between 1400 and 1200 BCE. Perfected around 1400 BCE, iron technology gave the Hittites access to a hard metal that was far more plentiful than the tin and copper used in making bronze.

Yet even though the Hittites held a Eurasian monopoly on the manufacture of iron after its discovery, they produced neither enough weapons nor farm tools to generate an increase in agricultural surpluses and prevent their fall. The reason the Hittites failed to expand their agricultural production is that they did not share their iron technology with the farmers they ruled; these farmers were subject peoples the Hittites did not trust with iron. Accordingly, once knowledge of iron manufacturing began to spread after 1400 BCE, a confederation of nomads that Herodotus called the Phrygians, a people who had moved into Anatolia from an unknown place, also learned how to produce iron weapons, shared the knowledge with their entire population, and overran the Hittite Empire. After 1200 BCE, once the Phrygians had risen up to destroy the Hittite kingdom, fleeing blacksmiths accelerated the spread of their once-secret techniques throughout the adjacent cultures. At the same time, their flight encouraged the discovery of iron-rich deposits throughout the ancient Eurasian commercial world and changed the lives of people everywhere.

Between 1200 and 1000 BCE, with the fall of the Hittites and the spread of iron technology, a new era of mass migration began based on iron farm tools and weapons. The nomads who acquired knowledge of iron did so just as they had learned about the wheel; trade with well-established urban centers spread the knowledge of blacksmiths to shepherd peoples. And since the beginning of sedentary civilization and the rise of cities, contact between farming and nomadic communities remained constant. Shepherd peoples had wandered through the best-defined agricultural regions on a regular basis. At the same time, no farming culture could raise enough food supplies to release the military resources needed to conquer the deserts or steppes where these nomads lived. As a result, a steady history of invasion and commerce belied the idea that a clearly defined border could be drawn between farming and herding cultures. Hence, valuable sedentary secrets like iron manufacture soon diffused to nomadic peoples.

Simultaneously, as mentioned above, in the case of iron, nomads such as the Phrygians had an advantage over their sedentary neighbors like the Hittites. Conquerors like the Hittites were foreign masters who ruled a subject people who spoke a different language and lived by a native traditions. As a result, these foreign masters did not dare to arm the rank-and-file of their agricultural tax base. Had they done so, armed native farmers might have turned on and attacked their alien masters rather than agree to fight a new nomadic invader. Therefore, nomads like the Phrygians who did not have to fear their own population had the advantage of being able to arm their entire pool of able bodied men for war. Accordingly, an iron-wielding population of nomadic tribes could sweep out of the deserts, or down from the steppes, with virtually every member of their community in support of the attack. As a result, the collapse of foreign occupying rulers like the Hittites signaled the beginning of the second great era of migration.

Shortly after the fall of the Hittites, the Mycenaeans also collapsed under pressures from Greek-speaking nomads who migrated from the north. Called "the Dorian Invasions," iron-wielding shepherds who spoke a different dialect of Greek from the Mycenaean city-states moved into Greece after 1100 BCE and disrupted the pirate kingdoms of the Achaeans (Homer's name for the Mycenaeans). Like India during the Aryan Invasions, the destruction of the Mycenaean urban culture was so complete at the hands of the Dorians that Greece descended into a Dark Age (1100–700 BCE). For the next four hundred years, the features of civilization disappeared: writing, art, and the wealth of goods created by an urban division of labor. In its place, shepherd kingdoms and tribal rule became the Greek norm.

With the collapse of the Mycenaean world, the "Sea People" began to raid the eastern coast of the Mediterranean. Armed with iron weapons, the Sea People began a cycle of assaults that ravaged the Levant Coast and Egypt. Some of these pirates may have been Mycenaeans who had fled the Dorians to the islands of the southeastern Aegean. Whatever their origins, the Sea People are believed to have settled at one point and learned the art of iron smelting. Armed with this new metal, they were joined by a people called the Philistines and together began a cycle of devastating raids along the Levant Coast and Egypt that led to the first naval battle in history recorded as an Egyptian victory during Ramses III's reign (Chapter Three).

Like the European Vikings of the Early Middle Ages (500–1000 CE), the Sea People had the ability to strike without warning, achieve their military objectives, and quickly retreat. Under the military strain of the exhaustive defense of their coast, the command of Egypt by native rulers eventually ended. Meanwhile, Kushite kings who invaded Egypt from the south be-

came the first foreigners to rule the Nile Valley since the reign of the Hyksos. Then Egypt fell to a series of other foreign monarchies, the Assyrians, the Persians, the Macedonians, and the Romans, all of which used iron to conquer the Land of the Nile. At the same time, the balance of power on the Levant Coast changed with the arrival of the Philistines.

One people who benefited from the invasion of Iron Age nomads like the Philistines were the Phoenicians. Settled on the Levant Coast in what today is Lebanon, the Phoenicians belonged to the previous era of migration that had begun around 2000 BCE. Living under the shadow of the great chariot empires that surrounded them, the Hittites, the New Kingdom of Egypt, and the Mycenaean pirate realms, the Phoenicians did not make their mark on world history until the Iron Age. Released to become a commercial society with the collapse of their more powerful neighbors, the Phoenicians began to move after 1000 BCE. Establishing some twenty to thirty great colonies along the Mediterranean coast, the Phoenicians created a commercial network that spread the artifacts of urban society wherever they went. One of their contributions to future urban civilizations was the development of the alphabet. This creation, which they shared with another Iron Age culture, the Hebrews, completely transformed writing in the ancient West.

Just as the power vacuum created by Iron Age invaders released the Phoenicians to make their mark on world history, so the Hebrews had a chance to establish an independent realm on the Levant Coast. As mentioned in Chapter Two, during the Bronze Age, the Hebrews, twelve tribes of Semitic nomads, wandered west from Sumeria into the Levant. Then they migrated into Egypt, perhaps as part of the Hyksos invasions. Sometime around 1400 BCE, those Hebrews still living in Egypt after the fall of the Hyksos, suffered from the New Kingdom's newfound xenophobia and found themselves enslaved. Then, according to *Exodus*, a leader named Moses engineered the liberation of the Hebrews and mounted a nomadic quest for a permanent homeland. After years of harsh living in the Sinai Peninsula, the survivors of Moses's exodus entered the land of Canaan and took up residence in the highlands opposite the Philistine coastal cities. There they learned the secrets of iron manufacture, developed agricultural skills, and challenged their eastern neighbors for command of the land. At this point the disruption of the great chariot powers like the Hittite Empire and the New Kingdom of Egypt had given the Hebrews the time they needed to secure their own territory. Named after the children of Israel, the twelve tribes who had followed Moses out of Egypt built their new kingdom around 1000 BCE and embarked upon a long, complex, and unstable history. The record of these events matured into the *Torah* (which Christians call the first five books of the Old Testament), a written document composed between the ninth and the second centuries BCE. This record combined historical events with literature, poetry, law, and religious principles to become the foundation for the first Eurasian monotheism. As a result, the Hebrews played a major role in this second episode of mass migration: they made significant contributions to the ongoing religious traditions of the West.

Two more Semitic groups migrated into the Fertile Crescent at the same time that the Hebrews and Phoenicians were establishing their respective realms on the Levant Coast. The Aramaeans and Chaldaeans moved up from the southern desert and branched off to occupy separate realms in the agricultural zones of Mesopotamia and Syria. Neither had iron weapons when they wandered into their new homelands, and, like the Hebrews, both of them had to learn the secrets of agriculture and metal smelting from their settled neighbors. The Aramaeans took over Syria in the eleventh century BCE, and the Chaldaeans occupied Babylonia. Once each had acquired their own iron weapons and farm tools, they developed the military resources to remain on the land they had captured.

A final mass migration recorded during the Iron Age is the appearance of the Celts. A shepherd culture first identified in what is now southwest Germany and eastern France in the second millennium BCE, the Celts derived their name from Herodotus. It was he who spoke of a large number of people living to the north of Greece, called the *Keltoi*, who herded livestock for a living. Spreading throughout Europe from the British Isles to the Balkans and the Baltic, the Celts occupied a land that ancient Western farmers had ignored. Acquiring iron technology between 1300 and 1100 BCE, the Celts developed a complex and warlike culture, occasionally slipping into the Mediterranean world to inflict severe damage.

As mentioned above, the centers of Celtic society occupied eastern France, southern Germany, and the western portion of the modern-day Czech Republic. Ruled by chiefdoms and supported by a military aristocracy, the Celts engaged in trade with the sedentary peoples to the south by finding, mining, refining, and supplying rich deposits of copper, silver, tin, and iron ore. Commanding some of Europe's main waterways, such as the Seine, the Saône and Rhône, the Rhine, and the Danube, the Celts developed a complex trade network that proved a key factor in the commercial development of the West.

As iron became an increasingly important metal after 1000 BCE, the Celts supplied Greek and Phoenician merchants with essential resources to meet farming needs. In fact, Celtic access to iron and silver mines motivated the Phoenicians, and later the Dorian Greeks, to set up colonies in the Western Mediterranean. Then, a major shift in climate that occurred sometime between the seventh and sixth centuries BCE caused an increase in humidity, which, in turn, transformed much of the land north of the Alps into a bog, forcing the Celts to migrate. Suffering from overpopulation, the Celts began to invade the sedentary cultures to the south; this migration included an episode in Roman history when Celtic warriors dealt early Rome one of its most severe defeats. Ironically, these migrations actually strengthened the commercial relations between the Mediterranean and Celtic centers of production; and increased cultural contact led to increased commercial exchange until the Romans felt compelled to capture the wealth of these districts located to the north when Julius Caesar (ca. 102–44 BCE) conquered Gaul.

Cavalry
The Third Wave of Migrations

Warfare underwent another revolution when Central Asian nomads learned how to ride the horse into combat. Well-coordinated cavalry units did not appear overnight. To fight from horseback required technical skills as well as the development of the saddle (the stirrup came much later near the end of the ancient era). Fighting from horseback actually took a long time to develop because the art of firing a bow from a fast-moving mount, without handling the reins required great skill. Since archery requires the use of both arms, a true cavalry rider had to command his horse with only his voice and his legs.

The equestrian arts originated in the Iranian highlands, the same location in which the Kassites had developed the first chariots. Practiced as a means of transport as early as 2000 BCE, the custom of riding a horse spread throughout the Fertile Crescent, Asia Minor, and the Aegean over the next thousand years. Yet a true cavalry force did not appear until the Scythians (Altaic nomads like the Turks and Mongols named by Herodotus) invaded the Assyrian Empire. Although the Assyrians themselves had developed a tiny cavalry unit of their own as early as 857 BCE, their reliance on infantry reflected the common problem of sedentary cultures: land invested to feed people could not be used to raise livestock. Hence, when the Scythians invaded the Assyrian Empire in the seventh century BCE, they arrived with far more cavalrymen than their sedentary opponents could mobilize.

Coming from the grasslands of Central Asia, the Scythians (perhaps really Turks or Mongols) had an abundance of horses. Spending most of their time tending livestock, the males of these tribes had little to do except refine their military skills to defend their pastures. Fighting endless blood feuds and local wars, these Scythians honed the ability of firing a bow from horseback into such a fine art that they became an irresistible force. Since the rider and the animal learned to function as one, when the Scythians invaded Assyrian territory with squadrons of mounted archers, the Assyrians had no way to respond. Attacking with raiding parties comprised only of cavalry, the Scythians cut a swathe through the Assyrian Empire that the might of this Iron Age civilization could not prevent. Uninterested in actually settling down, the Scythians took what they wanted and then retreated home. But the damage had been done; the Scythians had caused so much trouble for the Assyrians that they no longer had the resources left to face a major rebellion mounted against their empire at the end of the seventh century BCE. By being such harsh rulers, the Assyrians had inspired such a thirst for freedom in their subject peoples that they rose up en masse against their cruel occupiers once the Scythians had done their worst. The result was the fall of Nineveh, the Assyrian capital, in 612 BCE. Therefore, even if indirectly, the collapse of the last great Mesopotamian Empire resulted from chaos caused by the initial appearance of well-trained nomadic cavalrymen.

Following an already familiar pattern, the overthrow of the Assyrian Empire created another power vacuum that offered nomads the opportunity to invade. The Medes and Persians, like the Scythians, were skilled cavalrymen who migrated into present-day Iran. The Medes came first and developed a tribal confederation that joined the rebellious forces that overthrew the Assyrian Empire. Among the Medes, the Achaemenid clan, led by Cyrus the Great (559–530 BCE), launched his own rebellion, which replaced Median supremacy with Persian rule. Situated on the grasslands of the Iranian highlands, the Persians under Cyrus the Great then developed an excellent cavalry force that became the backbone of their army. Outnumbering the Neo-Babylonian horsemen, as well as every other sedentary culture to the west, Cyrus the Great began a conquest pattern that resulted in the establishment of the Persian Empire. Like the Scythians before them, the Persians relied on the horse, were ex-nomads originally from lands north of the Caucasus Mountains, and were a people who learned the art of cultivation from the cultures they came to dominate.

The people of the Ancient Near East who had endured the harsh rule of the Assyrians gladly accepted the Achaemenid clan as the new Persian rulers. For example, with the financial aid of the Persians, the Hebrews (the Judaic survivors of the Babylonian cap-

The "Mounted Archer Drawing a Bow" represented the power of cavalry. Swift and deadly, armed horsemen gave nomads the ability to hit and run, which could devastate any unprepared sedentary culture. From Austin Henry Layard's "Nineveh and Its Remains." Gorgias Press, www.gorgiaspress.com.

tivity now called "the Jews") were allowed to return to Jerusalem and rebuild their temple. This made the Jews a grateful ally of the Persians. Meanwhile, Cyrus the Great died shortly after the restoration of the Jews, while fighting Scythians, and his son, Cambyses, inherited the throne, conquered Egypt, and added perhaps some parts of Kush to the Persian Empire. The Persians also made inroads into Europe from Anatolia, invading their way into Thrace, in the Balkans, and coming into contact with Macedonia.

Unfortunately for Cambyses, when he exhibited signs of insanity his nobles assassinated him, and Darius I came to the throne. Known as Darius the Great (reigned 521–486 BCE), he became the new king of kings (a title Persian monarchs used to illustrate all the lands over which they had gained mastery). Darius divided the empire into twenty-three *Satrapies* (provinces), each of which was placed under a Persian *Satrap* (governor). Now the Persians constructed a 1600-mile-long road along which there were 111 way stations with supplies, fresh horses, and messengers waiting to take imperial decrees to the different parts of the Persian Empire. This is the earliest form of a postal system, in which communication was made easier and more reliable. For the first time "checks" were used as a monetary system which allowed the Persians to avoid transporting large amounts of precious metal through dangerous territory. Darius also brought about the standardization of weights and measurements to facilitate trade and the growth of the economy throughout his Empire.

By the time of Darius, Greek masons and Mesopotamian laborers, in a collaborative effort, had finished the famous capital of the Persian Empire, known as the Persepolis. Importing building materials from all over the empire—lumber from Phoenicia and gold from as far away as Africa—the Persians created a symbolic capital that awed their subject peoples with its splendor. Each year, during the Persian New Year at the Spring Equinox, emissaries from the different areas of the empire would bring gifts to the Persepolis, symbol-

Remains of the Persepolis, the palace of Darius. Courtesy of Touraj Daryaee.

izing the unity and the power of the Persian Empire. This ceremony is portrayed in reliefs on the walls of the Persepolis, which depict subjects bringing livestock, clothing, and other goods before the king on his throne.

Darius is also distinguished in that he left to posterity a personal biography written in three languages (Old Persian, Babylonian, and Elamite); this is important for several reasons. First, it is the longest surviving cuneiform inscription from the Ancient Near East. Second, it is through this inscription that scholars were able to decipher the cuneiform script and gain access to the rich literature of Mesopotamia. And third, Darius gives us a firsthand record of his achievements and his devotion to a universal god: Ahura Mazda (the chief deity of Zoroastrianism—a Persian religion).

In the Behistun inscription of Darius (a relief carved into the cliffs there), scholars can read a tale that stated his family had long been kings, and that a man by the name of Gaumata (*Smerdis* in the Herodotus account) had usurped the kingship. Consequently Gaumata had spread lies about Darius's lineage, prompting Darius and a small number of followers to kill the usurper and take back the throne for his family. Darius then put down many uprisings within his empire and became the absolute king of the Persian realm, which stretched from northern India in the east to Anatolia in the northwest and from Egypt in the southwest to Arabia in the south. Darius also tells us that he was successful because he worshiped Ahura Mazda, who aided him in his remarkable career.

Another important point that the Behistun inscription reveals is a basic understanding of the Persian dichotomy between good and evil. In the Zoroastrian school of thought, the world is a battleground between good and evil. Ahura Mazda, supreme god and champion of good, is the source of light that blesses the world. Ahriman, the prince of darkness and everything evil, fills the land with chaos. Every human being must

choose between these two opposites. All those who are good must join Ahura Mazda and help him vanquish Ahriman: good deeds, a love of the truth, and righteous conduct all serve the light and help to dispel the darkness. Those who belong on the side of Righteousness (*Arta*), and those who belong on the side of Lie (*Drūg*), represent this simple dichotomy between good and evil. Here Lie becomes personified as a demon whom Darius had met in Gaumata but was able to vanquish with the aid of Ahura Mazda.

The Persian society was aristocratic and their supremacy made them the elite of their vast empire. This meant the Persians, especially those of the upper classes, were exempt from paying taxes and lived a comfortable life, while others engaged in farming or entered the army. Herodotus and Strabo (a second famous Greek historian) give us detailed information regarding the training of the Persian youths. The "wise men" taught them reading and writing and the history of the Persian people, emphasizing the deeds of the great men. The young were initiated into the Zoroastrian religion, which was supervised by the priests known as the *Magi* (hence the etymology of the English world *magic*); the Magi had memorized the *Avesta* (the sacred text of the Zoroastrians) and knew well the secrets of the world. The young also had to learn how to plow the ground and gained knowledge of agricultural and other useful sciences. When they became older, the young entered military training, in which they learned to use a bow, ride a horse, and tell the truth. The military training was much more rigorous than anything else taught, except the lessons on good and evil. Finally, in the vast military system, the young Persians usually composed the cavalry, and the elite forces known as the Immortals, numbered 10,000 and served as the personal guards of the King. The rest of the army, the infantry and all the attendants, comprised subject peoples who served as allies in a system that gave them considerable autonomy.

Persian women, meanwhile, oversaw domestic affairs and childrearing. Since Persian society was bent on ruling Asia and Europe, it needed many sons to enter the army. Scholars have much more information on the royal women of the Achaemenid Dynasty that ruled the Persian court than other cultures. The Queen and Queen Mother were very influential and made decisions at the court, while others in the harem (the concubines of the king) plotted so that their sons had a chance to win the throne. Ambitious court women also followed the army to the battlefield and took initiatives on behalf of themselves and their husbands in advancing their careers in the service of the king of kings. Also, the worship of female deities such as Lady Anahita and the establishment of her cult across the empire by the Persian kings is another sign of female power in Persia. Anahita is a deity connected to waters in the Zoroastrian religion. Yet in the *Avesta*, Persian heroes, as well as villains, make sacrifices to her so that she would grant her favor to help them overcome their enemies in battle. Hence, she also took on a militaristic aspect, one in which the warriors worshipped her.

Meanwhile, in the Far East, the Xiong-nu and the Turks also developed a cavalry that went on to plague the Chinese. Both peoples formed vast confederations while living adjacent to one another on the grasslands north of China, roamed the vast steppes of Central Asia, and played key roles throughout world history at the end of the Ancient Era as well as during the Middle Ages. Finally, both represented a constant threat to their sedentary neighbors. The Turks, however, belonged to a different tribal confederation than the Xiong-nu and derived their name from *Tujueh*, the Chinese term used to distinguish them from Xiong-nu warriors. Closely related to the Scythians, a name used by Herodotus to describe the tribes that attacked Assyria, all three— Scythians, Turks, and Xiong-nu reflected the way sedentary people described the nomads rather than how they described themselves. All three in fact spoke variations of the same Altaic language and lived in close proximity to each other. Only time and migration drew them apart much later in world history.

Because they inspired fear in their sedentary neighbors, the role in world history of the Xiong-nu, Turks, and Scythians is punctuated with barbarities, a term used by the sedentary people who suffered their invasions. Each nomadic confederation developed practices that underlined their military prowess. Each enjoyed turning the skulls of defeated chiefs into drinking cups; the Xiong-nu, in fact, liked to line their drinking cups with gold to enhance the beauty of a fallen foe's skullcap. All three liked to slit the throats of the women in an opponent's harem, as well as slaughter the children and servants. Finally, all three developed such practices to ensure against the possibility of revenge—the most common way to settle differences among the tribes living within a nomadic confederation. Only survival defined virtue among these warlike people. Hence, these nomads represented a vast pool of people feared by all farmers.

As we have seen, the relationship between nomadic and sedentary cultures was a complex one. The nomads formed a violent community of migrating herdsmen who developed an uneasy but necessary relationship with sedentary peoples. The nomads needed the products of an urban division of labor; the sedentary people needed access to raw materials that they could not find for themselves. Since each group was essential to the other, contact was maintained. Yet the vast differences in culture inspired by extensive and intensive agriculture frequently led to sharp periods of violent warfare.

Successful cultures, whether sedentary or nomadic, created many of their own internal problems. Success based on agriculture fostered symbioses between humans, plants, and animals that caused all these populations to grow. Increased population created pressures within each successful society that required them to expand. Expansion, however, could only occur within the limits of compatible geographic sites. Eventually, survival of such expanding cultures created competition that led to violence.

Given the differences between the nomads and their sedentary neighbors, a basic pattern of interaction emerged. First, during eras of prosperity, trade dominated intercultural contacts; second, during eras of dearth, raids and warfare replaced trade and changed the face of ancient history by spawning mass migration of human groups, whence one group learned the skills of another. These exchanges punctuated ancient history with technical breakthroughs like the chariot, iron smelting, and the cavalry, as the nomads and the plant farmers worked out their disputes. The result was a history generated from the basic differences between two different styles of agriculture.

Suggested Reading

Buliet, Richard, *The Camel and the Wheel* (Cambridge: Harvard University Press, 1975).

De Crespigny, Rafe, *Northern Frontier Policies and Strategies of the Later Han Empire*, (Canberra, ACT.: Australian National University Press, 1996).

Grousset, René, *Empire of the Steppes: A History of Central Asia* (New Brunswick, N.J.: Rutgers University Press, 1970).

Jones, Thomas B., *From the Tigris to the Tiber: An Introduction to Ancient History*, Third Edition (Homewood, Ill.: The Dorsey Press, 1983).

Khazanov, A. M., and Julia Crookendan, *Nomads and the Outside World* (Cambridge: Cambridge University Press, 1984).

Malcolm, Todd, *The Early Germans* (Oxford: Blackwell Publishers, 1992).

Macquet, Jacques, *Civilizations of Black Africa* (New York: Oxford University Press, 1972).

McNeill, William H., *The Pursuit of Power*. See especially "Arms and Society in Antiquity," p. 1– 24. (Chicago: University of Chicago Press, 1982).

Steibing, William H., Jr., *Ancient Near Eastern History and Culture* (New York: Longman, 2003).

Weissleder, Wolfgang. *The Nomadic Alternative* (The Hague: Mouton, 1978).

VII

GREECE:
The Rainfall Zone

Greece presents a completely different type of sedentary history when compared to the other agricultural societies considered in prior chapters. Greece emerged as a system of city-states founded on a site with unusual geographical features that encouraged Greek migrants to move away from their mainland, into the Mediterranean Basin, rather than integrating their civilization around a government centered in one place. The Greeks built these city-states in isolated valleys, cul-de-sacs, and box canyons that never developed the overland communication system needed to pull their culture together in a single urban hierarchy. At the same time, blessed as they were with natural ports situated near sheltered waters adjacent to seemingly countless peninsulas and isthmuses, most all Greeks developed maritime skills as well as excellent sea-trade routes. The result was a system of cities that emerged in relative isolation from one another politically, but were connected by the sea through trade and travel. Meanwhile, since the foundations of Greek culture have already been discussed in Chapter Six—the discussion of the Mycenaean and Dorians who settled in Greece during the Bronze and Iron Ages respectively—the logical place to start this chapter is with the Dark Age (1200–700 BCE).

By 1200 BCE, signs of change in Greece were afoot. Evidence of immigration away from the mainland was common; the Mycenaean city-states had become heavily fortified with huge "Cyclopian Walls," and many people had fled to other regions outside Greece. This was a common pattern both on the Greek mainland and in the Eastern Mediterranean in general. And, as mentioned, by 1200 BCE the Phrygians already had destroyed the Hittite Empire in Anatolia and the Sea People had raided the Egyptian coast. Furthermore, the island of Cyprus and the Levant Coast, from Palestine to Syria, were under attack.

In Greece, writing disappeared and the culture entered a "Dark Age" (1200–700 BCE). While there is no one concrete reason to explain this occurrence in all of the Eastern Mediterranean, it is likely that a combination of factors such as the new Iron Age, climatic and geological events such as droughts and earthquakes, mass migrations of people in search of food, and the collapse of the local economies led to the chaos. Whatever the causes of the Dark Ages in Greece, the Dorian migrations pushed the remnants of Mycenaean culture away from the mainland—especially to the coast of Anatolia, known as *Ionia* (Ionia got its name from the Ionic dialect spoken by the Greeks who settled there).

By the eighth century BCE, one sees signs of recovery in Greece, such as the epic poetry of Homer. Homer lived before 700 BCE, probably came from the island of Chios, compiled poems in the Ionic dialect, and represented the legendary memory of the Mycenaeans who had fled the Dorians. Homer sang a massive collection of songs that were later compiled into "books" (twenty-five such books composed each poem). Yet during Homer's lifetime, these poems were only a small part of a larger oral tradition; as such they represented the absence of writing and the need to convey all the details of life through memory. Hence, they also reflected the complexity of life in the eighth century BCE as manifested by two epic tales that no one knew how to record in written form.

Homer was blind, and the narratives of his poems had been in circulation long before he integrated them into coherent poems. The two epic tales he compiled for the Greeks, *The Iliad* and *The Odyssey*, became one of the common elements that all ancient Greeks knew and shared. Hence, these poems gave the Greeks a common set of beliefs and practices, even if the Greek people remained divided politically. The poems, themselves, tell about the Mycenaean warriors (i.e., the Achaeans) who fought at Troy, and what they faced on their voyage and after their return home. Both tales relay a value system that praised courage in battle, self-sacrifice, love of one's comrades-in-arms, and the sanctity of the home. These basic ideas and beliefs, coupled with the wrath of the Greek gods—all of whom pop up here and there in the poems to twist people's fate—

80

gave the Greeks a unique understanding of the world and their place in it. These stories also created a common historical memory for the Greeks, one that happened to set their past in a poetic and beautiful manner that everyone could appreciate. Picking up the alphabet from the Phoenicians, the Greeks later set down both of Homer's epic poems in writing; thereafter these martial yet philosophical tales became part of the elementary education of every young Greek male.

Network Cities and the Special Case of Athens

Coming out of the Dark Ages (ca. 700 BCE), some cities on mainland Greece began to develop unique urban systems. Integrating the general commercial practices of the Mediterranean Basin with local agricultural circumstances, Greek *Poleis* (city-states) introduced Western Civilization to a new urban phenomenon, the network city. Geographers define network cities as high concentrations of people living in an urban setting but dependent more on long-distance trade than on local agriculture to feed their numbers. Hence, a network city relies more on exchanges generated in foreign markets by urban merchants and other businesspeople than on the local food production of the peasantry.

As mentioned above, the residents of the Greek mainland occupied a physically shattered landscape filled with box canyons, cul-de-sacs, isolated valleys, isthmuses, peninsulas, long bays, natural harbors, and local streams. Such a landscape criss-crossed by water discouraged travel by land but naturally encouraged sea voyages. As a result, Greek culture tended to look outward for the resources needed to build its cities rather than attempting to integrate the local geography through the political authority of a common urban hierarchy.

Each isolated valley situated close to a sheltered peninsula or isthmus had access to the Aegean, Adriatic, or Mediterranean seas as avenues of transport, while local streams or rainfall provided the moisture needed to sustain modest plant cultivation. Like the rainfall districts situated close to Mesopotamia's rivers, Greece also had to wait until regional trade networks had matured sufficiently to support an urban division of labor on its mainland. Accordingly, commercial links with Egypt via Crete, and with the Minoan civilization transferred the tools, ideas, seeds, livestock, and urban skills needed to change Mycenaean nomads into sedentary farmers during the Bronze Age (3500–1200 BCE).

The Greek Bronze Age (2200–1100 BCE) saw the rise of Mycenaean city-states in which local strongmen, supported by legions of chariot warriors, established successful urban sites. At first subordinate to Minoan leaders, these Mycenaean champions absorbed the techniques of plant cultivation from Crete before they felt powerful enough to claim independence for themselves. Then, in 1600 BCE, a major explosion on the volcanic island of Thera sent aftershocks across the Aegean Sea to Crete that damaged buildings there and disrupted food production on the island. Weakened internally, a sequence of local disasters followed that may have included widespread starvation, disease, and rebellion, but certainly caused the Minoan culture to lose command of the choice sea-lanes. Finally, the Mycenaean strongmen living on the Greek mainland took advantage of this weakness in Crete to capture the island and displace Minoan rule in the Aegean Sea.

After 1450 BCE, the cities of the Greek mainland therefore came to dominate Greece, the Aegean Islands, and present-day coastal Turkey. By 1200 BCE, these Mycenaean champions had perfected a highly distinctive and effective style of chariot warfare that became a permanent feature of Western Civilization through the artistic imagination of Homer's epic poetry. These Mycenaean strongmen rode their chariots to battle, dismounted, and fought the infantry engagements mentioned in Chapter Six. Relying heavily on their superior armor, these Greek champions could resist arrows fired at them by enemy archers, engage the enemy in hand-to-hand combat, and then strip the dead bodies of their precious weapons. Bronze was sufficiently rare that the ebb and flow of warfare depended on the prowess of a single man such as the hero warriors Achilles and Hector, the Achaean and Trojan protagonists of *The Iliad*, and the arms they captured in single combat.

The coming of the Iron Age completely changed the course of Greek history. Associated with the Dorian migration after 1100 BCE, iron delivered Greece into the hands of the nomads (Chapter Six). Speaking a different dialect of Greek than the Mycenaeans, these Dorians displaced the local strongmen and plunged Greece into the Dark Age mentioned above. Iron farm tools, local cities, and isolated valleys, however, combined to create the basis for a new era of urban history after 750 BCE. Paradoxically, iron farm tools expanded fields on the Greek mainland to stimulate food production, but the confined agricultural sites in isolated valleys soon created severe local population pressures. And these pressures motivated the newly strong Greeks to colonize the Mediterranean Basin.

Since, as mentioned, the Greek city-states could not provide food surpluses necessary to sustain their proportionately large urban numbers, periodically portions of a growing city's population had to immigrate into the Mediterranean Basin. The frequency with which these efforts took place over a two-hundred-year period (750–550 BCE) dotted the coastlines of the Mediterranean and Black seas with numerous cities that later functioned as a commercial network that sustained vastly expanded urban populations back on the Greek mainland. While each of these colonies led an independent political existence, each one also maintained strong cultural ties with their founder cities on the Greek mainland. These cultural ties later became a major factor in support of the emergence of network cities.

Each new Greek colony had to carve out a site for itself, quell local resistance, and organize a city. These activities linked military service with state formation and suggested to all Greeks the need to speculate about the ideal political constitution. So many efforts at state formation made Greek thinkers extremely imaginative, flexible, and creative in the process of designing these city-states.

The link between military service and state formation not only matured in these colonial efforts, but it also influenced politics at home on the Greek mainland. Central to this process was the *phalanx* (an infantry formation that arranged armored men in long parallel ranks that collided with the defending lines of the enemy). The phalanx created a concrete tie between the city and the farmer-soldier. As iron became plentiful in Greece, local farmers found themselves drawn into a city's markets and politics. Defending the town grew in importance and encouraged local farmers to acquire armor and join the wealthy in the protection of their cities. The cost of a suit of armor came to roughly the value of sixty sheep. Such an expense set the level of income needed for military service at about the harvest of a medium-sized farm. Thus, as farmers increased in number in the army, so did their military importance. Soon farmer-soldiers became the key military resource in the city's survival.

The culmination of this process occurred in the seventh century BCE. During the wars of that century, farmer-soldiers joined together in long ranks of heavily armored infantrymen, called Hoplites, who protected one another with their shields and increased their impact on the battlefield through the sheer weight of their numbers. The phalanx formation functioned as a wall of human flesh and metal that acted as a single body in the city's defense. In effect, the phalanx *became* the city-in-arms. From this moment on, Greek farmers connected military service with political responsibilities and privileges. Accordingly, each great city-state on the Greek mainland now worked out its own constitutional system to enhance and codify the ties between the farmer, military service, and citizenship.

At the heart of this link between the military and politics emerged the concept of "civic virtue" (the ethical and political obligations imposed by the city on its citizens and, conversely the rights the state owed each citizen). This ethical/political principle defined all civic responsibilities set by the state. Since military service determined the primary conditions of citizenship, only men could be active in politics. The type of military institution that matured reflected the constitutional design of the particular city. Sparta, for example, stopped its military development with the phalanx, formed an *oligarchy* (rule by the few), and dominated a slave population of Helots who worked the Spartan farms. These slaves fed the citizens, freed them for military training and warfare, and allowed them to define virtually every feature of Sparta's civic life in regard to military service. For Sparta, then, the phalanx became the basis of politics, public duty, and civic virtue. A Spartan male dedicated his entire life to military service, and a Spartan female committed herself to producing future soldiers for Sparta.

In contrast, Athens expanded the design of its military beyond the phalanx to include a naval force based on the *trireme* (ca. 500 BCE), a warship that required three banks of rowers on either side of the vessel to row in unison to propel the ship forward, ramming and sinking the enemy vessel. The oarsmen's survival required an identical level of discipline and stamina to perfect the coordinated movements of the ship. The trireme

The phalanx formation, a hallmark of ancient Greek warfare, was employed widely after the seventh century BCE. It consisted of a eight continuous ranks of heavily armed infantrymen wearing helmets and armor, and carrying shields to protect one another. This illustration represents the Macedonian variation developed during the fourth century BCE. Watercolour, 1981, by Peter Connolly (born 1935). akg-images, London.

Trireme model in bronze. The Athenian Trireme (Greek *trieres*) fighting ship was designed to cover long distances quickly under oar and sail and to ram enemy ships with devastating effect. Money from the new vein of silver in Laurion enabled Athens to buy timber from Italy to increase its *fleet from 40 in 489 BCE to 200 in 480. Note that this model shows only one bank of oars, but an actual trireme had three banks of oars. Photo courtesy Hellenic-Art.com.

generated the same group identity as that felt by the infantrymen in the phalanx. The cost of serving on a trireme, however, required only the price of an oar and a loincloth. This meant that even the poorest Athenian citizen could hope to provide valuable military service and validate his claim to citizenship. Hence, in Athens, unlike in Sparta, military service spread beyond farmers to include the poorest urban recruits.

The role of the navy in Athenian commerce and war, and the communal risk taken by oarsmen, seem to equal the demands placed on any infantryman in the Athenian phalanx. Athens evolved into a democracy that extended the concept of civic virtue to all its native-born males. As Athenian commerce spread and food came in from sources far beyond the local farms, a new urban-rural ratio emerged, with Athens as one of the first successful network cities.

The Role of Coins in Athenian History

The unique brand of Athenian democracy reveals the complex role that an urban market played in integrating political space in Greek history. Athens took its first steps toward becoming a network city when farmers there tried to cope with an expanding commercial system based on coin-money. First developed in Lydia in the Anatolian highlands during the seventh century BCE, the use of coins facilitated rapid exchanges by ensuring a standard of value for the price of any one item. Lydia's currency achieved this level of confidence by ensuring the purity and weight of the metal used in the coin through a royal stamp; the stamp protected the coin's value by offering a replacement on demand.

Coins migrated across the Aegean Sea to Greece through the Ionian colonies (those first Greek city-states founded on the coast of Turkey) bordering Lydia. They entered Greek trade and soon became part of the Athenian economy. With coin-money, the Athenian market began to see an increase of foreign goods, among them wheat from abroad that increased the local supply and created a new level of competition for Athenian farmers, naturally driving down the price of Athenian grain. Declining grain prices caused many Athenian farmers to fall into debt.

This debt endangered the political future of Athens because the only collateral for bankruptcy was the farmer's farm, his family, or himself. Since Athenian farmers could no longer calculate the shifting value of wheat in the Athenian market, an increasing number of them lost their families, their farms, and were themselves eventually sold into slavery. Enslavement of Athenian farmers threatened the very existence of that city. Should enough citizens become slaves, then who would buy armor, join the phalanx, and protect Athens?

This threat set in motion several political experiments that spanned the eighty-six years of change from 594–510 BCE. The Athenians granted a magistrate named Solon emergency powers to address the problem of debt and the enslavement of citizens, a process he began in 594 BCE. Solon examined the question of economic and political stability. He started by canceling existing debts, suspending speculation on the price of wheat, and outlawing enslavement for bankruptcy. He then reclassified citizens based on income using the amount of grain and olive oil harvested each year on a typical farm as a standard. Thus, income-level replaced birth as the sole criterion for status in the city.

Solon's flexible definitions of citizenship status recognized the way the import-export market had redefined the position of a family within society. Those who had become rich due to shifting market conditions owed it to the state to carry a heavier burden of political responsibility. Those who occupied the middle class, and bought the heavy armor needed for service in the phalanx, became the political-military backbone of the city. Since the poor could not even buy armor, they could not participate in politics. (Solon's actions occurred before the development of the trireme.) Finally, Solon completed the circle of democracy by allowing any ordinary citizen who defended the city onto juries that judged the behavior of the rich.

After Solon's reforms, Athens experienced a period of tyranny when an Athenian general named Pisistratus captured power. Pisistratus interrupted the process of constitutional development started by Solon. As a successful tyrant, Pisistratus managed the affairs of the Athenian city-state and generally kept the people happy. The typical Greek tyrant, Pisistratus was not the oppressive dictator implied by the modern meaning of the term "tyranny." Instead, the typical Greek tyrant captured power through political cunning, stayed in office as long as he had popular support, and left the city at death. Pisistratus held onto power, despite brief occasions when he was forced from office, and died of old age; this made him a political success. He then passed his rule to his two sons.

Less fortunate then their father, Hipparchus and Hippias did not keep enough Athenians happy to enjoy success. Hipparchus was assassinated for insulting the sister of his murderer. Following his brother's death, the oppressive rule of Hippias soon led to an uprising. With Hippias driven from power, Athens began another era of constitutional development. Yet these years of tyranny proved important because they disconnected Athens from its traditional past by a full generation and a half.

With the fall of Hippias, Athens dabbled in a brief period of oligarchy until the rise to power of a man named Kleisthenes. He was a wealthy Athenian from the ancient aristocratic clan called the Almaeonidae (the great Pericles also came from this clan) who used the political instability of the city after the tyranny to capture power. Kleisthenes noticed that political disputes in Athens mimicked the economic differences of people living on the coast, in the city, and among the farmers in the interior. To solve these conflicting interests, he created ten tribes comprised of members from each of these three areas: Athens itself, the coastal ports, and the interior farms. Thus, a tribe transformed three disputing economic factions into one political unit made

up of mutually dependent persons who fought as part of the Athenian phalanx. The survival of each tribe, therefore, depended on cooperation between these three factions, since each man protected his fellow man in the phalanx. Kleisthenes thus successfully unified the occupational elements of the city into a common interest group.

Next, each tribe sent fifty men to the Council of Five Hundred that ruled the city. These men were selected by lot, which ensured every male citizen would participate in government at one time in his life. Each tribe also elected a general who commanded it in the Athenian army. Since rivalries sometimes developed between the most charismatic of these generals, Kleisthenes created the punishment of ostracism, which forced one or the other disputing general into exile and ensured political stability under the leadership of the one who remained in the city. The term *ostracism* derived from *ostrakon*, or pot shard, the object used to select which politician or general would be expelled; the general whose name appeared most frequently on these pot shards had to leave Athens for ten years. Thus, Kleisthenes created a form of stable democracy that all Athenians could accept. Shortly after his success, the Athenians then developed the trireme, which transformed the city into a naval port, thus bringing their poorest citizens into politics.

The Limits of Democracy

While the idea of democracy took hold for the male citizens of Athens, not everyone had representation in Athenian politics. Women, foreigners, and slaves were excluded from the decision-making process. The women of Athens had few rights, were controlled by their parents, and then, once married, fell under the authority of the husband. The Athenians generally placed a low value on women; in fact, many Athenians argued that prostitutes existed solely for the sake of pleasure, concubines for the daily care of the body, and wives for the singular purpose of begetting legitimate children. Accordingly, "honorable" Athenian women lived in confinement at home.

The reason why "honorable" Athenian women, especially of those of upper classes, stayed at home and could not venture into the streets, was the fear that Athenian men had of ruining the family name. The family lost its good name even when confronted by the charge of adultery, much less by the commission of the act by any one of its women. Athenian men could not bear such dishonor and did everything in their power to prevent it. Hence these men defined the primary function of a "proper" woman as bringing healthy children, specifically sons, into the world, securing feminine chastity, and remaining secluded in the safety of the home.

The man of the house could disown any of his women and sell his children into slavery whenever he chose. Yet girls were kept when no boys were born to the family, for a daughter could be married to a close relative, bear a son, and carry on the family name. Consequently, such a daughter became an *epikleros*, which meant she would marry the nearest male relative to produce this desired child. Marriage for women began at the age of puberty (fourteen years); the families involved arranged the matrimonial contract. Cousins were often encouraged to wed. Women were not expected to know how read, but they could conduct funerals rites and serve as priestesses in cultic activities. Generally the women of lower-class families had much more freedom then their richer neighbors. Slave girls were used for the pleasure of their master, or as a source of income; they could be sent into the streets to function as common prostitutes or entertainers. Men who attended a *symposium*, an after-dinner drinking party in Athenian homes, could bring along expensive courtesans, or *hetairai*, which literally meant "female companions," while their wives stayed home. Some women, however, did not fit the Athenian or Greek mold. The most outstanding example of this is Sappho, who lived around the seventh century BCE in the city of Mitylene on the island of Lesbos. She was committed to the education of girls and women and established a school of erotic poetry composed for other women, which to this day affixed the name of her home island to female same-sex love.

Slaves, too, enjoyed few rights. They were made to work on the farms or given household assignments by their masters. They were allowed to marry, and set up a household with their master's permission, with the hope of producing future slaves. Also, foreigners were allowed to work in Athens, but they had to obtain official permission to stay in the city. If they stayed longer than one month they had to get a sponsor from the city to remain in residence. Aliens could not marry a citizen or own land, and they were welcomed only when there was a need for their labor. During the political troubles in the different city-states, people often immigrated to other cities and took on this status of noncitizen.

Greece, like all Mediterranean societies, based its diet on the triad of wine, olive oil, and grain. Athens was no exception. For the Greeks, eating well meant eating frugally. In fact, eating a simple meal represented the good life, as opposed to the habits of foreigners who were seen as being wasteful and extravagant. The study of food also brought about the discipline of nutrition

and medicine. Different types of foods were prescribed for men, women, and children to improve the health of each. Greek doctors also emphasized the moderate consumption of food along with regular exercise to retain good health.

Sparta

Sparta represented the opposite type of city-state when compared to Athens. Sparta shunned trade, refused gold and silver coins, developed its own native system of iron rings for use in exchange, and lived in economic isolation in Lakonia, the territorial valley in the eastern Peloponnesus. The Spartans began their political history by conquering the city-state immediately to their west: Messenia. Then they transformed the local inhabitants into the Helots, as mentioned above. Helots were state-owned slaves tied to the land, who did the work needed to feed the Spartan population, and freed the Spartan men to prepare for war. But while the Helots functioned as an economic caste in Spartan society, they also represented a constant threat because of their social, economic, and political oppression. Hence, the Spartan citizen always had to be vigilant against a possible Helot rebellion.

Between perceived threats from within and without, Spartan society was entirely geared for warfare and in a continuous state of battle readiness. The Spartan male was separated from his family at age six and put into a system of training known as *Agoge*, in which he learned to be a cog in the collective responsibility to defend Sparta. This system deliberately weakened family ties and emphasized the importance of the city as a whole, since young boys lived together and rarely went home. Young adult males supervised the military training of the younger boys, who were expected to learn all the military arts: marching, gymnastics, singing, carrying heavy weights (preparation for wearing armor), foraging, and reading—preferably inspirational literature such as Homer's martial epics. Once they reached the age of twelve, the boys attended the men's mess to select a military mentor, i.e., a young man who would carry one of them off to finish his education. This man and boy would leave for some place in the countryside for several months where the young boy formed a bond that linked the manly art of war to sexual activity.

Once these young boys were accepted into the Spartan male life, that is being able to attend the mess, they lived in groups of fifteen, eating and fighting together until they were thirty years old, at which point they were permitted to marry and set up a household and were considered full citizens. Nonetheless, they still

The Parthenon, the temple dedicated to Athena. The Athenian Empire provided Athens with an economic base that financed massive urban development. Yet, despite the beauty of such creations, the price paid for this urban development was the forced subordination of Athens' allies in its war with Persia. Courtesy Anne Lynne Negus.

continued to eat in the mess hall until the age of sixty. Women were also given physical training, were active in society, and met with the young men. They married relatively late by Greek standards, for they had to wait until they were eighteen years old, as opposed to other city-states in which girls were considered ready for marriage once they reached puberty. Even the courting and the marriage ceremony in Sparta had militaristic symbolism. In it, the young girl would be "stolen" from her family home, have her hair cut off, and then be dressed as a boy. Then she would wed and spend her "wedding night" in a windowless room. For the remaining days of the ceremony, the bride was left in this dark room, where her husband, who was still expected to go back to the mess hall to live and eat with the men, could visit her nightly. The custom of the Spartan men visiting their wives in the dark came about so that the pair would not become so emotionally attached as a couple as to lose sight of their military duty.

After marriage, Spartan women consequently remained at home and ran the household in the absence of their husbands. Spartan boys and girls were trained by their mother to focus constantly on their duty to the city. As we have seen, a Spartan boy left home at the age of six, while the girl remained with her mother. Spartan women and daughters were responsible for maintaining the household and, in fact, women were the ones who ran the farms and the domestic economy. In this way women were somewhat empowered and were free to engage in the Spartan economy and society. After all, the function of the Spartan society was collective; everybody did what he or she could for Sparta as a whole.

The Failure of Greek Politics

With two city-states as different from one another as Sparta and Athens, yet both members of the same culture, one might guess that a conflict between them was inevitable. All that one needed to occur was the right set of circumstances to touch off a flashpoint. This moment came soon after the ascendancy of the Athenian economy.

The strength of the Athenian navy, so important in the shaping of Athenian democracy, also tempted Athens to create a commercial empire, which emerged from a war with Persia between 499 and 468 BCE. As we saw in Chapter Six, Persia became a new cavalry power in the Near East and eventually took command of all the land between the frontier of India and Egypt. During their expansion, the Persians under Cyrus the Great had swept through much of what we call the Middle East today, conquering everything in their path from 539 to 530 BCE. Among the regions captured were Lydia and the Ionian coast of present-day Turkey.

By the time of Darius I (549–485 BCE), the third King of Persia, the people in Ionia revolted in an attempt to recover independence but in the process drew the Greek mainland into the struggle with Persia. At the forefront of the Greek defense, Athens distinguished itself as a great military power. It did so by defeating the Persians at Marathon, 22.6 miles north of Athens, in 490 BCE and orchestrating the Greek victory at Salamis, an island immediately to the south of Athens, in 480 BCE. Athenian leadership inspired the Ionians to again seek their independence and form a defensive alliance against Persia.

This alliance soon turned into a new source of wealth for Athens, seducing it into imperial adventurism. Success against Persia eliminated a common enemy to the Greek city-state system. But with Persia's sound defeat at Eurymedon in 468 BCE under Athenian leadership, the need for an alliance against a foreign foe also ended. Indeed, by this point Athens had gained so much income from its many client states through trade and tribute that the Athenians sought to force their former allies to submit to imperial economic control.

From 479 to 431 BCE, Athens honed a system of military and commercial power that forced reluctant allies to integrate into a market network that crossed not only the Aegean, but also penetrated deep into the Black Sea. Soon the urban population of Athens grew to 300,000—far more people than could be fed by the agricultural fields of Attica, Athens's rural territory, which comprised only 1,000 square miles of arable land. Athens therefore had to import food from allies and colonies alike. Given the unusually high concentrations of people living within the city itself, Athens enjoyed a vast quantity and quality of urban skills, which generated some of the richest intellectual and artistic artifacts of world history. These urban skills included literacy, computation, and critical thinking, the key intellectual agency that gave rise to classical Greek drama, history, and philosophy.

This emerging Athenian empire, however, ultimately challenged the Greek city-state system itself. Ironically, Athens began to replace Persia as the common enemy of its former allies. Now, Athens' neighbors and client cities banded together to seek independence from Athens based on the civic virtue that defined citizenship for all Greeks. Consequently, some of these disgruntled city-states formed a league with Sparta, starting a cycle of wars that ultimately destroyed classical Greece (431–338 BCE).

Known as the Peloponnesian Wars, this era of chaos first led to the defeat of Athens between 431 and 403 BCE. Then the victor, Sparta, tried to dominate pan-Greek affairs, ending up as the common enemy of the city-state system. This inspired Thebes to lead a league of Greek cities against the Spartans, win a war of independence, and repeat the same mistake of attempting to form an empire. Thebes too failed. Finally, in 338 BCE, the struggle for hegemony (imperial rule) in Greece ended when Philip of Macedon, using a redefined phalanx, defeated the combined armies of Athens and Thebes at Chaeronea. After 338 BCE, Macedonia ruled Greece, bringing meaningful citizenship to an end.

Nevertheless, Athens left an intellectual legacy that could only have been produced by a network city. Nowhere else in the ancient world, to date, had a culture generated such a high concentration of people living in cities. All other cultures had either a 9 to 1 rural-urban ratio or, at best, the 8 to 2 pattern witnessed in Egypt. Athens, however, had placed the majority of its people within the city itself. Its use of a vast seaborne trade and defensive alliances sustained a literate male population with the capacity to add and subtract, and the ability to ask abstract questions and draw meaningful conclusions to them. Hence, Athens had created a mass audience capable of sustaining a very productive urban intellect. This is one of the primary reasons Athens became the cultural center of Greece.

Philip of Macedon, Alexander the Great, and the Hellenistic World

Before a discussion of Athenian culture and Greek philosophy, drama, and history can take place, we must complete the cycle of the political events of ancient Greek civilization. The Peloponnesian Wars had weakened most of the Greek city-states and brought widespread chaos and destruction to the mainland. As mentioned above, another group of Greek-speaking people who lived to the north, in a region known as Macedonia, had redefined and improved phalanx warfare. Macedonian polity differed in many respects from that of the Greek city-states. The Macedonians used kingship to define politics, a principal perceived by the Athenians as barbaric. Most Macedonians were not urban dwellers. Still, they produced great military leaders.

One of these leaders became the king of Macedon in the fourth century BCE: Philip II (359–336 BCE). Philip's ability to reform the Macedonian military and redefine the phalanx was a product of his stay as a hostage in Thebes, where he witnessed a reinforced left flank in the Theban phalanx that had sixteen ranks of soldiers instead of the usual eight. Philip saw this redesigned phalanx defeat the Spartans in battle, which convinced him that he could use this same formation against all of Greece itself.

Once home, Philip drew all his nobles to court, exposed them to the luxuries of urban life, and convinced them that the wealth of Greece could be theirs if only they would unite with him in his purpose of conquest. He then reformed the Macedonian military creating a sixteen-rank phalanx each soldier armed with a *sarissa*, twenty-four-foot long spear. Using the vast resources of an entire kingdom, which far outshadowed those of a city-state, Philip mobilized a force far greater than any one city on the Greek mainland could match. And given the loyalty Philip had nurtured at his court among his young nobles, he had the time and the means to create a professional fighting force responsive to a central command.

Alexander the Great, detail of Battle of Issus, 310–300 BCE. The Battle of Issus is depicted in this Roman mosaic discovered in October 1831 in a house in Pompeii. Consisting of an estimated 3 million pieces, the work was based on a painting by Philoxenus of Eretria. Casa del Fauno, Pompeii, now Naples, Museo Archeologico Nazionale.

With the Greek city-states competing to fill the power vacuum created by the defeat of Athens in 403 BCE, none of them paid attention to the doings of their large neighbor to the north. Weakened by internal divisions and jealousies, the Greek states did not tear themselves away from conducting the Peloponnesian Wars until it was too late. By 338 BCE, Philip's defeat of both Thebes and Athens at Chaeronea left Greece open to his will. Two years later, his assassination brought his plans for the future—which included taking revenge against Persia for the Persian Wars (499–468 BCE)—to a halt. Now, however, Philip's enterprise landed in the hands of his son, Alexander.

Alexander of Macedon was only twenty years old when he became king and took control of one of the most successful and amazing military campaigns in history to date. In three successive battles, at Granicus, Issus, and Gaugamela, Alexander defeated the forces of Darius III, the Persian King, and by 330 BCE Alexander could call himself master of Asia. He took his armies to northern India and intended to press even farther east, but his tired soldiers wanted to go home. One of his problems was encouraging his army to venture into regions that they had not heard of, risk their lives, and continue to fight with no end to war in sight. They wanted to see their wives and children and their homeland of Greece, but Alexander kept pressing on—ever farther from home. Another problem was that once Alexander had defeated the Persian Empire, he wanted to receive the loyalty of his new subject people. He took several steps that were to have a lasting effect on the history of Asia.

During his conquest, Alexander made sure that he would always have the support of the oracles and deities to boost his aims. For example, he had himself represented as the son of the great god of Egypt, *Amun*

(the equivalent of Zeus). Consequently he was known as the "Son of God," and thus created one of the earliest references to the idea of a savior in the Western world. When he conquered Persia, Alexander married the two daughters of the last Persian king, Darius III, so that he would be seen as the successor to that king and his sons would become the legitimate Persian rulers. He also adopted Persian dress, married several other Persian women (one named Roxana bore him a son), and took part in their ceremonies. Probably, Alexander was trying to show his subject people that he was not there as a Greek conqueror but as a king of all people and the legitimate heir to Darius III.

Alexander's conquest and actions among his subject peoples effected a mix of Greek, Egyptian, Mesopotamian, Persian, and Indian religions and ideas, an amalgamation we now call *Hellenism*. The conquest also brought Greeks as far east as India and west to Egypt. Alexander encouraged Greek soldiers to marry Persian women, thus beginning an intermixing of different ethnic groups. This social, economic, and political integration introduced different peoples to new ideas and religions in an effort to create a universal culture. Greek became the dominant language and Egyptian and Persian religions became known to the Mediterranean region. Now deities from different regions were identified with one another until they began to merge as one (e.g., Amun in Egypt mixed with Zeus in Greece).

By 323 BCE, Alexander had died in Mesopotamia. His major generals who had campaigned with him now divided the conquered empire among themselves, Antigon (Antigonid Dynasty) received Greece; Ptolemy (Ptolemaic Dynasty) took over Egypt and Palestine; and Seleucus (Seleucid Dynasty) took over Asia. India was taken over by an Indian king, Chandragupta Maurya mentioned in Chapter Four, who brought unification to that region for the first time: the Mauryan Empire.

Greek Philosophy

Interestingly, the failure of Greek politics set the stage for the rise of Greek philosophy. But even before the Greeks responded to the Peloponnesian Wars and the collapse of the city-state system, Greek speculation about the universe had laid a scientific foundation for a blending of politics, ethics, and knowledge in a man named Socrates. Consequently, this pre-Socratic study of the universe must be analyzed before anyone can understand Socrates' response to the Peloponnesian Wars. Tellingly, this pre-Socratic worldview emerged from a weakness in the Greek religion.

The Greeks created a philosophical worldview in which the *divine* was an essence embodied not by any gods or goddesses, but by words, concepts, and forms. Called *logos*, these transcendental words, forms, and ideas were the compelling forces in cause and effect. Logos governed all natural phenomena in a rational way that could be analyzed through direct contact with nature by using the human intellect and articulating the product of critical thinking, *logic*, through speech. Accordingly, logos captured reason in the discipline of logic, as systematically developed by the Greeks. Logos also represented the transcendental (that which transcends human experience) as rational ideas captured by words and understood through objectively organized speech. In short, logos was the soul of the universe independent of any personification of a divine agency.

The Greek vision of logos combined all the basic trends of Greek philosophy that had developed from the first scientific thinker, Thales (636–546 BCE), to Aristotle (384–332 BCE), the founder of the western curriculum. Through their system of thought, the Greeks produced an integrated vision of the universe as a real, true, good, and beautiful entity. Each branch of philosophy explored an essential element of logos so that all the branches intertwined to become an extension of the others. Hence, the disciples of ontology and metaphysics considered the nature of reality and developed a correspondence with epistemology (the study of knowledge). At the same time, ethical and aesthetic thought sought to uncover the goodness and beauty buried in nature and integrate them with the real and the true in human life. Accordingly, if something was real, it also had to be true, good, and beautiful.

Greek thought began to evolve more thoroughly once philosophers from the city-state of Miletus stepped outside their religious tradition to discover an alternative way of explaining material phenomena in the universe. These philosophers felt that their gods and goddesses were inadequate to account for all the cosmic events that they had personally witnessed. In addition, the long history of Greek mythology spoke of three generations of divine beings, two of which overthrew their predecessors to establish the third under the command of Zeus, his siblings, and their offspring. Furthermore, Greek religion had postulated a physical reality that had existed even before the gods of Mount Olympus

had given order to the universe; perhaps conjecturing about this previous physical state would reveal more about reality than trying to comprehend the limited powers of the gods. Accordingly, this new wave of Greek philosophers set out to study nature and the human intellect independent of a reliance on the gods for the answers they sought.

The Pre-Socratics

The thinkers of Miletus, a city-state in Ionia on the Aegean coast of modern Turkey, originally launched their philosophical inquiry into the nature of reality when Thales proposed the idea that all physical events operated independently of the gods. Thales launched philosophy by asking: what is the world really made of? His assumption was that a fundamental substance underlay everything we see. Such a view required not only a grasp of the essence of matter itself, but also an understanding of the potential for change. Thales proposed the idea that all things where in reality made up of water, i.e., a substance that transformed itself into every other form of matter seen today. Hence, water changed itself into mist, and then air (i.e., the modern concept of gas), and condensed itself into ice and then earth (i.e., the modern concept of solids). In essence, water *was* alive.

Following Thales' lead, two other philosophers from Miletus—Anaximander and Anaximenes—agreed with Thales' thesis that the universe began with an original substance but disagreed as to what that substance was. Anaximander rejected water and argued that *apeiron*, the boundless, served as the material basis for all things and added sets of conflicting physical states to explain change: hot versus cold, dry versus wet, etc. Anaximenes thought air was the original substance, claiming that spirited matter contained within itself soul, will, and intelligence. But all three, Thales, Anaximander, and Anaximenes agreed on one thing: the original substance carried within itself a form of "living matter" that served as the agency to create all that we see around us.

Dissatisfied with an explanation that relied simply on living matter, Greek philosophers shifted gears abruptly at the beginning of the fifth century BCE by separating process from substance. Led by Heraclitus of Ephesus (ca. 535–475 BCE), a city-state north of Miletus and also on the Ionian coast, a new generation of philosophers developed a line of inquiry that they felt the Miletus school had failed to consider. This new group of thinkers wanted to know what natural laws governed the physical shape of things as substances changed throughout the universe.

Heraclitus believed that reality had no beginning or end. He argued that all things had always existed in a dynamic state of change. Thus, *flux* itself became the foundation of reality. Heraclitus communicated this idea of flux by asking metaphorical questions like: *can you step into the same river twice?* Since the river water continuously flowed, the answer was no.

Empedocles of Akraga (ca. 493–433 BCE) agreed with Heraclitus but argued that the animated hidden forces of attraction and repulsion explained flux. But Empedocles also included a concept of evolution that gave order and direction to flux. He argued that in the beginning crude forms of matter began to change and went through stages of development driven by attraction and repulsion to create superior objects.

Later Anaxagoras (500–428 BCE) of Clazomenae refined Empedocles' approach by postulating an all-pervasive mind called *nous* which had formed the universe. Nous assembled an infinite number of tiny particles that combined and recombined to compose physical objects. These tiny particles were the seeds of reality and explained such complex processes as digestion: the seeds of food disassembled in our intestines and reassembled in us through the power of nous.

Finally, Leucippus and Democritus of Adbera (ca. 460–370 BCE) refined Anaxagoras's theory by naming the seeds of reality: these tiny particles were called *atoms*. Unhappy with Anaxagoras's theory of nous, Leucippus and Democritus favored a purely mechanical explanation of process. They both argued that the physical qualities of each atom itself determined the natural processes in which it could participate. Thus, atoms carried within their makeup the elemental features of change itself. And even though this process of change anticipated modern atomic theory, the modern atom proved to be very different from the Greek concept; *atom* in Greek means *cannot cut* and denies the existence of the subatomic world of modern physics.

While one school of pre-Socratic philosophers explored the material world in a quest for explanations of all processes in nature, another school sought to ascertain the reasons the cosmos gave "shape," "form," and "design" to natural events. Their approach combined the math and logic of Pythagoras (582–507 BCE), Parmenides (493–433 BCE), and Zeno (490–430 BCE) to create a universal intelligence to account for the cosmic order of all living and inanimate things.

Pythagoras, Parmenides, and Zeno developed a line of study that differed from that of the previous thinkers. They focused on the realm of math and logic as models of thought that governed matter and process. For Pythagoras, Parmenides, and Zeno, the abstract nature of mathematics and logic opened the possibility of a transcendental realm, the source of an invisible reality that took precedence over physical events. The

power of these three thinkers resided not so much in what they had to say, as in their style of expression. Each argued that under reality lay a superior natural entity that ordered reason itself and determined the shape of existence.

Pythagoras proposed a vision of life based on a re-incarnating soul that existed in a system one could explain through numbers and music. Both numbers and music relied on the language of mathematics and served as a means to understand the essence of things. The purity of the soul could be understood by the use of numbers and music because both supposedly induced a memory of the transcendental substance. The purity of numbers could be seen by how they directed the heavens and created "the harmony of the spheres." Thus, the entire cosmos could be understood mathematically.

Parmenides and Zeno added to the Pythagorean vision by emphasizing the power of logic as an ally of mathematics. Logic was far superior to the senses as a source of discovering the truth. If logic contradicted sense data, then sensation was wrong. As a result, formulations of data supplied by the senses (empirical observation) had to submit to logic as the ultimate test of truth.

Using this approach, Parmenides tried to show that flux was impossible by denying motion—even though our *senses* told us that motion was indeed possible. He began his line of reasoning by arguing that space could not logically exist. He stated *"what is, is"* as a self-evident truth. Since the logic of this first statement could not be denied, then *"what isn't, isn't"* had to follow. Next, since substance "is," then substance had to exist. Yet, since space (meaning void) is the absence of substance (i.e., the *isn't*), space could not exist. Therefore, he concluded that the universe was fully occupied with substance. But without space, Parmenides thought that the resistance to substance would deny the logical possibility of motion. "Substance" was called "Being" by Parmenides, and he distinguished it from mere matter as the true stuff that held the universe together in an unchanging state. Matter, itself, offered a practical, physical reality, in which our bodies had to live, but matter was governed by Being and subordinate to the laws of logic.

Zeno agreed with Parmenides. He introduced a set of paradoxes that supported Parmenides' conclusions by also showing that motion was unnatural and could not exist. Zeno stated that the movement of anything could not be measured without time. He then demonstrated that to describe the motion of an object at any one moment in time was logically impossible. He began by saying that since all moments could be divided into an infinite number of temporal points, a moment had no dimensions. Like a spatial point in Euclidean geometry, a moment was a nondimensional concept. Hence, in the paradox of Achilles and the tortoise, Zeno demonstrated how time disappeared through an infinite division of moments in space. He argued that in a foot race between the two, if we give a tortoise a head start, Achilles could never catch or pass this animal. To cover the ground between the tortoise and the starting line, Achilles would have to divide the distance in half, and then half again, and then half again an infinite number of times. Thus, this process of division would never end. It would fall to later physicists to solve this problem.

The Socratics

The speculative philosophy of the pre-Socratics philosophers came to an abrupt halt during the fifth century BCE, when the Greek city-state system entered into the Peloponnesian Wars (432–338 BCE) that virtually destroyed citizenship. This cycle of suicidal wars created a hunger for order that inspired Socrates (469–399 BCE).

Socrates lived through the splendor and tragedy of his city's rise and fall. A citizen of Athens, he asked: where had his exquisite city-state gone wrong? His inquiry shifted philosophy from the realm of physics to that of ethics.

Socrates began by considering the work of Pythagoras, Parmenides, and Zeno. Following a line of dialectic (by *dialogue*) reasoning of his own creation, Socrates asked question after question until he came to a point where any theory contradicted itself. Dialectic reason itself used a dialogue, or a rigorous logical conversation governed by the rule of logic called "the law of contradiction." The dialogue determined the boundaries of what was true, actual, or real by stating that the truth must always be consistent with itself. This style of thought, and the law of contradiction, therefore, created a new standard for truth called *objectivity*, i.e., the truth is consistent with itself, corresponds to reality, and is universal, transcendental, and independent of human will and intellect.

Ascertaining that no one whom he had questioned really knew anything, Socrates concluded that "objective truth" must exist in a realm outside human experience. Hence, true knowledge must dwell in a place stripped of all personal or cultural biases, function independently of human will and intellect, but still be accessible to humanity through our capacity to reason by using logic, math, and language. This realm was a transcendental place governed by eternal thoughts independent of time and space. For Socrates, only the world of ethics offered access to such objective thoughts, so he concluded "if a thing existed in the universe, it had to exist for some *good*."

Plato (429–347 BCE) further explored the realm of existence defined by Socrates. According to Plato, this realm generated all the metaphysical *forms* (i.e., the transcendental models for all things in the universe as embedded in the ideas that named them, for example, "desk," "spear," "human," and "Earth," to list a few). Each form governed the material entity that it named and served as the basis for logos (the word, speech, and logic that explained the universe). Accordingly, each object in nature had to have its transcendental counterpart in the metaphysical realm in order to exist. This transcendental counterpart, in turn, constituted the basis for the good, the beautiful, the true, and the real. Finally, these forms combined to serve as the universal soul of the cosmos that anchored reality in a transcendental reference point that defined the shape and purpose of all things. This dual existence later caused Greek philosophers to praise transcendental existence for its eternal perfection while condemning the material world as a source of corruption and decay.

In contrast to Plato, his most famous student, Aristotle (384–322 BCE), reunited form with matter to function as the metaphysical element in causation. His theory of causation combined the concepts from the two branches of pre-Socratic thinkers with the philosophy of Socrates and Plato to develop an understanding of physical events as an integration of matter, process, and transcendental forms. Each of these features of the Greek worldview then became part of the Aristotelian model of reality. The first feature of causation Aristotle assigned matter was *material cause*, an idea he derived from the philosophers of Miletus.

Simply stated, material cause described change as a consequence of the matter involved. Things made up of earth had to conform to the nature of Earth itself as an element. In a similar manner, things comprised of water always behaved according to the nature of water; air like air; fire like fire. No object could change without taking into account its material composition as each element within the object set the physical limits of its capacity to change.

To material cause, Aristotle added *efficient cause*, the second feature of causation, as a natural process derived from the philosophy of Heraclitus, Empedocles, Anaxagoras, Leucippus, and Democritus. Aristotle felt that these thinkers had revealed the way natural events actually unfolded in the universe. According to Aristotle, efficient cause explained "how" things took place

Bust of Aristotle (384–322 BCE), Plato's most famous student. Courtesy Touraj Daryaee.

in nature. Now he had to try to explain "why" events followed natural paths of development.

The second half of Aristotle's theory of causation developed out of the separate and opposing philosophical traditions of Pythagoras, Parmenides, and Zeno plus the new objectivity offered by Socrates and Plato; both rejected matter and process as inadequate explanations. This second half of causation sought the "why" needed to explain completely change in nature. Like material and efficient cause, this second half had two parts: *form* and *end.* The logic and math of Pythagoras, Parmenides, and Zeno defined *formal cause,* the third element of causation, to explain the rational sequence of events that always conformed to the laws of nature. And since "cause" always preceded "effect" in time and space, an observer simply had to study all the circumstances that preceded an unknown phenomenon in order to understand how it had been "effected."

For Aristotle, *end* represented the fourth element of causation, *final cause.* Final cause used Plato's forms to describe the transcendental destination that governed the entire process of change. Final cause gave *purpose* to the *process* of change by making the transcendental essence of the thing embedded in its material composition the goal of the process of change itself.

To recap, an acorn contained within itself the *form* of oak tree that gave the acorn its purpose, end, and direction. Material cause defined the way matter from the earth assembled with the acorn as it grew. Efficient cause determined the process of growth itself. Formal cause outlined the logical steps each acorn took as it developed into a mature form. And final cause used the transcendental design of the ideal oak tree to define the destination of each acorn as it struggled to achieve its potential.

In Aristotle's universe, matter arranged itself according to the density of the elements it comprised. Earth sought the center. Water struggled to embrace and circle the Earth. Air fought to surround water. Finally, fire leaped up into the fourth sphere above the air. Each strove to occupy a location that matched its density, with this density being the ratio of matter to metaphysical form. At the same time, the density of matter caused imperfection, error, and corruption, while the form offered perfection, truth, and clarity.

Thus, the closer to the center of the universe one was, the greater the concentration of matter and corruption. Also since form gave expression to physical being, the greater the density of matter, the more imperfect the object became. Accordingly, the farther from the center of the universe, and the closer to the outer edge, the greater the concentration of pure form and hence, absolute beauty, goodness, truth, and reality. Once someone left the Earth and entered Heaven, each sphere found there also measured a degree of density that declined as this person approached the perfection of the outer edge.

Plato's separation of form from matter served to distinguish the idea of eternal perfection from the corruption of material existence. In contrast, Aristotle's reintegration of form with matter through his theory of causation helped to remind the observer to look at objects as things in themselves and to see them as sources of data. Yet, the use by both Plato and Aristotle of form as the ultimate cause, or reason, behind the existence of things created a conceptual bridge between the two philosophers. This conceptual bridge allowed Plato's emphasis on the dual universe of form and matter to support the theological inquiries that emerged in Christianity, while Aristotle's theory of causation led to a complementary scientific investigation.

Drama

Parallel to the development of philosophy in Athens, three great Athenian playwrights perfected tragedy as an art form while also addressing the key philosophical and religious questions of the day. Together, these three tragedians spanned the years from 525 to 406 BCE and reflected the Athenian spirit during this city-state's rise and fall from power. The first was Aeschylus (525–456 BCE) who wrote a total of ninety plays, of which nine survive, with seven completely intact. He lived during the period of Athens' greatest successes: the victory at Marathon, in which he participated; the victory at Salamis, which he witnesssed; and the creation of the Athenian Empire. A patriotic author, his plays reflected the grandeur of Athens with a religious underpinning. His greatest trilogy included *Agamemnon*, the *Choephoroe*, and the *Eumenides*, for which he won first prize in 458 BCE during the City Dionysia, the religious festival celebrated each spring in Athens in honor of Dionysius, the god of wine. These three plays follow the evolution of divine justice from a raging, blood-stained force in nature to a rational judgment. The first play, *Agamemnon* witnesses the murder of Agamemnon himself, the king of Mycenae, by his wife Klytemnestra in revenge for Agamemnon's sacrificing of their daughter Iphigeneia to Poseidon, the god of the sea, to acquire fair winds on his way to the conquest of Troy. The *Choephoroe* follows when Orestes, Agamemnon's son, finds himself trapped in a moral double bind in which he must avenge his father's death but can only do so by murdering his mother. Finally, the *Eumenides* resolves the issue of justice by having Orestes' case tried before the Athenian high court, the Aeropagus, found innocent of his crimes by the goddess Athena and the citizens of Athens, and released from the blood curse that has haunted his father's house. Hence, blood feuds and vengeance give way to true, sacred justice as all three plays unfold.

The second important tragedian was Sophocles (496–406 BCE) who wrote 120 plays of which only seven survive. He won twenty-four first prizes during the City Dionysia, Also, when he lost, Sophocles always came in second. Sophocles' plays reflected the doubt introduced into Athenian politics as the disasters of the Peloponnesians Wars (431–403 BCE) unfolded. Although he did not live to see the final defeat of Athens, Sophocles warned his fellow citizens of its eventuality with his most famous trilogy: *Oedipus Rex, Oedipus at Colonus*, and *Antigone*. *Oedipus Rex* tells of a young man whose ignorance of his true identity leads him to fulfill a tragic destiny. Cursed to kill his father and marry his mother, Oedipus begins his life under the threat of death. His father, the king of Thebes condemns his son to die, but a sympathetic shepherd saves Oedipus and sends him to live in Corinth where the king and queen there adopt him as their own. Discovering that he was to kill his father and marry his mother, Oedipus flees Corinth when he comes of age, travels north, confronts the king of Thebes in a dispute, kills him, and marries the Theban Queen. Thus Oedipus unknowingly has already fulfilled his destiny. The play opens when the city of Thebes suffers a plague caused by someone who has murdered his father and married his mother. Determined to find the guilty party, Oedipus launches a relentless search that leads him only to himself. Confronted with the reality of his crimes, his mother-wife commits suicide, he laments the fact that his children are also his siblings, and he blinds himself after discovering the truth.

Oedipus at Colonus is a quiet play that tells of Oedipus's final days and sets the stage for *Antigone*, the play that reveals trilogy's moral message. Antigone is one of Oedipus's two daughters. She is confronted with a moral dilemma when her two brothers kill one another in a war fought to determine which of them should be the rightful king of Thebes. With their deaths, the crown passes to her uncle who decrees that only one, the reigning brother, should be buried, while the other, the challenger, should become carrion for the birds. Forced by her sense of moral duty to bury the second brother, Antigone defies her uncle, is caught, and tried. At her trial she appeals to a moral code that transcends all city-states, i.e., an eternal set of laws that binds all humans to the universal ethic that became the backbone of Socratic philosophy. Hence, Antigone warns her uncle that the city's laws cannot obligate any citizen's sense of moral conduct if those laws violate a hidden, universal, and transcendental natural law. The play closes as Antigone is judged guilty and condemned to death, her lover (the king's son) commits suicide, the queen commits suicide after the death of her son, and the king's household collapses. Sophocles' message was clear: Athens, a city spiraling into defeat in the closing days of the Peloponnesian Wars, had to look to its current conduct and laws to see if its behavior as a polis conformed to the true conditions of justice buried in the laws of nature.

The last of the three playwrights, Euripides (480–406 BCE), was Sophocles' chief rival, but only won first prize five times. His plays lacked the majesty of both Aeschylus and Sophocles because Euripides focused on human conduct as an expression of personal will without any appeal to the gods or natural law. Tragedy for him was a human creation produced by people's reckless, thoughtless, and irrational conduct. None of his plays achieved the same stature as *Agamemnon*, *Oedipus Rex*, or *Antigone*, the three that both contemporary and modern critics hail as the finest dramas of the ancient Western world. Yet the power of Euripides' message was unmistakable in such plays as *The Trojan Women* and *Medea*. The former tells of the agony suffered by the victims of war; those powerless to stop the initiation of the struggle have to witness its bloodshed and mourn its losses, and become the vanquished who are sold into slavery once the last blow has been struck. The latter tells of a woman beguiled by a heartless seducer who uses his wiles to win the heart of this young princess, a woman willing to sacrifice her family and country for her faithless lover, while he abandons her for another. Driven insane with jealousy and the hopelessness of her plight, Medea kills her rival as well as her own children by her faithless lover. In both *The Trojan Women* and *Medea*, humans alone make their own tragedies, just as the population of Athens was suffering from the poor judgment of its leaders in the closing days of the Peloponnesian Wars.

The Origins of History

While tragedy enjoyed the vision of three outstanding playwrights, history developed as a discipline in the hands of two master chroniclers. Also, like Aeschylus, Sophocles, and Euripides, the two historians reflected the spirit of their times. Born in the city-state of Halicarnassus south of Miletus on the Ionian Coast, Herodotus spent his life traveling throughout the ancient Western world where he gathered stories that he compiled in a work call *The Histories* between 447 and 443 BCE. He lived in Athens during these four years, brought his work to a close with the Persian Wars (499–479 BCE), and told of the critical role Athens played in the salvation of Greece. The thesis that governed his work was the belief that a hidden, divine agency oversaw the outcome of all human events and judged each of us on the basis of the moral conduct that defined our decisions, great and small. States and people suffer the hubris (exaggerated pride) of kings and pay a heavy price for ill-conceived political and military projects. In the case of the Persian Wars, Persia suffered defeat due to the hubris of Darius and Xerxes, the Persian kings, while Greece, and especially Athens, prevailed due to its rational and moral demeanor.

In contrast to Herodotus, Thucydides (460–400 BCE) wrote of the *Peloponnesian Wars* (431–403 BCE), spoke with a purely secular voice, and assigned success and failure to the quality of the decisions people made. No divine agency operated behind the scenes in his history. Instead, Thucydides dedicated enormous energy to maintaining an objective perspective, getting his data right, and reporting events exactly as they happened. A failed Athenian general living in exile during the Peloponnesian Wars, Thucydides saw the struggle from both the Spartan and the Athenian perspectives. Although his history ended in 411 BCE, eight years before Athens' final defeat, Thucydides explained precisely why the war had unfolded the way it did, which provided his contemporaries with a clear understanding of how Greek culture had disintegrated during the twenty years of war he recorded. Buried in his history was a clear message: look to yourselves for the troubles that confront your lives.

Taken together, Greek philosophy, Athenian tragedy, and the development of the Greek historical voice reveal the level of high culture achieved by the city-state system in the fifth and fourth centuries BCE. The quality and diversity of these works, and the vast audiences that consumed them—some say as many as 30,000 witnessed a Greek tragedy during the City Dionysia—speaks to the unusual urban concentrations achieved by Greek network cities. As stated above, the most productive of them all, Athens, had 300,000 people living within one city on 1,000 square miles of arable land. Such a heavy concentration of city-dwellers on such a confined site, fed by the food production of foreign lands, fostered an unusually creative urban environment. Perhaps this is why so many fine works of science, philosophy, history, and drama appeared in such a short time in one location in Western history. Only the productivity of modern times would equal and surpass this extraordinary era.

Suggested Reading

Amos, H. D., and A. G. P. Lang, *These Were The Greeks* (Chester Springs, Penn.: Dufour Editions, 1982).

Austin, M. and P. Vidal-Naquet, *The Economic and Social History of Ancient Greece* (Berkeley: University of California Press, 1977).

Boardman, J., *The Greeks Overseas*, Revised Edition (London: Thames & Hudson, 1999).

Burkert, Walter, *Greek Religion* (Cambridge: Harvard University Press, 1987).

Clagett, Marshall, *Greek Science in Antiquity* (New York: Colliers, 1963).

Davies, J. K., *Democracy and Classical Greece*, Second Edition (Cambridge: Harvard University Press, 1993).

Farrington, Benjamin, *Greek Science* (Baltimore: Penguin Books, 1966).

Forrest, William George, *A History of Sparta, 950–121 B.C.*, Second Edition (New York: Norton, 1980).

Frost, Frank J., *Greek Society*, Fourth Edition (Lexington, Mass.: D.C. Heath and Company, 1992).

Guthrie, W. K. C., *A History of Greek Philosophy*, Volumes 1–6 (Cambridge: Cambridge University Press, 1962–1981).

McGregor, Malcolm F., *The Athenians and Their Empire* (Vancouver: Vancouver University Press, 1987).

Meiggs, Russell, *The Athenian Empire* (Oxford: Clarendon Press, 1972).

Osborne, R., *Demos: The Discovery of Classical Attica* (New York: Oxford University Press, 1977).

Starr, Chester G., *The Economic and Social Growth of Early Greece, 850–500 B.C.* (New York: Oxford University Press, 1978).

Taylor, A. E., *Socrates* (Boston: Beacon Press, 1953).

Taylor, Christopher, *Socrates* (New York: Oxford University Press, 1999).

VIII

ROME:
From Citizenship to Imperial Rule

The lessons of citizenship developed by the Greeks reached full maturity in Roman history. Yet ancient Rome experienced two distinct political episodes: the first revolved around the power of citizenship as developed in Greece and rejuvenated in Italy (ca. 509–31 BCE); the second around Imperial rule (31 BCE–476 CE). Both, however, revealed the political consequences of the use of iron technology as Rome shifted from a city-state to a great empire like those established by Assyria, Persia, and Macedonia. The two episodes of the Roman story, thus, represent both the complexity and the culmination of Western political culture during the ancient era as well as the power of iron and the dynamic energy of citizenship in Western history.

Part One: The Republic

Roman citizenship imitated the Greek model by combining the Greek concept of civic virtue with the Greek phalanx and iron technology. Yet in the first 244 years of the Roman Republic (509 to 265 BCE), Rome dramatically changed the Greek ideal of citizen conduct. This occurred when Romans did something that was unthinkable to the leaders of Greek city-states: they created a stable federation by establishing more than one level of citizen status within the empire. Rome produced the first version of this political innovation at the end of the Latin War (340–338 BCE).

Having won a hard-earned victory against its own allies who fought to achieve equality with Rome as members of the Latin League, Rome offered the vanquished Latin cities a generous peace treaty. Rome created a three-tiered system of political identity: fully incorporated cities, partially incorporated towns, and dependent allies. Fully incorporated cities were adopted into the Roman state; their inhabitants became equals of Roman citizens, including having the right to marry Romans, vote, and hold public office in Rome. The partially incorporated towns received limited citizenship; their inhabitants could intermarry with Roman citizens, but could not vote, nor hold office in Rome.

The dependent allies were subordinate states; they were not incorporated into the Roman Republic but allowed to retain their local governments and compelled by treaty to cede their public lands. Finally, Rome expected all three tiers of this new political federation to lend troops and material support during times of war and submit to Roman foreign policy.

The second critical moment followed the same circumstances as the first: it involved a war in which the Roman allies again demanded equality with Rome. Called the Social War, 91–88 BCE (from the Roman term for allies, *socii*), this struggle erupted when Rome's Italian allies, who had taken common risks to expand the Roman Empire, rebelled because they had not shared equally in the rewards. Prior to this war, Rome had developed a complex system of political designations: *cives Romani*, Roman citizens; *coloniae Romani*, Roman colonists with civil status; *municipia*, Latin cities with limited citizen status; and *latini*, dependent Latin allies of Rome. Since 338 BCE, Rome had added socii, or Italian allies, to the Roman federation; and *provinciales*, or free subjects of Rome (*peregrini*, or foreigners) living outside Italy.

Rome's socii, meanwhile, demanded equality with Rome just as its Latin allies had done in 340 BCE. Frustrated by Rome, the socii then declared their independence in 91 BCE, and rebelled to form a new state called *Italia*. Rome saved the empire by undercutting the enemy forces. Rome offered full cives status to any allied Latin or Italian state that remained loyal to Rome after hostilities had begun; Rome also offered cives status to any allied state that laid down its arms before a specified date. Then Rome defeated any state that refused these offers. When the Social War ended, 500,000 new cives had been added to the Roman rolls.

Rome's willingness to add new Latin and Italian cities to the citizen roles, or enlist allied states with the possibility of its citizens gaining Roman citizenship later, generated such a large military base that it produced an empire far more imposing than any Greek city-state ever was able to govern. Each Greek city that

Forum Romanum; daily life in the Roman Forum. Shown from left: Temple of the Dioscuri, Basilica Julia, Temple of Concordia, Triumphal Arch of Septimius Severus and Carcer Mamertinus; in the background is the Capitol. Woodcut, c. 1880, akg images, London.

had tried to expand its holdings ended up capturing more than its citizens could control. Accordingly, they all fell victim to counter-imperial military alliances designed to preserve the city-state system during the Peloponnesian Wars (431–338 BCE).

Rome, in contrast, had created a sufficiently flexible definition of citizenship to allow its military to expand at the same pace as its empire, so that Rome remained the political center of a growing social and economic system. Hence, unlike the great Greek network cities such as Athens, which had relied so heavily on long-distance trade to feed its urban population, Rome became the first centerplace city of the Mediterranean world.

Reinforcing Rome's role as the centerplace city of Western civilization, was a second major military innovation, the transformation of the Greek phalanx into the Roman *legion*. The massive design of the phalanx, with its continuous parallel ranks of men, lined up Hoplite citizen-soldiers that reached as far as their numbers would allow. Such a formation forced Greek armies to stage battles on whatever flatlands they could find. The Romans followed in this tradition until they confronted an enemy that took refuge in the Apennine Mountains, at which point they realized the need for more flexibility.

In the Samnite Wars (328–290 BCE), Romans had to modify the phalanx to create a sufficiently malleable military formation capable of fighting in rough terrain.

The legion broke the continuous ranks of the phalanx into separate units called *maniples* (handfuls). Each maniple functioned as a sub-unit of men whose commander coordinated with the general of the entire legion. With its maniples arranged in an infantry formation that resembled the dark squares in the first two rows of a checkerboard, a legion could confront an opposing force as a staggered line of resistance, making the line very difficult for the enemy to break completely through.

With each of its 120 heavily armored infantrymen toting two *pilia*, heavy spears made of iron and oak, a maniple formed a tightly packed and formidable unit. Rather than relying on the impact of a massive formation of all available men, as in the case of a phalanx, each soldier in a legion threw his two spears prior to waging combat at close quarters with a short iron sword. The two pilia when thrown weighed down the enemy's shields so that the Roman sword could penetrate the defenses. Furthermore, the shock of the staggered assault line proved far more effective than the even contact of the lengthy ranks marshalled by the phalanx. Finally, a top Roman commander usually had several legions at his disposal, which allowed him the ability to attack on more than one front at a time. As a result of this innovation, Rome won nearly all its land engagements.

Rome's military success eventually created an empire too large for a simple republic and the noble concept of civic virtue to rule effectively. Slow growth in Rome's first 244 years prepared it for its first great alien challenge when it confronted Carthage in three Punic Wars (264–241 BCE, 218–202 BCE, and 149–146 BCE). The Romans' ultimate success against Carthage allowed Roman civilization to expand beyond a cultural zone that understood Roman citizenship, civic virtue, the legion, and Rome's process of assimilating new allies. The massive numbers of subject peoples Rome added to its empire in merely 62 years (264–202 BCE) overwhelmed its own citizen population.

After 201 BCE, Rome's vast new acquisitions proved too much for it to handle. Victory over Rome's most-talented enemy in the second Punic War, the great general Hannibal, had added half the Mediterranean world to its empire. At the same time, the difficulty Rome faced in defeating Hannibal had included fourteen years of a virtual siege-like state during which the Carthaginians had occupied Italy. This long siege had separated Roman farmers from their land and eroded the backbone of the Roman army: the farmer-soldier.

The threat to Rome that Hannibal represented began when he crossed the Alps to invade Italy in 218 BCE. He followed this spectacular feat with a series of victories at Trebia, Lake Tassimire, and Cannae between 217 and 216 BCE. These victories drove Rome from the field with devastating losses. Having lost a generation of soldiers, the Romans could no longer face Hannibal, even as Hannibal discovered that he did not have enough men left to capture Rome itself and end the war. Thus, the Romans began an era of recovery under Fabius Maximus, the Great Delayer.

During the fourteen years that Hannibal wandered about in Italy without leaving but incapable of attaining a clean victory, Roman farmers had to live in Rome proper. There the cives grew accustomed to accepting military assignments and the generous support of Rome's leading families. When the war finally ended with Hannibal's defeat at Zama in 202 BCE, a generation of Roman farmers found it difficult to return to the land. Having developed dependent relationships on great Roman families, these farmers had become addicted to war. Therefore, between 201 and 133 BCE, they found themselves on campaign in Spain, North Africa, Macedonia, Greece, and Anatolia.

Abandoned farms in Italy came up for sale. Those who purchased these old farms used the estates to form latifundia (plantations), the most successful farming units in Italy after 201 BCE. Latifundia were large estates assembled by the great families of Rome, developed into commercial plantations, and worked by slaves captured in war. The Patricians, Rome's ancient aristocratic families, became the owners of these enormous farms and soon drove the remaining small farmers who had returned to the land out of business. According to Roman law, however, most of these new plantations exceeded the maximum legal size a Roman citizen could own.

The latifundia naturally concentrated power in the hands of the Patricians. The Patricians constituted Rome's original citizen families, the populous Romanus of the sixth century BCE, and they had watched their political authority erode under pressure from the Plebeians, the farmers from the rural population that fed Rome. Conversely, between the sixth and third centuries BCE, the Plebeians had struggled to achieve political equality with the Patricians and had succeeded in acquiring access to nearly all the major offices of the Roman magistracy due to their value as farmer-soldiers. But the Plebeians now faced a political crisis as Patrician-owned latifundia undercut the farmer-soldiers' role

in the Roman economy and politics. Thus, between 201 and 133 BCE, the Patricians had regained control of the magistracy, the Roman Senate, and foreign affairs. Also the Patricians had discovered that control over foreign policy allowed them to accumulate fresh spoils from war to fuel the continued erosion of Plebeian power. The Patricians imposed a war policy that took the Roman farmer-soldier (the Plebeian) away from his land for long periods, which increased the risk of the farmer's family sliding into bankruptcy, and reduced the willingness of the citizen body to serve in the military.

Among the Plebeians, rich families who had gone into business could compete with Patricians by using the office of Tribune. The ten Tribunes were state censors (guardians of morals) whose role allowed them to protect the interests of the poor against the Patricians. A man who sat as a Tribune was immune to prosecution, could veto a Senatorial law, and could declare a secessio—where the Plebeians withdrew from Rome when the Patricians grew too demanding. The office of Tribune served to secure the rights of the Plebeians within the constitution by forcing the Patricians to act with moderation. Yet in time, the spoils of war also undermined the ethics of Tribunes.

According to Roman tradition, Patricians should not engage in business; their income should derive solely from agriculture. This left the field of business open to rich Plebeians. At the same time, one of the most successful business ventures during these years of warfare was the issuance of war contracts. These contracts secured the supplies needed for Roman armies and collected a good share of the spoils won. Since this buying and selling meant profits at both ends, and since these contracts usually belonged to the rich Plebeians, the wealthiest Plebeian families tended to support those Senatorial policies that launched wars. Also, the richest Plebeians came from the same families who provided individuals who could afford to serve a year without pay as a Tribune. Hence, those Tribunes who should have censured corrupt Patricians increasingly had an incentive to join them in starting wars that might turn a profit.

What followed is one of the most studied eras of Western history: the Roman Civil War (133–31 BCE), in which generation after generation of Roman leaders came forward to claim control of Rome's politics only to set Patricians and their clients against rich Plebeians and their popular politics. Each generation saw a failed effort to resolve the conflict until Rome's republican form of government finally gave way to imperial rule.

The first generation that attempted to seize power, launching the political strife that led to civil war, were

Roman coins. Top, Head of Julius Caesar, ca. 46 BCE. At left, he is wearing a grain-ear wreath. On the reverse (right) are ceremonial emblems–the ladle, aspergillum (for sprinkling holy water), and jug. Bottom: Octavian, ca. 30–29 BCE. At left he is shown as the god Apollo. At right he is shown as the city founder, holding a whip and plowing with oxen. Images used by permission of Classical Numismatic Group, Inc.

the Gracchi brothers, Tiberius (d. 133 BCE) and Gaius (d. 121 BCE), who together formed the *populares* (Popular Party). Both held the office of Tribune and sought land redistribution in the hope of recovering Roman farmers as the military base of the legion. Their efforts led to the assassination of Tiberius and forced suicide of Gaius at the hands of Senators who would have lost their latifundia to these land programs. Their deaths divided Rome and defined the two poles in the contest: the populares versus the *optimates* (Senatorial Party).

The next generation pitted Gaius Marius (155–86 BCE) against Lucius Cornelius Sulla (138–78 BC). This generation saw Marius redefine the army so that twenty years of service led to retirement and a new farm. The result of this program transformed the Roman army into a political group loyal to a talented general. And such talented generals now took control of Rome's legions, paying their soldiers with the spoils of war. These generals became the leading political figures in Rome. Marius used this technique first to direct the populares, while Sulla developed the same strategy to organize the optimates. Since Sulla outlived Marius, the optimates took control of Rome at the end of this generation.

The third generation saw Gaius Julius Caesar (102–44 BCE), nephew to Marius, lead the populares and join Marcus Lucinius Crassus (d. 53 BCE), a rich land speculator among the Patricians who had as much ambition as money. Together they formed a power block that matched the military fame of Gnaeus Pompeius Magnus (or Pompey, 106–46 BCE), the conqueror of Armenia, Syria, and Palestine. Friendly rivals as long as all three were alive, Caesar, Crassus, and Pompey joined forces to offset the power of the Senate and the optimates. Their association was an uneasy one, but it lasted until Caesar developed a military reputation equal to that of the great Pompey with the conquest of Gaul, right about

the time that Crassus died in battle trying to capture Parthian Persia.

In the war that followed, this third generation finally resolved some the outstanding issues of Rome. Caesar defeated Pompey at Pharsala and followed him to Egypt. There the Macedonian Pharaoh, Ptolemy, murdered Pompey, which motivated Caesar to join with Cleopatra to secure control of Egyptian politics. Pompey's defeat at Pharsala also saw the death of most of the Senatorial families. Thus, when Caesar returned to Rome after a brief campaign in North Africa to eliminate the remnant of the Senatorial Party, the way was clear for him to form a dictatorship. His assassination in 44 BCE, however, prevented this outcome.

Before the civil war ended, however, one more generation of leaders took power. Now the conflict was a contest between Caesar's heirs: Gaius Octavius (63 BCE–14 CE) and Marc Antony (83–30 BCE). Gone were the optimates as rivals, meaning that the victor of this contest had a clear path to redefining the politics of Rome. Octavius defeated Antony and his ally Cleopatra at the battle of Actium in western Greece, drove Antony and Cleopatra to suicide, captured the riches of Egypt, and linked grain production in the Nile Valley with a new Roman government. Octavius' victory redefined politics in Rome by concentrating power in the hands of one man. Octavius solidified his position by carefully manipulating his public image to allow him to avoid assassination, as had befallen Julius Caesar. Thus, at the end of his career, it was Octavius who converted Rome to imperial rule.

With the fall of the Roman Republic, and the beginning of the Roman Principate, the next five hundred years of Roman history followed a line of political development that linked the resources generated by an iron technology to the ancient concept of kingship. This form of government had reached its apex in the Ancient Near East. Building on examples of monarchy that dated back to the first imperial ruler, Sargon the Great (2344–2279 BCE) during the Bronze Age, Rome instituted an iron-age empire like the Assyrians, Persians, and Macedonians. The Roman example, however, marked the end of political evolution in the West based on a process begun with the widespread diffusion of iron tools and the evolution of the Greek concept of citizenship. Thus, even though it borrowed heavily from the past, the Roman model became the largest hegemony in the West and developed the most elaborate empire based on a single centerplace city.

Ruled by a god-king that had served the ancient Near Eastern emperors so well, now Rome adopted a pattern of government that violated its original design based on citizenship. Professional armies replaced citizen-soldiers, as the military ceased to be a means of integrating the political loyalty of farmers with their city. An older pattern of submission and obedience returned as Roman farmers lost their sense of civic pride and political duty to serve their city. Once again, farmers came to distrust urban dwellers, seeing towns as composed merely of revenue-hungry parasites. Such an erosion of citizenship cut the bonds that held Western culture together.

Lost was the power that had launched the Roman Empire: that key integration achieved with the discovery of iron smelting that had set in motion the relationships between the farmer, citizenship, civic virtue, the phalanx, and the legion. The loss of civic virtue and citizenship, in turn, created a new hunger for social identity that only religion could fill. This hunger laid the foundation for Rome's experimentation with foreign faiths, as into the empire trickled Manichaeism, Egyptian cults, and Christianity. Among these rival faiths, Rome ultimately settled on Christianity.

Part Two: The Empire

The victory of Octavius (now Octavian Caesar) over Marc Antony at Actium in 31 BCE ended the Roman civil war (133–31 BCE) and left Rome with only one ruler. Fearful of Julius Caesar's fate, death by assassination, Octavian began a process of political innovation that preserved the institutions of the Republic while carefully constructing imperial rule. Rejecting any indication of being a king, yet ruling with the authority of an emperor, Octavian collected a series of titles bestowed upon him by the Senate that placed absolute power within his hands. Hence, he maintained the façade of Roman traditions, political forms, institutions, and public relations, while creating a new method of administering Rome's vast holdings.

Accepting the titles of *Princeps* (or "first citizen," from which comes the word Prince), Imperator ("victorious commander," from which we get Emperor), *Augustus* (great and holy one), *Pontifex Maximus* (high priest), and *Tribune* for life, Octavian set about establishing personal sovereignty. Preserving the Senate, Rome's aristocracy, the elected Roman magistracy, and Roman citizenship, Octavian managed to create the illusion of a *dyarchy* (the rule of two), but in fact all decisions of importance passed through his hands first. Over time, his paper title truly described the magnitude of his power. Eventually he ceased being known as Octavian Caesar and became Augustus Caesar. Also, to acquire Augustus's prestige, his heirs assumed the name of "Caesar" as a title until the Emperor Hadrian (117–138 CE) replaced it with "Augustus" and bestowed

"Caesar" on his heir apparent. All the remaining Roman emperors then followed Hadrian's example.

Augustus used the Senate to run the civil administration of Rome and the provinces. Yet, he was able to raise trustworthy supporters to the standards of honor, wealth, and conduct that the name "senator" required, given the death of so many of Rome's ancient families during the civil war. Accordingly, he knew he could "turn over decisions to the Senate," while in fact ruling through this now loyal, stabilized body. Meanwhile, he remained in command of the army, some twenty-six legions deployed along Rome's frontiers, maintained exclusive ownership of Egypt as a private imperial estate, and had a personal security force of 9,000 Praetorian Guards. Hence, Augustus had at his fingertips more than 350,000 soldiers, enough grain to feed Rome's poor so long as they had citizenship, and commanded a monopoly on coercion within Rome's 3.5 million square mile empire.

Casting himself in the role of Rome's military protector, high priest, and reviver of historical tradition, Augustus restored as much of Rome's past glory as he could. He paid particular attention to the worship of Venus (the name for the Greek goddess Aphrodite that the Romans used when they adopted the Greek Pantheon) because Julius Caesar had traced his ancestry to this goddess of love and passion. This attention to detail allowed Augustus to link Caesar's name to the ancient Trojan warrior Aeneas and sponsor such works of art as Virgil's *Aeneid*. To serve Augustus, Virgil (70–19 BCE) tried to imitate Homer and create a patriotic

Statue of Octavius (Octavian Caesar or Augustus Caesar). Courtesy Touraj Daryaee.

epic that told of the Trojan survivors who followed Aeneas (hence the title *Aeneid*) first to Carthage and then to Italy to lay the foundation for the origins of Rome. Also, Virgil instilled in Aeneas, the son of Venus, the virtues—stern rectitude, devotion to family, and care for the state—that became the backbone of Roman polity. The *Aeneid* described the origins of Rome as a product of a divine plan, made the Romans the heirs of Troy, and transformed Augustus from a mere human into the scion to an ancient prophecy, in other words the *genius* (divine spirit) of Rome. Accordingly, everything Augustus did fostered his power either directly or indirectly.

Imposing a peace that lasted until 180 CE, Augustus established a style of rule that sheltered the empire from profound internal disorder. He did so by encouraging the expansion of the economy, restoring fiscal stability, and securing empire-wide productivity. He knew that people everywhere were exhausted by war and hungered for peace and stability. He knew that 102 years of civil war had eroded the empire internally and left the Italian peninsula in chaos. And he knew that if he could provide the people the material security needed to recover the productive potential of Rome's vast holdings, Romans everywhere would be willing to accept citizenship in name only. Accordingly, he inaugurated an era of political stability, commercial prosperity, and agricultural productivity. At his death in 14 CE, the chaos of the past had become a distant memory.

But the one problem that Augustus could not solve was this: how would he choose a successor? Passing absolute power from one generation to the next, while maintaining the façade of the republic under the empire, proved to be too difficult even for someone of Augustus's abilities. Upon his death, he was left with no choice but to transfer authority to Tiberius Caesar (reigned 14–37 CE)—his most talented surviving heir. Using the principle of heredity, Tiberius then passed power to his nephew Caligula (reigned 37–41 CE). Yet insanity followed by his assassination soon removed Caligula from power and brought Claudius to the throne (reigned 41–54 CE); finally, Claudius's son Nero (reigned 54–68 CE) took over after the death of his father, thus marking the end of the first Roman imperial line.

These four men, plus Augustus, made up the Julio-Claudian line. Ironically, Augustus alone was the only major talent among them; Tiberius and Claudius were competent but uninspiring. Caligula and Nero were both deranged and had to be removed from office, the first by assassination and the second through forced suicide. Now the façade of republicanism so carefully constructed and maintained by Augustus, became increasingly less important. Hence, the material benefits associated with Roman citizenship also began to erode. Eventually, citizenship itself became a hollow shell, the legal and material advantages of this status having fallen victim to the harsh realities of imperial rule.

Following the death of Nero in 69 CE, came the Flavian line. One year of civil strife brought forward Vespasian (69–79 CE), founder of the line, and again Rome had a hard-working, conscientious, and competent professional soldier on the throne. Vespasian revived the economy, restored peace, and reasserted Augustus's administration of the provinces. But because he had two sons, Vespasian relied on inheritance as the means to pass on his power. Accordingly, Titus began his rule upon the death of his father, but this lasted only two years; a deadly fever cut short his reign (79–81 CE). Vespasian's second son, Domitian (81–96 CE) lasted longer and proved to be an able ruler, but in time he became paranoid. He created a system of secret police that terrorized his subordinates, which eventually led to his assassination fifteen years after he had taken office. Hence, the Flavian line did not fare much better than had the Julio-Claudian line.

One innovation, however, did come out of this flawed method of transferring power. The assassins who removed Domitian agreed to replace him with a man of unimpeachable character, Nerva (96–98 CE), who ruled quite briefly but who, notably, selected his own heir Trajan (98–117 CE). For the next eighty-two years, that is until the end of the *Pax Romana* (Roman Peace), the emperors of Rome had finally hit upon a method for selecting competent heirs: adoption. Trajan selected Hadrian (117–138 CE), who selected Antonius (138–161 CE), who selected Marcus Aurelius (161–180 CE); each of these men proved to be an effective and charismatic leader. Hence, Rome enjoyed an unbroken chain of command by men capable of inspiring loyalty and good will. Yet Marcus Aurelius failed to maintain this standard of rule because upon his death his son Commodus (180–193 CE) took over, with insanity once again infecting the imperial office.

Although the Augustan reign had been hailed as "the Golden Age of Rome," due to the peace, prosperity, and stability created by Augustus, something had died along the way. This sense of loss was lamented by Rome's intellectuals, historians, and artists. Each, in his own way, spoke of a sense of decay that had begun with the end of the republic. Each described a present world in which material success was unquestioned, but meaningless when compared to the loss of civic virtue, rigorous discipline, and political morality that once had marked Roman life. The imperial office brought forward great men, but only when lineage or inheritance was ignored. From Augustus to Commodus (31 BCE–196

CE), seven gifted rulers brought peace to Rome, but in between their reigns fell four competent, but uninspiring men, and three lunatics.

The wealth of the empire derived from an economy initiated by Augustus and maintained by the "good" emperors. This economy began with agriculture and centered on commerce. The heart of the empire, the Italian peninsula, held numerous latifundia and medium-sized farms large enough to diversify productivity. Since Egypt had become the granary of the empire under Augustus, Italian farmers could afford to produce a wider variety of crops designated for export as a hedge against bad agricultural years. Yet, those farmers who could not afford to experiment with different crops could instead specialize in such luxury items as wine and olive oil because of the high profit margins these products commanded. And during the prosperity of the Augustan Era, the demand for luxury goods in general grew so high that the raising of heretofore frivolous livestock such as poultry, pheasants, and peacocks became economically feasible. Finally, since all roads "led" to Rome at this time, it became the commercial center of the western world.

Italian industry also grew dramatically under Augustus's care. Since he used the equestrians (rich Plebeians) to staff the financial bureaucracy he had constructed to run the empire, he encouraged the formation of a new business class. In addition, since Augustus had launched a major reconstruction of Rome and the empire after the devastation caused by the civil war, the demand for building materials was great. Mass production based on slave-labor generated ceramics, bricks, tiles, and hard metals. Accordingly, the new business class grew as a needed imperial counterweight to offset potential senatorial corruption. At the same time, a vast new supply of building materials fueled a Roman economic revival.

In the provinces, meanwhile, prosperity followed on the heels of peace and stability. Egypt produced the grain needed to feed Rome as well as the fine sand needed to maintain its glass industry. At this time, Alexandria became the entrepôt for the Eastern Mediterranean. A new wave of trade in the Aegean and Black seas revived local economies and linked the Eastern Mediterranean with the West. Hence, Rome became a centerplace city in a growing economy, one whose prosperity generated its own momentum so long as the general population remained healthy. Despite the periodic rule of literally insane emperors, the Roman economy managed to survive well during the Pax Romana.

But, as mentioned, the material wealth of the empire could not compensate for the sense of spiritual loss that plagued Rome after 31 BCE. As a result, many Romans began to look for a new spiritual substitute to replace the real sense of citizenship they once nurtured. Many people turned to foreign religions and Greco-Roman philosophy as a means to recover what they felt was missing in their lives.

Roman Society

Roman society relied on the Roman family to form the backbone of the community. Romans lived in a complex household with a central bloodline, close relatives, multiple generations, free servants, and slaves. The head of the household, the *pater familias* (father of the family), governed the subordinate members with sufficient power to permit him to exact capital punishment on any member who might bring shame on the family. The pater familias made all the key decisions for the family: marriages, finances, politics, rights, duties, obligations, and punishments. Reinforcing the pater familias, but subordinate to him, was *manus*, the authority of a husband over his wife. Both pater familias and manus subjected Rome's women to the will of the male members of the family.

An example of the way the authority of the pater familias worked can be seen in the traditional Roman interpretation of rape. If a man raped a woman, he was guilty of a crime, but since the woman was a participant (even though unwilling), the family still held her partially responsible for the act. If she died as a result of the sexual assault, she was judged innocent, because she had given her life to protect her family's honor. If she were severely injured but survived, she was judged partially guilty and punished according to the evidence of her wounds—the more severe, the greater her degree of innocence. If she displayed few injuries, then the pater familias, acting on behalf of the family, judged her guilty of willfully participating in the act, probably because he believed she had incited it, and ordered her buried alive as if she were an adulteress. Such an oppressive authority over women, however, eroded as the Roman Republic acquired more wealth through conquest.

Between 265 and 31 BCE, women gained more freedom from male domination as their ability to supervise the family's household made them personally rich when the spoils of war poured into Rome. Although Roman law strictly limited the ability of women to inherit estates, the inconsistent application of these legal constraints allowed many women to become independently wealthy as their fathers and husbands died. Between 200 and 31 BCE, as Rome gained command of the Mediterranean world, clever individual females managed to procure massive estates that rivaled the wealth of the

The masses were distracted from their misery by bloody gladiatorial events. "Gladiatorial Combat," after Jean-Léon Gérôme "Pollice Verso," 1872, from "Roma," by Albert Kuhn, published in 1913. The VRoma Project, www.vroma.org.

At the very bottom of society were the slaves. Roman society ran on slave labor. By the second century CE, 33 percent of the Roman empire comprised slaves doing one form of work or another. Some 19.8 to 24.8 million of an estimated total 66 to 75 million people living within the empire were enslaved. Slaves worked the latifundia, formed the labor base of Roman factories, provided most of the household services, and were some of the best educated people of the Roman world. Women slaves commonly supplied domestic labor and sexual entertainment, while men did everything imaginable: they trained as gladiators (e.g., Spartacus, the man who led the slave revolt of 73 BCE); worked as teachers, craftsmen, or servants; and functioned as business agents. Yet most male and female slaves led such miserable lives that they failed to form families and reproduce their numbers, and could only be replaced by Rome's continued expansion against foreign foes. Hence, the total number of slaves began to decline as soon as Rome expanded to its maximum size.

richest families. Accordingly, such women even managed to escape the authority of the pater familias and manus to become heads of their own household.

Also newly rich families, who managed to survive the Roman civil war, and benefited from Octavius Ceasar's freshly instituted Pax Romana (31 BCE to 180 CE), swelled the growing ranks of the merchant, manufacturer, construction, and landowner classes. They represented the social fluidity of Rome's status system as those with talent, who could correctly estimate the direction of political and economic developments, prospered. Serving as a new source of consumer demand, these same newly rich families stimulated a new market in exotic luxury items, such as parrot-tongue pie, ice cream, and jellyfish, to name a few. Also they engaged in conspicuous consumption on a grand scale, which led to elaborate orgies punctuated with sumptuous banquets that included periodic vomiting to make room for more food.

At the other end of the social scale, a growing mass of urban poor became a major political problem after the second century BCE. Unemployed, rootless, and willing to sell their vote for the legal and political protection of any wealthy family, these indigent masses swarmed through the streets of Rome, rioting to ease their misery, and readily joining the army of any ambitious general during the civil wars. These same poor became a special concern of Octavius Caesar after his victory at Actium in 31 BCE; he used his newly won holdings in Egypt to feed any citizen in Rome who asked for free bread. To this benefit of free food, Octavius added the circus, which became an imperial monopoly so that he could supply ample entertainment to ease potential unrest and offer sufficiently blood-soaked gladiatorial contests to calm the urban masses.

At the height of Roman power, at Octavius Caesar's death in 14 CE, the empire comprised an estimated 4.9 million citizens. These people represented as few as 6.6 to as much as 8.3 percent of the total Roman population. This small percentage of the whole, however, constituted the empire's elite: nearly 3 million lived in Italy, with the remaining 2 million in the provinces. One-hundred-and-ninety-eight years after Octavius's death, in 212 CE, the emperor Caracalla officially proclaimed all freeborn males within the empire to be citizens; thus, by the third century CE, citizenship had become so common it was meaningless. No longer the political identity that gave purpose to public life, being a citizen now meant that all freeborn Roman men belonged to a vast, diluted pool of people with no real role in politics or society. Meanwhile, 85 percent or more or Rome's people made their living from agriculture; this meant that between 9 and 11.3 million Romans lived in its more than 1,000 cities. The Roman empire achieved an unusually high urban-rural ratio of 1.5 to 8.5. This was probably due to the productivity of Egypt, the Roman breadbasket, where the fertility of the Nile Valley never waned throughout its long history.

In summary, then, one could say that Rome's society was a fluid mass shifting with each passing year. Prosperity offered opportunity for the few who were competent and clever after the civil war. Fortune smiled on those with self-confidence and good economic and political judgment—including women. Yet if anyone guessed wrong as to the events of the day, especially during the reign of Rome's more unstable emperors, ruin soon followed. Near the bottom of society, the poor, the homeless, and the destitute teemed the streets of the Roman empire's major cities. They could be distracted by gladiatorial events and fed on free bread if they held Roman citizenship and lived in Rome, but there was no coherent policy to deal with the masses of urban poor. At the very bottom of society, the slaves represented a massive unstable labor pool whose misery denied the possibility of their replacing their own numbers. Hence the future of Rome rested on a cunning, self-absorbed elite capable of guessing the direction of political developments; the poor, urban masses unsure of what the future would bring; and a labor base that could only shrink once Rome had grown to its maximum size.

Roman Philosophy

The Roman philosophical perspective matured in an era of increasing demoralization as the Roman Empire first lost its sense of direction during the Pax Romana (31 BCE–180 CE), and then spiraled into chaos from 211 to 476 CE. The Pax Romana represented an era of both political stability and moral decay. The era of chaos that followed represented an age of social, economic, and political disintegration called "the fall of Rome," a gradual decline that the Romans seemed able to delay but powerless to stop (see Chapter Ten). Rome therefore proved fertile ground for Christianity, a faith whose history developed parallel to this growing sense of moral decay in the Western imagination.

As seen earlier in this chapter, the failure of Roman citizenship followed a pattern previously established by the Greeks. Just as Athens, Sparta, and Thebes had each grown beyond the limits of what its citizens could command by force during the Peloponnesian Wars (431–338 BCE), so Rome had expanded beyond the limits of what its form of citizenship could control. Roman socii status had allowed Rome to win its wars in Italy and had placed it in contact with Carthage by 265 BCE. Yet in Carthage, Rome found an enemy it could not assimilate. Furthermore, Rome's victories over the Carthaginians in three extremely difficult wars (264–241 BCE, 218–201 BCE, and 149–146 BCE) saw the Romans acquiring an enormous empire too quickly.

Accordingly, the command of so many subject people undermined the civic virtue that lay at the heart of Roman citizenship, and, just like that of Athens, Sparta, and Thebes, the internal design of Rome began to erode from the amoral political principle that "might is right." The consequences of such vast riches flowing into the Roman system caused its people to choke on their own wealth, initiating a greedy war policy that split the bonds holding the Patricians, Plebeians, and socii together. The fractures in Rome's politics saw the Roman Republic become embroiled in a civil war that lasted 102 years (133–31 BCE), destroyed the real meaning of citizenship, and created the political rule of the Principate.

Nonetheless, just as the decline of Greece inspired the valuable philosophies developed by Socrates, Plato, and Aristotle, the corruption of "this world" enhanced for Romans the beauty, goodness, truth, and reality of the transcendental realm developed by the Socratic philosophers. But, since the Romans had produced no philosophers of their own who could equal those of classical Greece, they became enamored with the Greek vision of a transcendental realm beyond everyday life. Thus, the Romans became consumers of the Greek worldview and merely added their own vision to the maturing concept of Platonic logos. Hence, even though citizenship had failed in both Rome and Greece, the standards of citizenship found in Socratic thought remained a beacon for the West to admire.

Romans consumed Greek philosophy in three forms: Stoicism, Epicureanism, and Neo-Platonism. Stoicism originated with a second Greek philosopher named Zeno (335–263 BCE; do not confuse him with the pre-Socratic Zeno of 490–430 BCE) who generated his theories while speaking from the so-called painted porch of Athens, the *Stoa Poikile*. His followers, the *Stoics*, or those who followed the ideas developed on the painted porch, emphasized Zeno's vision of the transcendental as conceived by the Socratics but carried that vision to such an extreme that they tried to withdraw from the physical world as much as possible. Far more popular then their Epicurean rivals (see below), the Stoics distanced themselves from the corruption of daily life through a detachment that protected them from pleasure as well as pain. The serenity they hoped to achieve was supposed to help them function effectively in public life, a public life that did not include real citizenship. The Stoics therefore believed that by achieving a state of *apatheia* (apathy), they could carry out their duty to other human beings through humanitarian and pacifist behavior. They hoped in this fashion to bring the divine cosmic order that governed the universe to earth, even though they were personally powerless to shape public events.

The antithesis of Stoicism, Epicureanism, was the product of a Greek thinker named Epicurus (341–270 BCE) who abandoned the Socratic vision of the transcendental to go to the opposite extreme and restore a pre-Socratic materialism. Building on the atomic theory of Leucippus and Democritus (mentioned in Chapter Seven), Epicurus developed a philosophy that argued change and growth resulted from the arrangement and rearrangement of the tiny particles alone. Rejecting any form of transcendental determinism as part of the process of change, Epicurus believed that all things were merely atoms going though physical transformations set in motion by their own material properties. The universe functioned on physical principles only; the gods existed but were indifferent to humanity. According to Epicurus, the absence of an eternal reward, and the lack of an immortal soul, made each human a mere combination of atoms; this suggested that life was merely an organization of matter spent in a universe filled only with more matter. Therefore one should enjoy life as much as possible by making those choices that prolonged one's material existence as long as conceivable. The ideal state for the Epicurean was *ataraxia*, (a withdrawal from politics, the marketplace, romantic love, and any form of stressful living that could upset one's atoms). A private life of serenity achieved through thought, mild exercise, and good food and wine represented the best that human beings could hope to achieve.

Independent of the Stoics and Epicureans, Neo-Platonism revived the metaphysics of Plato in the third century CE under Plotinus (204–270 CE). Plotinus transformed logos into "the One," i.e., a self-thinking universal entity that existed apart from and was superior to all events in the world. Accordingly, the One constituted "true Being" and served as a total, unitary, and simple existence that came before all other things. Reality itself was a series of levels of descending order, such as Intelligence, Soul, and Substance, that flowed from the highest state of existence (the One) to all other lower forms of being. Thus, the One generated Intelligence and Soul as eternal stages of "the real" (actuality) prior to mixing with matter to form Substance. Still, the One remained unaffected by anything other than its own existence.

In the human world, the One produced inferior forms of itself. The first was Intelligence. Intelligence emerged from the One to operate as a transcendental "simultaneity," a Being that existed at the same time as all other things but stood apart from them, as the source of the Platonic forms. The second aspect, the

Soul, generated conditions of time and received the Platonic forms as reasoned principles of existence from the Intelligence, which now functioned as the *logoi* (the forms, words, and speech that make all things make sense). The third aspect, Substance, occupied the three-dimensional world around us as the Soul projected itself into a negative field called "matter." Matter had no positive existence in itself; rather, it was simply the medium that received the logical impressions made by the Soul. By itself, matter was "evil" in the sense that it corrupted the transcendental perfection of the logoi to make up Substance. Together Intelligence, Soul, and Substance linked the One with the material world, while the corruption of matter became synonymous with the depravity of physical existence and filled the world with decay and error. Hence, like the Socratics, Plotinus tried to integrate everything within the One, but ended with a dichotomy between good and evil, form and matter, as part of everyday existence.

From Plotinus, Neo-Platonism diffused into the Roman world even as the barbarians invaded Rome, destroying the civilization. There, Neo-Platonism increasingly took on the features of magic and religion. One philosopher, St. Augustine, the bishop of the north African city of Hippo (354–430 CE), bridged the gap between Neo-Platonism and religion at the end of the Roman Principate by infusing the new universal faith, Christianity (see below), with its most enduring theology. As St. Augustine wrote his *City of God*, his vision of the fall of Rome as "the City of Man" represented a corrupt but necessary step in creating the Christian Church, or "the City of God." The City of Man, Rome, had served its purpose by offering a unified political empire in which Jesus could do his work. So once the Christian Church, the product of Christ's message, had taken firm root within the Roman Empire, its usefulness ended. Now the Divine Plan called for the dawning of a new age with "the City of God," the Christian Church; this new age would spread the "true faith" beyond the boundaries of the fallen Roman Empire into the entire world. Accordingly, St. Augustine emphasized the transcendental spirit of the Church over the corruption of the body as represented by Rome, arguing that the infinite potential of Christianity exceeded material limits. Thus, St. Augustine maintained the material and spiritual duality of Neo-Platonism within the confines of Christianity as a well-established problem of Western philosophy generated by Socratic thought.

Given the fact that the status of citizen eroded as the number of people honored with this legal designation increased, so the spiritual and emotional satisfaction derived from citizenship decayed, when, in 212 CE, every freeborn male had achieved such a distinction.

Christianity

Christianity began in Palestine, a place where everyone eagerly awaited the arrival of the Messiah. Who this Messiah might be, how he would appear, and how he would act, no one knew. One Jewish sect called the Pharisees expected a political leader who would rescue the Jews from the grip of Rome and reconstitute Jewish law. Another sect called the Zealots waited for a military leader who would lead a victorious army against Rome and overthrow its alien rule to establish a new Jewish state. A third sect called the Essenes sought a spiritual leader who would guide them in the repentance of their sins and create a means to experience a mystical union between humanity and God. Of these differing sects, Jesus Christ is more clearly aligned with the humble, peaceful, and spiritual goals of the Essenes rather than the political or military objectives of the Pharisees and Zealots.

Evidence of the existence of Jesus comes from the *Gospels*. These four accounts concerning Jesus, the kingdom of God, and salvation, however, bear witness more to the faith of their authors than serve as accurate records of history. They blend the way Jesus came into the world with a powerful message of redemption that obscures a clear picture of who Jesus really was. All that can be said with accuracy is: he was born in Judaea during the reign of Octavius Caesar (Augustus); as a Jew, he preached in the tradition of the prophets and was the most effective Rabbi of his day; he railed against sin and worldly concerns; and he offered access to a heavenly realm for the righteous. His success among the poor caused suspicion among the rich, and his criticism of the religious practices at the Temple in Jerusalem provoked the resentment of the religious establishment. The Roman Procurator (governor) of Judaea, Pontius Pilate, condemned Jesus as a dangerous revolutionary and subjected him to crucifixion some time around 30–33 CE. His followers, however, believed in his resurrection three days after his burial, which became the critical element in the new faith he generated.

More enduring than the story of Jesus was his ministry. He set out to establish his key religious themes sometime around 25–33 CE. These themes included: that God is the Father of all humanity; that the only way to the Father was through His son (Jesus); that we all should obey the Golden Rule (do unto others as we would have them do unto us); that everyone one of us is his or her brother or sister's keeper; that we should forgive those who trespass against us; that we should be forthright in our speech and actions and avoid hypocrisy, lies, and misdeeds; and, finally, that we should concentrate on our faith in God's infinite love for us and not become

hypnotized by ceremony or ritual. Jesus furthermore announced that the end of the world was at hand, and therefore, that we should free ourselves of sin in preparation for Judgment Day. Jesus concluded with the promise of the resurrection of the dead, which would establish the kingdom of Heaven for all the righteous.

The crucifixion of Jesus approximately three years after he began his ministry marked the critical moment for his followers at the beginning of the Christian religion. Stories of the resurrection of Jesus circulated among his followers, and the faithful became energized by a new confidence in his holiness, that he was, indeed, the hoped-for Messiah, the son of God and the savior of humankind. With their courage restored, these disciples, the core group known as his Apostles, began to venture out and spread the "good news" of humanity's potential salvation. The "good news" itself, or the *gospels*, was a compilation of the Apostles' memories of the deeds and teachings of Jesus.

The four gospels of Matthew, Mark, Luke, and John brought word of Jesus's ministry to the Greco-Roman world. Written between thirty and one hundred years after his death, the gospels bore witness to the passion of Christ as the son of God. The message provided by these four documents of faith was consistent with the image of Jesus as both a prophet and the son of God. Yet despite the legends that might have contaminated the historical accuracy of these accounts of Jesus himself, these gospels became the cornerstone of the new faith of Christianity.

The fourth gospel in particular reveals that the beginning of a union between Greek philosophy and Christianity had already begun. Here the author, the Apostle John, opened his "good news" with the sentence: "In the beginning there was the *word*, and the *word* was God." Written in *koine* Greek, the common language of the eastern half of the Roman Empire, the term for *word* was logos. Yet, as mentioned, in Greek, logos had a far greater meaning than merely "word" or speech; logos also meant reason, logic, or the logoi of the Neo-Platonists. In other words, "word, speech, and logic" were all part of the same concept and could not be separated from one another.

Since reason and logic in Greek philosophy identified the transcendental essences behind all existence, the use of the "word" to name God linked the Greek realm of eternal forms with the Hebrew vision of ethical monotheism. Thus, to these early Christians, most of whom were converted Jews, logos became a conceptual connection between transcendental reason and God's Divine Plan for the universe. Also, Jesus became the central player in this Plan so that when his message diffused into the Greco-Roman world, Greek philosophy became part of a heuristic device to develop a theology that communicated the ministry of Jesus to the pagans (nonbelievers).

At the same time that the gospels spread the news of Jesus, Saul of Tarsus (later St. Paul, ca. 10–67 CE) broadened the new faith's potential to embrace the entire world. Paul was not born in Palestine but was a Jew who lived in Tarsus, a Cilician city located near the frontier between modern Turkey and Syria. Originally a Pharisee, a person who insisted on strict adherence to Jewish law, and a persecutor of Christians, Paul had his first known contact with the followers of Jesus at the martyrdom of St. Stephen, the first Christian to die for his faith. Then Paul received a commission from the chief priest in Jerusalem to travel to Damascus to suppress Christianity. But on the road to Damascus, Paul had an intense religious experience, a vision that converted him to the new faith and turned him into a devout evangelist in 35 CE. It was through Paul's ministry that Christianity left the confines of Judaism and spread among the gentiles of the Roman world.

Denying that Jesus was merely the redeemer of the Jews, Paul made Christianity into a universal religion. He did so by placing an emphasis on the ideas of Jesus as the "Christ," or "the anointed one" in koine Greek; according to Paul, Jesus was a God-man sent to Earth by his Father to die for all of humanity's sins. Also, according to Paul, Jesus's sacrifice on the cross ushered in a new age in which Jewish ceremony and law ceased to be of primacy; in its place humanity could achieve salvation by having faith in God's infinite mercy. Paul argued that if God was willing to sacrifice His own son for the sin-ridden people who walked the Earth, then His mercy, as well as love for humanity, had no bounds. All each person had to do was acknowledge Jesus as the savior and join a growing community of the faithful.

Thus, while Jesus had proclaimed the imminent coming of the Kingdom of God, Paul's religious message became the means to define the gentle ceremonies that marked one's faith in God. Long after Paul's death as a Christian martyr in 67 CE, when he and the Apostle Peter became victims of Nero's persecutions. The ceremonies Paul instituted eventually became the sacraments of the Church as it grew in size and complexity over the years. These ceremonies would celebrate Jesus's message and bring the believer ever closer to Christ. Yet, ironically, the Church that served Christianity as its institutional vehicle to bring the message of Jesus to the world, also came to dominate the Western imagination. As the Church created an orthodoxy to define Christianity, it also ran contrary to Paul's original message: that one could achieve salvation through faith alone. Such a paradox, the conflict between an emerging orthodoxy and faith itself, would eventually cause major problems for the Church in the modern age (during the Reformation, 1517–1648 CE).

Meanwhile, in the second and third centuries CE, the degree of complexity in the growing Christian community resulted in questions about God, Jesus, and salvation. Each question generated a debate that resolved differences by introducing Greek philosophy and logic into a new discipline called *theology*. Theology developed the Christian understanding of God and His son Jesus Christ and generated the orthodoxy that received support from a growing Church hierarchy and authority system. At the same time, theological resolutions of these questions slowly melded logos with Christianity as both matured within the boundaries of the Church.

Men like Clement of Alexandria (ca. 150–215 CE) and his most famous student, Origen (185–253 CE), began this process of blending Greek philosophy with Christianity to create a nascent form of theology. Clement of Alexandria was among the first to formulate a relationship between Plato's vision of the universe and Jesus as the son of God. Clement espoused the belief that philosophy among the pagan Greeks was part of the Divine Plan because it served as a pedagogical preparation for the coming of Christ. He argued that Greek philosophy had created the proper mental constructs that allowed the world to acquire a clear understanding of God and His son. He also argued that the philosophers of his day had to rise above their pagan heritage and perfect their knowledge of reality through the revealed truth of Christ.

Like Clement, Origen was enthusiastic about Platonic concepts and borrowed heavily from Greek philosophy. Origen was among the first Christian thinkers to produce a systematic theology for the Christian Church. Though some of his ideas were later declared heretical, he helped lay the foundation for the blending of Greek and Christian beliefs. The most famous of his views, which was eventually rejected by the Church was *apocatastasis* (Greek for "re-establishment") or the universal salvation and restoration of all creation with God. Origen used the term apocatastasis to represent the restoration of all souls, including those condemned by God for their sins. Origen believed that, given his omnipotent and eternal nature, God would triumph over evil and all souls would eventually come to embrace Him. Thus, even those souls that had willfully violated God's laws would eventually see the errors of their ways and thus be saved. Ultimately, everyone in the universe was destined to seek the bliss offered by the pure goodness, beauty, truth, and reality of God. Yet such a view eliminated the threat of sin by reducing its punishment from eternal damnation to a lengthy but finite penance. As a result, the early Church rejected apocatastasis.

Between the third and fifth centuries CE, as the Church continued to grow and became legal under the Roman Emperor Constantine (ca. 288–337 CE), its size and complexity led to increasing disputes over the nature of Jesus and his role in the Divine Plan. These disputes refined Christian orthodoxy and condemned heresy, i.e., the Church's declaration that one view or another of Jesus was officially in error. Among these early heresies were those proclaimed by the Donatists (ca. 350 CE) who posited that sinners, once having sinned, might receive God's forgiveness but could not be re-embraced by the Church without causing contamination. Another heresy, Monophysitism (ca. 450 CE), declared that Jesus was not a God-man but God pure and simple; hence, Christ only appeared to have died on the cross; in reality he had ascended directly to Heaven as pure, uncorrupted Divinity. The single most important heresy, however, was the one started by Arius (ca. 250–336 CE).

Arius, a Libyan theologian who preached in Alexandria, declared Christ different from God since God had infinite existence before and after the beginning of time, while the life of Christ had begun at a finite moment in time. As a result, the *being* of Jesus was not identical to that of his Father, but only similar to it (*homoiousios*). Existing in a state of being less than God, the infinite divinity of Jesus then came into question. Yet, to limit Christ's infinite nature was to diminish his role in human history relative to God and lessen the quality of the mercy obtained by his sacrifice on the cross.

But Athanasius, the Patriarch of Alexandria (328–373 CE) argued the opposite: that Christ and God were the same (*homoousios*). And since Christ and God shared the same Being, Jesus represented God's infinite mercy in the form of self-sacrifice. Thus, the death of Jesus through crucifixion was a sign of God's Divine Plan for the salvation of humanity. Athanasius felt that Arius' challenge to Christ's nature threatened the very foundations of salvation itself and thus the Church.

Resolution to this debate came at the Nicene Council, which launched the idea of the Trinity. The Nicene Creed emerged from the first Church Council, the Council of Nicaea, a city in Asia minor southwest of Constantinople. In 325 CE, the emperor Constantine had called the Council to deal specifically with Arius and locked the concept of God and logos together along a path of synthesis that reached maturity in the fifth century CE. The Nicene Creed declared Christ to be God's equal because Jesus was merely God "conceiving" of Himself when he created His son. Accordingly, since

God "conceived" of Jesus before Christ's birth, then the "idea" (logos) of the son preceded the son himself. In addition, since the "idea" was a transcendental form that took precedence over any material manifestation of itself, then the infinite nature of Jesus preceded his birth as a God-man. Thus, Christ, the historical son, became a material expression of pure, infinite Being as expressed in the eternity of God's imagination. Consequently, the divinity of the son was the same as the divinity of the Father because both belonged in the same existence through *consubstantiation*, (existing as the same Being).

By the fourth or fifth centuries CE, the Greco-Hebrew-Christian synthesis achieved its complete form in St. Augustine's *City of God*. Mentioned above, this first medieval document combined Neo-Platonism, Christian, and Hebrew ideas. In it, God's function crystallized in a union with the Greek logos to create synthesis with ethical monotheism and Plato's Universal Soul, Aristotle's final cause and Prime Mover, and Plotinus's the One. For St. Augustine, failure to live a good Christian life was akin to nurturing the body while ignoring the soul. For one who led such a life, upon death only the body remained on Earth, for the soul had withered. These material remains soon became decaying matter without form, beauty, truth, or reality. Hence, the body returned to its constituent parts of earth, water, air, and fire, and eroded into an ugly, corrupt mass of chaotic, decomposing flesh. Those whose souls had died because they never embraced Jesus as Savior would never experience God in Heaven, which lay at the edge of a finite, geocentric universe. They would never understand pure reality, truth, beauty, and goodness and never know God. This became the ultimate punishment, or the equivalent of what became known as Hell.

St. Augustine wrote his work because he knew the fall of Rome was inevitable. The Visigoths had captured the city in 409 CE, and other nomadic tribes were entering the empire in seemingly endless waves (see Chapter Ten). The fall of Rome was at hand. To explain why God would visit barbarians upon the civilized, sacred world required the vision of a new age. And for St. Augustine, this explanation came with ease: the "City of Man" was the body of society and doomed to perish; its end could only signal the rise of the "City of God." The fall of Rome, therefore, marked the beginning of a new era: the Age of Christ.

St. Augustine assigned a Divine purpose to the process of change from the ancient to the medieval world. His *City of God* created a synthesis between the Hebrew, Greek, and Christian sense of reality that made every human experience a direct lesson from God and all souls equal to the task of salvation. The destruction visited upon the Roman world was merely part of the Divine Plan, just as the fall of Israel and Judah had prepared the Hebrews for the next age in their evolution. The actual fall of Rome must wait, however, until the collapse of the ancient Eurasian world is fully discussed in Chapter Ten.

Suggested Reading

Beard, Mary, and Michael H. Crawford, *Rome in the Late Republic*, Second Edition (Ithaca: Cornell University Press, 1985).

Boardman, John, Jasper Griffin, and Oswyn Murray, *The Oxford History of the Roman World* (Oxford: Oxford University Press, 1991).

Boren, Henry C., *Roman Society*, Second Edition (Chapel Hill: University of North Carolina; Lexington, Mass.: D.C. Heath, 1977).

Cary, M., and H. H. Scullard, *A History of Rome Down to the Reign of Constantine*, Third Edition (New York: St. Martin's Press, 1975).

Cochrane, C. M., *Christianity and Classical Culture* (Oxford: Oxford University Press, 1957).

D'Arms, John H., *Commerce and Social Standing in Ancient Rome* (Cambridge: Harvard University Press, 1981).

Frende, William H. C., *The Rise of Christianity* (London: Darton, Longman, and Todd, 1984).

Garnsey, P., and R. Saller, *The Roman Empire: Economy, Society, and Culture* (Berkeley: The University of California Press, 1987).

Kebric, Robert B., *Roman People* (Mountain View, Calif.: Mayfield Publishing Company, 1993).

Long, A. A., *Hellenistic Philosophy: Stoics, Epicureans, and Skeptics* (Berkeley: The University of California Press, 1974).

Macmullen, R., *Christianizing the Roman Empire* (New Haven: Yale University Press, 1983).

Sherwin-White, A. N., *The Roman Citizenship*, Second Edition (Oxford: Oxford University Press, 1973).

Syme, R., *The Roman Revolution* (Oxford: Oxford University Press, 1960).

Wells, C., *The Roman Empire*, Second Edition (Cambridge: Harvard University Press, 1984).

IX

PRE-ISLAMIC AFRICA
and the Americas

Unlike the Eurasian core that linked ancient Rome to Gupta India and Han China along a vast east-west land axis in the temperate climatic zone, most of Africa and all of the Americas developed outside the mainstream of human contact. The ways in which geographic and biological isolation shaped the history of both these cultural zones led to the formation in each of uniquely organized societies. As such, sub-Saharan Africa (exclusive of Egypt and the rest of North Africa) and the Americas developed agriculture, cities, and the common features of civilization on a completely different time scale.

Pre-Islamic Africa

Despite its proximity to the Eurasian core, sub-Saharan African civilizations reflected a significant degree of isolation. The Sahara Desert played a central role in this story but was not always a barrier to travel. The process of desiccation that slowly made the Sahara into a desert began about nine thousand years ago and created an enormous obstacle to cultural diffusion by 1000 BCE. Yet before this drying out, from 7500 to 2500 BCE, the Sahara was hospitable to human life.

Filled with lakes, rivers, trees, and grasslands, at that time, the region that became the Sahara Desert supported an abundance of mammals, fowl, reptiles, and fish fit for human consumption. The inhabitants of river and lake villages of considerable size made a relatively easy living in this region. Beginning around 7500 BCE, however, the region began to dry out rapidly. By 1000 BCE the desiccation process had advanced to the point that the Sahara cut off all occupied zones in Africa to the south. Now, only the corridor of the Nile River valley allowed access to the continent's interior.

As a result, the human inhabitants of much of the heartland of Africa led a separate existence from Eurasia. Yet this isolation was compounded by the fact that the interior of Africa does not enjoy easy access to the sea. Although three times the size of Europe, Africa lacked the isthmuses, peninsulas, and fiords of

the European coast that created natural breakwaters for ships. Instead, Africa below the Sahara has a much shorter coastline due to a simple, smooth, and direct contact between land and sea. This coastline includes numerous sandbars in both the Atlantic and Indian oceans that make navigation hazardous as one approaches the continent. In addition, since Africa rises sharply out of the ocean, the rivers in most of the region south of the Sahara feature violent waterfalls near the sea. Also, violent rapids make these rivers poor conduits for trade from the interior. Finally, the shape of Africa itself creates an average distance of 5,000 miles from coast to coast, both east to west and north to south, which produces a nonspecific land axis, as well as a landmass filled with rainforests, swamps, and other desert barriers in addition to the Sahara.

To the difficulties created by geography one has to add the unusual problems of climate and disease. Unlike Mesopotamia, Egypt, India, China, or Europe, all of which experienced predictable seasons, the climate of sub-Saharan Africa proved extremely irregular. Years of drought often followed years of prolonged downpour. Soil erosion became a major problem wherever humans used the land. Furthermore, like India, much of Africa suffered from hot and humid conditions that provided a natural breeding ground for pathogens of human disease.

Unlike India, Africa not only fostered the emergence of the human species but also the first parasitic relationships between people and germs. Africa carried numerous unique agents of infection that retarded human population growth. Mosquitoes that caused malaria, yellow fever, and dengue fever, the tsetse fly that caused sleeping sickness, the black fly (*simuliidae*) that caused river blindness (*onochocerciasis*), fresh water snails that carried cercariae and caused bilharziasis (schistosomasis) and other parasites filled the streams, rivers, lakes, as well as the hot and humid air of Africa. These pathogens killed populations in large numbers, both humans and their domesticated mammals.

As a result, sustaining healthy populations in one place was very difficult below the Sahara. Human and

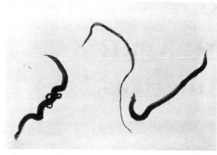

Schistosomiasis parasitic worms. Micrograph showing four *Schistosoma mansoni* parasites, (left to right) a pair, a male, and a female. Infestation is commonly due to poor sanitation and causes various tropical diseases. Courtesy of the CDC.

domesticated animal populations tended not to reach their critical mass that would permit a shift from nomadic to sedentary life until long after Eurasian civilizations had done so. And the impact of disease on large, imported domesticated mammals reduced the amount of labor that a specific species might provide as draft animals. Consequently, sub-Saharan Africa is noted for the general absence of the plow and the wheel in its formation of ancient cities.

Naturally, the absence of the plow and the wheel reduced the possibility of the large, regular food surpluses generated by agricultural labor. To explain why the plow did not diffuse into Africa in general, some scholars point to the prevalence of animal diseases. Others focus on Arabian camels and North African donkeys as the beasts of burden that worked best in sub-Saharan Africa, where they were not harnessed to any form of vehicle or tool. Still others point out that the soil of sub-Saharan Africa is both poor and thin, so it would not have responded any better to a plow than it did to a hoe because deep furrows did not change agricultural yields. And if these thin soils were plowed, they would rapidly erode in Africa's irregular climate. Finally, some authors emphasize Africa's isolation due to natural barriers that made this fringe region nearly inaccessible to Eurasia. Any one of these factors would have prolonged the development of both the wheel and the plow, but combined, they sharply cut into the possibility of either tool becoming common to sub-Saharan Africa. Thus, low agricultural yields and slow human population growth retarded the formation of civilization there.

Without large food surpluses, an urban division of labor had difficulty forming, so the region was largely denied further social, economic, and technical innovation. The only place on the African continent where such difficulties did not exist followed the line of diffusion up the Nile from Egypt to Kush and Axum. There, as we have seen, the fertility of the soil joined with a Mediterranean technology and the agricultural techniques of the Ancient Near East to generate significant food surpluses for large urban concentrations early in African history.

In contrast, the most hospitable places for humans in sub-Saharan Africa included three great grasslands. One such grassland extends across the continent south of the Sahara, comprising many modern nations today; it is known as the *Sudan* (Arabic for the "land of the black people"; do not confuse it with modern Sudan). A second grassland lies amid the mountains of eastern Africa, where humans also took up residence. Finally, a third is located across southern Africa above the Kalahari Desert, where civilization arrived quite late. In between these three grasslands lie the tropical forests that combined impenetrable jungles with a hot and humid climate that spawned numerous diseases capable of destroying both human and animal life.

But even though jungles and a rich disease environment created barriers to large concentrations of humans and domesticated animals, the hospitable grasslands of sub-Saharan Africa did offer two unique features. The first was a wide-open landscape that offered many potential sites for human habitation. And the second was the way that the disease barrier functioned as an agency that kept aggressive, alien cultures out of those sites for thousands of years, until the mid-nineteenth century.

The earliest Africans supported themselves by hunting and gathering. They began the domestication of plants and animals around 5000 BCE, probably because of contact with ancient Near Eastern farmers through North Africa. Farming began in three different sites—independent of one another: Ethiopia; the central Sudanese grasslands; and the upper Niger River valley. In Ethiopia, humans domesticated *tef* (a popular grain used to make a type of bread in Ethiopia today) and coffee. In the Sudanese grasslands known as the Sahel, Africans selected local cereal grains like sorghum and pearl millets from native grasses. And in the west, the Niger-Congo and Bantu Africans discovered useful omega varieties of rice, yams, kola nuts, and oil palms among the plants of the coastal rainforest. Domestication of animals spread into the Sahara before the desiccation had completely ruined that area. But as the arid zone continued to expand, herders and their cattle migrated north or south ahead of the advancing desert. Many settled in West Africa and Ethiopia, while their descendants trekked into eastern Africa between 1500 and 1000 BCE. South Africa experienced the development of agriculture much later.

Throughout all of Africa, the transition from hunting and gathering to herding and cultivation took place gradually. Only Egypt and the cultures shaped by contact with the Mediterranean by way of the Nile represented outstanding exceptions. In sub-Saharan Africa, combinations of hunting, gathering, herding, and gardening coexisted in many regions for long periods. Unpredictable climate and rainfall patterns, native food plants limited to the grasslands and rainforests within a narrow ecological range, and the absence of metal tools further slowed the spread of cultivation. The factors that finally overcame these limitations included the spread of new food plants and animals from Southeast Asia and the discovery and spread of an iron technology.

The migration of plants and animals from Southeast Asia into Africa is not too difficult to imagine when one considers the gentle waters of the Indian Ocean as compared to either the Atlantic or the Pacific. The relatively calm waters and predictable winds made travel on the Indian Ocean possible very early in world history. Typically the monsoon winds blow in one direction for six months out of the year, and then reverse themselves in the second six months. Moreover, coastal voyaging on this ocean required only small craft that could be dragged ashore after sailing. Visiting the shore nightly allowed voyagers to secure fresh water, supplement food supplies, and be protected from unexpected weather. Only hostile local natives might upset a gradual migration by sea on the Indian Ocean.

The appearance of a Southeast Asian language, Malagasy, in Madagascar around the time of Christ, reveals that such a trip was indeed possible. Furthermore, to move a language required the transference of a large group of people, while moving plants and animals required only a small number. The plants that made the trip include Asian rice, taro, a starchy root plant, sugarcane, bananas, and coconuts that arrived in the first millennium BCE and extended the range of cultivation. The animals include chickens, ducks, and geese from Southeast Asia, and pigs from Indonesia. These new plants and animals then spread into the habitable regions of Africa to expand the food base significantly.

Iron

Although native artisans developed bronze and copper manufacturing in West Africa, this technology did not spread. Iron, however, spread far and wide. The origins of iron manufacturing, however, are in dispute. Most scholars agree that iron entered Africa from Assyria and Phoenicia. They argue that Assyrian iron entered Egypt during Esar-Hadden's conquest (reign 681–668 BCE), traveled up the Nile into Nubia, and then crossed westward to Tibesti and the Sahel, reaching as far south as Lake Victoria by 250 BCE. They also argue that the Phoenicians founded the city of Carthage in the Bay of Tunis around 850 BCE, explored the northern coast of Africa, and introduced iron to Africa during the ninth century BCE. From Carthage, iron traveled south carried by Berber tribesmen to Aïr, and, from there, diffused into the Sudanese grasslands. Other scholars, however, point to a common and uniquely African smelting process, which suggests that the Africans developed iron manufacture on their own. Whether one or the other is correct is less important than the fact that both groups of disputing experts date the development of iron to roughly the same years.

As it had elsewhere, iron reshaped ancient sub-Saharan culture by transforming food production. An example of native iron manufacture comes from the Nok culture. The Nok people combined plant cultivation and cattle herding in the Jos Highlands of northeastern Nigeria and generated a stable food base. They cleared the forests of these highlands, as the production of a few pounds of iron required an estimated ten to fifteen trees. Their culture yielded stone tools, iron implements, and terra-cotta pottery dating from 800 to 400 BCE. The Nok mastered iron smelting during the sixth century BCE and spread their cultural artifacts into western and central Africa. They taught iron production to the Bantu, a Niger-Congo population who lived east of the Jos Highlands and migrated throughout sub-equatorial Africa over the course of 3,500 years (ca. 3000 BCE–500 CE). Nok technology, therefore, traveled to all the regions traversed by the Bantu whose mother-tongue spawned a reputed 500 daughter languages.

From their west-central African homeland in what is currently Nigeria and Cameroon, the Bantu migrated south and east until they covered nearly all of central and southern Africa except for the Kalahari Desert, which became the home of those peoples dislodged by the Bantu. Two factors account for the Bantu migration: population pressure resulting from the symbiosis developed between plants, animals, and humans; and the limited ability to raise food on the central African plateau, where the topsoil is thin and water is in short supply.

As the Bantu spread out over sub-Saharan Africa, they developed the same degree of cultural variation as found among Indo-Europeans in India and Europe. Yet the variations among the Bantu became even more pronounced than their European and Indian counterparts due to the sheer size of Africa and its numerous zones of isolation. As mentioned above, what emerged were an estimated five hundred closely related Bantu languages that reflected the independent development of different cultures in an enormous space. Diversity masked, however, a unique feature of Bantu culture that they shared with other sub-Saharan Africans: a strong emphasis on kinship ties. Extended families grouped themselves into corporate lineages whose numbers and patterns far exceeded the complexity of any-thing found elsewhere in the world. In time multiple layers of kinship linked families, villages, tribes, and peoples into a system of social organization that num-bered in the millions. These millions then became the basis for urban culture in sub-Saharan Africa.

Supreme loyalty belonged to the lineage first, the members of which ranked themselves according to age and created secret societies as secondary organizational bodies. With a slow but continuous increase of popula-tion due to the spreading success of agriculture in sub-Saharan Africa after the introduction of iron, chiefdoms in local villages gave way to kingships. At the same time, sedentary life anchored people in their respec-tive villages, so that various groups of allied extended families worked in support of their king. Permanent residence increased the complexity of kinship and gen-erated the first monarchies of West Africa ca. 100 CE.

To augment their claim to power, these kings be-gan a pattern of authority that survived for centuries. Claiming to be the offspring of divine ancestors with special powers of fertility, these monarchs grew power-ful enough to oversee hierarchies of public officials to spread their authority. Interlocking obligations of fa-milial ties with village alliances underlay this system. These villages then paid tribute to the king's court, through which the monarch used this supply of local products to begin a system of trade. Thus, monarchy and trade integrated into a functional basis for regional government. Yet the true power of these kings was not felt until the middle years of world history due to geo-graphic isolation, local disease history, the absence of the wheel and the plow, the need to import draft ani-mals, and the vast amount of land available below the Sahara, which dispersed human populations, slowing the ability of any one group to reach the critical mass necessary to conduct agriculture.

Nilotic Africa

Existing in sharp contrast to the corporate lineages of sub-Saharan Africa was the Nilotic culture of Kush, located south of Egypt in lower Nubia. As a Nilotic Civilization (one located on the Nile and its tributar-ies), this culture represented a society whose history reflected a commercial link with the Mediterranean world. Unlike West, Central, Eastern, or Southern sub-Saharan Africa, all of which had to develop organiza-tional principles separate from the experiences com-mon to Eurasia, Kush belonged to a history tied to Egypt. Kush, and later Axum, came to represent the familiar world of the Mediterranean because of the dif-fusion of tools, techniques, and foods common to Mesopotamia and Egypt. While the rest of sub-Saharan

Africa represented a unique human experience whose story reached maturity in the middle years of world his-tory, the Nilotic civilizations proved an exception.

Nilotic Africa links the Nile Valley with the Ethio-pian highlands. Here an Egyptianized culture arose from contact with the Mediterranean world to build a literate civilization that employed the agricultural and urban methods found in the north. Nilo-Saharan speak-ing peoples of Kush fell under the influence of the rich Egyptian culture.

Old Kingdom monarchs subjugated and colonized Nubia immediately to the south in the Fourth Millen-nium BCE. Egypt's hold, however, did not last. A power struggle between the Egyptian kings and a rising Egyp-tian nobility and priesthood during the First Interme-diate Period 2200–2000 BCE (discussed in Chapter Three) led to the Middle Kingdom: a new political align-ment in Egypt that reduced the king's power. With this erosion of royal power, the Egyptian king lost his abil-ity to control Nubia and Kush. Thus, by 2000 BCE Kush had won its independence and took control of its por-tion of the Nile Valley.

Kush gained command of southern Nubia from the third to the sixth cataract (rapids along the course of the Nile—hundreds of miles south of the first cataract that marked the boundaries of Egypt). This stretch of the Nile Valley tributaries comprised the Arbara River and the Blue and White arms of the Nile. Integrating this region was the capital of Kush, Kerma, which be-came a major trading partner for the Egyptian kings of the Middle Kingdom. Commerce became a basic eco-nomic theme in sub-Saharan Africa history; it gener-ated and sustained political organizations.

The early Kush kingdom reached its apex between 1700 and 1500 BCE. A wealthy culture that produced tombs, fortifications, and palaces, Kush used the plow and the wheel effectively to generate food surpluses. The plow and the wheel diffused south along the Nile into this region and later into Ethiopia, where their use in traditional sub-Saharan African history seemingly reached its limits.

At this time, the rise of Kush coincided with the relative weakening of Egypt. From 1730 to 1575 BCE the Hyksos occupied Egypt, removing Egyptian kings as a threat to Kushite independence. On the other hand, the later decay of Kush (1500 BCE) coincided with the new imperial ambitions of the New Kingdom, when the pharaohs reestablished Egyptian rule over the Upper and Lower Nile. During the most aggressive years of the New Kingdom, between 1570 and 1200 BCE, the pharaohs reasserted Egyptian power and created an empire to secure all its frontiers.

The New Kingdom pharaohs of Egypt extended cultural integration with Kush through aggressive ex-

Flooding from the Nile River in Egypt caused the surrounding lands to be ideal for agriculture, which supported the rise of early civilizations. The river also inspired their travel and commerce. Courtesy of Touraj Daryaee.

As intermediaries between Africa and the Mediterranean, the late Kushite monarchs exchanged animal skins, ebony, ivory, gold, oils, perfumes, and slaves for Roman goods. It was Kushite trade with the Roman world that finally linked the rest of Africa (Egypt, of course, excluded) to a much larger world system. Signs of prosperity included monuments and tombs, complex urban fortifications, elaborate palaces, and fine pottery and jewelry. As part of a larger world system, however, the Kushites also became dependent on successful trade. Once this trade failed, after disease eroded the movement of goods along the Silk Road and Indian Ocean sea lanes (see Chapter Ten), Meröe declined as a commercial center.

And the decay of this trade undermined the power of the late Kushites, the kingdom managing to linger only through the fourth century CE. Then, in 330 CE, a new kingdom emerged to replace Kush: Axum. The rulers of Axum finished off Kushite civilization and created a Christian kingdom centered in northern Ethiopia. In the rainfall zone of this region's highlands, Axum represented an ethnic and linguistic melting pot, the destination of migrants from far-away Yemen into Ethiopia. In the new kingdom, Axumites mixed with Kushites to create a culture that used Semitic speech and script; the people also acquired the dark complexion of sub-Saharan Africans.

With a new capital located at Adulis in a natural harbor along the Red Sea, Axum established a trade network that commanded the Indian Ocean in the waning days of the Roman Empire. Axum's trade routes linked it with India, the East Indies, Iran, the Arabic Peninsula, and the east African coast. African goods exported from Axum made their way as far west as Rome and as far east as Southeast Asia. During the fourth century CE, when Axum replaced Kush as the regional power base, Adulis commanded the Ethiopian plateau, Meröitic Kush, the rich Yemenite highlands, and much of eastern Nilotic Sudan. A king of kings ruled this large empire and held sway over subordinate princes in client states. Yet, like Kush, Axum depended largely on trade for prosperity.

The rise of Islam (see Chapter Eleven of Unit Two) in Arabia changed the condition of commerce for Axum. As a Christian kingdom, Axum began to decay with

pansion south. Yet once decay had again eroded Egyptian power after 1200 BCE, a new Kushite state emerged. Another period of Egyptian weakness, between 1090 and 945 BCE, re-encouraged Kushite monarchs to expand north. By 900 BCE, a new Kushite state had gained control over Lower and Upper Nubia and shifted its capital to Napata, near the fourth cataract. Closer to Egypt than Kerma, Napata revealed the imperial objectives of these new Kushite kings. In the eighth century BCE, the kings of Kush realized their ambition by conquering Egypt, ruling it as the twenty-fifth Egyptian Dynasty.

Yet Kushite control proved short lived as Assyrians wielding iron weapons expanded into Egypt. The Kushites did not yet have an iron technology, due to the fact that they relied on Egypt for contact with the Mediterranean, and the Egyptians did not adopt an iron-based agricultural technology since metal plows could not add more arable land to the Nile Valley. Consequently, iron did not filter into Kush until the Kushites made contact with Assyria. Hence, the Kushite Army was no match for the Assyrians.

Assyrian power swept the Kushites south, where they retreated beyond the reach of this Mesopotamian culture below the fifth cataract. There, the Kushite kings relocated their capital to Meröe. The eventual rise of the Persian Empire and the rejuvenation of Egypt held the Kushite kings in this remote region, but the vitality of their culture continued: Kushite kings extended their sway over Kordofan to the west and south along the Blue and White Nile into Abyssinia. As a centerplace city with an iron technology, Meröe became the key to the diffusion of this powerful metal into sub-Saharan Africa.

The apex of this late Kush kingdom in the first century CE coincided with the trade relations established between the Roman Empire and sub-Saharan Africa.

the fall of Rome in 476 CE. At the same time, the rapid expansion of Muslim power throughout the Middle East isolated Axum. Eclipsed by Islam, Axum's trade eroded in the sixth and seventh centuries CE. Then these conditions of isolation increased with the fall of Sassanian Persia (651 CE; see Chapter Eleven) and the invasions of the White Hun that destroyed Gupta India (535 CE; see Chapter Ten). Although Axum enjoyed cordial relations with the new Muslim domains in both Egypt and on the Red Sea, it ceased to be a center of foreign trade. Loss of commerce shifted the center of cultural gravity southward from the coast into the interior highlands. The continued spread of Muslim power from Egypt into Nilotic Sudan finally closed Axum off from access to the Mediterranean world, while the Indian Ocean became the domain of Islamic sailors and merchants.

Axum represented the last civilization to develop in the ancient sub-Saharan African world. The other sub-Saharan kingdoms of the Sudanese grasslands did not mature as successful civilizations until the middle years of world history. The village patterns already mentioned became common after the first and second centuries CE. They laid down the design for great commercial empires that would emerge during the middle years. A resumption of trade and politics had to wait in these grasslands until the caravan routes restored connections with the Mediterranean after the fall of Rome. Then trade linked the African kingdoms of the Sudanese savannas with the Islamic North African states. This trade served as the organizational basis of sub-Saharan monarchies, but that story belongs to the Middle Ages.

The Americas

As hunter-gatherers, the first people in the Americas most likely followed the migrations of large mammals from Siberia across an exposed land bridge some fifty miles wide on the Bering Straits during the last ice age. Such a trip remained possible until somewhere between 75,000 and 10,000 years ago, when the ice age ended, raising the water level of the world's oceans some 300 feet.

Spreading throughout the two continents to find food, the expanding population of the Native American ancestors developed into a complex set of cultures and economies. Supporting themselves by hunting and gathering, they found the Americas rich in resources. Yet the transition from nomadic life to cultivation proved far more gradual in the Americas than in Eurasia because of geographic isolation.

As mentioned in Chapter One, Eurasia has a broad east-west land axis that proved supportive to cross-cul-

tural communication and the diffusion of plants, animals, tools, and ideas. Travel along this east-west axis occurred through a temperate-zone that was generally hospitable to humans as they took their domesticated plants and animals as far as the climate would allow. In contrast, the Americas have a north-south land axis that discouraged human movement and delayed the communication of significant cultural discoveries. Migration north and south required travel through different climatic zones, which slowed the spread of plant and animal domestication as well as the development of new technology. The early Americans did learn how to control agricultural production, but they had great difficulty sharing this information with one another. Thus, the movement of human populations was possible, but the transfer of plants, ideas, and tools simply did not occur or took much longer than it did elsewhere in the world.

Around 5000 BCE, the people of present-day Mexico discovered how to germinate corn (maize) to acquire their most important symbiosis. To this staple, they added beans, pumpkins, squash, chili peppers, plums, and avocados. Also in 5000 BCE, the people of the Andean highlands domesticated cassava (or manioc) and potatoes to create a second food base for potential cities. To these two staples, the highland farmers added peanuts from the Amazon and quinoa. The spread of these domesticated plants took time.

Corn, however, seemed to travel farther than the numerous varieties of potatoes domesticated by the ancient farmers of the Andes. Corn traveled north from Mexico to become a food source for Native Americans living in what became the United States and Canada. Corn also moved south, crossing the Isthmus of Panama to reach South America. Cultivated around 1500 BCE, corn had reached what is now the southwestern United States, where the Pueblo Indians set up sedentary villages. By 300 BCE, corn had made its way to the forests of northeastern America. Native Americans in the Northeast, however, already knew of cultivation because they had domesticated sunflowers and artichokes before corn arrived.

With the domestication of plants, human populations grew dramatically. Three areas where these concentrations reached a critical mass included the central valley of Mexico, the humid coastal forests of the Gulf of Mexico, and the coast and highlands of the central Andes. Elsewhere, jungles and rainforests in South America, the deserts and arid interior mountain basins of northern Mexico, and similar arid zones in the North American West and Southwest created barriers to cultivation. Even with the fertility of the best sites, however, permanent villages did not appear in Mexico until ca. 2500 BCE, several thousand years after the beginning of agriculture in Eurasia. This delay resulted from the nature of corn: it took time for Native farmers to discover the method of soaking corn in lime dissolved in water (to release the niacin) and selectively breed it before corn provided a rich food supply.

Like the farmers of Mesoamerica, the first cultivators of the Andes on the South American continent had a very difficult time domesticating potatoes and beans. They selected beans and potatoes to supplement a very scarce food supply generated by local game, beginning this process around 5000 BCE. Living at 8,500 feet, the Guitarrero people gathered fruits, potatoes, beans, lima beans, and chili peppers to supplement their diet of deer and rabbit. In the process of selecting their foods, the Guitarrero gained control over the reproductive cycle of plants capable of living at high altitudes. Grown on small plots of land near rivers and streams, potatoes and beans soon became the most common foods in the Andean diet.

Eventually ancient farmers in the Andes developed different types of potatoes that could grow at various altitudes and in all kinds of soil and weather. As mentioned, some of the potatoes that they had chosen evolved into a rich starchy food highly preferred by humans. Others grew well at low altitudes, and farmers selected them because of the water they could store. Some grew fast enough so that they could adjust to the very short growing season found at the highest elevations of the Andes. Still others were selected because they could be easily stored after they had been pressed and frozen in the cold mountain air. In fact, experts believe that some three thousand varieties of potatoes exist today because of the careful selection process begun by these ancient South American farmers.

Accordingly, domesticated corn and potatoes produced so much food that Native American civilizations could emerge based solely on a Neolithic (New Stone Age) technology. Hence, ancient American farmers discovered gold, silver, copper, tin, and lead but did not develop metallurgy to create useful alloys like bronze (except for perhaps the Inca). As a result, the absence of bronze or iron throughout nearly all of Native American history reflected the severe conditions of isolation that separated the Americas from the rest of the world. The possibility of civilization developing without a bronze or iron technology becomes problematic when one considers the powerful role these metals played in shaping the cultures of Eurasia and Africa.

The disadvantages generated from cultivation without metal tools were compounded by the absence of the plow, the wheel, and large domesticated mammals. Like much of Africa, isolation and local conditions in the Americas created an agriculture that relied solely on hoes and pointed sticks. Could stone tools, hoes, and wooden cultivation sticks prove efficient enough to generate the needed food surpluses to produce great cities? Such restrictions placed on food production expanded the question of how civilization could have developed under such conditions. Nevertheless, civilization did occur in the Americas, which requires some explanation.

Given the low labor requirements and high caloric yields generated by corn and potatoes as compared to grains like wheat and rice, farmers producing corn and potatoes received substantial surpluses. These two plants had to have supplied sufficient food to release the urban division of labor needed to complete all the tasks necessary for both building and maintaining large cities despite hand-held tools and a stone technology. In fact, corn and potatoes calories must have proved so generous as to release far more people to urbanize than did wheat or rice when compared to the same expenditures of farm labor in food production. Finally, these generous food sources had to have supplied enough energy to allow Native Americans to satisfy their particular ambitions for building the richly decorated monuments found in both Mesoamerica and the Andes.

While corn and potatoes released urban labor in the Americas, geographic isolation allowed dense populations of Native Americans to concentrate in their cities without suffering the epidemics common to Eurasia and Africa. The early urbanites in the Americas led relatively disease-free histories. Infections occurred, but the absence of contact with Europe, Asia, and Africa quarantined the Native Americans, north and south, from the devastating epidemics that might have destroyed the internal balance of their civilizations. The quarantine enjoyed by the Native Americans allowed them to expand their numbers, even though it eventually created the disastrous disease diffusion that played a dreadful role in the Columbian Exchange (1492–1650 CE). This exchange took the lives of an estimated 90 percent of the Native American population and reveals how powerful this geographic quarantine must once have been.

Furthermore, Native Americans, like most Africans, did not have the impressive list of domesticable animals common to the Eurasian world. This lack of close association with animals reduced the animal protein consumed by Native Americans, but the absence of a close association with animals also reduced the possibility of a disease connection developing between humans and their herds; in the Eurasian world, this connection has generated an estimated 276 cross-species diseases that have developed over the course of human history.

At the same time, the scarcity of animal protein in the Native American diet (except for dogs, geese, ducks, fish, and even mice), has led some anthropologists to argue that Native Americans developed ritual cannibalism. These anthropologists explain the practice of human sacrifice, the Native American fascination with blood rituals, and the consumption of the bodies afterwards as a means of satisfying a craving for meat. Today, however, modern anthropologists and historians hotly debate the prevalence of this form of religious cannibalism. There is, however, sufficient evidence of fire-charred and split human bones to support the probability of humans having been used as a food source.

High-calorie yields from plants with low-labor requirements, low levels of lethal infections and few epidemics, and the possibility of using human beings as a food source sustained Native American urban numbers. Thus, Native American cities emerged despite the absence of a metal technology, the plow, or the wheel. And these cities proved very impressive as first efforts at building civilizations. As a result, the Native American cultures of Mesoamerica and the Andes equaled the accomplishments in Eurasia and Africa even through Native Americans lived in severe geographic isolation.

The Origins of America's First Cities

Just when the human history of the Americas actually began is the subject of scholarly debate. The disciplinary tools of anthropology and archaeology continue to provide us with ever-more refined and exact knowledge about early Native American communities, but the exact time frame remains murky, broadly defined and subject to disagreement. This is due to the absence of writing among most of the Native American cultures; hence, we do not have the benefit of the accounts of any eyewitnesses to help guide the inquiry.

As mentioned above, based on the growing body of evidence, it is clear that several human migrations began crossing into North America from Asia as early as thirty thousand years ago, although some scholars posit an even earlier entry. These nomadic hunters and gatherers used the temporary land bridge across the Bering Strait that appeared during the last major period of glaciation. This first group spread themselves thinly throughout the Americas, eventually reaching Chile, Argentina and southern Brazil. There, they found a terrestrial paradise of extensive plains, woodlands, and huge populations of large animals.

The migrations across the land bridge continued until about 9,000 BCE. As the climate changed and warmed, the bridge receded below the waters of the Arctic Ocean and the great movement of humans from Asia to America slowed to a trickle. The end of the ice age also introduced significant climatic changes, which dried out the grasslands and forced the Paleolithic (Old Stone Age) hunters to adapt. Also, evidence of overhunting helps explain the extermination of potentially useful large mammal species. Such evidence includes the abundance of American mammal bones with a common date of extinction (11,000 BCE), the discovery of numerous mammal skeletons with spear points in their ribs that coincide with this date, and the fact that hunters migrating southward found species that had never seen humans before and so had no fear of them. Whether climate, overhunting, or both killed these large mammals, from Canada to Peru, the people of the Americas largely turned to smaller animals, birds, fish, seeds, berries and roots for their livelihood as the larger huntable species died out. Necessity forced human communities to develop slowly the systematic cultivation of edible plants as their main food source.

It is important to reiterate that these great changes in the human condition took place in relative isolation in the Americas. While there may have been occasional contact with outsiders, the influence that Africa, Asia, and Europe exerted on each other due to their proximity has no parallel for the Americas. The centuries between 10,000 and roughly 3500 BCE witnessed a steady transition from primitive agriculture, to sedentary village life, to a gradual increase in human population. Hunting bands certainly co-existed in the same areas as the new villages for some time. Archaeologists working in the southern regions of the Western Hemisphere have uncovered evidence revealing the careful cultivation of maize, beans, and squash. Manioc (cassava), a tropical root that is a good source of carbohydrates, and the potato joined this basic group sometime later, probably by 5000 BCE. When these crops were added to hunting and the domestication of animals such as turkeys, llamas, alpacas, and dogs, by 3500 BCE it is clear that these early communities developed sufficient resources to sustain life and build complex societies.

Although the isolation of the Western Hemisphere allowed humans there to develop distinctive cultures, some disadvantages became clear the moment Europeans appeared. The region lacked large domesticated animals such as horses, cattle, sheep, goats, pigs, or water buffalo, all of which are valuable as beasts of burden and as food resources. Epidemic diseases such as smallpox and cholera were absent from the civilizations that developed in Mexico and the Andean highlands. This meant that Native American communities possessed no immunity to any such diseases when the Spanish, Portuguese, and other Europeans unwittingly introduced these killing agents to the Americas during the first period of contact. The mortality rates of Native Americans in the sixteenth century are so large as to be almost incomprehensible. The use of hard metals such as iron, commonplace in Europe and Africa, had no counterpart in the Americas. Although the artisans of civilizations from Mexico to Peru worked beautiful creations in gold and other soft metals, they lacked tools and weapons smelted from iron ore.

By 3500 BCE, two great cultural hearths emerged in Mesoamerica and the Andes. In the great central valley of Mexico, extending from the Pacific to the Caribbean coasts, complex cultures flourished and grew. Farther south, along the two-thousand-mile Andean highlands stretching from Peru to northern Chile, another great center evolved through the centuries, slowly developing a large agricultural base.

In the case of Mexico, the great central valley with its abundant lakes and rivers, rich volcanic soil, and agreeable climate offered the wandering human tribes and bands a large area of diverse landforms in which to settle. The valley became home to successive waves of migrating peoples. By the time the Spanish arrived in the early sixteenth century, scholars believe the great valley supported between 15 and 20 million inhabitants. As we shall see, similar population growth developed in the south, in present-day Central America, to the tropical Caribbean coastal area, and into the mountain ranges and arid lands of western Mexico, a broad geographic and cultural region often referred to as Mesoamerica.

Along the Andean highlands the steep rise from the coastal areas to the nearby mountain ranges created a narrow band crossed by numerous rivers that supplied developing human communities with enough fresh water to conduct extensive agriculture despite a natural aridity. Human communities there discovered an abundance of sealife along the coasts. The many valleys created by the mountain ranges offered ideal sites for the long and successful transition from nomadic wandering to sedentary village life. Maize, potatoes, quinoa, and various bean crops all flourished in this zone.

In both great regions, or cultural hearths, the transition to village life eventually influenced the emergence of tribal kingdoms. An ever-expanding population made it necessary for these formative cultures to develop surpluses from high-yielding crops. The ability of human communities in both areas to do this and then create trade and complex social, religious, and military organizations set the stage for greater advances in the centuries that followed.

As human communities grew in size and complexity throughout the Americas, the first cities began to

appear despite a vast diversity of cultures. The southern part of the hemisphere witnessed major changes in the centuries after 1000 BCE. The journey from nomadic hunting and gathering bands to villages of several hundred farmers producing maize, beans, and squashes varied in both time and intensity across the region. While the climate, soil, and resources of Mexico's central valley encouraged the concentration of people there early on, humans in the northern tropics of Brazil and the southern plains of Argentina hunted in nomadic bands for centuries, undisturbed by such changes. As scholars investigated the different regions of the continent before European contact in 1492, they discovered that local conditions and population density often determined how quickly communities moved from one stage of development to the next.

In analyzing these stages, specialists in the precontact history of the Americas use terms such as *archaic*, *formative*, and *classic* to describe the technology, social organization, and food production capabilities of various groups. The archaic stage, beginning around 9000 BCE, saw human communities slowly domesticate plants, gradually limit their movement to a particular area, and in some cases produce simple pottery. They thus evolved from food gatherers to food producers, leading to the next stage.

During the formative era, which began sometime between 2500 and 1500 BCE, communities developed high-yield crops, such as corn and beans, used irrigation systematically, brought pottery-making and weaving to advanced levels, and began to support urban groups such as priests and artisans.

Mesoamerica

In Mesoamerica (an area that includes the present-day southwestern United States, Mexico, and Central America), the most important stage of human history before the arrival of Europeans was the classic period. During this time, which coincided with the start of the Christian era in the Mediterranean world, indigenous peoples built large ceremonial sites and cities of immense complexity, both in their construction and political structures. These communities developed systems for counting their agricultural surpluses, developed writing, and recorded their observations and ideas in stone and on animal-skin manuscripts, and created sophisticated religious belief systems. They also made objects of enduring beauty using precious stones and soft metals.

The Olmecs

Growing populations led to the beginnings of village life along Mexico's gulf coastal lowlands. It is difficult, even with the recent archeological discoveries in Mexico and Central America, to say with absolute certainty which group led the way, but the *Olmecs* get credit for being the chief catalysts in the development of Mesoamerican civilization. Based on evidence gathered from archeological work, it appears that Olmecs developed ceremonial centers (between 1500 and 1200 BCE) at Tres Zapotes and La Venta, along the eastern coast of Mexico, which included pyramids, tombs, *stele* (stone columns inscribed with the names of gods, warriors, and kings) and sculptures. The innovations of writing and calendar-making probably originated at these Olmec sites, along with *Nahuatl,* one of the most important languages spoken throughout Mesoamerica. The Olmecs developed a high-yield agriculture based on corn, beans, squashes, and chili peppers. Each food item contributed to a balanced diet high in carbohydrates, protein, minerals, and vitamins.

This system produced a food surplus that allowed the Olmecs to free members of the community to take on special roles such as merchants, artisans, priests, soldiers, and political leaders. As the population increased and the sites grew in complexity, religious and social rituals emerged. Scholars can find traces of Olmec influence throughout the region. Carvings and masks representing a jaguar god, birds, serpents, and human beings making offerings to various elemental gods and goddesses indicate a rich cultural life. Although the Olmec cultures domesticated turkeys and small dogs, they did not possess cattle, horses, or other large animals.

Mexican calendar stone. From *Symbols, Signs, & Signets,* by Ernst Lehner.

In spite of the success enjoyed by this early cultural hearth, it began to collapse and disintegrate shortly after 400 BCE. Scholars are unable to say precisely why this happened, although the usual suspects of soil exhaustion, overpopulation, nomadic invasions, and drought and disease are all logical culprits. Olmec culture is recalled today by the stunning stone sculptures of gigantic human heads, some of which stand nine feet tall, mostly in the coastal lowlands of the Gulf of Mexico.

Other cultures that flourished during this time and after include Zapotec communities in Mexico's Oaxaca and Puebla regions. The extensive hilltop site at Monte Alban remained a viable Zapotec center of trade and culture until 1000 CE. Temples, marketplaces, monuments and elaborate stone dwellings indicate a high level of achievement. Even as Olmec culture declined, two important new cultures established themselves in different parts of Mesoamerica and emerged as centers of trade, agriculture, and artistic greatness. In central Mexico's great valley, Teotihuacan (the "city of the gods" as the Aztecs would later name it in awe of its builders), emerged as an agricultural village around 500 BCE and eventually became a vast ceremonial and artistic site (see below). To the east, more than sixty major sites supported a population of several million inhabitants.

The Maya

The culture of the *Maya* developed throughout an extensive region comprising southeastern Mexico (the Yucatan Peninsula), most of present-day Guatemala, parts of Belize, Honduras, and El Salvador. The core area of Mayan communities extended from the lowlands of Guatemala to the arid highlands of the Yucatan. Large sites such as Tikal probably had populations of more than 40,000, with dozens of smaller villages in their immediate vicinity housing thousands of farmers, artisans, and merchants. The smaller villages had strong clan, religious, and economic relations with the larger sites, supplying them with food, clothing, salt, labor, and other important commodities. In return, Tikal, Palenque, and Kaminaljuyu offered the villagers military protection from rival sites as well as serving as a center for religious ceremonies, food distribution, and marketplaces. Modern research makes it clear that people in these sites often warred with each other, boasting of their conquests on the walls of temples and palaces, sacrificing captured warriors, and engaging in political and social intrigues worthy of any modern state.

The most significant period of Mayan civilization spanned the centuries 300 to 900 CE, during which the artistic and social accomplishments of the individual sites were impressive. These included spectacular chartings of the heavens, elaborate calendars, sophisticated mathematics, the development of the concept of zero, complex ceremonial centers, and magnificent pyramids. Yet Mayan communities in Guatemala declined rapidly after about 800 CE. And while the sites enjoyed little political unity, the ceremonial and religious center at Chichen Itza gradually exercised some regional control in a loose imperial setting after 900 CE. Toltec invaders from central Mexico encouraged this development. They took control of Chichen Itza and introduced new types of warfare, an increased focus on large-scale human sacrifice to appease new deities, and more sophisticated forms of architecture and building. After 1200 CE Chichen Itza's influence declined and the site was abandoned. Mayapan emerged in the Yuca-tan as the new dominate site, controlling much of the peninsula for two centuries. This last great independent Mayan center was destroyed in 1441 CE, as local villages revolted against its authoritarian control. As fate would have it, the rapid decline of Mayan power and unity made the Spanish conquest relatively easy in the middle decades of the next century.

The success of the Maya in both the arid highlands of the Yucatan and the tropical lowlands of Guatemala and Belize stemmed from their ability to produce a reliable and consistent surplus in corn, beans and squashes, fish, small game and cotton over an extended period. In this they resemble many ancient cultures that relied on food and material surpluses to free members of their communities to engage in urban labors. And even though the Maya faced problems, such as reliable water supplies and rugged jungle terrain, depending on the location of their villages, the use of irrigation canals, raised fields, slash-and-burn agricultural techniques; and careful planning for planting and harvesting, as well as the conscious selection of which fields to plant or let lie fallow allowed the Maya to support a population of several million people.

By the middle of its classic period (300–900 CE), Mayan culture was highly stratified, with hereditary noble families ruling important sites and passing down control from one generation to the next. Priests, soldiers, merchants, artisans, farmers, and slaves all found their place in major centers such as Copan as well as in the smaller villages that ringed the great sites. Multistoried palaces, temples, public plazas, and marketplaces characterized sites like Copan. Priest-kings erected stele to record their civil, military, and religious accomplishments. (Only in the last few decades have scholars been able to decode these names, events, and dates.) Relatively few Mayan sites have been fully explored and studied in their complexity, leading specialists to predict that our understanding and knowledge of this dynamic culture will increase dramatically in the future.

One of the better-preserved examples of Mayan architecture, the Temple of Kulkulcan is the grandest structure at Chichen Itza. © 2006 Vagabum Mike Lopez (www.vagabum.com).

Among the accomplishments cited above, time was a central concern of the Maya and they constructed several calendars for religious and agricultural purposes. The agricultural calendar followed the solar year and contained 365 days, with key times for planting, watering, and harvesting carefully recorded. Months, days, and years were all named, and it was believed that being born on a fortunate day heavily influenced one's chances in life. Mayan priests developed the concept of zero, as part of a complicated mathematics that allowed them to manage, among other tasks, large calculations of time, and to track with precision the changing positions of the sun, the moon and the stars.

The Maya also developed a form of writing, using ideographic elements similar to those found in Egyptian hieroglyphics. This allowed them to record important events, religious ideas, prophecies, poems, stories, and legends. Unhappily, the Spanish conquerors destroyed almost all of the thousands of folded-bark paper books that Mayan priests had created over the centuries; only a handful remain for scholars to study.

The Maya worshipped hundreds of principal deities associated with nature. Gods and goddesses linked with rain, thunder, the heavens, corn, animals, fate, death, and birth populated the unseen world. Offerings of corn, animals, human blood and, eventually, people became necessary to appease these deities and guarantee success in this world and the next. Because the Maya believed there was always the possibility that this world might end suddenly in a mighty catastrophe, only a careful observation of the state of the world by priests trained to comprehend the order of things might stave off disaster.

Given all their attention to signs and wonders, the question arises: what accounts for the rapid decline of Mayan culture after 900 CE? As usual, scholars suspect soil exhaustion, overpopulation, internal warfare, outside invasion (from central Mexico, most probably

Toltec warriors) and disease. The precise cause awaits further exploration and study of this marvelous Meso-american culture.

Teotihuacán

Some thirty miles north of present-day Mexico City, another important culture flourished roughly during the same era as the Mayans. The city of Teotihuacán developed and rose to a "golden age" of classic civilization between 200 and 650 CE. The city featured huge temples honoring the Sun and the Moon and broad avenues flanked by palaces and marketplaces. The favorable climate and soil of central Mexico, combined with sophisticated social organization, allowed the farmers of Teotihuacán to support an ever growing urban population during this classic era. Centuries later when they encountered it, the Aztecs viewed Teotihuacán with great reverence.

As many as 200,000 people may have lived in this great center at its peak of influence around 650 CE. Its merchants and artisans dominated central Mexico, extending their reach north into the southwestern United States, and south into Guatemala. The Mayan sites in Guatemala most probably fell under the control of Teotihuacán at this time.

It appears from the archeological record that the people of Teotihuacán dominated central Mexico through trade, religious ceremonies, and resource development. Their tools made of fine obsidian (volcanic glass) and a distinctive orange-tinged pottery were highly sought and valued throughout Mesoamerica.

It appears that the people of Teotihuacán erected few defensive structures to ward off possible invasion or attack, at least until after 500 CE, and scholars believe that priests played a predominate role in this culture. Perhaps facing increased military pressure from nomadic invaders from the north, Teotihucán began to

Also known as "The Pyramid of the Sun," Teotihuacán was a prominent spiritual site long before the Aztecs. © 2006 Vagabum Mike Lopez (www.vagabum.com).

expand its influence through military means. Interestingly, just as the Maya and cultures to the west and south of central Mexico began to experience distress, Teotihuacán began a rapid decline. Although much of the artwork and descriptive books written on animal skins or bark-paper were destroyed in the conflicts that raged at the site, we do know that the people of Teotihuacán referred to the period 650–700 CE as the "time of troubles"; during those years Teotihuacán was invaded and ultimately destroyed.

Yet even as some areas of Mesoamerica slid into decline, other cultures rose to take the leading role. To the south, in the Andean highlands, hunter-gatherer groups evolved along similar lines, developing reliable cultivation techniques after 2500 BCE.

South America

In the Andean highlands, an area extending some 2,000 miles on a north-south axis from present-day Ecuador to northern Chile, human communities followed much the same pattern as their contemporaries to the north. Hunter-gatherers penetrated this area between 12,000 and 10,000 BCE, eventually settling into coastal villages around 2500 BCE. The villagers of this formative period cultivated crops such as beans and squashes and relied on the rich Pacific waters to supply them with fish and other edible marine organisms. Village life began developing in the coastal valleys after 2000 BCE, and in the highlands above the valleys shortly thereafter. Agricultural surpluses enabled these villages to begin producing pottery and textiles of locally grown cotton as well as building temples, storehouses, and ceremonial sites.

Researchers use the term *Chavin* to describe one of the earliest of these important centers (named after the modern town nearby). Chavin culture spread throughout what is now Peru from 900 to about 300 BCE and is characterized by its fine pottery, weaving, and stylized artwork. Over the next thousand years, numerous successful communities developed along coastal South America, the inland valleys, and nearby highlands. Corn became the important crop introduced through Central America, and populations expanded to fill the available land.

Although a limited exchange of ideas and crops occurred, regular trade and contact between the developing communities of South America and Mexico remained difficult at best, due to the daunting expanses of mountain ranges, jungles, and swamps that separate Central American countries such as Panama and Costa Rica from Columbia, Ecuador, and Peru. Despite these limitations, techniques for working soft metals such as gold, silver, and copper into tools and jewelry made their way north into present-day Nicaragua, Guatemala, and Mexico, just as new crops such as corn traveled south to the Andean highlands.

Another important Andean culture, the *Mochica*, built extensive irrigation systems in the highlands and developed regional economies based on exchanging products such as potatoes, llama wool and meat, cotton textiles, fish, and corn between roughly 300 and 700 CE. They did not, however, leave modern scholars a writing system to decode and study. Their major legacy is the beautiful and finely wrought ceramic vessels, plates, bowls, and vases that portray everyday people in a variety of common activities, from farming to war-making. Animals, gods and goddesses, kings and commoners decorate these rare treasures from the Andean past. During the time the Maya dominated the Yucatan Peninsula, while Teotihuacán controlled the economic and spiritual life of central Mexico, a number of large states rose to power in the Andean region. These states created a systematic agriculture based on irrigated fields of potatoes, grains, and vegetables, as well as employing the ocean resources of the nearby Pacific and grazing herds of llamas and alpacas. They learned to work gold and silver into decorative art, and weave exquisite cotton and wool textiles. The Mochica culture eventually collapsed, replaced after 1000 CE by a new and expanding society: the *Chimú*. None of these early cultures managed to create the complex social, political, economic, and military structures put into place by the greatest of the Andean states, the *Inca* (see Chapter Sixteen).

Although central Mexico, the Yucatan Peninsula, and the Andean region represent the most sophisticated human cultures in the period to about 700 CE, the Western Hemisphere included a wide variety of other human cultures. Along the interior rivers and coastal areas of Brazil, thousands of bands of Neolithic hunter-gatherers roamed the woodlands, fishing, hunting, and gathering. They gradually developed small villages, basic agriculture, and craftworks before the Portuguese arrived in 1500.

At the same time, the Caribbean islands offered shelter and food to millions of people, who apparently felt no need to build temples, palaces, and irrigation systems because local conditions did not demand or encourage any such effort. Fishing, gathering, and cultivating crops imported from coastal Mexico and South America provided sufficient resources to support large and successful human communities on these islands.

As we can see, it is quite possible to discover nearly every stage of human development within close geographical proximity at roughly the same time in the Americas. This fact underscores the incredible diversity of human communities in this region before much interaction with the rest of the world occurred.

Yet when compared to the Eurasian cultures of Rome, Han China, and Gupta India, the cities of Mexico and the Andes reveal how the absence of iron, large domesticated draft animals, and the plow and the wheel limited the develop of civilization. The cities of Mexico emerged on a different time scale and grew to a size restricted by food surpluses. Accordingly, each of the classical examples of cities in the Americas developed several thousand years after their Eurasian counterparts and supported about $1/5$ the number of people, which underscores the value of cultural diffusion, the flow of ideas, tools, plants, and animals between human communities that took place in Eurasia.

Suggested Reading

Berger, Iris, and E. Francis White, *Women in Sub-Sahara Africa: Restoring Women to History* (Bloomington: Indiana University Press, 1995).

Bohannan, Paul, and Philip Curtin, *Africa and Africans*, Revised Edition (Prospect Heights, Ill.: Waveland Press, Inc., 1995).

Burstein, Stanley, ed., *Ancient African Civilizations: Kush and Axum* (Princeton: Princeton University Press, 1998).

Collins, R. O., ed., *Problems in African History: The Precolonial Centuries* (Princeton, N.J.: Markus Wiener Publishers, 1993).

Curtin, Philip, et al., *African History*, Revised Edition (New York: Longman, Inc., 1984).

Davidson, Basil, *Africa: A History of a Continent* (New York: Macmillan Company, 1972).

Ehret, Christopher, *The Civilization of Africa: A History to 1800* (Charlottesville, Va.: University of Virginia Press, 2001).

Fage, J. D., *A History of Africa* (New York: Alfred A. Knopf, 1978).

July, Robert W., *A History of the African People*, Third Edition (New York: Charles Scribner's Sons, 1980).

Mokhtar, G., *Ancient Civilizations of Africa*, Volume II, *UNESCO General History of Africa* (Berkeley: University of California Press, 1981).

Oliver, R., *The African Experience* (New York: Harper Collins, 1991).

Shaw, Thurston, *Nigeria: Its Archeology and Early History* (London: Thames & Hudson, 1978).

Shillington, Kevin, *History of Africa* (London: Macmillan Company, 1989).

Turnbill, Collin M., *Man in Africa* (Garden City, N.Y.: Anchor/Doubleday, 1976).

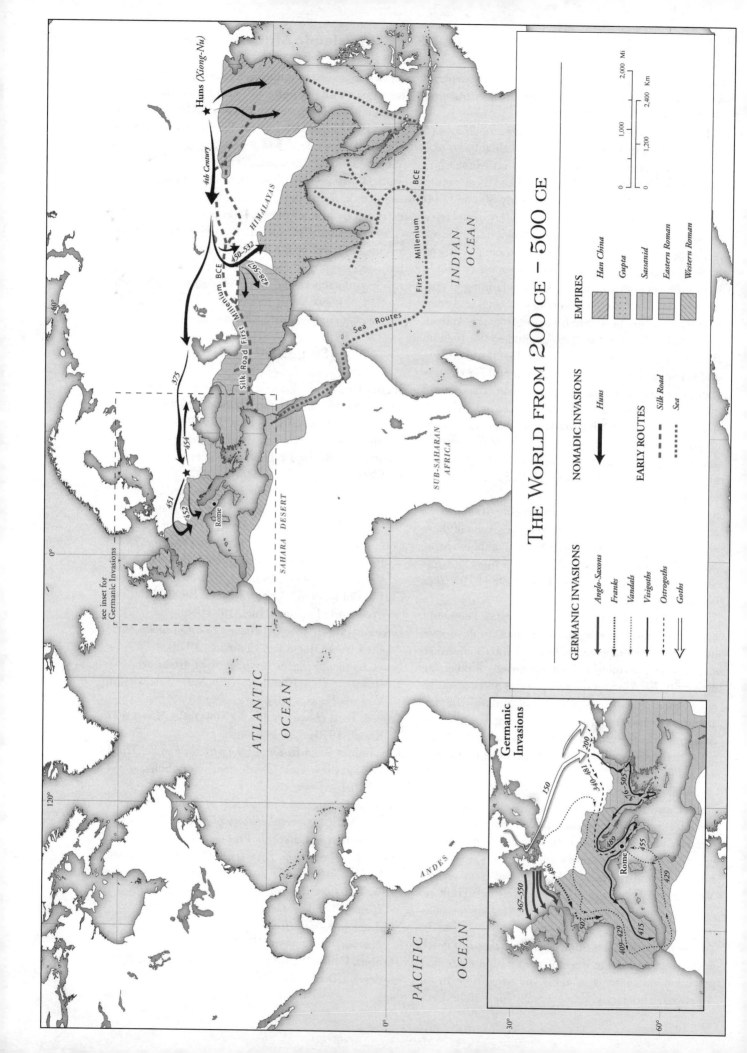

THE WORLD FROM 200 CE – 500 CE

GERMANIC INVASIONS

Anglo-Saxons
Franks
Vandals
Visigoths
Ostrogoths
Goths

NOMADIC INVASIONS

Huns

EARLY ROUTES

Silk Road
Sea

EMPIRES

Han China
Gupta
Sassanid
Eastern Roman
Western Roman

Huns (Xiong-Nu)

4th Century

HIMALAYAS

450–532

428–595

375

Silk Road First Millennium BCE

First Millennium BCE

Sea Routes

454

451

452

Rome

INDIAN OCEAN

SUB-SAHARAN AFRICA

SAHARA DESERT

ATLANTIC OCEAN

PACIFIC OCEAN

ANDES

see inset for Germanic Invasions

Germanic Invasions

200

340–481

516–565

489

455

429

150

367–550

507

686

409–429

415

Rome

2,000 Mi

2,400 Km

1,000

1,200

0

0

0°

0°

30°

60°

60°

120°

X

THE FALL
of the Ancient Eurasian World

The fall of the ancient civilizations of Rome, Han China, and Gupta India shared common features in part or in whole. The crises that brought Rome and Han China down involved a failure of leadership, a gradual internal disintegration, growing economic chaos, an inadequate labor force, epidemic disease, and a breakdown of loyalty to the centerplace city. Gupta India collapsed more swiftly due to the difficulties of organizing a stable central government on the subcontinent. At the same time, because each of these empires had developed a system of trade with the other two, the crisis alerted the nomadic confederations from Central Asia of the opportunities for quick conquests. Trade had enticed a vast sea of herding peoples into a system of contacts with the sedentary cultures living in the West, in China, and in India. Such trade had kept the warlike shepherds aware of the relative strength and health of their settled neighbors. Thus, internal disintegration combined with external military pressures to destroy the ancient Eurasian world. Internal collapse revealed how Rome's, Han China's, and Gupta India's methods of organizing their imperial systems had reached a point of exhaustion that none of them could address. External military pressures revealed how all three fell to nomadic invasions that exploited the chance to pillage the remains of the failing Eurasian system.

The internal problems of Rome, Han China, and Gupta India fit within a basic pattern of life that had troubled ancient civilizations from their inception. The methods used to develop ancient empires often carried within themselves internal flaws that set decay in motion. Ironically, success only nurtured the seeds of destruction. Success meant that human populations tended to grow to the limits of what the contemporary agricultural technology could support. In addition, the conquest of rival empires usually created problems of cultural assimilation that undermined loyalty to the centerplace city during times of crisis. Another consequence of empire was economic dependency on a vast

and frequently overtaxed peasant population, which made the centerplace city susceptible to financial instability. Finally, disease was a constant threat to sedentary societies and periodically cut deep swaths through the labor pool necessary to maintain the standing armies and tax base needed to defend the frontier.

At the same time, nomads sitting on the frontiers looked with envy at the wealth enjoyed by the privileged few who ruled settled civilizations. Eager to test their military prowess against the defenses of these successful sedentary cultures, mounted nomadic raiders determined when the time was ripe for conquest. Meanwhile, success among the nomads usually meant that their herds had grown beyond the limits of what their pastures could feed. Consequently, their own population pressures required that these nomads challenge rival tribes for control of their grasslands. And if these nomads turned to trade to supplement their income, they invariably increased their population to the point where they could no longer live on what their herds could produce. Accordingly, a combination of trade and success at herding often created a potential crisis for nomads that might spark war between whole tribal confederations. Should a disruption in trade due to internal problems suffered by sedentary cultures deny these nomads a source of wealth on which they had grown dependent, then waves of invasions might begin. Finally, a combination of both the quest for new pastures and the recovery of income caused by the loss of trade, might set in motion vast hordes of invaders to besiege agricultural societies.

The fall of the ancient Eurasian world revealed both sets of problems, internal decay and external nomadic threat. Just how this specific combination of crises caused the collapse of these three empires provides the key to understanding the way the ancient era came to an end. In addition, the specific circumstances that destroyed ancient Eurasia laid the foundation for the next great historical epoch: the Middle Years of world history.

Trade, Disease, and Religious Ideas

In the history of the collapse of the great ancient civilizations, the methods used to create a semiglobal trade network combined with a series of unexpected social, economic, and intellectual events that led to a general crisis. Rome and Han China had laid the foundation for the first trans-Asian trade system just as each center had reached its cultural apex. Rome decisively defeated Carthage, its most dangerous rival, in 202 BCE, while the Han Dynasty had established control over the settled provinces of China in the same year. Just as Rome continued its series of conquests to consolidate its hold on the rest of the Mediterranean world, so the Han Dynasty expanded both west and south to build an empire that became the traditional model for the Chinese until 1911 CE. In the process, Rome changed from a Republic based on citizenship into a Principate in which one man ruled with absolute power, while Han China extended imperial authority over a vast sea of peasant farmers. Each empire carved out a system of government that ruled populations of roughly equal number in regions also nearly equal in geographic space. The timing of these great political successes allowed both Rome and Han China to extend their commercial networks toward one another during this period of expansion. The result was the creation of the Silk Road and the sea-lanes of the Indian Ocean.

A system of trade began that exceeded anything the ancient world had seen before. Success by both Rome and Han China had drawn not only their own two empires into a pattern of commercial exchanges, but had also linked both with India. Accordingly, an immense trade network began, one that saw the three great cultural hearths join with one another in a process of exchange that accelerated diffusion to a degree as yet unknown. Goods, ideas, and germs began to travel with merchants from one point to another between the years 100 BCE and 300 CE. Each civilization bound up in this vast commercial system responded to the way these goods, ideas, and germs changed the course of their own specific histories over the next four hundred years. At the same time, nomads in Central Asia found themselves drawn ever closer into this semiglobal trade network as they developed a new level of dependency on the wealth that traveled through their territories. This curious mix of events created the external circumstances that eventually linked with the internal crises to bring the ancient era of world history to an end.

Trade provided a means to sustain human life beyond what a culture could normally produce for itself. Raw materials imported from nomadic territories into a sedentary culture created a livelihood for shepherds, manufacturers, and merchants that normally would not have existed. Should these raw materials be converted into farm tools that in turn allowed local farmers to expand their cultivation, then the production of new food surpluses could feed a growing number of people living in a sedentary culture. Conversely, should nomads engage in trade and acquire access to an external food source that sustained their local populations, then their numbers could soon grow beyond what their herds could feed. Accordingly, trade in general stimulated the growth of human numbers by integrating the productive potential of several foreign sedentary and nomadic cultures into a common matrix of exchanges.

As a result, a general dependency developed around trade that caused each culture involved to maintain or expand, whatever it could contribute. Yet if something should suddenly happen to erode a commercial network, then several populations of different peoples involved in the exchanges would suddenly become vulnerable to a loss of livelihood. Trade, once started, had to continue in order to feed those who had come to rely on it for making a living.

Meanwhile, traveling along with merchants were hidden agents of change that had nothing to do with trade itself. These agents were germs and ideas. As invisible passengers who accompanied merchants on their trips to distant markets, germs and ideas made trade between foreign cultures potentially very dangerous, and the way they affected human, plant, and animal populations in sedentary civilizations made them crucial in the wellbeing of the ancient Eurasian world. In other words, even as accidental byproducts of trade, periodic epidemics caused by the movement of germs and changes in religious beliefs caused by the introduction of new ideas played a central role in the fall of the ancient world. In telling this story, the history of disease must come first.

As we have seen, disease is a biological companion of intensive agriculture. To recap, disease history began the moment humans gave up a nomadic life, settled in one place, and could no longer escape the germs they and their attendant plants, animals, and waste products attracted. These germs thrived in the new environment sedentary agriculture created. Parasites that fed on domesticated animals evolved into organisms that infected humans. The plants that fed humans frequently attracted rodents, insects, and mollusks that not only transmitted disease, but also consumed potential calories that might have been used to maintain the strength that people needed to resist these pathogens. Finally, the rich supply of waste products created by the human consumption and digestion of food enticed scavengers such as flies, worms, bacteria, fungi, and viruses to take up residence with farmers, often inhabiting any available host. The combination of all three sources of disease generated a history of intragroup contagion that created local epidemics unique to every great sedentary civilization. Just as each cultural hearth had its own specific collection of domesticated plants and animals, so each sedentary agricultural society produced its own group of germs.

The way diseases develop over time is a process called microevolution. This process generated two biological histories: one for the germs, and the other for humans. The parasitic pathogens that fed off a sedentary society were those that had adapted to local conditions and, as opportunists, consumed whatever farmers could supply in terms of the nutrients these germs needed to survive. The infections produced by these parasites traveled from host to host via a series of disease vectors that these pathogens blindly refined as they adjusted to the life cycles of their successive hosts.

How specific cultures developed endemic diseases also reflected the way in which the human hosts adjusted to the invading parasites. Whenever a new infectious pathogen entered a sedentary culture, an epidemic erupted because the local human population had no immunities to it. The death rate jumped dramatically, but those people with the greatest resistance survived and some of them reproduced. Since humans use sexual reproduction, the mixed DNA of the father and the mother could make their offspring even more resistant to any new cycle of the disease. Hence, the second generation of humans proved more resistant than the first, but the death rate from the disease might still remain high. By the third generation, however, resistance in the local human gene pool had become common, and children seemed to be the only victims of infection. These children still died in large numbers because at birth they still had low immunity.

Meanwhile, the disease continued to adapt to their human hosts as the latter developed resistance. Those pathogens that killed their hosts died as well, not a successful strategy for the pathogen. Those that infected but did not kill their hosts, survived and reproduced. Accordingly, while the human population increased its resistance to this new disease, the pathogens evolved to become less fatal to their hosts. Since germs use an asexual strategy for reproduction, the DNA of the parents was the same as that of the offspring, and successful survivors pass their genetic inheritance to the next generation. As a result, only the less virulent parasites were available to infect host-children whose chances for survival at this point had improved; their recovery from the infection allowed even infants to build their own resistance to this disease. Thus, the human population recovered from its initial losses to this infection as the epidemics evolved into endemic childhood diseases.

Combined with sedentary agriculture, local disease history created a delicate balance of life and death that determined the potential number of people a civilization could sustain. Agriculture produced a symbiosis between humans, plants, and animals that provided the means for all three populations to grow. Parasitism generated a relationship between hosts and pathogens that reduced human numbers, either adults or children, when compared to the biology of agriculture. Together, the symbiosis of agriculture and parasites created a general equilibrium of life and death that sustained the basic number of survivors (and hosts) in a sedentary culture's gene pool of humans, plants, and animals.

The biological equilibrium between disease and food production laid a foundation for the political history of a civilization. If the symbiosis of agriculture prevailed in the balance of a culture's food production and diseases, human numbers tended to grow at a steady rate, and the labor force needed for food surpluses survived and reproduced. Also, with the steady increase of food surpluses, an urban population developed and supplied the skills needed to manage the politics of a prosperous agricultural community. If, however, disease frequently disrupted population growth, food supplies eroded, urban populations were devastated, and governments faced a crisis of survival. Of the three great ancient civilizations found in Eurasia (Rome, Han China, and Gupta India) two developed a stable history of centralized rule, while one did not. Rome and Han China produced the largest and most stable political systems of the ancient era; hence, the balance between symbiosis and parasitism in both must have favored agriculture rather than disease. Gupta India, however, comprised a region where political chaos was the norm and political unity was the exception; consequently, disease frequently disrupted the symbiosis of agriculture and eroded human organizational systems. Therefore, when contact between these three cultures finally occurred along the Silk Road and the sea-lanes of the Indian Ocean between 100 BCE and 300 CE, a sudden increase in epidemics swept through Rome and Han China.

Just as the pathogens that spawned new epidemics traveled with merchants, so did religious ideas. Indeed, new and similar concepts found in the monotheism of the Roman province of Palestine and the monisms that had evolved in India seem to have appeared at the same time, strongly suggesting an exchange of ideas. Situated in the middle of the new commercial network that had grown up between Rome, Han China, and Gupta

India, Judaism, Zoroastrianism, Brahmanism, and Buddhism had matured long before trade had linked them with one another. But once the Silk Road and the sea-lanes of the Indian Ocean created stable contacts between all three empires, these religious traditions began to change. Instead, the adherents of Christianity, Manichaeism, Hinduism, and Mahayana Buddhism emerged from Judaism, Zoroastrianism, Brahmanism, and what became Hinayana Buddhism. Each of these new variations on an old faith caused a new religious worldview when contact with one another allowed cultures to share powerful concepts. Between 200 BCE and 200 CE, the belief in a human-divine savior, salvation, the trinity, judgment day, and entry into an eternal paradise beyond this world emerged at the heart of several, if not all four, new creeds. At the same time, three of these new faiths broke with the most common practice found in ancient religious traditions: entry into the community of worshippers that could only occur by birth. Accordingly, the adherents of Christianity, Manichaeism, and Mahayana Buddhism sought converts and traveled to distant lands to proselytize. Furthermore, all four of these new religious traditions developed the belief that women too had souls, also needed to be saved, and had equal obligations with men to worship the savior.

The success of these new religious traditions also eased the agony of death and decay that accompanied an era of chaos brought on by disease, the internal collapse of ancient civilizations, and nomadic invasions. Christianity, Manichaeism, and Mahayana Buddhism more than Hinduism brought peace and hope to those Eurasian peoples surrounded by increasing instability. The promise of salvation and entry into an eternal paradise shifted the focus of human hope from this world to the next. The world beyond the grave grew in importance and soon ameliorated the pain of everyday life. Loyalty to the secular world gave way to a new loyalty, one that placed the heavenly realm at the heart of human conduct. Hence, while these religious changes helped people to cope with the imminence of death, they also undermined the commitment Eurasians needed to dedicate their lives to an existing and functional society. Therefore, while the evolution of new religious ideas prepared people for death, they also undercut the general allegiance that Roman, Chinese, and Indian peasants and urban laborers felt toward the state.

Internal Decay: The Roman Story

Each great civilization of ancient Eurasia faced an internal threat of decay that paved the way for nomadic invasion. The growing weaknesses within Rome and Han China, in particular, set the stage for invasion that eventually isolated Gupta India as the last remaining sedentary target for destruction. Hence, the story of internal decay, told in conjunction with the actual cycles of disease suffered by Rome and Han China, set in motion the critical conditions that invited barbarian invasion. The order of presentation here for, Rome, Han China, and Gupta India, reflects the availability of evidence to tell a complete tale.

Rome's slow descent into chaos reveals a number of internal weaknesses in the politics of the ancient West. To begin, Rome never established a clear manner of peacefully and successfully transferring authority from one emperor to the next. During the Pax Romana (31 BCE to 180 CE), the good emperors were those who selected competent heirs rather than allowing their sons to inherit the throne. When a son inherited the Imperial Office from his father, Rome's administration frequently suffered from incompetence. Furthermore, assassination and military usurpation frequently ended the career of one emperor and launched that of another.

Given this weakness in the shift of authority, Rome spiraled into chaos between the years 180 and 284 CE. The emperor Marcus Aurelius broke with the tradition established by the good emperors to select the most talented candidate as the successor, and instead allowed his vicious and incompetent son Commodus to become the next ruler of Rome. Commodus governed for the next twelve years by turning over state affairs to subordinates, personally indulging in gladiatorial combat, decreeing that he should be worshipped as Hercules Romanus due to his muscular physique, and seeking to rename Rome after himself. As if to mock Commodus, the conspirators who arranged his assassination had him strangled by a more powerful "Hercules" in 192 CE. Commodus, however, left no heir apparent, and his death evoked a civil war fought to decide who would be Rome's next emperor. A provincial general named Septimius Severus (193–211 CE) prevailed in this conflict, but he ruled as a military dictator whose only concern was to keep the army happy. Unfortunately, Severus's practices of lavishing rewards on his soldiers taught his military that they, not the emperor himself or lower government officials, controlled the emperor's fate; an era of assassination and invasion soon followed. From 235 to 284 CE no less than twenty-six men assumed the throne as emperor; all but one of them won this position by violence, meaning that their predecessors had met death at the hands of either a usurper or a barbarian challenger. Therefore, throughout this period, civil war and nomadic invasion plagued Rome.

In 284 CE strong rule returned to Rome with the Diocletian Reforms. A career soldier who won the support of the army, the emperor Diocletian held enough military power to reorganize the empire, postpone Rome's collapse, and solve the problem of transferring authority. But his solution of dividing the empire, sharing powers with a colleague, and freezing the occupational structure to prevent tax flight had come too late. Already set in motion were other factors that denied Diocletian's heirs the means to prevent the fall of Rome. For example, the consequences of civil war between 235 and 284 CE had severely eroded the economy of the empire. Not only did the civil war wear down trade and agriculture, but, at the same time, the rival aspirants to Rome's throne squandered vast amounts of wealth on their armies. Severus's maxim of keeping the army happy while virtually scorning the rest of the empire had destroyed imperial solvency while imposing a devastating tax burden on the civilian population. Landlords, peasants, and urban manufacturers alike now had little reason to produce goods for an empire they no longer trusted. At the base of society, the farmers suffered the most, and their role in supplying the food surpluses needed to feed Rome's urban hierarchy laid at the foundation of a healthy economy. Without a prosperous agricultural base, or a vibrant urban hierarchy, no emperor had the means to maintain Rome's imperial structure. Then, in the wake of civil war and economic decay, disease hit.

The epidemic cycles that joined the other factors to undercut Rome's labor base were spawned from the unintentional importation of pathogens from both India and Africa. Unlike Han China, Rome's empire included access to sub-Saharan Africa through trade with Egypt and North Africa. Since Africa already had a long history of exporting new diseases, Rome's contact with this massive continent involved the introduction of dangerous germs into Western civilization.

Like India, sub-Saharan Africa had a difficult time developing the human concentrations needed to produce urban cultures. Not only did this massive continent have a vast amount of land capable of sustaining human numbers without population pressures, but it also fostered a rich source of the germs that infected humans. Historically, these infections created a disease barrier to those who would travel below the Sahara; thus, disease had provided a form of protection to sub-Saharan Africans from invasion or colonization that lasted well into the late nineteenth century CE. Yet once trade with sub-Saharan Africans commenced, some of these pathogens escaped their original home; Rome proved to be one of the recipients of disease brought about by global commerce.

Malaria first appeared in the Italian Peninsula in the first century CE, a result of trade with Africa. Primarily restricted to the peninsula, especially in the districts surrounding Rome, malaria became a reoccurring problem that undercut the Roman political and military machines. Numerous eruptions of malaria plagued the city of Rome itself and depopulated the districts in the surrounding vicinity. Meanwhile, even those people who caught malaria but did not die from it, suffered from infertility, a high rate of stillborn children, and a shortened life span. Since Rome had long recruited its best soldiers and most talented officials from the Italian Peninsula, the sudden fall in the birth rate due to malaria forced the emperors of the second and third centuries CE to look to the outlying provinces for army replacements. Furthermore, in fertile regions such as Campania, malaria-carrying mosquitoes flourished and infected many farmers, costing Rome its due from some of its richest agricultural districts; hence, not only the population but also food production declined in Italy. As a result, a high death rate reduced food surpluses in Italy and eroded Rome's centerplace city status within the empire. From 100 to 476 CE, the Roman people found themselves caught in a slow process of geographic decentralization in which a declining population on the Italian Peninsula reduced Rome's

African Trade Goods. This unique find is evidence of a flourishing trade which took place between North Africa and Europe during the late sixteenth and seventeenth centuries. The collection contains coins struck during 1631–36 CE by Sharifs of the Sa'dian dynasty, pieces of gold jewelry, and ingots, as well as pewter, pottery shards, and a merchant's seal. Although late examples of the goods sent to Europe, this illustration displays the variety of items exchanged. Recovered in 1999 by divers in Salcombe Bay in Devon. © The Trustees of the British Museum.

Malaria

Malaria is a protozoan infection characterized by convulsive chills, fever, and sweating and by anemia, and a chronic relapsing of these symptoms. Malaria parasites come in four types: Plasmodium vivax, Plasmodium falciparum, Plasmodium malariae, and Plasmodium ovale. Infections occur through the bite of an infected female anopheles mosquito, which makes this disease one of the hitchhiker varieties.

The life cycle of the malarial parasite begins when the female anopheles mosquito, feeding on an individual with malaria, ingests the parasite. These parasites are gametocytes (cells that divide and produce gametes or sex cells) that then undergo sexual development inside the mosquito to end as sporozoites (parasitical protozoa with both a sexual and asexual reproductive phase) located in the insects salivary glands. The mosquito injects the sporozoites into a human victim while extracting blood, which stimulates the female mosquito to ovulate, thus reproducing thousands of future anopheles mosquito carriers. Meanwhile the sporozoites reproduce asexually within the human's liver. An asymptomatic phase of the disease begins in which the sporozoites mature over the course of two to four weeks, but in some cases they take up to several months. After this phase, the sporozoites in the liver release merozoites (a spore produced in the asexual phase of the malarial protozoa) that enter the blood stream, invade red blood cells, and reproduce until the red blood cells burst, which releases these merozoites back into the blood stream. The sporozoites continue to produce merozoites in the liver, while the merozoites continue to reproduce and occupy red blood cells. Gametocytes rather than merozoites are formed in some of the red blood cells and are released into the blood stream where they wait for the next female anopheles mosquito to bite the human malaria carrier.

After an untreated malarial infection, persistent and severe liver disease develops along with anemia. Also the spleen becomes soft and is saturated with malarial parasites as is any other tissue that comes in contact with red blood cells—especially the brain. Malaria caused by the P. vivax and P. ovale begins abruptly with a shaking chill followed by fever and sweats. Within a week the typical reoccurring pattern of the disease is established. The initial chill begins after a short period of malaise and a headache, then one to eight hours of fever follows, and the disease subsides; the attack follows a 48-hour cycle. P. falciparum malaria produces a chill that is more mild, but the temperature rises and fall sharply, reaching as high as 40 degrees Centigrade (105 degrees Fahrenheit). The attack cycle is 36 hours, which reduces the victim to a prostrated state. Also falciparum malaria produces severe headaches, drowsiness, delirium, and confusion, which indicates a cerebral crisis that will usually prove fatal. The P. malariae malaria attack begins abruptly, is more severe than P. vivax and P. ovale, and generates a 72-hour cycle. P. vivax, P. ovale, and P. malariae are chronic and slowly deplete the human host until weakness causes death by complications, while P. falciparum kills more swiftly.

Source: *The Merck Manual of Diagnosis and Therapy,* **Thirteenth Edition (Rathway, New Jersey: Merck and Co., Inc., 1977) p. 159–160.**

Smallpox

Smallpox is an acute (sudden onset), highly contagious viral (virus) disease that causes sudden, severe symptoms characterized by progressive skin eruptions that often result in permanent pits and scars. A virus related to cowpox, and other pustule-causing viruses, is the cause of smallpox. This virus is present through all stages of the disease—in the blistering phase, when the pustules crust, in nasal and throat secretions, and in feces. The virus resists drying and may be transmitted in the dried scales of the skin lesions, or may be airborne in the droplets from nose and throat secretions. The disease may be transmitted from person to person directly, or by contact with contaminated clothing or any household article. People without any recognizable symptoms frequently transmit the disease. Also, some infected people die before the symptoms appear when smallpox takes the severe hemorrhagic (uncontrollable heavy bleeding) form.

After a ten-to-fourteen day incubation period (time needed for the symptoms of a disease to appear after the original infection), onset of smallpox is abrupt with chills, high temperatures, and great prostration. Symptoms at first appear to imitate influenza, while vomiting and convulsions are common in small children. This phase of the disease may last up to two days with various rashes that are not suggestive of smallpox.

The characteristic eruptions, the pustules, appear after the third day, accompanied by a drop in temperature and a decrease in symptoms. Pink-red patches of skin generally appear first on the forehead, temples, and about the mouth, then spread over the scalp, ears, neck, arms, and hands, reaching the trunk after 24 hours. In severe cases, these patches become generalized and may be profuse on the palms and soles and in the armpits. The individual lesions enlarge, become deeply embedded in the skin, rather than on it, and feel hard to the touch. By the third day of the eruption, the lesions become deep pits, surrounded by a pinkish nipple, and filled with a clear serum and may flow. In the next day or two, the lesions become pustules and the fever returns with severe prostration. The characteristic pitted lesions may also be seen on the mucous membranes of the mouth, pharynx, larynx, vagina, urethral meatus, and rectum.

If the infected individual survives, by the eighth or ninth day of the eruption, most of the lesions have passed their peak, many have ruptured, and some are shrinking. The skin shows pus-saturated material that is crusting. There may also be extensive scaling of the skin and loss of hair, eyebrows, and nails. Healing is slow and may continue for two weeks with the deeper or multiple lesions leaving permanent pockmarks and deep pits.

The worst form of smallpox is the fulminant (sledgehammer) variety; this begins with a high fever, severe prostration, bone marrow depression, bleeding skin lesions, and progresses to death in three to four days. The mortality rate is 60 to 80 percent in both the fulminant and hemorrhagic variations of smallpox, but the fulminant form kills at the fastest rate. Some survivors both suffer gangrene to the skin and damage to the eyes and ears.

Source: Ibid., p. 30–31.

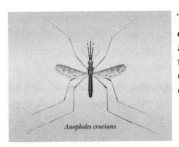

The *Anopheles crucians* mosquito is a common carrier of the malaria parasite. Courtesy of the CDC.

relevance as the center of a sprawling political system.

While malaria dominated Italy's disease history during the first century CE, another new disease broke out in 125 CE. Called the plague of Orosius, this new disease reflected a devastating famine-disease sequence, the undoing of a number of ancient civilizations. Launched by locusts that destroyed large areas of agricultural production in North Africa, famine easily killed hundreds of thousands of people. Pestilence soon followed, destroying a population already weakened by the lack of food. Erupting in Numedia (on the coast of modern Algeria and part of eastern Libya), the disease spread across North Africa and carried off an estimated 1 million victims. As yet unnamed, the infection then spread to Italy, presenting an awful fact: a disease that broke out in one province in a well-organized empire could easily travel to the rest of the civilization given the vast infrastructure built to facilitate communication.

Then, in the year 164 CE, the first empire-wide infection migrated from India to Rome. The disease first spread among Roman troops on the eastern frontier, where it remained for two years, at which point a Roman army sent by Rome to put down a rebellion in Syria caught the infection and commenced to march home. Commanded by Avidius Claudius, this army spread the plague throughout the east, introducing it to Rome in 166 CE. From Rome, this disease spread rapidly into all parts of the Western world, causing so many deaths that wagonloads of corpses had to be carried off in all the major cities. Producing symptoms described by Galen, Rome's most famous physician, the disease began with a high fever, inflammation of the mouth and throat and led to severe thirst and diarrhea. On the ninth day skin eruptions appeared and formed into pustules. Today, many historians believed that this was the first outbreak of smallpox in the Western world. At any rate, the plague then raged for the next twenty-five years, sweeping away a vast number of victims until it burned itself out in 189 CE.

Called the Antonine or Galen plague at the time, this infection was new to the Roman Empire, so the Romans had no natural resistance to it. As a result, this disease became pandemic. At the same time, the mortality rate was quite high. Records from the Roman cities whose officials chronicled the impact of these outbreaks tell of losses totaling 25 to 33 percent of the population. The countryside suffered similar losses. Overall, the Roman Empire saw enough people die to cause a serious breach in Rome's defenses, but this was merely the beginning of a cycle of diseases. The opening in Rome's frontier invited in the first the nomadic invaders: the Marcomanni from Bohemia and the Quadi from Moravia entered the empire. These two German tribes fought their way through the northeastern military barrier to Italy and found an undefended territory available for pillage. Rome could not mount an effective response, but it survived this initial onslaught because the invaders caught the dreaded disease as well. Ironically, the epidemic itself saved Rome, even though the infection had made the invasion possible in the first place.

After 189 CE, the Antonine plague seemingly disappeared. But a new disease broke out between 251 and 268 CE, sweeping across the empire for the next seventeen years. Called the Cyprian plague, after the Bishop of Carthage who described it, this disease devastated the Roman population as thoroughly as had the previous infection. Cyprius's description listed violent diarrhea and vomiting, an ulcerated sore throat, burning fever, and putrefaction of the hands and feet, but his lack of professional medical skills undermined the accuracy of these symptoms. Yet given the way in which it spread, and the number of people it killed, some historians believe it was either smallpox or measles.

The Cyprian plague spread throughout the vast expanse of the Roman Empire, from the frontier of Scotland to Egypt. It swept through the countryside using people as the primary disease vector. Once a region was infected, a lull in the disease usually followed until the next outbreak. There were also seasonal eruptions that began in the fall and lasted until the next spring. The rate of mortality was said to be higher than that caused by any other epidemic experienced to date. Given the dramatic impact of this infection, panic gripped the empire, as thousands of people fled, probably carrying the disease with them. Some reports reveal that this epidemic claimed as many as five thousand people per day in large urban areas. In addition, entire agricultural villages disappeared, which sharply reduced the food needed to build resistance, or stave off starvation. The impact of this plague created such a high mortality rate as to match the destructive power of the Black Death that hit Europe in the Late Middle Ages (1300–1450 CE).

While no satisfactory account of the actual mortality rate ever can be established, the sudden appearance of famine and nomadic invasions, the reports of depopulated lands no longer used to cultivate food, and the compounded death rates generated by war, infection, and starvation, speak to the weakness of Rome during this second cycle of death. Civil war, rebellion, and invasion punctuated the conjunction of the Cyprian plague with Rome's lack of effective leadership between 235 and 284 CE. Now Rome's legions fell back from Transylvania and the Black Forest to shorten its line of defense, and Rome began its policy of assimilation as the empire tried to recruit into the Roman army German tribes that had migrated to the frontier. In this manner, Rome hoped to convert a potential military threat into a resource to replace the many people who had died from disease. Yet throughout the next three hundred years, Rome lost so many potential workers and soldiers that it could no longer put up an effective resistance against the cycle of invasions that followed. In any event, since the Cyprian plague was probably Rome's second encounter with smallpox, or else a new infestation called measles, this epidemic most likely came from India. Measles and smallpox were endemic to India, traveled in the lungs of their hosts, and spread to others who happened to inhale the virus expelled through the respiration of a carrier.

The necessity of reorganizing the empire under Diocletian (reigned 285–305) mentioned above tells of a failing tax base and Roman weakness. The division of the empire into two halves, the creation of two rulers, and the explicit designation of two heirs reveal how Diocletian tried to deal with the politics of the era. Also, laws prohibiting farmers from leaving their farms, or artisans from migrating out of their cities, show that Rome's internal design had been severely damaged by the death rate. Reports of empty lands and attempts at tax flight tell of a vast empire in the thralls of what has been called a "die-off era." The necessity of attracting foreign people into the empire so that they could be used as a buffer against other hostile nomadic tribes merely underlines the desperateness of the measures taken to repopulate a system in decline.

While disease ultimately swept away somewhere between 25 and 40 percent of Rome's population, another fundamental internal problem exacerbated the death rate: both the rural and urban division of labor that fueled the Roman economy depended on a vast slave population. Segregated by sex, housed in barracks on Roman latifundia or in large urban "factories," slaves did not have the freedom to select mates or raise families. Troubled by a bleak existence and overworked, slaves had lost any hope of a future. Fresh conquests were an economic necessity in order to renew the number of slaves that Rome consumed. But the growth of the empire slowed after the establishment of the Principate under Augustus Caesar (63 BCE to 14 CE) because the Roman economy could not produce enough surplus food

to sustain the requisite number of men needed for the significant addition of territory after 150 CE.

Thus, a chronic case of labor shortages due to both epidemics and an eroding slave-labor base aggravated the economic problems brought on by Rome's lack of effective leadership during the era of civil wars from 235 to 284 BCE. Also, in the prior period, called the Pax Romana (31 BCE to 180 CE), when peace replaced expansion, the demands of the empire had required that the Roman people dedicate themselves to investing most, if not all, of their creative energies into productive enterprises just to maintain the supplies needed to fuel their imperial system. Yet, the Roman habits of luxurious living by its elite created yet another financial problem for the empire beyond its high death rate: Rome's elite had squandered potential capital on conspicuous consumption and robbed the Roman economy of potential investments in economic innovation. Rome's elite became accustomed to the luxury supplied by slave labor, which more than saturated the appetites of the elite and made most of Rome's wealthiest citizens indifferent to economic improvements. Yet nomadic invasions, plagues, rebellions, and civil wars that had replaced the Pax Romana begged the Roman elite to abandon its taste for luxury. Unfortunately for the empire, this shift in spending habits did not occur. The result was an indifference to the necessary economizing that might have compensated Rome for its declining labor and military force.

Another reason for the failure of the empire can be traced to the erosion of loyalty to the central government. Dedication to civic duty might have saved Rome, but few people living within the empire after 180 CE found the will needed to do the required work. In this case, a combination of new religious beliefs and the bankruptcy of ancient Western philosophy distracted most Romans' vision from the world of everyday life and redirected it toward an ideal realm like Christianity's Heaven. These new religious beliefs, as mentioned, offered commoners and elites alike an otherworldly paradise through belief in a savior, a mental escape from the day-to-day crises that confronted everyone. Furthermore, these new religious tenets made more sense than investing one's emotional energy in a political system that no longer seemed to have the individual's general welfare in mind. After all, why should the people of Rome have been expected to fight or work hard for Roman ideals of any sort when by this time the empire represented to them nothing more than crushing taxation and recurring civil war?

The philosophical problems facing the Western world that caused this separation of "the mundane world as it is" from "the ideal world as it ought to be" had started long before the appearance of Christianity. These problems began in classical Greece and then traveled to Rome. They reflected a growing gap between what Greco-Roman philosophy described as ethical conduct based on civic virtue and a contemporary political environment that seemed indifferent to moral behavior. The collapse of meaningful citizenship with the rise of the Principate, the general dilution of citizen status since after 212 CE every free-born male was a citizen, and the retreat from public life marked by a Roman hunger for new, foreign faiths signaled a change in Rome's moral compass.

As mentioned in Chapter Seven, while Socrates, Plato, and Aristotle had tried to save citizenship and civic virtue for Greece in the midst of its destruction during to the Peloponnesian Wars (431–338 BCE), the rise of Macedonia nullified their efforts. Philip of Macedon and his son Alexander the Great eliminated the possibility of salvaging Greek citizenship when both men laid the foundation for new kingdoms that came to dominate Greek politics during the Hellenistic era (322 to 149 BCE). Since monarchy relied on passive subjects rather than active citizens, Socratic philosophy had become politically irrelevant after 338 BCE. Also, as mentioned in Chapter Eight, when Rome revived citizenship during the Republican Era of Roman history (509 to 31 BCE), the Roman people, like the Greeks, repeated the process of self-destruction through civil war (133 to 31 BCE). Consequently, meaningful citizenship in Roman politics had ended when Augustus established the Principate (31 BCE to 14 CE). He too wanted passive subjects rather than active citizens. Thus, both Greece and Rome had created a political ideal in the concept of the "citizen" while, at the same time, both had failed to live up to the ethical standards prescribed by civic virtue.

The corruption that infected Greece and Rome, and laid the foundation for the destruction of meaningful citizenship, reinforced a separation of the "world as it is" from "the world as it ought to be." The ugliness of the world of politics only enhanced the beauty, goodness, truth, and desire for a reality found in the transcendental vision developed by Socrates, Plato, and Aristotle. Each philosopher had in his own way created a separation between an ideal life and the decadence of everyday existence by developing a system of ethics based on universal "oughts" that took precedence over what actually was. Also, since Rome produced no philosopher of its own who could equal the speculative powers of the Greeks, Roman intellectuals adopted the Greek worldview. Even though citizenship failed in the ancient Western world, the standards of citizenship found in Socratic thought remained a beacon for Ro-

man philosophy to admire. The use of Greek philosophy during the Roman era created a paradox that plagued the Western imagination: the world of politics seemed to have nothing to do with the world of ethics. This paradox manifested itself in the way Rome applied what it had learned from Greece.

As mentioned in Chapter Eight, Romans assimilated Greek philosophy in three forms: Stoicism, Epicureanism, and Neo-Platonism. These three philosophies bear witness to a crisis of faith in Roman public life. The apatheia of the Stoics and the ataraxia of the Epicureans revealed the meaninglessness of citizenship in Rome. Apatheia advocated withdrawal from the material world of sensation in favor of a realm of pure, dispassionate ideals that had no real outlet in Roman politics. Ataraxia acknowledged the absence of this political outlet by abandoning public life completely and retreating into a private, hedonistic realm of mild, stressfree pleasures. In contrast, Neo-Platonism emphasized the corruption of matter as the source of evil and drew Rome's elite into a mystical realm. Of these three philosophies, Stoicism initially attracted the greatest number of Roman followers but was eventually replaced by Neo-Platonism. None of the three, however, spoke well for the future, because all of them separated "the world as it is" from "the world as it ought to be." Clearly, Roman philosophy revealed a hunger for religion that laid a foundation for Christianity.

Christianity, in turn, gave new hope by preparing its worshippers for death. The new Christian faith filled an emotional, spiritual, and intellectual void that Greco-Roman philosophy could not satisfy. A savior, salvation, redemption, judgment day, and entry into the kingdom of Heaven reflected ideas shared along the Silk Road. These ideas helped Romans, as well as others confronted by plague, civil war, famine, and nomadic invasions, to compensate for the ugly truth of daily life that surrounded them with the possibility of paradise after death. Finally, Christianity, like Manichaeism, Mahayana Buddhism, and Hinduism elsewhere, helped people accept the collapse of the world that they knew.

Internal Decay: Han China

While Rome floundered, Han China exhibited similar signs of internal decay. Like Rome, the Han Dynasty experienced several hundred years of disintegration before its collapse actually occurred. Since Rome and Han China had required centuries to achieve fully mature empires, both required quite a bit of time to fall into disarray. This slow decay therefore began during the "Later Han," the second half of this dynasty's history.

After 57 CE, a political crisis began to form in Changan, the center of Han politics, that reflected a power struggle between several well-defined cliques: the hereditary aristocracy, wealthy landlords, relatives of the empress, the eunuchs, and the scholars. These cliques engaged in a power struggle that blossomed due to a failure of authority at the seat of government much like Rome's inability to transfer leadership from one generation to the next. In China's case, however, these well-defined cliques fought over access to power as each tried either to dominate a sitting emperor or place one of their candidates on the throne. This power struggle took place during an era of relative prosperity; consequently, Han China suffered from a decay of power at the center, while the Chinese work ethic, concepts of filial piety, and strong traditions allowed the people to carry on as if nothing was wrong. Accordingly, the Later Han Dynasty appeared to be a period of comparative peace: one in which the Chinese economy continued to expand even as a cancer began to grow in the Imperial Office.

The rise of such powerful cliques at the seat of government disrupted the Imperial Court because each group was more concerned with asserting its claims over the emperor rather than with considering the welfare of the state. The hereditary aristocracy comprised large landed families with well-established pedigrees that claimed a share of power based on their titles and past services to the First Han emperors. The wealthy landlords included the more recently established local magnates whose rise to power derived from the distinctions won by their sons in the Confucian examination system that had granted them powerful posts in the state bureaucracy. Relatives of the empress grasped at power based on the ability of the Imperial Consort to enthrall the emperor with her sexual favors. The eunuchs relied on a combination of personal talent, close contact with the emperor, and allies within the Imperial Harem to sway Chinese politics. Finally, the scholars comprised an intelligentsia whose dedication to and mastery of Confucian philosophy put them at odds with everyone else at court except their wealthy patrons.

Evaluating the role of each clique in government reveals how any one of them could cause so much trouble in a system that seemed capable of running itself. The families of the hereditary aristocracy produced a group of confident leaders who lived on enormous revenues derived from titled estates even though they personally spent all their time at Changan, the capital. As absentee landlords, they relied on the labor of tenant farmers, serfs, and slaves to free themselves to make time for their political intrigues. In the capital, they developed the skills of the courtiers: their membership comprised a number of famous poets and historians who produced a steady stream of art and literature rich in political commentary that bolstered their public position. Engaged in a life of luxury, they squandered wealth on hunting and entertainment in an effort to escape from boredom while they awaited the emperor's appointment. Arrogant and apathetic to others, they felt that only their pursuit of power had merit.

At the same time, a wealthy group of landlords in the countryside rose to power based on the Han Dynasty's first use of the Confucian examination system. Beginning with the Han era, Confucian philosophy evolved into an official state ideology as its social sanctions became the standards of conduct for the next twenty-one centuries (202 BCE to 1905 CE). Using the Classics and Confucian teachings to screen potential government officials, the Han emperors encouraged a career of study as an avenue for advancement. Successful candidates who won government appointments rewarded their patrons and fathers with the wealth they had earned while in office. The result was the rise of a new powerful clique of local magnates who aped the hereditary aristocracy by developing a sense of self-worth based on the success of their sons and protégés. These landlords, their families, their sons, and their protégés held a monopoly on access to a Confucian education, which made them act as if they were the sole guardians of an ancient, sacred tradition. Consequently, they tried to control entry to the bureaucracy, held valuable sinecures, and developed a strong sense of self-righteousness. Meanwhile, small farmers who began to suffer from an increasingly poor government apparatus endured local agricultural disasters that forced them to attach themselves to these regional land barons. As a result, the power of these local landlords waxed as the seat of government waned during the Later Han.

The third clique, the empress's relatives, exploited the influence she had won because of her intimate bonds with the emperor. This clique proved to be very powerful but had no security in its position. Since the emperor could easily be wooed into the arms of another, given the size of his harem, the empress's relatives could

Han Gaozu, first emperor of the Han Dynasty, reigned during the Eastern Han from 209–194 BCE. Born as Liu Bang, he gave his name to the Chinese: they call themselves "people of Han." Shelfmark: Or. 2231. Copyright © The British Library.

just as easily fall from power. They therefore took great pains to isolate him while exploiting their advantages. Once in power, they set about raising as many of their kin as they could to posts of authority while looting the empire. They were despised by the Confucian scholars for their lack of merit, hated by the aristocrats for their grasp on public offices, and envied by the local magnates for their access to imperial wealth. In addition, since the empress could become a powerful dowager or regent should the emperor die, her relatives played a major role in Chinese politics.

Numerous examples of such powerful regents and dowagers punctuate Han history. The Empress Lu rose to power in the "Former Han" (the first half of the dynasty's history). She was a favorite wife of Gao Di (206–195 BCE), and she became a regent to her son when her husband died in 195 BCE (see page 64). Later, she served as the dowager to her grandson when her son died, and later still as the dowager to an adopted grandson when her grandson died. She used her influence to place her relatives in key posts while deposing the Liu line as the rightful heirs to the throne; she ruled from 195 to 181 BCE. Under threat of disappearing, the Liu family launched a civil war, restored their claim to the throne, and slaughtered the empress's relatives.

In the Later Han, Empress Liang became a dowager when her husband Shun Di died in 147 BCE. Then, the head of the Liang Clan, Liang Ji, used the empress's new position to appoint the weakling Liu Zhi as Emperor Huan Di (147–67 BCE). Liang Ji easily dominated the court from 147 to 159 CE. During that time, Liang Ji amassed a great fortune, replaced Emperor Huan Di with two more puppet rulers, and swamped public office with his kin. Liang Ji's power remained unchecked until his assassination in 159 when Huan Di reclaimed the throne, at which point the whole Liang clan fell victim to slaughter.

Liang Ji's assassination had occurred in a palace plot engineered by Huan Di and the eunuchs, the fourth powerful clique. The eunuchs represented a unique power group in the Han capital. They came from all walks of life, including the aboriginal tribes of the south, and lived by their wits. As commoners, they had no social or economic distinctions except for what they could win for themselves while in office. Despised for having been castrated, their lack of social merit or prestige, and their access to royal power, the eunuchs, nevertheless, played a necessary role in palace life. They guarded the emperor's harem against other men who could impregnate the women sequestered there. Since the Imperial Court was secluded, and an emperor seldom left the palace grounds, the only people in close physical contact with him were his women and his eunuchs. For a young emperor raised in such seclusion,

the companionship of anyone besides his relatives proved greatly desirable. As such, the eunuchs could easily become his trusted friends, advisers, and confidants. Thus, a clever eunuch could gain influence over an emperor during his childhood and be raised to power once the boy became the ruler. Once in a position of power, this eunuch would appoint his companions to office and grasp at awards, titles, and honors. Usually, however, these eunuchs proved to be quite loyal because they had to serve as a buffer against sycophants such as their rivals, the aristocrats, the wealthy landlords, the empress's relatives, and the Confucian scholars.

The scholars comprised the last powerful clique at the seat of power. They were the educated sons who had won their posts through the patronage of the local landlords. Their role in government was to protect the principles of Confucian philosophy, staff the bureaucracy, and oversee the day-to-day affairs of government. Theirs was the voice of morality; they claimed the wisdom to read the signs of the future through omens and ancient texts, and they asserted that they had the ability to make philosophical speculations regarding the best course of action to take based on their reading of these signs. Although they represented the highest principles of good government, by the Later Han, these standards had given way to a system of patronage, networking, and personal connections. Those scholars who held Imperial Office gained their posts through their relatives, links to the imperial family, and prominent people at court. By this time, the Confucian examination system had lost its purpose: it no longer screened candidates based on academic excellence and character; instead, position, rank, and distinction could be bought. Nevertheless, one must keep in mind that the Han Emperors had never really developed a true bureaucracy based on Confucian principles; this was a feature of government that would make *later* dynasties famous. As a result, those scholars who won office, and later wrote the official history of the Han Dynasty, had become as corrupt as everyone else at court. Hence, when these scholars condemned the eunuchs for all the ills of the Later Han, one has to consider the corruption of the authors before accepting their reports at face value.

Given the power of these competing cliques, the Imperial Office floundered during the Later Han (25–220 CE). Weak emperors staffed the throne, influence peddling dissipated central authority, and revenues became a source of personal income instead of state funds. The taxes turned over to the throne during the last century of Han rule came to one-thirtieth the wealth enjoyed by the First Han emperors. Meanwhile, one-half of this earlier wealth fell into the hands of great landlords and aristocratic families as they continuously increased their rents during the era. One of the principle reasons for this weakness at the center of the Later Han Dynasty is that every emperor after 90 began his reign as a child; he therefore fell under the authority of a dowager empress and her family. As a result, the emperor did not have the means to effect change even if he wanted to save his dynasty. Furthermore, given the isolation of the Imperial Court, rivals at the center did not have access to the necessary information they needed to prevent the drift toward a paralyzed central government. Hence, although the Later Han began as an era of prosperity, ineffective leadership in the centerplace city gradually sapped the Imperial Office of the means to rule the empire.

By 165, open strife broke out between the cliques surrounding the emperor. Driving this struggle were all the signs of an enraged Heaven (i.e., the traditional signals the Confucian scholars recorded for the end of a dynasty mentioned in Chapter Five). Declining tax roles, increased demands for *corvée* services (a labor tax), and dwindling food surpluses to provide famine relief compelled the Imperial Office to increase the toll carried by the peasants to pay for government. Droughts, famine, tax flight, banditry, and peasant rebellions punctuated the last 65 years of Han rule as taxation began to exceed income. Now the increased revenues went primarily for defense against nomadic warriors who represented a new military threat along the northern frontier; the attack of these nomads signaled the transition from trade to raid as the marauders sensed weakness among their southern sedentary neighbors. Then, in a pattern that should by now be familiar, disease hit Han China; epidemics began to undercut the labor base.

Disease history in Han China is not as clearly reported as that in Rome. Although the Chinese have an excellent reputation for historical sensitivity, in the case of new diseases, they kept ambiguous records. The epidemics that entered China during the Han Dynasty did not appear among contemporary reports; rather they were catalogued some 700 to 1,500 years later. This makes reconstructing the role disease played during the Later Han period difficult.

According to the records, six great epidemics struck in the second and third centuries CE. Four came in rapid succession: 161–162, 173, 179, and 182, prior to the fall of the Later Han in 220; then two more hit after the collapse of the Han Dynasty in 310–312 and 322. The records hint that these epidemics exhibited symptoms very much like those produced by smallpox, which could have arrived in China as early as 37 CE. Of those epidemics reported, each reflected the impact of a new disease on a population without any significant immunity: at their worst, these plagues carried away somewhere between 75 and 100 percent of those infected.

Since fulminant smallpox has a mortality rate of 100 percent, and malignant confluent smallpox kills 75 percent of it victims, these reported figures have credibility. Of the four epidemics that struck before the fall of the Han, those infected were primarily soldiers on the northern frontier and peasants along the Yellow River. The mortality rates revealed a decline in population somewhere between 30 and 40 percent, which was sufficient to both open the frontier to nomadic invasion and spark two major peasant rebellions, which will be discussed below.

In China, as in the Mediterranean world, the outbreak of new diseases undercut the population, and the resulting massive die-off eroded the possibility of maintaining a successful central government. Just what role this die-off played in the fall of the Han Dynasty, however, remains unclear. The evidence indicates a major decline in human numbers: in 2 CE, the Han recorded a census of 12.3 million hearths (the Chinese record their census by family units rather than individuals); the next accurate census occurred 740 years later, during the Tang Dynasty: 8.9 million hearths. Each hearth represented a nuclear family, so 12.3 million hearths each comprising a family of five comes to 61.5 million people; 8.9 million hearths represent 44.5 million people, a figure that conforms to the recovery of China during the Tang Dynasty after centuries of chaos but is still smaller than the Han at its zenith. Meanwhile, since smallpox entered China sometime between 37 and 322 CE and had been imported in the same manner it had made its way to Rome (through contact with India), the lack of accurate reporting may be masking the role disease actually played at the end of the Han Era. Did disease undercut an already collapsing regime? Did it merely prolong the time it took China to recover its classical forms? Clearly, the four plagues that hit China before the collapse of the Han in 220 accelerated the spiraling chaos that changed the face of that empire just as the Antonine and Cyprian plagues had changed the face of the Roman Empire.

One thing concerning disease is certain. It facilitated the arrival of Buddhism in ancient China regardless of what impact the major epidemics may have had. The flowering of Buddhism in China is quite understandable given the increasing chaos caused by a collapsing central government and the arrival of new epidemics. Still, this imported Indian faith relied on tenets that were quite incompatible with basic, ancient Chinese beliefs.

Embracing several assumptions about life inconsistent with the Chinese experience, Buddhism held that existence here on Earth was essentially painful. It argued that our sense of "self" was really an unending series of false identities captured by the concept of "an individual" personality. This false "self" continued to exist through a process of reincarnation that trapped "a person" in this world because of karma. Sanskrit for "action," karma tricked the "individual" soul into believing that it was real by feeding this sense of "self" with the series of events "caused" by any act. Since one act seemed to cause another, karma accumulated, and projected the belief of the "self" into the next life. As a result, karma forced the "individual" personality to return to lead another existence filled with pain and misery. Birth led to death, and death led to further births, so that a chain of painful lives plagued a suffering soul. One could, however, escape this misery if one discovered the Four Noble Truths and followed the Eight-Fold Path mentioned in Chapter Four.

The Four Nobel Truths explicitly stated: life was suffering; the source of suffering was desire; one could end suffering by eliminating desire; and the way to end desire involved following the Eight-Fold Path. The Eight-Fold path was a series of disciplined stages of development that elevated the individual's understanding of his or her false "self." As people mastered each stage, they distanced themselves from their belief in their false existence, which prepared them for the rapture of a reunion with the universal, transcendental soul of the universe. Called nirvana, this reunion with the universal, transcendental soul meant that the false "self" ceased to exist, that the Buddhist had achieved enlightenment, and that the rapture experienced at the moment of enlightenment would last forever. Removal from this world, therefore, was the goal. Like a drop of water merging with the ultimate sea of reality, the agony of separation that constituted life here on Earth would no long plague the "individual."

As a universal religion, Buddhism traveled just as easily as did Christianity. Buddhism produced a series of religious principles that applied to everyone equally. Buddhists also proselytized and spread the evolving religion. In time it split into two branches, the Mahayana and Hinayana forms. The Mahayana form, or Greater Vehicle, was greater only in the fact that it influenced more people than did the Hinayana form. The Mahayana form was the version of Buddhism that traveled to China, Korea, and Japan. The Hinayana form traveled to Sri Lanka, Thailand, Burma, Cambodia, Laos, and Vietnam. The way the Mahayana form evolved, however, made it more compatible with foreign traditions because it could assimilate ideas from other cultures.

The Mahayana form distinguished between absolute and relative truths that allowed it to adjust to religious and traditional variations as it moved from culture to culture. It also developed a sense of tolerance to local beliefs that allowed traveling monks to adopt

new concepts into the vast pool of Buddhist metaphysics. In place of the Hinayana belief in a godless transcendental essence that embraced the "self" at the moment of enlightenment, the Mahayana form produced a series of godlike Buddhas who had lived and preached for eons. The Mahayana monks also developed a new type of deity, the Bodhisattva or "enlightened one," who chose to remain here on Earth even though he had achieved nirvana; he remained so that he could assist others in their salvation.

Functioning as a savior, the Bodhisattva dedicated his existence to helping weaker creatures in their quest to escape this world of pain. His role in Mahayana Buddhism changed the meaning of nirvana to one where a life after death in paradise began for those who had been saved. The "self" did not cease to exist; rather, it transcended this world with the aid of another. The Bodhisattva, as the being with strength, gave his strength to those who believed; all that was required was faith. In addition to the Bodhisattva, Mahayana Buddhism produced the *Lotus Sutra*, a popular scripture that claimed that eventually all creatures would be saved. In the *Lotus Sutra*, the Bodhisattva would remain here on Earth until all animal existence had entered paradise. Buddhism did not distinguish between humans and animals; each was a "self" in quest of salvation.

To the Chinese, who had developed a political philosophy based on Confucianism that placed them here on Earth and prescribed actions to enhance the quality of this life and celebrate the harmony that one could achieve by following the traditions found in the Classics, Buddhism's desire to escape this world was completely alien. Buddhism also clashed with Daoism. As mentioned in Chapter Five, Daoism expected a person (whose identity was real) to conform to the "Way" with a level of obedience appropriate to passive nonattachment that blended the "self" with the universal entity that preceded all things; the "self" linked with the entity to produce *chi* (the energy derived from a wedding of opposites that make up our existence). Even though Daoism acknowledged a universal entity—much like the sea that the Buddhist false "self" returned to during enlightenment—nonetheless, the Daoist "self" was a real and necessary part of the "Way."

Despite the differences between China's worldview and the one held out by Buddhism, the Chinese embraced this Indian religion with an enthusiasm unprecedented in their history. The assimilation of Buddhism into Chinese society represented one of the most complete and general borrowings of a foreign belief system ever exhibited by the Han people. But why would the Chinese reverse their own view of how to live in this world in order to accept the Buddhist principle that this life was filled with pain? One can only explain this reversal by visualizing the agony that the Chinese must have felt in the midst of political chaos, surrounded by disease, and threatened with nomadic invasions. Hence, the appeal of Buddhism must be seen as a response that was directly proportionate to the misery caused by a collapsing regime.

According to Chinese tradition, Buddhism appeared in China in 64 BCE during a dream experienced by Ming Di (57–75 CE), the second emperor of the Later Han; this was clearly an apocryphal tale manufactured to enhance the prestige of a popular new, but alien, faith. Evidence from India gives us a good sense of when Buddhism arrived in China. The grandfather of the founder of the Gupta Empire (320 to 535 CE) is known historically only because he built a place of worship for Chinese monks who had gone to India in order to learn more about Buddhism. Living in the mid-200s CE, Sri Gupta would have been lost to Indian history had he not constructed this Buddhist temple for the Chinese. Yet for the Chinese to have traveled back to India to learn more about Buddhism meant that the religion had already taken root in China. Since there was a Buddhist group living along the lower Changjiang (Yangtze) River valley in the second century BCE, this would place the arrival of Buddhism somewhere between 100 and 200 BCE. Thus, this religion began to shape Chinese beliefs in the midst of the decay of the Han Dynasty. As this chaos grew worse with the introduction of foreign epidemics and nomadic invasions, the appeal of Buddhism must have grown even more popular.

Like Christianity in Rome, Buddhism in China would have fed people's new hunger for spiritual reassurance. Also, like Christianity, Buddhism would have pulled Chinese loyalty away from a collapsing central government. Just as Christianity drew the Roman imagination to a heavenly realm beyond their present existence, so Buddhism created a spiritual distance to the events of this world. As a result, Buddhism made life tolerable for those Chinese who shifted their attention to a heavenly paradise just when the Han Dynasty needed all the support it could get.

Justification for abandoning the cares of this world was evident to the Chinese everywhere. Dissension had already begun in the Imperial Court as early as the reign of He Di (88–100 CE). During his reign, the relatives of ambitious empresses had struck several times as they tried to capture power. The Dou family won control of the Imperial Office briefly, but it soon fell to the might of the eunuchs in 89. Then the Deng family tried to control Emperor An Di (100–125 CE), but they too fell to eunuch influence. Finally, as already men-

tioned, Liang Ji ruled through several puppet emperors until Huan Di recovered power by exterminating the Liang family in the year 160. Next, an open struggle broke out among the Confucian scholars and the eunuchs in 165. The scholars began a campaign against the eunuchs by forming a political league designed to unite their powerful families and construct buffers against eunuch influence. A constant stream of complaints, memorials, and petitions flooded the Imperial Court demanding the removal of these "corrupting agents." The scholars' campaign against the eunuchs coincided with widespread peasant unrest in the countryside as mismanaged taxation had taken its toll on the small farmer. Meanwhile, provincial officials and government bureaucrats, representing the interests of the local landowners, joined in the scholar's complaints. Some 30,000 members of the intelligentsia mobilized to stifle eunuch power. These tactics succeeded in forcing some of the eunuchs to resign, a number of them committing suicide. The majority of eunuchs, however, mobilized, and struck back.

Already having formed a league of their own in 135, the eunuchs won the ear of Emperor Huan Di (146–167 CE) and forced the scholars to resign in 166. Huan Di then declared an amnesty for those eunuchs that had been dismissed and banished the remaining scholars from court. These reprisals, however, inspired another scholars' revolt, and the scholars grasped their opportunity when the emperor died in 167. Now they turned to the Dowager Empress who conspired with them in a plan to slaughter the eunuchs. The Dowager Empress, however, wavered at the last moment, the plan leaked out, and the eunuchs discovered their proposed fate. Instead of suffering a massacre, the eunuchs struck first. In 167–68, they engineered a palace *coups de état* (blows against the state) that led to a prosecution of scholars empire wide. Arresting members of the scholars' league, the eunuchs executed thousands of the intelligentsia. Triumphant, the eunuchs now held a monopoly on power. Their victory, however, would be short lived because they lacked the skills to run the empire. Indeed, the eunuchs had killed those who did have such skill. Thus, the Imperial Court fell into disarray: incompetence, extreme taxation, forced labor, epidemics, famine, and slavery swept through the empire.

An agrarian crisis marked the last few years of the Han Dynasty. From 170 onward, gangs of peasants took up banditry, fled to the protection of great landlords, or raised armed forces to protest their fate. Whole provinces were invaded by wandering ex-farmers seeking their next meal. Meanwhile, Daoism experienced a resurgence at the same time that Buddhism entered China as these peasants turned to rival faiths that opposed

Confucianism. Since Daoism preached that those who tried to control nature would suffer the wrath of the aboriginal forces of the universe, the peasants condemned the Confucian scholars who had failed to rule wisely or check the power of the eunuchs. Peasant leaders such as Zhang Jiao, Zhang Liang, Zhang Bao and Zhang Daoling used Daoism as a messianic message: they promised other peasants who joined in their rebellion that their efforts would end the chaos caused by the Imperial Court and restore the "Way" as the source of harmony on Earth. Movements like the Yellow Turbans (*Huang-jin*) under Zhang Jiao, and his brothers Zhang Liang and Zhang Bao, and The Five Bushels of Rice League (*Wu-dou mi dao*) under Zhang Daoling, sought to usher in a utopian paradise based on Daoist principles. (Incidentally, the Five Bushels of Rice League got its name from the tax it levied on those who joined its forces.) The combination of these two peasant movements organized a military force that by 184 numbered some 360,000 peasants in eight provinces.

On April 4, 184, Zhang Jiao agreed to stage a general rebellion against the Han, but the insurgents' plan leaked out. Fleeing to his provincial stronghold, he escaped the repression that followed and proceeded to organize local forces. When he launched a second revolt, all of rural China rose up with him. The Han Court was shocked at the degree of popular support Zhang Jiao had mustered, and they staged a massive reprisal. Five provinces, however, fell to the Yellow Turbans before the Han could mobilize. But once the Han forces did respond, some 500,000 Chinese peasants met their death. In the effort to meet this emergency, however, the aristocratic warlords overran the Chinese Empire. Massive armies marched through northern China trying to suppress peasant rebel forces, but local blame for the rebellion fell on the eunuchs. Now the aristocratic generals and surviving scholars, holding out the eunuchs as incompetent, banded together to slaughter the eunuch-league in 189. Meanwhile in the province of Sichuan, the Five Bushels of Rice League launched their revolt. By 190, the Five Bushels of Rice movement succeeded in establishing a kingdom under Zhang Lu, the grandson of Zhang Daoling. Now, however, the future of China belonged to the warlord-generals who had been put in charge of destroying the peasant rebellions.

And the final gasps of the Han Dynasty came at the hands of those aristocratic generals who had taken advantage of the peasant revolts as their opportunity to assert their power. Keeping the Han Court around as a symbol of unity, these generals were the true rulers of China. Four of these generals, Dong Cho, Yuan Shu, Cao Cao, and Sun De, were the men who had organized the slaughter of the eunuchs in 189 as a preliminary move to forge their own kingdoms from the remains of the empire. Dong Cho stands out among these men because he was the general who destroyed the Yellow Turbans. Meanwhile, immediately after the execution of the eunuchs, Dong Cho led his troops to Loyang to install the last Han emperor, Xian Di. But just as he planned to capture complete control over the remainder of the empire, his adopted son assassinated him.

With the death of Dong Cho, the greatest of all the warlords, Cao Cao, stepped forward to take the reins of power; his career coincided with the end of the Han. As a general, he had relied heavily on the recruitment of nomadic troops whom he settled within China as a source of military power. He became lord protector of the Imperial Court in 196 and oversaw the remainder of Xian Di's reign. He was a talented commander in a time of chaos; he was reputed to be willing to sacrifice anyone or anything for the sake of security. He was, at the same time, a respected poet, satirist, and intellectual. Cunning and unscrupulous, he was also witty, engaging, and charismatic. As a result, Cao Cao epitomized the age in which he lived: he was a completely corrupt and ruthless individual who nonetheless attracted a loyal and dedicated following.

As an expert commander and creative strategist, Cao Cao took control of the empire. One by one he eliminated his rivals in North China. Yet, with the death of Cao Cao in 220, the final break up of the Han Dynasty took place. His son, Cao-bei, forced the emperor Xian Di to resign and decided to rule on his own as the first Wei emperor. Out of the ruins of the Han, three kingdoms emerged: one forged by Cao-bei in North China called the Wei kingdom, and two others created by Liu-bei and Sun-juan. Liu-bei was a freebooter with a legitimate claim to the Han throne, given his Liu family connections; he built the kingdom of Shu located in the southwest. Sun-juan became the king of Wu in the southeast; he created a realm centered on Nanjing that controlled the lower Changjiang River. But trouble brewed on the frontier. By 307, the Ordos, an assimilated nomadic confederation to the north of China, saw no reason not to invade. They mounted an attack in 311, captured North China, commencing an era of internal division that lasted until 581.

Gupta India: The Great Exception

Unlike Rome and Han China, the Gupta Dynasty of India did not last a long time. Its official history stretches only from 320 to 535 CE, and yet this official era of rule is far too generous. The monarchs that governed as Gupta Emperors were: Chandra Gupta I (320–335); Sumudra Gupta (335–375); Chandra Gupta II (375–415); Kumara Gupta (415–455); and Skanda Gupta (455–467). Like the Han Dynasty, after Skanda Gupta, the remaining kings, Budha Gupta, his son, and his nephew, and finally his grandson, had such brief reigns that they could not effectively control the empire. Furthermore, all the Guptas spent their entire lives fighting either to build or maintain the empire. Chandra Gupta I controlled only a small kingdom some 375 miles long, and 180 miles wide along the Ganges River. His son Sumudra Gupta conquered the east coast of India, pushed the realm to the mouth of the Ganges in the northwest, and reached into the central highlands; he increased the realm eight-fold. Chandra Gupta II added the Shaka territories from the central highlands to the mouth of the Indus River and established a diplomatic alliance with the kingdoms of Madras Kartrpura, Yaudheyas, and Vakatakas using military pressure and a liberal intermarriage strategy. Chandra Gupta II married his daughters to these neighboring kings and used military campaigns to display his power and intimidate the others. The remainder of the Guptas rulers spent their entire careers either maintaining what had been won before them, or watching it slowly crumble before their eyes.

The Gupta Empire emerged in Indian history after a five-hundred-year gap between the first time the subcontinent had been unified and Chandra Gupta I's first campaigns. Also the Gupta Empire produced some remarkable parallels with India's first episode of unification. Both the Gupta Empire and the previous era of unity, the Mauryan Empire (see Chapter Four), began in the year 320—yet the former was 320 CE and the latter was 320 BCE. The founding monarchs of both empires were named Chandra Gupta, the former Chandra Gupta I, and the latter Chandragupta (one word) Maurya. Next, both founding monarchs only initiated the conquest process, while neither dynasty completed unification until the grandsons took the throne. Finally, both dynasties began disintegrating after the third generation, which produced two more eras of disorder in Indian history. In both cases, the two periods of complete unity lasted for only one generation, the third; after that, India reverted to its normal political condition—chaos.

Given the absence of an effective central authority, India remained divided throughout most of its history. Part of the reason for such political instability is likely due to the spread of disease. Given the heavy concentration of microparasites found in the Ganges River district, one should not be surprised at the problems that India faced in forming and maintaining an imperial bureaucracy. After 1500 BCE, the cities and

states that developed in India took root in a region very different from the semiarid environments found in the Mediterranean and North China. As mentioned in Chapter Four, the first kingdoms to appear after the Aryan invasions used a combination of rice and iron to provide the food surpluses needed to feed an urban hierarchy. Rice, however, did not grow in the dry districts of the Indus Valley; rather, it grew along the Ganges River Basin. Rice cultivation along the Ganges, however, proved to be dangerous.

In the Ganges River valley, the monsoons supplied an abundance of water during the six-month rainy season. With the Himalaya Mountains shielding it from the cold Arctic winds, the temperature in the Ganges Valley remained consistently warm. The combination of a wet and warm climate proved to be the perfect environment for breeding germs. Just as the Chinese experienced centuries of disease and hardship as they tried to colonize the wet and warm districts of the Changjiang River, China's rice basket, so the Indians suffered cycles of epidemics while settling the Ganges River. After centuries had passed, many of the farmers along both the Changjiang and the Ganges had built up immunities to local infections. Some diseases, however, were very unforgiving: smallpox and bubonic plague are two examples. Smallpox has produced some 450 varieties since it first made contact with humans; and, as mentioned above, fulminant smallpox is still 100 percent lethal to people without vaccinations. Bubonic plague remains dormant for many years, yet when it breaks out, only modern antibiotics like tetracycline will stop it. Such diseases were common in India, and they were joined by other major epidemics like measles and cholera. Living in the Ganges River Basin, these diseases infected the merchants who carried them off to their unsuspecting customers.

Ironically, while disease made India an easy target for invasion, many who tried could not stay long because of the danger of infection. A long succession of foreign rulers entered India from the northwest, but their capacity to rule the subcontinent depended on the balance struck between their military resources and local epidemics. From 1500 BCE to 1000 CE, most who invaded India suffered plagues; only the natives seemed to have sufficient immunities to rule portions of India for any length of time without succumbing to local infections. It was only after the end of the ancient era, when many of India's diseases had traveled throughout Eurasia, that foreigners began to share some of the immunities enjoyed by natives of the subcontinent. Only after this era of sharing, and the cycle of raids launched by Muslims, who had occupied Afghanistan ca. 1000 CE, did some of the invaders begin to rival the resistance enjoyed by native kings.

At any rate, the fall of the Gupta Empire did not affect the people of India in quite the same way that the fall of Rome and Han China had upset the imaginations of their respective peoples. Indians had long before given up relying heavily on political structures to organize their lives. Their religious traditions of Hinduism and Buddhism already played a far greater role in coping with the problems of the living than did allegiance to a political entity. Like Buddhism, Hinduism put forth the premise that life was suffering. Unlike Buddhism, however, Hinduism did not maintain that the "self" was a false identity; rather, it was a fragment of a larger universal whole. This universal whole, the all-suffering deity Brahma, served as a transcendental substructure to the body of society, which comprised all the various castes. Every caste represented a divine portion of Brahma, whose body had been divided by occupation, status, and conduct into the numerous functions required by the social structure. Karma trapped the soul bound within a caste to the wheel of life that represented all the lessons one had to learn before their journey in this world could end. Reincarnation reflected the way karma accumulated during one lifetime as one advanced from the feet of Brahma to his head; also, each life required a move from one caste to another. Everything a person sensed while living one of his or her various lives, however, was an illusion, for only the whole was real. As in Buddhism, the ultimate goal of every soul was to escape this world of misery at the end of the long journey on Earth.

Given both the religious traditions of Buddhism and Hinduism, Indians were well prepared for the end of a political era. Amazingly though, the fall of the Gupta represented the last time a native dynasty would rule the subcontinent until 1947. In the meantime, the destruction wrought by nomadic invasions, the internal squabbling that followed, and the arrival of Islam ensured the political division of India until the Mogul Empire in 1526.

For its part, the Gupta Dynasty began to decay after 450 CE, with external invasion and internal disloyalty quickly unravelling it. The White Huns, a branch of the Xiong-Nu (Mongols—see below), began by putting pressure on the remaining Gupta rulers. Focusing all their resources on defending the northern frontier, the Gupta Dynasty could not maintain its control over subordinate princes. More like a collection of quasi-independent *rajas* (kings) allied to a central government, than a true empire like Rome or China, Gupta India relied on the ability of its ruler to concentrate on domestic affairs. External invasions, however, allowed regional princes to break away from the façade of central rule. The result was that once the White Huns moved into and occupied the north, the rest of India collapsed into a system of independent fiefdoms. Even though one competent ruler, Harsha Gupta (616–657), made an attempt to reunite the empire, his efforts failed and the fragments of the old empire remained divided thereafter.

The Nomads

The nomadic invasions that destroyed what was left of Rome, Han China, and Gupta India reflected the age-old impulse to raid felt by shepherd peoples. Barbarian attacks were a constant threat throughout the history of the ancient world ; they could occur at any time. Their frequency increased, however, whenever a crippled civilization revealed its vulnerability to the warlike herdsmen living anywhere on its frontier. And as we have seen, trade itself could create the circumstances that encouraged nomadic invasions; commerce—especially of the magnitude that occurred along the Silk Road—usually gave the nomads two good reasons to invade. First, commerce supplied knowledge of the wealth available at each end of the trade routes. Second, trade itself involved exchanges, gifts, and even bribes by merchants that caused nomadic populations to grow beyond what their livestock could sustain. As a result, the enormous sea of grass that once fed the herds of Central Asia could no longer support the vast number of warlike tribes seeking new pastures to meet their needs. Movement, population pressures, and hunger provided the motivation needed to launch a major nomadic invasion.

As mentioned earlier in Chapter Six and again above, trade with nomads was a double-edged sword. While commerce created access to the resources needed by urban societies, it also diffused to shepherd cultures the skills, methods, and wealth of a sedentary civilization. Moreover, trade generated an alternative income beyond the food surpluses supplied by the livestock found in nomadic herds; as a result, trade drew shepherd societies into a dependent relationship with sedentary peoples. Thus, the numbers of people living in Central Asia between 100 BCE and 300 CE grew in response to the abundance supplied by the trade caravans that traveled through their territories. Therefore, once Rome, Han China, and Gupta India assembled the means to create the first semiglobal commercial network, these ancient sedentary civilizations had also set in motion a dangerous process of change. Not only had these great empires opened up avenues for the spread of goods, ideas, and germs, but they increased the number of the warlike nomads itching to attack their neighbors.

As trade faltered due to the increasing internal decay of Rome, Han China, and Gupta India, a vast number of nomadic peoples living in Central Asia had little choice but to search for the sources of wealth that had caused their numbers to grow. Tribes from one end of the Central Asian steppe to the other began to move in response to the population pressures caused by a loss of commercial income. At the same time, the quest for new pastures to supplement the loss of trade increased the use of violence. The result was new levels of warfare and movement among the nomads that led to yet another great migration. This migration, like earlier mass movements, culminated in cycles of invasion; the only difference here is that this migration destroyed the ancient Eurasian world.

The driving force behind this new nomadic movement proved to be the Xiong-nu. Named by the Chinese, the Xiong-nu were really the Mongols living on the porous frontier directly to the north of the Han Dynasty. Known as the Huns to Rome, and as the White Huns to Gupta India, the Xiong-nu (Mongols) supplied the military pressures that set in motion all other nomadic societies that took part in this new migratory episode. Living in the zone of exchange between China and the steppe, the Xiong-nu had suffered extensive attempts to control their movement by the Han Dynasty when it had been strong. But now the efforts at subjugation and relocation within China could not curb the military prowess of the Mongols. Thus, as the Han weakened, the Xiong-nu struck back. Since there was no longer anything between them and their goal, the Xiong-nu invaded China in 316, sacked Loyang, slaughtered 30,000 people, and sent northern China into a century of chaos. Only the mountains of Sichuan, and the large river systems of the Changjiang kept the nomads out of southern China. For more than three centuries, China remained divided: nomadic Mongol kingdoms in the north, and Chinese realms in the south.

From 316 to 386 CE, northern China became a battleground for nomadic tribal dynasties; during this period sixteen different states established brief kingdoms along the basin of the Huang He. Then, in 386, the Duo Ba Turks took up residence in north China, set up the Northern Wei Dynasty, and created an era of relative peace that lasted until 534. Their success, however, rested on the fact that they let the conquered Chinese manage agriculture, tax-collection, and administration for this new Turkish realm. Protecting the north from further invasions for 150 years, the Duo Ba Turks, however, suddenly broke into eastern and western factions after 534, and then could no longer secure political stability. Together, both factions generated three dynasties in quick succession, each plagued with numerous, but short-lived kings. The last of these, Emperor Bin, died under mysterious circumstances and opened the way for Yang Jian to grasp power. The son of a Chinese official to the Northern Wei with powerful connections, Yang Jian seized power in north China in 581 and then reunited it with the south. He was able to launch the brief Sui Dynasty (581–618) that laid the foundation for Chinese recovery and set up the circumstances for the next great era of political unity under the Tang (618–906).

Meanwhile, in north China, the surge of transitory nomadic kingdoms that dominated politics between 316 and 581 preserved Chinese institutions during the era of chaos that followed the fall of the Han. Each new group established a military state, encouraged the practice of Buddhism, and added a tough veneer of Confucian culture, for all those who invaded China recognized the value of what they saw. Group after group settled down, adopted Chinese ways, attracted immigrants from the south, and intermarried. Slowly a process of assimilation had begun despite the chaos of barbarian rule. Simply unable to rule an established agricultural region without aid from those that they had conquered, each wave of nomads left behind little beyond new military and economic institutions. Ironically, it was the combination of Chinese traditions and Buddhism that the nomads ended up preserving.

In terms of Roman history, another branch of the Xiong-nu marched west pushing all they encountered in the same direction. In the first century CE, the Hans Dynasty's efforts at pacification of its northern frontier (Mongolia) had set a portion of the Xiong-nu in motion seeking booty from easier victims. Moving at a leisurely pace, the Huns encountered the Ostrogoths (East-Goths) on the lands north of the Black Sea in 372 CE. After brutally conquering the Ostrogoths, the Huns, who used their access to a vast supply of horses and skilled archers in battle, then turned to the Visigoths (West-Goths) who fled to avoid devastation. An estimated 80,000 Visigoths—men, women, and children—sought refuge in Roman territory. Meanwhile, the Huns continued their westward migration driving still more Germans toward Rome. Beginning in the fifth century CE, the Hun occupied lands north of the Danube River, fed their horses on grasslands later called "Hungary," and lived comfortably with their German slaves, as long as both the Eastern and Western Roman Empires paid them a handsome tribute (see below).

Meanwhile the fleeing Visigoths arrived on the Roman frontier in 375. Tens of thousands of Visigoths entered the empire under Valens' protection, but poor treatment by frontier officials caused these Germans to attack their "protectors." Leading a force to deal with them, Valens met the Visigoths at Adrianople in 378. Instead of destroying these "barbarians," however, Valens himself suffered defeat and lost his life. Then, after 378, the Visigoths rampaged unchecked within the Roman frontier until they sacked the eternal city itself in 409. Right behind them were the Ostrogoths and the Huns as well as the flood of tribes that helped dismember the Western Roman Empire: the Franks, Burgundians, Saxons, Angles, Jutes, Danes, Alammani, Gepides, and Lombards.

Each of the nomadic tribes that entered Roman territory either settled on the land, or met with destruction. Of the twelve tribes mentioned above, only the Danes and the Franks produced a history that endured politically. The Danes occupied Denmark and remained there throughout the Middle Ages, while the Franks founded the feudal realms that became France and the principalities of Germany and Italy. All the other tribes experienced political or military defeat at the hands of their neighbors, or the second and third wave of nomadic invasions.

The Visigoths occupied much of Italy, southwestern Gaul, and settled in Spain. There they remained until the Ostrogoths drove them from Italy, the Franks expelled them from southern France, and the Arabs overran them on the Iberian Peninsula. The Vandals took up residence in North Africa, and sacked Rome a second time in 455, but suffered defeat at the hands of Emperor Justinian in 533 as he tried to reconstruct the old Roman Empire. The Burgundians occupied northern and western Europe, lending their name to Burgundy in France—but fell to the Franks in 543. The Gepides and Alammani suffered a common fate; they fought the Romans, the Huns, and the Ostrogoths, while their lands eventually became part of the Frankish Empire built by the Emperor Charlemagne (742–814). The Ostrogoths set up a kingdom in Italy, enjoying diplomatic contact with the Eastern Roman Empire, but it collapsed in 562 during Justinian's war to reunite the empire. The Lombards replaced the Ostrogoths on the Italian Peninsula, but suffered defeat at the hands of the Franks in 774 as the Carolingian (Charlemagne's) Dynasty constructed a new alliance with the Papacy in Rome to create the foundations of feudalism. The Saxons who remained in Germany experienced defeat at the hands of the Franks as Charlemagne expanded east between 772–804. Finally, the Danes, the Jutes, the Angles, and the Saxons who fought one another for control of Britain fell to the descendants of the Vikings at the battle of Hastings in 1066.

While the German tribes of the fourth and fifth centuries CE launched their attacks against Rome, the Huns ceased being content in Hungary. The Eastern Roman Emperor, Marian, refused to pay any further bribes in 451. The king of the Huns, Attila (ca. 433–53) began raiding, but he judged the Western Roman Empire an easier target than Constantinople (the capital in the east). Attila invaded Gaul and confronted a combined Roman and German army (the Germans

Attila the Hun, 406–53, King of the Huns, is shown here in a copperplate engraving, c. 1820, by Ludwig Buchhorn. Collection: Coll. Archiv f. Kunst & Geschichte, Berlin. Photo: akg-images, London.

feared the Huns as much as the Romans did). In 452, Aetius, a Roman general who had studied Hun military tactics, engaged them at the Battle of Châlon in Champagne, defeating Attila, but failing to destroy him. Attila regrouped his forces that same year, crossed the Alps into Italy, and confronted the Romans once again. Since Rome's German allies saw no reason to defend Italy, the Romans faced imminent destruction. But disease broke out among the Huns, and Pope Leo I (400–61) managed to persuade Attila to retreat, and Rome survived devastation. The following year, 453, Attila contracted a fatal illness, and when he died, the Huns left Europe, ending their pressure on both the Romans and the Germans.

Meanwhile Gupta India suffered the same fate as China and the West. During the reign of Kumara-Gupta (415–55), a group of *mleccha* (incomprehensible foreigners) entered India. These newcomers were another branch of the Xiong-nu (Huns) that had broken off from the main confederation and marched into Bactria (northern Afghanistan). These White Huns had become a constant threat to the Hindu-Kush region. Fortunately for the Gupta, a champion worthy of distinction stopped this early invasion; Skanda Gupta, Kumara's son, managed to repulse the White Huns. India enjoyed one more reign of peace, but with Skanda's death in 467, no other Gupta emperor had enough talent to step forward to prevent invasion. By 510, the fate of India was clear;

the White Huns under the leadership of Toramana, a Mongol as formidable as Attila, made their move. They overran Kashmir and the Punjab and defeated a Gupta army at Gwalior, after which they extended their control over Indian territory as far as Malwa. This signaled the weakness of the Gupta to the subordinate rajas who had accepted the leadership of this dynasty prior to the invasions. Now these regional rajas declared their independence from Gupta rule, broke the White Huns' hold on northwest India, and ended India's second great era of unification. One explanation for the success of India's rajas against a barbarian invader, when compared to Rome and China, is that the White Huns had entered a disease-rich territory. Infection thinned their ranks, and the armies of the newly independent Indian kings did the rest.

The fall of the Gupta Dynasty marked the end of the ancient era and the beginning of a new age. Since the nomads had used massive cavalry formations to defeat their foe, the nature of the new period would reflect the importance of the warhorse as a means of defense against future invasions. Furthermore, since the die-off era caused by horrific cyles of disease, famine, and nomadic invasions had greatly thinned human numbers in China and the West, land once dedicated to people could now be turned over to breeding horses. As a result, the Parthian Empire of Persia based on the warhorse, large landed estates, aristocratic warriors in armor, and a new fodder plant called alfalfa became a common model used to resist nomadic invasions (see Chapter Twelve, Unit Two for the details). Accordingly, the remnants of the Eastern Roman Empire that had survived the barbarian migration adopted the warhorse and aristocratic estates as an effective defense. While the Western Roman Empire that had fallen to invader after invader developed a system of feudalism, in which landed lords used large estates to enlist armored knights sitting on warhorses to defend their domains.

Thus, as one can see, the end of the ancient era laid a foundation for the middle years of world history. The old civilizations that surrounded the Central Asian steppe came to rely heavily on warhorses to hold nomads in check until infantry using combinations of the pike, the longbow, the crossbow, and eventually cannon and gunpowder finally neutralized the power of cavalry at the end of the Middle Ages. And these later military developments would mark the beginning of yet another major era in world history, the Modern Age.

Suggested Reading

Adams, Richard E. W., and MacLeod, Murdo J., *The Cambridge History of the Native Peoples of the Americas*, Vol. II (Cambridge: Cambridge University Press), 2000.

Bethel, Lesli., ed., *The Cambridge History of Latin America*, Vol. 1 (Cambridge: Cambridge University Press), 1984.

Bowker, J., *Problems of Suffering in Religions of the World* (Cambridge: Cambridge University Press), 1975.

Brown, Peter. *The World of Late Antiquity, A.D. 150–750* (New York: Harcourt Brace Jovanovich), 1971.

Diamond, Jared, *Guns, Steel, and Germs: The Fate of Human Societies* (New York: Norton), 1999.

Fairbanks, John King and Edwin O. Reischauer, *China: Tradition and Transformation*, Revised Edition (Boston: Houghton Mifflin), 1989.

Fairbanks, John King and Merle Goldman, *China: Tradition and Transformation* (Cambridge: Harvard University Press), 1999.

Gernet, Jacque, *A History of Chinese Civilization*, Translated by J. R. Foster and Charles Hartman, Second Edition (Cambridge: Cambridge University Press), 1999.

Hall, Thomas D., *Rise and Demise: Comparing World Systems* (Boulder, Colo.: Westview Press), 1997.

Harrison, J. A., *The Chinese Empire: A Short History of China from Neolithic Times to the End of the Eighteenth Century* (New York: Harcourt Brace Jovanovich), 1972.

Hopfe, Lewis M., *Religions of the World.* Revised Edition (Upper Saddle River, N.J., 2005).

Jones, A. H. M., *The Later Roman Empire, 284–605: A Social, Economic, and Administrative Survey*, Two Volumes (Baltimore: Johns Hopkins University Press), 1986.

Keen, Benjamin, ed., *Latin American Civilization*, 6th ed. (Boulder: Westview Press), 1995.

Keay, John, *India: A History,* (New York: Atlantic Monthly Press), 2000.

Krause, Enrique, *Mexico* (New York: Harper Collins), 1997.

McNeill, William H., *Plagues and People* (New York: Anchor Press), 1976.

Parinder, Geoffrey, ed., *World Religions, From Ancient History to the Present* (New York: Checkmark Books), 1971.

Reat, Noble Ross, *Buddhism: A History* (Berkeley: Asian Humanities Press), 1994.

Tainter, Joseph A., *The Collapse of Complex Societies* (Cambridge: Cambridge University Press), 1988.

Thaper, Romila, *Early India: From Origins to AD 1300*, Volume I (Penguin Books India), 2003.

The middle years of world history begin with the fall of Rome, Han China, Gupta India, and Kush Africa (ca. 200 to 600 CE). This period witnessed the consolidation of regional cultures, meaningful social transformation, and cultural diffusion that brought civilization to the remaining peoples living on the fringes of Eurasian sedentary life. For those communities who rose to domination over a region, the middle years of world history (500 to 1500 CE) were a golden age during which the original cultural hearths matured and spread outward to their neighbors. Such a cultural hearth existed in the Far East, as China recovered its ancient imperial design, underwent an era of cultural expansion, stimulating the emergence of civilizations in Korea and Japan, and inspiring the rise of the last great nomadic group in Central Asia—the Mongols. In contrast, a new era of social transformation began in Medieval Europe, post-Gupta India, West-Central Sub-Saharan Africa, and the Swahili Coast of East Africa. In all four cultural regions, the forces of military innovation, migrating religions, and unstable economic, social, and political institutions caused change. Finally, a new era of civilization began in the Middle East, Korea, Japan, Central and Southern Africa, Mesoamerica, and the Andean Plateau as new, original civilizations transformed the landscape and induced nomads to adopt a sedentary lifestyle. The best theme to explain the complex history of the middle years is *culture*, as seen within the context of the well-established sedentary hearths of the ancient era and their adjacent territories, as both adjusted to new conditions.

During any era, the definition of culture is itself complex, requiring several supporting ideas to explain its principle attributes. Culture is "learned, shared, symbolic," and "integrated." First, culture is *learned* because within a cultural group a rich pattern of conscious behavior is transmitted from one generation to the next, usually through the family, but often using other social institutions such as schools or churches to augment the learning process. Culture is *shared* because people within specific geographic locales produce a consensus on accepted beliefs and actions and encourage families within regional communities to form cooperative societies. Culture is *symbolic* because through it are transmitted abstract ideas—figurative representations that capture sounds, concepts, and numbers and convert them into spoken and written languages such as in mathematics; oral traditions; sacred texts and religious commentaries; literature, artistic expression, and music. Finally, culture is *integrated* because through it is formed a system of complementary institutions based on learned, shared, and symbolic experiences that generate the fabric of society, produce cooperative forms of labor, create religious and scientific explanations of the universe, and sustain political institutions that hold the entire society together. How well a culture is integrated explains whether social, economic, intellectual, and political institutions unify or undermine human communities.

In the middle years of world history, the way regional cultures integrated their principle institutions explains why some civilizations experienced a golden age, while others underwent unstable periods that required significant social change, and still others gave up a nomadic existence and accepted sedentary life through the sharing of ideas, tools, goods, and domesticated plants and animals from sedentary neighbors. How well a culture integrated its key institutions during the 1,000 years between 500 and 1500 CE determined how much geographic space this civilization would command, how many peoples such a society would influence, and how stable life would be within the community.

Since no one culture came to dominate the globe during the middle years, no single regional civilization created exactly the right mix of integrated cultural institutions to have an impact on the way everyone on Earth lived. Yet, since Europe spontaneously managed to create such a powerful integration of institutions that the West actually launched the process of modernization after 1500 CE (see Unit Three), historians know that the correct cultural potential existed in Western Eurasia to produce such a major shift during this time. Why Europe alone underwent such social, economic, intellectual, and political transformations that its civilization brought the world to the cusp of the modern age speaks to the power of culture itself.

Paradoxically, the more stable a culture's institutional fabric during the middle years, the less likely that society would change the integration of its key institutions to acquire the power needed to change the world. At the same time, the more unstable a culture's social fabric, the more likely that civilization would simply collapse internally. What was needed to reach beyond the regional patterns of cultural integration that dominated the middle years was to find the right institutional mix: one with sufficient instability to encourage internal change and sufficient stability to avoid complete cultural disintegration.

Keeping this issue of potential global change in mind, a quick assessment of the regional cultures of the globe during the middle years of world history offers some significant insights into human conduct between 500 and 1500 CE. During these 1,000 years, China enjoyed a golden age, repeated its behavior successfully, and maintained its classical forms; hence social continuity took precedence over change. India suffered severe internal disorder and could not achieve a stable form of internal coherence; hence political chaos was the norm. Korea, Japan, and the Mongols came in contact with sedentary life for the first time and had to spend years adjusting to their new lifestyle. Mesoamerica and the Andean Plateau were located in such complete geographic isolation from the rest from the world that their great sedentary civilizations could

only smelt soft metals and were still in the stone age; they had not really left the ancient era yet. The Middle East entered an age of religious expansion as the vitality of Islam sent armies of Muslims into North and sub-Saharan Africa and what had been the Ancient Near East: Persia, India, and Central Asia. But dedication to a theocratic form of government set limits on how much power the followers of Mohammed believed Allah had allowed humans to exercise on Earth. Finally, Europe produced a complex and intriguing cultural mix.

Medieval Europe combined a fragile, dysfunctional set of social, economic, and political institutions that did not sufficiently integrate to create a stable community. Instead, change became the norm for the various states, estates, and free cities that emerged during this time. Furthermore, some people in Europe began to see opportunity within change itself so that they participated in a spontaneous pattern of social transformation that made change tolerable within the context of a traditional society. This meant that Europe combined the right mixture of social dysfunction with sufficient internal coherence to allow Europeans to move through three different cultural integrations during the middle years. Europe also developed an institutional pattern of cultural integration that brought Europeans to the cusp of the modern age.

The concept of culture sheds light on the study of the various civilizations that are the subject of Unit Two. Each regional culture will be analyzed to explain how it functioned internally as well as how it related to adjacent civilizations and nomadic peoples. Also, using the concept of culture as the central theme of Unit Two will allow this text to explore the power of human creativity as an element of history in contrast with the limitations imposed by biological factors as studied in Unit One. Here the free range of humanity's potential to change the circumstances of life will be explored within the context of the institutional limits set by regional civilizations.

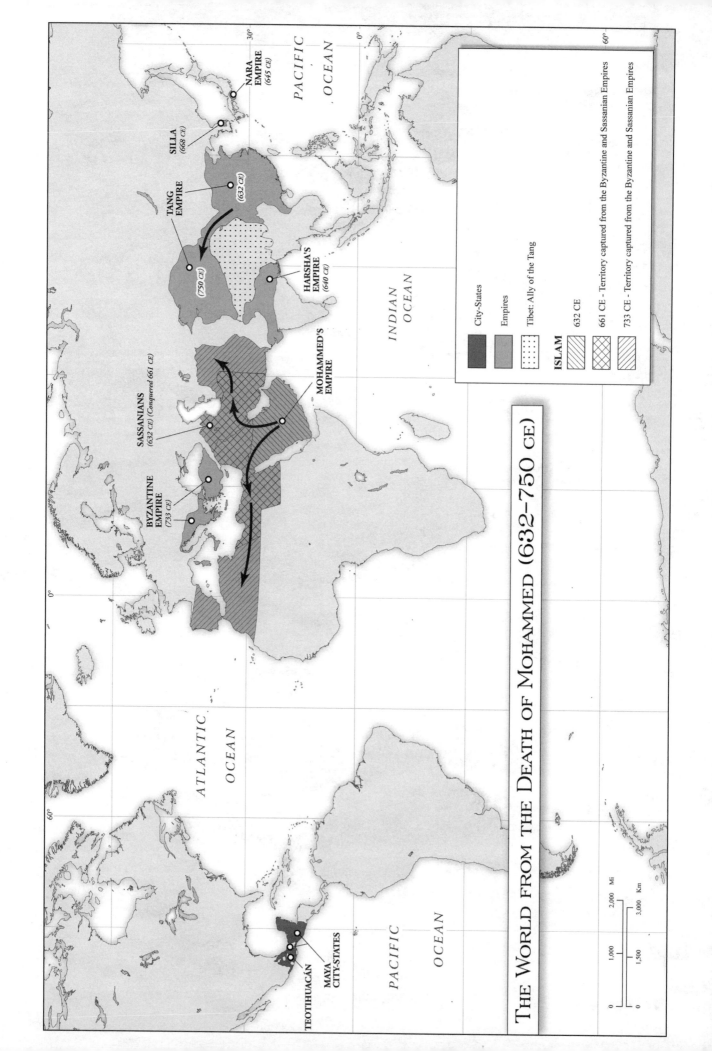

THE WORLD FROM THE DEATH OF MOHAMMED (632–750 CE)

NARA EMPIRE *(645 CE)*

SILLA *(668 CE)*

TANG EMPIRE *(632 CE)*

(750 CE)

HARSHA'S EMPIRE *(640 CE)*

SASSANIANS *(632 CE) (Conquered 661 CE)*

MOHAMMED'S EMPIRE

BYZANTINE EMPIRE *(733 CE)*

TEOTIHUACÁN

MAYA CITY-STATES

PACIFIC OCEAN

INDIAN OCEAN

ATLANTIC OCEAN

PACIFIC OCEAN

City-States

Empires

Tibet: Ally of the Tang

ISLAM

632 CE

661 CE - Territory captured from the Byzantine and Sassanian Empires

733 CE - Territory captured from the Byzantine and Sassanian Empires

0   1,000   2,000 Mi

0   1,500   3,000 Km

30°

0°

60°

60°

0°

XI

THE RISE
of Islam

The product of two Mediterranean religions that had migrated to the Arabian Peninsula, Islam emerged during the middle years of world history to become a potent force that helped to redefine Eurasia and Africa. Occupying the central land bridge between three continents, the followers of Islam played a major role in shaping the new era.

Having developed in the harsh environment of the Arabian desert, Islam borrowed heavily from Jewish and Christian concepts that had penetrated Arabia to find a Bedouin culture in transition. Comprised of nomadic herders, oasis agriculturists, and interregional merchants, the Bedouins organized themselves into tribes that required absolute loyalty. Bedouin tribesmen occupied themselves as nomadic herders, farmers, and merchants, moving back and forth between these occupations at will. Such occupational shifts forced Bedouins to adapt readily to cultural changes, and, at the same time, this shifting lifestyle eroded the power of the traditional deities the Bedouins had worshipped. As a result, Arabia was fertile ground for religious transformation.

When the tenets of Judaism and Christianity entered this new cultural environment the Arabs were receptive to these stimulating beliefs. Nonetheless, these religions were foreign and therefore did not speak fully to the Bedouin heart. This pattern of diffusion actually generated a new faith that took its vision from the prophecy of a Bedouin merchant named Mohammed. This prophetic vision, Islam, meant "submission," or the complete surrender of a person's will to God (*Allah*), while "Muslim" identified one who submitted.

Assuming the perspective of *Muslims*, the faithful were those who accepted Mohammed's worldview without question. His viewpoint sprang from a message that embodied the rapture Mohammed experienced when he accepted his role as the voice of Allah, the one true God. So successful was the prophet Mohammed at relaying the tremendous power of his vision to his followers, that in a remarkably short time Islam became a major religion, the passion of which transformed a marginal culture into a world power. The passion released by Islam mobilized Muslim society to expand from the Arabian Peninsula west and north into Europe, east into Asia, and south into Africa. From their central location on the land bridge astride the three continents, the Muslims set about redefining each society they encountered and transformed the entire region into a new geopolitical entity henceforth known as the "Middle East."

The Prophecy

Mohammed (570–632 *[from this point forward, all dates not marked BCE are CE]*) began life as an orphan in the Arabian Desert, where he learned what all Arabs typically had to discover in order to survive. Like all Arabs, he struggled to make his way in a huge, barren place of more than 1 million square miles, a place known to many in the world as the "vacant quarter." Thus, the Arabian Peninsula got its name from the vast wasteland it offered to humanity.

Mohammed learned the fundamental lesson of his culture: that to be an Arab meant being on the move. The word *Arab* itself derived from a Semite term meaning "to move." As an Arab, Mohammed traveled throughout Arabia, personally making numerous trips from Yemen to the Levant (what is today Syria, Lebanon, Palestine, and Israel) in his youth.

The crescent moon and star (divinity and sorrow), symbol of Islam. From *Symbols, Signs, & Signets*, by Ernst Lehner.

Like all Arabs of the day, Mohammed lived among a divided people whose traditions acknowledged few loyalties except the bonds of blood. These bonds tied each member of the tribe to the rest so thoroughly that only a blood feud could define justice. Each tribesman found himself linked by family to a narrow circle of fellow tribesmen, and Mohammed soon learned well the one rule of survival in a place with few resources: service to the tribe.

The harsh realities of the vacant quarter deprived Mohammed and his fellow Arabs of the luxury of kindness. In this cruel world, a male-dominated warrior society developed. The men of a particular tribe served a chief whose authority was absolute but whose wisdom required that he consult his followers. Tribes formed alliances with one another from time to time but never disobeyed the paramount social norm: do whatever it takes for your relatives and friends to survive. As a result, the very act of survival defined the successful male.

In such a harsh world with few sedentary sites, Mecca and Medina became highly regarded places. Mecca was a sacred city located on a crossroads where trade caravans often met. Though it had no industry or agriculture, Mecca was a city blessed with a shrine, the *Kaaba*. The Kaaba was a *haram*, or sacred enclave, controlled by powerful merchant tribesmen who enjoyed the commerce of those who came to the shrine to worship or seek refuge from a blood feud. The Kaaba drew many people into Mecca, sustained trade, guaranteed a person's safety while in town, and ensured the economic future of the city. In contrast Medina was an oasis center that enjoyed a self-sufficient existence based on its supply of well water, cultivation, and trade. Few other locations in Arabia offered sedentary residents the same degree of security or wealth.

The orphaned Mohammed found shelter among his relatives when his uncle took him in. As a boy, he worked as a shepherd and lived with his fellow nomadic Bedouins, traveling throughout Arabia from one end to the other before reaching the age of twenty-five. Though an ordinary man, Mohammed had the good fortune to marry a wealthy, loving widow, who bore him several children, and he enjoyed success in business. At the age of forty, however, his life suddenly changed.

A devout man, Mohammed regularly retreated to a cave in the hills near Mecca to pray. While on one of these retreats he heard a voice that proclaimed that he, Mohammed, was to be the messenger of Allah, the one true God. Mohammed believed that the voice he had heard was that of the Angel Gabriel. Mohammed knew that in doing God's work, Gabriel had previously visited numerous Jewish and Christian prophets. For three

years Mohammed struggled, uncertain how to execute the responsibility this voice insisted he take, to carry the word of Allah to his people.

Having no training as a minister, Mohammed suffered doubts about his qualifications, but the voice continued to insist that he act. Finally, he began to preach, at first unsuccessfully, but his passion helped him to perfect his skills. Eventually he won converts: first his wife, then the rest of his family, and then strangers. Those who accepted his message most readily were young people or those from families of modest means. Nonetheless, his ideas were revolutionary, and opposition to them soon formed.

This opposition became vocal as the powerful Omayyad tribe grew to fear Mohammed's influence. The Omayyads wanted their old animistic religion to continue, for it drew people, and thus commerce, to Mecca. Mohammed's new religion threatened their enterprise. Since the merchants of Mecca could ill afford the loss of their sacred shrine to this new faith, they began to persecute Mohammed's few followers. Fearing for his life, Mohammed fled north to Medina, where he set about with far more industry to win the hearts of his people to embrace Allah's word.

Mohammed's escape to Medina occurred one night in 622. Called the *Hegira* (the flight), this move marked the beginning of Islam. According to the Muslim calendar, which starts with the Hegira, the year 2007 of the Western calendar is 1385. Just as Christ's passion and sacrifice on the cross is sacred to Christians, so the Hegira is sacred to Muslims; not only did it launch the history that established Islam as a world religion, but it led to the creation of the cultural hearth known as the Middle East.

In the oasis city of Medina, Mohammed had fallen into the perfect environment to spread his faith. Due to his growing fame as a righteous man, and thanks to the advance work done by converts he had sent ahead, the prophet of Islam entered a city caught up in religious strife. Welcomed as a neutral arbitrator, Mohammed found himself confronted by five fractious tribes, three of which had converted to Judaism. Quickly forging bonds between his Meccan converts and those Medinans interested in his new faith, Mohammed soon gained control of the city. Converting a majority of the inhabitants to his faith, and obtaining the authority of a lawgiver, Mohammed then refined the principles needed to form the first Muslim community. As a result, he captured the hearts of the people of Medina and restored order there, Mohammed soon attracted many more Bedouin and foreign converts to this oasis city.

Conversion expanded the ranks of the Muslims in Medina until the city faced a crisis of having more residents than its resources could support. Resistance from those who had converted to Judaism continued until Mohammed concluded that the Muslims had to force the Jewish proselytes out of Medina. Though Mohammed allowed these Jews to keep their religion, he drove them from their property, turning the land he had confiscated over to his followers.

To expand on the principle of capturing wealth as needed, Mohammed launched raids against the legendary trade caravans coming into Mecca, which forced the merchant-tribesmen from Mecca to retaliate. Although a tiny one, the army Mohammed fielded comprised passionately religious soldiers who, along with their military knowledge gleaned from foreign converts to Islam, defeated Mecca's forces each time. Victory secured the future of both Medina and Islam and perpetuated the traditions of violence common to the vacant zone.

Islam's future derived from the faith Mohammed refined in Medina. As mentioned above, in Arabic Islam simply means *submission*; the Muslim by name was one who had *submitted*. This act of submission entailed following the five duties that Mohammed had imposed on his converts, the *Pillars of Islam.*

The first of the five pillars is the *Shahada*, the sincere profession of faith. Here, the Muslim declared with every fiber of his or her being that *there is no God but Allah, and Mohammed is His prophet.* This first act of acknowledging the authority of Allah and Mohammed began a Muslim's life as a follower of Islam. For a Muslim, the Shahada was in a sense a relief, for it contained no complex theological questions like those that plagued Christianity. Instead, it confirmed the existence of only one immediate and absolute God. Rejecting the complexity of theological debate like the one that spawned the Christian Trinity, Mohammed advanced a strict monotheism. Allah is eternal and infallible, the light of Heaven and Earth, and the Master of all things. Mohammed is merely Allah's prophet; one of many messengers that God had selected to teach the people. Of these messengers, only four had carried the word: Moses revealed the Ten Commandments, David composed the Psalms, Jesus advanced the Gospels, and now Mohammed presented the Qur'an. Of these four, however, only Mohammed's message contained a clear understanding of God's true Will.

The second Pillar, the *Salat*, required that the faithful pray five times a day. Before prayer, worshippers had to purify themselves by ritual bathing, turn to face Mecca from wherever they were in the world, and then move through a regimented cycle of standing, kneeling, bowing, and sitting. Done in groups of fellow Muslims, the regimented cycle of prayers created a strong

bond of union among the worshippers. This solidarity enhanced the power of the Salat and created in the individual Muslim the powerful sensation of being enveloped by the community as well as by Allah.

The third Pillar, the giving of alms, further reinforced the sense of community. Called a *Zakat*, this mandatory payment took the form of *Nisab* (minimum amount) or 85 grams of pure gold. Paid because all things belong to God, and wealth was therefore held by humans only in trust, the giving of alms purified the rest and justified the owner's possession. Like the Salat, the Zakat reinforced a sense of community and social obligation, a reminder that all wealth came from Allah alone. The estate that one acquired over the course of one's life was in fact on loan from God. The worshipper had to remember his duty to Allah and the community before he could take pleasure in the wealth he possessed at the moment.

The fourth Pillar, *Ramadan*, required a month of fasting to commemorate the first revelations of the Qur'an. The ninth month of the lunar year, Ramadan prescribed that no food, drink, medicine, or sensual pleasures occur during the daylight hours. The only people permitted exceptions to these rules were soldiers and the sick, for their duties, or weakness, required that they eat, drink, and take medicines. Ramadan was an annual renewal of one's commitment to Islam and drew together the expanding Muslim community.

The fifth Pillar, *Hajj*, required a pilgrimage to Mecca at least once in a Muslim's lifetime. The goal of the pilgrimage was to visit the *Kaaba*, the temple originally dedicated to the animistic deities that Allah had replaced. Mohammed had transformed the Kaaba from a place to worship pagan deities into one sanctified by Allah. He destroyed the idols located there and proclaimed the Kaaba a site dedicated to Allah.

Later Muslims came to believe that the Hebrew Patriarch Abraham and his son Ishmael had built the Kaaba. According to this legend, Ishmael was Abraham's first son by his wife's handmaiden, Hagar. Abraham had taken Hagar to his bed at the request of his barren wife, Sarah, because she could not bear a child. Yet, as Sarah's jealousy of Hagar grew, Abraham found himself forced to cast Hagar and her son out from among the wandering Hebrew tribes. Later built by the guilt-ridden father and his loyal son, the Kaaba housed a stone sent from Heaven by Allah.

The legend continues with an explanation of the Heavenly stone. Allah sent the stone to mark the Kaaba as a sacred place because He had created Hagar's well there to save her and Ishmael. God had saved them both because Ishmael was destined to become the father of all the Arabs. According to Islam, Allah's plans for the future of humanity included the origins of these tribesmen from the desert who were destined to change the faith of the world.

Finally, next to Hagar's well were the ancient blackstones that absorbed the sins of pilgrims who had fulfilled the Hajj. Allah had placed them near the Kaaba after Adam had been cast out of the garden of Eden. According to this legend, the stones were originally white but had gradually turned black as they absorbed the sins of the faithful. Consequently, the location there of the Kaaba, Hagar's well, and the blackstones combined to make Mecca the holiest of places in the Muslim imagination, the geographic focal point of Islam.

As the size of the Muslim world expanded after Mohammed's death, the Hajj functioned as a counterbalance to a potential and widespread decentralization. The Hajj served to remind all Muslims that their faith had a common center that demanded their personal loyalty. This fifth Pillar increased in significance given the eventual size of the Islamic world.

Some Muslims added *Jihad* as a sixth Pillar, for they felt that it kept the community pure. Jihad literally means *exertion* or *struggle* in Allah's service. Involving an internal as well as external effort, Jihad is a complex practice of maintaining spiritual purity within the individual and the community while endeavoring to spread Islam to the four corners of the Earth. Jihad is a reminder that keeps constant the degree of submission and obedience required of the faithful to Allah; this leads to internal personal and communal peace. At the same time, Jihad required conversion of the pagan world, which led to so-called holy wars. Accordingly, Jihad proved necessary to maintain the vigilance and vitality of the community through its commitment to Allah, while extending the faith as far as the prophecy could travel. Yet, over the course of many centuries, the definition of Jihad has narrowed and come to mean "holy war" for the more fanatical of Mohammed's followers.

Having firmly developed his religious vision, Mohammed expanded his new faith to other oases. This time, however, whenever he encountered converts to Judaism or Christianity, he did not drive them out as he had in Medina; rather he let them remain in place as a tax base. Their payment of the *jizya* (head tax) permitted the conquered to continue their own religious practices even as they submitted to Islamic authority. Then Mohammed added the jizya to the third Pillar, the alms paid by Muslims, to create a system of financial support for the rapidly growing Islamic community.

Under the aegis of this tax structure, Mohammed designed the first Islamic social system. This design involved a two-tier society that placed Mohammed's Arab converts at the top in purity and isolation, with the People of the Book (i.e., Jews and Christians), at the bottom. After Mohammed's death, when Islam reached beyond the Arabian Peninsula, this tax system expanded to include non-Arab converts.

This variation on Mohammed's original design kept Arab tribes as the ruling elite living at the top of an expanding community. Non-Arab converts, *mawali*, lived in the middle and paid a property tax, and occasionally had to pay the jizya as well. People of the Book continued to live at the bottom, obediently paying their head tax. This variation in community design allowed Islam to grow until it dominated the Middle East.

In 630, Mohammed's successes allowed him to return to Mecca in triumph. His entry into the city marked the end of his momentous task. Soon thereafter, in 632, he died of a fever while on a visit to Medina. His legacy was a tightly knit community that had consumed his vision and religious passion and captivated the imagination of Arabia in a mere ten years (622–632).

Mohammed's rapture now became the community's passion. His Five Pillars linked his simple, clear monotheism to a message of obedience that his followers accepted without question. Understanding the message became the central task of every Muslim's life. This task necessarily required capturing and preserving Mohammed's memory so that it could remain intact for future generations.

If his message remained only an oral tradition, the death of the great prophet threatened to end the spread of the new faith he had delivered. The generation that knew him best was slowly dying off, which could utterly destroy Islam unless something was done. Before the memory was lost, those surviving few who had lived closest to Mohammed set about recording his words and deeds.

The project, however, did not get started until 650, eighteen years after Mohammed had died. By that time, Muslim expansion had been dramatic. The size of the Islamic empire made recording Mohammed's memory and the purity of his message even more pressing. Only the survival of this message could hold together the enormous social edifice that Islam had constructed.

At the heart of this memory was the *Qur'an* (Koran). This sacred text contained the words of Allah as transmitted by Mohammed. Comparable to the New Testament, the Qur'an held 117 *sura* or chapters that represented the carefully reconstructed memory of the

Double page from the Qur'an. These pages are from chapter five of the Qur'an (called "al-Ma'ida, The Table Spread"), verses 75–77. The text speaks about Christ, who is described as an apostle, and Mary, who is referred to as "a woman of truth." Three styles of script are used in this case. While the main script and the Persian translations suggest an eastern Islamic source, an Indian (or even Anatolian) connection has been proposed for the style of the illumination. © The Trustees of the British Museum.

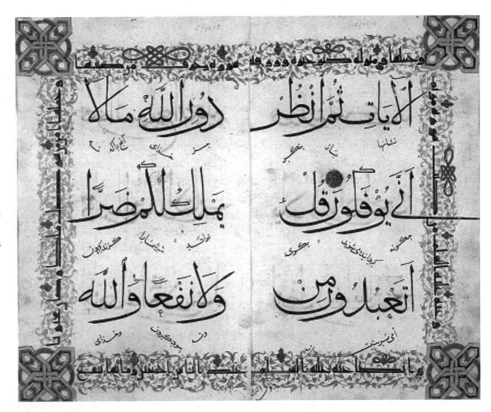

prophet's words. Arranged according to length, starting with the longest and ending with the shortest, all the sura represented the prophecy.

The Qur'an instructed the faithful in issues of social as well religious conduct. It defined inheritance, dowries, and marriage mixed with religious insights that guided Muslims in their daily lives. The faithful committed the Qur'an to memory to be able to apply its wisdom immediately. Only about one-sixth the length of the New Testament, the Qur'an became the living words of the prophet.

Combined with the Qur'an was the *Hadith*, a collection of writings that incorporates all of Mohammed's sayings and actions outside the Qur'an. Comprised of nonprophetic statements and deeds, the *Hadith* captured Mohammed's wisdom as a righteous man. Here, Mohammed's personal behavior as a mere human being held enormous value as a model of conduct for the faithful. This collection of thousands of Mohammed's statements and deeds, therefore, constituted a second guide to reinforce the Qur'an and flesh-out a much richer vision of Islam.

Finally, if the Qur'an or the *Hadith* did not directly address an issue that needed resolution, Muslims projected what they thought Mohammed might have done if confronted with the same dilemma. This last step in capturing Mohammed's memory represented the wisdom of the community, thereby completing the foundation for good conduct. All together, the Qur'an, the

Hadith, and the collective wisdom of the community became the basis of the *Shari'a* (the High Road).

The Shari'a created a standard of conduct that allowed Muslims anywhere in the world to maintain a level of purity in their behavior. The Shari'a became a Muslim's chief weapon in Jihad, or the exertion needed to maintain personal and communal purity. This purity of faith captured Mohammed's goals as he set out from the beginning to bring Allah's words to his people.

The tenets of Islam were now capable of holding together the vast community of people that Arabic expansion was about to encompass. The internal complexity of this vast community represented the extraordinary power of the new faith. Islam seemingly appealed to nearly every culture into which it was introduced, perhaps because it contained a straightforward model for obedience that linked politics with society and God. Developed by the *Ulama*, or the learned, the original message of the Shari'a grew into a rich legal tradition that extended the High Road into every facet of human life. Thus, Islam's uncompromising monotheism, highly developed legal codes, egalitarianism, and community focus served as the key principles to unite a geographic space that eventually stretched from Spain to the Philippine Islands.

Mohammed had taken two foreign religions, Judaism and Christianity, and transformed them into a new vision that stripped monotheism of any ambiguities. But, unlike Christianity, Mohammed's message did not synchronize with Greek philosophy, which had inspired the theological disputes among early Christians, as mentioned in Chapter Eight. Even though the Arabic world was fully aware of what the Greeks had achieved, Islam remained a simple and pure message untainted by foreign beliefs.

At the same time, since Islam required unambiguous obedience that reached back to prophetic Judaism, mentioned in Chapter Two, Mohammed had recovered the original image of God as developed by the Hebrew prophets. Muslims shunned theology as an irrelevant mental exercise; instead, they favored the simplicity of Allah as Mohammed presented Him through His Universal Majesty and Power. The secret to salvation resided with the individual Muslim who needed no other human to intervene on his behalf in his worship of Allah; complete submission and purity of heart was enough.

God was One Universal Being; there were no saints or Trinity. Angels merely served as Allah's messengers. Every person was his own priest, charged with the responsibility of maintaining the Five Pillars. The simplicity of this message crossed tribal boundaries to unite Arabs and allow them to curb their ancient tradition of intertribal warfare based on blood feuds. From this Arabic unity sprang an empire that reached out into the world to unite a strategic, central land bridge and allowed Islam to link Europe, Asia, and Africa. Islam became the centerpiece of the middle years in world history before the Mongols eventually took command of Central Asia.

The Umma

At the heart of Mohammed's message was the pattern of beliefs that made unity possible within a massive, singular community. The *Umma*, or community of faithful, sought to transcend all tribal and ethnic barriers. Within the Umma was the religious purity that Allah required; it defined political purpose and directed all humanity to achieve Jihad. With unity, the energy and genius of Islam could fulfill Allah's goals. To grasp the power of these ideas, one has to remember that Islam means submission, a Muslim is one who submits.

To submit as required by Mohammed's message, a person first had to have access to that message. Thus, the Arabic language became a key instrument of religious organization that cemented the Umma together. As the faithful learned Arabic to penetrate the mystery of Islam, Arabic spread far and wide to unify space in a way that never happened in the ancient world. Compared to Greek and Latin, Arabic carried a synthesis of the religious and secular authority in a single intonation of sound. More powerful than Chinese, Arabic comprised the Umma, and Mohammed's message.

Stressing the dignity of all believers, Islam created an ethical code that emphasized the immediacy of Allah in daily life. Every human accepted as his/her own personal responsibility: service to God. The rich and the poor alike belonged to the Umma, faced the same divine judgment, and carried out Jihad. Allah welcomed all who accepted His prophecy regardless of ethnicity or status. Humanity may divide the world by language, political states, and religious beliefs, but Allah ruled the universe and commanded the underlying truth of unity. Everyone would have to account for his or her own actions on the final day of judgment, when one's fate for all eternity would be decided.

Such a simple, pure vision of unity explains why this religion spread as far as it did and adjusted to the variety of local cultural conditions it met. Tolerating only The People of the Book, Muslims set out to convert all the rest to Mohammed's message. Spreading as far as its human resources would allow, Islam's unity was reflected in the way Arabic became the common language of the Middle East. Where other, older languages continued to survive, however, the unity of the Muslim community began to break down. Hence, language marked one of the frontiers of Islam.

Within its boundaries, Islam itself evolved. Starting first as Mohammed prescribed, the faithful stood apart from non-Arabs, Christians, and Jews. Converting the Arab town dwellers and the nomadic Bedouins that Mohammed had grown up with, the Umma originally existed above all the other cultures captured by Muslim armies.

As the use of the Arabic language spread along with Islam, the boundaries between Arabs and non-Arab converts blurred. The assigning of particular Arab tribes to command different provinces won by warfare eroded central authority, for on the frontier the occupiers tended to remember their original tribal bonds and forget their commitment to a central authority as they mixed with the local population. As a result, tribal loyalty combined with local cultural geography to create new regional identities within the Islamic world. As a result, when the Islamic community reached maturity by integrating Mohammed's faithful with local populations hundreds of years after the prophet's death, the Umma evolved to fit the goals established by the prophet's vision but still reflect specific local divisions marked by language, tribal affiliations, and geography.

The Caliphs

Since Islam is an immediate faith in which action represents worship, one must view the evolution of the Muslim world geographically. Mohammed launched the new faith, but his successors, the *Caliphs*, shaped its location on Earth. The shifts that occurred between Arabs and non-Arabs within the boundaries of Umma all have to be seen in relation to the link between belief and action. The first Caliphs (successors) took up their task soon after the death of Mohammed. Mohammed's ultimate victory and triumphant return to Mecca, had empowered him to convert his most strident opponents, the Omayyads, to the new faith. The Omayyads were the most powerful and outspoken opposition to the prophet and the primary cause of the Hegira in 622. In the eyes of the Omayyads, Mohammed's victories had made him a powerful enemy. Yet Mohammed's irresistible success had convinced other Bedouin tribes that his prophecy did come from the authority of Allah. Converted by the tens of thousands, these Arab tribes joined the prophet, and marched with him into Mecca, where he destroyed the idols of the Kaaba. This done, Mohammed converted his old enemies the Omayyad, preparing the world for the rise of Islam.

But Mohammed's sudden death in 632 threatened to destroy what the mighty prophet had built. Quick thinking on the part of his closest associates led them to select Abu Bakr as Mohammed's first successor. Abu Bakr was Mohammed's first male convert, his oldest friend, and one of the faithful sent ahead to Medina to prepare for the Hegira. As a surviving companion whom Mohammed had embraced as his chief advisor, Abu Bakr became the first Caliph, remained in Medina, and refused to allow any tribe to withdraw from the community Mohammed had constructed. Abu Bakr fought two hard campaigns to guarantee continued loyalty to the banner of Islam. He died in 634, but not before a tradition had been constructed that transferred power from Mohammed to the succeeding Caliphs.

Observing that Allah would not have taken Mohammed unless the message was complete, Abu Bakr did not claim the same powers of revelation as had belonged to the prophet. Rather, Abu Bakr created a concept of authority that survived him: he established that the Caliph held power only to enforce the prophet's message. This simple thesis preserved Mohammed's role as a living concept, which made his prophecy, his words, and his deeds a constant reminder of the necessity of submission to the will of Allah. Thus, when Abu Bakr died, the transference of power was easily understood: the next Caliph merely enacted the will of Allah through the message of His prophet.

Abu Bakr relied on talented generals who commanded his forces and demonstrated the power of Islam as a military faith. The morale of Muslim soldiers exceeded the fighting spirit of those who opposed Islam, suggesting that wholesale invasions north instead of simple raids might be the Muslims' best strategy. Initial probes revealed weakness in both the Byzantine and Sassanian empires. These two civilizations had been ravaged by years of disease and wars fought against one another, and both were vulnerable due to their general exhaustion and practice of creating landed aristocrats to finance their heavy cavalry. This practice had led to decentralization, which proved common to political societies based on raising warhorses through a landed nobility.

A smooth transition of power from Abu Bakr to Omar, the second Caliph (reigned 634–644), did not interrupt rapid expansion into the Fertile Crescent. Muslim armies defeated a Byzantine force at Yarmuk near the Jordan River in 636 to capture the Levant. The next year Omar turned on Mesopotamia and took this province from the Sassanian Empire. Egypt fell to the Muslims in 642, and they captured Persia as the Sassanian Empire collapsed seven years after Omar's death in 651. Each victory further convinced the Arabs that Allah had made them the instrument of His plans.

Rapid expansion required a military advantage. This advantage reflected the pure religious force that motivated the soldiers who composed the armies of Islam. The Muslim military had a fighting spirit that made morale the key difference in war; their opponents were exhausted and could not match their fervor. Within fifteen years, the Muslim world had expanded out of Arabia to encompass most of the Middle East except for Asia Minor, where Byzantine power still held sway. Yet such rapid success introduced an old problem among the Arabs: the issue of local versus central-state loyalty.

Omar decided to locate Arab tribes in captured provinces so as to preserve Mohammed's original design of Umma. As each tribe took up residence in its assigned province, it used the capital city as headquarters. There the Arabs lived off the taxes they collected from the non-Arab peoples. This design, however, created a conflict of loyalty: a provincial-tribal identity matured to motivate rivalry between provinces and the center of Islam in Medina. The distance between tribes on frontier outposts and the Caliph allowed the memory of the entire community of worshippers to fade. Omar's assassination in 644 at the hands of a slave made matters worse because the third Caliph was Othman (reigned 644–656), an Omayyad.

Their bitter defeat at the hands of Mohammed had not faded from the Omayyad's tribal memory. When Othman came to power, he deliberately placed members of his family in positions of responsibility, thereby elevating the Omayyads above other Arab tribes. Strategically located in Syria, the Omayyads occupied the geographic center of the Umma, while Othman's leadership in Medina raised the issue of tribal loyalty versus loyalty to the general community. Despite the fact that Othman commissioned the Shari'a to help central-ize the faith, rival tribes in Egypt and Mesopotamia revolted over his use of nepotism while a dedicated band of malcontents reached Medina to assassinate him.

Othman's assassination in 656 compounded the problem of division. Omar had died at the hands of an individual, but Othman's murder reflected the unruly will of warriors who claimed he had favored his family above the Umma; this raised the question of who should succeed to the office of Caliph after Othman. Widely scattered tribes living independently in provinces for-got the loyalty owed to the Caliph, so the next Caliph had to recover that loyalty if the Umma was to con-tinue. No one of the stature of Abu Bakr or Omar seemed available, so Mohammed's closest living relative seemed a likely choice. This relative was not, however, a direct descendant: Ali ibn-abi-Talib was the son of Moham-med's uncle and Mohammed's son-in-law.

Ali claimed the Caliphate after Othman's murder and immediately received the loyalty of tribal garri-sons in Mesopotamia. Yet the Omayyads rejected Ali's claim, believing the Caliphate should fall to their tribe. Only force could settle the issue. A civil war, however, contradicted the principle of the Umma, and the blood-shed that followed ended swiftly after Ali's victory at the battle of Siffin near the upper Euphrates River in 657. Ali's decision to accept arbitration instead of drive for outright total victory proved fatal. His opponent, Muawija, continued to resist and had himself declared Caliph in 660. Then Ali's death at the hands of one of his own followers in 661 reopened the question of suc-cession. This time a full-blown civil war erupted.

Ali's first son, Hasan, buckled under Omayyad pressure and rejected the Caliphate, allowing Muawija's claim to power to stand. Then, when Husain, Ali's sec-ond son, argued that his line should inherit the Caliph-ate, Muawija decided that this time the matter had to be settled completely. Leading the Omayyads in battle, Muawija defeated Husain after those from Iraq who promised to support him had abandoned him. Muawija was thorough: he killed Husain and all his relatives where they were camped at Karbala in 680. Loyalty by tribe and geographic location now increased in impor-tance; the Umma split along the lines of succession as the Muslim world divided into two factions: *Sunnis* (those loyal to Muawija) and *Shiites* (those loyal to Husain).

Muawija took command of the entire Muslim world, but beneath the surface were those who rejected Omayyad control. *Shia* followed the belief that Ali's claim to the Caliphate was just, and that his line should have continued in command. On the other hand, the Sunnis followed the Omayyads. Supporters of Shia had

come from those provinces captured during the war against the Sassanians. Supporters of the Sunni came from Byzantine provinces that had fallen to Islam.

In Persia, an underground but determined resis-tance to Omayyad rule continued. Since Persia was an ancient land with its own warrior traditions, language, and heritage, Shia Muslims took firm root in this re-gion and prepared to defend themselves. Thus, this division of succession became a permanent division in Islam, especially in Persia into which the Arabic lan-guage never penetrated or became the common tongue. Elsewhere Arabic carried Mohammed's message, but in Persia only the Arabic script crossed the frontier, as Shiites developed an independent intellectual tradi-tion based on Persian.

Shiite resistance to Sunni rule deepened as enthu-siastic and pious Muslims began to assert that the true Caliph remained hidden during these corrupt times. At some future date, a group of these Shiites claimed that this hidden *Imam* (the secret head of Allah's faithful ser-vants) would emerge. Until then, those who followed Shia resolved to remain patient and mourn Husain and his family while appearing to be obedient to the usurpers. Other Shiites claimed they could trace back Ali's de-scendents to the seventh, or even the twelfth generation. All agreed, however, that the day would come when they would crush Omayyad usurpation.

The only thing at issue was who should succeed to the Caliphate and lead the Muslim community. The purity of Islam remained intact. Only the relationship between political leadership and religious authority lay in doubt. For the moment the Omayyads had success-fully taken command. Through their Caliphate a uni-fied Muslim Empire emerged.

Under the Omayyads, Muslim expansion contin-ued. Moving across North Africa, the soldiers of Allah invaded Spain in 711. There they quickly destroyed the Visigoth kingdom, made themselves masters of the Iberian Peninsula, and advanced into France, where they finally were defeated in 732 by Charles Martel at Poitiers. In 705 Muslim armies reached India and over-ran the province of Sind along the lower Indus River. In Central Asia, Muslim soldiers followed the line of the Himalayas until they collided with Chinese forces at Talas in 751. The Muslims dealt the Chinese a de-feat that began a cycle of decline that eventually un-dermined the second great Chinese Dynasty, the Tang (618–907). The territories gained by war had made Is-lam the dominant force on the land bridge between the core civilizations of the ancient world.

The vast space that had fallen under Omayyad ruled made consolidation difficult to maintain. Any discon-tented group could hide successfully among the tribal provinces controlled by Arab garrisons. Omayyad ostensibly held central command, but elements of decentralization spread just as rapidly as their empire expanded. Locating their capital in Damascus, the Omayyads tried to build a bureaucracy that could hold together the vast empire that Islamic passion had forged. Yet only Arabia and parts of the Fertile Crescent actually had fully integrated communities. Elsewhere the divisions within each province continued to isolate an Arab elite that exploited a non-Arab population. Since the Omayyads tried to keep the Arab warrior elite concentrated in garrison towns, this empire floated on top of an unstable, unintegrated social base.

Despite Omayyad efforts to keep the Arab community separate, conversion blurred the differences between the Arab elite and their non-Arab/Muslim subordinates (Mawalis). Interaction and intermarriage followed quickly, as people acted on the egalitarian principles of Islam. Rapid conversion to Islam generated a homogeneous local image among worshippers that made separation seem unjust. The Omayyads insisted that the Mawali pay their taxes, even though in the eyes of Allah the non-Arab Muslim was the equal of the Arab. This payment often was the same as that made by non-believers, which only increased the Mawalis' sense of injustice. In addition, the Mawali did not share in the spoils of war, which went only to the Arab elite. Discontent against the Omayyads grew intense, especially after the Omayyad court became a luxurious center that rapidly consumed the pillage of victory after victory.

Rebellion against the Omayyads began among Arabic forces who had intermarried with local women in the eastern province of Merv along the Persian borderlands. There, a force of ten thousand warriors had developed a local sense of identity and resented paying for the luxuries enjoyed by the Caliphs in far-off Damascus. Joined by Shiites who had developed strength in Persia, this rebellious fever spread wide. Led by Abu-al-Abbas, these discontented warriors and their Shiite allies cleared the way for a new Caliphate.

As leader of the Abbasids, Abu-al-Abbas belonged to a rival tribe of the Omayyads who also had originally come from Mecca. Having a tribal name as ancient as that of the Omayyads, Abu-al-Abbas gained Persian and Shiite loyalty by asserting that he was a descendent of Mohammed's uncle. Mobilizing his Persian forces, Abu-al-Abbas launched an assault west that swept the Omayyads from power. His Persian soldiers had no difficulty with the idea of killing Arab Muslims as they followed Abu-al-Abbas's banner to victory. Apparently Abu-al-Abbas himself had no difficulty with the idea of killing Omayyads either, for he virtually eliminated the clan during a banquet he threw after his

victory that was set up under the pretense of reconciliation. His success changed the principles of organization behind the Muslim community. Now integration of all Muslims became official policy.

Removing the barrier between Arab and non-Arab, the Abbasids created a fully integrated local community among Muslims. While the People of the Book continued to live apart and pay their taxes, now Islam took firm root in the conquered provinces. The Abbasids ruled as Sunni Caliphs, while their claim to a lineage linked with Mohammed's uncle quieted the Shiites. Still, the division between the two forms of Islam continued as Abbasid authority increased in oppressiveness through a thoroughgoing absolutism that became more intense with each passing year.

Meanwhile, Arabic became the common language of Sunni territory, while their continued use of Persian kept the Shiites apart. This linguistic feature of Islam eroded ancient cultures and made the Middle East a common cultural zone. North Africa, Egypt, the Levant, and Mesopotamia joined Arabia to form a new cultural hearth. Persia remained apart, but it shared the passion of Islam, which drew it into Middle Eastern culture as well. Now the Eurasian core, and its contacts with sub-Saharan Africa, had a new world power with which to deal.

In the 508 years of Abbasid rule (750–1258), the Islamic world changed. A blending of cultures created a stable basis for traditional life to mature. Integration of local Muslim communities generated a broad cultural geography that made up the world of Islam. The different provinces, with their specialized production, secured material conditions that functioned smoothly beneath the political surface.

A vital economy sustained social and intellectual life as the Islamic world entered an era of great prosperity. In the center, Muslims bridged the gap between the ancient world and surviving Eurasian and African civilizations. Muslims, for example, reintroduced Europe to its classical heritage by developing Arabic commentaries on Greek texts that the Europeans could no longer read. Muslims also penetrated into India, where they began to reshape indigenous culture through a religious intolerance of Hinduism that further divided the subcontinent. Next, Muslims established the great trade caravan routes into sub-Saharan Africa, which fueled the commerce that supported emerging new monarchies there. Finally, Islam became a rival to Buddhism in Central Asia, a challenge to the nomadic tribes living there.

In Central Asia, numerous Mongol and Turkish clans readily absorbed the fierce religious passion encompassed by this new faith. Several of these nomadic

An Ottoman mosque, the main place of worship in Istanbul. It is a converted Greek Orthoxox Church called the Hagia Sophia, the principle cathedral for the Patriarch of Constaninople. Courtesy Touraj Daryaee.

son of an Omayyad Caliph had built the Caliphate of Cordoba. In Egypt Shiites had created the Fatimid kingdom ruling through the line of Fatima, Mohammed's daughter. In between, North Africa fell to the Aghilabi Emirate. All three challenged Turkish rule.

The Seljuk Turks became Sunni and tried to eliminate Shia as a potential opponent to their power. During the two centuries of their rule behind the scenes, they purged Shiites from the Caliph's domains. Their military prowess revived the dynasty as political order returned the military initiative to the Abbasid core. Rival Muslim realms suffered military defeat but could not be overrun. Furthermore, Seljuk victories against the Byzantine forces in Anatolia opened overland routes for more Turks to enter the Muslim empire. The new nomadic arrivals included the Ottoman Turks, who took up residence in Anatolia and renamed that region Turkey.

No step in these transitions of power touched the internal passion of Islam, disrupted the intense religious purity that Mohammed had created or undermined the material success and prosperity achieved by uniting the cultural space defined by Islam. The integration of the Islamic world as a religious, social, and economic experience continued despite shifts at the political level. The vitality of the religion remained fresh with each passing generation, for every Muslim made his or her own personal commitment to Allah through the Five Pillars and Jihad. Thus, the Middle East continued to develop despite the political realignments that occurred. Consequently, when the Mongols swept through the Abbasid Empire in 1258, killed the last Caliph, and ended the Caliphate, Islam as a religion endured.

Islam had transformed the Arabs, a recently settled nomadic people, from a fringe culture at the edge of civilization into one of the great pre-industrial world empires. Muslims had also laid the foundation for a truly global civilization that touched every corner of

warriors migrated into the Middle East seeking the source of this intoxicating new faith. Their arrival happened to coincide with severe internal strife suffered by Muslims contesting Abbasid rule. Taking advantage of these internal divisions, these Central Asian Turks rose as a powerful force in the Middle East.

Like the Omayyads, the Abbasids had developed into a luxurious dynasty, the oppulence of which offended the purity and austerity implied by Islam. Combined with severe absolutism and the extensive centralization of Abbasid authority, provinces that had undergone integration between Arabs and non-Arabs felt more local loyalty than commitment to the center. In 945, the armies of one of these regional opponents, the Buyids, invaded the center of Abbasid power, took their capitol at Baghdad, and converted the dynasty into puppet monarchs. This internal weakness signaled to other Islamic nomads that Muslim lands offered rich targets for raids.

The Buyids controlled the Abbasid court, but they could not prevent further disintegration of the empire. Marching into this political chaos in 1055, the Seljuk Turks captured Persia and replaced the Buyids in Baghdad. Allying themselves with Abbasid puppet governments, the Turks then took control over the core of Abbasid lands.

Muslim opponents in Spain, North Africa, and Egypt still contested Abbasid rule. In Spain a grand-

the Ancient Eurasian/African core, with only the Americas as the exception. At the same time, the sheer organizational energy released by Islam had the same kind of influence on Central Asian nomads like the Turks as it had originally had on Arabic culture.

Wherever Islam went, it left an imprint. There a new style of life emerged with sharp clarity. The mosques, prayer rituals, pilgrimages to Mecca, and Islamic law commanded loyalty from peoples stretching from Spain to Indonesia and the Philippines. Islam also reached from Central Asia into sub-Saharan Africa. The vitality of this new faith remained the same from the life of Mohammed to the present.

Suggested Reading

Ashor, E. A., *Social and Economic History of the Near East in the Middle Ages* (Berkeley: University of California Press, 1976).

Denny, F., A*n Introduction to Islam*, Second Edition, (New York: Prentice Hall, 1985).

Donner, Fred, M., *The Early Islamic Conquests* (Princeton: Princeton University Press, 1981).

Hodgson, Marshall G. S., *The Classical Age of Islam,* Three Volumes (Chicago: Chicago University Press, 1974).

Holt, P. M., et al., *The Cambridge History of Islam,* Two Volumes (Cambridge: Cambridge University Press, 1970).

Hourani, Albert, *A History of the Arab Peoples* (New York: Warner Books, 1991).

Perry, G. E., *The Middle East: Fourteen Islamic Centuries,* Second Edition (Englewood Cliffs, N.J.: Prentice-Hall, Inc, 1992).

Shaban, M. A., *Islamic History: A New Interpretation,* Two Volumes (Cambridge: Cambridge University, 1978).

XII

PERSIAN MILITARY INNOVATIONS
and India's Struggle with Islam

The end of the long-lived Parthian Empire of Persia (240 BCE–224 CE) marked the beginning of an important shift in the middle years of world history, even though this dynasty began during ancient times. The story of the Parthians belongs to the middle years of world history chiefly because they created an entirely new military system that greatly influenced the middle ages of many of their neighboring cultures. Technologically, then, the Parthians were on their own time scale. Only after the fall of Rome, Han China, and Gupta India did the rest of the Eurasian world catch up to these innovative people.

The Parthians hit upon their solution to "barbarian" raids that destroyed the other civilizations of the ancient Eurasian world because these Persian ex-nomads clearly understood the pastoral lifestyle of Central Asia. Although the Parthians had their solution in place before the fall of Rome and Han China, neither the Romans nor the Chinese were able to adopt these defensive measures because of a difficult choice doing so posed: either a civilization could dedicate large tracts of land to feeding massive warhorses, or it could use that land to feed its people. Neither Han China nor Rome could afford shifting a commitment of arable acres from people to horses prior to the collapse of their two empires. Persia, however, could.

Themselves once horse-based nomads, the Parthians had captured Persia in 240 BCE, displaced the local rulers, and established an empire based on a cavalry. Thereafter, they ruthlessly chose to feed their warhorses instead of their subject peoples and dedicated generous amounts of land to growing alfalfa to sustain their great horse herds. The Parthians had learned that by feeding their horses alfalfa during winter, when natural sources of fodder where in short supply, they could breed even more towering steeds. Not only did alfalfa offer their animals far greater nutrition than traditional grasses, but it belonged to a family of plants called *legumes*. Legumes such as alfalfa were salt tolerant and could actually restore fertility to land because these plants grew on soil that the evaporation

from irrigation had saturated with mineral salts. Also, alfalfa, like all legumes, increased soil fertility by capturing nitrogen in the air and fixing it in the ground through its root nodules. This made crop rotation possible, even if the Parthians knew nothing about the restorative powers of alfalfa as silage for their animals.

Alfalfa not only did a superior job of sustaining Persian horses, but it also increased the fertility of the Persian fields, which many centuries ago had been given up on as useless because of high salt content due to extensive irrigation. Alfalfa production allowed the Persians to select the largest and sturdiest of their animals and, by practicing animal husbandry, breed for size, bulk, and disposition—rendering exceedingly strong warhorses. These horses proved capable of carrying the weight of armored cavalrymen as well as their own armor. With such an unstoppable cavalry, the Persians were then capable of launching a force that could easily catch invading nomads, deflect their arrows, and turn them back. These horses, however, could not follow the raiders far out of Persia, to places where the native grasses proved too nutrient poor and scarce during winter to feed them. Hence, the Parthian solution to nomadic invasion remained only a defensive rather than an offensive tool capable of clearing the steppe of aggressive nomads and expanding their empire to greater size.

Having driven the raiders away from their territory, the Persians opened a new military era. But training soldiers to control the warhorses posed unique problems for cultures that later assimilated the Parthian solution. Professional cavalrymen had to be trained from childhood to master the massive animals as well as learn to fire a bow while in motion. Consequently, the Parthians set aside great parcels of land to create large estates capable of sustaining a new military aristocracy. The noblemen spent their lives preparing for war, wearing heavy, arrow-resistant armor, and riding aggressive steeds. True to a pattern we have seen many times now, the noblemen living in the countryside on large estates sustained by village cultivation eventually began to see their individual domains as mini-king-doms within the Parthian realm. The centralized Parthian ruler could never actually determine just how many soldiers would appear to defend the realm during any invasion. The resolution to the problem of strong loyalty to local lords, in contrast to ultimate loyalty to the central government, depended on the charismatic qualities of a Parthian ruler and his ability to reward his warriors. Accordingly, the Parthian solution included an element of decentralization that undermined the authority of the central governments, as cultures that borrowed Persian methods transferred power from one generation of rulers to the next.

The Parthians gained control of Persia and the adjoining regions by 240 BCE. They spoke an Iranian language (Indo-Persian), are believed to be the descendants of the Achaemenid Dynasty of Cyrus the Great, Darius I and Xerxes I, and practiced the Zoroastrian religion. At the same time, they used the Greek language for imperial and administrative purposes, greatly enjoyed Greek literature, built amphitheaters in which to perform Greek plays, and even used Greek legends on their coins. One might therefore say that the Parthians created the ultimate Hellenistic kingdom because they successfully blended Eastern and Western ideas, just as Alexander the Great had planned before his death in 323 BCE. In fact, the Parthians allowed their subjects to worship what deities they wished, whether Hellenic gods or the Zoroastrian *Ahura Mazda*, and each ethnic group within Persia was free to use its own language and customs as they had done before 240 BCE. The title that the great Parthian ruler chose to call himself, the "King of Kings," is emblematic of this system of rule, for it spoke of many local kings (aristocratic warriors and their heavy cavalry) in charge of their own domains within the Parthian Empire, all of whom were required to respond to the call to arms during the time of war. Otherwise they were independent of the Parthian King of Kings.

Among the greatest of the Parthian kings was Mithradates II (124–87 BCE). He expanded the Parthian Empire to its limits and successfully defended his realm from Roman aggression. Before his rise to power, Persia could be described as a region in which Hellenistic culture predominated in a patchwork of nearly independent military estates; after Mithradates II's rule, the Parthian Empire rose to become a great power that held the military initiative on Rome's eastern frontier. Mithra-dates II's heirs demonstrated that a new military age had begun. Persian forces typically numbered one quarter of the Roman legions sent against them; nonetheless the Persian use of mounted archers and *cata-phracts*, "fortresses," (i.e., men and horses

that functioned like heavy tanks) regularly defeated the Romans.

Now, the Parthians fought many battles with the Romans, who continued to view their increasingly sophisticated eastern neighbors as barbarians. Nevertheless, the Parthians' military innovations helped repel the Roman onslaught. The Parthian cavalrymen, their principal military force, were unsurpassed bowmen who had developed what became known as the Parthian Shot: while riding a horse at full gallop the Parthian horseman was able to turn and fire a volley of arrows against the enemy. In wars with the Romans, the mounted Parthians frequently managed to ride circles around the enemy foot soldiers and swiftly annihilate them with a volley of Parthian Shots. Several Roman generals, like Marcus Licinius Crassus of Julius Caesar's era (53 BCE), lost their lives fighting the Parthians. The Parthian military also forced the Romans to adjust their military tactics, giving more attention to the cavalry, even though the Romans never fully mastered the Parthian solution. Indeed, the failure to adapt to these methods eventually caused the fall of the Western Roman Empire, while the Byzantine world survived only because they did develop a heavy cavalry to ward off invading nomadic horsemen.

The Persian Sassanian Empire (224–651)

It seems that the Parthian Empire never went into decline. Instead it ended abruptly in the third century CE when a Persian known as Ardashir I (224–240) defeated the last Parthian ruler Artabanus VI in battle at Ardawan in 224. Ardashir I came from the province of Persis, the same province from which the Achaemenid Persians had risen. As a result, Ardashir I deliberately revived many of the original Persian traditions to distinguish his rule from that of his Parthian predecessors.

Ardashir I established the Sassanian Empire, which was different in many respects from that of the Parthian because Ardashir I was thoroughly committed to Persian culture and Zoroastrianism. He set about developing an anti-Hellenistic policy that returned Persia to its cultural roots and brought the entire region completely into the middle years of world history. During the Sassanian rule, a new vitality swept through Persia, one evidenced by the humiliating defeat Ardashir's heir dealt Rome in 260. Shapur I (241–72) defeated and captured the Roman Emperor Valerian, who spent the rest of his life as a prisoner of war. In his time, Ardashir I deliberately set about making Zoroastrianism the official religion of his expanding empire. He sought to create a fully integrated political system based

Zoroastrian Symbol. The Faravahar (a representation of a Guardian Spirit or possibly of the Creator of All) is one of the best-known symbols of the Zoroastrian religion. © **Walter S. Arnold, www.stonecarver.com.**

on his title: "The King of Kings of both Iran and non-Iran, whose origin is from the Gods."

The Sassanians called their Persian empire *Iran*, synonymous with the Indian term used to name them, *Aryan*. The Zoroastrian deity, Ahura Mazda of the Achaemenid period, thus became the most important deity, although now he was called *Ohrmazd*. The images on Sassanian coins capture the unity sought by Ardashir I: one side bore the monarch's name and full title as mentioned above; the other a picture of a fire-altar representing the Zoroastrian sacred light.

Church and state had united through Sassanian rule. Zoroastrian priests emphasized that neither religion nor the state could survive without the other and both institutions needed to support the people. At this time the priests recorded the sacred text of the Zoroastrians, the *Avesta*, in the Avestan Script and oversaw the construction throughout the empire of a network of fire-temples, in which people prayed daily. The Sassanians had developed a full-blown theocracy, one that many of their neighbors would later imitate.

Sassanian Society

Little is known about Sassanian social stratification due to the meager data made available to historians from Greek informants, royal Persian inscriptions, and carved rock reliefs. Even the traditional Indo-Iranian social division of priests, warriors, and farmers shifted with time to include scribes. Hence, only a broad image of Sassanian social organization has emerged.

Piecing together what historians have learned, the Sassanians combined a feudal system with a functional set of castes and foreign communities. Taking the feudal divisions first, the Sassanians continued the Parthian practice of relying on a small number of noble families who possessed vast holdings and supplied heavy cavalry to protect the empire. They fell into four

groups: 1) the *Sahrdar*, local semi-independent rulers and the sons of the King of Kings entrusted with regional power; 2) the *Vaspuhragan*, members of the Sassanian clan not directly related to the ruler; 3) the *Vuzurgan*, heads of the most important noble families; and 4) the *Azadan*, all the remaining Iranian nobility. Their role in Persian politics was to provide candidates for the top military and administrative posts. Magnates from all four groups commanded so much power that their estates became semi-independent realms within the Sassanian Empire; they would engage in private warfare unless the King of Kings proved strong enough to impose his will on all his subjects. On their vast estates, agriculture served as the basis for production during Sassanian times with free peasants and tenant farmers doing most of the planting while slaves provided labor for mining, construction, manufacturing, and the cultivation of temple estates.

The two most successful Sassanian rulers, Shapur I (240–70) and Khusro I (531–79), overawed the nobility and became the undisputed rulers of their realm. Both men extended royal authority by expanding agricultural production. Each invested heavily in irrigation to greatly increase Persian fields under cultivation. These expanded agricultural lands provided much of each monarch's surplus wealth; the fields were located on ancient Mesopotamian lands that had suffered extensive ecological damage during the third through first millennia BCE. By following the Parthian practice of using alfalfa as a salt-tolerant plant, a legume, and fodder for warhorses, these two Sassanian monarchs were able to regenerate field fertility.

Besides the feudal organization of Persian society, the second feature of the Sassanian community was the functional castes alluded to in the Avesta: the priests, the warriors, and the farmers—scribes were added later. The first was the *Asornan*, the priests, who busied themselves with many different occupational duties including the teaching and studying of the religion, tending to the sacred fires, performing marriages, and initiating the youth into Zoroastrianism. This formal initiation of the young into Zoroastrianism is called *Sedre Pushi*. During the ritual a cord was tied around the waist of the initiate to symbolize his pact with Ohrmazd. The young learned to accept three fundamental practices: good words, good thoughts, and good deeds. This remains the motto of the Zoroastrians today, and all adherents incorporate these simple precepts every day of their lives. Opposed to this concept, is "the Lie," which takes the character of a demon called Drūg (Persian for "the Lie"). Above all, *Ahriman* was the mastermind behind all evil that existed in the world, and it was the goal of a Zoroastrian to battle the forces of darkness in every way.

Sassanian dish showing a horse and rider. The use of large warhorses and riders trained to control them helped the Persians enter a new military era. Courtesy Touraj Daryaee.

3   The second caste comprised the *Arteshtaran*, or warriors. Their function was to keep the borders safe and fight the enemies of the King of Kings who himself came from this caste. He and his heavily armored cavalry were the backbone of the military, which included all the members of the landed aristocracy. The new emphasis on ancient Persian traditions had a tendency to reduce localism and provide the King of Kings greater loyalty under the threat of foreign invasion.

3   The third (sometimes called the third and fourth) caste comprised everyone else in Persian society; they were called "the farmers," the *Vastaryushan*, but they eventually comprised both the Vastaryushan and a group called the *Hutukhshan* (the "scribes"). The Vastaryushan practiced animal husbandry and planting, producing all of Persia's foodstuffs. They provided the material base of society by generating all the primary goods needed to feed the state and pay the taxes. The Hutukhshan were the secretaries, artists, medical practitioners, craftsmen, astronomers, singers, royal and noble servants, and retail and wholesale dealers of Sassanian society. They created durable goods or provided the basic urban services needed to run a complex realm. While their income exceeded that of actual farmers, the Hutukshan's social standing emerged slowly as a fourth caste.

Combining the functional castes of the Avesta with the feudal hierarchy of Sassanian society made the Iranian social fabric a very complex system. To add to this complexity, another feature of Sassanian society was the many foreigners who had settled in the empire as a result of war and conquest. Placed within the power structure as the "non-Iran" portion of the King of King's title, these foreign communities fit awkwardly within the feudal and caste systems. They included Germans, Goths, Romans, and probably even Slavs, among other peoples from the Near East who lived in the cities of the Sassanian Empire. These cosmopolitan inhabitants of the Persian cities brought foreign technology and unique skills to the empire. For example, one of the most important medical centers in the world in the fourth and fifth centuries was the Persian city of Jondi-shapur, one of seven major cities in Khuzistan, a province located on the western flank of the Zagros mountains near the Persian Gulf. There Persian, Roman, and Indian doctors lived and conducted research. Also, the development of new military tactics mixed Roman, German, Indian, and native Persian methods and weaponry to achieve a devastating impact on the battlefield. This military power can be seen in the fact that more Roman armies suffered defeat at the hands of the Sassanians than were achieved by any other civilization, proof that the Persians were far ahead of their Western neighbors in military technology.

As for women, caste affiliation determined their rights. According to Zoroastrian law, women had a set worth, like the price of a commodity, depending on their

Persian Court. A painting depicting a persian Shah surrounded by his courtiers. Reproduction of the original by Ostad Hadi Tadjvidi.

status and lineage. Furthermore, Zoroastrian literature dictated that a woman should be obedient to her husband and ask him three times a day if there was anything she should do to make him happy.

The subordination of women to men was borne out in both social mores and legal codes. If, for example, a woman committed adultery, she was put to death immediately. In addition, a man could divorce a woman if she could not bear him an heir. During menstruation, women were considered polluted and therefore isolated in a specific room. At this time, a woman could have no contact with other members of her family, no food, nor even glance at the sacred Zoroastrian fire. Since the Sassanians thought blood caused pollution, having sexual intercourse during a woman's period brought about a death sentence for both the man and the woman. Finally, women alleged to be sorcerers and prostitutes, common accusations in the medieval Persian world, were harshly punished. An ideal woman was one who refrained from gossip, who knew her prescribed limits, and who did not cause men to lose their heads; she was passive, obedient, and demure.

While these restrictions come from the Zoroastrian legal texts, scholars know that they belie many of the common practices of Sassanian society. Indeed, women of the nobility were quite powerful, with two such women, Puran (630–31) and her sister Azarmigdukht (631), becoming rulers briefly when there were no male candidates from the royal line; coins from the time bear their portraits and names. We also know that aristocratic women accompanied their men on hunts, owned land estates, and commanded the lives of numerous slaves. Furthermore, some women from

the Hutukhshan could create businesses, participate in international trade, and enjoy wealth independent of their husbands. Many of them successfully divorced their husbands, having shown just cause. There are hundreds of seals which, at the time, acted as signatures that bear the names and sometimes the images of women, further proof of the power and independence of women in trade and the economy. On the other hand, there is little explicit historical evidence pertaining to women living in poverty, but we can assume that their lack of material resources placed them at the mercy of the law. Hence, they were restricted and had to work in the fields as farmers, tend to the children, and keep up with the housework.

In contrast, a wealthy man could marry more than one woman, have several concubines, and have sex with his slaves so long as he could afford to care for them all. The children any of his women bore assumed the status of their father. Accordingly, the man had the power of the law behind his actions and did not have to create an exceptional space for himself to exercise the hard-won freedoms that strong-willed women had managed to gain for themselves.

The aspect of social life that concerned the Sassanian Persians perhaps more than any other was the issue of purity and the fear of pollution. The Earth and all water were to be protected from any kind of pollution, as they were deemed sacred. Once a human died, surviving relatives avoided handling the corpse for fear of pollution; gloves and special clothing were required while specialists alone took part in caring for the dead. When one died, the Zoroastrian religion dictated that he or she be exposed to vultures or dogs at designated enclosures, known as *Dakhma*, after which the bones were collected and placed in rock cut tombs. Great care was taken to clip the nails and hair of the deceased, after which the clippings were collected and placed in special receptacles in the ground. Because of these cultural practices, the Sassanians suffered few diseases that might have been spread from contact with corpses.

Meanwhile, rivers as well as seas had to be kept clean and free from humans. All bodies of water contained sacred substances that had to be kept pure. Bathing therefore could only occur in designated places, which were constructed in such a manner so that a specific amount of water would be used to clean the body. No one was ever allowed to jump into a river or sea to bathe. In the Sassanian imagination, there was not enough water in the world for it to be used in such a haphazard manner; furthermore, its sacred nature required great care and consideration.

Khusro I and the Height of the Sassanian Empire

Khusro I (531–579) succeeded his father, Kobad I (488–531), and reorganized the Sassanian Empire to create a new feudal order that proved far more responsive to central authority than anything prior to his reign. He was able to do so because he came to power during a time of extreme social unrest. While still crown prince, Khusro had to deal with the chaos caused by the *Mazdakites* (followers of Mazdak). Mazdak (d. 524) was a religious leader who preached a communal-style populist doctrine that involved a radical redistribution of wealth, property, and even women, which disrupted the Sassanian social order. Most influential during Kobad's reign, Mazdak represented the discontent of the peasants who had been overtaxed by the nobility and the previous King of Kings, Peruz I (459–484). At first Kobad I supported the Mazdakites to ease the misery of the poor and to quell the ambitions of his nobility. But Mazdak's followers soon began confiscating lands, opening granaries, and creating so much unrest among the nobility and Zoroastrian priesthood that they banded together to drive Kobad from power in 496. Relying on his son, Khusro, to recover the throne, Kobad approved a plan of execution that would eliminate the Mazdakites and their leader in 524. Khusro arranged a religious debate between Mazdak, his leading followers, and the Zoroastrian priests that was to take place in the royal gardens in the capital at Ctesiphon, located north of ancient Babylon. The debate was a ruse; Mazdak and his followers were captured and buried alive, and their movement suppressed. Seven years later, when Khurso inherited the throne, he consolidated his hold over Iran by initiating a redistribution of estates made available by the social chaos caused by Mazdak's movement.

Given the social instability caused by Mazdak, Khusro I was able to thoroughly reorganize the empire. He divided his kingdom into four military districts governed by *Spahbeds* (commander-in-chiefs) responsible to him. Within each of these military districts he redis-

tributed the land to the *Dehkanan*, a lesser nobility who served as heavy cavalry. Owning estates much smaller than the vast holdings owned by the Sahrdar, Vaspuhragan, Vuzurgan, or Aradan, these smaller landed aristocrats provided a far more stable social and military stratum for protecting the King of King's domain. Accordingly, Khusro I revitalized the empire, rejuvenated its sources of power, and made the Persians one of the most affluent civilizations in the world. Khusro I, displayed tolerance, allowing the Greek philosophers, whose schools had been shut down in the Eastern Roman Empire, to come to Persia and carry on their activity. But Khusro I's court also became one of the most distant and restrictive in the world.

Khusro I instituted an elaborate court pageantry wherein the Persian monarch sat behind a curtain so that a visitor could neither gaze upon the King of Kings, nor breathe the royal air. During the entire audience, the visitor had to prostrate himself before the King of Kings, not knowing if the Persian monarch was even present or listening to him. The King of King's crown became so large and heavy that it had to be suspended from the ceiling with chains above the monarch's head; this symbolized his power.

As far as his personal life was concerned, Khusro I had thousands of wives and concubines, constructed fabulous palaces, and became known as a man of enormous sexual potency, vast wisdom, and a keen sense of justice. To ensure the loyalty of his nobility, Khusro I reformulated the taxation system and reformed the army, which allowed the Persian empire to reach its apex of power. Khusro I also had the history of Iran rewritten so that it became a royal chronicle called the *Khwaday Namag*, (the Book of Kings), which was later translated into Persian and remains one of the most popular texts for the medieval period in Iran today, where it is called *The Shah Name*. Yet, within one hundred years of all these revisions, the Sassanian Empire collapsed with the sudden rise of Islam

The Sassanian Empire ended in 651, the consequence of a long and exhausting war with its immediate neighbor to the west, the Byzantine Empire. Evenly matched and trapped in perpetual wars of survival, both the Eastern Roman Empire and the Sassanian Dynasty were caught by surprise with the sudden rise of Islam. In imitation of their neighbors to the north, the Muslims developed a heavy cavalry and combined it with their religious fervor, which made them virtually unstoppable. Arab tribes swept out of the south and conquered the Persians in three major battles. The swift conquest of the Sassanian Empire gave the Muslims vast new resources. Yet it could not undermine completely the ancient Persian traditions and customs. The vitality of the new monotheistic faith generated by Mohammed proved attractive to the Persians, but it did not overwhelm their society as it did elsewhere in the new Middle East. Furthermore, the Shiite and Sunni split allowed the Persians to develop a dedication to Islam while maintaining their separate identity within the greater Muslim empire; the Persians chose to support the Imams who followed Ali's line. Hence, when the Abbasids displaced the Omayyads, using Shiite loyalists to create a new Caliphate in Baghdad, a Persian court took root there. In other words, the rise of Islam may have swept away a Persian Dynasty, but the power of the Parthian and Sassanian heritage lived on through a growing stronghold for Shia in Iran.

India and Islam

While Persia adjusted to Islam, India fell to the depths of chaos once the Muslims arrived. The fall of the Gupta Empire in 535 ushered in an era of internal division and external cultural isolation that eroded the achievements of the Classical Age (320–535). Surrounded by barbarians who cut India off from friendly civilizations, the Indians turned inward to try to recover political unity. Their efforts, however, failed.

Three hundred years after the fall of the Gupta Empire, a new force appeared on India's frontier: Muslim warriors who exposed India to a regular series of foreign invasions, internal divisions, and religious conflicts, the likes of which they had never experienced. These foreign assaults and a new level of religious intolerance, led to the destruction of Buddhism and the establishment of several Muslim overlords who produced a completely new cultural experience for India. The central question this new cultural experience posed for Indians was: how were they to deal with a people who denied, and even sought to destroy, the easy-going and tolerant nature of Hinduism? This question has never fully been answered, neither during the middle years of world history nor in the modern era.

The middle centuries of world history for India, therefore, represent chaos on a scale comparable to the anarchy experienced by the western portion of the Roman Empire as its provinces collapsed under nomadic invasions. After the Muslims invaded India and set up overlords on the subcontinent, the Indians lost command of their political destiny, which, incredibly, they did not recover until 1947.

The northern half of the Indian subcontinent took the brunt of these raids. There Buddhism had become a largely urban religion, practiced in cities that proved to be highly visible and vulnerable targets for the Is-

lamic onslaught. To the south, most Hindus continued their daily existence, doing their best to ignore the raids taking place to the north. Accordingly, they struggled with local political divisions while leading the lives prescribed by their caste system. Thus, India experienced two contradictory features of cultural existence during these middle years: political chaos and local Hindu survival.

The Muslim invaders to the north were components of the general expansion of Islam that used the religious passions of the Middle East as a springboard from which to expand in all directions. These Muslims carried with them the fury and passion of their new faith, one that brooked no compromise with pagans and idol worshippers. Treating Buddhists and Hindus as ignorant creatures worshipping false gods, the Muslims reflected the simplest forms of Islam. Comprised of Turks and Afghans, these servants of Allah took with them Islamic scribes, administrators, artists, and other educated persons to set up new states in India. They practiced a violent form of jihad and destroyed all that they felt represented the false deities of the Hindus and Buddhists, even as they tried to convert Indians to the new, true faith. Their bluntness and brutality reflected their simplicity.

Their brutal form of proselytizing created an ingrained hostility between faiths that Indians did not understand. For centuries Hindus and Buddhists had lived side by side successfully with one another, as well as with members of other religions, because both faiths claimed that all belief systems were manifestations of the same reality: the ineffable oneness of existence. Islam, however, would not tolerate any such claim.

The new invaders were attracted to India by the wealth of the cities and the rich landscape that differed substantially from the dry and barren homeland from which they had come. Bringing a Persian-style royal court with its isolation and luxury, the Muslim overlords at first lived apart from Indians, which probably had improved their chances of survival given the fact that they had unwittingly entered a disease-rich environment. Religious intolerance had created a social barrier that reduced direct contact between the Muslim ruling class and their Indian subjects, giving the newcomers even more time to gain some immunities.

In general the Muslims had followed the line of least resistance that made the Middle East and North Africa its easiest and therefore its first targets. Then they turned east to eliminate Sind, an Indian province at the mouth of the Indus River valley and a rival in trade, while they invaded Central Asia. Next, they turned to India itself. The Muslims who entered India were Turks from Central Asia, people who had been converted to the new faith and had joined the armies of Islam relatively late in the timetable of conquest set in motion by Islam.

The Turko-Afghani leader Mahmud of Ghazni (reigned 997–1030) launched seventeen raids into India from his kingdom in Afghanistan, vowing to convert or chastise all non-Muslims every day of his life. Attacking between 1001 and 1027, Mahmud targeted Hindu and Buddhist temples for destruction because they were both pagan centers of worship and the depositories of vast quantities of wealth. He invaded the upper Indus River Valley and the Punjab region to loot and to destroy, winning all his battles, and carrying off vast quantities of slaves, gold, and jewelry. Beginning with simple pillaging and advancing to the capture of the temple cities of Thanesar (1012), Mathura and Kanauj (1018), and finally Somnath (1026) in northeastern India, Mahmud killed or converted Hindus and Buddhists alike while stripping their places of worship of all portable treasures. Returning to his mountain stronghold in Afghanistan, he used his stolen riches to create a major Islamic center. Plunder and slaughter fit well within his definition of religious passion and left him with a clear conscience as he prepared to launch his next set of raids. When he died on April 30, 1030, he had established a Muslim dynasty that continued attacking India for the next century, while the Hindus and Buddhists who met these raiders developed a hatred for Islam that did not bode well for the future.

By 1200, these Turko-Afghani invaders had established a strong military base in much of northern India. Locating their capital at Delhi, they occupied a strategic site on the Jumma River whose mountains protected their southern flank and allowed them to consolidate their hold on the Ganges. To the north lay the Himalayas, to the west the Thar Desert, and to the east the Ganges River valley. Following the Ganges into the remainder of Hindustan, the Muslims occupied Bengal in 1202 and established a new sultanate in 1206. In Delhi a series of six dynasties ruled from 1206–1526: the Slave Dynasty (1206–90), the Khalji (1290–1321), the Tughlaq (1321–98), the Lodi (1413–14), the Sayyid (1414–51), and the Lodi again (1451–1526).

In their sweep through northern India, these Turko-Afghani rulers effectively destroyed Buddhism as an Indian religion. At Nalanda, east of Bengal, the Muslims found a rich target for their religious passion and destroyed a Buddhist monastery that housed some 10,000 monks and served as the principal intellectual center of this faith. During their assault they slaughtered everyone in sight, closed the center, and caused

the survivors to flee into Nepal and Tibet where Buddhism continued.

Hinduism did not fare much better. At Banares, just northeast of Nalanda, a similar Hindu intellectual center suffered the same fate. Yet Hinduism had a rural base in India, while Buddhism occupied most of India's northern cities. Being urban, Buddhism was highly visible and easy to target, but Hinduism blended into the Indian countryside where it could not be rooted out. Hence the Muslims could eliminate one of the Indian faiths but not the other.

Meanwhile, India's political tradition of chronic disunity left the Indians helpless to stop the Muslim invaders. Constant rivalry between Hindu *rajas* (princes) had reduced India's military effectiveness, so that they could not unite to mount sufficient resistance to check the invasions. Therefore, the Muslims faced tough local opposition, but only a feeble general defense against their onslaught as they defeated one Indian ruler after another. Only disease functioned as a natural barrier to Islam's advance; yet it could only slow, not stop, the attacks. Indeed, many of the native Indian pathogens had already been shared with the Eurasian world during the brisk sea trade conducted at the end of the ancient era.

As the Muslims sought to consolidate their hold on northern India, a new relationship between Islam and Hinduism matured. Recognizing the indispensable value of Indian farmers as a tax base, and Hinduism as far more sophisticated than simple paganism, the Delhi Sultanate came to terms with these idol worshippers by bestowing *Dhimmis* status (Arabic for "being cared for") on their new subjects.

All Dhimmis (non-Muslims living within a Muslim realm) were members of an officially tolerated religion such as Christianity and Judaism. As Dhimmis, Islamic law protected Hindus by bestowing specific rights, obligations, and restrictions on them. These rights included protection of life, wealth, and honor, the privilege of residing within Muslim territory, the power to choose their own religious leaders, to work, and trade, and the ability to remain free from slavery. The obligations required that they pay the *jizya* (head tax) and the *kharaj* (land tax). The restrictions denied them the right to build any new houses of worship, display their religious symbols outside their territories, engage in public prayer, perform their rituals, or wear visible signs of their faith, nor to publish or sell their religious texts, seek converts, or marry Muslim females.

Still, as Dhimmis, Hindus were not Christians or Jews; Hindus did not share a common religious text (the Bible) with the Muslims. Also, while indispensable as taxpayers, these unbelievers persisted in their stubborn determination to worship idols. Hence, the Hindus had to pay an especially heavy jizya and kharaj. As a substitute for forced conversion, these taxes allowed the Muslims to exploit India's productive energy to provide the food surpluses needed to rule their new territories. Yet unlike other Islamic provinces, where light taxes (that were less then the alms required of Muslims) allowed Christians and Jews to continue in their religions, the jizya and kharaj of India came to six percent of the Hindu total net annual worth.

Even Hindu rulers proved useful after their conquest. To administer the vast space of the subcontinent, the Delhi Sultans learned to exploit petty rajas as puppet monarchs in their local kingdoms to keep the Hindus quiet. This type of rule made tax collection more efficient, while Hindu monarchs could be weakened to the point where they did not represent a military threat. Thus, Muslim rulers slowly began to spread their influence south after the initial intolerance of Islam adjusted to the tenacity of Hinduism as the dominant religion of India.

At the same time, the Delhi Sultans proved too weak to command India as absolute rulers. Always too few in number, the slave-soldiers commonly used by Turk-Afghani adventurers did not provide the Delhi Sultans sufficient military resources to impose their power at will. This forced the Delhi Sultans to rely on their Hindu allies to maintain control. To this military weakness must also be added the court intrigues common to the history of the Delhi Sultanate.

The Delhi Sultanate had a history of instability in its court from 1206 to 1526. As absolute rulers, the Delhi Sultans felt they had to create an environment of fear to secure their power. Intolerant of any dissent, the Sultan classified criticism as treason and demanded obedience from submissive courtiers as a sign of loyalty. These courtiers swallowed their anger and harbored all types of slights as they eagerly plotted revenge. Assassination became commonplace in this Muslim realm as coups d'état, rebellions, and civil wars plagued its history. No agreed-upon method of selecting a new heir became standard in the long history of the Sultanate. Rather, transfer of power usually followed some palace plot wherein poison or the assassin's dagger became an ambitious usurper's modus operandi.

The Sultan's only hope of maintaining power lay in his military. In a style of recruitment also used by the Ottoman Turks and the Fatimite rulers of Egypt, the Delhi Sultans routinely captured young boys whom they raised as slave-soldiers. Called *Mamelukes* (meaning "slave" in Arabic), these recruits constituted a full-time professional military with no other loyalties than to the state. As a military force, their discipline grew

legendary under fire, but as a body they were easily corrupted. Periodically the military joined in partnership with courtiers who kept the throne open to ambitious and ruthless personalities.

Such a weak central authority made control over India fitful. The ruthlessness and frequent cruelty of a new Sultan often spread the idea of revolt outward. And the taxation required to maintain such an ambiguous political environment doubled the burdens of life among the peasants. Routine coups and countercoups, bribes and pay-offs, rebellion and civil war made life unsettling; only Hinduism gave solace to the long-suffering Indian population.

Indeed, the state seemed to be an instrument of karmic punishment for something India had done. Hindus felt that government in general, and Islam in particular, belonged to some hidden monistic message that one could only understand in a religious trance.

Turning deeper into themselves, the Hindus continued to tolerate the illusions of this world while they deepened their distrust of politics and government in general and learned to condemn Islam specifically for producing a hostile, oppressive state policy. Unlike anywhere else in the Middle East or North Africa where Muslim authority dominated, in India only a weak fusion of Islam and native culture occurred. The arts, poetry, music, architecture, and language saw Muslim influences penetrate, but a deep rift developed in politics and military affairs.

Meanwhile the Sultans of Delhi existed to maintain Islamic power in India. Ruling from 1206 to 1526, these Sultans produced numerous dynasties that managed to maintain only a semblance of control over the northern subcontinent while vying with one another to produce the next monarch. Power transferred violently and irregularly from ruler to ruler, which carried the Sultanate through to the modern era. Hence the Sultans ruled more as the first among equals rather then as the true sovereigns of the subcontinent because they never fully managed to compel the independent Hindu rajas to submit to Muslim rule.

To compound the problems of political instability and religious intolerance in India, the Sultans of Delhi could not effectively defend the frontier from a determined foe. In 1398–1399, the Mongol-Turkish adventurer, Tamerlane (or Timur the Lame, 1336–1405), plundered all of Central Asia and the Middle East, and then targeted India. Interested only in raiding territories in India rather than creating an empire, and sensing the weakness of the Delhi Sultanate, Tamerlane swept through the subcontinent leaving utter ruin in his wake. After plundering the Punjab and sacking Delhi, he slaughtered anyone he did not carry off. Taking vast supplies of wealth, food, and captives when he marched away, Tamerlane left behind famine and disease, while the Sultanate took decades to recover.

A second invader the Sultans could not handle was Baber the Tiger (1483–1530). He claimed to be a descendent of Tamerlane and lived off the same traditions of raid and plunder so cherished by his violent ancestor. Yet Baber's ambitions exceeded the simple goals of the pillage that seemed to satisfy Tamerlane. Baber wanted to create a realm of his own and jumped at the chance to enter India at the invitation of a Punjab ruler who had rebelled against the Sultanate. Once in the subcontinent, Baber began a conquest that he later claimed was always at the forefront of his mind: he captured Hindustan. India simply represented too much opportunity for this adventurer to ignore.

Baber took a small army into India and crushed whatever army the Sultan sent against him. As part of the sixteenth century "gunpowder" empires that included the Ottoman Turks, the Safavids of Persia, the czars of Russia, and modernizing states within Europe, Baber used cannon to great effect in his war of conquest. Defeating the Sultanate decisively at Panipat, Baber occupied Delhi in 1526 and began the Mogul Empire. The word *Mogul* itself is a name that came from the Persian word for Mongol to which Baber attributed the lineage of his new dynasty.

The Mogul Empire represented a new era of Indian unity. Mogul success seemed to equal that of the Mauryas and the Guptas. Belonging to a later story, the Moguls represent here the culmination of an era of political chaos. Before they came, India staggered through nearly a thousand years of internal division both in politics and religion. India's recovery from the fall of the Gupta Empire had not generated a new era of cultural order; rather India suffered the opposite extreme. India became a civilization with ancient faiths like Buddhism and Hinduism that tried to cope with the intolerant presence of the powerful new religion, Islam. The former ceased to exist on the subcontinent, and the latter survived under a new and heavy tax burden.

Islam's presence drove Indian civilization into the modern era with a new religious intolerance that compounded the tradition of political chaos common to India's ancient past. The destruction of Buddhism, and the subordinate of 75 percent of India's population as Hindus under Muslim rule, created a new internal division in India. Even after Baber established the Mogul Empire, India never bridged the gap between monism and monotheism.

Suggested Reading

Iran

Boyce, M., *Zoroastrians: Their Religious Beliefs and Practices* (Norfolk, Great Britain: Thetford Press, 1979).

Dandamaev, Mohammed and Vladimir G. Lukonin, *The Culture and Social Institutions of Ancient Iran*, P. L. Kohl, ed. (Cambridge: Cambidge University Press, 1989).

Frye, Richard, N., *The Heritage of Persia*, Revised Edition (Costa Mesa, Calif.: Mazda, 1993).

Ghirshman, R., *Iran: From Earliest Times to the Islamic Conquest* (London: Pelican, 1954).

Huot, Jean Louis, *Persia*, Two Volumes (Cleveland: World Publishing, 1965–67).

Irving, Clive, *Crossroads of Civilization: 3,000 Years of Persian History* (London: Weidenfeld and Nicolson, Ltd., 1979).

Widengran, Geo, *Mani and Manichaeism*, Translated by Charles Kessler (New York: Holt, Rhinehart, and Winston, 1965).

Wiesehöfer, Josef, *Ancient Persia from 550 BC to 650 AD* (London: I. B. Tauris Publishers, 2001).

Zaehner, R. C., *The Dawn and Twilight of Zoroastrianism* (New York: G. P. Putnam's Sons, 1961).

India

Chaudhuri, K. N., *Trade and Civilization in the Indian Ocean: An Economic History from the Rise of Islam to 1750* (Cambridge: Cambridge University Press, 1985).

Ikram, S. M., *Muslim Civilization in India* (New York: Columbia University Press, 1964).

Jackson, P., *The Delhi Sultanate* (Cambridge: Cambridge University Press, 1999).

Keay, John, *India: A History* (New York: Atlantic Monthly Press, 2000).

Lannoy, R., *The Speaking Tree* (Oxford: Oxford University Press, 1971).

Mandelbaum, D. G., *Society in India*, Two volumes (Berkeley: The University of California Press, 1972).

Murphy, Rhoads, *A History of Asia*, Fourth Edition (New York: Longham, 2003).

Singhal, D. P., *A History of the Indian People*, Third Edition (Boulder, Colo.: Westview, 1989).

Smith, V. A., *The Oxford History of India*, Fourth Revised Edition (Oxford: Oxford University Press, 1981).

Thapar, R. A., *A History of India*, Volume 1 (Baltimore: Penguin Books, 1969).

XIII

CHINA,
AN ERA OF RECOVERY
and Cultures on the Fringe:
Korea, Japan, and the Mongols

China's recovery came after four centuries of internal disorder. Divided into several kingdoms from 220 to 581, China experienced barbarian occupation in the north, and Chinese cultural expansion in the south. North China belonged primarily to the nomadic kingdom of Wei that controlled much of the Huang He valley region from 386 to 534. As mentioned in Chapter Ten, Buddhism spread rapidly as the new rulers sponsored this recently introduced Indian faith among their Chinese subjects. The Chinese embraced Buddhism, attracted to its ability to insulate people against the troubled times in which they lived.

In the south, Chinese culture survived the nomadic onslaught to absorb the many refugees from the north. With their swollen populations, the southern Chinese kingdoms expanded their territorial control of the Changjiang River system beyond the portion already colonized by the Han Dynasty. Although divided into several kingdoms, south China experienced a culturally rich era, one enhanced by the northern refugees, the arrival of Buddhism, and the opening of new agricultural lands. In time the region was prosperous enough to experience a revival in the arts, literature, and philosophy.

Despite their internal divisions and political weakness, the Chinese adopted many new features into their culture. Buddhism enjoyed rapid expansion as the Chinese sent pilgrims to India to facilitate a steady importation of the new religious and philosophical ideas. Furthermore, during this time the Chinese developed several innovations that would have a major impact on world history: gunpowder, paper, the magnetized needle used in compasses, and the use of coal as fuel. Simultaneously, the Chinese prepared their civilization for its next great era of unification.

Always present in the Chinese mind throughout the dark years was the image of a reunified state. Most Chinese expected the return of political unity once Heaven was ready to select the next imperial dynasty. Alongside the influence of Buddhism, the older Daoist

and Confucian beliefs still functioned in the Chinese imagination.

The moment of reunification came with the rise of the short-lived Sui Dynasty (581–618). The Sui came from the same northern region that had generated the ancient Qin Dynasty (221–206 BCE). Like the Qin, the Sui rulers had swept through China as a new military power, capturing the imperial office and imposing on the people a harsh and demanding centralized government, one that soon fell to a rebellion but gave birth to a long-lived, stabilizing dynasty.

Thus, like the Qin, the Sui Dynasty was a short, transitional one. Its greatest achievement was the re-establishment of national unity after some four hundred years of disunity, thereby laying the groundwork for the "Golden Age" of imperial China in the succeeding Tang and Song dynasties.

China's Second Empire:
The Golden Age of Imperial China

The Sui Dynasty (581–618) originated on the Wei River in the north, built its first capital at Chang'an, and later built a second center of power Loyang. Concentrating its political and military strength in the north, the Sui soon learned, however, that the south offered China its economic future. Along the lower Changjiang River, the central government successfully linked the rich rice-producing fields of the south with the tax hungry governmental offices in the north where years of agricultural abuse along the Huang He had severely eroded the land. Hence the Sui began a new productive era for China.

The Sui, as mentioned, proved to be a short-lived dynasty. Sui Wendi (541–604) came to power in 581 by displaying considerable military talents, exploiting the cavalry tactics of the nomads, and quickly reuniting the Chinese empire. He proved to be a competent administrator as well; he restored the empire's infrastructure, rebuilt the Great Wall, began the construction of the Grand Canal to connect the Changjiang with the Huang He, and completed a magnificent palace at Chang'an. His son, however, proved to be far less able as a ruler.

Consumed with imperial power, Sui Yangdi replaced his father in 604, continued work on the Great Wall, completed the Grand Canal, constructed a new capital at Loyang, began a magnificent palace there, and exhausted the Chinese with military campaigns in Vietnam, Sinkiang, Mongolia, and Korea. Heavy resistance in Korea, and the megalomania of his rule, however, drove the Chinese into rebellion. Sui Yangdi was killed by the commander of the palace guards in 618; frontier generals then competed for the throne and a long-lived dynasty soon replaced the Sui.

The Tang Dynasty

One of the competing frontier generals, Li Yuan, won the struggle for power, began a new era of benevolent rule in 618, and took the title Tang Taizong. He encouraged an open court, sought advice and criticism despite his proven personal abilities as a great soldier and administrator, and rewarded competence among his subordinates. He began a new era of prosperity unequaled by anything prior to his reign due to his extraordinary talents as a charismatic leader, and he earned the distinction of being called the best emperor of Chinese history by many historians.

To launch his new reign, Tang Taizong returned the capital to Chang'an, (present day Xi'an), and built an extraordinary administrative center. He laid out his capital on a on a grid, with the palace to the north of the city. Immediately to its south were the government buildings. Further south were the residential and commercial sections. Foreign merchants had separate sections where they lived and did business. When night fell the city was shut down as soldiers patrolled the streets and enforced a curfew. The capital was also the starting point of the Silk Road, which was by now a well-developed thoroughfare connecting China with India and Central Asia. People, goods, and ideas flowed along the road in both directions in great volume. Such a large urban complex speaks well for the abundance of food transported from the south using the Sui Dynasty's Grand Canal.

The Tang out-performed the Sui, developing an effective and balanced central government to run its vast empire. The emperor was powerful, but specialized offices headed by ministers were in place as a check on his authority. One office drafted his orders, another reviewed them, and still another implemented them. An order having missed any step of the process had no legal force. There was also an inspector general's office, a high court, and an office of punishment (law enforcement). All major issues had to be approved by a joint session of the ministers of the three offices.

Tang Taizong promulgated the *Great Book of Tang Law.* Unlike the harsh and cumbersome Sui legal system, Tang law strode for leniency and simplicity. It also took note of ancient Chinese history and wisely laid down standards and procedures intended to prevent the abuse of power. Tang law became a model for later Chinese dynasties and influenced the legal systems of Korea, Japan, and Vietnam.

The Tang imperial government reestablished Confucianism as the state ideology, even though Buddhist influence remained a secondary intellectual force. The Tang strengthened Confucian schools and the examination system for entrance into the civil service. The exams tested the candidates on how well they might solve current problems and interpret Confucian classics. As a result, individual merit began to replace the inherited privileges of aristocrats as the measurement of one's qualification for office. Once full-fledged, the imperial examination system served to recruit educated men to serve the emperor and staff his bureaucracy. These educated men had been trained in the basic skills of reading and writing, taught in the Confucian and Legalist schools of statecraft, and indoctrinated to be loyal to the emperor.

In theory, the imperial examination system was open to all men, rich or poor, of high or low birth. In practice, generally only the wealthy could afford to provide their children with an education that took a decade or two to complete. There were, however, the lucky few who, by a combination of circumstances, did rise from the very bottom of society to the top. In any case, the system strengthened the regime by bringing into its service the brightest young men. And by holding out the possibility of upward social mobility to all, it also preempted many capable men from forming a potential rebel force. Indeed, over the years, the Tang created a very efficient social service.

In a word, the Tang integrated Chinese culture on a level unprecedented in Chinese history. Tang Taizong began the process, but his heirs maintained a steady level of such competent rule that the Tang built the largest empire in Chinese history. The firm establishment of a revenue base and infrastructure built first by the Sui, and expanded by the Tang, the recruiting of talented men through the Confucian examination system, the formation of an efficient and professional bureaucracy, and the promotion of men based on competence rather than birth produced the most effective government in world history at that time. The integration of political, economic, and social institutions through a rational administrative program under Tang authority produced the material needs for a golden age in Chinese history. But the political achievements of the Tang were not confined to talented male rulers only; one woman in particular proved equally able.

That woman was Wu Zetian (624–705), one of Tang Taizong's favorite concubines. When he died, she became his son's wife and outlived him too. As empress dowager to Tang Taizong's grandson, she first held the reins of power from behind the scenes. Then she usurped the throne from the Li family to establish her own dynasty in 685. As empress, she was an iron-fisted ruler. She used troops to stamp out rebellion, spies and torture to crush opposition, and favoritism and an expanded examination system to foster absolute loyalty. Her long reign was stable and prosperous. A coup in her old age confined her to the rear quarters of the palace and returned the throne to the Li family. Chinese historians have attacked her for having less than aristocratic family roots and for her licentious lifestyle.

Though officially relegated as a subordinate intellectual force to Confucianism, Buddhism became a broad-based and deeply rooted religion during the Tang Dynasty. Buddhists came from all walks of life, from royals to commoners, from peasants to wealthy merchants. Tang royalty took a deep interest in this powerful foreign religion and commissioned the translation of original Buddhist texts into Chinese. Xuanzang (602–64), a Buddhist monk, made the ar-

Luohan Monk, disciple of Buddha (c. 907–1125 CE). Luohans, known for magical powers, remained immortal in order to preserve the teachings of Buddha. This stoneware figure, from the Liao dynasty follows the sculptural traditions developed in the Tang dynasty (618–906 CE). From Yi county, Hebei province, northern China. © The Trustees of the British Museum.

duous round-trip journey from Chang'an to India (629–45) where he studied Buddhism in its land of origin. He left India with 567 volumes of Buddhist dogma. Upon his return, the emperor ordered the formation of a translation bureau where Xuanzang and his followers devoted their lives to translating the Buddhist texts into Chinese.

Yet the expanded interest in Buddhism and a proliferation of Buddhist monasteries generated numerous enemies. The monks at the monasteries had amassed great fortunes, including large holdings of farmland and large workforces of peasants. And since these institutions enjoyed tax and labor-service exemptions, their gain was the state's loss. Accordingly, Buddhist teachings and Buddhist monasteries came under harsh attack by Confucian scholars, with Buddhism's foreign origin becoming a favorite target of its critics. The great essayist Han Yu (768–824) made this a major argument in his fierce assaults. After repeated anti-Buddhist onslaughts, Buddhist monasteries went into a sharp decline. Unlike their counterparts in the West, religious institutions in China never rose above the government. Over time, however, Buddhist metaphysical philosophy and religious practices were assimilated into Chinese doctrine: these Indian concepts integrated with and enriched traditional Chinese Confucian and Daoist culture.

Elsewhere, Chinese poetry also experienced its golden age during the Tang Dynasty. Imperial exam takers were required to write poetry as a measure of their talents, for the examiners believed that poetry and calligraphy (the art of writing Chinese characters) not only reflected a student's learning but also revealed his personal character. With this incentive, all educated people learned to write poetry, and poetry took on a wider social function. It was used in social communication, in entertainment, and as a personal pastime. Of the hundreds of accomplished Tang-era poets, two in particular stand out and are widely read and quoted to this day. Du Fu (712–70), deeply influenced by Confucianism, focused principally on the fate of the country and its people. Li Bai (701–62), inspired by Daoism, displayed a free-spirited individualism and wrote with a rich flare for imagery.

Decline of the Tang Dynasty

Many factors contributed to the decline of the Tang. The first involved a romance and a rebellion. The romance began in 745 when the Tang Emperor Xuanzong (685–762) became enamored with his son's concubine, Yang Guifei, took her into his harem, and began to neglect his royal duties. As her influence grew, he accepted her suggestions concerning royal appointments.

When his chief minister died, she had her second cousin, Yang Guozhong, assigned the post. His incompetence compelled a Turkic general named An Lushang, who commanded three provinces on the northeastern frontier to rebel in 755. An Lushang led 160,000 troops against Xuanzong, captured Loyang and Chang'an, and forced the emperor to flee to Sichuan. En route, Xuanzong's retinue blamed Yang Guifei for their predicament, and his guards strangled her. Xuanzong never recovered from her loss and soon thereafter abdicated.

But many other factors also contributed to the downfall of Tang Dynasty. They included rampant factional infighting at the highest levels of government, the malignant expansion of the power of families related to the emperor by marriage, the rise of eunuchs in the court and that of the warlords on the frontiers, widespread peasant uprisings, and invasions by non-Han peoples. These forces undercut the emperor's authority, sapped the state's vigor, and brought about its collapse. All the major dynasties in China's history fell due to some combination of these factors.

Following the collapse of Tang, China again entered a short period of disunity. Called the period of the "Five Dynasties and Ten States" by Chinese historians, this phrase described an era of rival warlords and kings seeking central authority that lasted only half a century (907–60). In the future, China would continue to undergo cycles of unity and disunity, but the periods of disunity would become increasingly shorter, indicating a coalescence of the peoples of the land. The gap between the Tang Dynasty and the Song, China's next dynasty, revealed the recuperative powers of China's classical values, culture, and standards. A pattern had been set by the Tang that consolidated Confucianism's and Daoism's hold on the Chinese imagination.

The Song Dynasty

The founder of Song Dynasty, Song Taizu, had been the commander of the palace guard in one of the rival states competing for power. He seized the throne after a military coup, set up his capital at Kaifeng, on the Huang He, and eventually unified China by 960. This experience made him highly sensitive to the potential danger of military coups and drove him to take extreme measures to restrict the powers of the military commanders under his rule. To prevent them from developing strong ties with their troops, he rotated their command and dispatched eunuchs to their command posts as his personal representatives to oversee their activities. He also staffed his government with well-paid civil servants who had risen through the examination system. These mea-

sures greatly restricted access to power by established military and aristocratic families, and thereby reduced the threat to the emperor.

Chinese science and technology reached a peak in the Song Dynasty. The Chinese claim credit for the "four great inventions"—the compass, gunpowder, paper making, and printing with movable type. Three of the four technologies were substantively improved in the Song Dynasty. As far back as the era of the Warring States (403–221 BCE), the Chinese had known that iron magnets had the ability to point north. They made iron spoons that would indicate north with their handles. Later, they magnetized needles and fish made of iron for purposes of orientation. By the time of the Song Dynasty, troops used a compass to determine direction on cloudy days or at night. Then ocean-going ships adopted the use of the compass, which Arab merchants who often traveled on Chinese ships introduced to Europeans.

Another of the four great inventions, gunpowder, became widely used early in the Song. Ancient alchemists had discovered the explosive quality of a mixture of nitrate, sulfur, and charcoal. In the late Tang era, gunpowder was attached to the heads of arrows, which would ignite upon impact and start fires. Later gunpowder was packaged in an iron case for delivery by catapults. The world's earliest tubular firearm was invented when the Chinese packed gunpowder and projectiles into bamboo tubes. When lighted, the gunpowder exploded, providing the pressure to deliver the projectile. During the Yuan (1279–1368) and Ming (1368–1644) dynasties, China developed the iron musket and cannon. Gunpowder was introduced into Persia in 1230 and then to Europe through Spain.

As for making paper and block printing, China had a long tradition of cutting characters into flat bones, bronzes, walls, boards, and commemorative stone slabs and pillars. Later, people wrote on strips of wood, bamboo, or silk. In the Han Dynasty, Cai Lun invented paper (104). Henceforth, the Chinese wrote on paper with a writing brush dipped in ink. In the Tang Dynasty, the Chinese began cutting the words of texts into wooden boards and then stamping them on paper to make identical copies. In the Song Dynasty a commoner named Bi Shen (?–1051?) invented movable type for printing. Now a small cube of baked clay bore a single character. This was a much more efficient printing method, for the same piece of type could be used repeatedly in different arrangements to print different texts. Printing with movable type on paper greatly facilitated the dissemination of knowledge. Now government documents, religious texts, agricultural manuals, and financial records could be kept and transmitted with much greater ease and reliability. Cai Lun's invention came four centuries before Guggenheim's similar invention in Europe. These three inventions and their application to the spread of information, the conduct of warfare, and ocean-going navigation caused profound changes in human civilizations. Their introduction to the West accelerated Europe's entry into modern times.

Southern China's New Role in the Economy

The shift of China's economic center from the Huang He to the Lower Changjiang River had begun during the Sui Dynasty but was completed in the Song. Rice lay at the heart of this new era of economic expansion. The popular image of China with its densely packed population working the soil to generate subsistence and taxable surpluses became a reality during the Sui-Tang-Song eras. The Tang expanded the process of internal colonization along the length of the Changjiang begun by the Sui to open the entire river and its tributaries to rice cultivation. This rich region became the new tax base for China and developed into the most populous portion of the empire. Most of China's food now came from the south, as the north suffered the ecological consequences of so many years of feeding and sustaining China's earlier civilizations (the Shang, Zhou, Qin, and Han). Recurrent droughts, soil erosion, siltation along vital irrigation canals, and violent periodic floods reaffirmed the Chinese nickname for the Huang He as "China's sorrow." The north was nearly exhausted agriculturally, but the land there was still useful in supplying the wheat found in the Chinese diet.

In the south, a steady application of peasant labor transformed the countryside. Thousands of small rice paddies developed on the landscape. These small farms both met the needs of subsistence and provided taxable surpluses from a very limited space. Unlike Europe, which expanded agricultural production by developing heavy plows, teams of draft animals, and large farms that covered great amounts of land, China invested in rice paddies worked by intense human labor. The hand-planted rice shoots in these paddies generated enough food to sustain the farmer's family and enough surplus to feed the rest of China. Each year Chinese farmers added a little more land to their concerns, so the area under rice cultivation in the south expanded slowly but steadily.

Ironically, the rapid acceleration of the symbiosis between humans and rice locked China into its well-established patterns of life. Rice yielded just enough food above what farmers and their families needed so that the new surpluses maintained a stable numerical balance between rural and urban populations: as farmers increased in number, so did the urban population.

Yet the urban population did not change in relative size compared to those living in the countryside. Thus, as China expanded food production, its urban component grew but remained roughly 10 percent of the total population. This 10 percent of China's population consumed the new surpluses generated by rice.

Meanwhile, a Commercial Revolution took place between the ninth and thirteenth centuries, one that shaped many aspects of a Chinese economic and social structure that remained unchanged into the nineteenth century. The capital during the Song Dynasty, Kaifeng, was located on the Huang He to the north and connected to the Huai and Changjiang rivers to the south using the Grand Canal. The markets in the capital had grains from the south; cattle and sheep from the west; seafood from the coastal east; silk, paper, books and tea from all over the country; and imported fans from Japan, writing ink from Korea, and spices from India. Scholars estimate Song Dynasty China had the largest volume of goods and currency in circulation in the world.

A beautifully painted scroll by the artist Zhang Zeduan depicts in detail a small but elegant fraction of the great variety of commercial activities in Kaifeng. The Song Dynasty teemed with traders in rice, tea, and salt. Merchants in precious metals and cotton fabrics did the largest volume of business. Restaurants, hotels, and inns were numerous. Merchants had their guilds, which often had their own restaurants where the merchants met to socialize, exchange information, examine goods, and negotiate transactions. These places often had performers of song and dance, courtesans, and prostitutes.

In the Song Dynasty, the Chinese were using the world's earliest form of paper money. In early Song, the main currency was copper coins, supplemented by iron coins. As commerce grew, pressure increased for a larger supply of currency. Sixteen rich merchants joined forces to issue the earliest paper currency, which was a natural extension of merchant credit certificates—light and convenient to carry. Soon the government monopolized the right to issue paper money. By the late Song, as the shortage of copper coins increased, paper money became the main currency. The government also coined gold into currency. In Europe, Sweden, the first state to issue paper money, did not do so until 1661, some six centuries later.

Non-Han tribes posed a constant threat to the Song Dynasty throughout its three centuries of existence. They mounted endless looting raids on China's northern frontiers, and formed the states of Xixia in the northwest and Liao (the Qidan tribe) in the northeast. Later, the Song allied with Jurzhen, who formed the state of

Jin, to defeat Liao. Now the Jin replaced the Liao as the Song's greatest threat, so the Song adopted a diplomatic policy of capitulation. It would repeatedly negotiate treaties with the Jin to give the aggressors gifts of silver, silk, tea, and copper coins in exchange for peace. This gift-giving diplomacy would buy a respite from fighting for a few decades but did not establish a lasting peace. At one point, the Jin captured the Song capital Kaifeng. Jin warriors looted the city and carried off the emperor, his wife, his concubines, his sons, and his ministers. One of his sons escaped and became the next emperor, having relocated his capital to Hangzhou, below the Changjiang River, far away from the reach of the Jin cavalry.

The new regime, called the Southern Song, entrenched itself in the south. Population, capital, and knowledge followed the regime in fleeing the north. Hangzhou became China's political, economic, and cultural center. It also became the world's largest city with a population of 1.24 million. So much wealth and luxury accumulated in Hangzhou, it won the reputation of being "heaven on earth."

As the Commercial Revolution continued, the central government of the Southern Song made unprecedented efforts to get the peasants to increase agricultural production. Government and private individuals compiled, printed, and circulated many books on new farming techniques. The focus was on intensive farming—to increase unit output by adopting better methods and making greater investments of labor and equipment. Output soared.

Handicraft also soared to new heights. At this time the government established agencies to make silk fabrics. These agencies typically housed hundreds of looms and thousands of workers. Private manufacturers of silk were numerous. Porcelain production also flourished. But commerce for the Southern Song became more difficult.

Centered in Hangzhou, the Southern Song had lost its access to the land route of the Silk Road. Therefore rulers of the Southern Song redoubled their efforts to develop a trade route by sea. This new sea route reached Southeast Asia, India, Persia, the Arab countries, Korea, and Japan. Quanzhou, Guangzhou, and Mingzhou quickly became major trading ports. Eager to prevent the outflow of Chinese currency, the Song government ordered the use of silks and porcelains as trade items in exchange for imports.

Philosophy

The Song witnessed another great period of philosophical creativity comparable to the Era of the Warring States (403–221 BCE), which produced "the hundred schools" mentioned in Unit One. Zhu Xi (1130–1200) reinterpreted Confucianism and added elements of Buddhism to it. This Neo-Confucianism was more systematic and had a deeper philosophical foundation. Removing the supernatural element of Dong Zhongshu's version of Confucianism, Zhu systematized Dong's principles of a hierarchical social structure and worked to popularize it. His model of a hierarchical society comprised four classes: scholar-officials, peasants, artisans, and merchants, in descending order. Yet one's place in life was not permanent: one could move up and down the social hierarchy, the imperial examination system being a channel for upward social mobility. Each person must act according to his station in life. How a person conducted himself was a question of morality. In a textbook Zhu wrote, for example, he laid out specific rules about how children should behave with regard to their dress, speech, conduct, reading, writing, and food and drink in a rigid social hierarchy. He relegated women to the confines of home. They were regarded as inferior to and dependent on men. Divorce and remarriage were heretical. The practice of foot binding (the painful folding and binding of a young girl's toes under her feet—a process that rendered the girl disfigured and barely able to walk) spread from the top to the bottom of society. The rationalization for foot binding was that tiny feet increased women's sex appeal. The work of Zhu Xi was quite influential, with his interpretation of Confucian classics becoming the standard answers used in imperial examinations; his version of Neo-Confucianism becoming the official orthodoxy throughout the rest of imperial China.

The Decline of the Song

Despite the wealth and sophistication of the Song Dynasty, the government suffered from a perennial shortage of revenue to sustain its overstaffed bureaucracy and ineffective armies. Appointed Prime Minister by Emperor Song Shen-Zong (1068–1085) Wang Anshi (1021–1086) made a historic attempt at solving the problem. His reforms (1069–85 with interruptions) were remarkable for their bold initiatives and ultimate failure. Essentially, his reforms were designed to expand government powers to intervene in all aspects of the people's lives. They included: 1) government low-interest loans to peasants; 2) government regulation of market prices; 3) fair distribution of land taxes; 4) government conversion of labor service into cash payments; 5) the collective security system (organizing households into units of 10, 50, 500, etc., wherein member households were collectively responsible for paying taxes, community security, and forming a militia); and 6) appointing generals to train troops (reversing the earlier practice of preventing strong ties between commanders and their troops). These reform efforts hurt the vested interests of the rich and powerful. For example, the attempts at redistributing taxes in accordance with the amount and quality of land a family owned hurt big landowners who had long enjoyed tax exemptions through legal or illegal means. Government regulation of market prices hurt big merchants who earlier had manipulated the market to their own benefit. Confronted by insurmountable opposition, the emperor gave up the reforms, after which the Song Dynasty was never able to solve its chronic problems of impoverished government and weak military. Eventually it fell prey to the unstoppable Mongol cavalry.

The Yuan Dynasty

The Mongols, who will be covered more thoroughly later in this chapter, overlap with the fall of the Song at this juncture in the story because they created the next Chinese dynasty, the Yuan (1279–1368). Kublai Khan (1215?–94) conquered the Southern Song as part of a larger subjugation pattern that the Mongols imposed on all of Central Asia (see below). Kublai Khan defeated the Song by first making an alliance with the Chinese to deal with the Jin. But the Song soon discovered that they had invited in a force too great for them to control. In due course, the Mongols invaded northern China, fought for forty years to occupy the south, and succeeded in defeating the Southern Song because divided council, factionalism, and inconsistent strategies at the Song court proved fatal.

To control a population vastly larger than its own, the Mongol regime adopted a policy of "divide and rule." They established an ethnic hierarchy, dividing people in China into four classes that were unequal as defined by law. Quite naturally, Mongols were perched at the top of the pyramid, the privileged ruling class. The non-Mongol, non-Han peoples living in the Mongol Empire, especially the Muslims from Central Asia, were next. The Han Chinese in North China, who had submitted to Mongol rule before Han Chinese in South China, occupied the third tier. Finally, the Han Chinese in South China lay at the bottom, as punishment for their long and tenacious resistance to Mongol conquest. The first two categories made up a scant 3 percent of all the households in China, the last two 97 percent.

Following their own tradition, the Mongols rewarded their followers with large grants of land. The recipients often converted farmland into pasture for their herds of livestock. This had disastrous consequences for the Han population. Having lost access to their rice paddies, Han farmers lost their livelihoods and became a roaming population while food production declined as herds replaced plant cultivation. The emperor's advisor, Yelu Chucai (1190–1244), an assimilated Qidan, saw the seriousness of the problem. He pointed out that turning farmland into pastures deprived the government of agricultural surpluses and created a large landless population that threatened the stability of society. He advised the Mongol rulers that it was in their best interest to make laws to keep land under government control, keep farmers on the land, and reestablish a Han-style government bureaucracy to collect taxes. The emperor was persuaded, and he modified the Mongol practice. Yet he was unable to free himself entirely from the tradition of his people, and he continued to allow Muslim tax collectors to extract food surpluses from Chinese peasants, a policy that was seriously flawed, for the tax collectors, who paid a fixed fee for the privilege, greedily took every grain of rice they could. The increased weight of the tax burden on the peasantry eventually led to revolts and rebellions.

The Mongols had a keen interest in artisans. Whenever they captured a city, they would take large numbers of craftsmen as prisoners. Under Mongol rule, craftsmen enjoyed certain privileges, such as exemption from taxes and labor service and the issue of rations and stipends, but they lacked personal freedom. The law required the son of a craftsman to work in his father's trade under government supervision. One of the products for which the Yuan craftsmen were best known were their excellent copper cannon.

The Mongols also had a keen interest in trade. Their far-flung empire with its well-developed road system greatly facilitated trade over a vast territory. The regime had a tendency to use the coercive powers of government to intervene in economics. One outstanding feature of Yuan trade was its government-run monopolies. The government managed direct monopolies of gold, silver, copper, iron, and salt; it sold some such monopolies to merchants. Many high government officials were also large-scale merchants. Wealthy Mongols often hired Muslim financial agents to manage their trading and money-lending businesses, with annual interest rates running as high as 100 percent. The Muslim merchants enjoyed government support and their privileged status often disrupted normal trading.

Intercultural trade throughout Eurasia was very active. The sea route of the Silk Road reached from the Pacific Ocean to the Persian Gulf and as far north and west as the Baltic Sea. China's chief exports were silk, tea, and porcelain. Imports included gold, copper, spices, jewelry, and ivory. The Yuan government enlarged the role of paper money to match its interest in trade. The currency was first based on a silk standard and later on a silver standard. But the Yuan were unable to restrain their appetite for printing more and more paper money. In the end, Yuan paper money became worthless as inflation became rampant.

The Yuan government made only sporadic, half-hearted efforts at reestablishing the status of Confucianism, the imperial examination system, and a national bureaucracy staffed by civil servants. This left large numbers of educated people outside the system and without a ladder of upward mobility. One consequence of this situation was that some of the restless but capable men of China were quick to join rebel forces when the opportunity appeared. Others turned their literary talents into a new subversive literary form—the Yuan poetic drama or Yuan Qu.

The Mongol armies were unstoppable on land, but all of their ventures at overseas conquest ended in failure. Most notable were their two attempts to conquer Japan. The Mongols launched their invasions of Japan from Korea first in 1274 and then in 1281. Japanese *samurai* (warrior aristocrats) resisted stubbornly. Moreover, the seasonal typhoons sank the Mongol ships during both attempts at landing in Japan and drowned Mongol troops, leading many Japanese to believe that Japan enjoyed the divine protection of the typhoon they called *kamikaze* (divine wind).

The government in late Yuan was riddled by factional strife and palace intrigue. It had eight different emperors in the twenty-five years between 1308 and 1333. The government was also corrupt and incompetent to the extreme, taxes and labor service became unbearably heavy, and peasant rebellions broke out all over the country, eventually bringing down the dynasty. A major rallying point for peasant rebellions was a secret peasant society called the White Lotus Sect and its military arm known as the Red Turbans.

Marco Polo (1254–1324) is widely known as the Italian merchant and world traveler from Venice who spent seventeen years in China. According to a book that Polo claimed was based on his oral account of his adventures, he went to the Yuan capital by way of the Silk Road in 1271, met with the Yuan emperor, and was appointed magistrate of Yangzhou, a great city at the confluence of the Changjiang and the Grand Canal. His memoirs give vivid descriptions of Chinese cities, ways of life, and unique practices. The Italian marveled at the Chinese use of coal, paper money, and

Marco Polo at the court of Kublai Khan. Marco Polo was a favorite of the Khan who employed him for seventeen years in a variety of duties: official envoy, advisor, and military expedition escort, to name a few. This miniature is taken from "Il milione," "The Travels of Marco Polo," an account of his travels to China, published during Polo's lifetime in 1298–99.

food—especially noodles. The book had a great impact in stirring the imagination of early modern Europeans.

Sinification:
The Influence of Chinese Culture
on Korea, Japan, and the Mongols

The cultures of Korea, Japan, and Mongolia played varied roles in world history, but all of them experienced the shift from nomadic herding to partial or total sedentary life during the middle years. Pulled into the web of civilization by contact with the Chinese, each of these three cultures occupied new lands, tried to manage plant cultivation, and experienced cultural diffusion from China—a phenomenon known as *Sinification*—as the shaping agent of their societies.

To illustrate China's power as an exporter of culture, ancient Rome offers a contrasting example. Rome allowed enough local autonomy within its empire to preserve cultural variations and sustain two basic languages, Latin and Greek. The use of these languages divided the Roman Empire into distinct western and eastern regions. The Chinese, in contrast, integrated everyone within their cultural boundaries into a cultural synthesis. Hence, China occupied the same sized landmass as Rome, but the Chinese created a far more powerful cultural system within their territory. Then, this massive system expanded outward.

This powerful impulse to assimilate partially explains the complete recovery of China after the fall of the Han Dynasty in 220 CE. In addition, it partly accounts for China's aggressive, imperialistic expansion during the Sui and Tang dynasties. Thus, for China's immediate neighbors—Korea, Japan, and Mongolia—to have undergone intense and sustained contact with China but maintain their own identity, speaks to the vitality of each of these peoples.

As these groups entered the mainstream of world history, they followed different paths. Each therefore generated a separate story that reflected local circumstances. Of the three countries, Korea and Japan followed the path of sedentary civilizations that developed sophisticated agriculture, unique traditions, and a rich urban history. As a pastoral people sampling the urban products of others, the Mongols released a burst of energy that led to the last great conquest pattern generated from the great grasslands of Central Asia, but then began to experience sedentary pressures that eventually ended the nomadic threat from the Eurasian steppe.

Korea

For the benefits of cultural diffusion, Korea had the advantage of close proximity to China. But this closeness also threatened Korea's absorption by the powerful Chinese imperial system. Yet even though Korea took many of its cultural practices from China, the Koreans managed to maintain a separate identity.

This feat reflected a combination of geography and the strong determination of the Koreans to maintain an autonomous political society. The Korean Peninsula had natural boundaries, a mountain range and the Yalu River at its northern end that helped to separate it from mainland Asia. At the same time, the determination of the Korean people to remain independent from China also stemmed from their preference for Buddhism over Confucianism as their intellectual basis of culture.

The people who occupied Korea in the middle years of world history probably had originally come there from Siberia or northern Manchuria. Once they settled on the peninsula they gave up a nomadic life of hunting and gathering to take up agriculture. Their spoken language is polysyllabic and completely unrelated to Chinese. They developed their own culture, but soon found themselves in numerous wars fought to prevent China from subjugating their land. Nevertheless, heavy Chinese influence enhanced Korea's life during the Han Dynasty without undercutting its identity as a separate culture.

The features of Chinese culture that pervaded Korea included rice and wheat cultivation, metallurgy, written symbols, paper manufacturing, printing, the art of producing lacquered objects and porcelain, and numerous other technical innovations. The material wealth generated by these Chinese innovations helped to refine political power and social order in Korea. At the same time, Korea's successful defenses against numerous Chinese invasions during the Han, the Sui, and the Tang dynasties suggested how persistent Koreans were in preserving their own cultural future.

Emerging from hunter-gatherer bands that migrated into Korea, the first sedentary cultures to develop on the peninsula did not reflect the Mongolian or Turkish patterns of life common to Siberia or Manchuria. Rather, these first Koreans learned cultivation instead of a pastoral lifestyle and developed metallurgy through their contact with China during the fourth century BCE. Based on the surplus generated by this agriculture, the Koreans began to form their first states by 200 BCE.

But the earliest Korean Kingdom, Choson, suffered defeat at the hands of the Han Dynasty in 109 BCE, and the Chinese colonized parts of the peninsula. These colonies naturally became conduits for the diffusion of Chinese culture and set in motion Sinification. At the same time, the Japanese created a small enclave at the southern tip of Korea that allowed cultural diffusion from there to the Japanese islands.

Despite these foreign presences, the Koreans still managed to keep their identity and rose in resistance to the Chinese, which led to the emergence of a northern kingdom called Koguryo. Koguryo grew to command the northern half of the peninsula, as the Han Dynasty in China weakened and finally collapsed in 220. Then Koguryo began to function as a political barrier to further Chinese penetration. At the same time, the middle and southern half of Korea developed into two additional monarchies: Silla and Paekche, respectively. All three kingdoms had became firmly established after 220.

The disunity in China between 220 and 581 allowed the Koreans to continue cultural importation while resisting Sinification. Thus, the Koreans further refined their civilization during this period and reached a level of sophistication that virtually guaranteed their separate identity. During this era of Korean strength, internal developments on the peninsula saw the Koreans actually become exporters of culture, as they helped to shape the Japanese civilization that lay across the narrow Korea Straits.

Renewed contact with China between the Han and Sui dynasties (220–581) saw the kingdoms of Korea adopt Buddhism, as this Indian religion continued to migrate into the Far East. Buddhism created a worldview that separated Korea's cultural vision from the dominant Confucian voice of China. Koreans now imported Master Kong's philosophy, the Chinese Classics, and ancestor worship without having to fear that the Chinese worldview would overwhelm the Korean imagination.

Buddhism created an independent vision in Korea that generated a distinct sense of self. Korean rulers patronized Buddhist monks, their intellectual pursuits, and their arts in order to perfect a vehicle to achieve high culture. Through Buddhism the Koreans learned about a transcendental reality that helped to shield them from their aggressive neighbors. The discipline and selflessness of Buddhism also functioned as a cultural armor that prepared the Koreans for the difficult years they soon would face. Hence, Korean scholars would travel into a divided China, pick up certain features of that society and then return home without fear of losing their cultural way.

Through Buddhism, Chinese writing, governmental forms, and educational systems entered Korea merely as conceptual models. Each of these imports enhanced Korea's command over its peninsula. Yet each had to be adapted to Korean needs. For example, writing posed special problems for the Koreans and Japanese; both used several sounds to form each word in their vocabulary. The Chinese, however, used only one sound per word. Thus, the monosyllabic Chinese developed a writing system in which pictographs evolved primarily into ideograms and ideographs to capture concepts rather than sounds. Hence, the language of the Chinese encouraged them to associate a symbol with a concept so that all the different dialects within their culture could read the same ideas despite the variations in the sounds each of them made when they spoke.

The Koreans and the Japanese, however, needed a phonetic system to capture the polysyllabic sounds for their words. Thus, they both had to alter the Chinese style of writing to meet their own linguistic requirements. Both the Koreans and Japanese solved this problem, but their solutions differed substantially. For most of their traditional history, the Koreans wrote and thought in Chinese while still remaining Korean. Only the most disciplined of minds could think in these two different styles. Finally, at the beginning of the modern era the Koreans abandoned this practice and developed a syllabary in which every consonant had five vowel sounds associated with it to create five symbols. This system replaced the Chinese ideograms that dominated most of Korea's history after the fifteenth century.

The Japanese went a bit further because they were both farther away from China and had not associated with the Chinese as long as the Koreans had. The Japanese mixed Chinese ideograms with two syllabaries early in their history to create a system of writing involving three levels. First, Chinese ideograms represented concepts that initiated Japanese sounds when reading Chinese symbols. Next, the Japanese developed a syllabary to capture Japanese sounds for Japanese words when Chinese symbols failed. Finally, the Japanese developed a separate syllabary for foreign words that they used both to incorporate alien ideas and identify them as such in their system of writing. These mental gymnastics reveal how the Koreans and the Japanese could grasp features of Chinese culture without becoming Chinese.

Chinese governmental forms and their educational institutions were concrete systems that Korea and Japan could assimilate as they pleased. Korea selected an assortment of these forms and made them Korean. Hence, the king of Koguryo created Chinese-style universities staffed by Korean professors who taught the Chinese Classics and Master Kong's philosophy as governmental forms to serve Korean objectives. Chinese history became an example of conduct to be studied and imitated through adaptation to Korean needs. A Chinese bureaucracy was imported and made to administer Korean territory for the Koguryo monarchy. Ironically, these Chinese techniques were most frequently used to defend Korea against Chinese invasions.

During this era of cultural diffusion, the three kingdoms of Korea fought one another while China remained divided. Consequently, centuries of war in Korea left the peninsula vulnerable just when reunification in China facilitated major new drives for cultural expansion. The rise of the Sui Dynasty (581–618) led to a massive Chinese invasion of Korea that threatened the people of the peninsula with complete Sinification.

The Sui emperor Sui Wendi viewed Korea as a future province of China and set about to conquer the peninsula. His invasion would have overwhelmed the Koreans if his son and heir, Sui Yangdi, had not taken on too many projects at once. As mentioned above, Sui Yangdi's domestic and foreign policies overburdened China and undermined Chinese military efforts to conquer Korea. Thus, before China could defeat Korea, the Sui collapsed to a general Chinese rebellion that saw the rise of the Tang Dynasty (618–907).

Like the Sui, the Tang included Korea on its list of places to conquer, yet the need to consolidate power in Tang China delayed an invasion for several decades. When the Chinese finally did launch their attack, Koguryo had to absorb the direct force of the Chinese military. At the same time, Chinese diplomats approached the kingdom of Silla and encouraged them to destroy the kingdom of Paekche on the southeast half of the peninsula—thus permitting the Chinese to focus on taking Koguryo. This strategy worked: both Paekche and Koguryo fell to military conquest, and the Tang Dynasty stood poised to absorb all of Korea. Then, quarrels with Silla over the division of the spoils gave the Tang the excuse they needed for war.

To the Tang's surprise, however, Silla proved strong enough to frustrate Chinese plans. And the stubborn resistance of Silla gave the Koreans a rallying point to defeat Tang ambitions. Korean rebellions against Chinese rule broke out in former Koguryo territory expanding the conflict. Thus, Korea survived under Silla's leadership.

Silla finally struck a deal with Tang China wherein Silla could remain independent if their kings acknowledged the Tang emperors as overlords. This created a relationship between Korea and China that endured for most of their shared history together. Thus Korea joined China's tributary trade system: the Koreans acknowledged the Chinese emperor as a "supreme but distant ruler" by paying a form of "tribute" to the Chinese court that allowed the Chinese emperor to match this "gift" and send back a far more valuable present representing his "magnanimous power." This created a fiction for China that allowed the emperor to declare himself king of kings at the center of civilization. The emperor seemed happy to pay for this privilege.

As a result, Korea remained politically and culturally independent as an autonomous state ruled by native dynasties. This strange relationship kept China at a distance. At the same time, it permitted the Koreans to continue their importation of Chinese culture without fear of Sinification.

Silla ruled the Korean peninsula into the 900s. Then a usurper within Silla's court displaced Silla's rulers in 935 to establish the Koryo Dynasty (918–1392). This new dynasty maintained the relationship established by Silla with China and kept Korean civilization on an even footing with the Chinese. Korea became a satellite state in orbit around China as a member of a cultural club that included other Chinese neighbors: Tibet, Vietnam, Thailand, Mongolia, and Manchuria. This cultural club defined the limits of Sinification and secured the future of all these independent societies.

Japan

Following a path similar to that taken by Korea, Japan had the seas of Japan and East China as additional geographic barriers between them and China. The Japanese, however, had further to go in terms of cultural assimilation before they could enter the ranks of a major civilization. Hence, diffusion from China had the added danger of engulfing the Japanese through the sheer power of cultural intoxication as high civilization literally transformed the Japanese imagination. Japan went through several cultural changes that mixed rapid assimilation from abroad with indigenous Japanese definitions of how to organize life.

What is striking about Japanese history is the capacity of this culture to absorb vast amounts of information from abroad in an amazingly short period without forgetting who they were. The Japanese developed this ability early in their history and exercised it more than once. Thus, Japan went through three major bursts of cultural assimilation—250 BCE, 604 CE, and 1853—yet the Japanese maintained their balance as a distinct people.

Starting in 250 BCE, Japan experienced the agricultural, bronze, and iron revolutions simultaneously. All three transformed a Stone Age culture into a vital grain-producing society in only 350 hundred years (250 BCE to 100 CE). Then, in the year 604, Japan undertook a deliberate policy of rapid cultural assimilation by absorbing Chinese practices. Over the next 150 years, this policy transformed the Japanese islands into a highly sophisticated civilization. Finally, in the year 1853, Japan entered the modern era when the United States dispatched a naval fleet commanded by Commodore Matthew C. Perry to force the Japanese to open their islands to foreign trade. Once again, the Japanese revealed their cultural flexibility by learning even from unexpected visitors, rapidly absorbing modern industry and nationalism within several decades. Each of these episodes speaks to the capacity of the Japanese people to borrow massive amounts of foreign cultural information while retaining their own identity.

Beginning with rice, and assimilating bronze and iron manufacturing at the same time, Japan emerged as a sedentary culture between 250 BCE and 100 CE. As part of the Yayoi period (250 BCE to 250 CE), this era of acculturation took Japan through a series of changes that civilizations like Egypt, Mesopotamia, and India experienced at their leisure over the course of some two thousand years. Like the Koreans, the Japanese developed out of bands of hunter-gatherers who leaped from a nomadic to a sedentary life in a single bound. Neither Korea nor Japan had much time in which to adjust to the powerful influences new technologies and rice cultivation had on their cultures. Consequently, Japan made this cultural shift in one thrust right behind the Koreans. Korea played a central role. The Korean peninsula provided the geographic avenue for the cultural diffusion that transformed Japan. Through Korea, Chinese institutions joined Indian beliefs as both migrated to Japan. Once there, both changed the Japanese way of life during the Yayoi period.

Organized into clans, the Yayoi people of Japan occupied Kyushu as their cultural headquarters. This location placed them in close contact with the Korean peninsula. In time a small enclave of Yayoi people at the southern tip of Korea developed in a tiny state called Mimana, through which the Japanese kept open access to new and valuable techniques coming down the Korean Peninsula from China. Soon, Mimana developed a close friendship with the Korean kingdom of Paekche.

Each Japanese clan in Yayoi society enjoyed the fruits of this association with Paekche. As the Japanese population grew, the Yayoi culture migrated north to transform the Japanese landscape. As a result of this movement, the Yayoi people occupied the main island, Honshu, displacing the older Jomon culture there, and generated the food surpluses that ensured Yayoi society's expansion over much of southern Japan.

Yayoi society itself comprised clans that traced their ancestry back to a divine parent called a *kami*. The kami itself was a god; the clan formed around a human founder who traced his lineage to the kami. Called the *uji-no-kami*, the clan leader ruled as a high priest and clan chief. The status of each clan reflected its lineage or familial proximity to the imperial clan through an association pattern with the principle kami, *Amaterasu*, the Sun Goddess. All clans, thus, marked their location in society as one of the original band of kami whose personal or familial relationships to Amaterasu explained what the Japanese believed to be the order of Heaven on Earth.

As chief kami, Amaterasu, turned command of the Japanese islands over to her grandson. The offspring of this grandson became the emperors and empresses of Japan. The other clans were the offspring of associated kami that had been the divine friends and relatives of Amaterasu's grandson. They had accompanied his children in their joint migration north to occupy Japan. Together they formed a community of clans and ancestors whose worship came to be called *Shinto* (the Way of the Gods).

Led by an uji-no-kami, each of these clans commanded a political and religious component of Yayoi society. Clans themselves were large sociopolitical units as complex as those extended families found in such places as Scotland. Together these Japanese clans formed the basis of Yayoi politics. Yet, like most clan systems, the uji-no kami seemed to reflect an element of decentralization, as the emperor or empress worked through these clan leaders to rule the people of Japan.

Continued association with Korea through Mimana gave the Japanese increasingly more Chinese features—but at a safe distance. Korea digested these features and gave them a Korean spin that further pro-

tected the Japanese from Sinification. Thus, due to the Koreans, the Japanese valued Buddhism over Confucianism as the intellectual vehicle for cultural development. Confucianism made the trip to Japan from the kingdom of Paekche in 513, but it was soon overshadowed by Buddhism, which arrived in Japan in 538. The relatively late arrival of these major cultural features speaks to the second sudden burst of Japanese cultural assimilation.

In 562 Paekche betrayed its friendship with Japan and joined Silla in a combined attack on Mimana, which cut off Japanese access to further cultural contact with Korea. Then, Korea's struggle to survive against the powerful Tang Dynasty all but erased the Korean peninsula as an avenue of cultural diffusion. Finally, Silla's ultimate survival through its victory over Paekche, and its war with a determined Tang Dynasty, turned Japan directly to China itself as the source of future changes.

Japan's relations with Silla had never been friendly. Silla's use of Paekche in the destruction of Mimana reflected this mutual hostility. Then when Silla betrayed Paekche, Japan watched as its old ally fell. These military and diplomatic moves by Silla confirmed Japan's distrust of this Korean kingdom and created a new barrier between the Japanese and Koreans. Silla's final victory and survival against the Tang permanently closed Korea to Japan.

Then, with the ascendancy in Japan of a charismatic leader, Prince Shotoku (574–622), Japan decided to bypass Korea and import culture directly from Chinese sources. Shotoku served the imperial clan as regent to the empress from 593–622. His regency gave him the authority to forge a direct link between Buddhism and Chinese culture in a series of reforms that would lift Japan into the ranks of a major civilization. He started this process in 604, and the Japanese achieved his objective within 150 years.

Prince Shotoku understood that his plan for cultural change would displace Shinto as the central religion of the islands. He expected that such a displacement would upset many powerful uji-no-kami who would no longer occupy their traditional locations in the structure of power that ruled Japan. Consequently, he sought allies in this enterprise.

He selected the Soga clan as his chief supporters because of their financial and military resources. Their association with the prince allowed him to defeat powerful clans that opposed the reforms he wished to implement. Yet when the Soga themselves threatened imperial rule through control of the succession, a later prince, Nara-no-Oe who became Emperor Tenchi (626–71), selected a new and more reliable ally, the Fujiwara clan. This shift to the Fujiwara allowed Nara-no-Oe to de-

The Great hall, Todaiji (747 CE), originally presented imposing dimensions to the world: 284 feet long, 166 feet wide, and 152 feet high. Destroyed in the civil wars of the Taira and the Minamoto, the present structure is smaller, but still impressive. Courtesy of Steven Wallech.

stroy the Soga and accelerate further cultural changes through the importation of Buddhism. The Fujiwara provided a stable partnership with the throne that would shape Japanese politics over the course of the next 585 years. Shinto continued as a form of worship, but in a subordinate role to Buddhism. Princes Shotoku and Nara-no-Oe set up intellectual centers in the city of Nara such as Horiuji and began Japan's transformation. This era became known as the Nara period (600–794).

Culminating in the *Taika* Reform (645), the Japanese looked to Tang China as an example of how to restructure their leadership into an imperial government. Property, inheritance, taxation, political authority, the conceptual order of society, writing, census reports, architecture, literature, philosophy, and the arts suddenly expanded as Japan underwent a second episode of profound change. Japan now sent embassies to China to note any cultural feature these diplomats considered valuable. The artifacts they brought back went into direct implementation.

From 600 to 800 Japan experienced the transplanting of Chinese culture. Yet even as the central government took on a Chinese appearance, the Japanese continued to use clans as the underlying basis of social organization. Buddhism spread everywhere, and Confucian concepts served to shape governmental design. Simultaneously, extended families ensured local stability as the basis of social order in the countryside.

Shinto remained in the background as a notion of clan association, while Buddhism served as the central intellectual tool transforming Japanese culture.

Buddhism explained the cosmic order of things and created the philosophical vocabulary necessary for the Japanese to grasp the subtle concepts of Chinese civilization. This mixture of religion and philosophy served to keep the Japanese focused on who they were even as they experienced a flood of Chinese imports, both material and conceptual.

By the year 794 a balance of Buddhism and Shinto had created a new basis for Japanese life. In that year the young Emperor Kammu moved the capital to Kyoto. The city of Nara had become so choked with Buddhist monasteries and temples that freedom of action at the imperial court became impossible. Hence, Emperor Kammu decided to start fresh in a new political center.

Kammu's move to Kyoto launched what became known as the Heian period (794–1185) in Japanese history. Yet, as in Nara, Kyoto soon became choked with Buddhist monasteries and temples. Nonetheless, Heian culture flowered into yet another magnificent expression of Buddhist-Japanese creativity.

In the countryside, however, a silent transformation was underway. Between 645 and 1185, Japanese communal life in rural districts had continued to follow the clan-based pattern of Japan's original social organization. Now the Japanese began to add to this clan system an element of military life as they completed the conquest of their home islands. Assigned the duty of protecting imperial and Fujiwara holdings in the provinces, the warrior-servants of the court (samurai) accepted the possession of estates as the basis of financing their local responsibilities.

These estates, called *Shoen*, had functioned as the tax base for the imperial court. Yet all of the estates owned by the imperial family and the Fujiwara clan had long enjoyed tax-free privileges. Thus, many Japanese clans had escaped taxation by giving the title of their lands to the Fujiwara clan. As a result, the Fujiwara grew more powerful than the imperial clan, even as their servants retained possession of the land. Consequently, a curious form of decentralization began, wherein the emperor lost income but his allies, the Fujiwara, became wealthy. At the same time, by retaining possession of the land the samurai began to feel the Shoen really belonged to them.

To confound the political system further, the Fujiwara practiced a marriage strategy by which they arranged for their daughters to wed the sons of the imperial family. This strategy gradually made the emperor more Fujiwara than an imperial offspring. Thus, the Fujiwara became the power behind the imperial throne, which kept the court together as a clan alliance.

But as the tax-base decentralized, the Fujiwara clan itself grew to unmanageable proportions. Given the long association between the emperor and the Fujiwara, the size and complexity of both clans began to generate so many branch families that they competed with one another in the selection of the emperor. Court intrigues to control this selection process made politics in Kyoto increasingly unstable. Emperors retired from office before dying, so that the next branch family could have its turn at authority.

While the court focused on the politics of imperial selection, no one paid much attention to the samurai in the countryside. Clans of samurai developed on the various farms that dotted the rich rice-producing plains to the northeast and southwest of Kyoto. In the northeast on the Kanto plain, branches of a samurai clan called the Taira developed strong local ties to the soil and began to think of their possessions as a private realm. Southwest of the Taira clan, the Minamoto clan developed the same attachment to scattered holdings around Nara, Nagoya, and the interior region just south of Mount Fuji. This sense of ownership developed over the course of the 585 years that marked the Nara and Heian periods.

Each samurai clan also developed an intense internal loyalty that took precedence over obligations to the central government. The isolation of the court, its internal struggles, its refined culture, and its indifference to the rest of Japan made the imperial and Fujiwara clans strangers to their servants. The samurai, on the other hand, shared risks alongside their charges, fought for their clan, and expected, even welcomed, death in battle as the natural end to the life of a soldier.

Reinforced by Buddhism, the samurai came to accept death as part of karma. This expectation allowed them to detach their sense of self from their conduct as they went into battle. Naturally, this selflessness improved their military skills because an empty mind freed them from fear of death during a military engagement. Thus, these samurai became selfless fighting machines capable of extraordinary deeds.

This feature of samurai life, their mental state, reflected the emphasis these Japanese soldiers placed on Buddhism as a worldview, one that allowed them to refine a link between this religion and the conditions of combat that shaped their daily lives. Buddhism also served as a tool for action that the samurai slowly developed into their own personal, artistic, and intellectual vehicle. Samurai culture matured outside the imperial court and lasted nearly six hundred years.

Late in the Heian period, Fujiwara rivals at the court made the mistake of ordering their samurai to Kyoto to settle disputes over the imperial succession. Once the samurai arrived, they reacted in a way that completely surprised their overlords. The refinement of the court offended these rough, rural soldiers. As a result, when the samurai clan leaders discovered that they controlled the sword, they also realized that they commanded the political destiny of Japan.

This discovery set the Taira and Minamoto clans at war with one another, as representatives of two rival branches of the Fujiwara clan. The struggle that ensued took place between 1156 and 1185. Victory meant the extermination of the defeated clan. At first the Taira prevailed, but their leader, Taira Kiyomori, made two mistakes: one, he tried to preserve the court as the center of Japan's political life without consolidating his hold over Japan's political future; and two, he failed to kill off the Minamoto completely.

Two surviving sons of the Minamoto clan, Minamoto Yoritomo and Minamoto Yoshistune, were held captive until they grew up and escaped. Their combined skills, Yoshistune's military leadership and Yoritomo's political sense, saw their clan prevail in the second episode of this war. The Taira lost ground militarily by letting court politics take up too much of their time. At the same time, the Minamoto regrouped in the countryside and prepared to counterattack. The Minamoto wiped out the Taira clan in their final engagement at the Battle of Dannoura in 1185.

The Minamoto victory ended the Heian period and began Japan's adventure with feudalism. Now the center of power shifted from the Fujiwara clan to the samurai as the basis of political authority. Yoritomo moved the seat of government to Kamakura and occupied old Taira estates to create a new political system. He called this new military state the *Bakufu* (tent government, which represented a military encampment) in which he alone commanded life and death in Japan. Yoritomo was so concerned with concentrating power in his hands that his insecurity forced Yoshistune to rebel; Yoritomo then hunted Yoshistune down and had him executed. This removed Yoshistune as a potential rival and clarified authority.

Yoritomo maintained an official connection to the imperial court by taking the title of shogun, one that had been used in the past as a rank to name "the barbarian quelling supreme general" (*Seii-Tai-Shogun*) who conquered the remaining Japanese islands for the Heian court. As shogun, Yoritomo generated a pattern of power that built upon the Fujiwara's association with the imperial clan. In forming this "shadow government," Yoritomo kept the imperial and Fujiwara clans in place, maintaining the fiction that he governed as their servant even as he ruled them with an iron hand.

What Yoritomo created became the basis of Japanese politics for nearly the next seven hundred years, 1185–1868. Locating power in the hands of a military clan guaranteed the political division of Japan through lineages trained in war. Rivalry between these clans continued even after power clearly belonged to one samurai family. Thus, any sign of weakness from the shogun set rival clans into motion, resulting in the civil wars that punctuated this part of Japanese history.

These wars generated three distinct eras of Japanese feudalism: the Kamakura (1186–1333), the Ashkaga (1333–1573), and the Tokugawa (1603–1868). The end of the first two eras saw Japan descend into military chaos as high-stakes military rivalry brought clans to the brink of absolute power only to see them destroyed. This history of sudden death enhanced Buddhism as the religion of the soldier and sustained morale throughout these military periods.

The Mongols: The End of Nomadism

As mentioned above, the Mongols conquered China and created the Yuan Dynasty (1279–1368). They did so as part of a larger conquest pattern that marked the last great episode of nomadic raids originating on the Central Asian steppes. Yet this raiding pattern also represented something new; it saw the end of an era when herding cultures threatened sedentary societies through the use of cavalry. Consequently, the Mongols set in motion a series of changes they themselves could not control.

Successful nomadic life had created a need for commercial exchange with sedentary people as the growing numbers of humans living on the Central Asian steppe required a means to secure new food sources. As mentioned in Unit One, during the ancient era, between 800 BCE and 200 CE, the steppe had become so fully occupied with people that the competing tribes located there found themselves locked into increasing warfare over rights to pastures. Their respective herds could no longer provide enough calories to feed all the new people. Consequently, nomads had exchanged animal products for urban surpluses to supplement their food supplies and acquire needed manufactured goods. Trade eased population pressures, but it had also slowly drawn nomads into the web of civilization.

The great barbarian raids that had destroyed the ancient world upset these trade relationships and eased population pressures temporarily. The conquest of Rome, Han China, and Gupta India had drawn off surplus people from the steppe to open up pastures for the remaining nomads. The numerous German tribes, the Persians, the Kushan, and the vast Xiong-nu (Mongol) confederation had moved into sedentary areas to occupy well-established civilizations. The issue of population pressure on the steppe, however, was not quelled for long.

Trade again appeared first as Islam filled the space between sedentary cultures. The Muslims facilitated the exchanges between Eurasia's civilizations as sedentary cultures began to recover from the shock that marked the end of the ancient world. With this recovery, key Eurasian cultures once again began to flourish during the middle years of world history. At the same time, this trade drew nomads back into the commercial web of plant-based agricultural societies.

Exchanges of meat and hides for grain and urban products caused nomadic populations to grow ever more dependent on trade. Herders became too numerous to substitute raiding for peaceful exchanges because such attacks interrupted the trade that sustained a growing reliance on a commercial life. By protecting caravans rather than destroying them, or securing civilization rather than invading such cultures, nomads ensured the mercantile contacts that supported their increased human numbers. Hence, the nomads began to settle down. In the midst of this process, the Mongols served as the pastoral culture that set this transition to sedentary life in motion.

In most histories written by sedentary peoples who encountered the Mongols during their raiding phase, the brutality of the attackers generated an image of "savage" hordes. The ferocity of a Mongol invasion became legendary, and their reprisals for resistance left thousands impaled in their wake. Their destruction of such urban centers as Abbasid Baghdad revealed the tendency of the Mongols to perpetuate violence after achieving victory. Finally, their mass slaughter of defeated enemies made fear of their hordes sufficient reason for many would-be targets to surrender simply to avoid this fate. These reports come from Muslim, Christian, Buddhist, and Confucian scholars alike, as all kinds of people fell victim to the destructive energy of the Mongol hordes.

Yet the Mongols had a second character, one too often left out of the chronicles of world history. At the peak of their power, when the Mongols occupied Russia, Mesopotamia, Persia, Afghanistan, Turkestan, Mongolia, Siberia, China, Korea, and Southeast Asia, they realized that they had to effect peace in order to safeguard the survival of all the people in the enormous realm they commanded. Thus, these once hostile nomads introduced a level of tolerance into their *khanates* (local princedoms) that made their geographic space a safe region to cross for merchants seeking profits through intercultural exchange. The strategic location captured by the Mongols by 1290 covered all of Central Asia with the Golden Horde of Russia, the Djagatai Khanate of the central steppes, the Ilkhan Empire of Persia, and Kublai Khan's command of Yuan China and Siberia. Located in the center of Eurasia, the Mongols carved out a place for themselves between Europe, China, the Middle East, and Africa. Like the Muslims before them, the Mongols had thus become the intermediaries of trade during the final years between the ancient and the modern world.

Hence, this episode of Mongol history combines the last great nomadic raids with the commercial history that trapped pastoral people in a dependency on trade. The Mongols ended a very long era of violence that had visited civilization on the steppe from as early as 650 BCE. The Scythians had launched this history by raiding the Assyrian Empire so frequently as to lay the foundation for a rebellion that destroyed Assyria's capital of Nineveh in 612 BCE. These raids signaled the future relationships between Central Asia and sedentary cultures: periodic violence that covered 1,900 years of history between 650 BCE and 1350 CE, as well as long eras of peace punctuated with extensive commercial exchanges.

Genghis Khan

The last nomadic raiding phase belongs to the great Mongol warlord Genghis Khan. The people he led into war had begun as hunter-gatherers who took up herding to secure a more regular availability of food as the supply of wild game declined. As pastoral nomads, the Mongols had belonged to that group of people who historically had fought over the control of the grasslands needed to feed their herds. Their survival depended on the well being of their horses, sheep, and goats. They drove these herds from pasture to pasture in an area they occupied and protected through waging war. Their

staples included milk products and meat that they supplemented with the grains and vegetables they gained through trade with farmers.

The Mongols used hides and dairy products as their most valuable commodities to purchase the grains, vegetables, jewelry, weapons, and tools they might acquire from sedentary cultures. They dressed in sheepskins, used hides to make boots, and lived in felt tents made of sheered wool. War was a central event in their lives, as intense competition for remaining grasslands led to a steady diet of conflict. A struggle to secure pastures for their animals became the dominant feature of their lives. Yet success as a pastoral people meant their numbers grew steadily over the years until, like other nomadic tribes, they eventually filled the steppe.

In the Mongolian world mobility and violence defined survival. Children learned to ride horses as soon as they could walk. Mongol warriors rode day in and day out without dismounting, often eating and sleeping in the saddle. Horses served as the foundation of life and were the most valuable animals in the Mongol herds. Stealing horses from other groups became a refined art that ensured the future of a Mongol tribe. In addition, horse thievery deprived a rival people of their

Genghis Khan was responsible for uniting the fractionalized tribes of Mongolia in 1206 CE. As a result, Mongolia became a powerful military force creating the largest land empire in history, lasting almost 175 years until the mid-fourteenth century. Imperial Palace Museum, Beijing.

mobility and access to pastures. Hence, for the Mongols aggression defined success.

Organized into tribal confederations, Mongol kinship was critical to life. Complex extended families identified clans whose intermarriages kept the various tribal units linked into a loose alliance of people. External threats drew the Mongol confederation together to produce a horde that could destroy a rival who ventured into Mongol territory. Leadership of the tribal units came through the election of the most talented males.

The leaders exhibited cunning and the necessary skills to command large numbers of men in raids for horses and securing pastures. Courage in battle, strategic and tactical abilities, organizational skills, and charismatic leadership were the features needed for a good commander. A man with such abilities could keep his horde alive. The Mongols found a leader of these qualities in the person of Genghis Khan.

Genghis Khan (1167–1227) forged the Mongol Empire from a growing nomadic culture into a mobile warring army bent upon conquering neighboring peoples. Born in Mongolia as Temjuin in 1167, this son of a tribal chief, forced by the murder of his father to wander, returned to his tribe, avenged his father, and became a tribal chief. By the age of forty, his people had elected him their great khan (leader). Using his charisma as a war chief, Genghis Khan organized his people for conquest, not just the skirmishes needed to maintain tribal grasslands.

The Mongols became the most successful nomadic confederation to herd horses, sheep, and goats on the steppe. Years of herding and conquering increasingly more grassland made Mongol men skilled equestrians and archers. But the winter pasturage and the thousands of felt tents of his wandering people were not enough for Genghis Khan. His vision was broader, and he organized his people for expansion.

First, he organized the army by dividing it up into units of ten men that ultimately generated a horde of tens of thousands. Each unit of ten had a leader and was part of the greater army. All these mounted archers were trained since childhood in equestrian and military skills and an elaborate signal system for maneuvers and fire control. All would, at a flag's command advance, retreat, turn a flank, and fire in concentration upon an enemy position. These warriors wielded the compound bow, and their mounts were accustomed to long hours feeding on grass alone and did not spook in battle. In addition the cavalrymen trailed with additional mounts, which enabled them to carry their own supplies and weapons and conduct mobile warfare over vast distances.

Using these impeccably trained soldiers—men who knew no other life besides riding and fighting—Genghis Khan initiated a pattern of conquests that captured the core of Central Asia. He began in 1206 commanding a mobile force estimated at 500,000. He also had a reserve of 1 to 2 million more soldiers who voluntarily allied themselves with him. With these resources, he set out to conquer the world he knew.

First he defeated the Tangut kingdom of northwest China in 1207. He converted this region into a vassal state. Next he conquered north China itself, which had fallen to nomads named the Jin (mentioned above). While fighting the Jin, he learned how to capture large cities by employing the siege weapons perfected by the Chinese artisan-prisoners the Jin used. Towns that put up stubborn resistance, he slaughtered to a man, or sold the entire population into slavery save for the intellectuals and artisans he needed. Towns that surrendered without a fight, he merely taxed.

Having established a bridgehead into China, Khan sent his armies west to capture the Kara-Khirai Empire established by other Mongols earlier. He completed this task in 1219. Then he turned his attention on Mohammed Shah II's Turkish kingdom, called Khwarazm, in western Persia and Afghanistan. Within two years, Mohammed Shah's empire belonged to Genghis Khan as he came to command all the land between north China and Persia. In 1227, Genghis Khan returned to northwest China to destroy the Tangut, who had failed to show him sufficient respect, but in this engagement he suffered severe wounds.

With his wounds infected, Genghis Khan fell mortally ill, but before he died he divided his holdings among his sons. Ogedei, Genghis Khan's third son, was elected as the next Khan and chose a career of diplomacy over warfare. Ogedei's manipulation of Russia, Eastern Europe, the Middle East, and China paved the way for the next generation of Mongols to extend the empire Genghis Khan had created.

Genghis Khan's Grandsons and Trade

All of Europe, Asia, and the Middle East now became targets for Genghis Khan's grandsons. The task of conquering Russia fell to the Golden Horde led by Batu, whose gold-colored tents gave his army its name. The task of tackling the Abbasids (of Chapter Eleven) fell to Hulegu, a second grandson of Genghis Khan, who established the Ilkhan Empire, which extended into Persia. The task of taking China (as mentioned above) fell to Kublai Khan, still another of Genghis Khan's grandsons whose empire eventually included Siberia, China, Korea, Burma, and Vietnam. Kublai Khan even considered the conquest of Japan, but the two typhoons, (also mentioned above) and the Kamakura Bakufu defeated these efforts.

Occupying the middle geographic position, these Mongol empires now created the commercial connections needed for the exchanges of food, tools, and ideas that brought the world to the brink of the modern era. At this point the Mongols shifted their attention from combat to peaceful exchange. This new, supercharged commerce saw large numbers of nomads on the Central Asian steppe become so completely dependent on trade that they could no longer revert to raiding without bringing famine upon themselves. This fundamental shift in Mongol history created the second part of the paradox buried within their story; this was the moment at which these pastoral herders had to change their behavior permanently and become a sedentary people. At the same time, the wealth stimulated by this trade generated so much cultural energy in places like Europe as to revive them and lay a foundation for the modern age.

The influence of the Mongol Empire on the Muslim world and Europe transformed military tactics in both places by introducing gunpowder to the Russians, the Turks, the Persians, Muslim warrior-adventurers like Baber the Tiger, and Europeans as mentioned in Chapter Twelve. This new military resource stimulated innovation. Europeans, Turks, and Persians alike developed a new technology based on the cannon that motivated political expansion in all three regions. The power this weapon created then redefined the political geography of Eurasia.

Ironically, the diffusion of gunpowder across Eurasia also neutralized the military advantages once enjoyed by the Mongol hordes. Based on cavalry, these hordes now became vulnerable to concentrated cannon fire, for even highly skilled and armored horsemen had trouble taking a city bristling with entrenched cannon. Gunpowder, therefore, severely reduced the ability of nomads to conduct raids. But gunpowder was only one of the important products in a trade that grew out of the commercial features of Mongol dominance toward the end of the middle years of world history.

As a result of their role in long-distance trade, the Mongols had trapped themselves and their descendents in a process that forced them to settle down while Europe unwittingly prepared for its new role in world history. The market-oriented behavior that the Mongols sustained now produced such population growth among all nomadic peoples that they had to secure lines of communication between civilizations to ensure new food sources. This could only be accomplished if the Mongols maintained a steady flow of trade goods. Raiding and warfare would only retard this process.

Thus, the Mongols helped to link China to Eastern Europe along the Silk Road by aiding any adventurer interested in crossing Central Asia. Now, men such as Marco Polo also recovered the Silk Road that tied Asia, the Middle East, and Europe into a vast new trade network that the Mongols could tax. This trade network brought all of the great land bridge spanning the civilizations of Eurasia under one political umbrella for a brief period, fueling a process of profound change.

Survival for nomads after 1300 now called for peaceful exchanges. Only through organized, regular commercial relations could the nomads secure the amount of food they needed. Once food was secured, nomadic numbers continued to increase, which further tightened the trap that ended their raids. But the regular supply of food and goods that trade secured them more than compensated for what they had lost by abandoning the haphazard mechanism of pillaging that always had destroyed more than it produced. Ironically, the Mongols—perhaps the best nomadic raiders in world history—had inadvertently planted the seeds of the destruction of their own lifestyle which had brought them to dominance in the middle years of world history.

Suggested Reading

China

Chaffee, John W., *The Thorny Gates of Learning in Sung China* (Cambridge: Cambridge University Press, 1985).

Dardess, John W., *Conquerors and Confucians: Aspects of Political Change in Late Yuan China* (New York: Columbia University Press, 1973).

Davis, Richard L., *Court and Family in Sung China, 9609–1279: Bureaucratic Success and Kinship Fortunes for the Shih of Ming-chou* (Durham, N.C. 1986).

Endicott-West, Elizabeth, *Mongolian Rule in China: Local Administration in the Yuan Dynasty* (Boston: Council of East Asian Studies, Harvard University, 1989).

Gernet, Jacques, *A History of Chinese Civilization* Second Edition (Cambridge: Cambridge University Press, Reprinted 1999).

Hsiao, Ch'i-ch'ing, *The Military Establishment of the Yüan Dynasty* (Boston: Council of East Asian Studies, Harvard University, 1978).

McMullen, David, *State and Scholars in Tang China* (Cambridge: Cambridge University Press, 1988).

McKnight, Brian, E., *Village and Bureaucracy in Southern Song China* (Chicago: University of Chicago Press, 1971).

Reichauer, Edwin O., and John K. Fairbanks, *China: Tradition and Transformation,* Revised Edition (Boston: Houghton Mifflin Company, 1989).

Sinor, Denis, ed., *The Cambridge History of Inner Asia* (Cambridge: Cambridge University Press 1990).

Smith, Paul J., *Taxing Heaven's Storehouse: Horses, Bureaucrats, and the Destruction of the Sichuan Tea Industry, 1074–1224* (Boston: Council of East Asian Studies, Harvard University, 1991).

Twitchett, Denis C., *Financial Administration under the Tang Dynasty,* Second Edition (Cambridge: Cambridge University Press, 1970).

———— and Michael Loewe, eds., *The Cambridge History of China,* Volume Three, Sui and Tang China 589–906 (New York: Cambridge University Press, 1986).

Wechsler, Howard J., *Mirror to the Son of Heaven: Wei Cheng at the Court of Tang Tai-tsung* (New Haven, Conn.: Yale University Press, 1974).

Korea

Hang, W., *Ancient Korean and Japanese History* (Seoul: Kudara International, 1995).

Henthorn, G., *History of Korea* (Glencoe, Ill.: Free Press, 1971).

Lee, K. B., *A New History of Korea,* Trans. By E. Wagner (Cambridge: Harvard University Press, 1986).

Pai, H., *Constructing Korean Origins* (Cambridge, Mass.: Harvard University Press, 2000).

Takashi, Hatada, *A History of Korea* (Santa Barbara, Calif.: ABC-Clio Press, 1969).

Tenant, R., *A History of Korea* (New York: Columbia University Press, 1996).

Japan

Dunn, C. J., *Everyday Life in Traditional Japan* (London: Batsford, 1969).

Duus, Peter, *Feudalism in Japan,* Second Edition (New York: Alfred A. Knopf, 1972).

Eisenstadt, S. N., *Japanese Civilization: A Comparative View* (Chicago: University of Chicago Press, 1995).

Farris, William Wayne, *Heavenly Warriors: The Evolution of Japan's Military, 500–1300* (Cambridge, Mass.: The Council on East Asian Studies, Harvard University Press, 1995).

Hall, John Whitney, Keiji Nagahara, and Yamamura Kozo, eds.. *Japan Before Tokugawa: Political Consolidation and Economic Growth, 1500–1650* (Princeton, N.J.: Princeton University Press, 1981).

Hane, Mikiso, *Japan: A Historical Survey* (New York: Charles Scribner's Sons, 1972).

Hane, Mikiso, *Premodern Japan,* Second Edition (Boulder, Colo.: Westview Press, 1990).

Reischauer, Edwin O., *The Japanese* (Cambridge Mass.: The Belknap Press of Harvard University, 1981).

Sansom, G. B., *Japan: A Short Cultural History,* Revised Edition (New York: Appleton-Century-Crofts, Inc., 1962).

The Mongols

Adshead, S. A. M., *Central Asia in World History* (New York: Macmillan Press Ltd., 1993).

Allsen, Thomas T., *Mongol Imperialism: The Policies of the Grand Qan Möngke in China, Russia, and the Islamic lands, 1251–1259* (Berkeley: University of California Press, 1987).

Barfield, Thomas J., *The Perilous Frontier; Nomadic Empires and China* (Cambridge, Mass.: Blackwell Publishers, 1989).

Grousset, Réne, *The Empires of the Steppe: A History of Central Asia,* Trans. by Naomi Walford (New Brunswick, N.J.: Rutgers University Press, 1994).

Morgan, David, *The Mongols* (Oxford: Blackwell Publishers Ltd., 1986).

Prawdin, Michael, *The Mongol Empire: Its Rise and Legacy,* Second Edition, Trans. By E. and C. Paul (London: George Allen and Unmin Ltd., 1961).

Rossabi, Morris, *Khublai Khan: His Life and Times* (Berkeley: University of California Press, 1988).

Saunders, J. J., *The History of the Mongol Conquests* (Philadelphia: University of Pennsylvania Press, 2001).

XIV

EUROPE
in the Middle Ages

When the western part of the Roman Empire disintegrated under the pressures of nomadic invasion and internal decay, it set in motion the transition to a new era. Then, when most of the Byzantine world also fell to the Muslims, the geographic foundations of the ancient West ceased to exist. No longer would the Mediterranean serve as the middle sea of western history. Now the geographic center of western civilization shifted north to include lands that Rome either had ignored or only partially colonized. This space included the Germans: the collection of warring tribes that had invaded the Roman Empire, occupied many of its old provinces, and transformed its culture.

To the south, Muslims had captured about a third of the old empire. The Ancient Near East, North Africa, and much of the Iberian Peninsula would remain closed to the new German kingdoms and the Byzantine world for the next several centuries. Furthermore, the Muslim presence along the southern and eastern shores of the Mediterranean would pose a new military threat both to the emerging states of Europe and Constantinople, capital of the Eastern Roman Empire (the Byzantine world). Yet, during the High Middle Ages (1000–1300), these same Muslims would serve as a conduit for the recovery of commerce and ancient knowledge in medieval Europe as the Crusades temporarily opened access to the Holy Lands. Thus, warfare, trade, and the diffusion of ideas would permit extensive cultural exchanges between the Islamic and Catholic worlds.

But given the complexity of the new cultural setting in the Mediterranean, a complete recovery of the glory of the ancient past proved to be impossible for Western Civilization. While China managed to reassemble its old imperial structure, first under the Tang (618–906), and then under the Song Dynasty (960–1279), neither Europe nor the Byzantine Empire could reconstruct the old Roman world. The religious and political differences between these two Christian realms made such a union unworkable, and the constant threat posed by the Muslim presence in the south was an enduring distraction to both sides. Therefore, in Europe

the eclectic mix of a German, Catholic, and Greco-Roman heritage produced medieval culture, an extremely unstable, evolving, and volatile new social setting that drove Europe both toward the modern world and away from its Greek Orthodox neighbor to the east.

In the east, the survival of this part of the ancient Roman Empire led by Constantinople followed its own evolutionary path. Ironically, the Greek Orthodox theocracy that emerged in the Byzantine Empire evolved into something so different from its ancient roots that it would have looked entirely alien to an old Roman citizen. Also, as seen in Chapter Eleven, the presence of Islam in the south created a new cultural hearth called the Middle East, the permanence of which ensured the separation of the old Western world into its new constituent parts.

The Early Middle Ages, 500–1000

Beginning with Germanic Europe, medieval civilization generated a combination of institutions that survived into—and shaped—the modern era. Albeit unintentionally, these institutions produced a culture that replaced tradition with innovation. To trace the evolution of this profound transformation, which eventually gave birth to the modern era, one first must have an understanding of the failure of medieval political, religious, economic, and social institutions to integrate and then reintegrate sufficiently to work well together. Ironically, it was the dysfunctionality of these institutions that forced each one to change continuously, resulting in the foundations of modernization.

The key institutions in play in Europe in the Early Middle Ages were the Volk (the German tribe), the Catholic Church, kingship, lords and vassals, and private property. The way these institutions related to one another, their pattern of overlapping authority, and their rivalry for ultimate control marked the tensions that shaped medieval culture. During each era of the Middle Ages, one of these institutions came to dominate the rest, thereby creating the major episodes of this part of

Europe's story. During the Early Middle Ages (500–1000), the Volk defined the conditions of life in medieval Europe; during the High Middle Ages (1000–1300), it was the Catholic Church; and during the Late Middle Ages (1300–1450), it was kingship that became the most powerful of these institutions.

1

The Volk

In the Early Middle Ages, the Volk represented numerous German tribes; each became the dominant institution in its locale because it comprised all the practices one would expect to find in a state. Yet each German Volk did not function like a government per se. Rather, these German tribes were kinship systems that relied on customs instead of laws, the leadership of a chief instead of a king, and on warfare instead of diplomacy in their dealings with the outside world. As a kinship system, each Volk comprised individuals of unequal value whose roles derived from what they could contribute to the tribe's military prowess. Young men— because of their utility as potential soldiers—were deemed more important than women, but women were not dismissed, as it was recognized that without female fertility, the Volk had no future. Custom defined the way one person related to another. If a dispute arose, custom prescribed combat as the final means to resolve differences, but these violent solutions often disrupted the internal harmony of the tribe when personal vengeance led to a blood feud. The chief served as the military leader responsible for the luck (good fortune) of the Volk. Selected from among the strongest and bravest sons of a royal family, the chief got his job by election. The chief determined when his people would go to war, settled quarrels between members of the tribe in order to avoid blood feuds, and served as a high priest who spoke to the gods. War itself functioned as the normal state of affairs between the Volk and the outside world, for war determined whether the Volk could stay in one place or had to relocate.

Called *comitatus* by the Romans, the young men of the tribe made up the "war band" or companions of the chief. As a war band, these young men swore loyalty to their chief, followed his direction in battle, and remained at his side until he retreated. Agreed-upon social sanctions made the warriors prefer death to cowardice in combat, fueling their resolve. The same type of agreed practices also made each warrior equally responsible for the welfare of the Volk since their behavior decided the outcome of combat. Like the ancient tribes of Israel, or the Greek soldiers that made up the city-state, the survival of the Volk took priority over the life of any one member.

During the great migrations that destroyed the western half of the Roman Empire, the Volk's membership defined its own boundaries. Contact with strangers invariably meant conflict, so constant warfare was the norm for the tribe. Whether the Volk was on the move, or had settled down, military prowess became its central function. Meanwhile, once the Volk inhabited a new domain, its members took up agriculture, and the chief gave the best land to those with the greatest military skills, who then worked the soil and spent the rest of their time defending their new territory.

Slowly a system of stratification evolved within the internal makeup of the Volk. Warriors of the highest value continued to specialize in war, while their militarily less-talented neighbors became the labor base that worked the land. Full-time soldiers slowly began to inherit a special social distinction that set them apart from ordinary farmers. Royal families also emerged from among the chief's kin who offered up candidates for leadership in the next generation. At the same time, Catholic missionaries infiltrated the tribe and began to introduce classical ideas about property, the law, and inheritance that reinforced the new social strata. Slowly a crude form of state began to emerge that took the first long stride toward the birth of feudalism.

The Church, Community, the "King," and the Law   *2*

Community, the law, kingship, and the lords began to replace the older notions of the blood feud, custom, chiefdom, and an egalitarian companionship in war that governed human interaction. The Catholic Church served as the principal institution that taught the German Volk the idea of community, advancing this concept by defining the social bonds that existed between families. The church argued that these relations would allow members of the German tribes to settle their differences by discussion rather than violence. The church instructed that the community functioned as a medium to establish the borders between the Christian and pagan worlds; the community, communication, and communion all belonged to the same basic idea within the emerging society. In this social space, quarrels could be resolved efficiently; nevertheless beyond it, warfare should be expected. In time, the idea of community as the place for peaceful intercourse became an intellectual outpost on a frontier of chaos.

The Catholic Church itself became part of the Germanic Volk when heroic missionaries braved death in an effort to "save souls" by converting them to Catholicism. Before the conquest of Rome, Saint Martin of Tours (316–97), an ex-soldier turned bishop after he converted, traveled through Gaul and Britain baptizing those willing to receive the Word of God. In Ireland, Saint Patrick (385–461) converted the Celts, one tribe after another, until Pope Leo I welcomed the entire island into the fold. Following Saint Patrick's example, after the fall of Rome, Saint Columba (521–97) took the message of Christ to the Picts of Scotland, changing this land into a Christian domain. In England, Pope Gregory I sent a delegation of monks to the island under their abbot, Augustine of Canterbury (d. ca. 605), to save the realm; Augustine experienced rapid success because he converted the kings first who, in turn, converted their people. Both closer to Rome, and earlier than Scotland or England, the conversion of Clovis, king of the Franks, set up a fundamental relationship between the Catholic Church and kingship in 496 that not only explained the emerging history of the medieval community, but also gave shape to the origins of feudalism, first in Clovis's realm and then elsewhere.

The conversion of Clovis laid a foundation for community that spread as the Franks expanded to the east and south. Clovis began his career as a petty war chief living in Tourai, Belgium. Then he invaded Gaul where he won a decisive victory over the Gallo-Roman General Syagrius, and gained command over the Loire region (in France). His conversion to Catholicism then secured for him both the support of the pope and the French bishops, sharply enhancing his power. The wedding of an emerging Frankish State under Clovis and the Catholic Church provided the necessary foundation to produce the origins of a stable realm. From this point forward, Clovis became the defender of the church against pagan and heretical Christian Germans who rejected the Nicene Creed of 325. For example, the Visigoths who occupied southern France had learned of Christianity from those monks who had spread the Aryan heresy among the nomads before the beginning of the Germanic invasion. As mentioned, this heresy violated the Catholic tenet that Jesus and God were of the same substance, which was a religious principal established at the Council of Nicaea in 325. As a result, the pope felt that the Arian heresy threatened the existence of Catholicism; this made Clovis's military support against all such heretical tribes vital to the church's survival. Hence, the alliance between Clovis and the papacy allowed the king, the church, and the community to expand in step with one another.

After Clovis, the Merovingian Dynasty (Clovis' lineage) began a long and slow decline. In its place, however, the Carolingian family of nobles who served as the chief retainers to Clovis's heirs rose to dominance and maintained the alliance between the church and

state on Frankish lands as both gave shape to the growing community. The rise of the Carolingians accelerated the conversion of the German Volk to Roman Catholicism, as these nobles actively supported missionary efforts. Chief among the missionaries was Wynfrith, or Saint Boniface (680–754), who spread Christianity into Central Europe. Using the church as a preliminary step to invasion, each of the Carolingian nobles who rose to power in Frankland exploited the alliance between the church and the state by drawing more and more pagans into an expanding Catholic community. Since victory in war meant nothing unless an enduring peace followed, the expansion of Catholicism increased the chances that the concept of *community* would provide the needed stability. Therefore, the pacification of the pagans by conversion to Catholicism made the assimilation of Central Europe into an expanding Frankish realm a real possibility.

The increasing stability of this realm and the emerging sense of community created by the alliance between the church and state fostered the emergence of a system of rudimentary laws. Since neither the state nor the community represented clearly defined concepts in the German Volk's imagination as yet, neither existed as an actual legal entity. Accordingly, the victim of a crime was not the public; therefore, the prosecutor who faced the accused did not represent the tribe. Instead, he was the plaintiff himself. The crime therefore represented a dispute between two persons: the injured party and the perpetrator. To preserve the idea of peace within the tribe, a third party, the "king," had to intervene. The king (the Roman concept that the chief had bestowed upon himself) judged the crime by determining the value of the injury suffered by the victim. In order to avoid violence, the accused had to pay the victim in silver the value stated by the king. Called the *wergeld*, or "man-money," the amount paid represented the "price" of the crime as judged by the king. In this system, an injury to a man of fighting age would cost more than damage done to a woman during her fertile years: some 2,800 versus 2,400 *denarii* (small Roman silver coins). In addition, injury to persons of high status required a greater compensation in silver than the price paid for injury to the lowborn; these different values reflected the emerging concept of rank. Finally, during the Early Middle Ages, an injury to a person was still considered more damaging to the tribe than the destruction of property.

With the practice of law came the records it produced. These records reflected the importance placed on writing by the church as it encouraged the formation of community. Kings and their tribes felt comfortable with an oral tradition since that was all they had known; as a result, the church had to urge them to keep records. The church supported written accounts of legal decisions because it wanted to standardize judicial practices. Slowly, tribal customs grew into lists of judgments that set the value of an injury and standardized the wergeld. And with the refinement of these lists, the idea of the community slowly began to emerge as well.

By 800, or about halfway through the Early Middle Ages, the sense of community had grown to the point where the punishment prescribed by law included the abstract principle that crime injured an entity larger than the individual: this larger entity was the Volk, the tribe. The tribe, as the larger entity, came to rely on the *ordeal* and *oath-helpers* to settle disputes. While the ordeal applied only to common people, the oath-helper (a peer of the accused willing to swear to his innocence) assisted the king in cases where a valuable member of the Volk stood charged with a crime. In the case of commoners, the law assumed the accused to be guilty before the trial began. The trial itself would determine innocence. What the accused had to do was swear an oath of innocence before a priest to place his or her soul in jeopardy prior to the ordeal. Then, either the ordeal of cold water, hot water, or a hot iron determined the veracity of the oath. A trial by cold water saw the accused bound and cast into a pool of water; if the person sank, he or she was innocent, for the purity of water had embraced them; if the person floated, he or she was guilty. In the case of trial by hot water, stones were boiled in a caldron until judged sufficiently hot; the accused then had to pluck one of them from the caldron, carry it three steps, and lay it down; the accused then had three days in which to recover from the wounds to determine innocence. In the case of the hot iron, metal was heated until red-hot; the accused then had to pick it up, carry it three steps, and lay it down; once again, he or she had three days in which to heal. Obviously, in all three cases, since only a miracle would have saved the accused, God's intervention alone determined innocence and thereby proved the veracity of the oath before the priest.

Since men of rank were far more valuable than commoners, no such ordeal was required when one of them stood accused of a crime. Such men belonged to the emerging noble caste, whose refinement of military skills set them apart, they enjoyed a new social distinction as "gentlemen," whose honor among the band of brothers, called "the companions," placed them beyond the reach of the ordeal. They merely needed oath-helpers, men of equal rank willing to place their souls in jeopardy in order to swear to the innocence of their comrades. Since gentlemen came to be judged by one or more of their peers, the body of oath-helpers slowly gave birth to the concept of a jury. Many centuries would pass, however, before this idea would be applied to commoners as well.

As the law replaced the blood feud and created a new internal stability within the tribe, so the community slowly replaced the Volk as the social medium that defined how families should interact. The law matured with the development of the community, and it enhanced the role of the king, for he accepted new social responsibilities as defined by the church. Hence, the law represented the influence of kingship on the notion of a kingdom as both became part of the German world.

Carolingian Kingship

The ideas of kingship and kingdom took a long step forward with the rise of the Carolingians. Coming to power during the decline of the Merovingian Dynasty, the Carolingians began to rule the Frankish realm before they had actually acquired the title of "king." Heirs to the office of Mayor of the Household, the Carolingian nobles had access to the executive authority of the Frankish throne, while the Merovingians became known to history as the "do-nothing-kings." Using this power, one Carolingian Mayor after another took steps to consolidate his hold on royal authority, while systematically pushing aside the Merovingian monarchs. Starting with Pepin of Landen (d. 639?), who used his service to the king to secure his hold over Austrasia (the eastern half of Frankland), the Carolingians began the process of supplanting Merovingian rule as they passed the office of Mayor from father to son. Pepin of Héristal (d. 714) became the third Mayor who extended Carolingian control to Nuestria (the western half of Frankland).

Then, Pepin of Héristal's illegitimate son, Charles Martel (714–41) initiated a sequence of events that greatly expanded Carolingian power. First, he won the office of Mayor by exploiting his use of the warhorse, armor, and the hammer in battle to crush all opposition to his claims over his father's estates. Second, using this same military skill, Charles conquered the modern-day provinces of Burgundy, the Aquitaine, and Provence to enlarge Frankland. Third, Charles invaded eastward in a war against a pagan German tribe called the Saxons to quell this fierce threat to the expanding Catholic/Frankish community. Fourth, Charles always improved his hold over newly conquered territory by encouraging the conversion of all of the Germans under his authority to Catholicism. Accordingly, Charles supported St. Boniface's efforts to convert the tribes living east of the Rhine to make the assimilation of these future lands easier for the growing Carolingian realm. Fifth, in the midst of all this military activity, Charles turned to face a new threat invading from the south, the Muslims. At the Battle of Tours (732) he won a decisive victory that stopped the spread of Islam farther north than the Pyrenees Mountains of the Iberian Peninsula, using heavy cavalry as the new weapon of choice. The warhorse, armored horsemen, the lance, the mace, and the sword prevailed over Muslim warriors whose lines of communication from Damascus had finally become too long.

Like all Franks, Charles divided his estates between his sons, Pepin the Short (reigned 714–68) and Carloman. Both brothers chose to work together to select the last Merovingian king, Childeric as the nominal ruler of the Franks. Then, Pepin persuaded Carloman to retire to a monastery in 747. Next, Pepin turned to Pope Zacharias (reigned 741–52) to claim the Frankish throne for himself by engineering an agreement between the papacy and the Carolingians. Pepin was to use his army to invade the Italian Peninsula and remove the Lombards, an Aryan heretical tribe threatening Catholicism: in exchange for his military efforts, he would gain the crown. Named "King of the Franks" in 751 by the pope, Pepin the Short attacked the Lombards, captured northern Italy, and created the Papal Estates to keep his end of the bargain.

Following Pepin's death, his son, Charlemagne (reigned 768–814), began his career as king by sharing the throne with his brother Carloman, but Carloman's sudden death in 771 freed Charlemagne to rule on his own. Now sole master of Frankland, Charlemagne spent the rest of his life building what became known as the Holy Roman Empire.

A man of boundless energy, Charlemagne used war to construct a domain that united Western and Central Europe under one ruler. Although this realm did not survive beyond the lives of Charlemagne's grandsons, it did provide a strong enough sense of community to ensure the spread of the warhorse, armed warrior, and feudalism throughout Charlemagne's estates. Adding Bavaria, Venetia, and Lombardy, and securing the Papal States by 788, Charlemagne turned his attentions east and south. In the east he conquered Saxony in 804, and in the south he captured the Spanish March in 811. At the same time, he struck an alliance with all the Slavic tribes on his eastern frontier to close this avenue of invasion from Central Asia during his lifetime.

Building a state that comprised numerous tribes and seminomadic peoples, Charlemagne used each of his major towns to house a bishop in order to secure local stability in an era of constant violence. Thus, wherever he went, Charlemagne expanded the role of

Generally considered the first Holy Roman Emperor, Charlemagne (Charles I or Charles the Great) consolidated a large portion of Europe under his rule, promoted learning, and instituted innovative administrative concepts. "Karl de grosse" by Albrecht Dürer.

the church in an effort to unify his massive new realm. Believing that a strong alliance between church and state was essential, Charlemagne used Catholicism's practices of record keeping, acting on precedent, and resolving disputes by discussion as a means to weld together all his estates. The reward for these efforts won him the support of Pope Leo III (reigned 795–816); as a result, Leo III crowned Charlemagne "Emperor of the Romans" on Christmas Day in the year 800.

While Charlemagne built his enormous kingdom, political power within his realm rested on the Frankish nobility. As an emerging aristocratic caste of warrior-Christians, this Gallo-Frankish elite filled the countryside with fortified villas. Based on the Roman concept of *villa* and *coloni*, where villa stood for a fortress-estate, and coloni represented a population of peasant-serfs who worked the soil, each feudal holding provided the food surpluses needed to free soldiers to refine their martial skills. Commanding local units in a larger army comprised of heavy cavalry, these noblemen supplied the mosaic of regional forces that made up the expanding feudal order. Each aristocrat displayed his family colors to represent his claim to local authority, and reinforced his rank by bonds of marriage with a daughter from another noble family of equal status. Rewarded with lands won during the years of military expansion, this Gallo-Frankish aristocracy remained loyal to the Carolingians so long as they added new territory to their realm. Although this loyalty began to wane after the death of Charlemagne, the concept of a feudal estate was in place, as was the idea of a local community based upon this feudal holding.

After Charlemagne's reign, the Carolingian Dynasty began to disintegrate. The son of Charlemagne, Louis the Pious (reigned 814–40), inherited the throne but failed to expand the Holy Roman Empire. Well-educated, and deeply religious, Louis was not a soldier like his father, grandfather, and great grandfather, and he did not take an active part in warfare, which soon lost him the respect of his great nobles. Lacking the energy of Charlemagne and failing to add new lands to reward his subordinates, Louis simply could not hold the Holy Roman Empire together.

Since the Carolingian Empire lacked an internal administration and was filled with tribes whose command over regional loyalties outweighed the authority of a central government, warrior-aristocrats now had a much better chance of creating a stable local community than a weak ruler trying to command the realm from the center. Thus, the nobility and the church, rather then his immediate heirs, became the principal beneficiaries of Charlemagne's successful reign. As a result, Louis the Pious did not pass a durable kingdom on to his three sons: Lothair, Louis the German, and Charles the Bald.

When he died in 840, Louis had already faced the fact that his three sons could not tolerate one another, since all three had entered into a war of accession. This, however, was a war that no one could win. As a result, Lothair, Charles, and Louis eventually struck an agreement between themselves. At the Treaty of Verdun in 843, the western portion of Charlemagne's Empire, now called West Francia, passed to Charles the Bald, and the eastern portion, East Francia, went to Louis the German, while a geographic jumble of estates in the center fell to Lothair. Lothair's realm did not survive beyond his grandson, Louis II (reigned 855–75). Charles the Bald and Louis the German agreed to divide Louis II's estates among themselves at the Treaty of Meersen in 870, while Louis stopped a second attempted Muslim invasion of Europe through Sicily. Between them, Charles the Bald and Louis the German then created what eventually became France and Germany. Meanwhile, separated to the south, Italy's story would from this point forward belong to Central European history, and a revived Holy Roman Empire under Otto I (reigned 962–73).

The Byzantine Empire: The Eastern Half of the Empire that Survived the Fall of Rome

As mentioned in Chapter Ten, the Diocletian Reforms (284–305) had divided the Roman Empire into two halves, a step taken in response to the increasing nomadic pressures along the eastern and the western frontiers. Since the Germans were infiltrating the west (see Chapter Ten), and the Parthian Empire (see Chapter Twelve) caused no end of troubles in the east, the Ro-

man Empire had split to meet both threats. Thus, even though Emperor Constantine had briefly reunited the empire during his reign (306–37), the division made by Diocletian became a permanent feature of late Roman politics. Furthermore, once wave after wave of nomads followed on the heels of the invading Visigoths (374) and the west collapsed; the east began to develop its own unique culture. Hence, no amount of effort would be able to reassemble the old Roman Empire after the year 455.

In fact, the last of these efforts, the one made by Emperor Justinian (reign 527–65), destroyed much of what was left of both the eastern and western halves. Justinian fought these wars to dislodge the Ostrogoths, and he temporarily captured Italy and North Africa, but at a horrible cost. Not only did this military venture drain the Byzantine treasury, destroy the Italian and North African economy, and kill countless numbers of people, it also laid the foundation for a major epidemic. Reported by Procopius, the most celebrated historian of the Byzantine world, an invasion of black rats from India followed the trade routes up the Red Sea into the Mediterranean and hit the Eastern Roman Empire at its moment of greatest exhaustion. These rats carried fleas, and the fleas harbored an internal parasite that was to have a devastating impact on human history.

Appearing in the Mediterranean world in 542, the black rat transferred its fleas to human hosts, thereby launching what became known as the Bubonic Plague. Traveling by ship, these rats usually followed the food source from culture to culture whenever famine hit. Since prolonged warfare destroys the human organization needed to produce food, and the official fall of the Gupta Empire started an era of protracted political chaos on the Indian subcontinent after 535 (see Chapter Twelve), the appearance of the black rat in the Eastern Roman Empire is not surprising. In addition, since rats normally do not venture far from their nests unless they are desperate to find food, major migrations of these rodents have not been recorded except during periods of agricultural crisis. Such a crisis set in motion a devastating epidemic that maintained a steady appearance of the Plague in the Mediterranean world for the next two hundred years (542–750). Hence, after Justinian's reign, the Byzantine Empire was in no shape to reassemble the old Roman world.

Meanwhile, the strong military system that had successfully protected the Eastern Roman Empire from the same nomadic invasions that had destroyed the west was refined by the Byzantine rulers. While the west had to rely on the kinship patterns of the German Volk, the Byzantine Empire had maintained the administration needed to assemble and deploy a highly mobile army. At the heart of this administration lay Constantinople, not only the capital of the Eastern Roman Empire, but the staging ground for mobilizing resistance to constant threats of invasion. Constantinople was able to withstand the countless attempts made to capture it during the Middle Ages because no foreign power could mount a simultaneous land and sea attack on it. As a result, Constantinople fell only twice: once when betrayed by its Christian allies in the Fourth Crusade (1202–04) and a second time to Turkish cannon fire in 1453. Thus, between 400 and 1453, Constantinople remained the nerve center of a successful administration that held at bay both the nomads and Muslims.

The second and third factors that underlay the military success of the Eastern Roman Empire included a combination of heavy cavalry and Greek fire. Heavy cavalry, developed out of the Parthian solution described in Chapter Twelve, emerged in both feudal Europe and the Eastern Roman Empire and was used to stop constant nomadic raids. In the case of the Eastern Roman Empire, mounted archers, using specially bred warhorses fed on alfalfa, lived in the households of great nobles stationed throughout the realm. Ready to ride at a moment's notice, the Byzantine warriors successfully defended the empire until the Muslims attacked. Once Islam launched its assault, however, only the use of "Greek fire" could save the Eastern Roman Empire from destruction.

Like napalm, Greek fire—believed to be a secret mixture of sulphur, quicklime, and liquid petroleum—stuck to whatever it hit and burned furiously. Used by Byzantine forces primarily as a naval weapon, Greek fire proved to be a significant threat in the Eastern Roman Empire's military arsenal. Greek fire was carried on ships, ignited when mixed with water, and pumped out of a bronze syringe called a *siphonarios*, Its use ensured the security of the trade routes whenever the Muslims attacked by land. The use of Greek fire also protected the Mediterranean sea-lanes, safeguarding them as a way to supply food during times of siege. The combination of using heavy cavalry on land and Greek fire on the seas provided sufficient military prowess to secure the Balkans and Asia Minor—the only portions of the Eastern Roman Empire that survived the German invasions and initial Muslim attack after 634.

Beyond these new military technologies, however, the Byzantine Empire's primary contribution to the middle years of world history was its preservation of the ancient Greco-Roman culture. This intellectual treasure fueled the Arab and European imagination from 634 to 1453. Found in Roman law, especially in the Justinian Code, and in the maintenance of the Greek language and philosophy, the Byzantine Empire supplied a wealth of ancient achievements to both Muslims and Catholics alike. Yet, only after a sufficient recovery of the idea of community had occurred in the west, could the emerging German states begin to exploit the subtlety and wealth of this classical treasury. Hence, each time new material filtered into Europe from the Middle East after the year 1000, a *renaissance* (a rebirth of ancient Greco-Roman knowledge) would also begin.

Meanwhile, during the Early Middle Ages (500–1000), the western and eastern halves of the old Roman worlds drifted apart. With the loss of the west to the Germans, the capacity to administer the community broke down; with the loss of this administration came the collapse of the state, which began an era some still call the Dark Ages. Only the slow reconstruction of society over the next five hundred years restored any semblance of order in Europe. In contrast, the Byzantine Empire in the east maintained a continuity of order. While the west foundered, the east preserved Roman institutions, the law, science, and philosophy. Consequently, the Byzantine Empire did not experience the severe loss of literacy, bureaucracy, and urban culture as did the west. Accordingly, with the Eastern Roman emperor, the senate, and a legal structure all well in place, the Byzantine world maintained a rich civilization, a durable military, and a real government.

And while the church and state had combined to produce a theocracy in the east, in the west they remained separate institutions, even though they had formed an alliance. As a result, while the pope would challenge the Holy Roman emperor politically, such practices could not occur in the east. Instead, the Greek Orthodox Church functioned as an arm of the state with which the emperor could meddle whenever it proved necessary. Thus, while the Roman Catholic Church steadily grew independent of the kings of Europe, especially after the Early Middle Ages, the opposite occurred in the east.

In the Byzantine world, the emperor's jurisdiction over the church was a political fact, and he looked upon Christianity as a branch of the state to be protected, nurtured, and used. The emperor nominated the Patriarch of Constantinople as the highest church official and interfered in church policy as he saw fit. As a key element to ensure the loyalty and obedience of the people, the emperor sustained the church as an essential feature of political authority. In fact, the vigilant attention showered on the church by the emperor to secure it against alien as well as heretical influences created issues of intolerance that eventually made the

Byzantine Empire vulnerable to the infiltration of Islam. Because of a split in the Greek Orthodox Church over the nature of Jesus—whether he was a man and the son of God or simply had one divine will—the Byzantine emperor persecuted many of his subjects. Since the emperor claimed that Jesus had two natures, human and divine, he alienated many of his people living in Syria and Egypt. They believed Jesus was one pure divine being and suffered for their belief in this "heresy." Accordingly, both provinces fell easily to Muslim expansion when the Christians there preferred a less-stringent foreign rule to the strict theocracy emanating from Constantinople.

Meanwhile, differences in the way the Latin and Greek churches viewed the world created an even greater barrier between the Eastern Roman Empire and Medieval Europe. Seeing ancient Rome as a finite, corporeal, and corrupt urban center condemned by St. Augustine in his *City of God*, explained why an all-powerful and loving Deity would send barbarians to destroy civilization, so the Western clergy lived apart from their ancient past. They accepted the fall of Rome as a necessary step in the Divine Plan leading to the creation of the Holy Church. They therefore felt a sharp emotional and spiritual separation from the old Roman world, one that allowed them to build a new community in an alliance with the Germans. Thus, such deliberate religious, social, and political actions gave the heads of the Roman Catholic Church a sense of the future that resulted in cultural optimism.

In contrast, the Eastern Roman Empire viewed the fall of Rome as a tragedy: a loss of an ancient past that God had constructed in the interest of protecting His faithful. Consequently, the Eastern Church decried the fall of Rome as the beginning of a communal retreat that the Byzantine Empire seemed unable to stop. Hence, Greek Christians living in the East suffered from a sense of embattlement that resulted in cultural pessimism.

Also, in the east a holy man belonged to the general community as a hero of daily life. He might come from any level of society to manifest the true faith as part of a rich brotherhood of Christians. He lived and died to preserve the purity of doctrine. He represented the ideal of someone who had abandoned the flesh in the service of his Savior, as he was both a monk and a priest simultaneously. Finally, "saints" came from among those who had wandered into the desert as hermits only to return to society after having been cleansed by isolation.

In contrast, in the west, the holy men of Christianity grew out of a small core of surviving priests and monks who had helped to weld the Germans into a community even while surrounded by the illiterate Volk.

Kept apart from the tribe, in a separate and special enclave where they practiced celibacy, these priests and monks evolved into a unique group of individuals with the competence to bestow the gift of salvation on the unwashed. Since they were selected primarily from the socially prominent, a person who became a churchman lived with the nobility, held real power apart from the king, and was not to be trifled with by even the greatest figures in the realm. As a churchman, if he should lead an exemplary life filled with miracles due to his service to the community, he achieved sainthood, and his body became a holy relic whose power lived beyond his death. Finally, a churchman committed his life to one of two distinct callings: either he served humanity as a priest in the secular clergy (those churchmen who lived with the laity), or he became a member of the regular clergy (those churchmen who retreated from the world and followed a common set of "rules or regulations" as dictated by their order). Consequently, while the Western churchman served an institution that existed "apart" from the laity, the eastern churchman remained very much a part of the community.

Finally, the fragmentation of the Mediterranean world because of Islam's expansion thoroughly divided the east from the west. Having lost most of its wealthiest provinces to the Muslims after 634, the Eastern Roman Empire suffered from a severe sense of isolation that only grew worse. At the same time, military necessity forced the pope to seek out allies among the Germans, while the Muslim threat to the Eastern Roman emperor precluded his ability to come to the defense of theWest. Furthermore, constant military pressure from the Muslims worsened with the arrival of the Turks during the reign of Caliph al-Mutasim (833–42) and increased the sense of separation that divided the two parts of the European world. As a result, by 1000, the east and west had drifted so far apart that a critical break eventually occurred during the High Middle Ages.

Europe and the High Middle Ages, 1000–1300

The transition from the Early (500–1000) to the High Middle Ages (1000–1300) saw feudalism replace empire as the Carolingian Dynasty waned in power. As a system of local defense, feudalism made sense due to the chaos caused by the wars between the heirs of Louis the Pious and the sudden appearance of the Vikings and Magyars. Originating in Scandanavia and the Ural and Northern Caucasus Mountains respectively, the Vikings and the Magyars represented the last wave of barbarians to attack Europe. Because of their threatening presence, they ensured the success of feudalism since only the local lord seemed to be able to offer the commoners any real protection. Thus, the various Volk living within a kingdom preferred to invest their loyalty in a count or a duke rather than in an ineffectual king in a distant center.

Feudalism

Imposed on medieval Europe by nineteenth-century historians, the term *feudalism* defined a type of government that linked landed estates to the legal concepts of "state" and "status." Derived from the medieval terms, *feodum, fief,* and *fee,* feudalism defined the "rights of possession" granted by a king to his nobility in exchange for military service. Creating the system of lords and vassals, feudalism helped to organize the interior of a kingdom by developing the concept of "Real Estate." Since "Real" referred to "actual" or "legitimate," and "Estate" defined "state and status," land became the sole form of property with a legal identity during the Early Middle Ages. Hence, feudalism created a new set of institutional distinctions besides that of kingship, the church, and community and thereby generated an intermediate state and status between the king and his Volk. At the same time, feudalism divided the kingdom three ways. First, the king's right to bestow landed estates on his lords as his chief vassals derived from his "allodial title" to the realm granted to him by God (i.e., the king "owned" the realm as a product of conquest, election, or inheritance). Second, a lord, as a vassal of the king held "rights of possession," which he could then subdivide among his own retainers in order to recruit a needed supply of local soldiers. And third, "Real Estate" distinguished wealth produced on the land as "legitimate," in contrast to the "incorporeal property" that described the riches generated by a city or trade. "Incorporeal property" was a legal phrase that identified the illegitimacy of money and goods in contrast to the legitimate state and status bestowed upon a nobleman by his Real Estate.

Feudalism survived the fall of the Carolingian Dynasty and served as the communal bridge that led to the formation of France and a revived Holy Roman Empire. Feudalism also explains the function of the government of Medieval Europe at two different levels. At the local level, an effective government, or state, belonged to the lord; he possessed the land, the status, and the authority to impose the rule of law on his fief. At the central level, great lords who served as royal officials on their estates provided the link between the king and his realm. Hence, at the central level, decentralization marked feudalism before it even began. A duke who was the master of a "duchy," or a count who was the master of a "county," was not only an agent of

the king, but also a ruler in his own right. Each therefore embodied an internal tension: on the one hand, they wanted to participate in royal decisions; on the other, they had to fight the urge to separate their estates from the kingdom.

At the same time, each nobleman oversaw his estates with an iron hand thanks to the refinement of heavy cavalry during the Early Middle Ages. Indeed, the powerful men of estate who comprised the nobility had evolved out of the Carolingian bodyguard. Chief retainers in the Frankish army, these soldiers fought from horseback in a manner that proved irresistible from 700 to 1300. The tools that made these men so powerful derived from a combination of innovations imported from both Asia and Persia. The stirrup—a device to secure the seat of a rider and bolster the unity of purpose between a man and his horse—had developed in China before making its way into Central Asia, and from there into Europe. The idea of breeding a warhorse, and feeding it a special fodder, had developed in the Parthian Empire (see Chapter Twelve), and traveled from Persia into the Eastern Roman Empire, and from there into Europe. These special horses bred for war grew to such a size that they were capable of supporting an armored warrior. Thus, the link between a heavily armored soldier, seated on a warhorse, and using a saddle reinforced with stirrups convinced Charles Martel that a new military age had dawned. From Charles Martel's reign through that of Charlemagne, each new province added to the Carolingian Empire saw the spread of the estate-system that supported both these warriors and their warhorses. In time, the warhorse, armor, and the professional soldier—all sustained by large-landed estates—became the backbone of the new political and social structure called feudalism.

Linked by bonds of *fealty* (faithfulness), the soldiers of the king found themselves stationed throughout the realm. Sworn to support the monarch as payment for a grant by him of land, every nobleman served as a knight ready for war within his own district, or at the beck and call of the king. Reinforced by the sanctity of the Catholic Church, each knight took an oath that indentured his soul to God as security against all faithless claims of service when estates were handed out. Bound by honor, and their soul, each knight served as a *vassal* (an Old German word for "child") within a surrogate family designed to replace the Volk with a new militaristic community. Linked to the church in a manner similar to a "Father" and his parish, or an *Abbot* (Aramaic for "father") and his monks, the king became the parent of his realm who possessed all the bonds of loyalty within his domain.

As the system spread, however, the oath of fealty became confused. *Infeudation*, which linked the king to his vassals, was clear and simple. But *subinfeudation*, which occurred when a great noble like a duke or a count gave out estates to his own retainers to secure the regional forces the king failed to provide him, created cross-currents of loyalty that confused feudalism. Dukes commanded duchies, or provinces, that made up a vast numbers of estates within a king's realm. As mentioned, counts held counties with fewer estates than a duke, but their holdings still comprised enough land to make subinfeudation necessary. Each case of subinfeudation saw a knight swear loyalty to an intermediate lord instead of the king. The king was the *liege lord*, or first among equals, but if a monarch failed to win the respect of his nobility, then decentralization became a reality, with the great lords breaking away from their obligations to the crown. Hence, embedded within feudalism was a tendency to splinter the kingdom.

Western versus Central Europe

To further compound the confusion of loyalty generated by oaths of fealty, the feudal system varied from Western to Central Europe. In Western Europe, a conquered Gaulic people joined with a German Volk to generate clear lines of subordination within a master-servant contract. The Franks, who had captured the Roman Province of Gaul, had also acquired a Latin-speaking peasant population loyal to the Catholic Church. To rule their new domain, the Frankish kings had learned to accept Catholicism and build new military estates based on the Roman concept of patrimony (an estate inherited from one's father). Under patrimony, the Franks allowed the transfer of land from a father to his sons, so that an estate could stay within one family. Hence, the kingdom passed from a king to his sons, just as a duchy or a county remained within the same family. Yet with each passing generation a new oath of fealty was required to reaffirm the bonds of loyalty between a lord and his vassals. And at the same time that the legitimate heirs inherited their estates, they also acquired all the peasants needed to work the soil. Called *serfs*, these Gaulic peasants supplied the labor required to release the German noblemen from agriculture so that they could perfect the military skills they needed to discharge their martial duties to the king. Feudalism described the bond between a lord and his vassal; "manorialism," a variant of feudalism, described the contracts of service between a knight and his serfs.

Central Europe, however, did not have a conquered Gaulic population to exploit. Instead, the Volk who occupied estates in Germany lived in a frontier zone exposed to fresh nomadic invasions coming from the east.

Thus, the manorial system common to Western Europe, which placed one knight on one estate, did not work in Central Europe, for it failed to provide a sufficient concentration of soldiers to mount an effective defense against new barbarian invasions. Therefore in Germany a system of feudalism clustered knights together in large duchies so that powerful dukes could house independent armies on their *demesnes* (domains). In addition, since the Germanys comprised only the Volk, rather than a conquered serf population, patrimony did not take root as easily there. As a result, kingship was not inherited; instead, the monarch had to be elected by his "companions," (i.e., his great lords). Hence, these powerful dukes became the primary levers of power in Germany, which eventually divided into several German states as each duke had retained his own army of knights living in his household and gradually became the most powerful lord.

Given the different styles of feudalism in Western and Central Europe, kingship in both places developed along distinct lines. To understand these differences, one has to link the history of specific monarchies with that of the Catholic Church. Since both the king and the pope sought to define the concept of community according to their own ends, the one who held sway in a particular realm determined the way the idea of society took hold. Since Western Europe used the principle of patrimony to generate a tradition of inheritance that transferred estates from a father to his sons, Gaulic kings had a distinct advantage compared to Germanic rulers in their dealings with the pope. In Germany, the tradition of electing the ruler eventually allowed the pope to win his struggle for supremacy with the ruler of the new Holy Roman Empire after 962. In the first place, each election compelled the new Holy Roman emperor to appease the demands of his great lords, which created a trend of decentralization in his realm that he could not stop. Second, the pope soon discovered that he could occasionally excommunicate an emperor and draw upon immediate military support from those ambitious dukes who wanted to break the power of their feudal overlord in order to win independence. Thus, in Central Europe, kingship faced far more problems than it did in Western Europe.

In the meantime, the role of conquest in the development of the kingdoms of England, Spain, and Portugal reinforced the institution of kingship in Western Europe. And these new realms built during the High Middle Ages all imported the legal principle of patrimony from France. As realms won by direct conquest, each of these new kingdoms created a fresh balance of power between the pope and the local monarch that tended to favor the monarchy. All three, therefore, joined with France to create a story of centralization in Western Europe that stood in sharp contrast to the history of Germany, and eventually Italy, in Central Europe.

Politics of the High Middle Ages

The alliance between the Carolingian monarchy and the church defined the emergence of community during the Early Middle Ages (500–1000). But the dysfunctional nature of medieval cultural gradually pitted the authority of the pope and the king against one another as both tried to define their control over society. Each sought ultimate power as the best expression of how their offices should function within local politics. Accordingly, the king grasped at the ability to appoint his candidates to religious posts within his realm while the pope tried to win independence for the church from royal control. Thus, this struggle encouraged both to pronounce their view of how the medieval community should be run.

Developing Petrine Theory, as first articulated by Pope Leo I (reigned 440–61), the popes of the Early Middle Ages claimed that (St.) Peter was the heir of Jesus as the chief Apostle of Christ. Although they fully realized that they could not enforce this idea, each successive pope repeated Petrine Theory by arguing that Jesus had wanted His Church to follow the decisions of Peter's heirs. Claiming to be Peter's heirs through Apostolic succession, the popes argued that since each Bishop of Rome was a celibate, all who took this office had inherited the authority of Christ according to the Biblical passage Matthew 16:18: "Here is Peter [i.e., *Petros*, or stone, in koine Greek], and on this *rock* I will build my Church." Interpreting Peter, Petros, and rock to be the same thing, the popes who followed Leo I's reasoning claimed that the Bishop of Rome was the cornerstone of Christ's church. In other words, the papacy was the "rock" Christ had meant when He identified those who would take charge of constructing Christendom.

Supporting Leo I's claims were the remarks made by Pope Gelasius I (reigned 492–96) in his dispute with the Eastern Roman emperor, Anastasius I (reigned 491–518). Since the Eastern Roman emperor had the power to appoint the patriarchs, Anastasius I was quite surprised when Gelasius I objected to royal interference in local church affairs. Gelasius I insisted that the bishops, and not civil authorities, were responsible for administering the church. He maintained that only two institutions governed the world: the sacred offices of the church and the royal authority of monarchs. Because prelates had to answer to God for the conduct of all of Christendom, their duties took precedence over

those of kings. Hence, Anastasius should not interfere in the appointment of churchmen. This dispute with the Eastern Roman emperor drove a wedge between the Byzantine world and the papacy that simply grew worse with time.

One reason this wedge grew ever wider was the fact that the Muslims had confined the Byzantine Empire to the Balkans and Asia Minor. As mentioned above, unable to help the pope in his struggle to survive against fresh pagan and heretical German invasions, the military impotence of the Byzantine emperor forced the papacy to turn to the Franks for protection. Allied to the most successful monarchy of the Early Middle Ages, the papacy grew in power as the Carolingians spread Catholicism across the continent. Yet, with the breakup of the Carolingian monarchy after 843, the role of the church, as well as that of the papacy, began to change again. This time, the division of Charlemagne's realm into Western and Central European kingdoms coincided with the third and final invasion of nomadic tribes and caused the pope to seek new royal friends to ensure his continued existence. These new kings gave shape to France, the Holy Roman Empire, the Duchy of Normandy, and England and finally stopped the nomadic threat. Since the Duchy of Normandy was part of the kingdom of France, and spawned the ruling house of England; the role this province played in the politics of Europe is a good place to start the account of how the dysfunctional nature of medieval culture transformed the Early into the High Middle Ages (1000–1300).

Civil war and Viking raids during the two hundred years following Charlemagne's death (814) had left West Francia a divided and chaotic realm. Provinces and counties had broken away from a weak central authority to begin an era commanded by great lords. One such lord was a Viking chief named Rollo who had occupied Normandy in 911. This Viking warlord proved to be so powerful militarily that the king of West Francia, Charles the Simple (879–929), could not dislodge him. As a result, Charles decided to make Rollo the Duke of Normandy in exchange for his willingness to stop any further raids along France's northern coast. Keeping his promise to Charles, Duke Rollo protected France from Viking assaults and reigned as duke from 911 to 927.

Meanwhile, following the death of the last Carolingian monarch in 987, the French nobility decided to meet and select a new king. They settled on Hugh Capet, whose extraordinarily long-lived and fertile line of heirs managed to hold France together for the next 341 years (987–1328). Building on the continuity offered by this line of legitimate heirs, the Capet Dynasty deliberately selected and installed the next king while his predecessor still occupied the throne. In this manner, the Capets slowly built a precedent for inheritance that ultimately replaced Hugh's original election to office by his chief nobles. Although weaker than the Dukes of Normandy, the Capets held onto the office of kingship long enough to establish the dignity of their monarchy beyond the power of their great lords. Through this slow but patient process, and in close alliance with the church, the Capets created the kingdom of France.

At the same time, Duke Rollo's heirs welded Normandy into one of the most powerful domains in Europe. As Rollo's direct descendent, and the son of Robert the Magnificent (reigned 1027–37), William the Conqueror (reigned 1035–87) inherited the Duchy of Normandy despite his illegitimate birth. Given his father's skill in raising him as an heir, and his own iron will to take control of his domain, William, originally known as "the Bastard," took command of his duchy. Then he forged his domain into a realm capable of winning a kingdom. As a result, William not only crossed the channel to conquer England in 1066, but he also gained the right to change his name from William "the Bastard" to "the Conqueror."

Between 1014 and 1042, England had belonged to a Scandinavian realm built out of Viking conquests. Stretching from Norway to Denmark to Normandy, Iceland, Greenland, and briefly Vinland (the coast of Canada), this Scandinavian patchwork of lands connected a Viking Volk who shared bloodlines with Canute, the King of Denmark and England. When Canute became king of Norway as well in 1030, he made England the center of his realm. Canute tried to integrate the diverse elements of his complex realm by encouraging assimilation between all his peoples. This assimilation policy produced Edward the Confessor (1042–66), King of England and son of an Anglo-Saxon father and a Norman mother.

Dying without an heir in 1066, Edward the Confessor spawned three claimants to his throne: Duke William of Normandy, Harold, the Earl of Wessex, and Harold III, the King of Norway. The most powerful man in England, Harold of Wessex gained the throne upon the death of Edward despite a promise he had made to William of Normandy to forego such a claim to royal office. Breaking his promise to William on the grounds that he had issued it under duress while held prisoner after having been shipwrecked off the French coast, Harold of Wessex immediately prepared to defend his throne. Harold III invaded from the north, and Harold of Wessex marched to meet the invader, defeating him at Stamford Bridge. Having killed Harold III in battle, Harold of Wessex then turned south to meet William of Normandy at Hastings. This time, however, Harold of

Wessex died in battle, and his crown passed to William who became the King of England with the blessing of the pope. For England, this power struggle yielded complex results. First, French feudalism had crossed the English Channel and taken root in the island realm. Second, now the King of England was also the Duke of Normandy, a vassal of the King of France. And third, a new and complicated relationship began between the King of England and the rising Capet House in France. Years of warfare followed, as both the King of England and the King of France tried to determine who had the greatest amount of power on the continent and over England. These years of warfare helped to define the role of kingship and the papacy in both realms.

Meanwhile, in Central Europe, Otto I (936–73) destroyed the Magyar threat at the Battle of Lechfeld near Augsburg in the duchy of Swabia in 955 and reconstituted a new Holy Roman Empire. This battle marked the end of the nomadic menace from the east, as Central European feudalism firmly established heavy cavalry on massive noble estates along the frontier. Accordingly, Otto became the savior of Christendom and seemed to his people to be a reincarnation of Charlemagne. Since he had secured both the German territories as well as the Italian Peninsula, the pope therefore decided to elevate Otto I to the rank of Holy Roman Emperor.

Imitating Charlemagne deliberately, not only was Otto enthroned at Aachen, the old Frankish Capital, but he also built his realm on a direct alliance with the church. Relying on his authority to appoint the bishops of his realm, Otto planned to use the church as a counterweight to the power of his dukes. Since one of the bishops of the Holy Roman Empire was the pope himself, control of such appointments would have made Otto the most powerful man in medieval politics. And reasoning that since celibacy denied the possibility of a family dominating the office of a prelate, Otto hoped that if he controlled the selection of the great churchmen in his domain, he alone would receive their loyalty. Finally, since bishops and abbots rose to their positions of authority based solely on their abilities, securing such loyalty would guarantee that the most talented men in the Holy Roman Empire supported the crown. At the same time, Otto turned over much of the land he had acquired by conquest to his bishops to ensure that these estates remained loyal to his heirs. Although his plan seemed an air-tight one, what Otto could not have anticipated was that a struggle for power would begin between his descendents and the papacy that would further redefine politics in the High Middle Ages.

The role of the church with regard to kingship began to change when a major intellectual movement at

Cluny, a powerful French Monastery, questioned the right of monarchs to appoint bishops. At the same time that the new kings in France, England, and the Holy Roman Empire were winning control of their realms, these Clunaic monks advanced the principle that the church should function autonomously in order to ensure that salvation remained available to all of Christendom. Fearing the sin of *simony* (the assigning of a church office to a man of secular interests, which perverted the religious function of that office), these monks felt that the royal appointment of bishops endangered all the souls of Europe. Claiming that the pope alone should control the assignment of bishops as a means to guarantee freedom from simony, these monks promoted the independence of the papacy.

At this point, a simple accident of papal succession in Central Europe released the pope to make good on the claims of Cluny. After five generations of the Holy Roman emperors following Otto I's plans for control of the church, Henry III (reigned 1039–56), Otto's great-grandson, had allowed his cousin Leo IX to become the pope (served 1049–54). Leo IX was part of the Clunaic reform movement and supported regional synods (church legal assemblies) that condemned simony. Leo IX proceeded to place outspoken Clunaic monks in key administrative posts in Rome, and together they began to reform the papacy. Then, following Leo IX's death, and Pope Stephen IX's brief reign (1057–58), Pope Nicholas II (reigned 1059–61) took the unprecedented step of creating the College of Cardinals to advise the papacy on church matters. To this new College, Nicholas recruited even more Clunaic reformers.

Even as Leo IX began his reforms, Henry III died, leaving his infant son, Henry IV (reigned 1056–1106), as heir to the throne of the Holy Roman Empire. Since Henry was a minor child, his authority as emperor belonged to a board of regents comprised of his electors. These regents, however, failed to keep the power of the papacy in check. They were Henry's great lords, and as such, they only stood to profit from the weakness of the imperial office. Consequently, as long as Henry IV remained a minor, the pope and the regents were free to secure the autonomy of their own estates at the expense of the monarchy. Thus, the Clunaic reformers who staffed the College of Cardinals took this opportunity to liberate the papacy from imperial appointments, declaring that henceforth only the cardinals would elect the pope.

Using this electoral technique while Henry IV remained a child, the College of Cardinals elected Alexander II (reigned 1061–73) to the papacy. Upon Alexander II's death in 1073, the College of Cardinals then elected a radical Clunaic reformer named Hildebrand as pope. Taking the name of Gregory VII (reigned 1073–85), the new pope permanently changed the relationship between the Bishop of Rome and the Holy Roman emperor. Gregory VII declared the independence of the papacy and implemented sweeping reforms that challenged Henry IV's control over the empire. Thus, in the same year as Gregory's election, 1073, by which time Henry IV was twenty-three years old and capable of managing his own affairs, the Holy Roman emperor tried to reverse the changes that had been implemented during his childhood. By then, however, it was too late.

The papacy had functioned as an independent authority from 1056 to 1073, during which time Henry IV grew up and reached adulthood. Now the struggle between the Holy Roman emperor and the pope over who would control the remainder of the church began. Building on the precedents laid down by Leo I and Gelasius I, as mentioned above, Gregory VII held significant advantages in his claim over an independent church: and, as indicated, many of Henry IV's great lords had little interest in his recovery of imperial power. Furthermore, many of Italy's cities had allied themselves with the pope, hoping to profit from the freedom they might win from royal interference. Hence, a conflict began that would last the next two hundred years, one in which the papacy would succeed in establishing its control over the Central European Church.

Simultaneously, the question of who controlled the appointment of all the bishops in Central Europe was linked to the question of who controlled the Holy Roman Empire. The Clunaic reformers had claimed that all appointments had to be a function of an independent church. Hence the Holy Roman emperor faced a major political crisis: if the pope gained control over the appointment of the bishops, then Otto I's original plan for his monarchy and his heirs would collapse, for the pope instead of the emperor would command the richest estates in Central Europe, win the loyalty of the most talented men of the region, and command an institution backed by the realm's greatest lords and richest cities. If the papacy's power over these appointments remained unchecked, then the pope would become the most powerful man in Europe.

During the High Middle Ages, this scenario became a reality as the struggle between kings and the papacy unfolded. Only after the transition to the Late Middle Ages did the pope begin to lose ground to Western European kings in their struggle over control of the church. Hence, the politics of the Middle Ages after the year 1000 focused on a persistent rivalry between the kings and the pope.

In Central Europe, the pope prevailed. Pitting the great lords of Germany as well as the commercial centers of Italy against the emperor, the papacy won a difficult victory, making it the dominant political institution in Central Europe. At the same time, this victory broke the power of kingship in Central Europe and split the territories of Germany and Italy into principalities allied to papal independence. This fracturing of political space saw Central Europe form into a subculture quite different from Western Europe. These differences in turn laid a foundation for state formation that later made the Germans and Italians envious of the military power western European kings could mobilize in far more centralized realms during the Late Middle Ages (1300–1450). During the High Middle Ages, however, cen-tral Europeans celebrated the independence of their church, in the midst of their fragmented political landscape.

In the years following the rule of Gregory VII, the papacy pressed for the reforms that he had initiated. Pope Urban II (reigned 1088–99) reorganized the central administration of the Catholic Church to ensure an efficient system of keeping records and maintaining papal finances. He used the College of Cardinals as it was intended: a body of talented advisers. Around their recommendations, Urban II built a new papal court called the *curia*, which he assembled whenever he faced a major problem. Once established, the curia slowly evolved into an efficient governing body that gave the pope the most-advanced state in Europe.

Using the curia as a springboard, the eleventh- and twelfth-century papacy refined church law into a system of authority that medieval kings later imitated. Developing into the highest legal council of the church, the curia used the law to press for internal coherence within the church hierarchy. Sending legates throughout Christendom, the pope developed the capacity to intervene in all matters of church business in every realm of Europe. Establishing similar councils in the various parts of the continent and England, the curia cloned itself to create a legal pyramid of lesser courts. Using a system of appeals similar to the modern court system found in nation-states today, those who objected to lower-court decisions could have their cases reviewed at a higher level. As a result, a true administrative structure began to reappear in Europe.

Utilizing this court system to ensure the separation of church and state, the papacy maintained its control over issues it felt belonged to papal jurisdiction. Hence, church land, income, services, elections, and lawyers served as the arms and legs of the pope as his reach spanned all the territories of Christendom. Able to cross political boundaries like no king, the pope had

Magna Carta Seal, Seal-die of Robert Fitzwalter, approx. 1213–19. Seal-die are engraved stamps used to impress a design onto hot wax to seal documents. Made of silver, this example relates to the career of Robert Fitzwalter and is inscribed : + SIGILLVM: ROBERTI: FILII: WALTERI. Fitzwalter was one of the most influential barons of the early thirteenth century and played a significant part in the baronial revolt which resulted in the signing of the Magna Carta in 1215 by King John (1199–1216). © The Trustees of the British Museum.

access to all the souls of Europe. Accordingly, he developed a monopoly over belief that lasted until the Renaissance (1300–1600). The extent of papal authority during the High Middle Ages is personified by the reign of Pope Innocent III.

Pope Innocent III (reigned 1198–1216) was the most powerful man in Europe, able to impose his will on medieval kings whenever and wherever he chose. Extending Gelasius I's theory concerning the two institutions that governed Christendom, the sacred office of the church and royal authority of kings, Innocent III claimed that the church always took precedence. Asserting that since the church nurtured the eternal spirit of every Christian in the realm, while the king only ruled the temporal body, the papacy was the final arbiter in political matters. Therefore he frequently and freely told Europe's kings what to do. For example, Innocent III forced Philip II, King of France, to take back a wife he could not abide—Ingebord of Denmark; Innocent III involved himself in the complex politics of Germany, serving as the final judge in the election of the Holy Roman emperor; and in England, Innocent III's opposition to King John first led to an interdict against the realm, and then to the deposition of John as

The Magna Carta

The Magna Carta is a document that serves as an exam-ple of the dysfunctional nature of medieval culture; but one that produced positive, if accidental, results. Written as the claims of English men of estate (men of state and status due to their Real Estate or offices held) against an auto-cratic monarch, the Magna Carta secured the rights of the English nobility, the clergy, and corporate towns against their king. Designed to reverse the centralizing impulses of power of the ruling house of England (the Plantagenets), the Magna Carta served as a contract to create an internal balance of authority within English medieval society as it struggled with the issue of justice. Given the multilayered politics of feudalism, with its infeudation, subinfeudation, separation of church and state, and thirst for domination within the midst of a multitude of special rights and privileges, the Magna Carta tried to capture a sense of what it meant to be "English" in a society governed by a king. Out of this conflict came balance: the monarchy remained intact, the legitimate powers and rights of England's notables were duly recognized, and the idea of a realm shared by all as a community of diverse interests differentiated the English experience from the fragmentation that occurred in the Holy Roman Empire. While the church, noble, and urban claims to power against the monarchy in the Germanys and Italy humiliated the Holy Roman Emperor, and undid his efforts at centralization, the Magna Carta achieved a balance that drew the English people together in what eventually became known as a "commonwealth" (a kingdom whose wealth was held in common by its distinguished members). Hence, the Magna Carta resolved an immediate conflict of interests while laying down a precedent for future discussions of how to resolve internal disagreements over where the authority of the state ended and freedom of its people began.

Source: Frederic Youngs, Jr. Henry L. Snyder, and E. A. Reitan, *The English Heritage, Volume I to 1714* (Arlington Heights, Illinois: Forum Press, Inc. 1988), p. 51–52.

King when he refused to accept Innocent's candidate for the Archbishop of Canterbury. Innocent III reinstated John when he capitulated, but with the stipulation that the pope was now the overlord of England. Furthermore, Innocent backed John again when his great lords forced their incompetent ruler to sign the Magna Carta (see insert for a discussion of this document). Finally Innocent III nullified the Magna Carta as a promise forcibly extracted from a king without the knowledge of his overlord, the pope. Finally, Innocent III made himself the liege lord of Spain, Scandinavia, Hungary, and the Latin East.

The Crusades

Beyond the capacity of Innocent III to impose his will on the monarchs of Europe, the power of the pope during the High Middle Ages was most evident in his ability to launch the Crusades, a series of religious wars designed to recover the Holy Lands for Christendom and defeat heresy and the infidels (unbelievers) wherever they might be found in Europe. Beginning with the most successful military adventure of 1095–99 and ending in failure between 1271 and 1272, the Crusades spanned most of the eleventh, twelfth, and thirteenth centuries. The Crusades represented the charismatic force of the papacy, as pope after pope inspired a multitude of Christians to invade the Middle East, as well as fight heresy at home, in an effort to bear witness to their faith. In addition, the Crusades represented an era of cultural vitality when the younger sons of noble families sought land outside Europe because they could no longer inherit Real Estate at home. Furthermore,

the Crusades established lucrative commercial links across the Mediterranean that opened medieval Europe to a sudden increase in money and goods as a form of property that existed outside the legal boundaries of feudalism. Finally, the Crusades reintroduced Europe to its classical past, as contact with the Arab world allowed knowledge preserved by the Byzantine Empire to reshape the medieval imagination and bring forth a major intellectual revival during the High Middle Ages.

The enormously popular response to papal calls for the Crusades revealed the power the pope possessed to sway events during the High Middle Ages. The papacy launched eight invasions with the intent to regain and secure the cradle of Christendom. It called another to destroy heresy in southern France, and yet another against Emperor Frederick II (reigned 1220–50) in a struggle to resolve finally the question of who controlled the appointment of bishops in Central Europe. Still another began as an invasion of the Holy Lands but ended with a surprise attack on Constantinople that both captured the city and created a Catholic kingdom that lasted from 1204 to 1261. Finally, the pathetic adventure called the Children's Crusades saw thousands of youthful Christians embark for the Holy Lands from Marseilles only to be sold into slavery by unscrupulous merchants. Underlying all these Crusades, however, were layers of motives that combined a sincere sense of service to God with less savory incentives including material greed and political power.

The Crusades had grown out of an ongoing struggle with Islam that had begun with Charles Martel's victory at Tours in 732. Since Charles Martel's grandson,

Charlemagne, had driven the Muslims back across the Pyrenees and had recaptured the Spanish Marches, the early focus of Christendom's war with Islam had been waged on the Iberian Peninsula. There, the concept of a Holy War emerged in which Spanish and Portuguese Christians began a struggle against the Moors (Spanish Muslims) called the *Reconquista*, which would last until 1492. Spanning more than 700 years, the Reconquista wedded the papacy to the Castile, Aragon, Navarre, and Portuguese monarchies in a common cause that ultimately resulted in the creation of two powerful Western European kingdoms, Spain and Portugal. The slow but deliberate progress of Catholicism on the Iberian Peninsula created the *cortes* (Spanish Parliament), the *presidio* (garrison town), missions (local churches designed to propagate the Catholic faith), and *pueblos* (villages), which led to the recovery of about 90 percent of Spain and Portugal from Islam by 1250. Also, these same institutions prepared Spain for rapid expansion after 1492 when the Reconquista ended with a Catholic victory and Christopher Columbus sailed to the Americas. Parallel to these political and religious developments in Spain and Portugal, a Holy War in the Middle East seemed like a logical consequence.

While the papacy supported the Reconquista, the Muslims to the east gave the pope a second motive for wanting to recover Palestine/Israel—one involving domestic politics rather than religion. Still entangled in a bitter struggle with the Holy Roman emperor over who controlled the appointment of bishops in Germany and Italy, the papacy wanted to demonstrate its ability to raise its own armies. The popes reasoned that if they could mobilize a major military force to strike down the enemies of Christ abroad, then they had a legal as well as religious precedent to use the same type of power at home. Hence, each of the Crusades represented a way of reminding all recalcitrant kings in Europe of their duty to the church.

A third reason for launching the Crusades was the complex relationship between the papacy and the Byzantine Empire. A slow integration of Catholicism with the German Volk over the course of the Early Middle Ages had drawn popes away from their original alliance with the Eastern Roman emperor. This gradual separation had deepened as the isolation of the papacy from its eastern roots allowed for doctrinal issues to split the Latin Church from its Greek neighbor. For example, the Eastern Orthodox Church rejected Pope Leo I's fifth-century claim to supremacy over all of Christendom as the heir of Peter based on his interpretation of Petrine Theory (see Matthew 16:18 mentioned above). Also, during the eighth and ninth centuries,

the Eastern Roman emperors had begun a campaign to destroy the power of religious images (icons) in the Byzantine world and insisted that all churchmen participate; the papacy had refused. Finally, the Greek Orthodox Church developed the doctrine that the Holy Ghost sprang from God the Father rather than God the Son, which led to a theological dispute that saw both the pope and the patriarch of Constantinople excommunicating one another in 1054. The result of this final confrontation led to a division between the Roman Catholic and Greek Orthodox churches that the pope hoped to repair by initiating a war against a common enemy, Islam.

Finally, the Crusades rested on practical political and economic considerations. They offered an opportunity for kings and great lords to export surplus knights. A mild climate and an abundant food supply during the High Middle Ages had generated too many surviving sons. Since feudalism proved unforgiving in terms of inheritance, only a few noble slots were available to fill each generation. If a kingdom followed the practice of *primogeniture*, one heir alone could receive the estate. If a kingdom followed Salic Law, which allowed every son to inherit, then all the male offspring in a family could become heirs, a practice that soon divided an estate to the point of military uselessness. Hence, great families that tried to ensure that the inheritance of an estate stayed within their bloodline often produced too many sons for their land to support. The best solution, therefore, was to train these boys for war and then send them on their way. Accordingly, the pope had an abundance of land-hungry young men available for service, each one eager to win his fortune by invading the Middle East or driving away heretics at home.

The energy produced by the Crusades established temporary outposts on the Levant coast that lasted from 1099 to 1291—the dates marking Europe's capture of Jerusalem to the fall of Acre, the last Christian stronghold in the Holy Land. At the same time, the eight officially sanctioned Crusades against the infidels allowed the monarchs of Europe, and their Italian commercial suppliers, to establish diplomatic contacts with Islamic rulers. These diplomatic links led to a revival of trade, which in turn stimulated a process of change that took medieval Europe well beyond the cultural boundaries prescribed by the papacy, feudalism, or the Crusades.

Trade, Real Estate, Incorporeal Property, and Towns

Trade across the Mediterranean—and eventually along the Silk Road and Indian Ocean—reintroduced to Europe the general uses of money and goods in an economy. Ironically, this use of money and goods did not fit within the legal definitions of Real Estate as prescribed by feudalism. Instead, Real Estate identified land as the only legitimate, or legally sanctioned, form of ownership/possession. Hence, surplus wealth in the form of money and goods belonged to what English Common Law called "incorporeal property," (wealth *without body*). Hence, money and goods did not bestow "status or state" on its owner, and they did not enjoy any legal protection from "men of estate," (i.e. legitimate rulers of "states" as defined by their possession of land).

Accordingly, money and goods represented a cultural paradox: on the one hand, incorporeal property was economically valuable; on the other, it did not exist in the eyes of the law. Thus, if incorporeal property did not have legal protection from men of estate, then these aristocrats could attack, rob, or tax with impunity any merchants transporting moveable wealth across their lands. As a result, to accumulate surpluses of incorporeal property within feudal Europe produced a real risk of personal danger. Consequently, incorporeal property required its owners to develop a social system that legally functioned beyond the boundaries of feudalism.

Indeed, between the Early and High Middle Ages, as these surpluses began to accumulate, so did the extralegal space for them in society. Paradoxically, the peace produced at the local level by the general introduction of heavy cavalry based on Real Estate had also generated enough stability to create incorporeal property on those lands possessed by knights. The goods that these professional soldiers did not personally need they exchanged with other estates. Slowly, the reintroduction of trade created a pattern of local commerce that led to regional fairs and market towns. Around these fairs or market towns people gathered to take advantage of the livelihood made possible by moveable wealth.

During the Crusades, the accumulation of incorporeal property accelerated rapidly. Soon trade on a grand scale connected local market towns with great commercial centers along the medieval trade routes. These trade routes linked European lands bordering the Baltic and North seas with commercial centers in Flanders. Goods collected in the north were sent to Flanders, from which they would then travel up the Rhine River to the Alps. Crossing the Alps, these goods next entered North Italy, where they arrived in cities on the eastern and western shores of the Mediterranean; there they were sent both south and east. Crossing the Mediterranean, these same European goods now made their way to either Constantinople, Aleppo, Alexandria, or Tunis, where diplomatic contacts forged by the Crusades facilitated trade with Asia and sub-Saharan Africa. Finally, these same trade routes were used on the return trip when merchants from the Muslim world introduced Europe to the gold transported from North Africa, the spices from India, and goods from China such as the wheelbarrow, coal, rag paper, moveable woodblock type, the crossbow, silk, and gunpowder.

Still, neither the richest commercial centers situated directly on the medieval trade routes nor the less well-placed towns that only served as depots for local goods enjoyed any legal protection from men of estate. Thus, towns everywhere developed a sense of isolation and fear peculiar to the Middle Ages. For any town to exist, grow, and prosper, it had to develop some form of legal identity or military protection in order to defend its amassed incorporeal property from aristocratic warriors. For the less wealthy towns—those not directly on the medieval trade routes—the legal identity used to shield these cities from men of estate emerged with the concept of a "corporation." Forming a corporation required a charter granted by a king that transformed a commercial center into a legal entity.

In the so-called corporate towns, men pointed to their charters to prove the legal existence of their towns. By paying taxes in the form of moveable wealth, these men provided their kings a revenue stream that existed outside feudalism. Such an income had no traditional or legal sanctions on its use. Hence, the more corporate towns a king chartered, the more he stepped outside the boundaries of legitimate feudal conduct, and the richer these chartered towns made him through his "bodiless" contact (illegitimate, nontraditional behavior) with them.

On the other hand, if a town was rich enough, it was also strong enough to defend itself against any man of estate. Such a city could ignore all kind of lords, kings included, and create a political entity independent of all legitimate medieval institutions, except the papacy. Such towns commanded the trade routes, tapped into its enormous wealth, and developed the military technology needed to secure their existence outside the feudal hierarchy. Their long-distance trade with cultures like China introduced Europe to weapons that could kill armored knights in open battle. Such towns now began to feel a general hostility toward the countryside; they felt that the rural landscape threatened their existence and forced them to reside in a legal no-man's-land. As a result, they sought political, economic, and social autonomy, encouraging a process known as *decentralization*.

For chartered towns, the royal creation of a corporation produced a separate, legal definition of urban space that divided the kingdom's forms of wealth into what the French called *Domaine* and *Proprietas*. As in English Common Law, Domaine was Real Estate and identified a legal personality called a man of estate. Domaine could not be taxed without the consent of its owner. Also, as in English Common Law, Proprietas was incorporeal property with no legal existence. Proprietas, however, could acquire legal identity through the specific terms of a charter. Thus, French chartered towns, like their English counterparts, supplied a king both with an income that existed outside the boundaries of medieval tradition and with the means to develop a new command over geographic space. Such towns were later called centerplace cities by geographers because of the way they linked with other urban centers within a kingdom to begin a process called *centralization*.

If a town ignored kings and lords, it had to rely on its own ability to defend its independence from men of estate. Existing without legal identity, however, was dangerous. As a result, these autonomous towns had to defend themselves constantly and therefore devised whatever means necessary to separate themselves from Real Estate. Such towns required the wealth that only a great trade network could provide. Thus, these towns became what geographers called "network cities." As the richest cities in medieval Europe, these commercial centers could only exist in places where kings or great lords were weak.

The great network cities of the High Middle Ages emerged between the years that marked the end of the nomadic invasions and the ascendancy of the pope in Central Europe. These towns sided with the papacy in his struggle with the Holy Roman emperor and helped to break the power of a centralizing state. Located in the decentralized territory of Central Europe, these cities dominated the medieval trade routes and developed into three very wealthy trade centers: North Italy, Flanders, and Germany. All three commercial zones featured urban centers capable of defending themselves against men of estate while introducing Europe to knight-killing weapons.

North Italy was far more important than Flanders or Germany during the High Middle Ages due to the central position it occupied in Mediterranean trade. Rising to wealth during the Crusades, northern Italian merchants from Venice, Genoa, Florence, Milan, and Pisa forged links with the Jews and Christians of the Middle East to sustain intercultural commerce even as Catholic and Muslim soldiers killed each other on battlefields. The trade produced by these Mediterranean exchanges soon became so valuable that even religious warfare itself could not block its further expansion. In time, Italian city-states grew wealthy enough to seek and win their independence from the Holy Roman emperor.

The cities of Flanders, Ypres, Ghent, and Bruge sought political freedom as well, but the merchants of these comparatively less wealthy towns had to form alliances with the local counts in order to create a pocket of power in which they could conduct trade autonomously. This freedom of action, however, made Flanders a political question mark in the minds of the rulers of the royal houses of Europe. England, France, and the Habsburgs of Austria acquired and lost this commercial zone as a result of shifting alliances during the Middle Ages. Today, Flanders belongs to Belgium, a nation-state like Holland that eventually won its independence through the wealth earned by trade.

In Germany, the Hanseatic League generated an assembly of more than one hundred cities to control the commercial trade lanes of the Baltic and North seas. Supplying the goods that were collected in Flanders—and then sent to North Italy—the Hanseatic League represented an organization of cities designed to protect themselves from the Holy Roman emperor and local Baltic kings. Thriving from the thirteenth to the sixteenth centuries, the Hanseatic League did not construct a political base similar to the network towns in Flanders or North Italy. As a result, the league did not survive the Middle Ages; nevertheless, its formation and function reflects the hostility of towns to the countryside in Central Europe.

In contrast, those towns that encouraged centralization were the corporate cities of Western Europe. Integrated into regional urban hierarchies, these cities linked with local towns, villages, and agricultural hamlets to create a new geographic coherence within a Western European kingdom. While all towns facilitated commercial transportation, only chartered towns encouraged the development of a kingdom's roads and waterways, which in turn allowed a medieval monarch to integrate his Domaine. At the same time, these chartered towns supplied the most competent and ambitious of these medieval kings with the means to change feudalism—the income needed to purchase the latest knight-killing weaponry from abroad and thereby subdue any unruly nobles. Military technology imported by the Italian city-states, such as the crossbow and gunpowder, joined with local arms like the Welsh longbow and Swiss pike to redefine warfare in the Late Middle Ages. Hence, trade and chartered cities changed the balance of power within Western European kingdoms; both eventually gave the king the means to enforce his will over the Real Estate of his realm.

Meanwhile, the legal distinctions between Real Estate and incorporeal property that had caused the internal tensions between the rural and urban portions of feudal Europe had also encouraged a general state of dysfunction within medieval culture. This dysfunction eventually set in motion the historical process called "modernization" based on the habits of innovation, risk, and change inspired by making a living outside the legitimate spheres of tradition. These habits derived from the urban skills one had to acquire in order to survive in a medieval city, including literacy, computation, and critical thinking. Reading and writing were essential because one had to keep records in order to succeed in trade. Computation was necessary because one had to maintain the accounts in order to measure the profitability of any given venture. Critical thinking was imperative because of the questions one had to ask, and the risks one had to take, to engage in trade as well as live beyond the legal boundaries of feudalism. Each of these skills encouraged learning. Each, in turn, also stimulated a curiosity about Europe's ancient Greek and Roman heritage. Thus, the revival of trade, and the development of medieval cities, stimulated a great intellectual renaissance in Europe.

The Awakening of the Medieval Mind: Colleges and Universities

This intellectual revival combined a general desire for learning with a quest for ancient beliefs that coincided with the newly won power of the papacy. The desire for learning elevated Latin as the universal language of the Catholic Church into the ubiquitous tongue of medieval Europe. Prior to the High Middle Ages, a small number of churchmen had struggled to preserve and interpret the ancient Greco-Christian worldview using Latin. With time, and the continued destruction of cities caused by each new nomadic assault, much of the rest of Europe's ancient heritage had been lost. Included in the casualties was the ability to read, write, and speak Greek. Thus, Latin alone survived as the language of the Roman Catholic Church. As a result, Latin helped to define the boundaries between Western Christendom, the Byzantine Empire, and the pockets of "vulgar" languages spoken by the German Volk. Among the unburied treasures of the past were St. Augustine's *Confessions* and *The City of God* as well as the writing of Ancius Manlius Severius Boethius (480–525). Both authors had provided the primary sources of Christian theology that had survived the barbarian invasions of the Early Middle Ages.

After centuries of chaos during the Early Middle Ages, a series of exceptional clerics stepped forward to help the church revive theology and philosophy during the High Middle Ages. These exceptional scholars stressed God's all-powerful nature, which they believed was made accessible by the reason and speech found within the ancient Greek concept of logos (see the Greco-Roman philosophy of Chapters Seven and Eight). These scholars revived logos as the idea behind Plato's forms and Aristotle's final cause that permeated the nature of God as both the Creator and the Soul of the universe. They argued that since logos meant "logic, word, and speech," and facilitated an understanding of universal knowledge, it could also help humanity rediscover God's will.

Emerging alongside the recovery of urban life that had accompanied the revival of trade during the Crusades, scholarship developed out of Cathedral and secular schools of the Early Middle Ages to become new colleges and universities; these new institutions then joined with the exceptional clerics to distinguish the High Middle Ages from the violence of the earlier era. Students everywhere welcomed the new knowledge available in the institutions of higher learning, which chartered towns that specialized in reviving the "sacred" truths of the church. Each incorporated college and university, therefore, encouraged the resurrection of Latin as "the word, speech, and logic" found within the universal voice of the Catholic Church.

Formed by student guilds seeking this universal knowledge, colleges in Salerno, Naples, Rome, Florence, Bologna, Padua, Grenoble, Basel, Heidelberg, Cologne, Vienna, Prague, and Leipzig represented the intellectual life of Central Europe. At the same time, Seville, Salamanca, Toulouse, Avignon, Montpellier, Bordeaux, Poitiers, Bourges, Orleans, Paris, Oxford, Cambridge, Glasgow, and St. Andrews constituted the scholarship bases of Western Europe. Both sets of chartered colleges and universities attracted talented individuals. Accordingly, each college or university tried to entice the best teachers in the arts, theology, law, and medicine to join with students to develop institutions of higher learning as part of the new fabric of society.

The universal acceptance of a college degree also required some form of legitimate recognition, the acquisition of which caused students and instructors alike to seek a charter from a king, or the church, that transformed both into *universitas*, or academic guilds. Yet since the church was in the process of developing a universal worldview for Christendom, anyone receiving a degree had to swear loyalty to *dogma*, (Roman Catholic doctrine). Thus, all graduates from these new educational guilds had in effect become the agents of the church as these new institutions spread across Europe. Typically, however, students formed university guilds in southern Europe, while professors took the initiative in northern Europe.

The Late Middle Ages, 1300–1450

While the papacy rose to prominence the High Middle Ages, kingship began its ascent during the last medieval period. This rise in royal power, however, emerged from a set of circumstances that should have destroyed civilization rather than stimulate a new era of cultural vitality. A biological crisis swept through Europe that normally would have resulted in social collapse; instead, an era of consolidation began that ushered in the modern age. At the heart of this process was a cycle of death that first undermined the papacy, then inspired a major renaissance, and ended with the kings of Europe stepping into the power vacuum left by the diminished popes. Thus, while death was everywhere, and the Apocalypse seemed to be at hand, medieval Europe produced a new era of cultural integration that ultimately changed world history.

Ironically, the Late Middle Ages reintroduced Europe to a major die-off era that linked warfare to famine and the Bubonic Plague but failed to destroy Western culture completely. Each cause of mass death reflected the consequences of three extraordinary events. First, a major climatic shift nearly destroyed Eurasian agriculture while triggering a global famine. Second, the use of the trade routes established during the Crusades carried the disease vector of the Bubonic Plague which swept across Eurasia. And third, warfare followed when the powerful men living at all levels of medieval society decided to fight over what was left.

Victims of the Bubonic Plague, commonly known as "Black Death" (due to the blackening of the skin from subdermal hemorrhaging). The disease spread north across Europe, killing a third of the population within three years. The plague was eliminated in Europe at the onset of the nineteenth century, but outbreaks continue to be reported today (see Chapter I vector diagram). Illustration of the Black Death from the Toggenburg Bible (1411).

Famine

Famine struck first. A mini Ice Age changed the Eurasian growing season by eliminating fourteen days of mild temperatures just before the harvest. Simultaneously, a shift in the Jet Stream suddenly brought cold air from the Arctic Circle down into China, Central Asia, and Europe. Starting in 1302, Europe lost the warm air that preceded each year's reaping; suddenly, freezing temperatures caused moisture trapped in clouds to fall as sleet and hail rather than as rain. Thus, frozen water plummeting from an altitude of 30,000 feet smashed down onto Europe's crops, killing most of the plants. The wet earth then saturated the fallen wheat, barley, or rye, destroying Europe's food supply before farmers could harvest it.

Hitting after centuries of warm weather, this mini Ice Age eliminated the agricultural abundance to which medieval Europeans had grown accustomed. In addition, by 1300 Europe's population had grown to its maximum limits based on the years of bounty and relative peace produced by the High Middle Ages. Now, these enlarged human numbers faced a major food crisis that replaced prosperity with the terror of starvation and raised new questions concerning God's will. No longer did the people of Christendom seem assured of God's reward; rather, they appeared to be facing His wrath. Thus, the sudden drop in the food supply created a cultural emergency that threatened the very existence of medieval Europe.

Plague

As if general famine was not bad enough, the Bubonic Plague, or Black Death, made matters far worse. Traveling along the Silk Road from China to Europe, starving rats sought the same sources of food that fed humans. Rats rarely venture far from their nesting areas, but famine drove these tiny migrants from China to the Middle East, and then from the Middle East into Europe. The Bubonic Plague, caused by the bacillus, *Yersinia Pestis*, lived in the digestive tracts of fleas that fed on the blood of these rodents. Striking Europe between 1347 and 1352, in its first cycle of destruction the Plague claimed the lives of as many as 25 million people, or an estimated 40 percent of the population of medieval Europe.

Once active, the Plague continued to take its victims locally until 1665, when the last episode hit London. Many took the Plague, called *arta mors* (dreadful death), as a sign of God's rage. The impact of the Plague reflected the terror it created in the human imagination. The Black Death took its victims in one of three ways: first, it could cause septicemia, take the Bubonic form, or imitate pneumonia (see insert).

The Bubonic Plague

The Bubonic Plague is an infection caused by the bacillus Yersinia pestis, *sometimes called* Pasteurella pestis. Yersinia pestis *is a short bacillus, which has a "safety pin" like shape as it appears to fold in on itself when viewed under a microscope. Carried by wild rodents such as rats, mice, squirrels, and prairies dogs,* Yersinia pestis *causes an acute (sudden onset), subacute (slower onset), or chronic (always present) infection.* Yersinia pestis *produces a "hitchhiker" style disease: it is transmitted by a bite from a flea carrying* Yersinia pestis *in its digestive tract that has hitched a ride on an infected rodent. Once transmitted to human victims through the fleabite, the disease takes on several forms.*

Bubonic plague is the most common form. The incubation period (time needed for the symptoms of a disease to appear after the original infection) varies from a few hours to twelve days, but most commonly occurs within two to five days after the flea bite. Onset is abrupt. Symptoms include chills and a rapid rise in temperature (39.1 to 41 degrees Centigrade, or 103 to 106 degrees Fahrenheit). The pulse becomes rapid and thready (lacking fullness). High blood pressure may occur. Enlarged lymph nodes (buboes) appear shortly before or during the rise in the temperature. The lymph nodes located in the thighs and groin are most commonly involved. The lymph nodes in the armpits and the neck may follow. All these nodes become sensitive to the touch and are firm and fixed; they can swell to the size of tangerines. The overlying skin becomes stretched until its is smooth and reddish in color. Occasionally a primary skin lesion appears at the flea bite site varying from a small blister to a large scab. The infected person will then most likely become restless, delirious, confused, and uncoordinated. His/her liver and spleen will enlarge and can be felt by an examining physician. The white blood cell count

rises, then these cells die trying to protect the body, and form pus collected in the lymph nodes; this is what caused them to swell in the first place. These nodes will then discharge pus into the blood stream and throughout the body usually within two weeks of the infection. This discharged pus pools beneath the skin and forms large, discolored bruises. Internal organs may then become infected. If a person is not treated, the mortality rate is 60 percent with most people dying from sepsis, a toxic reaction to the spread of bacteria and the accumulation of pus within the body.

Primary pneumonic plague begins when a bubonic patient coughs and sprays attending people with infected sputum (spit). The cough is not noticeable initially, but appears within twenty to twenty-four hours after the infection. The sputum is thick with mucus at first, then rapidly shows blood specks, and finally becomes uniformly pink or bright red and foamy. Symptoms include high fever, chills, rapid heartbeat, and a severe headache. Shortly thereafter the lungs become congested with fluid and the infected person drowns within 48 hours after the onset of the disease. Ninety-nine to 100 percent of all untreated patients die.

Other forms of the Plague include septicemia. The septicemic plague usually evolves from the bubonic form. Those infected with septicemia die of blood poisoning within hours after the infection because their blood is saturated with pus. The mortality rate is 100 percent, but the patient dies so quickly that they do not infect anyone else. Hence, the septicemic plague is the least damaging of the three forms of Black Death when considered in terms of the impact on population during a massive die-off era.

Source: *The Merck Manual of Diagnosis and Therapy*, **Thirteenth Edition (Rathway, New Jersey: Merck and Co., Inc., 1977) p. 101–102.**

Killing virtually whomever crossed its path, the Black Death caused China's population to drop from 125 to 95 million. In the Middle East, major urban centers reported similar devastation: Constantinople and Alexandria lost 1,000 people per day; in Cairo 7,000 died per day, and the death toll for the Muslim world reached an estimated 33 percent of its entire population.

The story in Europe was no different. The Black Death became pandemic within four years of its arrival in 1347. In Paris, it killed 800 a day, and in Florence it took 50 percent of the population on three separate occasions. Arriving in Italy, it marched north across the Alps to the Rhine, and from there it spread to Flanders and to the rest of Europe and Russia.

War

Occurring at the same time as famine and Plague, and taken as yet another sign of God's anger, the last

major killer of the Late Middle Ages was warfare. Over the next 150 years war erupted sporadically, killing people at all rungs of society. At the royal level, the Hundred Years War (1377–1453) pitted France and England in a final struggle to determine the role of the English king in French politics. At the local level, peasant rebellions in France, England, Spain, Sicily, and the Germanys reflected the economic consequences of famine and Plague, as local lords tried to increase their income by imposing new rents and taxes on their surviving farmers. Furthermore, in Flanders and North Italy, guild wars erupted when masters and journeymen fought over wages and profits as the rising demand for labor caused by the die-off changed the conditions of production. Finally, intercultural conflict increased as the Turks began a major push to capture Southern and Central Europe.

The Hundred Years War and State Formation

While all of these conflicts reflected the political, economic, and social consequences of a major die-off era, the Hundred Years War was the most dramatic example. This conflict pitted Edward III of England (reigned 1327–77) against Philip VI of France (reigned 1328–50) as both tried to claim the French throne. Edward III was Queen Isabella's son, while Queen Isabella was the daughter of Philip IV (reigned 1268–1314) and a royal princess of France. Philip VI was the son of Charles, Count of Valois, and brother to Philip IV. Yet, since Salic Law (the law of the Franks) mandated that only male heirs could inherit an estate, Philip VI's claim to the French throne proved to be superior to that of Edward III. Accordingly, an assembly of French nobility elected Philip VI as their next king even though Edward was a direct descendent of Philip IV. Thus, Philip VI acquired the French throne when the last Capet king, Charles IV, died in 1322.

Beyond this set of royal claims, however, the kings of England and France had been fighting one another for centuries trying to determine what role the English monarchy should play in French politics: the king of England remained both an equal to, and a vassal of, the French king. William the Conqueror had begun his career as the duke of Normandy before capturing the English throne in 1066. As mentioned, becoming the king of England had made William both a royal brother to and a subordinate of the king of France. But since William's heirs had engaged in a series of royal marriages that had made the king of England a greater landholder in France than the French king, the question of who really ruled on the continent became a major political issue. Then, wars between France and England during the High Middle Ages had eliminated many of England's French possessions after the incompetent reign of John (reigned 1199–1216), William's great great grandson. By 1328, however, Edward III still held vast claims to the French province of the Aquitaine that were very good. Thus, war began once again between England and France when Philip VI tried to impose his will on the Aquitaine as overlord, an act Edward would not tolerate. The war itself led to thousands of deaths, increased England's command over French lands temporarily after the victories at Crécy (1346), Poitiers (1356), and Agincourt (1415), but ultimately resulted in a French victory. Meanwhile, throughout the entire struggle, the royal authority in both kingdoms consolidated.

In England and France the respective king had manipulated taxation, as well as the passions of his people, to mobilize the military resources needed for victory. The impact of these maneuvers welded together a sense of territorial integrity that gave the English and the French a feeling of unity that was unprecedented in the Middle Ages. The nobility, the clergy, the counties, and the corporate towns of each medieval realm assembled in either England's Parliament, or France's Estates General, to bestow new taxes on their royal overlords. These medieval assemblies of men of estate and centerplace cities met frequently as the struggle passed from one generation to the next. In England, the regular gathering of Parliament during the Hundred Years War created a sense of law in the English imagination that later played a major role in defining sovereignty for that kingdom. In France, the generosity of the French church, nobility, and corporate cities, as the three estates of the Estates General, virtually granted their king a free hand to raise money so that he could finally win the war. This license to tax also played a major role in defining sovereignty in France after 1453.

The war itself assembled unprecedented armies. The English mobilized an estimated 10 percent of their total male population to fight the three times more populous France. The French, in turn, enlisted more men than the English but lost most of the early battles. The English won these initial victories because the king of England was willing to use new weapons in his quest for victory. Hence, England deployed infantry using the Welsh long bow, which broke the monopoly on coercion held by France's heavy cavalry. Also, this bow changed the face of warfare itself; now the infantryman began to replace the far more expensive cavalryman as the principal soldier in royal armies. Simultaneously, mercenaries who fought for money began to replace men of estate who fought for land. Furthermore, commanders of royal blood led their armies personally into combat and fought engagements that released such passions on the battlefield that the desire for victory led to new styles of killing that completely ignored chivalry. Military triumph at any cost, while using any weapon, suddenly seemed far more important than maintaining a noble, Christian level of traditional behavior. Finally, great heroes like Joan of Arc (see insert below) emerged to spark a sense of protonational emotion that completed the picture of consolidation in France and later resulted in a final French victory. Yet the separation of England from France after 1453 did as much for the English as it did for the French to clarify the politics in both states: thereafter the kings in each realm became the principal rulers of their respective countries.

Peasant Rebellions

Even as the Hundred Years War drew men-in-arms into mortal combat from 1337 to 1453, peasant revolts that swept across Europe expressed the rage that rural

Joan of Arc

Joan of Arc (1412?–31) was the daughter of a French peasant from Domrémy in Lorraine who was raised as a devout and obedient girl. At sixteen, she nonetheless began to hear the voices that claimed to be St. Michael, St. Catherine, and St. Margaret. All three exhorted her to aid the dauphin (the French crown prince), Charles VII (1403–61), to become the King of France by liberating Orléans and Rheims—the traditional seat of the French coronation. Met with considerable skepticism, Joan managed to win the support of Robert de Baudricourt, the military governor of Vaucouleurs, who helped her get an interview with the dauphin. She met Charles at Chinon castle in 1429 and overcame his incredulity about her mission by using her religious sincerity, while French desperation to achieve any type of military victory helped her claims immensely.

Furnished with troops, she succeeded during that same year in relieving Orléans, liberating the surrounding countryside, and winning a string of military victories. Her success derived from her ability to give the French people and armies something neither the French nobility nor crown had managed to do: a unique sense of divine inspiration that offered a type of mystical confidence in her mission. With Orléans liberated, and, with considerable efforts at persuading Charles that it was now safe to travel to Rheims, Joan participated in his coronation.

At the height of her popularity, Joan wanted to press on with the military campaign, but Charles's indolence lost the French the momentum she had gained with her victories.

Also in 1429, Joan tried to liberate Paris but failed. Then, in the following spring, she led a military force to the relief of Compiègne, but the Burgundians, allies of England, captured her. Charles was in a good position to secure her release, but he forgot about Joan as quickly as he had embraced her. He simply allowed her to languish in prison while the Burgundians sold her to the English for a handsome ransom. The English held her at Rouen, part of France that was still in their hands, put her on trial for heresy, and broke her in ten weeks of unrelenting torture. She died a relapsed heretic in May 1431, but Charles then reopened her case and had her declared innocent on July 7, 1456, twenty-five years after her execution. Four years after her execution, Charles made peace with England in 1435, and a united France, thanks to the inspiration of Joan's mission, now had the means to progressively drive the outnumbered English from French soil. By 1453, the war came to an end, Charles was still king, and the English were confined to one French port: Calais.

Barbara W. Tuchman, *A Distant Mirror: The Calamitous 14th Century* (New York: Ballantine Books, 1978) p. 588–89).

people felt toward the excessive new taxes and rents that landlords forced farmers to pay. The combination of nearly continuous warfare and the rising demand for agricultural labor saw this form of rebellion spread from Western to Central Europe. France and England experienced most of these rural uprisings, for both realms had imposed an enormous demand on agricultural productivity during the Hundred Years War. The events that drove these desperate farmers to rebel, however, went far beyond the immediate cause for new taxation.

Men of estate everywhere suffered economic hardship due to the great die-off era; they experienced financial misfortune one of three ways: first, those aristocrats who received rents in the form of agricultural labor lost these services when their peasants died in large numbers; second, those landlords who obtained a moneyed rent in lieu of agricultural labor saw these payments end with the death of their farmers; and third, the cost of living for aristocrats suddenly increased. This final change in the finances for men of estate reflected the rising cost of producing goods in corporate towns and network cities as laborers died. The die-off took skilled journeymen as well as farmers, so the increase in the demand for surviving urban labor generated an increase in wages; this, in turn, caused the masters of guilds to increase their prices in order to maintain profits. Consequently, men of estate experi-

enced financial exigency for the first time in their otherwise untroubled economic lives. They suffered a financial crisis as they found themselves caught in a classic double bind: on one hand they had a shrinking income; on the other they suffered a rising cost of living.

To recoup their financial losses, some landlords converted their estates into grazing land for sheep, hoping to sell wool at a better price than the rents they could receive from their peasants. Other aristocrats gave up cultivation altogether, rented their land to the highest bidder, and saw their fields converted into commercial farms. Still other men of estate used their access to local legislatures to freeze wages, convert manorial services into money rents, and set all rents higher. Finally, wherever possible, aristocrats created new taxes or new labor obligations in order to pass the burden of their financial misery onto their farmers. The result of all these actions were peasant rebellions—acts of violent desperation that invariably failed.

As stated above, these peasant revolts occurred most frequently in France and England. In France, the crushing burden of taxation imposed from above fomented a general peasant rebellion in 1358. The expenses of the Hundred Years War placed the French throne in jeopardy, and it prompted the Estates General to raise the *taille*—a direct tax paid by farmers. At the same time, whole regions of France suffered from sprees of aristocratic crimes wherein armed bands of men simply extorted goods and services from the defenseless. Finally, English military successes in the face of heavy French taxes caused the French peasantry to explode spontaneously.

No longer willing to live under these oppressive conditions, these angry French farmers launched a massive uprising know as the *Jacquerie*. Concentrated in the provinces of Picardy and Champagne, the French peasants (Jacques) stormed onto the estates, killing every nobleman they could find, raping women, and slaughtering livestock. This violent rampage may have eased the anger the rural people felt, but it hardly solved their problems. Meanwhile, the French nobility outside the rebellious districts organized a counterattack, in which they slaughtered thousands of peasants, many of whom had not been directly involved in the atrocities against the nobility. After this initial outburst, France suffered regional peasant rebellions periodically: in 1363, 1380, 1420, and 1484. Each one, however, ended predictably, with the state crushing the peasantry.

In England, peasant rebellions reflected a response to legal measures practiced by men of estate to ensure their high standard of living. Taking advantage of their privileged position as lawmakers, English landlords and representatives from corporate towns met in Parliament to pass the Statute of Laborers in 1351, which froze wages at a pre-1347 level, before the Black Death had killed so many workers. In this manner, England's wealthy hoped to freeze the cost of their luxuries. Then they began a process of converting rents from services into cash payments so that they could take advantage of the rising value of labor. Finally, the men of estate set the price of their new moneyed rents at a level equal in value to the services performed before famine and plague had swept through England. Now trapped with rents that exceeded their means to pay, English peasants rebelled in 1381. The results of this rebellion matched those in France; an initial rampage threatened the established order, led to a counterattack, and ended in wholesale slaughter.

Outside the lands directly involved in the Hundred Years War, peasant uprisings reflected a general rise in the demand for rural labor. In Spain, aristocrats tried to impose a new form of serfdom on their peasants to secure higher rents. As in England and France, peasant rebellions followed in 1391. Spanish farmers led massive attacks on urban centers and aristocratic estates near Barcelona. These assaults marked a rural rage equal to anything seen in France and England. Also met with the same determined noble resistance, these Spanish episodes ended with an equal level of slaughter as practiced on the rebellious poor by Spain's northern neighbors.

Guild Wars

In contrast to rural violence, the general demand for urban labor led to the guild wars. These conflicts reflected a struggle between journeymen and their masters over setting the price of labor. Guild masters had managed to gain a voice in city government as their windfall profits from the increased price of manufactured goods had elevated their status to a level equal to that of the ruling merchant and patrician families of network and corporate towns. Using their newfound political power to produce restrictive legislation, these guild masters fixed wages low, limited the production of their goods, and prevented the rise of journeymen above the rank of laborers. Many journeymen, however, had hoped to profit from the increased demand for their work and organized resistance to this new legislation. The result was intra-urban warfare.

The skilled but propertyless workers of Florence, in Italy, Ghent, Bruge, and Ypres in Flanders, and Brunswick, Lübeck, and Danzig in Germany, rose up like their peasant counterparts to seek new incomes. Also like their rural counterparts, the urban artisans faced organized resistance. Swinging back and forth between attacks on masters, followed by employer retribution, the guild wars had a way of consolidating power in the hands of local strongmen. In Florence, it was the De Medici family; in Flanders, the Habsburg Dynasty; in Germany, the city councils of the Hanseatic League. In all three places, stability was imposed from above while the poor paid a heavy price in blood.

The Ottoman Turks

The final military threat faced by late medieval Europe came from the Turks. Founded by Osman (reigned 1260–1326), the Ottoman Turks began a long history of expansion that resulted in the Ottoman Empire. The Ottoman Sultans began this expansion after 1453. In 1453, Mohammed II achieved what was long considered impossible; he captured Constantinople with the use of a new weapon: cannon. Launching a combined land and sea assault, Mohammed II destroyed Constantinople's defenses—ending the one-thousand-year history of the Eastern Roman Empire—and began an invasion of the Balkans. Riding the passion of Islam, and with the use of new slave soldiers—the Janissaries, Mohammed II's heirs swept through the Balkans all the way to the gates of Vienna. Posing a new military threat to Europe at the end of the Late Middle Ages, the Turks became symbolic of a general question on the minds of every Catholic: why had God decided to punish Christendom with so many lethal instruments?

The Papacy in an Apocalyptic Age

Death seemingly everywhere inspired Apocalyptic images that filled the medieval mind with horror. Responsible for dealing with questions about God, an overwhelmed papacy floundered. As the ongoing struggle with European kings over who took precedence in medieval politics distracted the pope from his Christian duties, the papacy itself suffered from two extremely embarassing episodes: the Babylonian Captivity (1309–77) and the Great Schism (1378–1415). At the same time, a popular demand for church reform inspired a major intellectual movement known as the Renaissance (1300–1600), encouraged a drive to revive primitive Christianity according to Christ's original principals, and bestowed the instruments of secular power on kings.

Between 1309 and 1377, the papacy relocated from Rome to Avignon, France, due to a dispute between the French monarchy and the pope over church taxes; this move began the "Babylonian Captivity" (a reference to the forty years of enslavement of the Jews in Babylon after the fall of Jerusalem in 586 BCE). Philip IV of France (reigned 1285–1314) had claimed the right to tax the French church as he prepared to go to war with England over the old question of who had ultimate authority over the French estates held by the English crown, the king of France or England. Pope Boniface VIII (reigned 1294–1303) had rejected Philip's claim to the right to tax the French church by issuing a papal Bull entitled Unam Sanctum. Like Pope Gelasius I (reigned 492–96), Boniface had argued that there were two authorities recognized by God: the church and the state. Since the church took responsibility for the soul, the authority of the pope exceeded that of the state. Thus, the king of France should not challenge the pope's authority in deciding any matter concerning the church. Philip responded by creating the Estates General in an effort to mobilize a general consensus among France's men of estates in support of his plan to tax the French church. Upon receiving this support, Philip decided to send a force to Italy to kidnap the pope in 1303. An outraged Boniface VIII was aghast at the audacity of Philip's actions, but, powerless to deal with this affront, Boniface VIII soon went into a decline and died that same year.

In an attempt to thwart any further military assaults against the papacy, the College of Cardinals decided to elect a French pope, Clement V (reigned 1305–14), to mollify Philip. However, in moving the church administration to Avignon, Clement created a crisis for the papacy by staffing his bureaucracy with Frenchmen.

With a French pope and a College of Cardinals dominated by French appointees, the papacy developed a strong French bias and ceased to represent all of Catholic Christendom. Shortly after the papacy moved to Avignon, the Hundred Years War (1338–1453) erupted, turning England and all its allies into enemies of the pope due to his blatant support of France. Thus, so long as the papacy remained in France, the church suffered from a secular bias. At the same time, this bias coincided with the famine, plague, and warfare that raged across Europe and seemed to signal God's anger.

To ease the criticism leveled against the Avignon papacy, Pope Gregory XI (reigned 1370–78) decided to return to Rome. Making this decision in 1377, he did not complete the move until 1378. His sudden death that same year, however, created a new crisis for the church: who should be the next pope? The people of Rome were determined to keep the papacy within their city, but the majority of cardinals were French. The tension was extraordinary but resulted in the compromise election of Urban VI (reigned 1378–89).

A Neapolitan by birth, Urban VI took an immediate dislike to his French cardinals and purged the College. Such a high-handed action against those who had elected him caused the College of Cardinals to leave Rome, venturing first to Anagni and then to Fondi, where they reconvened, nullified Urban's election, and selected Robert of Geneva as Clement VII. Now Europe had two popes; both of whom tried to staff the church. Called the "Great Schism," this extraordinary state of affairs lasted from 1378 to 1415. During this entire time, the die-off continued, seemingly indicating that God's anger at Christendom had actually increased. This anger raised a central question: if the pope was unable to keep his own house in order, how was the papacy supposed to save Europe from sin? The great flowering of intellectual thought and art known as the Renaissance (1300–1600), and a general desire to restore Christ's original message to the Universal Church, served as responses to this question.

The Renaissance, 1300–1600

The Renaissance, the period that marks the end of the Middle Ages and the dawn of modernity, reflected a fascination with ancient science, philosophy, and human studies. Unlike any other similar period of recovery, however, this final Renaissance exceeded anything the Crusades in Spain or the Holy Land had generated. This final Renaissance inspired Europeans to plunge into their monasteries and libraries, seeking out dusty old texts to help them answer the questions raised by the crises that God's anger forced all Christians to face.

The Renaissance represented a study of humanity itself, both as a manifestation of the way people should relate to God and as a way to discover how people should relate to one another. First expressed in Latin, and then in Greek, authors of the Renaissance looked to Cicero, Livy, Plato, and Aristotle to grasp the meaning of life as a secular and religious experience. Resurrecting the concept of *civic virtue*, the ancient Greek conceptual basis for social and political conduct, Renaissance authors tried to integrate human conduct on Earth with the type of behavior that gained one entry into Heaven. Free will, personal choice, individual conduct, and human history became the foundations for understanding the "Good," as the original Greek and Roman philosophies had intended.

First to take this approach, Francesco Petrarch (1304–74) served the Avignon papal court as a minor official. He used the leisure his office provided to produce a body of literary work in Latin of such quality that he inspired a revival of the language. At the same time, he developed the Humanist perspective, i.e., a focus on human conduct consistent with ancient Greek and Roman standards that changed the value of time: the ancient era was the age of "light," while the Middle Ages had ushered in "darkness." Authors inspired by Petrarch's example began a search for ancient texts that would enhance their command of Latin as an ancient Roman language rather than as a tool of the church. In the process, the *Humanitates* emerged.

The Humanitates, or Humanities, produced such men as Leonardi Bruni (1361–1444), Lorenzo Valla (1406–57), Leon Battista Alberti (1404–74), Pico della Mirandola (1463–94), Benvenuto Cellini (1500–74), and Niccolò Machiavelli (1469–1527) from Italy; and Desiderius Erasmus (1466–1536), Jacque Lefèvre d'Étaples (1455–1536), John Colet (1466–1519), and Sir Thomas More (1478–1535) who came from realms north of the Alps. Each belonged to a complex intellectual movement that caused a transformation of belief in Europe. Each revived history, reinforced Petrarch's concept of time, restored ancient standards of conduct, and released the medieval imagination from church dogma. All of those listed above felt that a fresh look at the world and salvation was essential to the well-being of Christendom. Thus, each Renaissance author fueled a desire to return to the past to see how humans should act, and what Christ was really like. Finally, each asked fundamental questions of the church that the pope could not answer. For the details of this movement, see Chapter Eighteen, in Unit Three in Volume Two.

Aiding in this process, the final days of Constantinople added the Greek language as a tool with which the Renaissance men might restore a Greco-Roman past. With the Ottoman Turks closing in on Constantinople, Byzantine scholars left the crumbling Eastern Roman Empire to seek their fortunes in Europe; these Greek intellectuals brought with them everything they knew. Thus, their very use of the Greek language—the original tongue of Plato and Aristotle—helped Renaissance scholars penetrate far deeper than what Arabic commentaries had revealed. This recovery of an ancient language revealed to the West the mystery of how pagan wisdom could work in a non-Christian context. Thus, European scholars could finally see Greek and Roman science, philosophy, and the arts in their own context, independently of an Arabic or Catholic interpretation.

Thus the Renaissance created a new intellectual energy that challenged the pope just at the time when the kings of Europe seemed most eager to increase their authority. Simultaneously, the frequency of death in the midst of an Apocalyptic age raised questions of salvation that Renaissance scholars seemed better equipped to answer than the pope. The result was a new intellectual challenge to the papacy that broke the pope's monopoly on belief. Accordingly, the church's command over orthodoxy began to erode, and in its place Greco-Roman solutions began to surface.

Western European Kings

Even as the papacy floundered, the kings of Western Europe redefined politics by perfecting the art of war. England and France used one another as targets in their 116-year struggle that saw them develop very determined and effective armies. At the same time, the Spanish and Portuguese had also developed a very efficient military as their seven-hundred-year-old war against the Moors continued until the 1390s for Portugal and 1492 for Spain. Each kingdom had refined their methods of raising armies, financing warfare, and unifying a consensus that justified their various causes. All of these royal actions welded these four kingdoms into very powerful monarchies just as the papacy went into a sharp decline.

To finance these wars, the kings of France, England, and the Iberian Peninsula had turned to the banks of north Italian network cities for ready cash. Now these Italian cities enjoyed a banking bonanza as the Bardi, Peruzzi, Di Medici, Pitti, and Strozzi families developed lending houses that used branch offices and letters of credit to supply each king's demand for money. Simultaneously, the Estates General of France, Parliament of England, and the cortes system of Spain assembled the church, the nobility, and the corporate towns of each realm in order to increase taxes and support royal war efforts. Using these new sources of income the kings of France, England, Spain, and Portugal purchased knight-killing weapons to drive away their enemies.

The cannon, the long bow, the Swiss pike, and the crossbow swept across Europe, changing the relationship between the king and his nobility. Now the monopoly on coercion passed from the great lords of Europe into the hands of the monarchy, as each king developed the financial means to mobilize the armies he needed to dispose of his enemies. Hence, the office of the king became the center of the respective realms as new mercenary forces responded to the demand for men-in-arms and kings developed the means to pay for them. As a result, kingship became the only institution with the ability to assemble a kingdom's great estates, mobilize the support needed to fight a general war, and pay for these military efforts with a reliable financial base.

And as the power of kings waxed, that of the papacy waned, and the Middle Ages drew to a close. The five key institutions that underlay the shifting foundation of power from the Early Middle Ages through the High Middle Ages to the Late Middle Ages reveal a complex cultural system that never really worked. Poorly integrated, the Volk, the Catholic Church, kingship, lords and vassals, and private property may have provided the institutional design that carried Europe through the Middle Ages, but these same institutions proved to be dysfunctional and never really produced a stable social order.

Suggested Reading

The Early Middle Ages

Collins, Roger, *Early Medieval Europe: 300–1000* (Basingstoke: Macmillan Education, 1991).

———, *Early Medieval Spain: Unity in Diversity, 400–1000* (New York: St. Martin's Press, 1983).

Campbell, James, ed., *The Anglo-Saxons* (Oxford: Phaidon, 1982).

Hussey, J. M., *The Byzantine World* (Westport, Conn.: Greenwood Press, 1982).

Magoulias, H. J., *Byzantine Christianity: Emperor, Church, and the West,* (Detroit: Wayne State University Press, 1982).

Riche, Pierre, *The Carolingians: A Family Who Forged Europe* (Philadelphia: University of Pennsylvania Press, 1993).

Wolfram, Herwig, *History of the Goths* (Berkeley: University of California Press. 1987).

Wood, Ian, *The Merovingian Kingdoms 450–751* (London: Longman, 1994).

The High Middle Ages

Bartlett, Robert, *The Making of Europe: Conquest, Colonization, and Cultural Change, 950–1350* (Princeton, N.J.: Princeton University Press, 1993).

Berman, H., *Law and Revolution: Formation of the Western Legal Tradition* (Cambridge: Harvard University Press, 1983).

Bisson, Thomas N., ed., *Cultures of Power: Lordship, Status, and Process in Twelfth Century Europe* (Philadelphia: University of Pennsylvania Press, 1995).

Clanchy, M. T., *England and Its Rulers, 1066–1272* (New York: B & N Imports, 1983).

Dunbabin, Jean, *France in the Making, 834–1180* (New York: Oxford University Press, 1985).

France, John, *Western Europe in the Age of the Crusades, 1000–1300* (Ithaca, N.Y.: Cornell University Press, 1999).

Finucane, Ronald C., *Soldiers of the Faith: Crusaders and Muslims at War* (New York: St. Martin's Press, 1984).

Fuhrmann, Horst, *Germany in the High Middle Ages, 1050–1200* (New York: Cambridge University Press, 1986).

Ferruolo, S. C., *The Origins of the University,* (Stanford: Stanford University Press, 1985).

Hanawalt, Barbara A. and Kathlyn L. Reyerson, eds., *City and Spectacle in Medieval Europe* (Minneapolis: University of Minnesota Press, 1994).

Lopez, Robert, *The Commercial Revolution of the Middle Ages, 950–1350* (New York: Cambridge University Press, 1971).

Lynch, Joseph H., *The Medieval Church: A Brief History* (New York: Longman, 1992).

Semaan, Khalil, *Islam and the Medieval West: Aspects in Intercultural Relations,* (Binghamton, N.Y.: State University of New York Press, 1980).

The Late Middle Ages

Allmand, C., *The Hundred Years War: England France at War, c. 1300–1450,* (New York: Cambridge University Press, 1988).

Aries, P., *The Hour of Death,* (New York: Oxford University Press, 1983).

Duffy, Eamon, *Saints and Sinners: A History of the Popes* (New Haven, Conn.: Yale University Press, 1997).

McNeill, William H., *Plagues and People* (New York: Anchor Press, 1976).

Mollat, Michel and Philippe Wolff, *Popular Revolutions of the late Middle Ages* (London: Allen and Unwin, 1973).

Oakley, F., *The Western Church in the Later Middle Ages,* (New York: Cornell University Press, 1985).

Ozment, Stephen, *The Age of Reform, 1250–1550* (New York: Yale University Press, 1980).

Zieger, Philip, *The Black Death* (New York: Harper and Row, 1969).

XV

ISLAMIC
Africa

Prior to the seventh century CE, before Islam had swept over the African continent transforming the way of life there, an earlier mode of subsistence had developed characteristics that persist to this day. During the ancient era, West African trade settlements had dotted the banks of the Niger and Senegal rivers. Clustered around the trading centers were thatched huts swarming with children and chickens, the outlying fields planted with vegetables, millet, and sorghum. A few towns of reddish mud-brick buildings on the banks of these rivers featured towering leafy green trees, the shade from which cooled potters who displayed their ceramics on local beaches. Salt blocks brought from the hot, arid interior of the Sahara by Berber nomads were also on display. Gold mined from alluvial deposits on the Niger River dotted the ground, while traders deftly guided their pirogue skiffs around the stray hippopotmus or crocodile as they traveled up and down the rivers. In the weekly markets erected near the town centers, then as now, brightly attired and bejeweled women displayed homegrown produce and family handiwork of beads, glass, and metal. In this highly organized and competitive environment, the women drove the hardest bargains, their loud and firm voices informing even the casual observer that female hands held the purse strings. Enjoying an economic power unusual in other parts of the world, the women of the region dominated the marketplace. A few steps down one of the many dusty streets off the market plaza brought one to the ironmongers, women included, who produced some of the most valuable trade items available.

Once back home, these same market women would start the long process of cooking and serving dinner. They also took over the care of their children, whom siblings and other relatives had watched in their absence. Thus in the pre-Islamic sub-Saharan Africa, women were the stable center of the family, though not its head. That role belonged to fathers in what is still a patriarchal society. Indeed, every man in the culture aspired to head a large family. From the nuclear center to the extended family, the clan, and the tribe of the corporate lineage, all descended from the common sacred ancestor who demanded loyalty so that all members of the family understood their duty.

From their youth, men competed with remarkable intensity for the attention of the future mothers of their children. Many times, it became necessary to abduct women from other tribes to find these men wives. Male virility and female fertility were the overarching topics of concern in all African homes. Children were adored and pampered; in the ideal, they were considered most precious, for they defined the family's future. And in practice they were essential to household production and social status.

This emphasis on male virility and female fertility, and the desire for numerous children, speaks to the difficulty of sustaining a large human population in sub-Saharan Africa. As stated in Chapter Nine, in much of sub-Saharan Africa, soils were poor, the jungle thick, and diseases rife—malaria, sleeping sickness, leprosy, smallpox, and guinea worms, to name a few. Famines occurred on the average of every seventy years, killing one-third to one-half of the local population. Death was so common that in the eighteenth century a general decree went out stating that only a woman's fourth dead child had the right to a funeral. With the warfare and plagues attendant upon drought, even basic foods like animal milk to feed babies nearly disappeared. Relying on breast-feeding for up to four years of age to compensate for limited supplies, African women reduced their fertility, limiting the number of conceptions and actual births. Simultaneously, the average life expectancy at birth for a sub-Saharan African was barely over twenty years.

Under these circumstances, only a few densely populated areas punctuated an enormous expanse of unsettled territories, the "bush." Understandably, the residents of these exceptional areas lived under clouds of danger, as their centers became targets for breakaway families or nomads seeking to kidnap women and children. In dire circumstances, such as we see today in the Sudan, warlord gangs fought over food, water, and power, with people selling themselves into slavery for a bowl of millets or sorghum.

Corporate Lineage and State Formation after 500

Corporate lineage served as the primary unit of government in sub-Saharan Africa prior to 500. Political discipline and order were enforced by the regulations of family, clan, tribe, age-set, and shamanic rituals. These early "stateless" societies were just as efficient at governing as were the more familiar kingdoms appearing for the first time after the fall of the ancient world (500). A village or group of villages fell under the rule of the oldest male, who took advice from a ranking queen mother or council of elders. Evidently, women shared power with men and enjoyed significant political positions. They led age-set organizations and participated in conciliation and peacemaking, healing and divining, and above all, in business and marketing.

With respect to religion, ritual, and sacred rites, native Africa was "animistic" (i.e., from *anima* Latin for *alive*). Nature was seen as animated by divine spirits whose cult objects might be ancient baobab trees or sacred crocodiles or even a mysterious iron pillar set in the earth. Disorderly spirits resided in the bush or uncultivated forest and had to be appeased. Shamans served as intermediaries between the divine powers and humans, between the wild bush and the tame village. Each village might have a male or female gifted in shamanic lore. Within a wide region, one shaman usually gained renown and stayed busy with the needs of the local residents, since evil sorcerors or witches could wreak havoc on a community. Women, especially unfortunate ones, were often suspected of being witches; as outcasts, those who were suspect were usually the barren, the poor, and the powerless.

Ceremonies of passage into adulthood—which included male and female circumcision—and initiation into social membership involved suffering and pain. Nevertheless, the culture felt that these rituals were a necessary transition from the bush (wild) into the village (society). Ideally one was born and died in a domestic area. The corpses of those who suffered "abnormal" deaths—by execution, suicide, or drowning—were considered taboo and were left to rot in the wild.

Just as in ancient North Africa, especially Egypt, in sub-Saharan Africa the cosmos and nature were considered as one seamless unit. Natural, physical phenomena and social-moral metaphysical phenomena were held as intertwined parts of the same reality. Nevertheless, there was a tendency to juxtapose order with chaos, the wild with the civilized, in the same way that the modern Western imagination framed good with evil. Much of Africa, both North and sub-Saharan, produced ritual and myth that involved the movement from one side of this juxtaposition to the other, or required the integration of the two. Most African groups acknowledged a single creative power with many spirit manifestations. In addition, they believed that their ancestral spirits could and did intervene in the lives of mortals.

Unlike the later medieval and Renaissance European view, African thinkers were open, practical, and theoretically eclectic and tolerant. Given the lack of authoritative texts and a highly developed orthodoxy, many native and alien ideas and practices were welcomed as long as they mixed and worked well with local beliefs.

Muslim Africa: Islam's General Impact

After 650, Muslims spreading Allah's recently revealed message swept across Africa starting near Cairo. They proceeded from Egypt southeast through East Africa, westward through North Africa, and southwest through West Africa, knitting the residents of the top half of the continent and the coasts into the new dynamic religion.

Islam's astounding success in the rapid and peaceful conversion of Africans was due in part to an effective combination of intellectual, moral, and economic incentives that they valued as well as a willingness by these Africans to assimilate foreign ideas. Islam also offered the Africans a degree of political savvy as yet unknown on the continent and a high level of the religious passions needed to organize armies. Economic and moral factors predominated in Africa, while ancestor worship, which proved necessary for managing the politics of corporate lineages that pre-dated Islam, continued. Islam also proved to be a religion admirably suited to the commercial societies of Africa, while Africans reconciled Mohammed's strict monotheism to the persistent belief that African kings had descended from divine parents. Accordingly, Islam enhanced the prosperity and intensified the political and social processes that led to the fabled African trading kingdoms and empires of the middle years of world history.

As economic and moral considerations were important, Islam was a religion admirably suited to Africa's commercial societies. Muslim traders and warriors integrated Arabia and the commercial sectors of Africa into a larger economic system based on the land bridge that united the three major continents of Eurasia; this facilitated the commercial connections needed to sup-

This modern-day camel caravan, hardly changed from those centuries ago, is transporting salt from Lac Assal to Ethiopia. Photo courtesy Djibouti Lafforgue.

port the rise of great African trade kingdoms and empires between 500 and 1000. Proceeding across North Africa, Muslims reached Kairwan, Tunisia, and named the new province *Ifriqiya* (from which the word *Africa* derives) and then spread south.

Muslim Sahara

The fervor of Muslims to spread the word of Allah and the allure of trade gave a new vigor to the old desire to cross the centuries-old long-distance Saharan trade routes. The nomadic Tuareg nobles of Berber ancestry eventually converted to Islam and joined with Moors, Mauritanian nobles of Arab ancestry, to act as caravan conductors and guards. As such, these Tuareg intermediaries coordinated business details at each stop of a planned trade caravan, procuring the needed camels, trade goods, and camel drivers. Commonly, caravans comprised as many as 20,000–30,000 camels and stretched fifteen miles across the desert. One caravan was reputed to have as many as 50,000 camels. The great trans-Saharan trade caravans went from one town to another in a chain-link pattern. Yet it was impossible to cross the Sahara in one stretch. At key transit points, camel loads were transferred to donkeys and then to humans, since in certain sub-Saharan regions one entered dense rainforests where only human porters could carry goods through the narrow, winding paths.

Hence, the Sahara Desert ceased to be a barrier to trade and culture. These elaborate and well-organized trips eventually converted the Sahara's vast sea of sand into a well-traveled highway. In time, the new ideas launched by Mohammed began to make as deep an impression in the sub-Saharan grasslands of Africa as they had in the north coastal regions. African history was about to change dramatically.

Muslim West Africa

Muslim merchants and nomadic Berber converts followed ancient trade routes across the Sahara, their camels piled high with the diversified products of North Africa and of the rest of an expanding Muslim world. En route, the merchants loaded heavy slabs of salt

mined by slaves from the blisteringly hot and dry pits of Tagaza and the northwest Sahara. Salt, necessary for human and animal nutrition as well as the preservation of food, was the chief mineral export sent south. So important was this mineral that the people living in the city-states of Hausa in Central Africa supposedly had fifty different words for salt. At the southern edge of the desert, the caravans entered the city gates of thriving sub-Saharan trade towns like Old Jenne and Timbuktu. There they exchanged their products for millet, kola nuts, iron, and, above all, gold, some of it taken from nearby Wangara and Bambuk, an eight-day's journey from Ghana's capital, and some from Senegal and Faleme riverbeds.

Slaves became one of many commodities for sale in African societies very early in their history. Given the vast amount of land on the continent and the relatively tiny number of people available, each human being was precious, and therefore a potential target for the slave trade. The people sold as slaves had usually committed capital crimes, or were prisoners of war, debtors, or abandoned women and children. For many such persons, enslavement was preferable to certain death. Even slave soldiers were common. In addition, since the Muslims of the Ottoman and Fatimid Empires as well as the Slave Sultanate of India had used slavery as one of the steps in the process of conversion, the creation of human bondage did not carry any social stigma. Furthermore, women slaves had the potential of bearing many children, which made them especially valuable. Finally, the physical beauty, strength, and exotic qualities of black slaves placed them in high demand in the Muslim world, slave raids and kid-nappings becoming routine ways to provide wealthy households with domestic workers and concubines.

In contrast, gold became the property of kings. Legend has it that one nugget unearthed in Africa at this time was large enough to hold a roped horse in place. Gold was usually traded in the form of dust, gravel, pebbles, and nuggets, and was so abundant that it was said to carpet the Sahara. In fact, the gold traded across the Sahara became the chief source of precious metals used in the vast trade system of Europe during the High Middle Ages. Yet precisely where and how gold was obtained remained a guarded secret in the kingdoms with knowledge of the mines.

Less valuable than gold, but still highly prized, were kola nuts. Regarded as an aphrodisiac, stimulant, and thirst-quencher kola nuts sold extremely well in African markets. To this day, they are offered in hospitality on the street corners in the towns of West Africa.

Even after the arrival of Islam, African women continued to rule the marketplace. Their bold behavior,

Abu Abdullah Mohammed ibn Battuta

Abu Abdullah Mohammed Ibn Battuta (1304–69) began exploring Europe, Africa, Asia, and the Middle East in 1325 at the age of twenty-one. He spent thirty years (1325–55) in his travels, visited what are today some forty-four countries, and traversed an estimated 75,000 miles. He was an excellent observer, tireless chronicler, and major contributor to medieval geography.

Born in Tangiers, Morocco, Ibn Battuta spent the next twenty years planning his extensive journey. Gone for thirty years, he finally settled in Fez, Morocco, where he dictated an account of all he had seen. Dead at the age of 65, he left a geographic legacy more impressive then Marco Polo's travels.

Over the course of the thirty years that he was abroad, Ibn Battuta traveled through Algiers, Tunis, Egypt, Pales-tine, Syria, Arabia, Shiraz, Mesopotamia, and then returned to Mecca to perform the Hajj. Next he trekked to Jeddah and sailed to Yemen, Aden, and Mombasa, East Africa. After this trip, he returned to Oman and Mecca in 1332 via Hormuz, Siraf, Bahrain, and Yamama. And after a brief break, and a false start for India, Ibn Battuta returned to the Middle East, revisiting Cairo, Palestine, Syria, Anatolia, and Sinope in preparation for a voyage across the Black Sea to Constantinople, a trek through southern Ukraine, and a trip across the Hindukush where he entered Afghanistan, visiting Ghani, and Kabul, and crossing into India.

Visiting most of the major urban centers of the Slave Sultanate, he passed through central India where he embarked on a ship at Malabar to reach the Maldive Islands and Ceylon. Returning to the Maldives, he made for Bengal and visited Kamrup, Sylhet, and Sonargaon. Next on his list was Sumatra, Malaya, Cambodia, and China. In China he visited Canton, Beijing, and Hangzhou. Returning along the same route he had taken going to China, he set out for the Middle East to reach Mecca once again in 1348. Crossing North Africa to Morocco, he prepared for a trek to Spain and another into sub-Saharan Africa where he visited Mali in 1352–53. On his return to Fez, Morocco, Ibn Battuta was ready to settle down; then he dictated the results of his journey.

Ibn Battuta's voyages and overland travel produced one of the most remarkable accounts of his era. His contribution to our modern understanding of medieval geographic is priceless. He has taken modern scholars where no medieval Christian could have gone in the Middle Ages. He has also covered lands that Marco Polo had visited and reinforced the power of that traveler's observations. Added to these extensive trips is an intelligence that distinguished Ibn Battuta's accounts of what he had seen. Tireless, careful, thorough, exhaustive, and detailed, Ibn Battuta filled in blanks about the past that no one else could have. No contemporary observer came close to the distances he traveled, or the care he took in his chronicles.

Ibn Battuta, *Travels in Asia and Africa, 1325–1354*, Translated by H. A. R. Gibb, (London: Routledge. 1929).

however, scandalized many visiting Arabs who believed women had no place in business. Then as now, in the hot climate African women went around only partly clothed and spoke their own minds with dignity and conviction. The Arab traveler and writer Ibn Battuta who had explored and commented on China, the Middle East, Europe, and Africa, was critical of the lovely, unveiled women "lacking in humility." Despite his worldly sophistication, he disapproved of their husbands who had allowed all these females to take lovers and join men in intellectual debate.

As the new Islamic trade system grew, it generated new levels of wealth but became monopolized by African families, who extended their control over ever wider territories. By 800, New Jenne administered some sixty-five neighboring settlements and enjoyed the protection of towering city walls and gates. In Nigeria's Igboukwe, artifacts from the graves

Since Muslims of the Ottoman and Fatimid Empires as well as the Slave Sultanate of India had used slavery as one of the steps in the process of conversion, the creation of human bondage did not carry any social stigma. A convoy of captured slaves in the East African Sudan. © Mary Evans Picture Library / The Image Works.

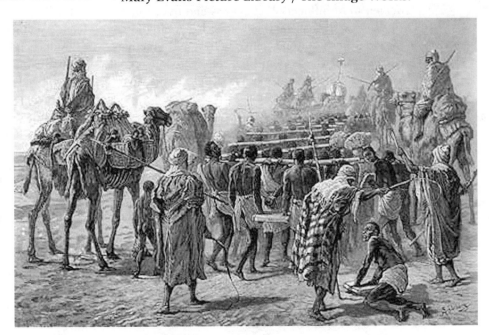

of the elite included highly refined bronze goods and wares from Egypt and India. In these growing urban centers the heads of communities and the upper class converted to Islam not only to serve Allah, but also for trade benefits, the business networks, literacy and culture, and egalitarian treatment of merchant households. Islam offered access to a sophisticated new lifestyle so that high culture rapidly became Islamic culture. In rural villages and the hinterland, on the other hand, manufacturers and providers of trade goods were largely left out of the lucrative commerce system and remained non-Islamic, native animists who still placed religious value on ancestor worship, which kept them loyal to the court cities that served as trade centers for African kings.

Around 800, the first of the famous medieval West African kingdoms emerged. One of the war kings of the Soninke people, whose territory ranged from Soninke to Mande, formed a village federation around the upper Niger and Senegal rivers that became known as the *Ghana* (sacred king). Of necessity, he developed a bureaucracy and army under his sway as "sacred king." From the earliest written accounts by the Arab writers like the Spanish Moor turned geographer Al Bakri (ca. 1067), we learn that the sacred king ruled from Kumbi-Sahel, where he commanded a market rich in iron goods, especially swords and spears, and gold.

Ghana, like the later kingships of Mali and Songhai, was a sacred kingship or paramount chiefdom relying on the loyalties of subchiefs all bound together in a divine corporate lineage. In these kingdoms the warrior function was pervasively ritualized; daily cult action linked the living to the dead and their powers through the animistic bonds of heaven and earth. Their women were influential as queens and queen mothers, and as shamans and advisers; Islam offered access to a world beyond native beliefs and practices, but the sacred king could not afford to convert for fear of losing the loyalty of his people to his divine ancestors.

As is often the case in highly centralized monarchies, the strengths of Ghana were also its weaknesses. Rigid control at the level of the divine king, along with the delegation of power to subchiefs, eventually resulted in loose oversight at the periphery of the kingdom, the borders of which were unclear in the first place. Subchiefs and warlords fomented rebellion among villagers and conquered peoples farther afield. These warlords retained animist and native African culture and saw themselves left out of the prosperity enjoyed by their Islamic overlords. A general drying of the Sahara and advancing sands made agriculture increasingly difficult and opened the door to ambitious Berbers who

invaded Ghana in the 1000s and sparked a civil war. Called the *Almoravids*, these Berbers swept through Ghana taking Kumbi-Sahel in 1076. Thereafter, they forced the sacred king to convert to Islam. This conversion broke the bonds of the divine corporate lineage and Ghana began to disintegrate. The winner of this disintegration was the smaller state of Mali.

Mali means "where the king dwells"; the people were southern Mandinke, which included lands that stretched from the west coast through Ghana to Songhai. In the thirteenth century their great magician king, Sundiata Keita, took over Ghana's position in African and world trade to Europe and the East. In the process his kingdom grew larger, spread beyond Ghana, and became more sophisticated and more prosperous than its predecessor. Part of the reason for this was the opening of a new gold field in thirteenth century Bure.

As Mali rose to prominence, African trade items became ever more crucial to the functioning of medieval Europe. In the thirteenth century, gold surpassed silver as Europe's main currency, and most of the gold in fourteenth-century Europe came from Mali. Accordingly, Mali's gold was essential to medieval Muslim commerce and is credited for the revival of European trade.

In the report of the Arab traveler and tireless commentator Ibn Battuta (1352), Mali's enlightened and effective laws guaranteed the traveler's safety, while medical care ensured his health and comfort. He also praised standards of sanitation and food preparation in the kingdom, as well as the physical beauty of the architecture. These were features of culture that could be attributed to Islamic influences, which he recognized, for they reflected the discipline of a Muslim ethic. He was less impressed with what he observed in the bush villages where the wild dancing of animistic ceremonies continued to be practiced.

At its height early in the fourteenth century, Mali's famed Muslim king, Mansa Musa, oversaw an empire of 8 million people from Morocco to Timbuktu, a larger, more organized, and richer entity than any European state of the same period. The victories of Mansa Musa's royal army were respected in Egypt and Morocco, and they generated elaborate foreign ministries and diplomacy. In 1324, Mansa Musa took one hundred camels loaded with a ton of gold dust and five hundred slaves, each carrying a six-pound gold staff, and threaded his way across the Sahara to Mecca. Upon reaching Cairo, Egypt, the king magnanimously gave away so much gold that the value of this precious metal remained depressed in that region for a generation thereafter. After this demonstration of wealth, Mali became known as the land of gold and never failed to appear on any world map.

In returning to Timbuktu, Mansa Musa brought back with him architects, engineers, and artists who helped turn his city into the greatest Muslim African center of learning and culture. He built palaces, mosques, and *madrassas* (universities), installing and subsidizing scholars and other experts. The biggest business in Timbuktu were said to be bookstores; visitors to Mali today can see some of those very books in private homes. In 1500 Timbuktu lay in the midst of vast cultivated fields and cattle pastures, lakes, and wells of sweet water. Inside its great walls stood homes for 25,000 cosmopolitan people—Muslims, animists, Berbers, and sub-Saharan peoples all lived together. Timbuktu's markets displayed salt, gold, cloth, copper, iron, ivory, ebony, ostrich plumes, slaves, glass, and beads.

The history of the third great West African state paralleled that of Mali. In the fourteenth century, the Malian empire frayed due to palace infighting, quarrels over the succession to the throne, the rebellious actions of subchiefs, and attacks by nomadic invaders. Soon vassal states began to break away from Mali's rule; one of these followed the tributary warlords of Gao who established a new kingdom called Songhai. By the late fifteenth century, the most successful of these warlords, Sunni Ali Ber (1464–92), challenged Timbuktu and began to expand through Malian territory using the combined forces of heavy cavalry and a river-based navy. He assembled an empire that not only incor-porated Mali, but also expanded the trade zone farther east to Lake Chad. Yet, Sunni Ali Ber became infamous because when he attacked Timbuktu, he slaughtered the Muslim scholars at the university there because they had loyally supported Mali. Accordingly, Muslim hostility toward Sunni Ali Ber mounted due to the brutality of this act. Then, when he accidentally died in 1492, the Muslims sought revenge by supporting a slave officer of Ali's army, Askiya Mohammed Touré (1493–1528). Mohammed Touré usurped the throne from Ali's son and renewed Songhai empire by using a new Islamic passion that expanded on Sunni Ali's chain-mailed cavalry and river navy. Like Mansa Musa before him, Mohammed piously endowed the university center of Timbuktu with a giant new mosque, subsidized Muslim scholars, and went on a pilgrimage to Mecca, where he distributed huge amounts of gold to the poor. Under Mohammed Touré, Songhai was a remarkable world state until his death in 1528.

Despite this highly structured form of government, Mohammed did not end his days as ruler of Songhai, for his own sons toppled him from power in 1528, signaling the weakness in this newly established empire. While Songhai remained a key part of the trade network into the sixteenth century, its rivals already had begun to pick away at the periphery of this kingdom.

The fall of Songhai came at the hands of the Moroccans, who used a mercenary army and gunpowder to penetrate south and defeat the Songhai army in 1591 but continued resistance, and disease prevented the Moroccans from creating a new empire. Morocco's victory, however, did eliminate Songhai as a trading empire, which, in turn, led to the collapse of West Africa as a unified commercial region. The gold fields now belonged to several rival kingdoms that could not organize this region into one political system.

Second only in importance to gold, slaves also became a principal item of exchange in the middle years. And it was the high demand for slaves from sub-Saharan Africa that created a tragic precedent that later drew many thousands of Africans into the Atlantic world's (Europe, Africa, Latin America, and North America) early modern commercial system (1492–1763). Leading the way in slavery as a business was the kingdom of Kanem-Bornu.

Muslim Central Africa and Its Non-Muslim Frontier

The big three African kingdoms of the middle years of world history—Ghana, Mali, and Songhai—were spectacular kingdoms, but there were others of unique character: Kanem-Bornu, Hausa, Kongo, Yoruba, and Benin.

In the fourteenth century on the fertile agricultural plateau around Lake Chad, the kingdoms of Kanem-Bornu rose to prominence under the leadership of a flamboyant Muslim elite that exploited the slave trade and dispatched their mounted cavalry on violent military raids. They maintained their elite status by special dress and dialect. Ruthless, brandishing swords and thrusting spears, their pride was legendary. Like medieval knights, they held to a code of chivalry, courage, and an indifference toward suffering, their own and that of their victims. Due to the military skills of this elite cavalry, two slave-based kingdoms arose: first Kanem and then Bornu.

Kanem raided villages in the western Sudan, captured and transported their human cargo to markets in North Africa, and exchanged these slaves for warhorses in order to maintain a 40,000-man cavalry. With these mounted horsemen, the warriors of Kanem could easily attack their neighbors and keep up a steady flow of humans north. Unfortunately, the trek into North Africa required crossing the Sahara, which proved to be a harrowing journey for the thousands of people trapped by Kanem in bondage. Accordingly, thousands died.

Justifying these slave raids as Jihad, the warriors of Kanem kept the Middle East supplied with bondspeople. Despite their Muslim faith, they maintained that their king, whom they called a *mai*, was a divine being. And, as a god, he lived in seclusion in a royal court whence power emerged in an absolute form, his divinity. This contradiction with the absolute power of Allah as the one true God, existed side by side, just as it did in Ghana's and Mali's monarchies, and it helped to hold the loyalty of Africans to the court of the mai. Aided by a centralized bureaucracy that implemented his will, the mai of Kanem embraced Islam as a valuable tool in his relations with Muslim states to the north.

The mai's principle trade route followed the caravans through the Sahara to Tripoli, on the Mediterranean coast some 1,500 miles to the north. Two secondary routes directed caravans in opposite directions: one to the east that led to Morocco, and one to the west that ended at the Red Sea. Both, however, added more than 1,000 miles to the trip for slaves forced to travel north. Every such caravan transported thousands of these slaves to markets.

Kanem dominated the slave trade for two centuries, reaching the zenith of its power early in the thirteenth century. At that time, the mai commanded a mobile force of 40,000 men. Yet that power waned rapidly as a bitter dispute developed in the court between rival factions of the ruling family. Bornu to the southwest broke away as a vassal state to become autonomous in the fifteenth century. As the century unfolded, Bornu's power expanded and Kanem fell to tributary status. Now Bornu took up where Kanem left off.

As specialists in the slave trade, both Bornu and Kanem brought the exchange in humans to a level second only to gold. Since slaves were their most important commodity, the rulers of Kanem-Bornu adopted attitudes toward other human beings that included a level of brutality, which turned people into chattel and established destructive commercial practices that would shape African history when Europe became interested in purchasing slaves after 1492. Kanem and Bornu's kings were divine; as such they bestowed divinity on their lineage. Those outside that lineage, however, were reduced to a status of a simple object or commodity found in nature. Thus, one lineage could raid another and sell its members without a qualm. Added to this mix was Islam and a distorted notion of Jihad that combined religious passion to carry out the morally questionable acts of enslaving others. Thus, a kingdom specializing in slave sales had no problem attacking weaker neighbors and carrying off people as property.

While Kanem and Bornu specialized in slavery, they were not the only ones to sell people. Slaves had been a part of trade in Africa reaching back to Kush and Axum and were among those items sold by Ghana,

Mali, and Songhai. The difference between the commercial empires to the west of Kanem-Bornu, and the Kanem-Bornu itself, was the degree and intensity of the slave trade. This feature of Kanem-Bornu's commerce, and the general participation of African monarchies in slave exchanges, did not bode well for Africa's future.

From an average of 1,000 slaves sold per year in the late seventh and early eighth centuries, the number grew to 4,300 per year during Bornu's prime, circa 1400. Captured in armed raids, most slaves came from families not organized into states or simply too weak to defend themselves against ambitious monarchs. A monarch who wanted to increase his power captured humans from neighboring families, traded them as slaves for horses, and built a mobile army. Kanem-Bornu proved to be the most adept in applying this systematic technique. The exchange rate was estimated at seven to fifteen humans per horse; the speed of these animals then became a tool to expand the range of this monarch's raids.

This early development of the slave trade created major problems for Africa after 1500. The acceptance of a practice of selling humans as a normal item in commerce created habits of trade that exposed Africa to a destructive new demand. When Europe began its commercial expansion after Christopher Columbus and Vasco da Gama made their voyages of discovery, African monarchs became willing partners in the export of humans from their continent. These African habits opened the sub-Saharan world to a human loss that no one could anticipate, and yet, those habits were already well established by 1500.

To the southwest of Kanem-Bornu were the Hausa city-states. Like Ghana and Mali, Hausa's commercial centers emerged from a federation of villages that coalesced into powerful commercial cities. Unlike Ghana and Mali, however, Hausa did not form a single kingdom; rather, the people who occupied these villages generated several major trading centers that took command of the local territory. A king governed each of these trading centers, but none of them proved strong enough to unite the entire region, despite their fabulous wealth.

Hausa's city-states proved to be self-sufficient because each produced food from a fertile region that supported local horticulture, allowed herds to graze on rich grasslands, and provided merchants access to the major trade routes leading north. Like Kanem-Bornu, Hausa participated in the slave trade, but not to the same extent, or with such a singular focus. Yet, the people of Hausa were willing to sell humans, including other Muslims, despite the fact that this practice of selling their co-religionists was contrary to Islamic tradition.

The most important cities in Hausa were Zaria, Kano, and Katsina; these represented the principle centers of trade. Zaria took the lead as the southern most commercial center that became known for its slave raids in the fifteen century. Kano rose to power second to become the wealthiest city of Hausa in the sixteenth century; situated in the center and to the east of Zaira, Kano continued to sell humans, but did not specialize solely in slaves. Kano also sold leather and textile goods. Finally, Katsina replaced Kano as the wealthiest commercial center in Hausa near the end of the sixteenth century. Katsina was situated northwest of Kano and had better access to Hausa's chief customers located the Middle East. The reason for this shift from south to north had to do with access to the Muslim markets in North Africa and Arabia. Yet, after the seventeenth century, with the arrival of European ships off the African coast, the momentum of trade began to move south again.

Already, the cost of the slave trade was enormous. Violent raids undertaken to capture people killed numerous potential slaves. The subsequent confinement and brutal forced march to the north over the caravan routes killed even more enslaved people before any of them had been sold. Much more destructive per capita than the trans-Atlantic trade, this overland trade "killed per sold ratio" made each slave the representative of a figure believed to be five to ten times larger than his or her personal loss to their family. Then the Atlantic trade expanded the total demand for people so much as to make the human drain far more damaging to Africa's population, but the "killed per sold ratio" leveled off at one sold for every two killed in capture and transport. Speaking of humans in this fashion, however, reveals just how destructive it is to think of a person as a commodity available for sale.

Farther removed from the well-traveled trade routes across the Sahara, the Kingdom of Kongo occupied a fertile, well-watered plateau south of the Congo (Zaire) River along the western coast of Africa. Bordered by the grasslands to the north, and surrounded by the equatorial rainforest, Kongo controlled a commercial zone that exchanged goods between the coast and the hilly interior. Situated between the coast, the interior, the grasslands, and the forest, the kings of Kongo built a central government based on taxes and tribute extracted from villages that participated in these local exchanges. With these local exchanges, the kings of Kongo founded a society based on the awe they inspired from the common belief that they functioned as intermediaries between the gods and his divine ancestors. Hence, Kongo was the first society in central Africa to mature just beyond the reach of Islam.

The Mwissikongo, a Kongo royal clan, unified several small chiefdoms during the fourteenth century, built a centralized army, and spread outward by conquest. Captives taken for this military expansion served as slaves who cultivated the rich soil surrounding Mbanza Kongo, a capital constructed on land just south of the Congo River. Concentrated on this fertile soil, the enslaved captives from these wars of conquest produced the food surpluses that fed the court living in Mbanza Kongo. Royal kinsmen administered Kongo's sparse rural population using a system of provincial governors. Although the central government offered social recognition for those who loyally paid their taxes, the king of Kongo struggled with the tendency of outlying villages to break away from the center and migrate into the interior. Still, by the end of the sixteenth century, Kongo boasted a well-administered government that controlled lands about half the size of England, and manufactured such local products as iron, woven goods, and pottery that joined salt production, fishing, and local cultivation.

Farther into the rainforest, beyond the reach of Kongo, human numbers declined relative to the available land. Here political evolution developed much more slowly than on the more populous coast. Stateless village societies clustered around ad hoc local communal councils in which politically astute "big men" could claim the charisma needed to command authority. These big men built small, cohesive, but isolated communities too remote from the trade centers to generate the wealth or power needed to form stable states. Consequently, there were no records of their activities; only tradition and artwork attest to the achievements of these people.

Two of the most artistically notable of these small states were Yoruba and Benin. The Yoruba people had founded a state at Ife by 1000, basing their prosperity on a limited trade in agricultural products, some gold, and the especially impressive humanistic and naturalistic terra cotta sculptures and brass and copper castings of everyday life—beautiful works crafted by skilled artisans in the twelfth and thirteenth centuries.

Benin succeeded Ife in the fifteenth century but maintained the distinct traditions of the latter. The renowned healing and ritual powers of the enlightened and temperate King Ewuare had formed the Benin state out of some two hundred villages. He erected a huge palace at the capital, also called Benin, with courtyards and quarters adorned with native masterworks. Broad, miles-long avenues and mighty defensive walls attracted to the city masters of brass and gold casting and ivory and ebony sculpture. As in the rest of Africa in the middle years, in Benin the queen mother wielded considerable power along with her son. A standing army and trustworthy provincial governors stabilized Benin.

Muslim East Africa and Christian Ethiopia

A thousand years before Christ, during the Egyptian New Kingdom, East African coastal towns had benefited from limited trade with Egyptian pharaohs like Hatshepsut, who risked the perilous Red Sea voyage to Punt (modern Eritrea and Somalia) or with Arabian rulers like the Queen of Sheba (Saba in modern Yemen). By the time of Christ, Greeks, Romans, and Indians had joined the Red Sea trade network, connecting with vessels from the mysterious east sailing into the Persian Gulf and Indian Ocean. The earliest Greek record of this maritime activity dates from the first century CE, *Periplus of the Erythrean Sea*. It lists typical African products as being: rhinoceros horns, tortoise shells, beads, ivory, oils, incense, pearls, coral, amber, fragrant woods, animal skins, grain, brass, copper, iron, gold, and above all, slaves. For these goods, Africa received silk, brocade, glassware, porcelain, and other exotica.

Islam's arrival in Africa in the eighth century accelerated commercial activity along the east coast and provided the economic basis for political and social development. After establishing their foothold in Egypt and North Africa, Muslim Arabs turned their attention south towards partly Christianized Nubia. Islam was not so well embraced by the Nubians, especially now that the latter had converted to the rival religion of Christianity. Accordingly, military encounters there between the followers of the new religions proved to be ferocious.

Yet the spread of Islam proved irresistable elsewhere. As the Arabs swept down the Nile corridor through Nubia, and across to the Red Sea, they simultaneously moved down the west coast of the Arabian Peninsula. This expansion caught largely Christian Axum in a pincer action, which choked off its life-supporting commerce. Axum's leaders withdrew into the central interior highlands, and by the 1100s the area had evolved an even more colorful blend of cultures, one that now included Judaic features.

The Zagwe dynasty of Christian Axum that had survived the Muslim onslaught exploited Jewish symbols in claiming to have descended from Moses and founding a new city called Zion next to a stream named Yordanos and a hill they called Calvary. Much of Ethiopia's celebrated religious architecture came from this dynasty. The dozen or so cathedrals at Roha, carved out of volcanic rock in the reign of King Lalibela (1181–1221), purportedly were erected by stonemasons during the day and by angels at night. Though Christian, the leaders of Axum found no problem trading slaves for imported Islamic luxuries.

Following the Zagwe dynasty, the Solomonid family, which rose to prominence during the late thirteenth and fourteenth centuries, continued to emphasize a Jewish heritage. Lasting right up until 1970, when the last Solomonid emperor, Haile Selassie, died, the dynasty supposedly had begun in a circa 1000 BCE liaison between King Solomon of Israel and Queen Makeda of Sheba in Arabia. According to legend, the royal couple had installed their son, Menelik, in Axum as *Negus Negusti* (King of Kings). He then began a new family of Christian rulers. A full royal account is the *Kebre Negast* (Glory of Kings), which explains how the Ark of the Covenant (which bore inside it the Ten Commandments) got from Jerusalem to Addis Ababa, Ethiopia, where it reputedly stands housed and guarded to this day.

These Solomonid kings were determined to maintain their Judeo-Christian traditions against those of the Muslims. As the Crusades were going on in Europe, something of the same type of conflicts were threatening Ethiopia. One creative move on the part of the Solomonids to preserve their power and culture involved *Mount Geshen* (Mountain of Kings). As the year 1300 approached, the Solomonid king Yikunno-Amlak conceived of an unusual plan to ensure stability of rule. Relatives and exiles who might challenge him for the throne were sent to live in the palaces atop Mount Geshen. There, living in splendor and absorbing high culture, they were instructed in scholarship, the arts, or theology, each to his or her own taste, to deflect an interest in politics. Some four hundred years later Louis XIV of France would devise a similar plan at Versailles.

In their geographically, religiously, and ethnically diverse land, the Solomonid kings tried to rule with absolute power through vassal monarchs and nobles, with even their daughters and close female relatives serving as governors. The Ethiopian Christian church was the unifying force in society, but only the royal court was truly Christianized, and it was generally intolerant of other belief systems. A unique feature of this court was that it traveled about the country, staying in one area for six months or so at a time while it settled disputes, reinforced royal authority and orthodoxy, oversaw schools and lands, and encouraged trade. In medicine, Ethiopia, like all of Africa, was a crucible for difficult diseases, but only priests were acknowledged as healers. In the long run, since Christianity was in effect a court religion, it was not widely embraced by the rural population nor did it seem to address their problems, much as Islam would fail to appeal to country people hundreds of years later.

The East African Christian kings were really a military dynasty, their warhorses costing up to one-third of the tax revenue they collected from peasants. Constant expansion to extract more taxes, brutal punishments against rebels, and self-discipline to the point of masochism reinforced the area's theme of civilization against nature. Competition with the Muslims over the control of religion and trade continued into the brilliant reign of King Zarayakob (1434–68). This ruler from a family of fabulously wealthy Ethiopians unknown to Europeans during his life gave rise to the medieval legend of Prester John, supposedly a Christian king possessing an African treasure of gold. In the fifteenth century Europeans braved dangers of intercontinental travel to find him.

Farther south, beyond Nubia and Ethiopia, signs of the first Muslim presence are eighth-century postholes of a tiny Kenyan wooden mosque oriented towards Mecca. From there, the Islamic Arab culture took rapid hold in the many trade cities, which boasted fine harbors and safe entry. Arab *dhows* (ships rigged with a triangular or lateen sale) plied the Red Sea, Indian Ocean, and Persian Gulf at three times the speed of a trans-Saharan camel and carried a thousand times the cargo. Arabs were envied middlemen in an opulent worldwide market.

In the eleventh and twelfth centuries, along the eastern coast of Africa, yet another cultural zone matured, this one on the shores of the Indian Ocean and under the influence of Islam. City-states dotting this eastern shore soon found themselves drawn into the Muslim trade network. Because this region already had a long history of foreign contacts with Eurasia based on ocean-going commerce, Arabs merely joined a long list of earlier travelers that included Indonesians, Southeast Asians, Indians, and the peoples of the Greco-Roman world. As mentioned in Chapter Nine, these earlier contacts accelerated cultural growth in Africa by introducing new foods that included Southeast Asian rice along with several valuable root plants such as yams and sweet potatoes. These foods diffused throughout Africa to feed the millions of people that participated in the civilizations there.

The value of trade with the port cities on the East African shoreline to the Arabic world is revealed by how frequently Arab traders touched down in them. This frequency could be seen in the term *al-Zanj*, used to describe the valuable contacts made there. Al-Zanj referred to the black people of the coast that led to a commercial zone called Zanzibar. Gradually, such contact led to a conversion of the al-Zanj to Islam, just as it had in the west sub-Saharan grasslands. Muslims, thus, became so numerous in these port cities as to dominate them as well as in towns inland, prompting the beginnings of a profound linguistic shift. In time, Arabic mixed with Nilo-Saharan languages to create *sawahil*, the Arabic term to describe the emerging language. Later changed to *Swahili*, this term identified a language that diffused throughout the city-state system and became the name of the new culture that developed there.

Written in Arabic script like Persian, Urdu, and Turkish, Swahili reflects another frontier of linguistic penetration so common to Islam as a religion based on a sacred tongue. As mentioned in Chapter Eleven, Arabic carried the prophetic message of Islam, and could be used to measure the penetration of Muslim culture into foreign, non-Arab lands. Hence, Islam had completely won over those people who adopted Arabic, while Persian, Urdu, and Turkish represented regional cultures where non-Arab secular traditions had blended with Mohammed's prophecy to produce a frontier zone in the Middle East. Now the Swahili coast of Africa became another of these cultural frontiers. The hybrid character of Swahili mirrors how Arabic penetrated the African world to transform the east coast city-states.

Combining an African base with Arab, Persian, and other Indian Ocean influences, Swahili represented the network of trade and beliefs that synthesized along the east coast. Like its grammar and vocabulary, those who spoke Swahili made up a mosaic of cultures that mixed together in one population through cross breeding. More complex than Ethiopia to the north, that combined Yemeni and African elements, the Swahili cities included African, Indian, Persian, Arab, and Asian contributions. Together, this mix represented the commercial contact points of the Indian Ocean.

Stretching from the Horn of Africa in the north to the Cape of Africa in the south, Islam shaped politics and trade along 75 percent of the east coast of Africa. By the thirteenth century, Swahili city-states included Mogadishu (on the Horn), Lamu, Malindi, Gedi, Mombasa, the Sofala (on the Cape), the Pemba Islands, the Zanzibar Islands, and Kilwa, examples of some of the larger urban centers. In general, however, more than forty Swahili city-states dotted the east coast of Africa.

Regular wind patterns generated by the seasonal monsoons drove ships south from November to February, and north from April to September along the African coast. Reaching their zenith in the 1300s and 1400s, these Swahili city-states became fortified towns that secured the movement of goods at the western end of a complex Indian Ocean trade system. From each port, merchants made their way into the interior to extract the precious natural resources and craft items available in the rainforest and jungles to the west. These items, exchanged for goods manufactured in the Middle East, produced the wealth that helped to define the urban markets of each town.

Because they were distribution centers housing great wealth, each city was a fortress made of cut and dressed stone. Within a city, mosques and palaces dominated the skyline. Walled houses, port facilities, and fortified prominent points and peninsulas underlined the security measures taken in the interest of safeguarding and conducting trade. The energy that went into this style of construction reveals the riches generated by commerce and, evidently, the constant threat of piracy.

Ruled by Africans, these city-states remained focused on the coast. Local agriculture came from farmers who lived in a world set apart from the wealth enjoyed in the towns. These farmers made up the backbone of the population, lived in mud huts, and populated villages that supplied the city with food. The African Plateau to the east cut off easy access into the interior so that these villages, and the cities they served, occupied a thin strip of culture along the coast. Simply stated, then, wealth and power derived from trade.

South Africa

The people of South Africa lived beyond the reach of Islam, or any other foreign influence, until the arrival of the Europeans off the coast during the sixteenth century. A product of the Bantu migrations, those who occupied subequatorial Africa spoke an amalgamation of languages that reflected the movement of a vast number of people over a long period of time. Like the Indo-European languages mentioned in Chapter Nine, the Bantu represents a very complex family of peoples in subequatorial Africa whose ancestry is as tangled as the many different peoples of Europe. Starting somewhere near the Benue River that feeds the Niger, the Bantu marched south from 3000 BCE to 500 CE.

The Bantu covered a vast area ranging from the Kingdom of Kongo in Central Africa through the highlands of East Africa and into the savanna of South Africa. Into these different geographic zones, the Bantu brought their domesticated plants, agricultural techniques, and iron tools. In their new homelands, the Bantu displaced the local hunters, the Pigmies and the Bushmen, just as European farmers later displaced Na-

tive Americans in the British colonies and the United States. Over the course of several centuries near the end of their migration, the Bantu began to generate complex new kingdoms in the Transvaal of South Africa that became the hallmark of their cultural achievement.

One result of this achievement is the striking example of Great Zimbabwe. A magnificent civilization that generated an urban population of 18,000, Great Zimbabwe also had massive structures and buildings, using cut stone and a sturdy plaster called *daga*. In that urban complex, Great Zimbabwe produced one of the most impressive examples of African architecture, including a cone-shaped tower some 200 feet wide by 300 feet long that stood 32 feet high and was 17 feet thick. Such a construction speaks to the engineering skills and wealth of the Bantu.

Great Zimbabwe generated a large urban complex based on a trade system that commanded a wide area. Controlling a major portion of the interior around South and Central Africa, Great Zimbabwe developed a powerful commercial state between 1000 and the 1400s that expanded to the coast. As a trading culture, Great Zimbabwe dominated regional gold production, giving it the same kind of economic advantages enjoyed by Ghana, Mali, and Songhai.

The wealth of trade developed by this civilization can be seen in the products archaelogoists found at its capital: glass from western Asia, porcelain from China, ceramics from Persia, and salt and copper from other parts of Africa. Great Zimbabwe acquired all of these goods from trading partners located on the East Coast of Africa. In exchange, Great Zimbabwe itself produced and exported gold, tin, iron, pottery, carved soapstone and ivory, and spun cloth. Like other African systems, trade clearly played a key role in the accumulation of power and political organization.

After the fifteenth century, Great Zimbabwe began to decline. The combined effect of declining trade, soil depletion, overgrazing, and loss of wild game eroded the resource base used by this kingdom. Late in the 1400s a new dynasty tried to salvage the political situation by moving the capital off its Limpopo River site. Thus, they left behind the magnificent urban center of Great Zimbabwe and migrated to the Zambezi River.

It was at this time that the people of Great Zimbabwe made first contact with a European people: the Portuguese. Gold deposits had attracted the Portuguese as infighting at the new Zimbabwe court centered on the selection of the next heir to the monarchy. Sensing the court's weakness, the Portuguese encroached on Zimbabwe's territory and accelerated its disintegration into smaller regional cultures.

Besides the achievements of Great Zimbabwe, the Bantus spread out to make up a complex system of cultures and kingdoms. Each of these new Bantu communities imposed their language in the places in which they settled. How this linguistic shift occurred is not actually known. Most likely, the people who spoke one of the Bantu languages probably derived their local variation from the way they tended to intermarry with indigenous peoples. Thus, the Bantu simply seemed to have absorbed different cultures and peoples or push them aside, as they did the Bushmen and Pigmies they encountered along their trek south.

The Bantu developed a wide array of economic styles: some practiced hunting and gathering, while others engaged in the cultivation of sorghum and millet. Those who grew these grains generated urban systems that ranged from villages to massive cities like Great Zimbabwe. Their strategy for assimilating newcomers, or driving off those who resisted their authority, involved encouraging some and excluding others from becoming part of local corporate lineages. Over the course of their long history of migrating into sub-equatorial Africa, the Bantu generated some five hundred languages, which speaks to the cultural complexity of the regions they occupied.

From all the accounts of cultures, societies, and civilization cited in this chapter, one can see that Africa in the middle years of world history was an extremely complex human environment. Broad geographic concentrations of different peoples found in North, West, Central, East, South-Central, and South Africa provide recognizable patterns that make comprehending this vast variation of civilizations manageable. Yet the degree of cultural diversity on the continent reveals how much the word *African* cloaks when studying African history. That same kind of diversity existed in Asia and Europe and reveals the problematic use by scholars of such ethnic terms as *Asian* and *European*; like the term *African*, these hide more than they reveal.

Still, at the heart of Africa in the middle years of world history one can see the power of Islam. The way this religion penetrated the continent, and its slow growth and limited contact with African people living under Muslim-animistic monarchs, speaks to a form of Islam specific to the African experience. The aggressive conversions found elsewhere in the expansion of Islam generally did not exist in Africa; only the slave-generating practices of Jihad used by Kanem-Bornu came close, punctuated as it was by the sale of humans, but it did not shape the conversion pattern. Otherwise, Islam as practiced in Africa proved to be an extremely tolerant religion.

Meanwhile, Islam's value to Africa can be appreciated by a consideration of the sophisticated ideas it introduced to people living there. Thanks to the strategic geographic position the Middle East occupied on the land bridge between Africa and Eurasia, Islam was able to defeat some of the consequences of isolation that slowed cultural development below the Sahara. Hence, Islam (as mentioned above) changed the military and commercial history of much of Africa while also introducing literacy, accounting, scholarship, architecture, and the management skills needed to rule massive new kingdoms and complex societies.

Suggested Reading

Berger, Iris and E. Francis White, *Women in Sub-Sahara Africa: Restoring Women to History* (Bloomington: Indiana University Press, 1995).

Bohannan, P. and P. Curtin, *Africa and Africans,* Revised Edition (Prospect Heights, Ill.: Waveland Press, 1995).

Bovill, E. W., *The Golden Trade of the Moors: West African Kingdoms in the Fourteenth Century,* Second Edition (Princeton, N.J.: Markus Wiener Publishers, 1995).

Burstein, Stanley, ed., *Ancient African Civilizations: Kush and Axum* (Princeton, New Jersey: Marcus Wiener Publishers, 1998).

Collins, R. O. ed., *Problems in African History: The Precolonial Centuries* (Princeton, N.J.: Markus Wiener Publishers, 1993).

Curtin, P., et al., *African History,* Second Edition (London: Fage, J. & W. Tordoff, 1995).

Ehret, Christopher, *The Civilizations of Africa: A History to 1800* (Charlottesville, Va.: University Press of Virginia, 2002).

July, Robert, *A History of the African People, Fourth Edition* (Prospect Heights, Ill.: Waveland Press, 1992).

Middleton, J., *The World of the Swahili: An African Mercantile Civilization* (New Haven, Conn.: Yale University Press, 1992).

Oliver, R., *The African Experience* (New York: Harper Collins Press, 1991).

Pouwels, Randall and Nehemia Levtzion, eds., *The History of Islam in Africa* (Columbus: Ohio University Press, 2002).

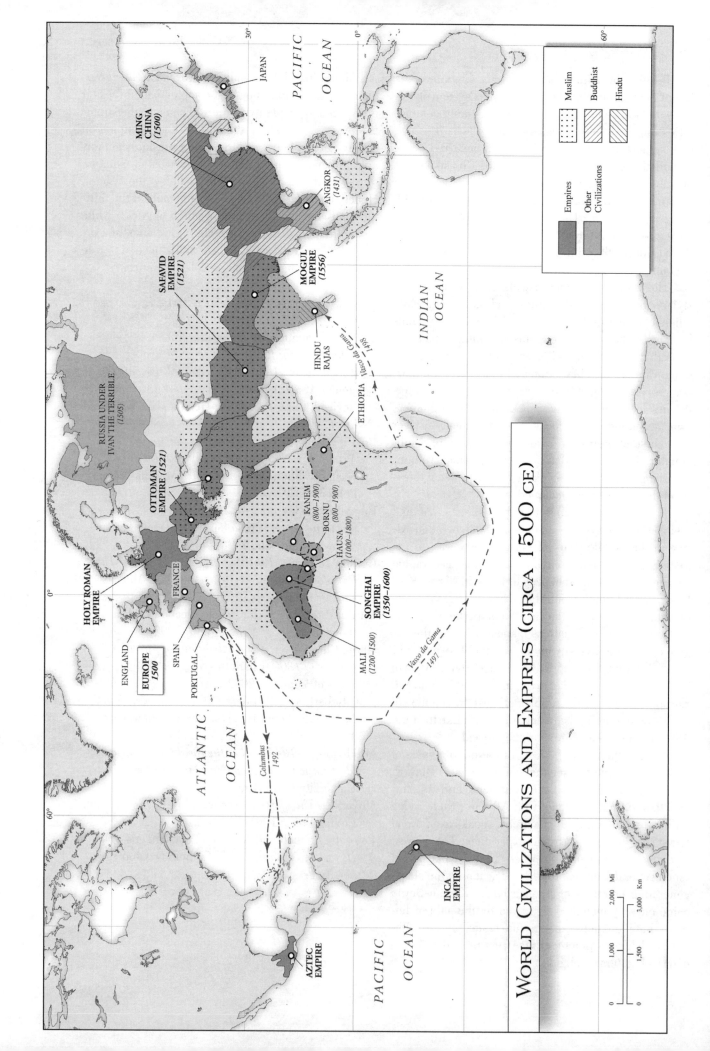

WORLD CIVILIZATIONS AND EMPIRES (CIRCA 1500 CE)

Legend:
- Muslim
- Buddhist
- Hindu
- Empires
- Other Civilizations

JAPAN

PACIFIC OCEAN

MING CHINA (1500)

ANGKOR (1431)

SAFAVID EMPIRE (1521)

MOGUL EMPIRE (1556)

HINDU RAJAS

INDIAN OCEAN

Vasco da Gama 1498

RUSSIA UNDER IVAN THE TERRIBLE (1505)

ETHIOPIA

OTTOMAN EMPIRE (1521)

KANEM (800–1900)

BORNU (800–1900)

HAUSA (1000–1800)

HOLY ROMAN EMPIRE

FRANCE

SONGHAI EMPIRE (1350–1600)

ENGLAND

EUROPE 1500

SPAIN

PORTUGAL

MALI (1200–1500)

Vasco da Gama 1497

ATLANTIC OCEAN

Columbus 1492

PACIFIC OCEAN

INCA EMPIRE

AZTEC EMPIRE

0   1,000   2,000 Mi
0 1,500 3,000 Km

XVI

THE AMERICAS:
A Time of Troubles

As mentioned in Chapter Nine, the Western Hemisphere imposed strict biological and geographic limits on human creativity that placed Native American cultures living in the Americas at a developmental disadvantage when compared to civilizations found in Eurasia and Africa. These local biological and geographic conditions isolated the human societies in the Western Hemisphere from the powerful stimulus of external cultural diffusion that provided Eurasians and Africans access to new domesticated plants and animals, new ideas and tools, and, occasionally, new germs. Accordingly, such isolation had so restricted the opportunities available to Native Americans for cultural development that their societies were still in the stone age, had only developed the ability to smelt soft metals, and had only generated one literate culture on two continents: the Maya. Yet, a generous food base led by corn and potatoes overcame the absence of a metal technology and a general state of illiteracy to produce several major urban civilizations. These foods required less labor to raise than wheat or rice and supplied significant agricultural surpluses capable of feeding large cities despite the fact that Native Americans also did not have the plow, the wheel, or a wide variety of large domesticated mammals. Only camelets like the domesticated llama and the wild alpaca in South America were useful as beasts of burden and for wool, while Mesoamerica had no large mammal resources: instead they had small hairless dogs (the Chihuahua), exotic birds, and turkeys.

Despite the local technical and biological circumstances that restricted agricultural potential in the Western Hemisphere, civilizations developed and flourished in the Americas anyway. Each produced a significant urban population that generated impressive stone monuments, or created elaborate engineering feats in irrigation, terrace cultivation, and road building. Still, none of these cultures could overcome the powerful influence of geographic isolation, which denied them access to the external cultural diffusion enjoyed by Eurasians and Africans.

Also mentioned in Chapter Nine, this isolation resulted from two great oceans and a north-south land axis that hampered human movement. The Atlantic and Pacific oceans quarantined the Western Hemisphere from Eurasia and Africa. The north-south land axis created topographic and climatic barriers that reduced the possibility of human and domesticated plant movement. Together, these natural conditions reduced human contact and the inspiration associated with seeing how others lived.

Besides the two oceans and land-axis, the principal topographic feature that also restricted migration was a narrow land bridge at Panama situated in a dense jungle between North and South America. The land bridge tended to confine humans to their respective continents by preventing or delaying movement north or south. Next, climate divided the Americas into numerous weather zones that upset the comfort humans felt by remaining in regions where rainfall and temperature matched what their culture had trained them to manage. Finally, all these conditions combined to deny the Western Hemisphere access to major new human migrations from Eurasia that might have brought the stimulating impact of new plants, animals, tools, and ideas transmitted by a combination of trade and cultural diffusion.

Geographic and biological factors, however, also combined to limit disease history in the Western Hemisphere as well. Reduced human movement north and south restricted the transference of pathogens. Quarantining the Western Hemisphere by two great oceans cut off access to Europe, Africa, and Asia and their rich catalog of diseases. Light labor requirements and generous domesticated plants overcame limited productive technology while generating enough food to create a healthy population. Finally, the general absence of domesticated animals broke the disease link between mammals, their infections, and the dependent human population.

All these factors kept Native Americans relatively disease free as a people. Yet, these same conditions also made this human population vulnerable after Christopher Columbus came to the Americas. Bringing their plants, animals, and germs with them, Europeans created a biological catastrophe that profoundly altered human life in the Americas after the first contact was made in 1492.

Prior to the Columbian exchange, geography, biology, and technology limited the development of urban societies in the Western Hemisphere. Nevertheless, large concentrations of humans occurred in major cities, and Native American urban systems could rival those in Eurasia. Their achievements occurred on a great scale that speaks to Native American creativity as well as the value of culture as a means to generate cooperative, industrious labor.

The absence of domesticated animals added one more feature to Native American culture that proved unique to Mesoamerica (i.e., Mexico, Central America, and the Caribbean Islands). With only a limited number of animals to provide meat, Native Americans substituted plants as the primary source of protein in their diet and seem to have developed a craving for human flesh and blood. The absence of large mammals in the Native American diet can be correlated to the development of religious beliefs that encouraged ritual and gustatorial cannibalism.

The gustatorial form of cannibalism is the exception and not the rule in the history of Mesoamerica. Gustatorial cannibalism refers to the eating of other humans as a preferred source of food. Such practices occurred on Caribbean islands where Native Americans called Caribs developed a preference for the flavor of human flesh. In fact the Caribs not only lent their name to the Caribbean in general, but also to cannibalism itself. Coined by the Spanish in 1553, the term cannibalism derived from a corruption of the word *Carib*.

The ritualized form of cannibalism found in Mexico and Central America emerged from a fascination with blood and human sacrifice that functioned at the heart of Mesoamerican religions—a prominent feature of Native American culture during the middle years of world history. In Mesoamerica the absence of animal protein in their diet led Native Americans to include human blood, hearts, skin, and flesh as sacred substances needed to feed the gods. Without this flesh and blood as part of religious ritual, Mesoamericans believed that their the gods would grow weak from hunger. These gods needed human nourishment to keep up their divine strength and ensure order in the universe. Seeking humans to feed the gods forced Mesoamericans to capture victims in increasingly violent cycles of warfare.

Once the blood had been drained from a human sacrifice, the heart removed, or the body flayed for its skin, the remaining meat and organs were then made available for human consumption as part of the ritual. The flesh supplemented a meat-poor diet. Most likely, the fascination with blood and flesh, therefore, generated habits of ritual cannibalism used in religious ceremonies. To what degree ritual cannibalism blended with gustatorial preferences is still hotly debated among Latin American scholars.

Despite the fascination with human blood and flesh, as well as the limits set by geography, biology, and technology, Native American culture flourished. As we have already seen in Chapter Nine, the native populations of Mexico, the west coast of South America, and Andes Highlands generated numerous civilizations. In the middle years of world history, these peoples produced three more urban cultures that reflected the power of human creativity: the Toltecs, the Aztecs, and the Incas. Each of these urban-based civilizations pulled the boundaries of the Native American world together to make impressive political systems. Consequently, their three stories complete the pre-Columbian picture in Meso and South America. Yet, beyond these three major urban cultures is a rich history of Native Americans in North America who had begun the transition to sedentary life. The history of the peoples in Mesoamerica, the Andean Plateau, and North America must be examined to illustrate how human creativity in the Western Hemisphere dealt with the limits imposed by geography and biology.

A Time of Troubles: The Toltecs

In Mesoamerican historiography, there is a consensus among scholars that the years after the destruction of Teotihuacán and the beginning of the Mayan decline, (around 700), mark an ominous period of incessant warfare, soil exhaustion, and internal revolt. Overpopulation, misuse of cultivated fields, depleted soils, and shifts in climate increased the competition for food surpluses, which in turn stimulated rivalry between cities and social and political unrest. As local economies broke down, and large-scale food production failed, famine began and the social fabric disintegrated. Although new and more complex empires arose on the ashes of vanished Mesomerican cultures, a new set of challenges faced Native Americans during the middle years.

Like a geographic magnet, Mexico's great central valley drew wave after wave of nomadic wanderers, as both invaders and desperate migrants, seeking a place rich in water, game, and fresh soil. The lure of plush lands, adequate water supplies, and a hospitable climate gave the valley an irresistible appeal to peoples forced by drought, famine, or invasion to migrate. It is a familiar human story, played out across the world's great river valleys. For a time, Teotihuacán created order and stability in central Mexico, fostering trade and producing an agricultural surplus that allowed artisans, priests, and merchants to flourish. As the great center collapsed, tribes hovering on its northern frontiers rushed in, establishing successor states that relied on military power, conquest, and tribute to strengthen themselves. Scholars often use the term *militarist* to describe this era, which extends to the time of the Spanish arrival in Mexico in 1519.

One of these invading tribes, the Toltecs, entered the valley during the eighth century, eventually establishing their capital at Tula, some thirty-five miles north of present-day Mexico City. The Toltecs probably traded with Teotihuacán, and most certainly absorbed the culture and religious ideas of their southern neighbors. When Teotihuacán weakened, however, and could not defend itself, the Toltecs joined the attack and eventually built a successful empire that controlled most of central Mexico from coast to coast between 750 and 950. Although called an "empire," the political system the Toltecs built was really a collection of semi-independent city-states governed by priest/kings who found themselves subject to the might of the Toltec army. The Toltecs, therefore, relied on force of arms to support their political center, Tula, which grew into a city of some thirty to sixty thousand people. As a major urban site in Mesoamerica, Tula became a regional commercial center that replaced Teotihuacán. Jade, turquoise (acquired through long-distance trade with northern peoples in the present-day Southwest United States), feathers, textiles, and foodstuffs filled Tula's market. The Toltecs built temples, storehouses, and palaces along broad avenues. They traded with Mayan cities in the Yucatan Peninsula as well as to the Gulf of Mexico. The Toltec reached the apex of their power by the end of the tenth century, when their influence stretched across central Mexico, south into Guatemala, and north into New Mexico.

The Toltec's best-known ruler is Topiltzin (reigned ca. 980–99) who came to power just as Tula entered its zenith. A revered monarch who had functioned as a high priest, Topiltzin represented the god Quetzalcoatl, the "feathered-serpent," god of civilization, of the planet Venus, of the wind, and of good and light as pitted against evil and darkness. Topiltzin's fame derived from the fact that he led a campaign to reform religion and abolish human sacrifice. He faced fierce opposition, however, because human sacrifice offered the needed blood and hearts to keep order in the Toltec universe. The Toltecs believed that human sacrifice provided the divine substances required to feed their gods, give them power over the forces of nature, and make the Toltecs the rulers in a very unstable world. Quetzalcoatl, however, did not require blood and hearts; he was a gentle god who needed only token sacrifices: butterflies and the plumage of quetzal birds. Hence, Topiltzin's reforms, though consistent with Quetzalcoatl's nature, threatened the military vision the Toltecs had developed to explain order in heaven and on Earth.

Driven from power by the opposition at the very end of the tenth century, Topiltzin promised to return and reclaim his throne. At this point in Toltec history, Topiltzin assumed Quetzalcoatl's attributes and name, making himself into the deity and thereby creating a direct link between himself and the immortal powers of nature. The story of Topiltzin-Quetzalcoatl then enlarged beyond history and became legend. His departure for the east included the vow that upon his return, he would alter the order of the universe to match the requirements of his reforms. He stated that he would arrive in the year *Ce Acatl* (one Reed), the same year that, according to legend, Queztzalcoatl, the bearded white-faced god, was born. This expanded legend based on a historical figure then grew into a powerful, enduring myth that resurfaced in the later history of the people who followed the Toltec Empire.

The great king's successors proved unable to stop the familiar pattern of the rise and fall of empires in world history: internal dissension, agricultural failures, and military revolts. The pressure never lessened at the margins of the Toltec Empire, with rival tribes, derisively called *Chichimecs* (barbarians) always pressing at the gates of civilization. Emboldened by the obvious internal problems faced by the rulers of Tula—there were numerous revolts in the twelfth century—the Chichimecs stormed into the sagging empire in the 1170s, occupying Tula itself by 1225. Although having been invaded and burned, the area around the great city remained a population center when the Spanish arrived some three centuries later. Later kingdoms, including that of the Mexica or Aztecs, looked to the Toltec Empire as a direct link with the glorious past of the great Central Valley. Invading speakers of *Nahuatl* (the language of the Toltecs, the Central Valley, and the Aztecs) absorbed the culture and practices of the vanquished empire and even claimed direct descent from the Toltecs.

Over the next century and a half, tribal cultures developed to fill the political and economic void left in the wake of the collapse of the Toltec Empire. The most successful and important kingdoms formed around the edges of Lake Texcoco, a large, shallow lake and marsh complex at the southern end of the great valley. Divided into political units, these independent kingdoms often warred with each other over resources, political squabbles, and failed alliances. A city on the western shore, Azcapotzalco, ruled as the most powerful state. The kingdom of Texcoco flourished as a coalition of towns that united to challenge the Azcapotzalco in the late thirteenth and early fourteenth centuries. Both of these competing states spoke Nahuatl and sought to preserve much of the heritage and culture of previous empires. A late arriving group, the Mexica, would soon begin the last great cycle of native conquest, empire building, and cultural expansion.

The Aztecs

Following the lead of many previous groups, the Mexica, as the Aztecs referred to themselves, began a long and difficult migration from the north into the Central Valley. Most scholars cite 1111 as a probable date for their departure from Aztlán, a place of uncertain origin. A series of caves in northwestern Mexico, or perhaps an island in the Gulf of California or even the mouth of the Colorado River as it enters the gulf, have all been cited as possible locations of Aztlán. Certainly the Aztecs wandered for generations. According to surviving Aztec pictographs, a woman carrying the symbols of their tribal deity, Huitzilopochtli (the Aztec war god), led them. Drought, military pressure, or possibly famine forced them to depart from Aztlán, wherever that may have been. They most probably entered the valley early in the thirteenth century and settled in the marshy swamps of Lake Texcoco, where they endured hard-

Huitzilopochtli, the Aztec war god. From *Symbols, Signs, & Signets*, by Ernst Lehner.

ships, rejection, and attacks from the established kingdoms over the next century.

An aggressive culture, the Aztecs understood the political environment they had moved into. They distrusted and disliked the dominant powers of the region, Azcapotzalco and Texcoco, but used the Mexica's excellent military skills as mercenaries to win favor and secure the opportunity to settle down. For a century, the Aztecs had wandered around the shore, being allowed to settle at one moment, and then being driven off the next. During that time, the Aztecs developed a reputation as tough warriors who worshipped their gods passionately by offering many humans as sacrifice. By 1345, their value as mercenaries finally won them the opportunity to settle on the island in the lake that belonged to Azcapotzalco where the Aztecs built Tenochtitlán.

Acting out a legend that stated their home would be marked by an eagle perched on a cactus with a snake in its beak, the Aztecs took command of their island. From the security of this island, the Aztecs then took a more active role in regional politics. Supporting first their partnership with Azcapotzalco, the Aztecs picked the stronger side and won access to more land and tribute as mercenaries. By 1428, however, the Aztecs felt secure enough to rebel against Azcapotzalco and joined the Texcoco alliance to destroy their old partner. From this victory, the Aztecs then emerged as an independent power and soon came to rule the lake.

Throughout the fifteenth century, Tenochtitlán grew in size and complexity, eventually reaching a population of 150,000, and was filled with temples, palaces, and storehouses—the equal of any constructed by human communities in Mexico. Rocks, lake-sediment, earth, and wood became the building blocks for the island city. The Aztecs eventually constructed three retractable causeways that linked the city to the mainland. Streets, canals, and irrigated fields took shape in the decades following the Aztecs' decision to build where their religious traditions prophesied that they would be safe from their enemies.

Year-round crops of maize, chilies, and beans, plus fish, frogs, and fowl from the lake allowed the population to grow. Later conquests and alliances expanded Aztec agriculture into surrounding lands, providing food for the rapidly growing culture.

Itzcoatl, the Aztec war leader, was the architect of the 1428 victory. Within a generation the Aztecs constructed a series of profitable and strategic alliances, gradually becoming the dominant partners. These alliances stretched over most of central Mexico, running from the Caribbean to the Pacific coast. Scholars estimate that more than 20 million people lived under Aztec control by the time the Spanish arrived in 1519.

The great island city of Tenochtitlán now became the hub of a complex political and commercial empire. The Aztecs demanded the right to trade and send their merchants into the cities of their alliance partners. Gradually they added tribute to the cost of doing business. Tenochtitlán became a marketplace for all of central Mexico, with food, textiles, animal skins, jade, and myriad other commodities bought and sold on the great market days. Aztec merchants brought back news of outlying regions, often actively spying for the state. This could be a dangerous duty, as angry "allies" sometimes murdered Aztec merchants. Later, the Spaniard Hernán Cortés would write several letters to his king in which he openly admired the great marketplace at Tenoch-titlán. "This city has many public squares, in which are situated the markets and other places for buying and selling. There is one square twice as large as that of the city of Salamanca, surrounded by porticoes, where are daily assembled more than sixty thousand souls, engaged in buying and selling; and where are found all kinds of merchandise . . . articles of food, as well as jewels, gold and silver, lead, brass, copper, tin, precious stones, bones, shells, snails and feathers."[1]

By 1450, the rulers of Tenochtitlán felt secure enough to order scholars to rewrite the chronicles of their civilization to provide the Aztecs with a more heroic past, including a fictional direct relationship to the Toltec Empire. Society became highly stratified, with a ruling elite of powerful landowners, noble clans, and a priestly class controlling virtually every aspect of life. Schools were established for the sons and daughters of both the elite and commoners, and a strong sense of duty to the state and religious deities became a central goal of the education system.

The success of the Aztec culture fostered the idea that their war god, Huitzilopochtli, favored them above all others. The practice of offering sacrifices to honor and appease gods and goddesses was well established throughout the great valley. In accordance with their growing success, the Aztecs began to offer greater and greater blood sacrifices, eventually engaging in large-scale ceremonies in which thousands of prisoners from tributary states were ritualistically slaughtered at the great temples in Tenochtitlán.

1 Irwin Blacker, *Conquest* (New York: Grosset and Dunlap), p. 56–61.

Aztec Human Sacrifice. One of many religious rituals, the act of human sacrifice was often recorded in art such as this, showing a vivisection. From an ancient Mexican drawing. akg-images, London.

The Aztec offered so many human sacrifices because they thought that their command over their empire and the universe was only temporary. Believing they held power in trust for the Toltecs, the Aztecs accepted the legend of Topiltzin-Quetzalcoatl who had claimed he would return. Offering humans in sacrifice to their patron deity, Huitzilopochtli, served as a method to postpone that day when the Aztecs would have to surrender their command of the world to Topiltzin-Quetzalcoatl. Accordingly, the Aztecs produced a cosmology that synthesized their deities with previous native gods to explain the passage of power from one civilization to the next. Thus, the Aztec worldview complemented their understanding of political power: the rise and fall of civilizations matched the rise and fall of different worlds as the universe went through cycles of creation and destruction.

The world had not existed just once but several times. Four such world-cycles had come about. Each was an era of the sun that had suffered destruction. Each cycle of the sun had existed in consecutive order with every passing age improving on the last. A primordial force had directed these different epochs: first from the earth, then from the wind, next from water, and finally from fire—these four forces accounted for the first four cycles. Now the universe was in its fifth and most perfect cycle: the age of the moving sun. Although the best of all the ages, this fifth cycle too would come to an end.

Expecting a cataclysm that would terminate their world, the Aztecs set about postponing this eventuality

Ixiptla: An Aztec God-Representative

Each year the Aztecs worshipped the forces of nature during September that provided them with their harvest. This festival, "Sweeping of the Road," was devoted to Chicome-coatl, "Seven Serpents," the Aztec goddess of maize. The "sweeping" referred to the effects of the winds that brought the winter rains, which marked the end of the growing season, the harvest, and the beginning of the season for war— and the acquisition of captives. The broom symbolizes female excellence, which pleased Chicomecoatl. The Aztecs believed that the performance of this twenty-day celebration ensured a bountiful year so the participants had to pay very close attention to the sacred details.

The Sweeping of the Road began with a five day lull in any religious activity. On the afternoon of the sixth day, warriors marched in a phalanx-like form-ation carrying flowering branches, solemnly ushering in a sacred event. For the next eight days, these warriors repeated their grave parade and maintained an ordered silence as they marched. Following the eighth day, four days of frenzied activity began with a more vivacious crowd of midwives, female physicians, and women wearing sacred tobacco pouches forming two ranks and engaging in a mock skirmish while casting flowers, reeds, and tree mold at one another. These were the escorts of the Ixiptla for Chicomecoatl. They were there to beguile the Ixiptla, a doomed woman, who needed to be distracted so that she would not cry and cause misfortune for the Aztecs in the coming year.

On the evening of a final fifth day, the women escorted the Ixiptla to the temple of Chicomecoatl where one of the priests carried her on his back up the steps with her face turned toward the night sky. At the top of the temple pyramid, another priest cut off her head, flayed her body, and draped her skin over the naked flesh of yet another priest. Also, her blood was drained and poured over a figurine of Chico-mecoatl. The priest who wore the skin, breasts, and genitalia of the Ixiptla was selected for his powerful masculine body, which was now hidden underneath the feminine form of the dead woman to create an ambiguous being—both male and female. From this point on, the priest in his female skin became the goddess of plenty and the female aspect of corn.

He/she then descended the steps of Chicomecoatl's pyramid and confronted the chief warriors and bravest men of the Tenochtitlán. She chased the fearless warriors who fled before the her to the War God's (Huitzilopochtli) temple. Once at Huitzil-opochtli's pyramid more captives were sacrificed with the incarnation of Chicomecoatl performing four of these sacred executions. During the last two days of the celebration, symbols of war were passed around the gathered crowd at the foot of Huitzilopochtli's pyramid and squash and maize seeds were thrown from the temple to represent the bounty of next year. On the final day, the Aztecs chose an enemy city for that year and declared war so that they could acquire more captives to continue to feed the gods.

Inga Clendinnen, *Aztecs: An Interpretation* **(New York: Cambridge University Press, 1991), p. 99–110.**

for as long as they possibly could. Only sacrifices to the gods could supply the sacred substances they needed to maintain the fifth world order. Thus, human blood, hearts, and flesh alone provided the necessary divine energy to maintain the movement of the sun. Taking responsibility for supplying this sacred stuff, the Aztecs sought out as many people as were needed to release the vitality trapped within their bodies. Their sacrifice as well as ceremonial warfare supplied the needed blood that maintained the world order. Hence, like the Toltecs, the Aztecs produced a level of violence within their empire that they believed was a necessary feature of religion to keep the universe together.

The history, rituals, and ideas of the Aztecs, recorded in deerskin books filled with pictographs, were taught and interpreted to successive generations. These deerskin books provided the Aztecs with their cosmology and the justification for war. Sadly, the Spanish destroyed most of these materials (as mentioned) when they demolished Tenochtitlán, but a few survived.

In the meantime, a few powerful native cities managed to resist the pull of an alliance with the Aztecs. The Tarascans and Tlaxcalans, although encircled, were never fully dominated by the Aztecs. Indeed, they became willing allies of Cortés when his arrival changed the military dynamic in central Mexico.

Despite the failure of the Aztecs to control all of their neighbors, their powerful empire was well equipped to extract wealth from both friends and subject states, from which they demanded maize, cotton, cacao beans, and many other goods. Most complied; the few who resisted faced dire consequences. The Aztecs occasionally attacked and destroyed cities unwilling to deliver their tribute, or who foolishly murdered or turned away Aztec merchants. These forays kept most in line, although the possibility of sectional revolt remained a constant fear of Aztec emperors.

In 1502 Montezuma II became the ruler of Tenochtitlán. He was both a soldier and a highly educated priest who studied the history and legends of his people. As mentioned above, one such legend relayed the long-awaited return of the fair-skinned god Topiltzin-Quetzalcoatl. The chronicles told the story of Topiltzin-Quetzalcoatl's abrupt departure from Mexico during the collapse of the Toltec Empire. His return, usually calculated in the calendar system as one Reed, would signal the end of the reign of whoever held the throne and the destruction of the state, for Quetzalcoatl would reclaim his empire and throne. Among his other mundane concerns, Montezuma always kept watch for signs that foretold the return of the great god. As fate would have it, one Reed occurred in the European calendar during 1519, the year Cortés arrived in Mexico.

The Incas

Meanwhile in South America, the Andean region experienced a pattern similar to that of Mexico in the centuries after 1000 CE. Several powerful states, such as Chimú, on the northern coast of Peru, and Tiahuanaco, thirty-four miles from the southern shore of Lake Titicaca, dominated the highlands and coastal areas but failed to create a centralized empire capable of exercising control over the entire region. Chanchan, Chimú's capital, boasted a population of more than 60,000 residents based on large-scale agriculture and trade. Impressive buildings, extensive irrigation systems, and the accumulation of significant individual wealth characterized Chimú during the thirteenth and fourteenth centuries, while Tiahuanaco collapsed in 1300 creating a powerful vacuum for competing cultures in the region around Lake Titicaca. By the 1430s a new, powerful state constructed a regional empire that stretched more than two thousand miles through the Andes and soon rivaled the Aztecs and the Mayans (See Chapter Nine) as the most sophisticated and successful empire of the Western Hemisphere.

The Incas (a name derived from the ruling elite in the valley of Cuzco, located northwest of Lake Titicaca) emerged as an imperialistic state under the inspired leadership of three successive rulers from the 1430s to the 1520s. The first of these, Pachacuti Inca, created a bureaucratic empire that eventually controlled a population of between 10 and 12 million people, re-organized the food production system of the Andes to feed these ever-growing numbers, and initiated construction of a system of paved roads that ensured the efficient movement of food, goods, and soldiers throughout the empire. Upon arriving in Peru in the 1530s, the Spanish conquerors marveled at the workmanship of these "royal roads" which reached more than 14,000 miles in total length. Modern-day visitors to the Andes still walk and ride over sections of the roads the Incas built five hundred years ago.

The Incas created a highly organized system whereby the ruling elite of empire's capital, Cuzco, extracted from the many provinces—areas as diverse as the highlands of Ecuador and the coasts of central Chile—wealth in the form of textiles, animals (mainly llamas), gold, and foodstuffs. By the time of the reign of Huayna Capac, in the 1520s, the ruling clans of Cuzco were wealthy landowners, merchants, and military leaders who siphoned off the surplus produced by millions of ordinary cultivators. This wealth, in turn, built the great buildings of Cuzco, the palaces of the great Inca, the gold-encrusted temples honoring Inti, the sun god, and the thousands of miles of roads that traversed the empire.

The Incas built the sophisticated centralized empire in a relatively rapid span of about a century despite a modest population base. They also created this level of organization without a written language. Precise record keeping finally became possible with the use of the quipu, a series of knotted strings of different colors tied to a small piece of wood. Each color represented a commodity, such as potatoes or woolen cloth. The strings allowed local administrators to keep track of goods produced and taxes owed to the royal estates in each province. Labor was also an important commodity. The Incas taxed labor (the *mita*), which required subjects to work in food production, manufacturing, mining, building roads, maintaining royal estates, and creating the surpluses that drove the social order. Records of the mita and its products also allowed central officials to respond to periodic problems such as floods, drought, and famine by shifting animals and textiles from one part of the empire to another. Finally, the Incas extended their control over their subjects by making their language, *Quechua*, the dominant tongue of the Andes.

The Incas encouraged local populations to keep their own customs and invited their chieftains to become officials of the empire through civil or military service and marriage. Although the ultimate power lay with the ruling clans in Cuzco, provincial leaders exerted a degree of influence when the Inca clans quarreled amongst themselves.

The empire produced a wide variety of crops including maize, potatoes, chilies, quinoa (a wheat-like grain), beans, and squashes. Llamas, alpacas, and vicunas (different but related species of mammals) and other small animals populated the region as well. Although smaller than a horse or a camel, llamas were used as beasts of burden throughout the empire while alpacas and vicunas supplied wool. Farmers utilized irrigation canals, terracing, and crop rotation to ensure maximum production. Scholars consider the Inca Empire to have been the most productive and centralized of the Western Hemisphere before the arrival of the Europeans. Also, the Inca integrated the regions they conquered into the most stable and extensive realm of the Americas. Despite the lack of a written language, complex religious traditions flourished. These tended to focus on gods and goddesses associated with the natural world, including the sun, the moon and other celestial bodies. The Inca maintained schools that trained a priestly class, merchants, and administrators who ruled the empire. Taxes, land titles, labor demands, and construction schedules demanded the oversight of numerous educated and dedicated bureaucrats.

Problems did surface despite the success of the Incas. Subject populations sometimes proved restive, even rebellious. One response taken by the central government was to force relocation of problem groups to different areas of the empire. Another technique involved settling Inca populations in far-off areas to assure stability and loyalty in the outlying empire. Also, the death of an Inca emperor could result in fierce rivalries between competing clans jostling for power. To solve this problem, the Great Inca (the ruler) usually selected his heir apparent before death. The reigning emperor then required that the young ruler-to-be build his own palace and set up his own household. And, finally, upon the death of the Great Inca, his executioner killed his widows, concubines, and many of his servants after they celebrated the dead ruler's entry into heaven; this reduced challenges to the new ruler. Yet, upon the death of the Great Inca, still another problem surfaced that his people could not solve.

When the Great Inca died, his body underwent mummification so that it could be used as a conduit to communicate with the gods. Since Pachacuti had claimed to be the descendent of Inti, the sun god, then all Great Inca were divine because they all sprang from Pachacuti's bloodline. Also, since they were all divine, when one died, it was not difficult to imagine that his spirit lived on and had to be appeased. From this conclusion, the Inca developed a cult of royal ancestor worship. This cult mummified the old ruler, kept his body in his palace, and the surviving members of his family, except for the new Great Inca, used the deceased ruler's lands, buildings, chattel, and property to serve the mummy. During special ceremonies, these mummies sat in royal wall niches in Inti's temple in Cuzco, participated in the celebration, sat in the order of seniority, and received offerings of food cooked in special fires.

While the new Great Inca inherited his predecessor's powers as a ruler, his symbols of authority, right to govern, raise taxes, and wage war, the new Great Inca did not receive any of the surplus wealth from his father's estate; his father had retained these riches. Hence, the new Great Inca had insufficient immediate

resources to maintain order, or build a future unless he wished to raise taxes or wage war. Consequently, the new Great Inca had to worry about how to secure his own palace, his own wealth, and his own lands in preparation for the afterlife.

Since raising taxes was out of the question in an already heavily burdened empire, the best solution was for the new Great Inca to capture new lands through warfare. This way he could establish a new income and meet the needs of the state while preparing for the afterlife. But enough new wealth had to be taken from conquered peoples so as to provide the splendor needed to demonstrate his power in accordance to the divine dignity of his office. Hence, each new monarch had to spread the empire to provide for his administration and prepare for his life in the next world. Yet, there was a limit to the available lands to be conquered; eventually one of these Great Inca would not be able to satisfy the requirements of his office.

It was precisely this problem that created a crisis of power at the death of Huayna Capac (1493–1527), the third Great Inca. Two brothers fought over the throne: Huáscar (1525–32) and Atahualpa (1532–33). Huáscar had the best claim to the throne and became the next Great Inca, but he attempted a land reform to by-pass the problems of having to create his own income through conquest. His great grandfather, grandfather, and father had already conquered all the known sedentary cultures and there was nothing left to take. Yet, land reform would take wealth from his progenitors and undermine the mummy cult. This gave Atahualpa the fuel he needed to challenge his brother's claim to power.

Atahualpa fed on this discontent and split the empire. He took the north and Huáscar led the south. Huáscar had more men, but Atahualpa had better generals. The results of their struggle left thousands of soldiers dead or wounded, Huáscar imprisoned in Cuzco, and Atahualpa wounded, but still the unquestioned new ruler of the Inca Empire. Yet, the same year of Atahualpa's victory was the year when Francisco Pizzaro, his brothers, and a troop of Spaniards arrived, signalling the end of the great Inca Empire.

North America

Although the Toltecs, Aztecs, and Incas represent what might be termed the high cultures of the Western Hemisphere during the middle years of world history, other human communities had developed sophisticated lifestyles based on the good soil, animal populations, and abundant resources that North America possessed.

Along the Mississippi River valley numerous communities developed; some had even taken up sedentary cultivation and produced urban centers. Still, these Native American cultures existed on a time scale of their own; their technology placed them more in the ancient era rather than in the middle years.

By the fifteenth century, however, none of these emerging cultures approached the size and complexity of the Toltec, Aztec, and Inca civilizations. Today, demographers estimate that the bulk of Native Americans lived south of the Rio Grande, which provided a home for some 40 to 50 million people. The numbers were smaller for the area north of this great river: perhaps only 10 to 14 million by current estimates. Nonetheless, a population base of 50 to 65 million people compared favorably with the great cultural hearths of Europe, Africa, and Asia. Yet, those living in the Western Hemisphere had to generate their numbers while still living in a stone age, with few societies developing rudimentary writing, cultivating few domesticate plants, raising even fewer large mammals as tame animals, and growing crops without a plow and wheel. Despite these material handicaps, Native American did very well in contrast to their more fortunate counterparts in Eurasia and Africa.

In the lands north of the Rio Grande, small bands of hunters had explored most of North America between 10,000 and 1500 BCE, establishing communities from the shores of California to the deep woodlands of the Carolinas. These communities utilized what their regions offered. On the west coast of North America, groups fished in coastal waters, hunted marine mammals, gathered pine nuts, seeds, and acorns, and harvested other local plants. These great natural resources supported a diverse population that reached at least 300,000 people in California alone before the Spanish appeared at San Diego Bay. Communities stretching farther north to Alaska eventually crafted canoes to harvest fish and small whales from the rich Pacific waters. The great salmon fisheries of the Columbia and Snake rivers fed thousands along their banks and helped to create a huge trading network in that part of the continent.

Farther east, the abundance of large mammals first encountered by hunters from Asia allowed nomadic immigrants a plentiful food supply that could be harvested by a diverse but effective set of strategies to trap and kill large mammals. But mastodons, mammoths, ancient horses, and giant bears soon disappeared because they did not recognize the danger these new human hunters represented. Yet, when these species declined, or disappeared completely, due to excessive

hunting and, perhaps, the changing climate of the Great Plains, these nomads turned to bison, deer, caribou, and other herd animals that prospered on the drier, grassier plains. Communal hunting encouraged cooperation and innovation as the bands developed new and more effective stone tools, gradually adapting the bow and arrow of the Artic hunters. The introduction of European horses by Spanish soldiers after 1520 dramatically altered the mobility and strategies of these groups and furthered their capacity to harvest nature's bounty.

Other communities, notably along the eastern river valleys and in the arid southwest, turned to farming, in some cases constructing elaborate irrigation canals to bring water from great distances. The pueblo cultures (so named by Spanish conquerors), the Anasazi, cultivated beans, squash, and corn, the Mexican Trinity they acquired by a slow diffusion of domesticated plants north across the Rio Grande. The Hohokam communities also cultivated the Mexican Trinity along the Arizona-Mexico border. These farming peoples often traded food with the hunters of the Plains, creating commercial patterns that persisted well after the Spanish took control. Food, pottery, baskets, animal skins, and many other items flowed across a wide expanse from the Mississippi River to the Rio Grande and south into Mexico. After 1000, the Pueblo people of New Mexico and Arizona constructed hundreds of villages in their river valleys, all sustained by corn, beans, and squash.

The great rivers of eastern North America, the Ohio, the Tennessee, the St. Lawrence, and the Mississippi, all facilitated the development of corn cultivation as the crop came north from the Mexican highlands with human migration. Europeans often commented on the large and well-tended fields of Native American maize they found as they encountered villages along the coasts and riversides of North America, which represented an unexpected sophistication among a pagan people.

The general picture of the immense area north of the Rio Grande that emerges in the centuries leading up to the encounter with European explorers is that of a rich and diverse geographic region of great rivers intersecting extensive mountain ranges, grassy plains, arid highlands, deserts, and sub-Artic tundra. Across this huge space, uncounted herds of large animals roamed, complemented by vast quantities of migratory birds, coastal waters abundant with fish and marine mammals, and interior rivers teeming with salmon and other important species. Humans flourished in this setting, some still engaged in hunting and gathering, others beginning to experiment with new sources of food such as corn, and still others involved in a well-established sedentary life. Where local conditions encouraged such a wide range of activities, sedentary populations built impressive towns, storehouses, and religious places of worship. Anyone can see examples of such building in the southwest Pueblo areas if they travel to that region today. The diversity of economic activities, religious practices, and social structures in the Americas is staggering, as the following three examples will demonstrate.

Cahokia

Near the confluence of three great rivers, not far from present-day St. Louis, a large, complex, and successful human community developed sometime before 750. The marshy wet lowlands flooded during certain times of the year and encouraged the growth of Cahokia, which scholars often associate with the Mississippian, or Hopewell, culture that flourished in that region for the eight centuries leading up to the arrival of the Europeans in eastern North America. Farming large fields of corn, beans, and other vegetables as well as fishing and hunting allowed Cahokia to support an estimated population of between 15,000 and 30,000. During its greatest stage of growth, usually calculated at between 900 and 1200, the site functioned as a center of trade and worship. Well-established trading networks linked Cahokia to the Atlantic coast, the Rocky Mountains, the Great Lakes to the north, and, most probably, to the Gulf of Mexico via the Mississippi River. Shells, volcanic obsidian, copper, perhaps textiles, and furs all made their way through this great site. Food surpluses allowed some of the people to become artisans who sculpted and carved statues, jewelry, and other or-naments. Religious, military, and political leaders emerged to govern and protect Cahokia by 900 CE. Their importance can be judged by the amount of labor the community utilized to construct the many large mounds that dot the site. The largest example is known as Monk's Mound, measuring nearly one hundred feet high and over one thousand feet long. Thousands of inhabitants must have labored years to construct such a structure.

Hundreds of smaller mounds stretch from Illinois to Alabama, a testament to the influence and success of Mississippian culture. Despite its great importance and obvious success, Cahokia went into serious decline by the thirteenth century. The usual culprits: soil exhaustion, a growing population, climate changes, and political in-fighting all contributed to its decline. The wealth and success of Cahokia may have attracted unwanted attention from enemies. By the time the Spanish began to explore and map the Caribbean, the metropolis was abandoned, its people scattered to the forests to the east, and to the plains to the west. A state park now protects the remains of this great site, its visitor center interpreting the past for amazed guests.

The Chumash

Along the coast of southern California a dynamic human community grew that sprawled from present-day Santa Barbara south to Los Angeles. The Chumash were part of the on-going southward migration from the Bering Strait region discussed above. By 10,000 BCE they constituted one of the hundreds of different communities fishing and harvesting marine mammals on the coast of California. Adapting to environmental changes that produced a drier local climate by 1000 BCE, the Chumash began to gather seeds, nuts, and wild plants, hunt smaller game, and live in larger, more structured bands. Scholars note that as many as 20,000 to 30,000 Chumash may have occupied the southern coastal region and divided into five or six tribal groups when the Europeans first appeared.

Chumash villages became the center of a vast trading network extending throughout California and into Mexico and Arizona. Chumash artisans produced baskets, wooden bowls and tools, shell beads used for

A Native American site of the Mississipian culture, Cahokia Mounds was first settled around 650 CE. This painting is a view of the community circa CE 1150–1200, with Monks Mound (the largest man-made mound in North America) at the center, overlooking the Grand Plaza and the Twin Mounds. The central area is enclosed by a log defensive palisade, or stockade wall, and agricultural fields surround the city for many miles. Located near Collinsville, Illinois. Cahokia Mounds State Historic Site, painting by William R. Iseminger, 1990.

Many California Indian communities constructed houses of rigid poles and woven grasses, often using tule reeds, illustrated here by a reconstructed Chumash dwelling at the La Purisima Mission State Park in California. Photo by Carol Hendricks.

exchange purposes, and ocean-going canoes. Village life functioned around clans, with groups of families taking on specialized tasks, as well as harvesting plants, and collecting and processing seeds such as acorns. Scholars write of elaborate ceremonies involving birth, death, puberty, marriage, and child naming, all indicating a complex and sophisticated worldview. Religious ideas and rituals were of central importance to Chumash communities, as the elaborate hierarchy of deities embedded in their oral tradition attest. By the time of the encounter with exploring Spanish soldiers, the Chumash were a vigorous, expanding community, poised for the next level of human development: cultivation. The arrival of the Spanish, however, sent their culture off on another, more ominous direction: residence in disease-ridden missions.

The Iroquois Confederacy

Along the dense river valleys of New York, southern Maine and eastern Pennsylvania, a superbly organized and successful culture developed in the centuries before the English and Dutch settled their Atlantic colonies. The Iroquois peoples, grouped into five, and then later, six tribes, took control of the eastern woodlands and created a dynamic and aggressive empire that stretched to the Mississippi River. With roughly 100,000 people, the Iroquois Confederacy was able to hold off European domination of their lands until well into the eighteenth century.

According to legend, a saintly statesman named Deganawidah (son of the virgin mother) and a highborn councilor, Hiawatha, put an end to intertribal warfare and established a universal peace among the five tribes. The purpose of the new union was to promote harmony, justice, and government based on law. The success of this new political organization created such a stable communal bond that the Iroquois generated a longer history of military success then their far more numerous neighbors, the Algonquians.

Cultivating corn, squash, and beans, which arrived along the north coast by 300, the Iroquois represented a culture in transition from hunting and gathering to sedentary life. Engaged in careful slash-and-burn style cultivation, they transformed their woodland territories into a park-like environment that the Europeans admired and exploited in the seventeenth and eighteenth centuries. Careful land management defined a society well prepared to exploit the wealth that nature offered in North America.

Led by powerful tribes such as the Mohawks and Senecas, the Iroquois lived in villages scattered throughout the northeast. Iroquois men engaged in long-distance trade, taking furs and animal skins south and west to exchange for shells, copper, obsidian, and other such useful items. Even before the Europeans arrived, the Iroquois fought prolonged wars with their Algonquian-speaking neighbors to the north and east over hunting grounds and trade. The Dutch, English, and French soon learned to exploit this weakness in the fabric of indigenous life in North America. For their part, the Iroquois learned how to play the Europeans off against one another for political advantage and to acquire European metal goods, especially firearms.

By the time of the first English colonies, the Iroquois were the masters of the eastern forest woodlands. Their orderly and productive villages, elaborate religious and family rituals, and, above all, their powerful political and military confederacy, excited both the admiration and fear of the arriving Europeans. Yet, given these major cultural successes, the Iroquois were still a people living in transition from hunting and gathering to a Neolithic lifestyle several millennia after the Eurasians had first taken up residence in cities.

Hence, the Iroquois, like all of the Native American cultures living north of the Rio Grande represent societies progressing on a time scale all their own. Like their brethren in the Central Valley of Mexico and the Andean Plateau, these Native American cultures struggled with the conditions of life that geography and biology offered for them. Their capacity to produce as many people as found in Europe, Asia, and Africa, without similar material resources, speaks well of the Native American ability to cope with the physical circumstances of their existence.

Yet, these geographic and biological disadvantages cannot be ignored; all these cultures of the Western Hemisphere found themselves on a time scale far different than their neighbors in Eurasia and Africa. Native Americans had to struggle against a restrictive symbiosis of plants and animals due to a limited biological supply of domesticated species, a geography that discouraged diffusion due to different climatic zones that ran north and south along the dominant land axis, and the quarantining of two continents by the Atlantic and Pacific oceans. Native Americans prospered under the good fortune of suffering few pathogens, but paid a very heavy price with the arrival of the Europeans (see Unit Three). And as a result, symbiosis far outweighed parasitism to generate numbers that rivaled the Old World (Europe, Asia, and Africa). Early humans' existence in the Western Hemisphere illustrates their creativity in coping with widely varied biological and geographical conditions of life.

Suggested Reading

Bethel, Leslie, ed., *The Cambridge History of Latin America,* Vol. II (Cambridge: Cambridge University Press, 1984).

Burns, E. B., *Latin America,* 7th ed. (Upper Saddle River, N. Y.: Prentice-Hall, 2002).

Calloway, Colin G., *First Peoples: A Documentary Survey of American Indian History* (Boston: Bedford-St. Martin's Press, 2004).

Leon-Portillo, Miguel, *Aztec Thought and Culture* (Norman: University of Oklahoma Press, 1970).

INDEX

Ulama (religious leaders), 151, 458
Umma (community of the faithful), 152, 154–55
United Arab Emirates, 493
United Arab Republic, 507
United Kingdom. *See also* England; Great Britain
United Nations
    admission of People's Republic of China to Security Council, 481
    creation of, 474, 487
    creation of Israel, 493–94
    intervention in East Africa, 491, 492
    role in Korean War, 478
    World Health Organization, 520
United States
    Civil War, 346, 352, 383, 439
    concerns about population control, 521
    containment policy, 474–75, 478–79, 518
    dependence upon oil, 495
    détente, 510
    development as a nation-state, 346–53, 374
    diplomatic relations with People's Republic of China, 509, 510, 515
    effects of World War I, 424, 425, 441
    exploitation of African labor, 401
    government of, 412, 472
    Great Depression and New Deal in, 441–43
    immigration into, 440
    imperialism of, 241, 417, 440
    Industrial Revolution in, 351, 439
    influence in Egypt, 489
    influence on developing nations, 477
    involvement in Vietnam War, 508–10
    Islamist's view of, 496
    isolationism of, 432, 441, 514
    Japanese aggression and, 448
    land grant programs, 439
    loans to Germany, 433
    as mediator in China, 477
    migrations to, 512
    as new world power, 411, 425, 439, 440–43, 464
    occupation of Japan, 481–82
    opening of Japan to global trade, 353, 355
    racial inequality in, 440, 472, 515–17
    relationships with Latin American countries, 449, 497–99, 500
    relationship with Cuba, 502–3
    relations with Iran, 495
    role in Arab-Israeli conflict, 494
    role in Cold War. *See* Cold War
    role in Korean War, 478–79
    role in Sino-Soviet split, 481
    September 11, 2001, terrorist attacks, 519
    signing of NATO pact, 475

Spanish-American War, 418–19, 420, 440, 497
    trade with China, 387–88
    transcontinental railroad, 440
    two-party system in, 472–73
    Versailles Treaty and, 432
    view of India's independence, 486
    women's movement in, 517–18
    World War I, 421, 423, 425, 440–41
    World War II, 465, 467, 470–72
United States Central Intelligence Agency (CIA), 498, 503, 508
United States v. *Harris*, 352
Universal Geist, 338
universe, 285–86
universities
    in Africa, 403
    development of in High Middle Ages, 205
    in Iran, 455
    in Japan, 357
    in Latin American colonies, 376
    in sub-Saharan Africa, 219
Upanishads, 53–54, 55
Ur, 26, 33, 70
Urabi (Egyptian colonel), 402
urban division of labor
    absence of in sub-Saharan Africa, 110
    in Babylonia and Assyria, 70
    development of in Andes region, 120
    establishment of in Americas, 117–18, 119
    in Great Britain, 240
    in modernizing nations, 321
    production of revolution through, 321
    of Sassanian Empire, 160–61
    Smith's view of, 297–98
urban hierarchies
    agriculture and development of, 1, 2, 13–14, 16–17, 23
    commercial zones of in Middle Ages, 204
    created for commerce in Great Britain, 327
    creation of nation-states and, 320, 342
    development of in ancient Mesoamerica, 1, 14
    development of in ancient sub-Saharan Africa, 1
    development of in China, 14
    development of in Mesopotamia, 23, 69–70
    development of in the ancient Andes, 1
    development of military in, 18
    development of trade in, 18
    diffusion of into Aegean region, 73–74
    in Germany, 333
    in Great Britain, 240, 319
    history of disease and, 19–21
    impact of chariot on, 71
    in independent India, 486
    lacking in emerging Middle Eastern

countries, 493
    in Medieval Europe, 203–4
    nomads raiding/trading relationship with, 17–18, 69, 74, 79
    Phoenicians' spread of, 75
    religious beliefs concerning, 30
    in South Africa, 225
Urban II (pope), 200
urbanization, 255–57, 319, 325–27, 512
urban skills
    acquisition of in European nation-states, 416
    acquisition of in Japan, 357
    creation of nation-states and, 240, 319, 342
    lacking in emerging Middle Eastern countries, 493
    lacking in Latin America, 376, 462
    as necessary precursor to communism, 426–27
Urban VI (pope), 211
Ur III, 26
Uruguay, 500
Uruk, 14, 26
Urwat al Wuthqa (The Indissoluble Bond), 457
Urzababa, 26
U.S.S.R., *See* Soviet Union
Usuman dan Fodio, 396
Utopia (More), 277

Valen, 140
Valerian, 159
Valla, Lorenzo, 212, 275–76
Valois Dynasty, 304–5
Vandals, 141
Vargas, Getulio, 497, 500–501
Vaspuhragan, 160
vassals, 187, 195, 196
Vastaryushan (farmers), 161
Vedantas, 53
Vedas, 48, 52–53, 72
Velazquez, Diego, 247
Venetia, 191
Venezuela, 374, 375, 458, 494
Venus, 99
Verdun, Treaty of, 192
Versailles, Treaty of
    drafting of, 432, 441, 446
    failure of, 439, 441, 465
    German violations of, 437
    German war indemnities, 425, 433
    protests against in China, 450–51
Vespasian, 100
Vespucci, Amerigo, 246
viceroys, 373, 374
Victor Emmanuel II (king of Italy), 330
Victor Emmanuel III (king of Italy), 435
Victoria, Guadalupe, 375
Viera, Antonio, 250
Vietnam
    Chinese invasion of, 169